THE
MACMILLAN
PORTABLE
WORLD ATLAS

MACMILLAN • USA

Table of Contents

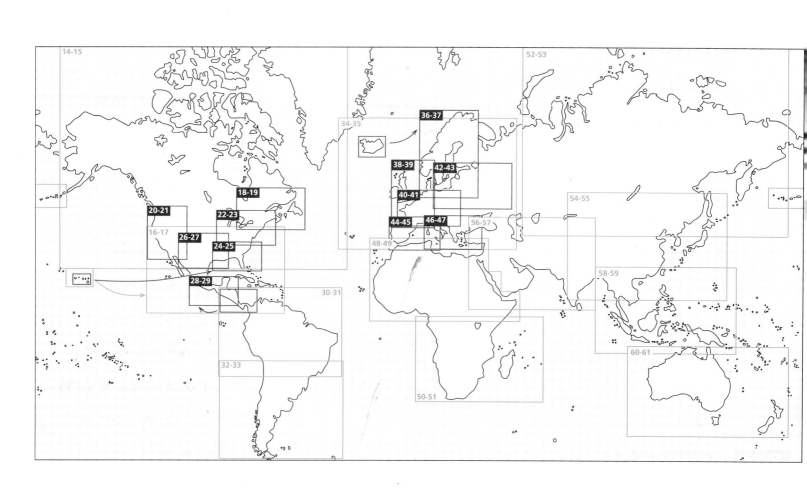

Explanation of Map Symbols

All Scales

- Freshwater lake
- Seasonal lake
- Lake with variable shoreline
- Salt lake
- Perennial stream or river
- Intermittent stream (wadi, arroyo)
- Navigable canal
- Non-navigable canal
- Mean pack ice limit in summer
- Mean pack ice limit in winter
- Ice shelf
- Marsh, moor
- Flood plain
- Salt swamp
- Coral reef
- Spring, well
- Reservoir with dam
- Waterfall, rapids
- International boundary
- Disputed international boundary
- Administrative boundary
- 1365 Mountain (with elevation)
- 1014 Pass (with elevation)
- Railway ferry
- Car ferry
- Shipping line
- International airport
- Domestic airport
- **OTTAWA** Capital of a sovereign state

Scale 1:15,000,000

- Superhighway or expressway
- Trunk road
- Main road
- Main railroad
- Other railroad
- over 5,000,000 inhabitants
- 1,000,000 to 5,000,000 inhabitants
- 500,000 to 1,000,000 inhabitants
- 100,000 to 500,000 inhabitants
- 50,000 to 100,000 inhabitants
- 10,000 to 50,000 inhabitants
- Population less than 10,000 inhabitants
- Reservation
- National park, national monument
- Restricted area
- *Chichén Itza* Interesting cultural monument
- *Devils Tower N. M.* Interesting natural monument

Scale 1:5,000,000

- Superhighway or expressway - under construction
- Highway - under construction
- 23 Main road with number
- Other road - Unpaved road, track
- Main railroad
- Other railroad
- 259 Distances in kilometers
- Urban area
- over 5,000,000 inhabitants
- 1,000,000 to 5,000,000 inhabitants
- 500,000 to 1,000,000 inhabitants
- 100,000 to 500,000 inhabitants
- 50,000 to 100,000 inhabitants
- 10,000 to 50,000 inhabitants
- 5,000 to 10,000 inhabitants
- Population less than 5,000 inhabitants
- Settlement, hamlet, research station (in remote areas often seasonally inhabited only)
- Reservation - Restricted area
- National park or national monument - Boundary of a time zone
- Camino de Santiago UNESCO World Cultural Heritage Site
- *Trakošćan* Cultural monument of special interest
- **A CORUÑA** Place of special interest
- **TOURS** Place of interest
- *Rock of Cashel* Interesting cultural monument
- *Milet* Ancient monument or excavation
- La Scandola UNESCO World Natural Heritage Site
- *Gullfoss* Natural monument of special interest
- *Riisitunturin kans. puisto* Interesting natural monument

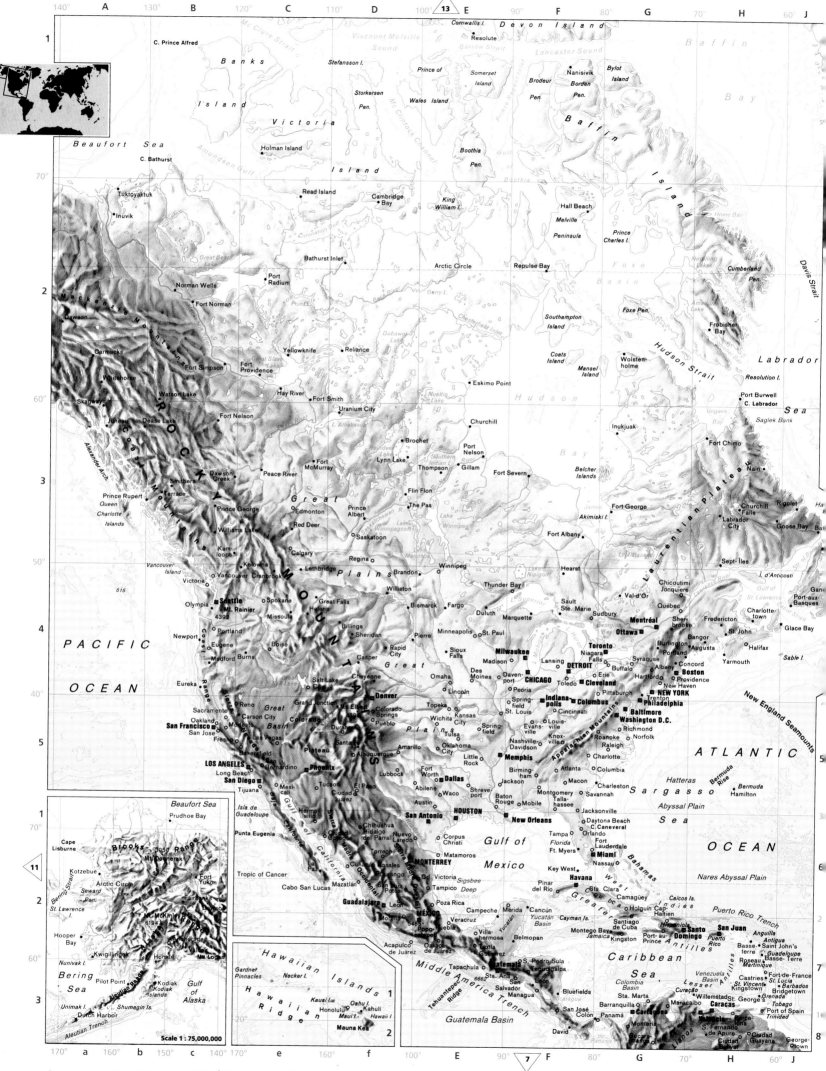

Scale at the equator 1 : 44,500,000

South America

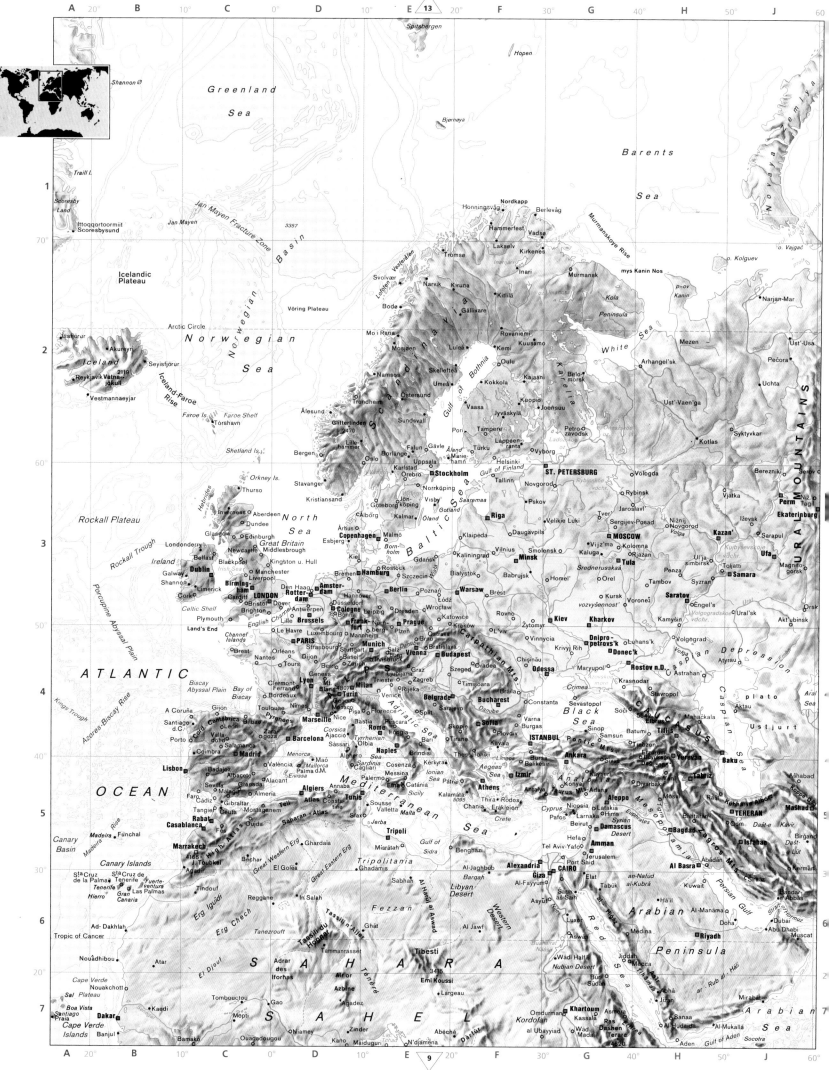

Scale at the equator 1 : 44,500,000

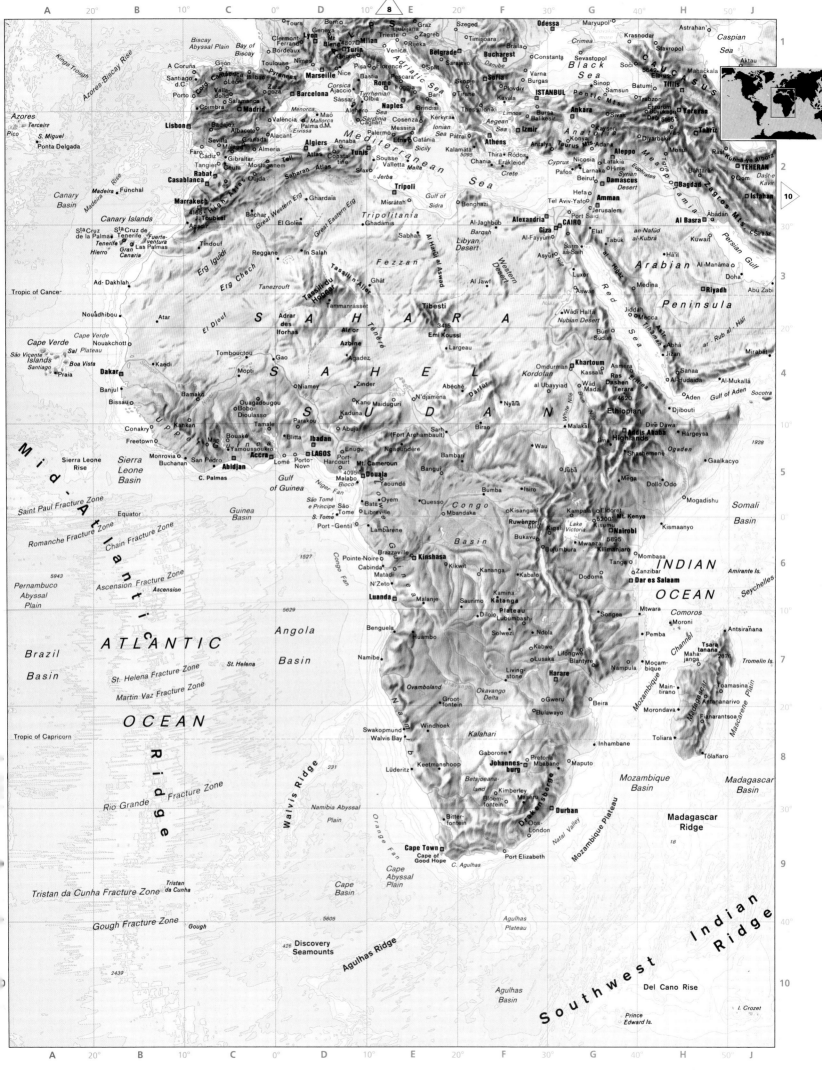

Scale at the equator 1 : 44,500,000

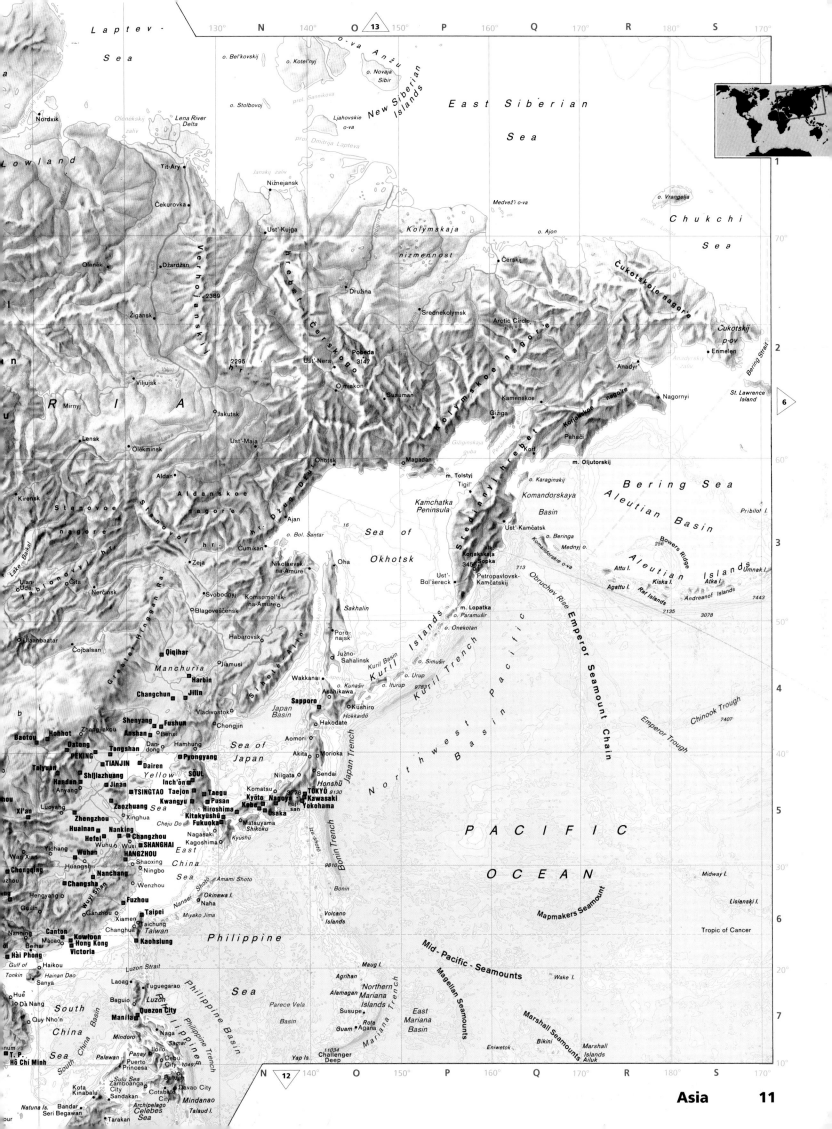

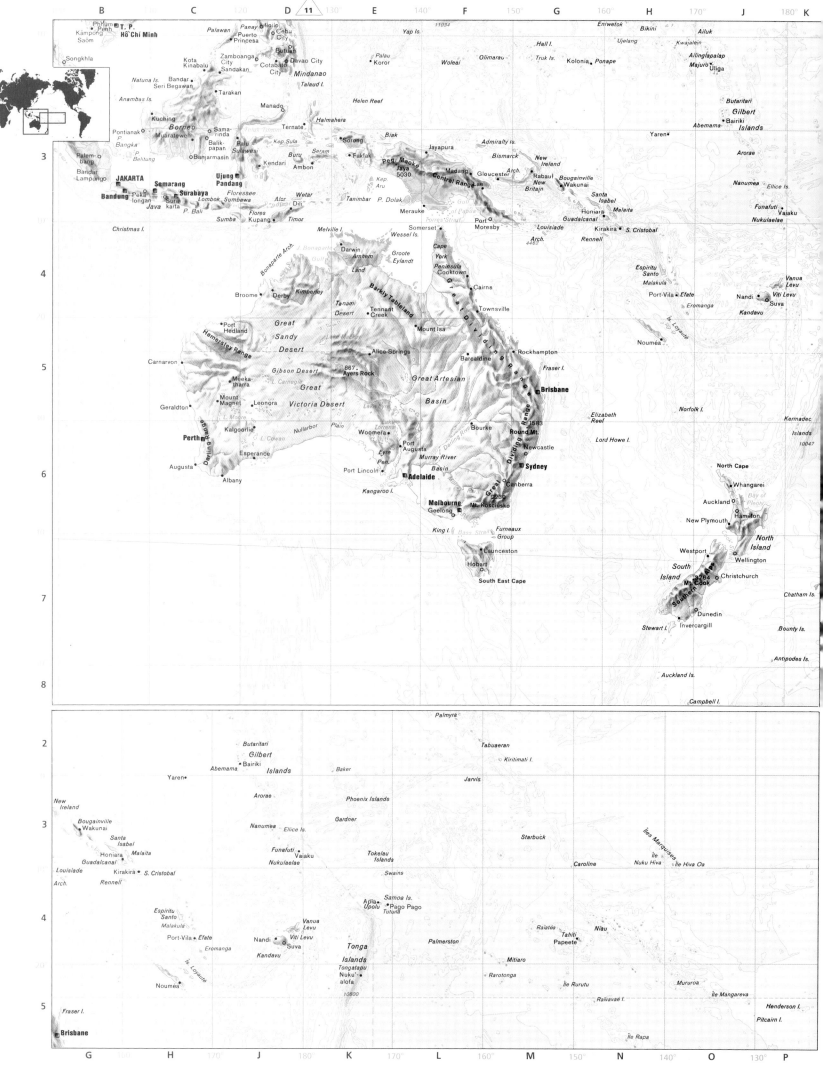

The Arctic · Antarctica

1 : 30,000,000

13

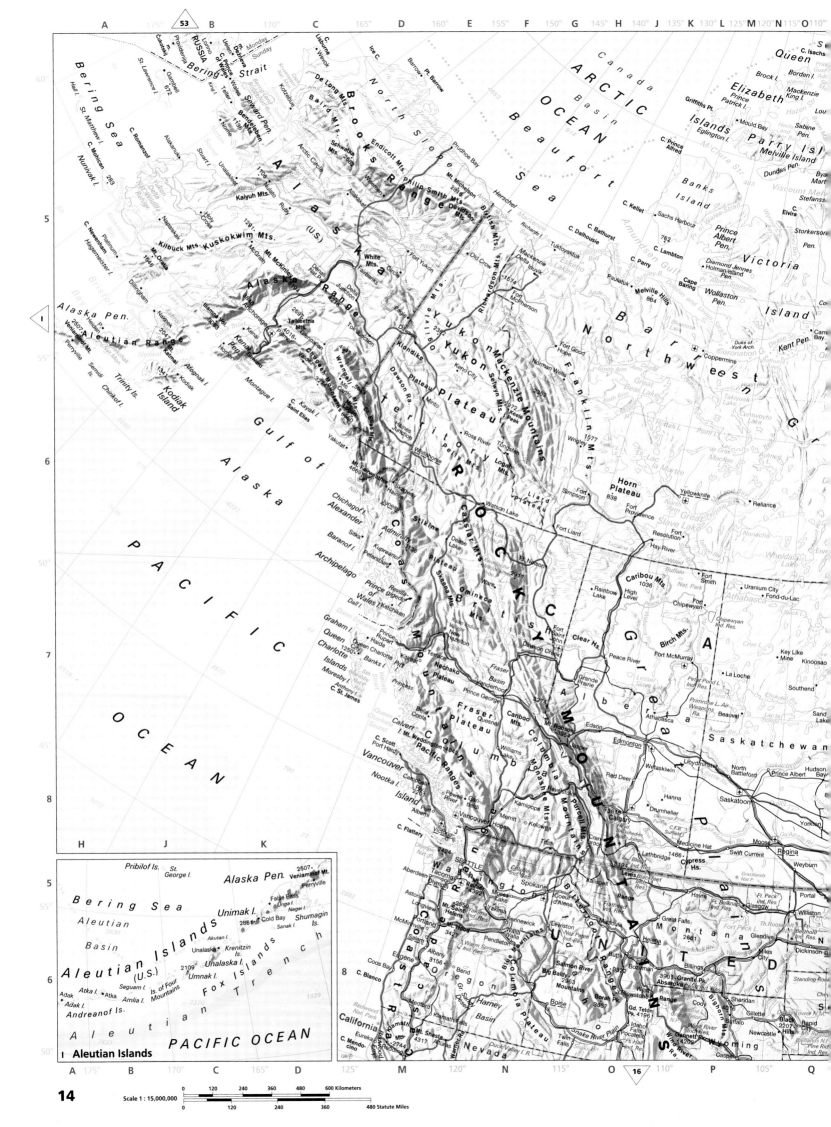

Alaska Islands

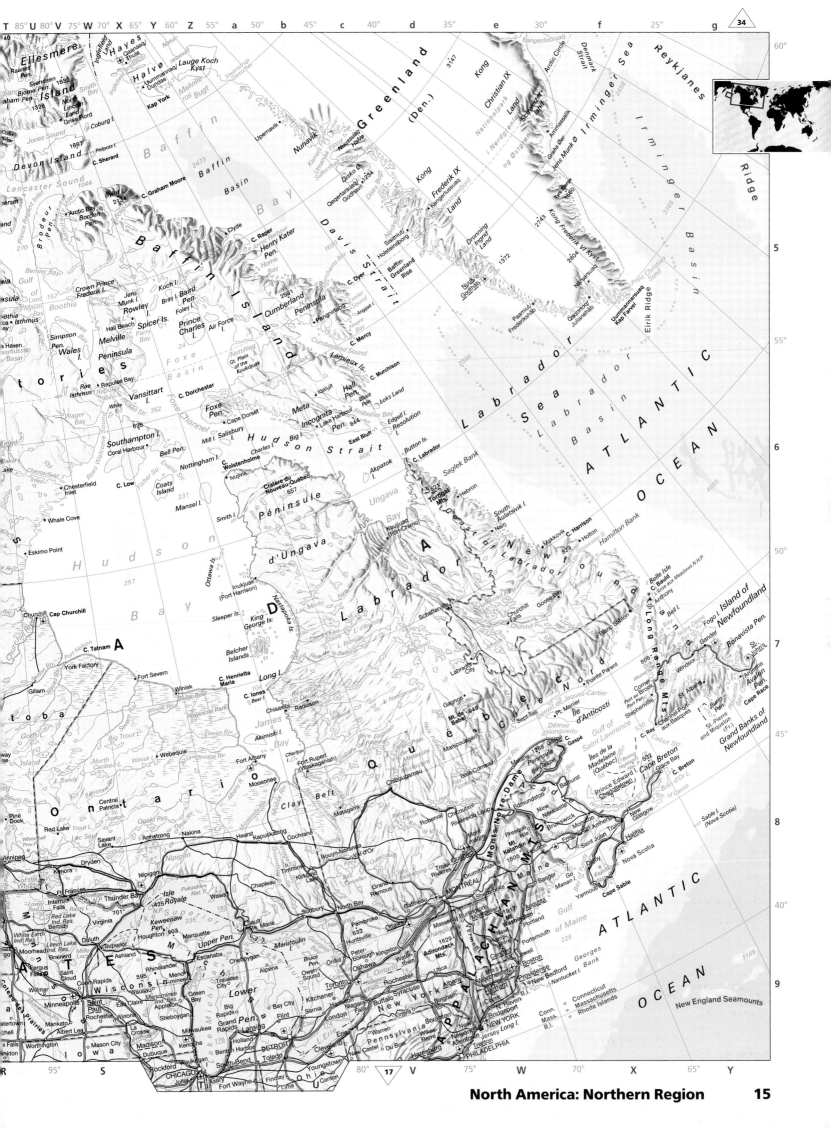

North America: Northern Region 15

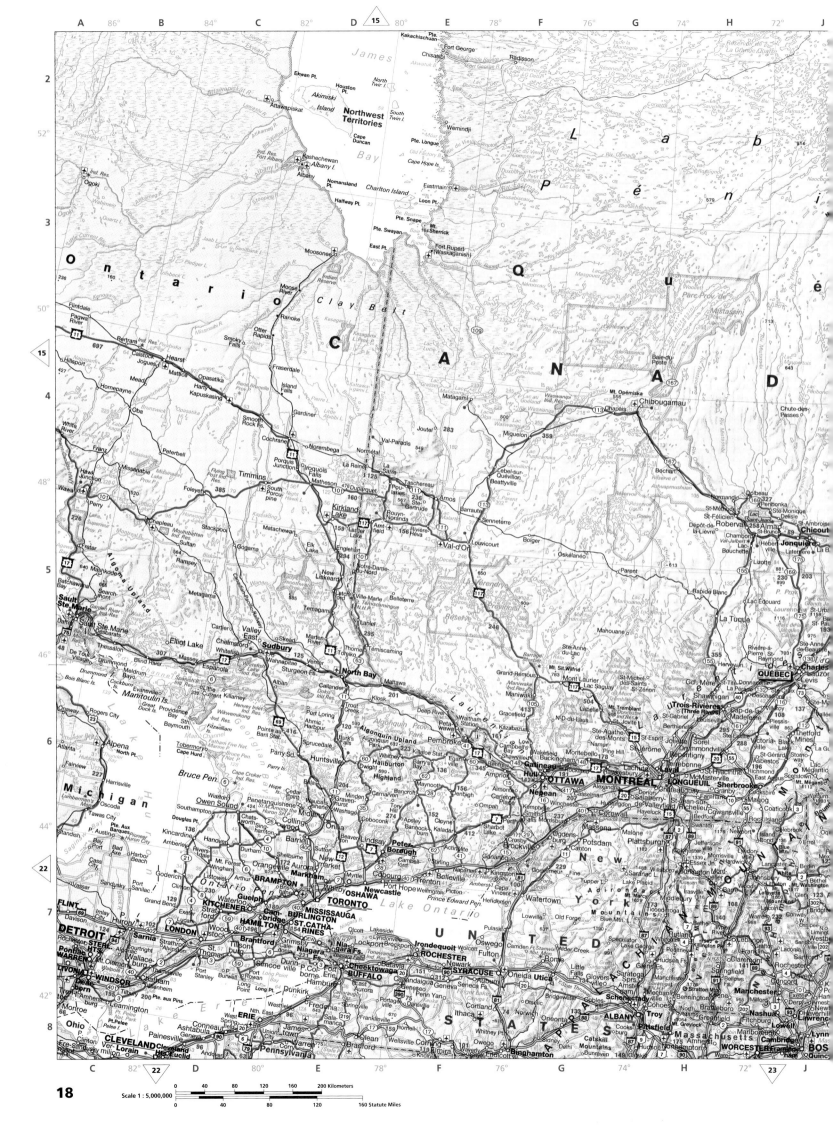

Scale 1 : 5,000,000

0 40 80 120 160 200 Kilometers

0 40 80 120 160 Statute Miles

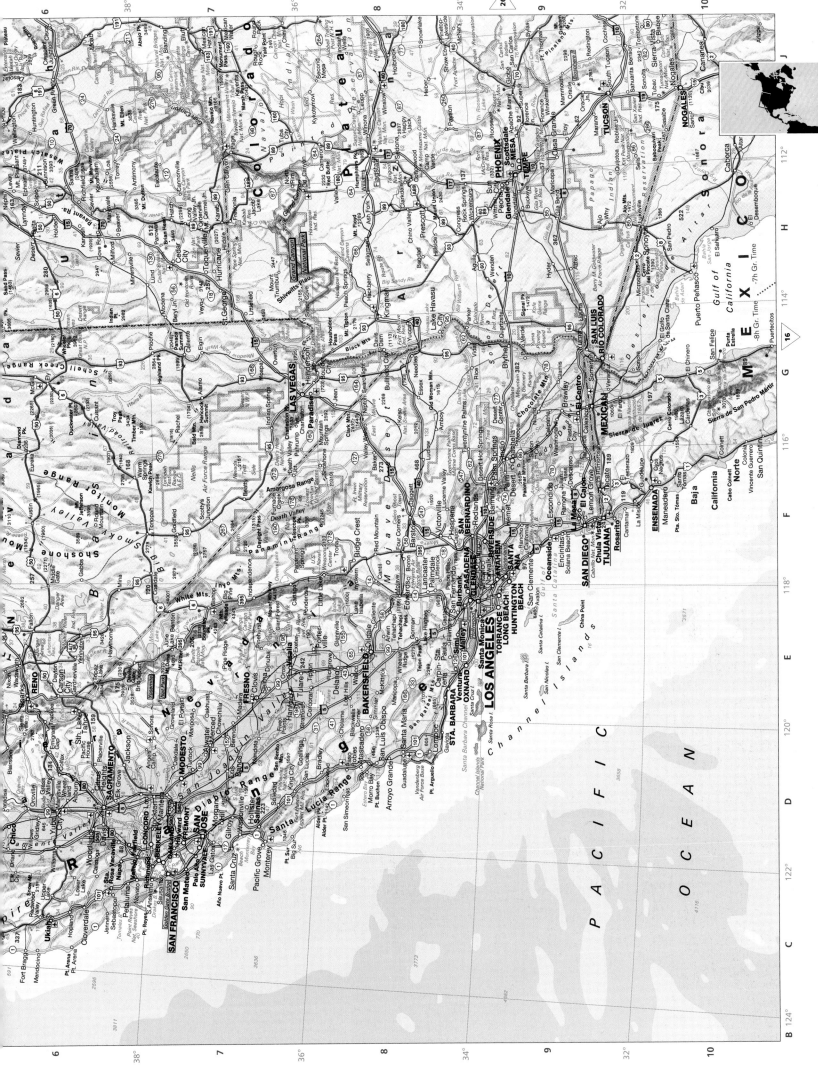

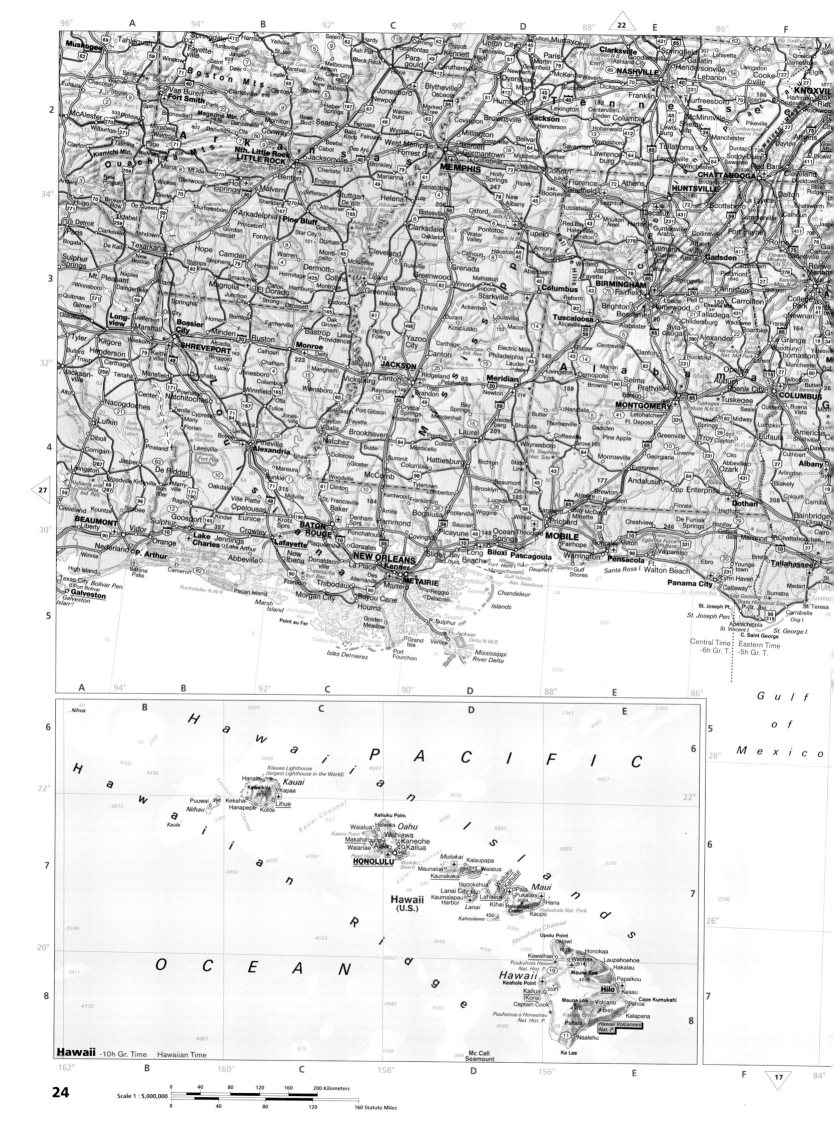

Muskogee
Tahlequah
Fort Smith
Springdale
Harrison
Yellville
Salem
Hardy
Pocahontas
Corning
Piggott
Blackham
Fulton
Murray
Dover
Clarksville
Springfield
Lafayette

NASHVILLE

Tennessee

Memphis

LITTLE ROCK

Arkansas

Texarkana

SHREVEPORT

Louisiana

Mississippi

Alabama

BIRMINGHAM

MONTGOMERY

JACKSON

Meridian

MOBILE

Pensacola

BATON ROUGE

NEW ORLEANS

Mississippi
River Delta

Gulf of Mexico

Central Time
-6h Gr. T.

Eastern Time
-5h Gr. T.

CHATTANOOGA

HUNTSVILLE

COLUMBUS

Panama City

Tallahassee

Hawaii -10h Gr. Time Hawaiian Time

PACIFIC

OCEAN

Hawaiian Ridge

Kauai

Lihue

Oahu

HONOLULU

Molokai

Maui

Lanai

Kahoolawe

Hawaii
(U.S.)

Hilo

Kailua
(Kona)

Mauna Kea
4205

Mauna Loa
4170

Ka Lae

Hawaii Volcanoes
Nat. P.

Scale 1 : 5,000,000

0 40 80 120 160 200 Kilometers

0 40 80 120 160 Statute Miles

17

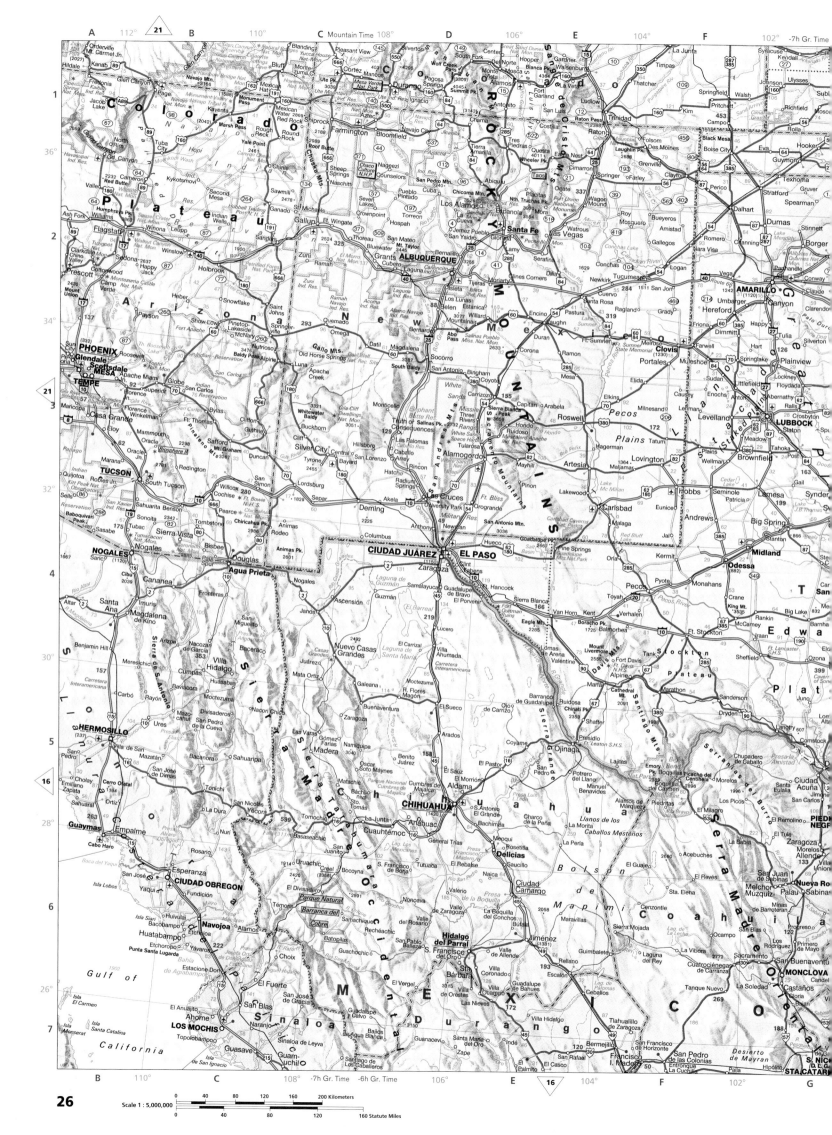

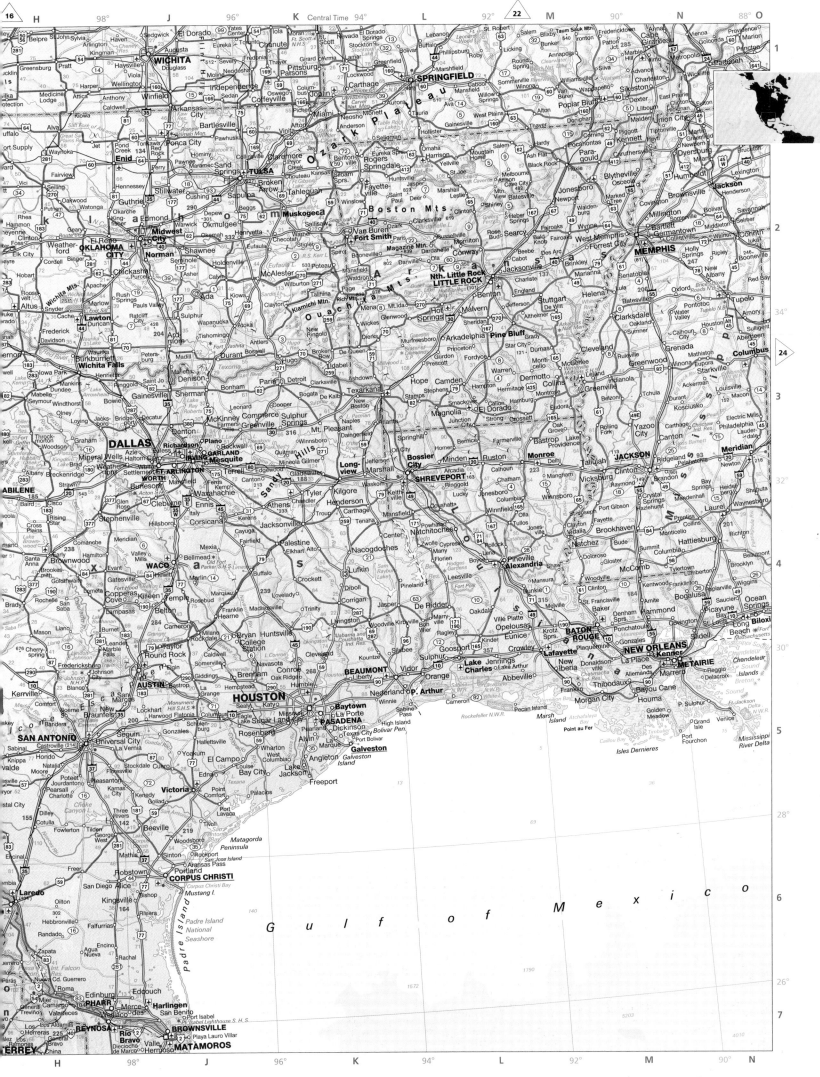

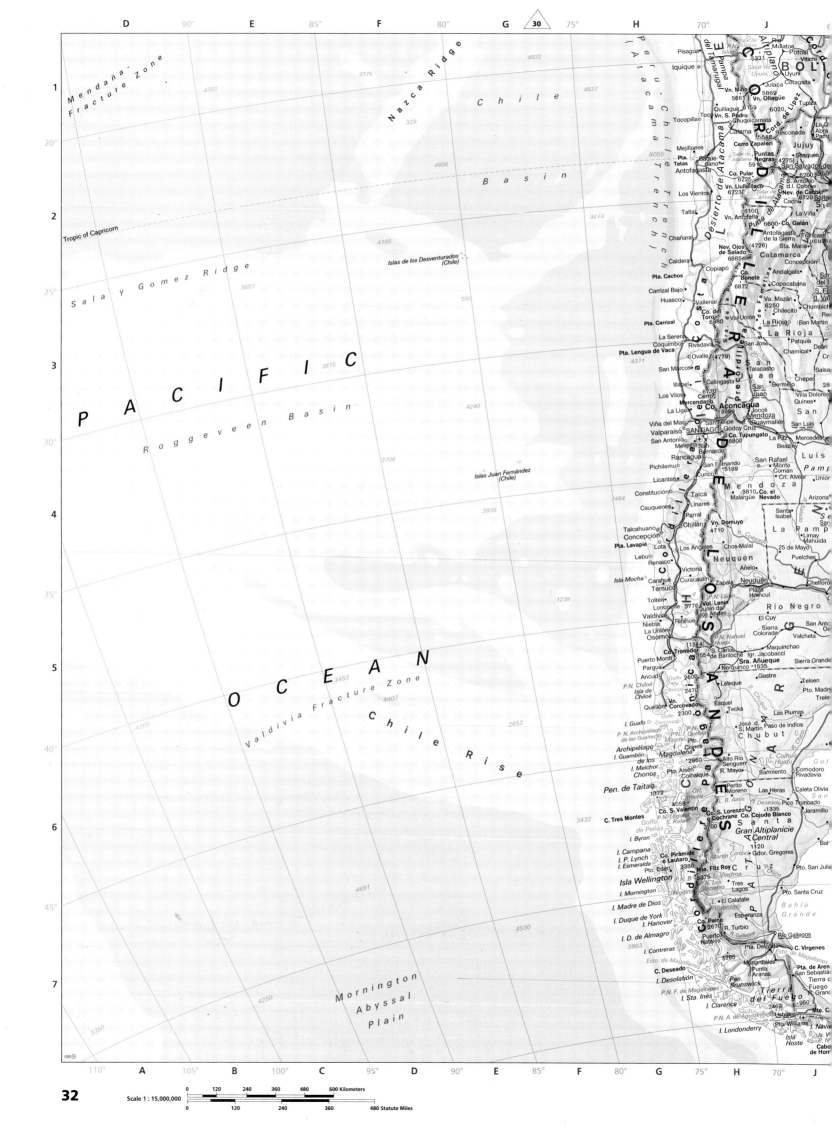

Europe 35

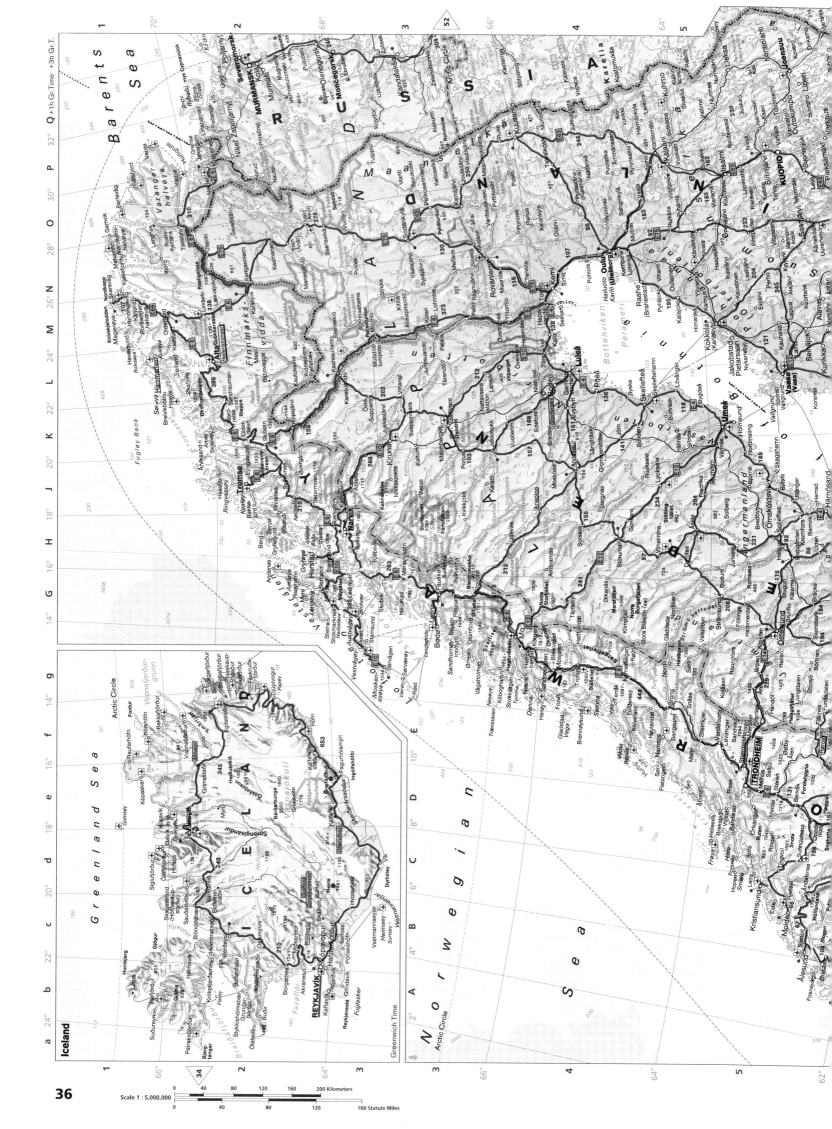

Scale 1 : 5,000,000

0   40   80   120   160   200 Kilometers

0   40   80   120   160 Statute Miles

Iceland

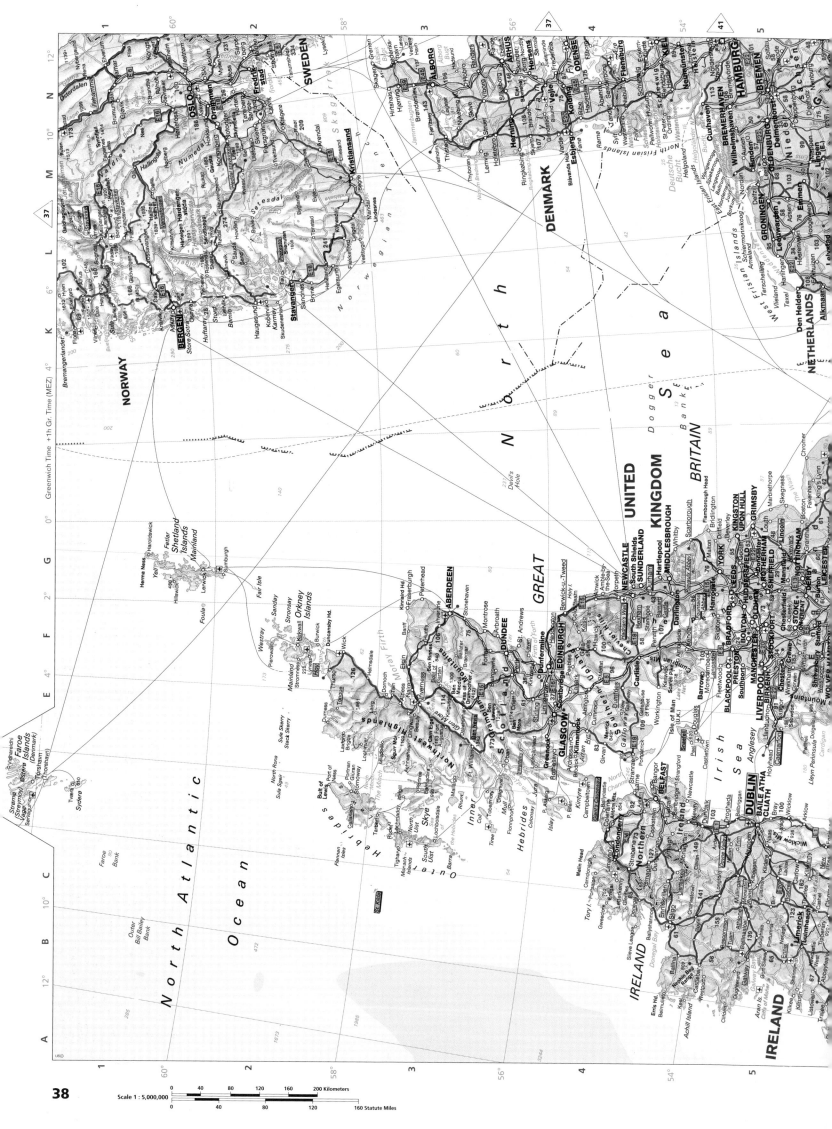

Scale 1 : 5,000,000

| 0 | 40 | 80 | 120 | 160 | 200 Kilometers |

| 0 | 40 | 80 | 120 | 160 Statute Miles |

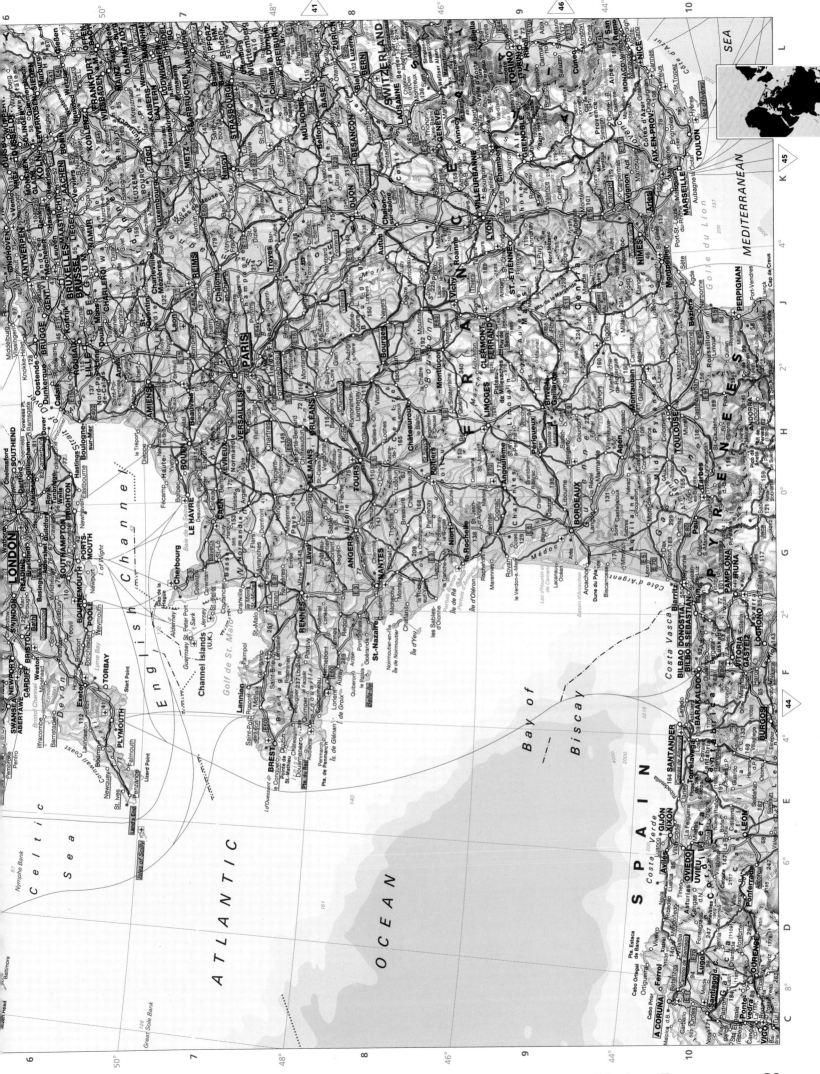

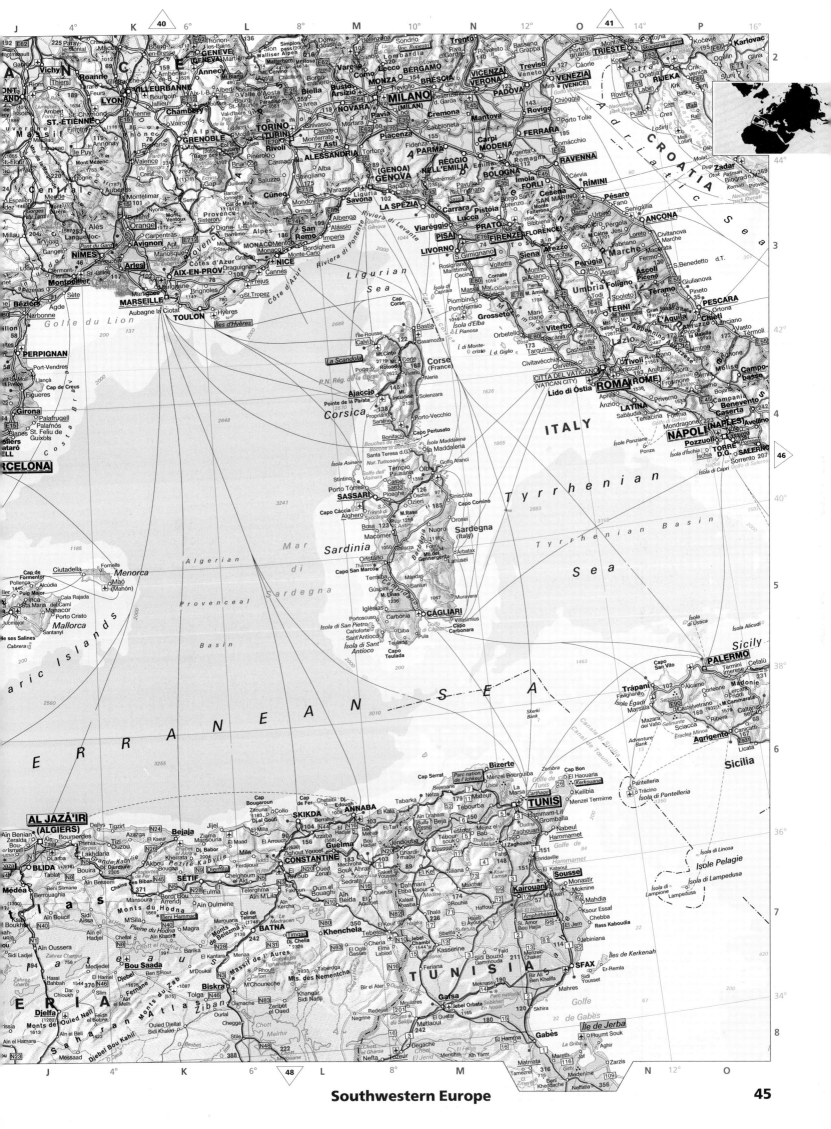

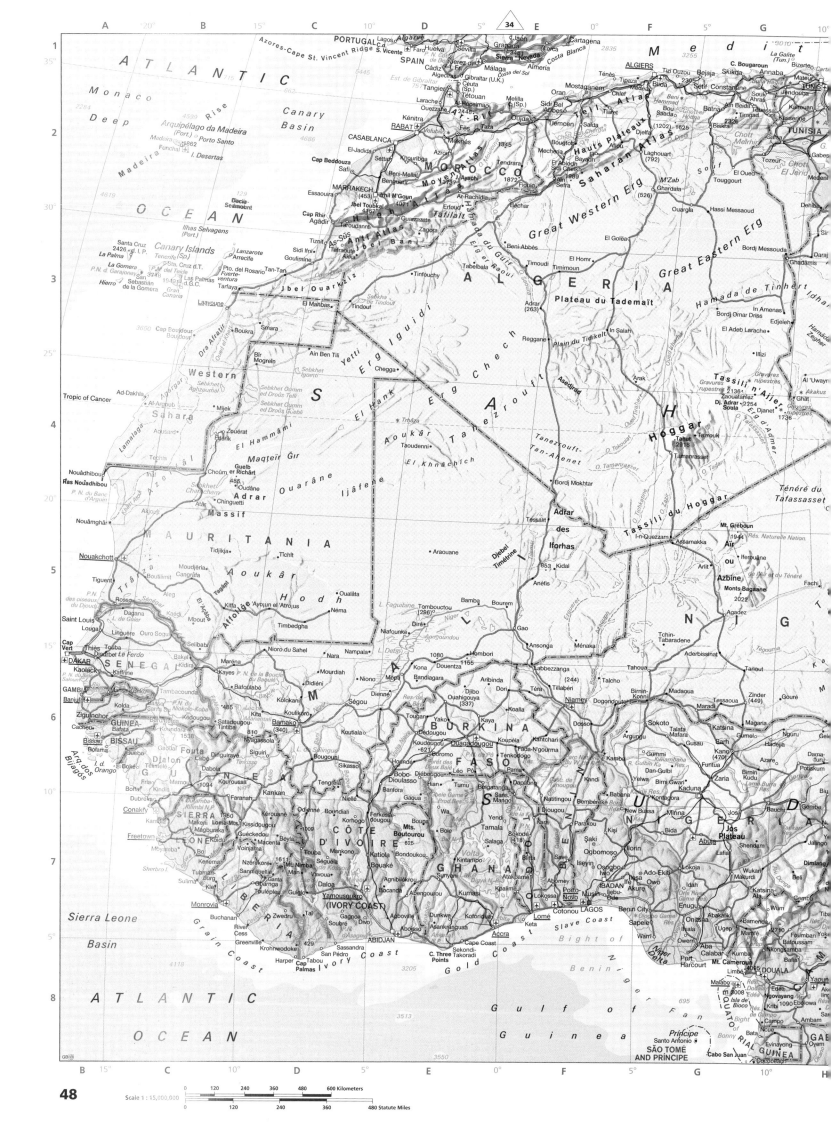

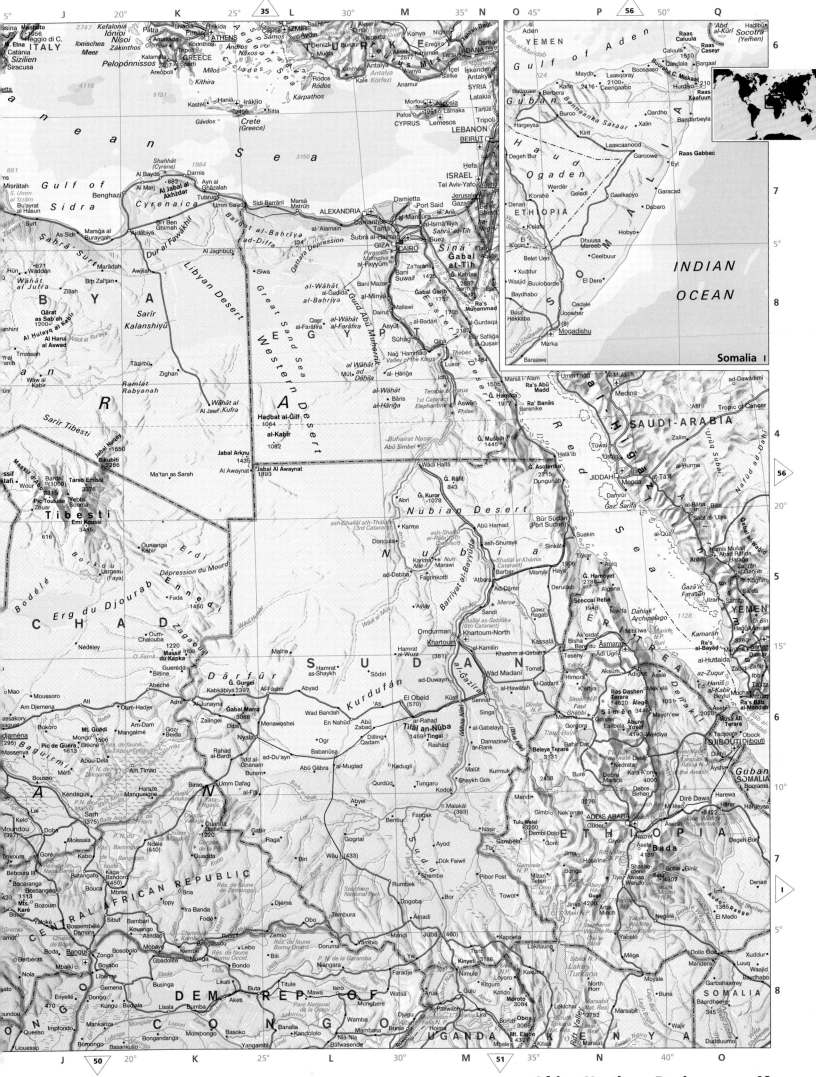

Africa: Northern Region 49

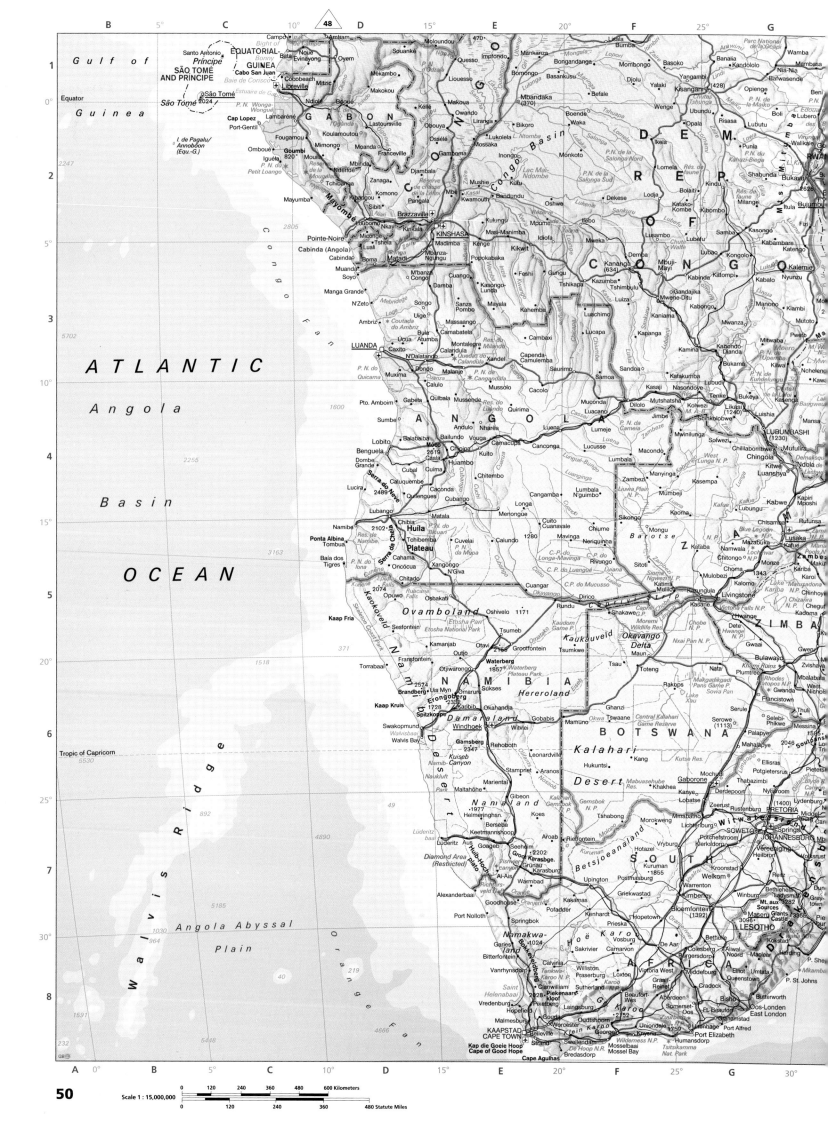

Africa: Central and Southern Region

Scale 1 : 15,000,000

0   120   240   360   480   600 Kilometers

0   120   240   360   480 Statute Miles

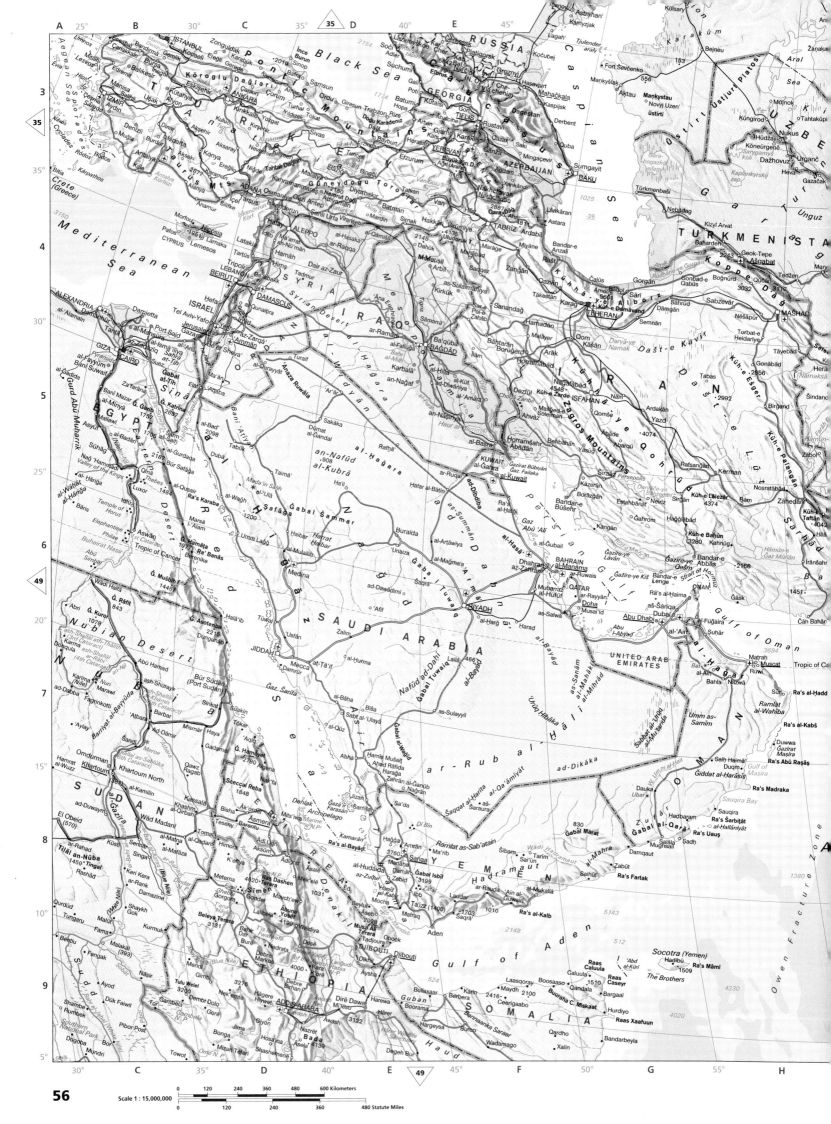

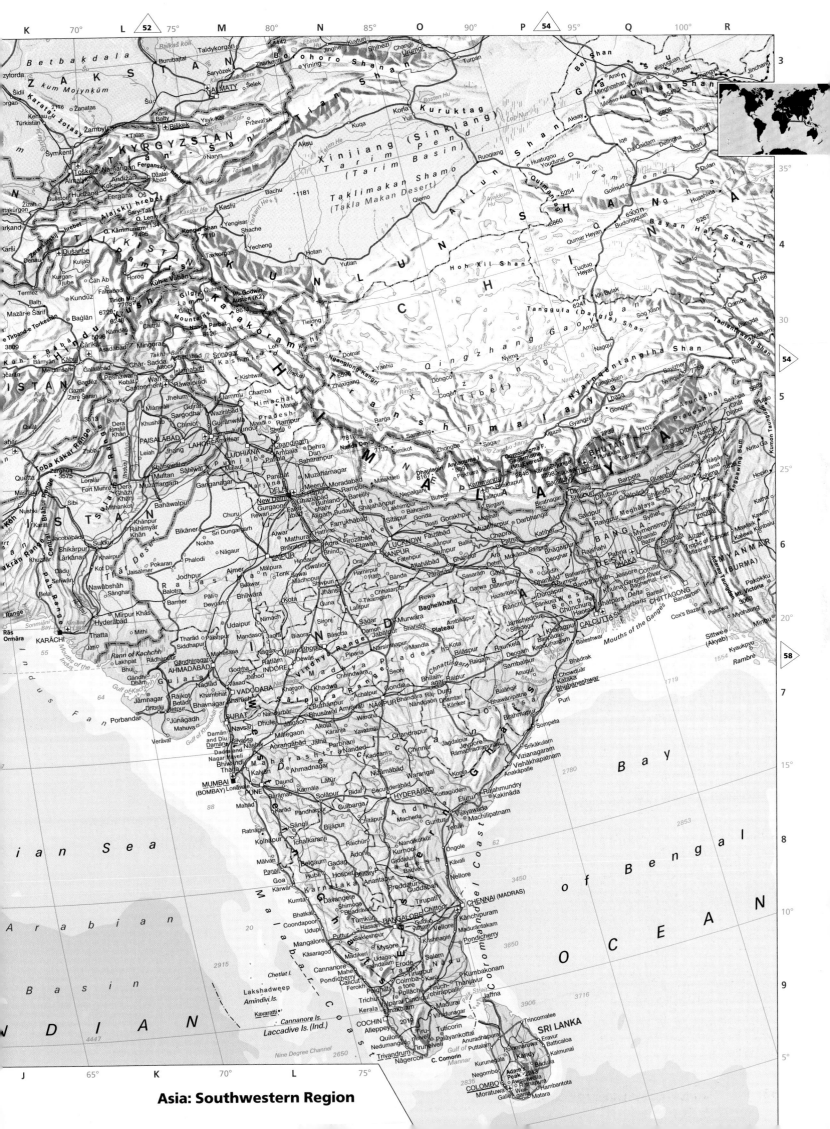

Asia: Southwestern Region

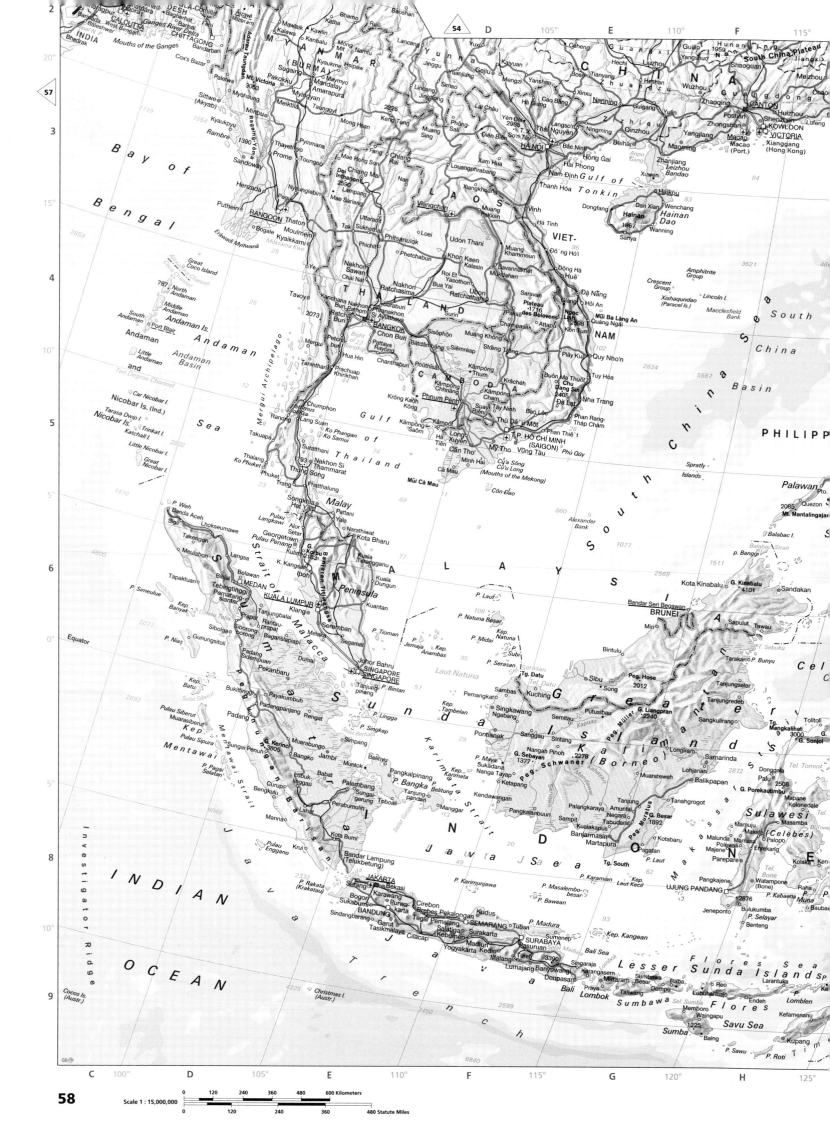

Selected References

Abbreviations

A

A.	Alm (Ger.) mountain meadow
Abb.	Abbaye (Fr.) abbey
Abor.	(Engl.) aboriginal
Aç.	Açude (Port.) small reservoir
Ad.	Adası (Turk.) island
A.F.B.	(Engl.) Air Force Base
Ag.	Agios (Gr.) saint
Á.I.	Área Indígena (Port.) Indian reservation
Ald.	Aldeia (Port.) village, hamlet
Arch.	(Engl.) archipelago
Arch.	Archipiélago (Span.) archipelago
Arh.	Arhipelag (Rus.) archipelago
Arq.	Arquipélago (Port.) archipelago
Arr.	Arroyo (Span.) brook
Art.Ra.	(Engl.) artillery range
Aut.	(Engl.) autonomous
Aut.Dist.	(Engl.) autonomous district
Aut.Reg.	(Engl.) autonomous region

B

B.	Baie (Fr.) bay
B.	Biológica, -o (Span.) biological
Ba.	Bahía (Span.) bay
Bal.	Balka (Rus.) gorge
Ban.	Banjaran (Mal.) mountains
Bel.	Belo, -yj, -aja, -oe (Rus.) white
Bk.	Bukit (Mal.) mountain, hill
Bol.	Boloto (Rus.) swamp
Bol.	Bolšoj, -aja, -oe (Rus.) big
Bot.	(Engl.) botanical
B.P.	(Engl.) battlefield park
Brj.	Baraj (Turk.) dam
Buch.	Buchta (Ukr.) bay
Buh.	Buhta (Rus.) bay

C

C.	Cap (Fr.) cape, point
C.	Cabo (Port., Span.) cape, point
Cab.	Cabeça (Port.) heights, summit
Cach.	Cachoeira (Port.) rapids
Cal.	Caleta (Span.) bay
Can.	Canalul (Rom.) canal
Can.	Canal (Span.) canal
Cast.	Castello (Ital.) castle, palace
Cd.	Ciudad (Span.) city
Cga.	Ciénaga (Span.) swamp, moor
Ch.	Chenal (Fr.) canal
Chr.	Chrebet (Ukr.) mountains
Co.	Cerro (Span.) mountain, hill
Col.	Colonia (Span.) colony
Conv.	Convento (Span.) monastery
Cord.	Cordillera (Span.) mountain chain
Corr.	Corredeira (Port.) rapids
Cpo.	Campo (Port.) field
Cr.	(Engl.) creek
Cs.	Cerros (Span.) mountain, hill

D

D.	Dake (Jap.) mountain
Dağl.	Dağlar (Turk.) mountains
Dist.	(Engl.) district
Df.	Dorf (Ger.) village
Dl.	Deal (Rom.) heights, hill

E

Ea.	Estancia (Span.) ranch
Ej.	Ejido (Span.) common
Emb.	Embalse (Span.) reservoir
Ens.	Enseada (Port.) small bay
Erm.	Ermita (Span.) hermitage
Ero.	Estero (Span.) estuary
Esp.	España (Span.) Spain
Est.	Estación (Span.) railroad terminal
Estr.	Estrecho (Span.) straight, sound
Ez.	Ezero (Bulg.) lake

F

Faz.	Fazenda (Port.) ranch
Fk.	(Engl.) fork
Fn.	Fortín (Span.) fort
Fr.	(Engl.) France
Fs.	(Engl.) falls, waterfall
Ft.	(Engl.) fort

G

Ğ.	Ğabal (Arab.) mountain
G.	Gawa (Jap.) lagoon
G.	Gitul (Rom.) pass

G

G.	Golfo (Span.) bay, gulf
G.	Gora (Rus.) mountain
Gde.	Grande (Span.) big
Gds.	Grandes (Span.) big
Glac.	Glacier (Fr.) glacier
Gos.	Gosudarstvennyj, -aja (Rus.) national
Gr.	(Engl.) Greece
Gr.Br.	(Engl.) Great Britain
Grd.	Grand (Fr.) big
Grl.	General (Span.) general

H

H.	Hora (Ukr.) mountain
H.	Hütte (Ger.) mountain hut
Harb.	(Engl.) harbor
Hist.	(Engl.) historic
Hm.	Heim (Ger.) home
Hr.	Hrebet (Rus.) mountains
Hte.	Haute (Fr.) high
Hwy.	(Engl.) highway

I

I.	(Engl.) island
Î.	Île (Fr.) island
I.	Ilha (Port.) island
I.	Isla (Span.) island
Igl.	Iglesia (Span.) church
In.	Insulă (Rom.) island
Ind.	(Engl.) Indian
Ind.Res.	(Engl.) Indian reservation
Int.	(Engl.) international
Is.	(Engl.) islands
Is.	Islas (Span.) islands

J

Jaz.	Jazovir (Bulg.) reservoir
Jct.	(Engl.) junction
Jez.	Jezero (Slovenian) lake
Juž.	Južnyj, -aja (Rus.) southern

K

Kan.	Kanal (Ger.) canal
Kep.	Kepulauan (Indon.) archipelago
Kg.	Kampong (Indon.) village
K-l.	Köli (Kazakh.) lake
K-l.	Kūli (Uzbek.) lake
Kör.	Körfez (Turk.) gulf, bay
Kp.	Kólpos (Gr.) gulf, bay
Kr.	Krasno, -yj, -aja, -oe (Rus.) red

L

L.	(Engl.) lake
L.	Lac (Fr.) lake
L.	Lacul (Rom.) lake
L.	Lago (Span.) lake
Lag.	Laguna (Rus.) lagoon
Lev.	Levyj, -aja (Rus.) left
Lim.	Liman (Rus.) lagoon
Lim.	Limni (Gr.) lake
Lte.	(Engl.) little

M

M.	Munte (Rom.) mountain
M.	Mys (Rus.) cape, point
Mal.	(Engl.) Malaysia
Mal.	Malo, -yj, -aja, -oe (Rus.) little
Man.	Manastir (Bulg.) monastery
Man.	Manastır (Turk.) monastery
Măn.	Mănăstire (Rom.) monastery
Mem.	(Engl.) memorial
Mgne.	Montagne (Fr.) mountain, mountains
Mi.	Misaki (Jap.) cape, point
Mil.Res.	(Engl.) military reservation
Milli P.	Milli Park (Turk.) national park
Min.	(Engl.) mineral
Mñas.	Montañas (Span.) mountains
Moh.	Mohyla (Ukr.) tomb
Mon.	Monasterio (Span.) monastery
M.P.	(Engl.) military park
Mt.	(Engl.) mount
Mte.	Monte (Span.) mountain
Mti.	Monti (Ital.) mountains
Mtn.	(Engl.) mountain
Mtns.	(Engl.) mountains
Mtn.S.P.	(Engl.) mountain state park
Mts.	(Engl.) mountains
Mts.	Montes (Span.) mountains
Munț.	Munții (Rom.) mountains
Mus.	(Engl.) museum

N

N.	Nehir/ Nehri (Turk.) river, stream
N.	Nudo (Span.) peak
Nac.	Nacional (Span.) national
Nac.	Nacional'nyj, -aja, -oe (Rus.) national
Nat.	(Engl.) national
Nat.Mon.	(Engl.) national monument
Nat.P.	(Engl.) national park
Nat.Seas.	(Engl.) national seashore
Naz.	Nazionale (Ital.) national
N.B.P.	(Engl.) national battlefield park
N.B.S.	(Engl.) national battlefield site
Ned.	Nederland (Neth.) Netherlands
Nev.	Nevado (Span.) snow-capped mountain
N.H.P.	(Engl.) national historic park
N.H.S.	(Engl.) national historic site
Niž.	Niže, -nij, -naja, -neje (Rus.) lower
Nizm.	Nizmennost' (Rus.) lowlands
N.M.P.	(Engl.) national military park
Nördl.	Nördlich (Ger.) northern
Nov.	Novo, -yj, -aja, -oe (Rus.) new
N.P.	(Engl.) national park
N.R.A.	(Engl.) national recreation area
Nsa.Sra.	Nossa Senhora (Port.) Our Lady
Nth.	(Engl.) north
Ntra.Sra.	Nuestra Señora (Span.) Our Lady
Nva.	Nueva (Span.) new
Nvo.	Nuevo (Span.) new
N.W.R.	(Engl.) national wildlife refuge

O

O.	Ostrov (Rus.) island
Obl.	Oblast (Rus.) district
Ö.	Östra (Swed.) eastern
Öv.	Övre (Swed.) upper
Of.	Oficina (Span.) office
Ostr.	Ostrov (Rom.) island
O-va.	Ostrova (Rus.) islands
Oz.	Ozero (Rus.) lake

P

P.	(Engl.) port
P.	Passe (Fr.) pass
P.	Pico (Span.) peak
P.	Pulau (Indon.) island
Peg.	Pegunungan (Indon.) mountains
Pen.	(Engl.) peninsula
Pen.	Peninsula (Span.) peninsula
Per.	Pereval (Rus.) pass
Picc.	Piccolo (Ital.) little
P-iv.	Pivostriv (Ukr.) peninsula
Pk.	(Engl.) peak
Pkwy.	(Engl.) parkway
Pl.	Planina (Bulg.) mountain, mountains
P.N.	Parque Nacional (Span.) national park
Po.	Paso (Span.) pass
Por.	Porog (Rus.) rapids
P-ov.	Poluostrov (Rus.) peninsula
Pr.	Proliv (Rus.) strait, sound
Pr.	Prohod (Rus.) pass
Presq.	Presqu'île (Fr.) peninsula
Prov.	(Engl.) provincial
Prov.P.	(Engl.) provincial park
Pso.	Passo (Ital.) pass
Psto.	Puesto (Span.) outpost
Pt.	(Engl.) point
Pta.	Ponta (Port.) point
Pta.	Punta (Span.) point
Pte.	Pointe (Fr.) point
Pto.	Pôrto (Port.) port
Pto.	Puerto (Span.) port, pass
Pzo.	Pizzo (Ital.) point

Q

| Q.N.P. | (Jap.) quasi national park |

R

R.	Reka (Bulg.) river
R.	Reserva (Span.) reservation
R.	Rio (Port.) river
R.	Rio (Span.) river
Ra.	(Engl.) range
Rch.	Riachão (Port.) small river
Rch.	Riacho (Span.) small river
Rdl.	Raudal (Span.) stream
Rep.	(Engl.) republic
Repr.	Represa (Port.) dam
Rère.	Rivière (Fr.) river
Res.	(Engl.) reservoir

Res.

Res.	Reserva (Port.) reservation
Resp.	Respublika (Rus.) republic
Rib.	Ribeira (Port.) shore
Rib.	Ribeiro (Port.) small river
Rif.	Rifugio (Ital.) mountain hut
Riv.	(Engl.) river
Rom.	(Engl.) Romania
Rom.	Romano, -na (Span.) Roman
Rus.	(Engl.) Russia

S

S.	San (Jap.) mountain, mountains
S.	San (Span.) saint
S.	São (Port.) saint
Sa.	Saki (Jap.) cape
Sa.	Serra (Port.) mountains
Sal.	Salar (Span.) salt desert, salt lagoon
Sanm.	Sanmyaku (Jap.) mountains
Sd.	(Engl.) sound
Sel.	Selat (Indon.) road
Sev.	Sever, -nyj, -naja, -noe (Rus.) north
Sf.	Sfintu (Rom.) holy
Sh.	Shima (Jap.) island
S.H.P.	(Engl.) state historic park
S.H.S.	(Engl.) state historic site
S.M.	(Engl.) state monument
Sna.	Salina (Span.) salt flat
Snas.	Salinas (Span.) salt flats
Snia.	Serrania (Span.) ridge
S.P.	(Engl.) state park
Sr.	Sredne, -ij, -aja, -ee (Rus.) middle, central
Sra.	Sierra (Span.) mountains
St.	(Engl.) saint
St.	Saint (Fr., Span.) saint
Sta.	Santa (Span.) saint
Sta.	Staro, -ij, -aja, -oe (Rus.) old
Ste.	Sainte (Fr.) saint
Sth.	(Engl.) south
St.Mem.	(Engl.) state memorial
Sto.	Santo (Port.) saint
Str.	(Engl.) strait
Suh.	Suho, -aja (Rus.) dry
Sv.	Svet, -a, -o (Bulg.) saint
Sv.	Sveti (Croatian) saint

T

T.	Take (Jap.) peak, heights
Tel.	Teluk (Indon.) bay
Tg.	Tanjung (Indon.) cape
Tg.	Tōge (Jap.) pass
Tte.	Teniente (Span.) lieutenant

U

Ülk.	Ülken (Kazakh.) big
U.K.	(Engl.) United Kingdom
U.S.	(Engl.) United States

V

V.	Vallée (Fr.) valley
Va.	Villa (Span.) market town
Vda.	Vereda (Port.) path
Vdhr.	Vodohranilišče (Rus.) reservoir
Vdp.	Vodospad (Ukr.) waterfall
Vel.	Veliko, -aja, -oe (Rus.) big
Verh.	Verhnie, -yj, -ee (Rus.) upper
Vf.	Vîrf (Rom.) peak, heights
Vill.	(Engl.) village
Vis.	Visočina (Bulg.) heights
Vjal.	Vjalike (Belarus.) big
Vlk.	Vulkan (Ger.) volcano
Vn.	Volcán (Span.) volcano
Vod.	Vodopad (Rus.) waterfall
Vol.	Volcán (Span.) volcano
Vul.	Vulcano (Philip.) volcano

W

| W.A. | (Engl.) wilderness area |

Y

| Y. | Yama (Jap.) mountain, mountains |

Z

Zal.	Zaliv (Rus.) gulf, bay
Zap.	Zapadne, -ij, -aja, -noe (Rus.) west
Zapov.	Zapovednik (Rus.) protected area

ndex of Map Names

The index contains all names found in all three map scales (44.5 mill., 15 mill., only North and Central America in 5 mill.). Names which occur in more than one scale have, therefore, a separate page reference for each scale. The index's alphabetical listing corresponds to the sequence of letters in the Roman alphabet. Diacritical marks and special letters have been ignored in alphabetizing, e.g.:

A ....Á, À, Â, Ã, Ä, Ą, Á, Ã, Ä, Æ

The ligatures æ, œ are treated as ae and oe in the alphabetical listing.

Names that have been abbreviated on the maps are generally written in full in the index.

Generic concepts follow geographic names, e.g. Mexico, Gulf of; Ventoux, Mont. Exception: colors (e.g. Mont Blanc) and adjectives (e.g. Big, Little) come first. Official additions (e.g. Frankfurt am Main)

are included in the alphabetizing.

To a certain degree, the index also includes official alternate forms, linguistic variants, renamings and other secondary denominations. In such cases, the index refers to names as they appear on the maps, e.g. Bolzano = Bozen, Leningrad = Sankt-Peterburg.

Abbreviations in parentheses help distinguish between places bearing the same

names. Abbreviations as used on international motor-vehicle license plates have been given priority; where this is insufficient, administrative information like federal lands, provinces, regions, etc. are indicated.

Icons, which immediately follow the names, are used to indicate fundamental geographic concepts.

New York	○••	**USA**	(NY)	◇	22-23	M 5
①	②	③	④	⑤	⑥	⑦
Search concept	Icon	Nation	Administrative unit	Scale	Page	Search grid designation

② Icons

..................Sovereign nation	⌄ ....Depression	⊂ ....Glacier	✦ ....Airport
◻ ....Administrative unit	▲ ....Mountains	⊄ ....Dam	∴ ....Ruins, ruined city
★ ....Capital city (national capital)	▲ ....Mountain	≃ ....Undersea topography	
☆ ....State (provincial) capital	▲ ....Active volcano	⊥ ....National park	⋯ ....World cultural or natural heritage site
○ ....Place	≈ ....Ocean, part of an ocean	入 ....Reservation	•• ....Point of major interest
⊥ ....Landscape	o ....Lake, salt lake	xx ....Military installation	• ....Point of interest
⌒ ....Island	~ ....River, waterfall	‖ ....Transportation construction	

③ Sovereign States and Territories (Abbreviations in *italics*; abbreviation not official)

A ....Austria	ER ....Eritrea	LV ....Latvia	RT ....Togo
AFG ....Afghanistan	ES ....El Salvador	M ....Malta	RUS ....Russia
AG ....Antigua and Barbuda	EST ....Estonia	MA ....Morocco	RWA ....Rwanda
AL ....Albania	ET ....Egypt	*MAI* ....Marshall Islands	S ....Sweden
AND ....Andorra	ETH ....Ethiopia	MAL ....Malaysia	SCV ....Vatican City
ANG ....Angola	F ....France	*MAU* ....Mongolia	SD ....Swaziland
ANT ....Antarctica	FIN ....Finland	MC ....Monaco	SGP ....Singapore
AR ....Armenia	FJI ....Fiji	MD ....Moldova	SK ....Slovakia
ARU ....Aruba	FL ....Liechtenstein	MEX ....Mexico	SLO ....Slovenia
AUS ....Australia	FR ....Faroe Islands	MK ....Macedonia	SME ....Suriname
AUT ....Autonomous region	*FSM* ....Micronesia	MOC ....Mozambique	SN ....Senegal
AZ ....Azerbaijan	G ....Gabon	MS ....Mauritius	*SOL* ....Solomon Islands
B ....Belgium	GB ....United Kingdom	*MV* ....Maldives	SP ....Somalia
BD ....Bangladesh	GBA ....Alderney	MW ....Malawi	STP ....São Tomé and Príncipe
BDS ....Barbados	GBG ....Guernsey	MYA ....Myanmar (Burma)	*SUD* ....Sudan
BF ....Burkina Faso	GBJ ....Jersey	N ....Norway	SY ....Seychelles
BG ....Bulgaria	GBM ....Isle of Man	NA ....Netherlands Antilles	SYR ....Syria
BH ....Belize	GBZ ....Gibraltar	NAM ....Namibia	TCH ....Chad
BHT ....Bhutan	GCA ....Guatemala	*NAU* ....Nauru	THA ....Thailand
BIH ....Bosnia and Herzegovina	GE ....Georgia	*NEP* ....Nepal	TJ ....Tajikistan
BOL ....Bolivia	GH ....Ghana	NIC ....Nicaragua	TM ....Turkmenistan
BR ....Brazil	*GNB* ....Guinea-Bissau	NL ....Netherlands	TN ....Tunisia
BRN ....Bahrain	GQ ....Equatorial Guinea	NZ ....New Zealand	*TON* ....Tonga
BRU ....Brunei	GR ....Greece	OM ....Oman	TR ....Turkey
BS ....Bahamas	*GRØ* ....Greenland	P ....Portugal	TT ....Trinidad and Tobago
BU ....Burundi	GUY ....Guyana	PA ....Panama	*TUV* ....Tuvalu
BY ....Belarus	H ....Hungary	*PAL* ....Palau	UA ....Ukraine
C ....Cuba	HN ....Honduras	PE ....Peru	UAE ....United Arab Emirates
CAM ....Cameroon	HR ....Croatia	PK ....Pakistan	US ....Uzbekistan
CDN ....Canada	I ....Italy	PL ....Poland	USA ....United States
CH ....Switzerland	IL ....Israel	*PNG* ....Papua New Guinea	*VAN* ....Vanuatu
CHN ....China	IND ....India	PY ....Paraguay	VN ....Vietnam
CI ....Côte d'Ivoire (Ivory Coast)	IR ....Iran	Q ....Qatar	WAG ....Gambia
CL ....Sri Lanka	IRL ....Ireland	RA ....Argentina	WAL ....Sierra Leone
CO ....Colombia	IRQ ....Iraq	RB ....Botswana	WAN ....Nigeria
COM ....Comoros	IS ....Iceland	RC ....Taiwan	*WB* ....West Bank
CR ....Costa Rica	J ....Japan	RCA ....Central African Republic	WD ....Dominica
CV ....Cape Verde	JA ....Jamaica	RCB ....Congo	WG ....Grenada
CY ....Cyprus	JOR ....Jordan	RCH ....Chile	WL ....Saint Lucia
CZ ....Czech Republic	K ....Cambodia	*RG* ....Guinea	WS ....Western Samoa
D ....Germany	*KA* ....Kazakhstan	RH ....Haiti	*WSA* ....Western Sahara
DJI ....Djibouti	*KAN* ....Saint Kitts and Nevis	RI ....Indonesia	WV ....Saint Vincent and the Grenadines
DK ....Denmark	*KIB* ....Kiribati	RIM ....Mauritania	*Y* ....Yemen
DOM ....Dominican Republic	KS ....Kyrgyzstan	RL ....Lebanon	YU ....Yugoslavia
DVR ....North Korea	KSA ....Saudi Arabia	RM ....Madagascar	YV ....Venezuela
DY ....Benin	KWT ....Kuwait	RMM ....Mali	Z ....Zambia
DZ ....Algeria	L ....Luxembourg	RN ....Niger	ZA ....South Africa
E ....Spain	LAO ....Laos	RO ....Romania	ZRE ....Democratic Republic of Congo
EAK ....Kenya	*LAR* ....Libya	ROK ....South Korea	ZW ....Zimbabwe
EAT ....Tanzania	*LB* ....Liberia	ROU ....Uruguay	
EAU ....Uganda	LS ....Lesotho	RP ....Philippines	
EC ....Ecuador	LT ....Lithuania	RSM ....San Marino	

⑤ Scales

◇ ....scale 1:5.000.000	◆ ....Scale 1:15.000.000	◆ ....Scale 1:44.500.000

1st Cataract ~ **ET** 48-49 M 4
3rd Cataract = ash-Shallāl ath-Thálith ~
SUD 48-49 M 5
4th Cataract = ash-Shallāl ar-Rābi' ~ **SUD**
48-49 M 5
5th Cataract = ash-Shallāl al-Khámis ~
SUD 48-49 M 5
6th Cataract = Shallai as-Sablúkah ~ **SUD**
48-49 M 5
15 de Septembre, Embalse < **ES**
28-29 K 5

A

Aachen o ··· **D** 40-41 J 3
Aar, De o **ZA** 50-51 F 8
Aba o **WAN** 48-49 G 7
Abaco Islands ⌒ **BS** 16-17 L 5
Ábádán o **IR** 56-57 F 4
Ábáde o **IR** 56-57 G 4
Abaj Takalik · **GCA** 28-29 J 4
Abakaliki o **WAN** 48-49 G 7
Abakan ☆ **RUS** 52-53 P 7
Abakan ~ **RUS** 52-53 P 7
Abancay ☆ **PE** 30-31 E 7
Abapo o **BOL** 30-31 G 8
Abarqú o **IR** 56-57 G 4
Ábaya Hâyk' o **ETH** 48-49 N 7
Abay Wenz ~ **ETH** 48-49 N 7
Abaza o **RUS** 52-53 P 7
Abbeville o **F** 38-39 H 6
34-35 M 5
Abbeville o **USA** (AL) 24-25 F 4
Abbeville o **USA** (GA) 24-25 F 4
Abbeville o **USA** (LA) 26-27 G 4
Abbeville o **USA** (SC) 24-25 G 2
Abbotsford o **USA** 22-23 C 3
Abbottábád o **PK** 56-57 L 4
'Abd al-Kúri ⌒ **Y** 56-57 G 8
Abéché o **TCH** 48-49 J 6
Abemama Atoll ⌒ **KIB** 12 J 2
Abengourou ☆ **CI** 48-49 E 7
Aberdare National Park ⊥ **EAK**
50-51 J 2
Aberdeen o **GB** 38-39 F 3
34-35 L 4
Aberdeen o **USA** (MD) 22-23 K 6
Aberdeen o **USA** (MS) 24-25 D 3
Aberdeen o **USA** (SD) 14-15 H 3
Aberdeen o **USA** (WA) 20-21 C 2
14-15 M 7
Aberdeen o **ZA** 50-51 F 8
Aberdeen Lake o **CDN** 14-15 H 4
Abernathy o **USA** 26-27 G 3
Abhā o **KSA** 56-57 E 7
Abidjan ☆ **CI** 48-49 E 7
Abilene o **USA** 26-27 H 3
16-17 G 4
Abingdon o **USA** 22-23 H 7
Abiquiu o **USA** 26-27 G 1
Abitibi, Lake o **CDN** 18-19 E 4
14-15 V 7
Abo, Massif d' ⌐ **TCH** 48-49 J 4
Åbo = Turku ☆ **FIN** 34-35 Q 3
Aboisso o **CI** 48-49 E 7
Abomey ☆ **DY** 48-49 F 7
Abong Mbang o **CAM** 48-49 H 8
Abo Pass ⌐ **USA** 26-27 D 2
Abou-Deïa o **TCH** 48-49 J 6
Abou-Telfân, Réserve de faune de l' ⊥
TCH 48-49 J 6
Abraham's Bay o **BS** 16-17 M 6
Abrams o **USA** 22-23 D 3
Abra Pampa o **RA** 32-33 J 3
Abri o **SUD** 48-49 M 4
Abrolhos Bank ⌣ **BR** 30-31 M 8
Absaroka-Beartooth Wilderness ⊥ **USA**
20-21 J 3
Absaroka Range ⌐ **USA** 20-21 J 3
14-15 O 7
Abú 'Ali, Ğazirat ⌒ **KSA** 56-57 G 5
Abu Dhabi = Abú Zabi ★ **UAE**
56-57 G 6
Abú Hamad o **SUD** 48-49 M 5
Abuja ★ **WAN** 48-49 G 7
Abú l-Abyad ⌒ **UAE** 56-57 G 6
Abulug o **RP** 58-59 H 3
Abú Madd, Ra's ⌒ **KSA** 56-57 D 6
Abuná o **BR** 30-31 F 6
Abuña, Rio ~ **BOL** 30-31 F 7
Ábune Yoséf ▲ **ETH** 48-49 N 6
Abú Rasás, Ra's ⌒ **OM** 56-57 H 6
Abú Simbel ·· **ET** 48-49 M 4
Abú Zabi o **SUD** 48-49 L 6
'Açâba, El ⌐ **RIM** 48-49 C 5
Acadia National Park ⊥ **USA**
22-23 O 3 14-15 X 8
Acadian Historic Village · **CDN**
18-19 M 5
Acadie ⌐ **CDN** 18-19 L 4
14-15 X 7
Acajutla o **ES** 28-29 K 5
Acala o **MEX** 28-29 H 4
Acámbaro o **MEX** 28-29 D 1
Acanceh o **MEX** 28-29 K 1
Acapetagua o **MEX** 28-29 H 4
Acaponeta o **MEX** 16-17 E 6
Acapulco de Juárez o **MEX**
28-29 E 3 16-17 J 7
Acará o **BR** 30-31 K 5
Acara ou Acari, Serra ▲ **BR**
30-31 H 4
Acaraú o **BR** 30-31 L 5
Acarigua o **YV** 30-31 F 3
Acatic o **MEX** 28-29 C 2
Acatlán o **MEX** 28-29 F 2
Acatlán de Osorio o **MEX** 28-29 F 3
Acayucan o **MEX** 28-29 G 3
Accomac o **USA** 22-23 K 6
Accra ★·· **GH** 48-49 E 7
Achacachi o **BOL** 30-31 F 8

Achaguas o **YV** 30-31 F 3
Achalpur o **IND** 56-57 M 6
Acinsk = Acínsk ☆ **RUS** 52-53 P 6
Ačinsk o **RUS** 52-53 P 6
Ackerman o **USA** 24-25 D 3
Acklins Island ⌒ **BS** 16-17 M 6
Acoma Indian Reservation ⋊ **USA**
26-27 D 2
Aconcagua, Cerro ▲ **RA** 32-33 H 4
Açores, Arquipélago dos ⌒ **P**
34-35 S 8
Acre o **BR** 30-31 E 6
Acre, Rio ~ **BR** 30-31 F 6
Actinolite o **CDN** 18-19 F 6
Acton State Historic Site ·· **USA**
26-27 J 3
Actopan o **MEX** 28-29 E 1
Acula o **MEX** 28-29 G 2
Acultzingo o **MEX** 28-29 F 2
Acuña, Ciudad o **MEX** 16-17 F 5
Adak o **MEX** 26-27 J 2 16-17 G 2
Adrak o **USA** 14-15 A 6
Adak Island ⌒ **USA** 14-15 A 6
Adam, Mount ▲ **GB** 32-33 L 8
Adamaoua, Massif de l' ▲ **CAM**
48-49 H 7
Adams, Cape ▲ **ANT** 13 F 30
Adams, Mount ▲ **USA** 20-21 D 2
Adam's Peak ▲·· **CL** 56-57 N 9
'Adan ☆ **Y** 56-57 F 8
Adana ☆ **TR** 34-35 T 8
Adarau Taungdan ▲ **MYA** 54-55 G 7
Adare, Cape ▲ **ANT** 13 F 18
Ad-Dakhla o **WSA** 48-49 B 4
Ad-Dâr'al-Bayda o **MA** 48-49 D 2
ad-Dauha ★ **Q** 56-57 G 5
Addis Ababa = Ädis Äbeba ★·· **ETH**
48-49 N 7
Adel o **USA** 24-25 G 4
Adelaide ☆ **AUS** 60-61 H 6
Adelaide Island ⌒ **ANT** 13 G 30
Adelaide Island ⌒ **ANT** 13 F 30
Adelaide Peninsula ⌣ **CDN** 14-15 R 3
Adelaide River o **AUS** 60-61 G 2
Adélie, Terre ⌐ **ANT** 13 G 15
Aden = 'Adan o **Y** 56-57 F 8
Aderbissinat o **RN** 48-49 G 5
Adi, Pulau ⌒ **RI** 58-59 K 7
Adigrat o **ETH** 48-49 N 6
Adin o **USA** 20-21 D 5
Adirondack Mountains ▲ **USA**
22-23 L 3 14-15 W 8
Ádis Äbeba ★·· **ETH** 48-49 N 7
Adi Ugri o **ER** 48-49 N 6
Adjuntas, Presa de las < **MEX**
16-17 G 6
Adler o **RUS** 34-35 T 7
Admer, Erg d' ⌐ **DZ** 48-49 G 4
Admiralty Gulf ≈ **AUS** 60-61 F 2
Admiralty Inlet ≈ **CDN** 20-21 C 1
14-15 U 2
Admiralty Island ⌒ **USA** 14-15 K 5
Admiralty Islands ⌒ **PNG** 58-59 N 7
Admiralty Range ▲ **ANT** 13 F 17
Ado-Ekiti o **WAN** 48-49 G 7
Ádoni o **IND** 56-57 M 7
Adour ~ **F** 38-39 G 10
34-35 L 7
Adrar ☆ **DZ** 48-49 E 3
Adrar Massif ▲ **RIM** 48-49 C 4
Adrar Soula, Djebel ▲ **DZ** 48-49 G 4
Adré o **TCH** 48-49 K 6
Adrian o **USA** 22-23 F 5
Adriatico, Mare ≈ **I** 46-47 D 2
34-35 O 7
Adriatic Sea ≈ **I** 46-47 D 2
34-35 Q 8
Affollé ⌐ **RIM** 48-49 C 5
Afghanistan ■ **AFG** 56-57 J 4
'Afif o **KSA** 56-57 E 6
Aflou o **DZ** 48-49 F 2
Afmadow o **SP** 50-51 K 1
Afognak Island ⌒ **USA** 14-15 F 5
Afton o **USA** 26-27 K 1
Afyon ☆ **TR** 34-35 S 8
Agadem o **RN** 48-49 H 5
Agadez ☆ **RN** 48-49 G 5
Agádir o **MA** 48-49 D 2
Agalega Islands ⌒ **MS** 50-51 N 4
Agalta, Sierra de ▲ **HN** 28-29 M 4
Agana ☆ **USA** 58-59 M 4
Agargar ⌐ **WSA** 48-49 B 4
Agartala ☆ **IND** 56-57 O 6
Agboville o **CI** 48-49 E 7
Agdam o **AZ** 34-35 V 7
Agde o **F** 38-39 J 10 34-35 M 7
Agen o **F** 38-39 H 9 34-35 M 7
Aghzoumal, Sebkhet o **WSA**
48-49 C 4
Aginskoe ☆ **RUS** 52-53 T 7
Agnes Lake o **USA** 22-23 C 1
Agnew o **AUS** 60-61 E 5
Agnibilékrou o **CI** 48-49 E 7
Agra o **IND** 56-57 M 5
Ağri ☆ **TR** 34-35 U 8
Agrigento o **I** 46-47 D 6
34-35 O 8
Agrihan ⌒ **USA** 58-59 N 3
Agrinio o **GR** 46-47 H 5
Agua Azul o **HN** 28-29 L 4
Agua Azul Cascades · **MEX**
28-29 H 3
Agua Azul Falls ~ **BH** 28-29 K 3
Agua Caliente Indian Reservation ⋊ **USA**
20-21 F 9
Água Clara o **BR** 32-33 M 2
Agua Dulce o **MEX** 28-29 G 2
Aguaduce o **PA** 28-29 D 7
Agua Fria River ~ **USA** 20-21 H 8
Aguán, Rio ~ **HN** 28-29 L 4

Agua Nueva o **USA** 26-27 H 6
16-17 H 3
Aguanus, Rivière ~ **CDN** 18-19 N 3
Agua Prieta o **MEX** 16-17 E 4
Aguaro-Guariquito, Parque Nacional ⊥ **YV**
30-31 F 3
Aguascalientes ☆·· **MEX** 16-17 F 6
Aguateca ⋊· **GCA** 28-29 J 3
Aguila o **USA** 20-21 H 9
Aguilares o **ES** 28-29 K 5
Aguililla o **MEX** 28-29 C 2
Aguja, Punta ▲ **PE** 30-31 C 6
Agulhas, Cape **ZA** 50-51 E 8
Ahad Rāfida ~ **KSA** 56-57 E 7
Ahaliche o **GE** 34-35 U 7
Ahar o **IR** 56-57 F 3
Ahmadābád o **IND** 56-57 L 6
Ahmic Harbour o **CDN** 18-19 E 6
Ahoskie o **USA** 24-25 K 1
Ahtubinsk o **RUS** 34-35 V 6
Ahuacatlán o **MEX** 28-29 F 1
Ahuachapán ☆ **ES** 28-29 K 5
Ahualulco de Mercata o **MEX**
28-29 C 1
Ähväz ☆ **IR** 56-57 F 4
Ai-Ais o **NAM** 50-51 E 7
Aiea o **USA** 24-25 D 7
Aigle, l' ⌐ **F** 38-39 H 7
34-35 M 6
Aigles, Lac-des- o **CDN** 18-19 N 5
Aigues o **F** 38-39 K 9 34-35 N 6
Aiken o **USA** 24-25 H 3
Ailigandi o **PA** 28-29 E 7
Ailinglapalag ⌒ **MAI** 12 J 2
Ain ~ **F** 38-39 K 8 34-35 N 6
'Ain, al- o **UAE** 56-57 G 6
'Ain al-Gúwairi o **Y** 56-57 F 8
Ain Beida o **DZ** 48-49 G 1
Ain Ben Tili o **RIM** 48-49 D 3
Ain Sefra o **DZ** 48-49 E 2
Aiquebuena Provincial Park ⊥ **CDN**
18-19 E 4
Aire o **BOL** 30-31 F 8
Aire o **F** 38-39 K 7 34-35 N 6
Aire-sur-la-Lys o **F** 38-39 J 6
34-35 M 5
Air et du Ténéré, Réserve Naturelle
Nationale de l' ⊥ **RN** 48-49 H 4
Air Force Island ⌒ **CDN** 14-15 W 3
Airmadidi o **RI** 58-59 H 6
Aïr ou Azbine ▲ **RN** 48-49 G 5
Aisne, l' ~ **F** 38-39 K 7
34-35 N 6
Aix-en-Provence o **F** 38-39 K 10
34-35 N 7
Aix-les-Bains o **F** 38-39 K 9
34-35 N 6
Áizawl ☆ **IND** 56-57 O 6
Ajaccio ☆ **F** 44-45 M 4
Ajacuba o **MEX** 28-29 E 1
Ajakó o **KZ** 52-53 N 8
Ajalpan o **MEX** 28-29 F 2
Ajana o **AUS** 60-61 C 5
Ajax Peak ▲ **USA** 20-21 H 3
Ağdâbiyá o **LAR** 48-49 K 2
Ajgir ~ **LAR** 48-49 H 3
Ajmer o **IND** 56-57 L 5
Ajo o **USA** 20-21 H 9
Ajo Mountains ▲ **USA** 20-21 H 9
Ajon, ostrov ⌒ **RUS** 52-53 e 4
Akademii, zaliv ≈ **RUS** 52-53 Y 6
Akagera, Parc National de l' ⊥ **RWA**
50-51 H 2
Akakus ⌐ **LAR** 48-49 H 4
Akčatau o **KZ** 52-53 L 8
Ak-Dovurak o **RUS** 52-53 P 7
Akela o **USA** 26-27 D 3
Aketi o **ZRE** 48-49 K 8
Akhdar, Al Jabal al ▲ **LAR** 48-49 K 2
Akimiski Island ⌒ **CDN** 14-15 U 6
Akita ☆ **J** 54-55 R 4
Akjoujt o **RIM** 48-49 C 5
Akka o **MA** 48-49 D 3
Akmola ☆ **KZ** 52-53 L 8
Akonolinga o **CAM** 48-49 H 8
Ak'ordat o **ER** 48-49 N 5
Akpatok Island ⌒ **CDN** 14-15 X 4
Akron o **USA** 22-23 H 5
Aksaj ⌐ **KZ** 34-35 W 5
Aksaray o **TR** 34-35 S 8
Aksay o **CHN** 54-55 G 4
Akşehir o **TR** 34-35 S 8
Akseki o **TR** 56-57 C 3
Aksoran tauy ▲ **KZ** 52-53 M 7
Aksu o **CHN** 54-55 E 3
Aksu ☆ **KZ** 52-53 M 7
Aksum o ··· **ETH** 48-49 N 6
Aktobe ☆ **KZ** 34-35 W 5
Aktöbe ☆ **KZ** 34-35 X 5
Akumal o **MEX** 28-29 L 1
Akure o **WAN** 48-49 G 7
Akureyri ☆ **IS** 36-37 d 2
Akutan Island ⌒ **USA** 14-15 C 6
Akwatuk Bay ≈ **USA** 18-19 N 2
Alabama ⬚ **USA** 24-25 E 4
16-17 J 4
Alabama River ~ **USA** 24-25 E 4
Alabama and Coushatta Indian Reservation
⋊ **USA** 26-27 J 3
Alabaster o **USA** 24-25 E 3
Alaçam o **TR** 34-35 S 7
'Alamain, al- o **ET** 48-49 L 2
Alamo o **MEX** 28-29 F 1
Alamo o **USA** (NV) 20-21 G 7
Alamo ~ **USA** 20-21 G 7

Alamogordo o **USA** 26-27 E 3
16-17 E 4
Alamo Navajo Indian Reservation ⋊ **USA**
26-27 D 2
Alamos, Los o **USA** 26-27 D 2
Alamosa o **USA** 26-27 E 1
16-17 E 3
Åland ⌒ **FIN** 34-35 P 3
Alanntika Mountains ▲ **WAN**
48-49 H 7
Alanya o **TR** 34-35 S 8
Alaotra, Farihy o **RM** 50-51 L 5
Alapaha o **USA** 24-25 G 4
Alapaha River ~ **USA** 24-25 G 4
al-Arab, Bahr ~ **SUD** 48-49 L 6
al-Bahr al-Azraq = Blue Nile ~ **SUD**
48-49 M 6
Alban o **CDN** 18-19 D 5
Albanel o **CDN** 18-19 H 3
Albania ■ **AL** 46-47 G 4
34-35 P 7
Albany o **AUS** 60-61 D 7
Albany o **USA** (GA) 24-25 F 4
Albany o **USA** (OR) 20-21 C 3
Albany o **USA** (NY) 22-23 M 4
14-15 W 8
Albany River ~ **CDN** 14-15 U 6
Albatross Island ⌒ **MS** 50-51 N 5
Albatross Bay ≈ **AUS** 60-61 J 2
Al Bayda o **LAR** 48-49 K 2
Albemarle o **USA** 24-25 H 2
Albemarle Sound ≈ **USA** 24-25 K 1
16-17 L 3
Albert o **F** 38-39 J 6 34-35 M 5
Albert, Lake o **USA** 20-21 D 4
Albert, Lake = Lac Mobutu-Sese-Seko o
EAU 50-51 H 1
Allegany State Park ⊥ **USA** 22-23 J 4
Allegheny River Reservoir < **USA**
22-23 J 5
Allemands, Des o **USA** 26-27 M 5
Allendale o **USA** 24-25 H 3
Allende o **MEX** 16-17 F 5
Allentown o **USA** 22-23 L 5
16-17 L 2
Alleppey o **IND** 56-57 M 9
Alliance o **USA** 22-23 H 5
Allier ~ **F** 38-39 J 8 34-35 M 6
Allison o **USA** 26-27 C 2
Alma o **CDN** 18-19 J 4
Alma o **USA** (NB) 18-19 M 6
Alma o **USA** (QUE) 24-25 G 4
Alma o **USA** (MI) 22-23 F 4
Alma-Ata = Almaty ☆ **KZ** 52-53 M 9
Almalyk o **UZ** 56-57 K 2
Almanor, Lake o **USA** 20-21 D 5
al-Mansúra o **ET** 48-49 M 2
Al Marj o **LAR** 48-49 K 2
Al-Mausil ☆ **IRQ** 56-57 E 3
Almeirim, Serra do ▲ **BR** 30-31 J 5
Almenara o **BR** 30-31 L 8
Almería o **E** 44-45 F 6 34-35 L 8
al-Minyá o **ET** 48-49 M 3
Almirante Brown o **ANT** 13 G 30
Almirante o **PA** 28-29 C 7
Almonte o **CDN** 18-19 F 6
al-Muñá o **Y** 56-57 E 8
Al-Mukallá o ··· **Y** 56-57 F 8
Alor, Pulau ⌒ **RI** 58-59 H 8
Alor Setar ☆ **MAL** 58-59 D 5
Alotau o **PNG** 58-59 O 9
Alpena o **USA** 22-23 G 3
14-15 U 7
Alpha o **USA** 22-23 C 5
Alpha Cordillera ⌣ **13** A 30
Alphonse Group ⌒ **SY** 50-51 M 3
Alpine o **USA** (AZ) 26-27 C 3
Alpine o **USA** (TX) 26-27 F 4
16-17 F 4
Alpine Lakes Wilderness ⊥ **USA**
20-21 D 2
Alps ▲ **40**-41 J 6 34-35 N 7
al-Qáhira ★ **ET** 48-49 M 2
al-Qusair o **ET** 48-49 M 3
Alsace ⌐ **F** 38-39 L 8 34-35 N 6
Alsace* ⌐ **F** 38-39 L 8 34-35 N 6
Alta o **N** 36-37 L 2
Alta Floresta o **BR** 30-31 H 6
Altaj o **KZ** 52-53 O 8
Altaj ☆ **MAU** 54-55 G 2
Altajn Caadah Gov'ⁱ ⌐ **MAU**
54-55 G 3
Altamaha River ~ **USA** 24-25 H 3
16-17 K 4
Altamira o **BR** 30-31 J 5
Altamonte Springs o **USA** 24-25 G 5
Altar, Desierto de ⌐ **MEX** 16-17 D 4
Altar de Sacrificios ⋊· **GCA**
28-29 J 3
Altavista o **USA** 22-23 J 7
Altheimer o **USA** 24-25 C 2
Altai Tikuna Evare, Áreas Indígena ⋊ **BR**
30-31 F 5
Altiplano ⌐ **PE** 30-31 F 8
Alto Araguaia o **BR** 30-31 J 8
Alto Garças o **BR** 30-31 J 8
Alto Longo o **BR** 30-31 L 5
Alto Molócuè o **MOC** 50-51 J 5

Alton o **USA** (IL) 22-23 C 6
16-17 H 3
Altona o **USA** (MO) 26-27 M 1
Altoona o **USA** 22-23 J 5
16-17 L 2
Alto Parnaiba o **BR** 30-31 K 6
Alto Purus, Rio ~ **PE** 30-31 E 7
Alto Quiel o **PA** 28-29 C 7
Alto Turiaçu, Área Indígena ⋊ **BR**
30-31 K 5
Altun Ha ·· **BH** 28-29 K 3
Altun Shan ▲ **CHN** 54-55 F 4
Aluturas o **USA** 20-21 D 5
14-15 M 8
Altus o **USA** 26-27 H 2
16-17 G 4
Al-Ubayyid = El Obeid ☆ **SUD**
48-49 M 6
al-Uqsur o ··· **ET** 48-49 M 3
Alva o **USA** 26-27 H 1
Alvarado o **MEX** 28-29 G 2
Alvarães o **BR** 30-31 G 5
Alvin o **USA** 26-27 K 5
Alvinston o **CDN** 18-19 D 6
Alvord Lake o **USA** 20-21 F 4
Alvord Valley ⌣ **USA** 20-21 E 4
Alwar o **IND** 56-57 M 5
Alxa Gaoyuan ⌐ **CHN** 54-55 J 3
Ama o **USA** 26-27 H 6
Amacuzac, Río ~ **MEX** 28-29 E 2
Amadeus, Lake o **AUS** 60-61 G 4
Amadi o **SUD** 48-49 M 7
Amadjuak Lake o **CDN** 14-15 W 4
Amahai o **RI** 58-59 J 7
Amajac, Río ~ **MEX** 28-29 E 1
Amalāda o **GR** 46-47 H 6
34-35 P 8
Amamapare o **RI** 58-59 L 7
Amambay, Sierra de ▲ **PY** 32-33 L 2
Amami-shotó ⌒ **J** 54-55 O 6
Amaná, Lago o **BR** 30-31 G 5
Amanab o **PNG** 58-59 M 7
Amankaragaj o **KZ** 52-53 J 7
Amantenango del Valle o **MEX**
28-29 H 3
Amapá o **BR** (APA) 30-31 J 4
Amapá o **BR** 30-31 J 4
'Amára, al- o **IRQ** 56-57 F 4
Amarante o **BR** 30-31 L 6
Amarapura o **MYA** 54-55 H 7
Amargosa Range ▲ **USA** 20-21 F 7
Amargosa River ~ **USA** 20-21 F 7
Amarillo o **USA** 26-27 G 2
16-17 F 3
Amasya o **TR** 34-35 T 7
Amata o **AUS** 60-61 G 5
Amates, Los o **GCA** 28-29 K 4
Amatique, Bahía de ≈ **GCA** 28-29 K 4
Amatitlán o **GCA** 28-29 J 4
Amatitlán de Cañas o **MEX** 28-29 B 1
Amazonas ⬚ **BR** 30-31 G 5
Amazon Canyon ⌣ **30**-31 K 4
Amazon Fan ⌣ **30**-31 K 3
Amazônia, Parque Nacional de ⊥ **BR**
30-31 H 5
Amazon Shelf ⌣ **30**-31 K 4
Ambala o **IND** 56-57 M 4
Ambam o **CAM** 48-49 H 8
Ambanja o **RM** 50-51 L 4
Ambargasta, Salinas de o **RA**
32-33 K 3
Ambato ☆ **EC** 30-31 D 5
Ambatolampy o **RM** 50-51 L 5
Ambatondrazaka o **RM** 50-51 L 5
Ambatosoratra o **RM** 50-51 L 5
Ambatry o **RM** 50-51 K 6
Ambazac o **F** 38-39 H 9
34-35 M 6
Ambelau, Pulau ⌒ **RI** 58-59 J 7
Ambergris Cay ⌒ **BH** 28-29 K 2
Ambérieu-en-Bugey o **F** 38-39 K 9
34-35 N 6
Amberley o **CDN** 18-19 D 6
Ambert o **F** 38-39 J 9
34-35 M 6
Ambikápur o **IND** 56-57 N 6
Ambilobe o **RM** 50-51 L 4
Ambohitra ▲ **RM** 50-51 L 4
Amboise o **F** 38-39 H 8
34-35 M 6
Ambon o **RI** 58-59 J 7
Ambondromamy o **RM** 50-51 L 5
Ambositra o **RM** 50-51 L 6
Ambovombe o **RM** 50-51 L 7
Amboy o **USA** (CA) 20-21 G 8
Amboy o **USA** (IL) 22-23 D 5
Ambrim = Île Ambrym ⌒ **VAN**
60-61 O 3
Ambriz o **ANG** 50-51 D 3
Ambriz, Coutada do ⊥ **ANG**
50-51 D 3
Ambrym, Île = Ambrim ⌒ **VAN**
60-61 O 3
Am-Dam o **TCH** 48-49 K 6
Amderma o **RUS** 52-53 J 4
Amdo o **CHN** 54-55 G 5
Amealco o **MEX** 28-29 B 1
Ameca o **MEX** 28-29 B 1
Ameca, Río ~ **MEX** 28-29 B 1
Amenia o **USA** 22-23 M 5
American Falls o **USA** 20-21 H 4
American Falls Reservoir < **USA**
20-21 H 4
American Fork o **USA** 20-21 J 5
American Highland ⌐ **ANT** 13 F 8
Americus o **USA** 24-25 F 3
Amery Ice Shelf ⌐ **ANT** 13 F 8
Ames o **USA** 22-23 J 7
Amesbury o **USA** 22-23 N 4
Amga o **RUS** (SAH) 52-53 X 5
Amga ~ **RUS** 52-53 Y 5
Amguèma o **RUS** 52-53 h 4
Amgun' ~ **RUS** 52-53 Y 7
Amherst o **CDN** 18-19 M 6
Amherst o **USA** (MA) 22-23 M 4
Amherst o **USA** (VA) 22-23 J 7
Amherstburg o **CDN** 18-19 C 7
Amherst Island ⌒ **CDN** 18-19 F 6

Amiens o ··· **F** 38-39 J 7
34-35 M 6
Amindivi Islands ⌒ **IND** 56-57 L 8
Amirantes Group ⌒ **SY** 50-51 M 3
Amistad o **USA** 26-27 G 2
Amistad, Parque Internacional La ⊥ ··· **CR**
28-29 C 7 16-17 K 9
Amite o **USA** 26-27 L 4
'Ammán ★ ··· **JOR** 56-57 D 4
Ammassalik o **GR0** 14-15 d 3
Ámoi o ··· **RI** 58-59 G 8
Amoltepec o **MEX** 28-29 F 3
Amores, Los o **RA** 32-33 K 3
Amory o **USA** 24-25 D 3
Amos o **CDN** 18-19 G 4
Amozoc o **MEX** 28-29 F 2
Ampanihy o **RM** 50-51 K 6
Ampasimanoloitra o **RM** 50-51 L 5
Ampato, Nevado ▲ **PE** 30-31 E 8
Amphithéâtre (El Jem) ··· **TN**
48-49 H 1
Amphitrite Group = Xuande Qundao ⌒
CHN 58-59 F 3
Amqui o **CDN** 18-19 L 4
'Amrán ☆ **Y** 56-57 E 7
Amrávati o **IND** 56-57 M 6
Amritsar o **IND** 56-57 L 4
Amsterdam ★ ··· **NL** 40-41 H 2
34-35 M 5
Amsterdam o **USA** 22-23 L 4
Am Timan ☆ **TCH** 48-49 K 6
Amudarė o **UZ** 56-57 J 2
Amund Ringnes Island ⌒ **CDN**
14-15 R 1
Amundsen, Mount ▲ **ANT** 13 G 11
Amundsen o **RI** 13 G 5
Amundsen Glacier ⌐ **ANT** 13 E 0
Amundsen Gulf ≈ 14-15 M 2
Amundsen havet ≈ **13** G 26
Amundsen-Scott o **ANT** 13 E 0
Amuntai o **RI** 58-59 F 7
Amur ~ **RUS** 52-53 V 7
Amurang o **RI** 58-59 H 6
Amursk o **RUS** 52-53 Y 7
'Ána o **IRQ** 56-57 E 4
Anabar ~ **RUS** 52-53 S 3
Anabarskoe plato ▲ **RUS** 52-53 S 3
Anaco o **YV** 30-31 G 3
Anaconda o **USA** 20-21 H 2
Anaconda-Pintler Wilderness ⊥ **USA**
20-21 H 2
Anacortes o **USA** 20-21 C 1
Anadyr' ☆ **RUS** (CUK) 52-53 g 5
Anadyr' ~ **RUS** 52-53 f 5
Anadyr' o **RUS** 52-53 e 4
Anadyrskij liman ≈ **RUS** 52-53 g 5
Anadyrskiy zaliv ≈ **RUS** 52-53 g 5
Anadyrskoe ploskogor'e ~ **RUS**
52-53 e 4
Anadyrskoye Ploskogor'e = Anadyrskoe
ploskogor'e ▲ **RUS** 52-53 e 4
Anaheim o **USA** 20-21 F 9
Anajás o **BR** 30-31 K 5
Anakápalle o **IND** 56-57 N 7
Anamã o **BR** 30-31 G 5
Anambas, Kepulauan ⌒ **RI** 58-59 E 6
Anamosa o **USA** 22-23 C 4
Anamur ☆ **TR** 34-35 S 8
Anantapur o **IND** 56-57 M 8
Anápolis o **BR** 32-33 N 2
Anastácio o **BR** 32-33 L 2
Anatahan ⌒ **USA** 58-59 N 3
Añatuya o **RA** 32-33 K 3
'Anaza Ruwála ▲ **KSA** 56-57 D 4
Ancenis o **F** 38-39 G 8
34-35 L 6
Anchorage o · **USA** 14-15 G 4
Ancona o · **I** 46-47 D 3
34-35 O 7
Ancud o **RCH** 32-33 H 6
Ancud, Golfo de ≈ **RCH** 32-33 H 6
Anda o **CHN** 54-55 O 2
Andalgala o **RA** 32-33 J 3
Andalusia o **USA** (AL) 24-25 E 4
16-17 J 4
Andalusia o **USA** (IL) 22-23 C 5
Andaman and Nicobar Islands ⬚ **IND**
58-59 B 4
Andaman Basin ≈ **58**-59 C 4
Andaman Islands ⌒ **IND** 58-59 B 3
Andaman Sea ≈ **58**-59 C 4
Andamooka Opal Fields o **AUS**
60-61 H 6
Andelys, les o **F** 38-39 H 7
34-35 M 6
Anderson o **USA** (IN) 22-23 F 5
Anderson o **USA** (MO) 26-27 K 1
Anderson o **USA** (SC) 24-25 G 2
Anderson River ~ **CDN** 14-15 L 3
Andersonville National Historic Site ··· **USA**
24-25 F 3
Andes ▲ **30**-31 D 4
Andhøy o **AFG** 56-57 K 3
Andhra Pradesh ⬚ **IND** 56-57 M 7
Andira o **BR** 32-33 M 3
Andirá-Marau, Área Indígena ⋊ **BR**
30-31 H 5
Andižan o **UZ** 56-57 L 2
Andoany o **RM** 50-51 L 4
Andong o **ROK** 54-55 O 4
Andorra ■ **AND** 44-45 H 3
34-35 M 7
Andover o **USA** 22-23 F 5
Andradina o **BR** 32-33 M 2
Andriba o **RM** 50-51 L 5
Androka o **RM** 50-51 K 7
Androscoggin River ~ **USA**
22-23 N 3
Andros Island ⌒ **BS** 16-17 L 6
Andulo o **ANG** 50-51 E 4
Anefis o **RMM** 48-49 F 5
Anegada, Punta ▲ **PA** 28-29 D 8
Anegada, Punta o **I** 10 O 7
Añelo o **RA** 32-33 J 5
Aneto, Pico de ▲ **E** 44-45 H 3
34-35 M 7

Angangueo ○ **MEX** ◇ 28-29 D 2
Angara ∼ **RUS** ◆ 52-53 Q 6
Angarsk ○ **RUS** ◆ 52-53 R 7
Angarskij krjaž ∸ **RUS** ◆ 52-53 R 6
Angaur Island ∩ **USA** ◆ 58-59 K 5
Ángel de la Guarda, Isla ∩ **MEX** ◆ 16-17 D 5
Angeles ○ **RP** ◆ 58-59 H 3
Angeles, Los ○ **RCH** ◆ 32-33 H 5
Angelina River ∼ **USA** ◇ 26-27 K 4
Angels Camp ○ **USA** ◇ 20-21 D 6
Ångermanälven ∼ **S** ◇ 36-37 H 5 ◆ 34-35 P 3
Angers ○ **F** ◇ 38-39 G 8 ◆ 34-35 L 6
Angijak Island ∩ **CDN** ◆ 14-15 Y 3
Angleton ○ **USA** ◇ 26-27 K 5
Angoche ○ **MOC** ◆ 50-51 J 5
Angola ■ **ANG** ◆ 50-51 D 4
Angola ○ **USA** ◇ 22-23 F 5
Angola Abyssal Plain ≃ ◆ 50-51 B 7
Angola Basin ≃ ◆ 50-51 B 5
Angoram ○ **PNG** ◆ 58-59 M 7
Angostura, Presa de la < **MEX** ◇ 28-29 H 3 ◆ 16-17 H 7
Angoulême ☆• **F** ◇ 38-39 H 9 ◆ 34-35 M 6
Angpawing Bum ▲ **MYA** ◆ 54-55 H 6
Anguilla ∩ **GB** ◆ 16-17 O 7
Anguille, Cape ▲ **CDN** ◇ 18-19 P 5
Anguille Mountains ▲ **CDN** ◇ 18-19 P 5
Anhui □ **CHN** ◆ 54-55 M 5
Aniakchak National Monument and Preserve ⊥ **USA** ◆ 14-15 E 5
Anie, Pic d' ▲ **F** ◇ 38-39 G 10 ◆ 34-35 L 7
Animas ○ **USA** ◇ 26-27 C 4
Animas, Las ○ **HN** ◇ 28-29 L 4
Animas Peak ▲ **USA** ◇ 26-27 C 4
Animas River ∼ **USA** ◇ 26-27 D 1
Aniva, mys ▲ **RUS** ◆ 52-53 Z 8
Aniva, zaliv ≈ ◆ 52-53 Z 8
Aniwa Island = Île Nina ∩ **VAN** ◆ 60-61 O 3
Anjou ∸ **F** ◇ 38-39 G 8 ◆ 34-35 L 6
Anju ○ **KOR** ◆ 54-55 O 4
Anjuj, Boľšoj ∼ **RUS** ◆ 52-53 d 4
Anjuj, Malyj ∼ **RUS** ◆ 52-53 E 4
Anjujskij hrebet ▲ **RUS** ◆ 52-53 d 4
Ankang ○ **CHN** ◆ 54-55 K 5
Ankara ★• **TR** ◆ 34-35 S 8
Ankasa National Park ⊥ **GH** ◆ 48-49 E 7
Ankazoabo ○ **RM** ◆ 50-51 K 6
Ankazobe ○ **RM** ◆ 50-51 L 5
Ankobra ∼ **GH** ◆ 48-49 E 7
Ann, Cape ▲ **USA** ◇ 22-23 N 4
Anna ○ **USA** ◇ 22-23 D 7
Anna, Lake ⬭ **USA** ◇ 22-23 K 6
Annaba ○ **DZ** ◆ 48-49 G 1
Annapolis ○ **USA** (MO) ◇ 22-23 C 7
Annapolis ☆ **USA** (MD) ◇ 22-23 K 6 ◆ 16-17 L 3
Annapolis Royal ○ **CDN** ◇ 18-19 M 6
Ann Arbor ○ **USA** ◇ 22-23 G 4
Annaville ○ **CDN** ◇ 18-19 H 5
Annecy ○ **F** ◇ 38-39 L 9 ◆ 34-35 N 6
an-Nil ∼ **ET** ◆ 48-49 M 5
Anniston ○ **USA** ◇ 24-25 F 3 ◆ 16-17 J 4
Annonay ○ **F** ◇ 38-39 K 9 ◆ 34-35 N 6
Año Nuevo Point ▲ **USA** ◇ 20-21 C 7
Anpo Gang ≈ ◆ 54-55 K 7
Anqing ○ **CHN** ◆ 54-55 M 5
Anshan ○ **CHN** ◆ 54-55 N 3
Anson ○ **USA** ◇ 26-27 H 3
Ansonga ○ **RMM** ◆ 48-49 F 5
Antalaha ○ **RM** ◆ 50-51 M 4
Antalya ☆ **TR** ◆ 34-35 S 8
Antalya Körfezi ≈ ◆ 34-35 S 8
Antananarivo ★• **RM** ◆ 50-51 L 5
Antarctica **ANT** ◆ 13 F 28
Antarctic Circle **ANT** ◆ 13 G 3
Antarctic Peninsula ∪ **ANT** ◆ 13 G 30
Antarctic Sound ≈ ◆ 13 G 31
Antelope Island ∩ **USA** ◇ 20-21 H 5
Anthony ○ **USA** (KS) ◇ 26-27 H 1
Anthony ○ **USA** (NM) ◇ 26-27 D 3
Anthony Island ∩··· **CDN** ◆ 14-15 K 6
Anti Atlas ▲ **MA** ◆ 48-49 D 3
Anticosti, Île d' ∩ **CDN** ◇ 18-19 M 4 ◆ 14-15 Y 7
Antigo ○ **USA** ◇ 22-23 D 3
Antigonish ○ **CDN** ◇ 18-19 N 6
Antigua ○• **MEX** ◇ 28-29 F 2
Antigua and Barbuda ■ **AG** ◆ 16-17 O 7
Antigua Guatemala ☆··· **GCA** ◇ 28-29 J 4
Antigua Island ∩ **AG** ◆ 16-17 O 7
Antimony ○ **USA** ◇ 20-21 J 6
Antipajuta ○ **RUS** ◆ 52-53 M 4
Antipodes Islands □ **NZ** ◆ 12 J 7
Antlers ○ **USA** ◇ 26-27 K 2
Antofagasta ☆ **RCH** ◆ 32-33 H 2
Antofagasta de la Sierra ○ **RA** ◆ 32-33 J 3
Antofalla, Volcán ▲ **RA** ◆ 32-33 J 3
Anton ○ **USA** ◇ 26-27 F 3
Antongila, Helodrano ≈ ◆ 50-51 L 5
Antonito ○ **USA** ◇ 26-27 D 1
Antón Lizardo ○ **MEX** ◇ 28-29 F 2
Antsalova ○ **RM** ◆ 50-51 K 5
Antsirabe ○ **RM** ◆ 50-51 L 5
Antsiranana ☆ **RM** ◆ 50-51 L 4
Antsohihy ○ **RM** ◆ 50-51 L 4
Antwerpen ☆·· **B** ◇ 40-41 H 3 ◆ 34-35 M 5
Añueque, Sierra ▲ **RA** ◆ 32-33 J 6
Anugul ○ **IND** ◆ 56-57 O 6
Anuradhapura ○··· **CL** ◆ 56-57 N 9
Anvers, Île ∩ **ANT** ◆ 13 G 30
Anxi ○ **CHN** ◆ 54-55 H 3
Anxious Bay ≈ ◆ 60-61 G 6
Anyang ○ **CHN** ◆ 54-55 L 4
Anza-Borrego Desert State Park ⊥ **USA** ◇ 20-21 F 9
Anzali, Bandar-e ○• **IR** ◆ 56-57 F 3
Anžero-Sudžensk ○ **RUS** ◆ 52-53 O 6
Anzhero Sudzhensk = Anžero-Sudžensk ○ **RUS** ◆ 52-53 O 6
Anžu, ostrova ∩ **RUS** ◆ 52-53 Y 2
Aomori ○ **J** ◆ 54-55 R 3
Aougoundou, Lac ⬭ **RMM** ◆ 48-49 E 5
Aouk, Bahr ∼ **TCH** ◆ 48-49 J 7
Aoukâr ∸ **RIM** ◆ 48-49 C 5
Aoukâr ∸ **RMM** ◆ 48-49 D 4
Aousard ○ **WSA** ◆ 48-49 C 4
Apache ○ **USA** ◇ 26-27 H 2
Apache Creek ○ **USA** ◇ 26-27 C 3
Apache Junction ○ **USA** ◇ 20-21 J 9
Apalachee Bay ≈ ◇ 24-25 F 5 ◆ 16-17 K 5
Apalachicola ○ **USA** ◇ 24-25 F 5
Apalachicola River ∼ **USA** ◇ 24-25 F 4
Apan ○ **MEX** ◇ 28-29 E 2
Apaporis, Río ∼ **CO** ◆ 30-31 E 4
Apatity ○ **RUS** ◆ 34-35 S 2
Apatzingán de la Constitución ○ **MEX** ◇ 28-29 C 2
Apaxtla de Castrejón ○ **MEX** ◇ 28-29 E 2
Apennines ▲ **I** ◇ 46-47 B 2 ◆ 34-35 N 7
Apiaí ○ **BR** ◆ 32-33 N 2
Apitpac ○ **MEX** ◇ 28-29 H 3
Apolo ○ **BOL** ◆ 30-31 F 7
Apopa ○ **ES** ◇ 28-29 K 5
Apopka ○ **USA** ◇ 24-25 H 5
Aporé, Rio ∼ **BR** ◆ 30-31 J 8
Apostle Islands ∩ **USA** ◇ 22-23 C 2
Apostle Islands National Lakeshore ⊥ **USA** ◇ 22-23 C 2
Appalachian Mountains ▲ **USA** ◇ 22-23 J 6 ◆ 16-17 K 3
Appleton ○ **USA** ◇ 22-23 D 3
Appomattox ○ **USA** ◇ 22-23 J 7
Appomattox Court House National Historic Park • **USA** ◇ 22-23 J 7
Apsley ○ **CDN** ◇ 18-19 E 6
Apt ○ **F** ◇ 38-39 K 10 ◆ 34-35 M 7
Apucarana ○ **BR** ◆ 32-33 M 2
Apuka ○ **RUS** (KOR) ◆ 52-53 e 5
Apuka ∼ **RUS** ◆ 52-53 f 5
Apura ○ **SME** ◆ 30-31 H 3
Apure, Río ∼ **YV** ◆ 30-31 F 3
Apurimac, Río ∼ **PE** ◆ 30-31 E 7
'Aqaba ☆ **JOR** ◆ 56-57 D 5
Aqaba, Gulf of = 'Aqaba, Ḫaliğ al- ≈ ◆ 56-57 C 5
'Aqaba, Ḫaliğ al- ≈ ◆ 56-57 C 5
'Aqiq ○ **SUD** ◆ 48-49 N 5
Aqtaū = Aktau ☆ **KZ** ◆ 56-57 G 2
Aqtöbe = Aktöbe ☆ **KZ** ◆ 34-35 X 5
Aquila ○ **MEX** ◇ 28-29 C 2
Aquitaine □ **F** ◇ 38-39 G 10 ◆ 34-35 L 7
Ara ○ **IND** ◆ 56-57 N 5
Arab ○ **USA** ◇ 24-25 E 2
Arabela ○ **USA** ◇ 26-27 E 3
Arabian Basin ≃ ◆ 56-57 J 8
Arabian Peninsula ∸ **KSA** ◆ 10-11 C 6
Arabian Sea ≈ ◆ 56-57 J 7
Aracá, Área Indígena X **BR** ◆ 30-31 G 4
Aracaju ☆• **BR** ◆ 30-31 M 7
Aracati ○ **BR** ◆ 30-31 M 5
Araçatuba ○ **BR** ◆ 32-33 M 2
Araçuaí ○ **BR** ◆ 30-31 L 8
Arad ☆• **RO** ◆ 34-35 Q 6
Arafura Sea ≈ ◆ 58-59 K 8
Arafura Shelf ≃ ◆ 12 E 4
Aragua de Barcelona ○ **YV** ◆ 30-31 G 3
Araguaia, Parque Indígena X **BR** ◆ 30-31 J 7
Araguaia, Parque Nacional do X **BR** ◆ 30-31 J 7
Araguaia, Rio ∼ **BR** ◆ 30-31 J 7
Araguaína ○ **BR** ◆ 30-31 K 6
Araguari, Rio ∼ **BR** ◆ 30-31 J 4
Araguatins ○ **BR** ◆ 30-31 K 6
Arak ○ **DZ** ◆ 48-49 F 3
Arāk ☆• **IR** ◆ 56-57 F 4
Aral ☆ **KZ** ◆ 56-57 J 1
Aral Sea ⬭ ◆ 56-57 H 1
Aral teņízí ⬭ ◆ 56-57 H 1
Aramac ○ **AUS** ◆ 60-61 K 4
Aranda de Duero ○ **E** ◇ 44-45 F 4 ◆ 34-35 L 7
Arandas ○ **MEX** ◇ 28-29 C 1
Aranib, Umm al ○ **LAR** ◆ 48-49 H 3
Aranos ○ **NAM** ◆ 50-51 E 6
Aransas Pass ○ **USA** ◇ 26-27 J 6
Araouane ○ **RMM** ◆ 48-49 E 5
Arapiraca ○ **BR** ◆ 30-31 M 6
'Ar'ar ☆ **KSA** ◆ 56-57 E 4
Arara, Área Indígena X **BR** ◆ 30-31 J 5
Araranguá ○ **BR** ◆ 32-33 N 3
Araraquara ○ **BR** ◆ 32-33 N 2
Araras ○ **BR** ◆ 30-31 J 6
Ararat ○ **AUS** ◆ 60-61 J 7
Araribóa, Área Indígena X **BR** ◆ 30-31 K 5
Araripe, Chapada do ▲ **BR** ◆ 30-31 L 6
Arauca ☆ **CO** ◆ 30-31 E 3
Arauca, Río ∼ **YV** ◆ 30-31 F 3
Arawa ☆ **PNG** ◆ 58-59 P 8
Arawale National Reserve ⊥ **EAK** ◆ 50-51 K 2
Araweté Igarapé Ipixuna, Área Indígena X **BR** ◆ 30-31 J 5
Araxá ○ **BR** ◆ 30-31 K 8
Arba Minch ☆ **ETH** ◆ 48-49 N 7
Arbil ☆ **IRQ** ◆ 56-57 E 3
Arcachon ○ **F** ◇ 38-39 G 9 ◆ 34-35 L 6
Arcadia ○ **USA** (FL) ◇ 24-25 H 6
Arcadia ○ **USA** (LA) ◇ 26-27 L 3
Arcata ○ **USA** ◇ 20-21 B 5
Arcelia ○ **MEX** ◇ 28-29 D 2
Arc-et-Senans ○··· **F** ◇ 38-39 K 8 ◆ 34-35 M 6
Archer Bay ≈ ◆ 60-61 J 2
Arches National Park ⊥ **USA** ◆ 16-17 E 3
Archipiélago de las Guaitecas, Parque Nacional ⊥ **RCH** ◆ 32-33 H 6
Arco ○ **USA** ◇ 20-21 H 4
Arcos ○ **BR** ◆ 32-33 N 2
Arctic Bay ○ **CDN** ◆ 14-15 U 2
Arctic Circle ◆ 14-15 R 3
Arctic Harbour ≈ ◆ 14-15 X 3
Arctic Institute Range ▲ **ANT** ◆ 13 F 16
Arctic National Wildlife Refuge ⊥ **USA** ◆ 14-15 G 3
Arctic Ocean ≈ ◆ 52-53 V 2
Arctic Red River ∼ **CDN** ◆ 14-15 K 3
Ardabil ○• **IR** ◆ 56-57 F 3
Ardakān ○ **IR** ◆ 56-57 G 4
Ardmore ○ **USA** ◇ 26-27 J 2 ◆ 16-17 G 4
Arecibo ○ **USA** ◆ 16-17 N 7
Areia Branca ○ **BR** ◆ 30-31 M 5
Arena, Point ▲ **USA** ◇ 20-21 C 6
Arenal, Volcán ▲ **CR** ◇ 28-29 B 6
Arenas ○ **PA** ◇ 28-29 D 8
Arenas, Punta de ▲ **RA** ◆ 32-33 J 8
Arendal ☆ **N** ◇ 36-37 D 7 ◆ 34-35 N 4
Arenosa ○ **PA** ◇ 28-29 E 7
Areópoli ○ **GR** ◇ 46-47 J 6 ◆ 34-35 Q 8
Areõs, Área Indígena X **BR** ◆ 30-31 J 7
Arequipa ☆• **PE** ◆ 30-31 E 8
Arezzo ○ **I** ◇ 46-47 C 3 ◆ 34-35 O 7
Argahtah ○ **RUS** ◆ 52-53 b 4
Arga-Muora-Sise, ostrov ∩ **RUS** ◆ 52-53 V 3
Arga Sala ∼ **RUS** ◆ 52-53 T 4
Argent, Côte d' ∪ **F** ◇ 38-39 G 10 ◆ 34-35 L 7
Argentan ○ **F** ◇ 38-39 G 7 ◆ 34-35 L 6
Argentia ○ **CDN** ◇ 18-19 S 5 ◆ 14-15 a 7
Argentina ■ **RA** ◆ 32-33 J 6
Argentine Abyssal Plain ≃ ◆ 32-33 M 7
Argentine Basin ≃ ◆ 32-33 N 5
Argentine Islands ○ **ANT** ◆ 13 G 30
Argentino, Lago ⬭ **RA** ◆ 32-33 H 8
Argentino, Mar ≈ ◆ 32-33 L 6
Argenton-sur-Creuse ○ **F** ◇ 38-39 H 8 ◆ 34-35 M 6
Argonne ○ **USA** ◇ 22-23 D 3
Argoub, Al- ○ **MA** ◆ 48-49 B 4
Arguello, Point ▲ **USA** ◇ 20-21 D 8 ◆ 16-17 B 4
Argun' ∼ **RUS** ◆ 54-55 M 1
Argungu ○ **WAN** ◆ 48-49 F 6
Argyle, Lake ⬭ **AUS** ◆ 60-61 F 3
Arhangel'sk ☆ **RUS** ◆ 34-35 U 3
Århus ○ **DK** ◇ 36-37 E 8 ◆ 34-35 O 4
Aribinda ○• **BF** ◆ 48-49 E 6
Arica ○ **RCH** ◆ 30-31 E 8
Arichat ○ **CDN** ◇ 18-19 O 6
Ariège ∼ **F** ◇ 38-39 H 10 ◆ 34-35 M 7
Ariḥāl ☆·· **AUT** ◆ 56-57 D 4
Arinos ○ **BR** ◆ 30-31 K 8
Arinos, Rio ∼ **BR** ◆ 30-31 H 7
Aripuanã ○ **BR** ◆ 30-31 H 6
Aripuanã, Área Indígena X **BR** ◆ 30-31 H 7
Aripuanã, Parque Indígena X **BR** ◆ 30-31 G 7
Ariquemes ○ **BR** ◆ 30-31 G 6
'Ariš, al- ☆ **ET** ◆ 48-49 M 2
Arismendi ○ **YV** ◆ 30-31 F 3
Arizaro, Salar de ⬭ **RA** ◆ 32-33 J 2
Arizona □ **USA** ◇ 20-21 H 8 ◆ 16-17 D 4
Arjona ○ **CO** ◆ 30-31 D 2
Arkadelphia ○ **USA** ◇ 26-27 L 2
Arkalyk ☆ **KZ** ◆ 52-53 K 7
Arkansas □ **USA** ◇ 26-27 L 2 ◆ 16-17 H 3
Arkansas City ○ **USA** ◇ 26-27 J 1
Arkansas Post National Memorial ∴ **USA** ◇ 26-27 M 2
Arkansas River ∼ **USA** ◇ 26-27 M 2 ◆ 16-17 H 4
Arkhangel'sk = Arhangel'sk ☆ **RUS** ◆ 34-35 U 3
Arknu, Jabal ▲ **LAR** ◆ 48-49 K 4
Arktičeskogo instituta, ostrova ∩ **RUS** ◆ 52-53 N 2
Arlee ○ **USA** ◇ 20-21 G 2
Arles ○··· **F** ◇ 38-39 K 10 ◆ 34-35 M 7
Arlington ○ **USA** (GA) ◇ 24-25 F 4
Arlington ○ **USA** (KS) ◇ 26-27 H 1
Arlington ○ **USA** (OR) ◇ 20-21 D 3
Arlington ○ **USA** (TX) ◇ 26-27 J 3
Arlington ○ **USA** (VA) ◇ 22-23 K 6 ◆ 16-17 L 3
Arlington ○ **USA** (WA) ◇ 20-21 C 1
Arlit ○ **RN** ◆ 48-49 G 5
'Armā' ▲ **KSA** ◆ 56-57 F 5
Arma ○ **USA** ◇ 26-27 K 1
Armagnac ∸ **F** ◇ 38-39 H 10 ◆ 34-35 M 7
Armavir ○ **RUS** ◆ 34-35 U 6
Armenia ■ **AR** ◆ 34-35 U 7
Armenia ☆ **CO** ◆ 30-31 D 4
Armería ○ **MEX** ◇ 28-29 C 2
Armidale ○ **AUS** ◆ 60-61 L 6
Armstrong ○ **CDN** ◆ 14-15 T 6
Arnaud (Payne), Rivière ∼ **CDN** ◆ 14-15 W 4
Arnett ○ **USA** ◇ 26-27 H 1
Arnhem Aboriginal Land X **AUS** ◆ 60-61 G 2
Arnhem Land ∸ **AUS** ◆ 60-61 G 2
Arnold ○ **USA** ◇ 22-23 E 2
Arnprior ○ **CDN** ◇ 18-19 F 6
Arntfield ○ **CDN** ◇ 18-19 E 4
Aroab ○ **NAM** ◆ 50-51 E 7
Aroostock River ∼ **USA** ◇ 22-23 O 2
Arorae ∩ **KIB** ◆ 12 J 3
Arpajon ○ **F** ◇ 38-39 J 7 ◆ 34-35 M 6
Ar-Rachidia ☆ **MA** ◆ 48-49 E 2
ar-Rahad ○ **SUD** ◆ 48-49 M 6
ar-Rahad ∼ **SUD** ◆ 48-49 M 6
Arraial do Cabo ○ **BR** ◆ 32-33 O 2
ar-Rank ○ **SUD** ◆ 48-49 M 6
Arras ☆• **F** ◇ 38-39 J 6 ◆ 34-35 M 5
Arrecife ○• **E** ◆ 48-49 C 3
Arreti ○ **PA** ◇ 28-29 F 8
Arrey ○ **USA** ◇ 26-27 D 3
Arriaga ○• **MEX** ◇ 28-29 H 3 ◆ 16-17 H 7
Ar-Ribāt ★·· **MA** ◆ 48-49 D 2
Ar-Rif ▲ **MA** ◆ 48-49 D 2
Arrowhead, Lake < **USA** ◇ 26-27 H 3
Arrowrock Reservoir ⬭ **USA** ◇ 20-21 G 4
Arroyo Grande ○ **USA** ◇ 20-21 D 8
Arsen'ev ○ **RUS** ◆ 52-53 X 9
Artāwiya, al- ○ **KSA** ◆ 56-57 F 5
Arteaga ○ **MEX** ◇ 28-29 C 2
Artem ○ **RUS** ◆ 52-53 X 9
Artesia ○ **USA** ◇ 26-27 E 3
Arthur ○ **CDN** ◇ 18-19 D 7
Arthur, Lake ⬭ **USA** ◇ 22-23 J 5
Arthur's Pass National Park ⊥ **NZ** ◆ 60-61 P 8
Arthur's Town ○ **BS** ◆ 16-17 L 6
Artigas ☆ **ROU** ◆ 32-33 L 4
Artois ∸ **F** ◇ 38-39 H 6 ◆ 34-35 M 5
Arturo Prat ○ **ANT** ◆ 13 G 30
Artvin ☆ **TR** ◆ 34-35 U 7
Artyk ○ **RUS** ◆ 52-53 a 5
Aru, Kepulauan ∸ **RI** ◆ 58-59 K 8
Arua ☆ **EAU** ◆ 48-49 M 8
Aruanã ○ **BR** ◆ 30-31 J 7
Arunāchal Pradesh □ **IND** ◆ 56-57 P 5
Arusha ☆ **EAT** ◆ 50-51 J 2
Aruwimi ∼ **ZRE** ◆ 50-51 G 1
Arvajhèèr ☆ **MAU** ◆ 54-55 J 2
Arwin ○ **USA** ◇ 20-21 E 8
Arwin Island ∩ **PNG** ◆ 58-59 M 7
Arzamas ○ **RUS** ◇ 42-43 S 4 ◆ 34-35 U 4
Arzon ○ **F** ◇ 38-39 F 8 ◆ 34-35 L 6
Asadābād ☆• **AFG** ◆ 56-57 L 4
Asagny, Parc National d' ⊥ **CI** ◆ 48-49 D 8
Asahi-dake ▲ **J** ◆ 54-55 R 3
Asahikawa ○ **J** ◆ 54-55 R 3
Āsalē ○ **ETH** ◆ 48-49 O 6
Asankranguaa ○ **GH** ◆ 48-49 E 7
Asbestos ○ **CDN** ◇ 18-19 J 6
Asbury Park ○ **USA** ◇ 22-23 L 5
Ascención, Bahía de la ≈ ◇ 28-29 L 2
Āseb ○ **ER** ◆ 48-49 O 6
Asedjrad ▲ **DZ** ◆ 48-49 F 4
Āsela ☆ **ETH** ◆ 48-49 N 7
Aşfi ☆ **MA** ◆ 48-49 D 2
Ašgabat ★• **TM** ◆ 56-57 H 3
Ašhabad = Ašgabat ★• **TM** ◆ 56-57 H 3
Ashburn ○ **USA** ◇ 24-25 G 4
Ashburton ○ **NZ** ◆ 60-61 P 8
Ashburton River ∼ **AUS** ◆ 60-61 D 4
Ashdown ○ **USA** ◇ 26-27 K 3
Asheboro ○ **USA** ◇ 24-25 J 2
Asher ○ **USA** ◇ 26-27 J 2
Asheville ○• **USA** ◇ 24-25 G 2 ◆ 16-17 K 3
Ash Flat ○ **USA** ◇ 26-27 M 1
Ash Fork ○ **USA** ◇ 20-21 H 8
Ashgabat = Ašgabat ★• **TM** ◆ 56-57 H 3
Ashkum ○ **USA** ◇ 22-23 E 5
Ashland ○ **USA** (IL) ◇ 22-23 C 6
Ashland ○ **USA** (KS) ◇ 26-27 H 1
Ashland ○ **USA** (KY) ◇ 22-23 G 6
Ashland ○ **USA** (ME) ◇ 22-23 O 2
Ashland ○ **USA** (OH) ◇ 22-23 G 5
Ashland ○ **USA** (OR) ◇ 20-21 C 4
Ashland ○ **USA** (WI) ◇ 22-23 C 2 ◆ 14-15 S 7
Ashland City ○ **USA** ◇ 24-25 E 1
Ashley ○ **USA** ◇ 22-23 D 6
Ashmore Reef ∩ **AUS** ◆ 60-61 E 2
ash-Shallāl al-Khāmis = 5th Cataract ∼ **SUD** ◆ 48-49 M 5
ash-Shallāl ar-Rābi' = 4th Cataract ∼ **SUD** ◆ 48-49 M 5
ash-Shallal as-Sablūkah = 6th Cataract ∼ **SUD** ◆ 48-49 M 5
ash-Shallāl ath-Thālith = 3rd Cataract ∼ **SUD** ◆ 48-49 M 5
Ashtabula ○ **USA** ◇ 22-23 H 5
Ashton ○ **USA** ◇ 20-21 J 3
Ashuanipi Lake ⬭ **CDN** ◇ 18-19 L 2
Ashuapmushuan, Réserve Faunique d' ⊥ **CDN** ◇ 18-19 H 4
Ashuapmushuan, Rivière ∼ **CDN** ◇ 18-19 H 4
Asia, Kepulauan ∩ **RI** ◆ 58-59 K 6
Asientos, Los ○ **PA** ◇ 28-29 D 8
Asinara, Ísola ∩ **I** ◇ 46-47 B 4 ◆ 34-35 N 7
Asino ☆ **RUS** ◆ 52-53 O 6
Asir □ **KSA** ◆ 56-57 E 7
Āsmara ★• **ER** ◆ 48-49 N 5
Āsmera = Āsmara ★• **ER** ◆ 48-49 N 5
Asoteriba, Ğabal ▲ **SUD** ◆ 48-49 N 4
Aspermont ○ **USA** ◇ 26-27 G 3
Aspy Bay ≈ ◇ 18-19 O 5
Assam □ **IND** ◆ 56-57 P 5
Assamakka ○ **RN** ◆ 48-49 G 5
Assateague Island ∩ **USA** ◇ 22-23 L 6
Assateague Islands National Seashore ⊥ **USA** ◇ 22-23 L 6
As-Sawirah ☆• **MA** ◆ 48-49 D 2
As Sidr ○ **LAR** ◆ 48-49 J 2
Assiniboine River ∼ **CDN** ◆ 14-15 Q 6
Assinica, Lac ⬭ **CDN** ◇ 18-19 G 3
Assinica, Réserve Faunique ⊥ **CDN** ◇ 18-19 G 3
Assis ○ **BR** ◆ 32-33 M 2
Assomption ∩ **SY** ◆ 50-51 L 3
As-Sūs ∸ **MA** ◆ 48-49 D 2
Astara ○ **AZ** ◆ 34-35 V 8
Astoria ○• **USA** ◇ 20-21 C 2 ◆ 14-15 M 7
Astove Island ∩ **SY** ◆ 50-51 L 4
Astrahan' ☆ **RUS** ◆ 34-35 V 6
Astrakhan' = Astrahan' ☆ **RUS** ◆ 34-35 V 6
Asunción ○ **CR** ◇ 28-29 C 7
Asunción ★• **PY** ◆ 32-33 L 3
Asuncion ∩ **USA** ◆ 58-59 N 3
Asunción Nochixtlán ○ **MEX** ◇ 28-29 F 3
Aswa ∼ **EAU** ◆ 48-49 M 8
Aswān ☆·· **ET** ◆ 48-49 M 4
Asyma ○ **RUS** ◆ 52-53 W 5
Asyūṭ ☆• **ET** ◆ 48-49 M 3
Atacama, Puna de ∸ **RA** ◆ 32-33 J 3
Atacama, Salar de ⬭·· **RCH** ◆ 32-33 J 2
Atacama Trench ≃ ◆ 30-31 E 8
Atafi, Massif d' ▲ **RN** ◆ 48-49 J 4
Atakpamé ☆ **RT** ◆ 48-49 F 7
Atalaya ○ **PE** ◆ 30-31 E 7
Atâr ☆ **RIM** ◆ 48-49 C 4
Atascadero ○ **USA** ◇ 20-21 D 8
Atasta ○ **MEX** ◇ 28-29 H 2
Atasu ☆ **KZ** ◆ 52-53 L 8
Atauro, Pulau (Kambing) ∩ **RI** ◆ 58-59 J 8
'Atbara ∼ **ETH** ◆ 48-49 N 6
'Aṭbara ☆ **SUD** ◆ 48-49 M 5
Atbasar ☆ **KZ** ◆ 52-53 K 7
Atchafalaya Bay ≈ ◇ 26-27 M 5
Atenango del Río ○ **MEX** ◇ 28-29 E 2
Atencingo ○ **MEX** ◇ 28-29 E 2
Atequiza ○ **MEX** ◇ 28-29 C 1
Athabasca ○ **CDN** ◆ 14-15 O 6
Athabasca, Lake ⬭ **CDN** ◆ 14-15 P 5
Athabasca River ∼ **CDN** ◆ 14-15 O 5
Athens ★··· **GR** ◇ 46-47 J 5 ◆ 34-35 Q 8
Athens ○ **USA** (AL) ◇ 24-25 E 2
Athens ○ **USA** (GA) ◇ 24-25 G 3 ◆ 16-17 K 4
Athens ○ **USA** (OH) ◇ 22-23 G 6
Athens ○ **USA** (TN) ◇ 24-25 F 2
Athens ○ **USA** (TX) ◇ 26-27 K 3
Atherton Tableland ∸ **AUS** ◆ 60-61 K 3
Athi ∼ **EAK** ◆ 50-51 J 2
Athol ○ **USA** ◇ 20-21 F 2
Áthos ▲··· **GR** ◇ 46-47 K 4 ◆ 34-35 Q 7
'Ati ○ **SUD** ◆ 48-49 L 6
Ati ☆ **TCH** ◆ 48-49 J 6
Atico ○ **PE** ◆ 30-31 E 8
Atikonak Lake ⬭ **CDN** ◇ 18-19 M 2
Atitlán, Lago de ⬭ **GCA** ◇ 28-29 J 4 ◆ 16-17 H 8
Atitlán, Volcán ▲ **GCA** ◇ 28-29 J 4
Atka ○ **USA** ◆ 14-15 B 6
Atka Island ∩ **USA** ◆ 14-15 B 6
Atlacomulco ○ **MEX** ◇ 28-29 E 2
Atlanta ○ **USA** (MI) ◇ 22-23 F 3
Atlanta ○ **USA** (TX) ◇ 26-27 K 3
Atlanta ☆ **USA** (GA) ◇ 24-25 F 3 ◆ 16-17 K 4
Atlantic ○ **USA** ◇ 24-25 K 2
Atlantic City ○ **USA** ◇ 22-23 L 6 ◆ 16-17 M 3
Atlantic Ocean ≈ ◆ 7 E 2
Atlasova, ostrov ∩ **RUS** ◆ 52-53 c 7
Atlasovo ○ **RUS** ◆ 52-53 c 6
Atlin Lake ⬭ **CDN** ◆ 14-15 K 5
Atlixco ○ **MEX** ◇ 28-29 E 2 ◆ 16-17 G 7
Atmore ○ **USA** ◇ 24-25 E 4
Atoka ○ **USA** ◇ 26-27 J 2
Atomic City ○ **USA** ◇ 20-21 H 4
Atotonilco ○ **MEX** ◇ 28-29 E 2
Atotonilco el Alto ○ **MEX** ◇ 28-29 C 1
Atotonilco El Grande ○ **MEX** ◇ 28-29 E 1
Atoyac, Río ∼ **MEX** ◇ 28-29 F 3
Atoyac, Río ∼ **MEX** ◇ 28-29 E 2
Atoyac de Alvarez ○ **MEX** ◇ 28-29 D 3
Atoyatempan ○ **MEX** ◇ 28-29 F 2
Atrato, Río ∼ **CO** ◆ 30-31 D 3
Atrek ∼ **TM** ◆ 56-57 G 3
Attalla ○ **USA** ◇ 24-25 E 2
Attapu ○ **LAO** ◆ 58-59 E 4
Attawapiskat River ∼ **CDN** ◆ 14-15 U 6
Attica ○ **USA** (IN) ◇ 22-23 E 5
Attica ○ **USA** (KS) ◇ 26-27 H 1
Attica ○ **USA** (OH) ◇ 22-23 G 5
Attock ○• **PK** ◆ 56-57 L 4
Atwater ○ **USA** ◇ 20-21 D 7
Atwood ○ **USA** ◇ 22-23 D 6
Aua Island ∩ **PNG** ◆ 58-59 M 7
Auasbila ○ **HN** ◇ 28-29 B 4
Aubagne ○ **F** ◇ 38-39 K 10 ◆ 34-35 M 7
Aube ∼ **F** ◇ 38-39 K 8 ◆ 34-35 M 6
Aubenas ○ **F** ◇ 38-39 K 9 ◆ 34-35 N 6
Aubigny-sur-Nère ○ **F** ◇ 38-39 J 8 ◆ 34-35 M 6
Auburn ○ **USA** (AL) ◇ 24-25 F 3
Auburn ○ **USA** (CA) ◇ 20-21 D 6
Auburn ○ **USA** (IN) ◇ 22-23 F 5
Auburn ○ **USA** (ME) ◇ 22-23 N 3
Auburn ○ **USA** (NY) ◇ 22-23 K 4
Auburn ○ **USA** (WA) ◇ 20-21 C 2
Aubusson ○ **F** ◇ 38-39 J 9 ◆ 34-35 M 7
Auch ☆• **F** ◇ 38-39 H 10 ◆ 34-35 M 7
Auckland ○ **NZ** ◆ 60-61 P 7
Auckland Islands □ **NZ** ◆ 12 H 8
Aude ∼ **F** ◇ 38-39 J 10 ◆ 34-35 M 7
Audierne ○ **F** ◇ 38-39 E 7 ◆ 34-35 L 6
Audo Range ▲ **ETH** ◆ 48-49 O 7
Augathella ○ **AUS** ◆ 60-61 K 5
Augrabies Falls National Park ⊥ **ZA** ◆ 50-51 F 7
Augsburg ○·· **D** ◇ 40-41 L 4 ◆ 34-35 O 6
Augusta ○• **AUS** ◆ 60-61 D 6
Augusta ○ **USA** (GA) ◇ 24-25 H 3 ◆ 16-17 K 4
Augusta ○ **USA** (MT) ◇ 20-21 H 2
Augusta ☆ **USA** (ME) ◇ 22-23 O 3 ◆ 14-15 X 8
Augustus, Mount ▲ **AUS** ◆ 60-61 D 4
Aurangābād ○ **IND** ◆ 56-57 M 7
Auray ○ **F** ◇ 38-39 F 8 ◆ 34-35 L 6
Aurillac ☆ **F** ◇ 38-39 J 9 ◆ 34-35 M 7
Aurora ○ **CDN** (ONT) ◇ 18-19 E 7
Aurora ○ **CDN** (ONT) ◇ 18-19 E 6
Aurora ○ **USA** (IL) ◇ 22-23 D 5
Aurora ○ **USA** (MO) ◇ 26-27 L 1
Auroraville ○ **USA** ◇ 22-23 D 3
Aus ○ **NAM** ◆ 50-51 E 7
Au Sable River ∼ **USA** ◇ 22-23 G 3
Ausangate, Nudo ▲ **PE** ◆ 30-31 E 7
Austin ○ **USA** (NV) ◇ 20-21 F 6 ◆ 16-17 C 3
Austin ○ **USA** (TX) ◇ 26-27 J 4 ◆ 16-17 G 4
Austin, Lake ⬭ **AUS** ◆ 60-61 D 5
Australes, Îles ∩ **F** ◆ 12 M 5
Australia ■ **AUS** ◆ 60-61 E 5
Australia ∸ **AUS** ◆ 60-61 E 5
Australian-Antarctic Discordance ≃ ◆ 12 D 7
Australian Capital Territory □ **AUS** ◆ 60-61 K 7
Austria ■ **A** ◇ 40-41 N 5 ◆ 34-35 O 6
Autlán de Navarro ○ **MEX** ◇ 28-29 B 2
Autun ○• **F** ◇ 38-39 K 8 ◆ 34-35 M 6
Auvergne □ **F** ◇ 38-39 J 9 ◆ 34-35 M 7
Aux Barques, Pointe ▲ **USA** ◇ 22-23 G 3
Auxerre ☆• **F** ◇ 38-39 J 8 ◆ 34-35 M 6
Auyuittug National Park ⊥ **CDN** ◆ 14-15 X 3
Ava ○ **USA** ◇ 26-27 L 1
Avallon ○ **F** ◇ 38-39 J 8 ◆ 34-35 M 6
Avalon ○ **USA** ◇ 20-21 E 9
Avalon Peninsula ∪ **CDN** ◇ 18-19 S 5 ◆ 14-15 a 7
Avare ○ **BR** ◆ 32-33 N 2
Aveiro ○ **BR** ◆ 30-31 H 5
Aveiro ☆• **P** ◇ 44-45 C 4 ◆ 34-35 K 7
Aveiro, Floresta Nacional ⊥ **BR** ◆ 30-31 H 5
Avellaneda ○ **RA** ◆ 32-33 L 4
Avenne of the Giants • **USA** ◇ 20-21 C 5
Avery ○ **USA** ◇ 20-21 G 2
Aves Ridge ≃ ◆ 16-17 O 8
Aveyron ∼ **F** ◇ 38-39 J 9 ◆ 34-35 M 7
Avignon ○·· **F** ◇ 38-39 K 10 ◆ 34-35 M 7
Avissawella ○ **CL** ◆ 56-57 N 9
Avoca ○ **AUS** ◆ 60-61 J 7
Avon ○ **USA** ◇ 20-21 H 2
Avondale ○ **USA** ◇ 20-21 H 9
Avon Park ○ **USA** ◇ 24-25 H 6
Avon River ∼ **AUS** ◆ 60-61 D 6
Avranches ○ **F** ◇ 38-39 G 7 ◆ 34-35 L 6
Awanui ○ **NZ** ◆ 60-61 P 7
Awar ○ **PNG** ◆ 58-59 M 7
Āwasa ☆ **ETH** ◆ 48-49 N 7
Āwash ○ **ETH** ◆ 48-49 O 7
Āwash National Park ⊥ **ETH** ◆ 48-49 N 7
Āwash Reserve ⊥ **ETH** ◆ 48-49 N 7
Āwash Wenz ∼ **ETH** ◆ 48-49 O 6
Awaynat, Al ○ **LAR** ◆ 48-49 K 4
Awaynat, Jabal Al ▲ **SUD** ◆ 48-49 L 4
Awbāri ☆ **LAR** ◆ 48-49 H 3
Awjilah ○ **LAR** ◆ 48-49 K 3
Ayachi, Jbel ▲ **MA** ◆ 48-49 D 2
Ayacucho ☆ **PE** ◆ 30-31 E 7
Ayacucho ○ **RA** ◆ 32-33 L 5
Ayakkum Hu ⬭ **CHN** ◆ 54-55 F 4
Ayden ○ **USA** ◇ 24-25 K 2
Aydın ☆ **TR** ◆ 34-35 R 8
Ayers Rock ▲·· **AUS** ◆ 60-61 G 5
Aylmer Lake ⬭ **CDN** ◆ 14-15 P 4
Ayn al Ghāzalah ○ **LAR** ◆ 48-49 K 2
Ayod ○ **SUD** ◆ 48-49 M 7
'Ayoûn el 'Atroûs ☆ **RIM** ◆ 48-49 D 5
Ayr ○ **AUS** ◆ 60-61 K 3
Āysha ○ **ETH** ◆ 48-49 O 6
Ayu, Kepulauan ∩ **RI** ◆ 58-59 K 6
Ayutla ○ **MEX** (JAL) ◇ 28-29 B 1
Ayutla ○ **MEX** (OAX) ◇ 28-29 F 3
Ayutla de los Libres ○ **MEX** ◇ 28-29 E 3
Ayutthaya ○··· **THA** ◆ 58-59 D 4
Azangaro ○ **PE** ◆ 30-31 E 7
Azaough ∼ **RIM** ◆ 48-49 F 5
Azare ○ **WAN** ◆ 48-49 H 6
Az Bogd ▲ **MAU** ◆ 54-55 H 2
Azeffâl ∸ **RIM** ◆ 48-49 B 5
Azerbaijan ■ **AZ** ◆ 34-35 V 7
Azle ○ **USA** ◇ 26-27 J 3
Azogues ☆ **EC** ◆ 30-31 D 5
Azores-Biscaya Rise ≃ ◆ 34-35 G 7
Azores-Cape Saint Vincent Ridge ≃ ◆ 34-35 J 8
Azov, Sea of = Azovskoe more ≈ ◆ 34-35 T 6
Azovskoe more ≈ ◆ 34-35 T 6
Azrou ○ **MA** ◆ 48-49 D 2
Aztec ○ **USA** (AZ) ◇ 20-21 H 9
Aztec ○ **USA** (NM) ◇ 26-27 D 1
Aztec Ruins National Monument ∴• **USA** ◇ 26-27 D 1
Azuero, Península de ∪ **PA** ◇ 28-29 D 8 ◆ 16-17 K 9
Azul ○ **RA** ◆ 32-33 L 5
Azul, Cerro ▲ **CR** ◇ 28-29 B 7
Azul, Río ∼ **MEX** ◇ 28-29 E 3
Azul, Río ∼ **MEX** ◇ 28-29 K 3
Azúl Meambar, Parque Nacional ⊥ **HN** ◇ 28-29 L 4
Azurduy ○ **BOL** ◆ 30-31 G 8

B

Baardheere ○ **SP** ◆ 48-49 O 8
Bābā, Kūh-e ▲ **AFG** ◆ 56-57 K 4
Bāb al-Mandab ≈ ◆ 56-57 E 8
Babana ○ **WAN** ◆ 48-49 F 6
Babanūsa ○ **SUD** ◆ 48-49 L 6
Babaomby, Tanjona ▲ **RM** ◆ 50-51 L 4
Babar, Kepulauan ∩ **RI** ◆ 58-59 J 8
Babar, Pulau ∩ **RI** ◆ 58-59 J 8
Babat ○ **RI** ◆ 58-59 D 7
Babati ○ **EAT** ◆ 50-51 J 2
Babb ○ **USA** ◇ 20-21 H 1
Babel, Mont de ▲ **CDN** ◇ 18-19 K 3 ◆ 14-15 X 6
Babelthuap ∩ **PAL** ◆ 58-59 K 5
Babinda ○ **AUS** ◆ 60-61 K 3
Babine Lake ⬭ **CDN** ◆ 14-15 L 6
Bābol ○• **IR** ◆ 56-57 G 3
Baboquivari Peak ▲ **USA** ◇ 20-21 J 10
Baboua ○ **RCA** ◆ 48-49 H 7
Babrujsk ☆ **BY** ◇ 42-43 L 5 ◆ 34-35 R 5
Babruysk = Babrujsk ☆ **BY** ◇ 42-43 L 5 ◆ 34-35 R 5
Babuškina, zaliv ≈ ◆ 52-53 b 6
Babuyan Channel ≈ ◆ 58-59 H 3
Babuyan Island ∩ **RP** ◆ 58-59 H 3
Babuyan Islands ∩ **RP** ◆ 58-59 H 3
Bacabal ○ **BR** ◆ 30-31 K 5
Bacaja, Área Indígena X **BR** ◆ 30-31 J 5
Bacalar ○ **MEX** ◇ 28-29 K 2
Bacan, Pulau ∩ **RI** ◆ 58-59 J 7
Bacău ☆• **RO** ◆ 34-35 R 6
Bachbone, Mount ▲ **USA** ◇ 22-23 J 6
Bachu ○ **CHN** ◆ 54-55 D 4
Back River ∼ **CDN** ◆ 14-15 Q 3
Bắc Ninh ☆ **VN** ◆ 58-59 E 2
Bacolod ☆ **RP** ◆ 58-59 H 4
Bad', al- ○• **KSA** ◆ 56-57 C 5
Bada ▲ **ETH** ◆ 48-49 N 7
Badajós, Lago ⬭ **BR** ◆ 30-31 G 5
Badajoz ○·· **E** ◇ 44-45 D 5 ◆ 34-35 K 8
Badāri, al- ○ **ET** ◆ 48-49 M 3
Bad Axe ○ **USA** ◇ 22-23 G 4
Baddeck ○ **CDN** ◇ 18-19 O 5
Baddo ∼ **PK** ◆ 56-57 J 5
Badger ○ **CDN** ◇ 18-19 Q 4
Badgingarra ○ **AUS** ◆ 60-61 D 6
Badlands National Park ⊥ **USA** ◆ 14-15 Q 8
Bado ○ **RI** ◆ 58-59 L 8
Bad River Indian Reservation X **USA** ◇ 22-23 C 2
Badu Island ∩ **AUS** ◆ 60-61 J 2
Badulla ○ **CL** ◆ 56-57 N 9
Badvel ○ **IND** ◆ 56-57 M 8
Bafata ☆ **GNB** ◆ 48-49 C 6
Baffin Basin ≃ ◆ 14-15 X 2
Baffin Bay ≈ ◆ 14-15 W 2
Baffin Bay ≈ ◇ 26-27 J 6
Baffin-Greenland Rise ≃ ◆ 14-15 Z 3
Baffin Island ∩ **CDN** ◆ 14-15 V 2
Bafia ○ **CAM** ◆ 48-49 H 8
Bafoulabé ○ **RMM** ◆ 48-49 C 6
Bafoussam ☆ **CAM** ◆ 48-49 H 7
Bafra ☆ **TR** ◆ 34-35 T 7
Bafwasende ○ **ZRE** ◆ 50-51 G 1
Bagaces ○ **CR** ◇ 28-29 B 6
Bagansiapiapi ○ **RI** ◆ 58-59 D 6
Baġdād ★·· **IRQ** ◆ 56-57 E 4
Bagdad ○ **USA** ◇ 20-21 H 8
Bagdarin ☆ **RUS** ◆ 52-53 T 7
Bagé ○ **BR** ◆ 32-33 M 4
Baghdad = Baġdād ★·· **IRQ** ◆ 56-57 E 4
Baghelkhand Plateau ▲ **IND** ◆ 56-57 N 6
Bagherhat ○··· **BD** ◆ 56-57 O 6
Baġlān ☆ **AFG** ◆ 56-57 K 3
Bagnères-de-Bigorre ○ **F** ◇ 38-39 H 10 ◆ 34-35 M 7
Bagoé ∼ **RMM** ◆ 48-49 D 6
Bagomoyo ○• **EAT** ◆ 50-51 J 3
Baguio ○·· **RP** ◆ 58-59 H 3
Bāḥa, al- ☆ **KSA** ◆ 56-57 E 6
Bahamas ■ **BS** ◆ 16-17 L 5
Bahamas, The ∩ **BS** ◆ 16-17 L 5
Baharampur ○• **IND** ◆ 56-57 O 6
Baharden ○ **TM** ◆ 56-57 H 3
Bahariya Oasis = Baḥrīya, al-Wāhāt al- ∸• **ET** ◆ 48-49 L 3
Bahāwalpur ○• **PK** ◆ 56-57 L 5
Bahia □ **BR** ◆ 30-31 L 7
Bahía, Islas de la ∩ **HN** ◇ 28-29 L 3 ◆ 16-17 J 7
Bahía Blanca ○ **RA** ◆ 32-33 K 5
Bahía Grande ≈ ◆ 32-33 J 8
Bahía Laura ○ **RA** ◆ 32-33 J 7
Bahías, Cabo dos ▲ **RA** ◆ 32-33 J 6
Bahía Solano ○ **CO** ◆ 30-31 D 3
Bahir Dar ○ **ETH** ◆ 48-49 N 6
Bahla ○··· **OM** ◆ 56-57 H 6
Bahraich ○ **IND** ◆ 56-57 N 5
Bahrain ■ **BRN** ◆ 56-57 G 5
Baḥr al-Azraq, Al- **SUD** ◆ 48-49 M 6
Baḥr al-Milḥ < **IRQ** ◆ 56-57 E 4
Baḥrīya, al-Wāhāt al- ∸• **ET** ◆ 48-49 L 3
Baḥrīya, Barqat al- ∸ **ET** ◆ 48-49 K 2
Bāḫtarān ☆• **IR** ◆ 56-57 F 4
Baḫtegān, Daryāče-ye ⬭ **IR** ◆ 56-57 G 5
Baía dos Tigres ○ **ANG** ◆ 50-51 D 5
Baia Mare ☆• **RO** ◆ 34-35 Q 6
Baião ○ **BR** ◆ 30-31 K 5
Baïbokoum ○ **TCH** ◆ 48-49 J 7
Baicheng ○ **CHN** ◆ 54-55 N 2
Baie, La ○ **CDN** ◇ 18-19 J 4
Baie-à-la-Loutre ○ **CDN** ◇ 18-19 N 4
Baie-Comeau ○ **CDN** ◇ 18-19 K 4 ◆ 14-15 X 7
Baie-des-Sables ○ **CDN** ◇ 18-19 L 4
Baie-du-Poste ○ **CDN** ◇ 18-19 H 3
Baie Johan-Beetz ○ **CDN** ◇ 18-19 N 3
Baie-Sainte-Claire ○ **CDN** ◇ 18-19 M 4
Baie-Saint-Paul ○ **CDN** ◇ 18-19 J 5
Baikal, Lake ⬭ **RUS** ◆ 52-53 S 7
Baile Átha Cliath = Dublin ★·· **IRL** ◇ 38-39 D 5 ◆ 34-35 K 5
Băileşti ○ **RO** ◆ 34-35 Q 7
Bailleul ○ **F** ◇ 38-39 J 6 ◆ 34-35 M 5
Bailundo ○ **ANG** ◆ 50-51 E 4
Baimka ○ **RUS** ◆ 52-53 d 4
Bainbridge ○ **USA** ◇ 24-25 F 4
Baing ○ **RI** ◆ 58-59 H 9
Baiquan ○ **CHN** ◆ 54-55 O 2
Baird ○ **USA** ◇ 26-27 H 3
Baird Mountains ▲ **USA** ◆ 14-15 D 3
Baird Peninsula ∪ **CDN** ◆ 14-15 V 3
Bairiki ★ **KIB** ◆ 12 J 2
Bairin Zuoqi ○ **CHN** ◆ 54-55 M 3
Bairnsdale ○ **AUS** ◆ 60-61 K 7
Bairūt ★ **RL** ◆ 56-57 D 4
Baiš, Wādi ∼ **KSA** ◆ 56-57 E 7
Baïse ∼ **F** ◇ 38-39 H 10 ◆ 34-35 M 7
Baiyin ○ **CHN** ◆ 54-55 J 4
Baja California ∪ **MEX** ◆ 16-17 C 4
Bajanaul ○·· **KZ** ◆ 52-53 M 7
Bajanhongor ☆ **MAU** ◆ 54-55 J 2
Bajdarackaja guba ≈ ◆ 52-53 J 4
Bajkal ○ **RUS** ◆ 52-53 R 7
Bajkal'sk ○ **RUS** ◆ 52-53 R 7
Bajkal'skij zapovednik ⊥ **RUS** ◆ 52-53 S 7
Bajkoņyr ○ **KZ** ◆ 52-53 K 8

Angangueo — Bajkoņyr 67

Burnie-Somerset ○ **AUS** ◆ 60-61 K 8
Burnpur ○ **IND** ◆ 56-57 O 6
Burns ○ **USA** ◇ 20-21 E 4
Burnside ○ **CDN** ◇ 18-19 S 4
Burnside, Lake ⊖ **AUS** ◆ 60-61 E 5
Burns Indian Reservation X **USA** ◇ 20-21 E 4
Burns Junction ○ **USA** ◇ 20-21 F 4
Burntbush River ~ **CDN** ◇ 18-19 E 4
Burnt Lake = Lac Brûlé ⊖ **CDN** ◇ 18-19 N 2
Burnt Ranch ○ **USA** ◇ 20-21 C 5
Burqin ○ **CHN** ◆ 54-55 F 2
Burra ○ **AUS** ◆ 60-61 H 6
Bursa ☆ ·· **TR** ◆ 34-35 R 7
Būr Safāğa ○ **ET** ◆ 48-49 M 3
Būr Saʿīd ☆ **ET** ◆ 48-49 M 2
Būr Sūdān ☆ · **SUD** ◆ 48-49 N 5
Buru, Pulau ⌒ **RI** ◆ 58-59 J 7
Burubajtal ○ **KZ** ◆ 56-57 L 2
Burundi ■ **BU** ◆ 50-51 G 2
Buruntuma ○ **GNB** ◆ 48-49 C 6
Bururi ○ **BU** ◆ 50-51 G 2
Buryatia □ **RUS** ◆ 52-53 T 7
Būšehr, Bandar-e ☆ · **IR** ◆ 56-57 G 5
Businga ○ **ZRE** ◆ 48-49 K 8
Busselton ○ **AUS** ◆ 60-61 D 6
Buta ○ **ZRE** ◆ 48-49 K 8
Butare ○ · **RWA** ◆ 50-51 G 2
Butaritari Island ⌒ **KIB** ◆ 12 J 2
Butler ○ **USA** (AL) ◇ 24-25 D 3
Butler ○ **USA** (GA) ◇ 24-25 F 3
Butler ○ **USA** (PA) ◇ 22-23 J 5
Buton, Pulau ⌒ **RI** ◆ 58-59 H 7
Butte ○ **USA** ◇ 20-21 H 3 ◆ 14-15 O 7
Butterpot Provincial Park ⊥ **CDN** ◇ 18-19 S 5
Butterworth ○ **ZA** ◆ 50-51 G 8
Button Islands ⌒ **CDN** ◆ 14-15 X 4
Butuan ☆ **RP** ◆ 58-59 J 5
Butwal ○ **NEP** ◆ 56-57 N 5
Buulobarde ○ **SP** ◆ 48-49 P 8
Buur Hakkaba ○ **SP** ◆ 48-49 O 8
Buyo, Lac du < **CI** ◆ 48-49 D 7
Büyükağrı Dağı (Ararat) ▲ ·· **TR** ◆ 34-35 U 8
Buzău ☆ · **RO** ◆ 34-35 R 6
Búzios, Cabo dos ▲ **BR** ◆ 32-33 O 2
Buzuluk ☆ **RUS** ◆ 34-35 W 5
Bwagaoia ○ **PNG** ◆ 58-59 O 9
Byam Martin Channel ≈ ◆ 14-15 P 1
Byam Martin Island ⌒ **CDN** ◆ 14-15 Q 1
Bydgoszcz ☆ · **PL** ◇ 40-41 P 2 ◆ 34-35 P 5
Bylas ○ **USA** ◇ 26-27 B 3
Bylot Island ⌒ **CDN** ◆ 14-15 V 2
Byrd ○ **ANT** ◆ 13 F 25
Byrd Land ∸ **ANT** ◆ 13 E 0
Byron, Cape ▲ **AUS** ◆ 60-61 L 5
Byron, Isla ⌒ **RCH** ◆ 32-33 G 7
Byrranga, Gory ⛰ **RUS** ◆ 52-53 N 3
Bytantaj ~ **RUS** ◆ 52-53 X 4
Bytom ○ **PL** ◇ 40-41 P 3 ◆ 34-35 P 5

C

Caala ○ **ANG** ◆ 50-51 E 4
Caatingas ∸ **BR** ◆ 30-31 L 7
Caballo ○ **USA** ◇ 26-27 D 3
Caballo Reservoir < **USA** ◇ 26-27 D 3
Cabano ○ · **CDN** ◇ 18-19 K 5
Cabimas ○ **YV** ◆ 30-31 E 2
Cabinda □ **ANG** ◆ 50-51 D 3
Cabinda ☆ **ANG** ◆ 50-51 D 3
Cabinet Mountains ⛰ **USA** ◇ 20-21 F 1
Cabo de Hornos, Parque Nacional ⊥ **RCH** ◆ 32-33 J 9
Cabonga, Réservoir < **CDN** ◇ 18-19 F 5
Cabool ○ **USA** ◇ 26-27 L 1
Cabo Orange, Parque Nacional do ⊥ **BR** ◆ 30-31 J 4
Cabora Bassa, Lago de < **MOC** ◆ 50-51 H 5
Cabo San Lucas ○ **MEX** ◆ 16-17 E 6
Cabot ○ **USA** ◇ 26-27 L 2
Cabot Strait ≈ ◇ 18-19 O 5 ◆ 14-15 Y 7
Cabrillo National Monument · **USA** ◇ 20-21 F 9
Caçapava do Sul ○ **BR** ◆ 32-33 M 4
Cáceres ○ **BR** ◆ 30-31 H 8
Cáceres ○ ⋯ **E** ◇ 44-45 D 5 ◆ 34-35 K 8
Cache ○ **USA** ◇ 26-27 H 2
Cache Peak ▲ **USA** ◇ 20-21 H 4
Cacheu ☆ **GNB** ◆ 48-49 B 6
Cachi ○ · **RA** ◆ 32-33 J 2
Cachí, Nevado de ▲ **RA** ◆ 32-33 J 2
Cachimbo, Serra do ⛰ **BR** ◆ 30-31 H 6
Cachoeira do Sul ○ **BR** ◆ 32-33 M 4
Cachoeiro de Itapemirim ○ **BR** ◆ 32-33 O 2
Cachos, Punta ▲ **RCH** ◆ 32-33 H 3
Cacolo ○ **ANG** ◆ 50-51 E 4
Caconda ○ **ANG** ◆ 50-51 E 4
Caculé ○ **BR** ◆ 30-31 L 7
Cadale ○ **SP** ◆ 48-49 P 8
Caddo Lake ⊖ **USA** ◇ 26-27 K 3
Cadillac ○ **USA** ◇ 22-23 F 3
Cádiz ○ **E** ◇ 44-45 D 6 ◆ 34-35 K 8
Cadiz ○ **USA** (KY) ◇ 22-23 E 7
Cadiz ○ **USA** (OH) ◇ 22-23 H 5
Caen ☆ · **F** ◇ 38-39 G 7 ◆ 34-35 L 6
Caesaera Scugog, Lake ⊖ **CDN** ◇ 18-19 E 6
Caetité ○ **BR** ◆ 30-31 L 7
Cafetal ○ **MEX** ◇ 28-29 K 2
Cagayan de Oro ☆ **RP** ◆ 58-59 H 5
Čağčarān ○ · **AFG** ◆ 56-57 K 4
Cágliari ○ **I** ◇ 46-47 B 5 ◆ 34-35 N 8
Caguas ○ **USA** ◆ 16-17 N 7
Čāh Āb ○ **AFG** ◆ 56-57 K 3
Cahabón, Río ~ **GCA** ◇ 28-29 K 4
Cahama ○ **ANG** ◆ 50-51 D 5
Čāh Bahār ○ · **IR** ◆ 56-57 J 5
Cahokia Mounds ⋯ **USA** ◇ 22-23 C 6 ◆ 16-17 H 3
Cahors ☆ · **F** ◇ 38-39 H 9 ◆ 34-35 M 7
Cahuapanas ○ **PE** ◆ 30-31 D 6
Caia ○ **MOC** ◆ 50-51 J 5
Caicos Islands ⌒ **GB** ◆ 16-17 M 6
Caicos Passage ≈ ◆ 16-17 M 6
Caillou Bay ≈ ◇ 26-27 M 5
Cairns ○ ·· **AUS** ◆ 60-61 K 3
Cairo ○ **USA** ◇ 24-25 F 4
Cairo = al-Qāhira ★ ⋯ **ET** ◆ 48-49 M 3
Caiundo ○ **ANG** ◆ 50-51 E 5
Cajamarca ☆ · **PE** ◆ 30-31 D 6
Čajbuha ○ **RUS** ◆ 52-53 d 5
Cajcara del Orinoco ○ **YV** ◆ 30-31 F 3
Cajon ○ **USA** ◇ 20-21 F 8
Cajon, El ○ **USA** ◇ 20-21 F 9 ◆ 16-17 C 4
Cajon, Embalse el < **HN** ◇ 28-29 L 4
Cajones, Río ~ **MEX** ◇ 28-29 F 3
Calabar ☆ **WAN** ◆ 48-49 G 8
Calabozo ○ **YV** ◆ 30-31 F 3
Calafate, El ○ **RA** ◆ 32-33 H 8
Calais ○ · **F** ◇ 38-39 H 6 ◆ 34-35 M 5
Calais ○ **USA** ◇ 22-23 P 3
Calama ○ **RCH** ◆ 32-33 J 2
Calamar ○ **CO** ◆ 30-31 E 4
Calamba ○ · **RP** ◆ 58-59 H 4
Calamian Group ⌒ **RP** ◆ 58-59 G 4
Calamuya ∴ · **HN** ◇ 28-29 L 4
Calandula ○ **ANG** ◆ 50-51 E 3
Calandula, Quedas do ~ ·· **ANG** ◆ 50-51 E 3
Calapan ☆ **RP** ◆ 58-59 H 4
Calatayud ○ **E** ◇ 44-45 G 4 ◆ 34-35 L 7
Calayan Island ⌒ **RP** ◆ 58-59 H 3
Calbayog ○ **RP** ◆ 58-59 H 4
Calbore ○ **PA** ◇ 28-29 D 7
Calcasieu Lake ⊖ **USA** ◇ 26-27 L 5
Calcasieu River ~ **USA** ◇ 26-27 L 4
Calçoene ○ **BR** ◆ 30-31 J 4
Calcutta ☆ ·· **IND** ◆ 56-57 O 6
Caldera ○ **CR** ◇ 28-29 B 7 ◆ 16-17 K 9
Caldera ○ **RCH** ◆ 32-33 H 3
Caldwell ○ **USA** (ID) ◇ 20-21 F 4
Caldwell ○ **USA** (KS) ◇ 26-27 J 1
Caldwell ○ **USA** (OH) ◇ 22-23 H 6
Caldwell ○ **USA** (TX) ◇ 26-27 J 4
Caledonia ○ **CDN** ◇ 18-19 E 7
Caledonia ○ **USA** ◇ 22-23 C 4
Caledonia Hills ⛰ **CDN** ◇ 18-19 M 6
Caleta Olivia ○ **RA** ◆ 32-33 J 7
Calexico ○ **USA** ◇ 20-21 G 9
Calgary ○ **CDN** ◆ 14-15 O 6
Calhoun ○ **USA** (GA) ◇ 24-25 F 2
Calhoun ○ **USA** (LA) ◇ 26-27 L 3
Calhoun City ○ **USA** ◇ 24-25 D 3
Calhoun Falls ○ **USA** ◇ 24-25 G 2
Cali ☆ **CO** ◆ 30-31 D 4
Calico Ghost Town ∴ · **USA** ◇ 20-21 F 8
Calicut ○ · **IND** ◆ 56-57 M 8
Caliente ○ **USA** (CA) ◇ 20-21 E 8
Caliente ○ **USA** (NV) ◇ 20-21 G 7
California □ **USA** ◇ 20-21 D 5 ◆ 16-17 B 2
California, Gulf of ≈ ◆ 16-17 D 4
California Aqueduct < **USA** ◇ 20-21 D 7
Calingasta ○ **RA** ◆ 32-33 J 4
Calion ○ **USA** ◇ 26-27 L 3
Calipatria ○ **USA** ◇ 20-21 G 9
Calistoga ○ **USA** ◇ 20-21 C 6
Calkiní ○ **MEX** ◇ 28-29 J 1 ◆ 16-17 H 6
Callahan ○ **USA** (CA) ◇ 20-21 C 5
Callahan ○ **USA** (FL) ◇ 24-25 H 4
Callahan, Mount ▲ **USA** ◇ 20-21 F 6
Callander ○ **CDN** ◇ 18-19 E 5
Callao ○ **PE** ◆ 30-31 D 7
Callao ○ **USA** ◇ 22-23 K 7
Callaway ○ **USA** ◇ 24-25 F 4
Calmar ○ **USA** ◇ 22-23 C 4
Cal Miskaat, Buuraha ⛰ **SP** ◆ 48-49 P 6
Caloosahatchee River ~ **USA** ◇ 24-25 H 6
Caloundra ○ **AUS** ◆ 60-61 L 5
Calpulalpan ○ **MEX** ◇ 28-29 E 1
Caltanissetta ○ **I** ◇ 46-47 E 6 ◆ 34-35 O 8
Calulo ○ **ANG** ◆ 50-51 D 3
Caluquembe ○ **ANG** ◆ 50-51 D 4
Čālūs ○ · **IR** ◆ 56-57 G 3
Caluula ○ **SP** ◆ 48-49 Q 6
Caluula, Raas = Ilaawe ▲ **SP** ◆ 48-49 Q 6
Calvert Island ⌒ **CDN** ◆ 14-15 L 6
Calvert River ~ **AUS** ◆ 60-61 H 3
Calvin ○ **USA** ◇ 26-27 J 2
Calvinia ○ **ZA** ◆ 50-51 E 8
Camabatela ○ **ANG** ◆ 50-51 E 3
Camacupa ○ **ANG** ◆ 50-51 E 4
Camagüey ☆ · **C** ◆ 16-17 L 6
Camagüey, Archipiélago de ⌒ **C** ◆ 16-17 L 6
Camana ○ **PE** ◆ 30-31 E 8
Camaquã ○ **BR** ◆ 32-33 M 4
Camarata ○ **YV** ◆ 30-31 G 3
Camarones ○ **RA** ◆ 32-33 J 6
Camaruã ○ **BR** ◆ 30-31 G 6
Cà Mau ○ **VN** ◆ 58-59 E 5
Cambaxi ○ **ANG** ◆ 50-51 E 3
Cambellford ○ **CDN** ◇ 18-19 F 6
Cambodia ■ **K** ◆ 58-59 D 4
Cambrai ○ · **F** ◇ 38-39 J 6 ◆ 34-35 M 5
Cambridge ○ **CDN** ◇ 18-19 D 7
Cambridge ○ ·· **GB** ◇ 38-39 H 5 ◆ 34-35 M 5
Cambridge ○ **USA** (ID) ◇ 20-21 F 3
Cambridge ○ **USA** (MA) ◇ 22-23 N 4
Cambridge ○ **USA** (MD) ◇ 22-23 K 6
Cambridge ○ **USA** (OH) ◇ 22-23 H 5
Cambridge Bay ○ **CDN** ◆ 14-15 Q 3
Cambridge Gulf ≈ ◆ 60-61 F 2
Cambutal ○ **PA** ◇ 28-29 D 8
Camden ○ **USA** (AL) ◇ 24-25 E 4
Camden ○ **USA** (AR) ◇ 26-27 L 3
Camden ○ **USA** (NY) ◇ 22-23 L 4
Camden ○ · **USA** (SC) ◇ 24-25 H 2
Cameia, Parque Nacional da ⊥ **ANG** ◆ 50-51 F 4
Cameron ○ **USA** (AZ) ◇ 20-21 J 8
Cameron ○ **USA** (LA) ◇ 26-27 L 5
Cameron ○ **USA** (TX) ◇ 26-27 J 4
Cameroon ■ **CAM** ◆ 48-49 H 8
Cametá ○ **BR** ◆ 30-31 K 5
Camiguin Island ⌒ **RP** (CAG) ◆ 58-59 H 3
Camiguin Island ⌒ **RP** (MSO) ◆ 58-59 H 5
Camilla ○ **USA** ◇ 24-25 F 4
Camisea ○ **PE** ◆ 30-31 E 7
Camocim ○ **BR** ◆ 30-31 L 5
Camooweal ○ **AUS** ◆ 60-61 H 3
Campamento ○ **HN** ◇ 28-29 L 4
Campana, Isla ⌒ **RCH** ◆ 32-33 G 7
Campana, Monte ▲ **RA** ◆ 32-33 J 8
Campbell Island ⌒ **NZ** ◆ 12 H 8
Campbell Military Reservation, Fort xx **USA** ◇ 22-23 E 7
Campbell Plateau ≃ ◆ 12 J 7
Campbell River ○ **CDN** ◆ 14-15 L 6
Campbell's Bay ○ **CDN** ◇ 18-19 F 6
Campbellsville ○ **USA** ◇ 22-23 F 7
Campbellton ○ **CDN** ◇ 18-19 L 5
Campeche □ **MEX** ◇ 28-29 J 2
Campeche ☆ · **MEX** (CAM) ◇ 28-29 J 2 ◆ 16-17 H 7
Campeche, Bahía de ≈ ◇ 28-29 G 2 ◆ 16-17 G 7
Campinas ○ **BR** ◆ 32-33 N 2
Campo ○ · **CAM** ◆ 48-49 G 8
Campo ○ **USA** ◇ 26-27 F 1
Campo, El ○ **USA** ◇ 26-27 J 5
Campo, Réserve de = Campo Reserve ⊥ **CAM** ◆ 48-49 G 8
Campo Belo ○ **BR** ◆ 32-33 N 2
Campo Grande ☆ **BR** ◆ 32-33 M 2
Campo Grayling Artillery Range xx **USA** ◇ 22-23 F 3
Campo Maior ○ **BR** ◆ 30-31 L 5
Campos ○ **BR** ◆ 32-33 O 2
Campos Belos ○ **BR** ◆ 30-31 K 7
Camp Pendleton Marine Corps Base xx **USA** ◇ 20-21 F 9
Camp Point ○ **USA** ◇ 22-23 C 5
Camp Verde ○ **USA** ◇ 20-21 J 8
Camp Wood ○ **USA** ◇ 26-27 G 5
Canada ■ **CDN** ◇ 18-19 D 3 ◆ 14-15 M 5
Canada Basin ≃ ◆ 14-15 H 1
Canada Bay ≈ ◇ 18-19 Q 3
Cañada de Gómez ○ **RA** ◆ 32-33 K 4
Canadian ○ **USA** ◇ 26-27 G 2
Canadian River ~ **USA** ◇ 26-27 E 2 ◆ 16-17 F 3
Canaima, Parque Nacional ⊥ ⋯ **YV** ◆ 30-31 G 3
Çanakkale ☆ · **TR** ◆ 34-35 R 7
Canal de Tūnis ≃ ◇ 46-47 C 6 ◆ 34-35 O 8
Canalí ○ **MEX** ◇ 28-29 E 1
Canandaigua ○ **USA** ◇ 22-23 K 4
Canarias, Islas □ **E** ◆ 48-49 B 3
Canary Basin ≃ ◆ 34-35 J 9
Canary Islands ⌒ **E** ◆ 48-49 B 3
Cañas ○ **MEX** ◇ 28-29 D 2
Cañas, Las ○ **CR** ◇ 28-29 B 6
Canaveral, Cape ▲ **USA** ◇ 24-25 H 5 ◆ 16-17 K 5
Canavieiras ○ **BR** ◆ 30-31 M 8
Cañazas ○ **PA** (Pan) ◇ 28-29 E 7
Cañazas ○ **PA** (Ver) ◇ 28-29 D 7
Canberra ★ · **AUS** ◆ 60-61 K 7
Canby ○ **USA** ◇ 20-21 D 5
Canconga ○ **ANG** ◆ 50-51 E 4
Cancuc ○ **MEX** ◇ 28-29 H 3
Cancuén ∴ · **GCA** ◇ 28-29 J 3
Cancún ○ · **MEX** ◇ 28-29 L 1 ◆ 16-17 J 6
Cancún, Isla ⌒ **MEX** ◇ 28-29 L 1
Candelaria ○ · **MEX** ◇ 28-29 J 2
Candelaria, Río ~ **MEX** ◇ 28-29 J 2
Cangamba ○ **ANG** ◆ 50-51 E 4
Cangandala, Parque Nacional de ⊥ **ANG** ◆ 50-51 E 3
Çangrâfa ○ **RIM** ◆ 48-49 C 5
Cangzhou ○ **CHN** ◆ 54-55 M 4
Caniapiscau, Réservoir < **CDN** ◆ 14-15 W 6
Caniapiscau, Rivière ~ **CDN** ◆ 14-15 X 5
Canindé ○ **BR** ◆ 30-31 M 5
Çankırı ☆ · **TR** ◆ 34-35 S 7
Cannanore ○ · **IND** ◆ 56-57 M 8
Cannanore Islands ⌒ **IND** ◆ 56-57 L 8
Cannes ○ · **F** ◇ 38-39 L 10 ◆ 34-35 N 7
Cannonville ○ **USA** ◇ 20-21 H 7
Cann River ○ **AUS** ◆ 60-61 K 7
Caño, El ○ **PA** ◇ 28-29 D 7
Caño, Isla de ⌒ **CR** ◇ 28-29 C 7
Canoa ○ **HN** ◇ 28-29 K 4
Canoas ○ **BR** ◆ 32-33 M 3
Cañoncito Indian Reservation X **USA** ◇ 26-27 D 2
Cañon del Sumidero, Parque Nacional ⊥ **MEX** ◇ 28-29 H 3
Cañon de Río Blanco, Parque Nacional ⊥ **MEX** ◇ 28-29 F 2
Canso ○ **CDN** ◇ 18-19 O 6
Canso, Strait of ≈ ◇ 18-19 O 6 ◆ 14-15 Y 7
Canterbury Bight ≈ ◆ 60-61 P 8
Cần Thơ' ○ · **VN** ◆ 58-59 E 4
Cantil ○ **USA** ◇ 20-21 F 8
Canto do Buriti ○ **BR** ◆ 30-31 L 6
Canton ○ **USA** (GA) ◇ 24-25 F 2
Canton ○ **USA** (MO) ◇ 22-23 C 5
Canton ○ **USA** (MS) ◇ 26-27 M 3
Canton ○ **USA** (NY) ◇ 22-23 L 3
Canton ○ **USA** (OH) ◇ 22-23 H 5 ◆ 16-17 K 2
Canton ○ **USA** (PA) ◇ 22-23 K 5
Canton ○ **USA** (TX) ◇ 26-27 K 3
Canton = Guangzhou ☆ ·· **CHN** ◆ 54-55 L 7
Canutama ○ **BR** ◆ 30-31 G 6
Čany ☆ **RUS** ◆ 52-53 M 6
Čany, ozero **RUS** ◆ 52-53 M 7
Canyon ○ **USA** ◇ 26-27 G 2
Canyon Chelly National Monument ∴ **USA** ◇ 26-27 C 1
Canyon Creek ○ **USA** ◇ 20-21 H 2
Canyon Ferry ○ **USA** ◇ 20-21 J 2
Canyon Ferry Lake ⊖ **USA** ◇ 20-21 J 2
Canyonlands National Park ⊥ **USA** ◆ 16-17 E 3
Cao Bằng ☆ · **VN** ◆ 58-59 E 2
Čapaevo ☆ **KZ** ◆ 34-35 W 5
Capanema ○ **BR** ◆ 30-31 K 5
Cap-aux-Meules ○ **CDN** ◇ 18-19 O 5
Capbreton ○ **F** ◇ 38-39 G 10 ◆ 34-35 L 7
Cap-de-la-Madeleine ○ **CDN** ◇ 18-19 H 5
Cape Anguille ○ **CDN** ◇ 18-19 P 5
Cape Arid National Park ⊥ **AUS** ◆ 60-61 E 6
Cape Barren Island ⌒ **AUS** ◆ 60-61 K 8
Cape Basin ≃ ◆ 50-51 C 8
Cape Borda ○ **AUS** ◆ 60-61 H 7
Cape Breton Highlands National Park ⊥ **CDN** ◇ 18-19 O 5 ◆ 14-15 Y 7
Cape Breton Island ⌒ **CDN** ◇ 18-19 O 5 ◆ 14-15 Y 7
Cape Byrd ▲ **ANT** ◆ 13 G 8
Cape Canaveral ○ **USA** ◇ 24-25 H 5
Cape Canaveral Air Force Station xx · **USA** ◇ 24-25 H 5
Cape Charles Lighthouse · **USA** ◇ 22-23 L 7
Cape Coast ☆ · **GH** ◆ 48-49 E 7
Cape Cod Bay ≈ ◇ 22-23 N 5
Cape Cod National Seashore ⊥ **USA** ◇ 22-23 O 4
Cape Cod Peninsula ∸ **USA** ◇ 22-23 O 5
Cape Colbeck ▲ **ANT** ◆ 13 F 21
Cape Coral ○ **USA** ◇ 24-25 H 6
Cape Crawford ○ **AUS** ◆ 60-61 H 3
Cape Croker Indian Reserve X **CDN** ◇ 18-19 D 6
Cape Dart ▲ **ANT** ◆ 13 F 24
Cape Dorset ○ **CDN** ◆ 14-15 V 4
Cape Fear River ~ **USA** ◇ 24-25 J 2 ◆ 16-17 L 3
Cape Flying Fish ▲ **ANT** ◆ 13 F 26
Cape Freshfield ▲ **ANT** ◆ 13 G 16
Cape Girardeau ○ **USA** ◇ 22-23 D 7 ◆ 16-17 J 3
Cape Hatteras National Seashore ⊥ **USA** ◇ 24-25 L 2
Cape Hope Islands ⌒ **CDN** ◇ 18-19 E 2
Cape Horn ▲ **RCH** ◆ 32-33 J 9
Cape Krusenstern National Monument ⊥ **USA** ◆ 14-15 D 3
Cape Le Grand National Park ⊥ **AUS** ◆ 60-61 E 6
Capella ○ **AUS** ◆ 60-61 K 4
Capelle, la ○ **F** ◇ 38-39 J 7 ◆ 34-35 M 6
Cape Lookout National Seashore ⊥ **USA** ◇ 24-25 K 2
Cape May ○ **USA** ◇ 22-23 L 6
Cape Moore ▲ **ANT** ◆ 13 F 17
Capenda-Camulemba ○ **ANG** ◆ 50-51 E 3
Cape of Good Hope ▲ · **ZA** ◆ 50-51 E 8
Cape Palmer ▲ **ANT** ◆ 13 F 27
Cape Race ○ **CDN** ◇ 18-19 S 5 ◆ 14-15 a 7
Cape Sable Island ⌒ **CDN** ◇ 18-19 M 7
Cape Smiley ▲ **ANT** ◆ 13 F 29
Cape Tormentine ○ **CDN** ◇ 18-19 N 5
Cape Town ☆ ·· **ZA** ◆ 50-51 E 8
Cape Vincent ○ **USA** ◇ 22-23 K 3
Cape York Peninsula ⌣ **AUS** ◆ 60-61 J 2
Cap-Haïtien ☆ **RH** ◆ 16-17 M 7
Capim, Rio ~ **BR** ◆ 30-31 K 5
Capitan ○ **USA** ◇ 26-27 E 3
Capitán Pablo Lagerenza ☆ **PY** ◆ 30-31 G 8
Capitol Reef National Park ⊥ **USA** ◇ 20-21 J 6 ◆ 16-17 D 3
Caponda ○ **MOC** ◆ 50-51 H 4
Capoto, Área Indígena X **BR** ◆ 30-31 J 6
Capps ○ **USA** ◇ 24-25 G 4
Capricorn, Cape ▲ **AUS** ◆ 60-61 L 4
Caprivi Game Park ⊥ **NAM** ◆ 50-51 F 5
Caprivi Strip ∸ **NAM** ◆ 50-51 F 5
Cap-Seize ○ **CDN** ◇ 18-19 L 4
Captain Cook ○ **USA** ◇ 24-25 E 8
Capulin Mountain National Monument · **USA** ◇ 26-27 F 1
Caquetá, Río ~ **CO** ◆ 30-31 E 5
Čara ~ **RUS** ◆ 52-53 U 6
Caracarai ○ **BR** ◆ 30-31 G 4
Caracaraí, Estação Ecológica ⊥ **BR** ◆ 30-31 G 4
Caracas ★ · **YV** ◆ 30-31 F 2
Caracol ∴ · **BH** ◇ 28-29 K 3
Carajás, Serra dos ⛰ **BR** ◆ 30-31 J 6
Carapán ○ **MEX** ◇ 28-29 C 2
Caraquet ○ · **CDN** ◇ 18-19 M 5
Caratasca, Laguna de ≈ ◆ 16-17 K 7
Caratinga ○ **BR** ◆ 30-31 L 8
Carauari ○ **BR** ◆ 30-31 F 5
Caraúbas ○ **BR** ◆ 30-31 M 6
Caravelas ○ **BR** ◆ 30-31 M 8
Caraveli ○ **PE** ◆ 30-31 E 8
Carazinho ○ **BR** ◆ 32-33 M 3
Carbonado ○ **USA** ◇ 20-21 C 2
Carbondale ○ **USA** (IL) ◇ 22-23 D 7 ◆ 16-17 J 3
Carbondale ○ **USA** (PA) ◇ 22-23 L 5
Carbonear ○ **CDN** ◇ 18-19 S 5
Carcassonne ☆ ·· **F** ◇ 38-39 J 10 ◆ 34-35 M 7
Cárdenas ○ · **MEX** ◇ 28-29 H 2
Cardiel, Lago ⊖ **RA** ◆ 32-33 H 7
Cardiff ○ **GB** ◇ 38-39 F 6 ◆ 34-35 L 5
Carefree ○ **USA** ◇ 22-23 E 6
Careiro ○ **BR** ◆ 30-31 G 5
Carentan ○ **F** ◇ 38-39 G 7 ◆ 34-35 L 6
Carey ○ **USA** ◇ 20-21 H 4
Carey, Lake ⊖ **AUS** ◆ 60-61 E 5
Cargados Carajos Islands ∸ **MS** ◆ 50-51 N 5
Carhaix-Plouguer ○ **F** ◇ 38-39 F 7 ◆ 34-35 L 6
Caribbean Sea ≈ ◆ 16-17 L 8
Caribe, Río ~ **MEX** ◇ 28-29 J 2
Cariboo Mountains ⛰ **CDN** ◆ 14-15 M 6
Caribou ○ **USA** ◇ 18-19 L 5
Caribou Mountains ⛰ **CDN** ◆ 14-15 N 5
Čārīkār ☆ **AFG** ◆ 56-57 K 4
Carinhanha ○ **BR** ◆ 30-31 L 7
Caripito ○ **YV** ◆ 30-31 G 2
Carleton ○ **CDN** ◇ 18-19 M 6
Carleton, Mount ▲ **CDN** ◇ 18-19 L 5
Carleton Place ○ **CDN** ◇ 18-19 F 6
Carlin ○ **USA** ◇ 20-21 F 5
Carlinville ○ **USA** ◇ 22-23 D 6
Carlisle ○ **GB** ◇ 38-39 F 4 ◆ 34-35 L 5
Carlisle ○ **USA** (PA) ◇ 22-23 K 5
Carlisle ○ **USA** (SC) ◇ 24-25 H 2
Carlota, La ○ **RA** ◆ 32-33 K 4
Carl Sandburg Home National Historic Site · **USA** ◇ 24-25 G 2
Carlsbad ○ **USA** (NM) ◇ 26-27 E 3 ◆ 16-17 F 4
Carlsbad ○ **USA** (TX) ◇ 26-27 G 4
Carlsbad Caverns National Park ⊥ ⋯ **USA** ◇ 26-27 E 3 ◆ 16-17 F 4
Carlsberg Ridge ≃ ◆ 50-51 M 1
Carlyle Lake ⊖ **USA** ◇ 22-23 D 6
Carmanville ○ **CDN** ◇ 18-19 R 4
Carmaux ○ **F** ◇ 38-39 J 9 ◆ 34-35 M 7
Carmelita ○ **GCA** ◇ 28-29 J 3
Carmen, Ciudad del ○ · **MEX** ◇ 28-29 J 2 ◆ 16-17 H 7
Carmen, Isla del ⌒ **MEX** ◇ 28-29 J 2
Carmen, Laguna del ≈ ◇ 28-29 H 2
Carmen de Patagones ○ **RA** ◆ 32-33 K 6
Carmi ○ **USA** ◇ 22-23 D 6
Carmona ○ **CR** ◇ 28-29 B 7
Carnarvon ○ **AUS** ◆ 60-61 C 4
Carnarvon ○ **CDN** ◇ 18-19 E 6
Carnarvon ○ **ZA** ◆ 50-51 F 8
Carnegie ○ **USA** (PA) ◇ 22-23 H 5
Carnegie ○ **USA** (PA) ◇ 22-23 J 5
Carnegie, Lake ⊖ **AUS** ◆ 60-61 E 5
Car Nicobar Island ⌒ **IND** ◆ 58-59 B 5
Carnot ○ · **RCA** ◆ 48-49 J 8
Carnot, Cape ▲ **AUS** ◆ 60-61 H 6
Carnot Bay ≈ ◆ 60-61 E 3
Carol City ○ **USA** ◇ 24-25 H 7
Carolina ○ **BR** ◆ 30-31 K 6
Carolina ○ **USA** ◆ 16-17 N 7
Carolina ○ **ZA** ◆ 50-51 H 7
Caroline Island ⌒ **KIB** ◆ 12 M 3
Caroline Islands ⌒ **FSM** ◆ 58-59 M 5
Caroline National Memorial, Fort ∴ · **USA** ◇ 24-25 H 4
Caroline Seamounts ≃ ◆ 58-59 M 5
Caron Brook ○ **CDN** ◇ 18-19 K 5
Caroni, Río ~ **YV** ◆ 30-31 G 3
Carpathian Mountains ⛰ ◆ 34-35 Q 6
Carpentaria, Gulf of ≈ ◆ 60-61 H 2
Carpentras ○ **F** ◇ 38-39 K 9 ◆ 34-35 N 6
Carpinteria ○ **USA** ◇ 20-21 E 8
Carrabelle ○ **USA** ◇ 24-25 F 5
Carreta, Punta ▲ **PE** ◆ 30-31 D 7
Carrington Island ⌒ **USA** ◇ 20-21 H 5
Carrizal, Punta ▲ **RCH** ◆ 32-33 H 3
Carrizal Bajo ○ **RCH** ◆ 32-33 H 3
Carrizo Creek ~ **USA** ◇ 26-27 F 1
Carrizo Springs ○ **USA** ◇ 26-27 H 5 ◆ 16-17 G 5
Carrizozo ○ **USA** ◇ 26-27 E 3
Carrollton ○ **USA** (GA) ◇ 24-25 F 3
Carrollton ○ **USA** (KY) ◇ 22-23 F 6
Carson City ☆ **USA** ◇ 20-21 E 6 ◆ 16-17 C 3
Carson Sink ⊖ **USA** ◇ 20-21 E 6
Cartagena ☆ ⋯ **CO** ◆ 30-31 D 2
Cartagena ○ **E** ◇ 44-45 G 6 ◆ 34-35 L 8
Cartago ☆ **CR** ◇ 28-29 C 7
Cartago ○ **USA** ◇ 20-21 E 7
Carter ○ **USA** ◇ 20-21 J 2
Cartersville ○ **USA** ◇ 24-25 F 2
Carthage ∴ ⋯ **TN** ◆ 48-49 H 1
Carthage ○ **USA** (IL) ◇ 22-23 C 5
Carthage ○ **USA** (MO) ◇ 26-27 K 1
Carthage ○ **USA** (MS) ◇ 24-25 D 3
Carthage ○ **USA** (TX) ◇ 26-27 K 3
Cartier ○ **CDN** ◇ 18-19 D 5
Cartier, Port- ○ **CDN** ◇ 18-19 L 3
Cartier Islet ⌒ **AUS** ◆ 60-61 E 2
Carti Suitupo ○ **PA** ◇ 28-29 E 7
Carúpano ○ **YV** ◆ 30-31 G 2
Caruthersville ○ **USA** ◇ 22-23 D 7
Cary ○ **USA** ◇ 24-25 J 2
Casablanca = Ad-Dār-al-Bayda ☆ **MA** ◆ 48-49 D 2
Casa Grande ○ **USA** ◇ 20-21 J 9 ◆ 16-17 D 4
Casa Grandes Ruins National Monument ∴ **USA** ◇ 20-21 J 9
Casa Nova ○ **BR** ◆ 30-31 L 6
Casares ○ **NIC** ◇ 28-29 L 6
Cascade ○ **USA** ◇ 20-21 J 2
Cascade Caverns ∴ **USA** ◇ 26-27 H 5
Cascade Range ⛰ **USA** ◇ 20-21 C 5 ◆ 16-17 B 2
Cascade Reservoir ⊖ **USA** ◇ 20-21 F 3
Cascapédia, Rivière ~ **CDN** ◇ 18-19 L 4
Cascavel ○ **BR** ◆ 32-33 M 2
Cascumpeque Bay ≈ ◇ 18-19 N 5
Caseyr, Raas = Cap Gwardafuy ▲ **SP** ◆ 48-49 Q 6
Casiguran ○ **RP** ◆ 58-59 H 3
Casilda ○ **RA** ◆ 32-33 K 4
Casino ○ **AUS** ◆ 60-61 L 5
Casma ○ **PE** ◆ 30-31 D 6
Casper ○ **USA** ◆ 16-17 E 2
Caspian Depression ⌣ ◆ 34-35 V 6
Caspian Sea ≈ ◆ 34-35 V 7
Cassai ~ **ANG** ◆ 50-51 F 4
Cass City ○ **USA** ◇ 22-23 G 4
Casselman ○ **CDN** ◇ 18-19 G 6
Cassiar Mountains ⛰ **CDN** ◆ 14-15 L 5
Cass River ~ **USA** ◇ 22-23 G 4
Castaic ○ **USA** ◇ 20-21 E 8
Castanhal ○ **BR** ◆ 30-31 K 5
Castaños ○ **MEX** ◆ 16-17 F 5
Casteljaloux ○ **F** ◇ 38-39 H 9 ◆ 34-35 L 7
Castella ○ **USA** ◇ 20-21 C 5
Castelló de la Plana ○ **E** ◇ 44-45 G 5 ◆ 34-35 L 8
Castelnaudary ○ · **F** ◇ 38-39 H 10 ◆ 34-35 M 7
Castelnau-Magnoac ○ **F** ◇ 38-39 H 10 ◆ 34-35 M 7
Castelsarrasin ○ **F** ◇ 38-39 H 9 ◆ 34-35 L 7
Castelvetrano ○ **I** ◇ 46-47 D 6 ◆ 34-35 O 8
Casterton ○ **AUS** ◆ 60-61 J 7
Castillo de San Felipe · **GCA** ◇ 28-29 K 4
Castillo de San Marcos National Monument · **USA** ◇ 24-25 H 5
Castle Island ○ **CDN** ◇ 18-19 R 3
Castlemaine ○ **AUS** ◆ 60-61 J 7
Castle Peak ▲ **USA** ◇ 20-21 G 3
Castor, Ruisseau du ~ **CDN** ◇ 18-19 E 2
Castres ○ **F** ◇ 38-39 J 10 ◆ 34-35 M 7
Castries ★ **WL** ◆ 16-17 O 8
Castroville ○ **USA** ◇ 26-27 H 5
Casuarina Coast ⌣ **RI** ◆ 58-59 L 8
Catacamas ○ **HN** ◇ 28-29 B 4
Catahoula Lake ⊖ **USA** ◇ 26-27 L 4
Catalina ○ **CDN** ◇ 18-19 S 4
Catamarca □ **RA** ◆ 32-33 J 3
Catandica ○ **MOC** ◆ 50-51 H 5
Catanduanes ⌒ **RP** ◆ 58-59 H 4
Catanduva ○ **BR** ◆ 32-33 N 2
Catánia ○ **I** ◇ 46-47 E 6 ◆ 34-35 P 8
Catanzaro ○ **I** ◇ 46-47 F 5 ◆ 34-35 P 8
Cataratas del Iguazú ~ ·· **RA** ◆ 32-33 M 3
Catarina ○ **USA** ◇ 26-27 H 5
Catarman ☆ **RP** ◆ 58-59 H 4
Cat Arm River ~ **CDN** ◇ 18-19 Q 3
Catazaja ○ **MEX** ◇ 28-29 H 3
Catemaco ○ **MEX** ◇ 28-29 G 2
Catemaco, Laguna de ⊖ · **MEX** ◇ 28-29 G 2
Cateté, Área Indígena X **BR** ◆ 30-31 J 6
Cathedral Mountain ▲ **USA** ◇ 26-27 F 4
Cathedral Valley ∴ **USA** ◇ 20-21 J 6
Cathlamet ○ **USA** ◇ 20-21 C 2
Catia la Mar ○ **YV** ◆ 30-31 F 2
Cat Island ⌒ **BS** ◆ 16-17 L 6
Cat Island ⌒ **USA** ◆ 16-17 J 5
Catoche, Cabo ▲ **MEX** ◇ 28-29 L 1 ◆ 16-17 J 6
Cato Island ⌒ **AUS** ◆ 60-61 M 4
Catrilo ○ **RA** ◆ 32-33 K 5
Catrimani, Rio ~ **BR** ◆ 32-33 G 4
Catskill ○ **USA** ◇ 22-23 M 4
Catskill Mountains ⛰ **USA** ◇ 22-23 L 4
Cattaraugus Indian Reservation X **USA** ◇ 22-23 J 4
Caucasia ○ **CO** ◆ 30-31 D 3
Caucasus ⛰ ◆ 34-35 U 7
Čaunskaja guba ≈ ◆ 52-53 e 4
Caupolican ∸ **BOL** ◆ 30-31 F 7
Cauquenes ○ **RCH** ◆ 32-33 H 5
Causabiscau, Lac ⊖ **CDN** ◇ 18-19 F 2
Causapscal ○ **CDN** ◇ 18-19 L 4
Causapscal, Parc Provincial ⊥ **CDN** ◇ 18-19 L 4
Causey ○ **USA** ◇ 26-27 F 3
Cavalla River ~ **LB** ◆ 48-49 D 7
Cave City ○ **USA** ◇ 26-27 M 2
Caverns of Sonora ∴ · **USA** ◇ 26-27 G 4
Caviana de Fora, Ilha ⌒ **BR** ◆ 30-31 J 4
Caxias ○ **BR** ◆ 30-31 L 5
Caxito ☆ **ANG** ◆ 50-51 D 3
Caxiuaná, Reserva Florestal de ⊥ **BR** ◆ 30-31 J 5
Cayambe ○ **EC** ◆ 30-31 D 4
Cayambe, Volcán ▲ **EC** ◆ 30-31 D 4
Cayce ○ **USA** ◇ 24-25 H 3
Cayes, Les ☆ · **RH** ◆ 16-17 M 7
Cayman Islands □ **GB** ◆ 16-17 K 7
Cayman Ridge ≃ ◆ 16-17 K 7
Cayman Trench ≃ ◆ 16-17 K 7
Cayo Nuevo ⌒ **MEX** ◇ 28-29 H 1
Cayos Arcas, Isla ⌒ **MEX** ◇ 28-29 J 1
Cayuga ○ **USA** ◇ 26-27 K 4
Cayuga Lake ⊖ **USA** ◇ 22-23 K 4
Cazorla ○ **YV** ◆ 30-31 F 3
Ceara Abyssal Plain ≃ ◆ 30-31 L 4
Čeboksary ☆ **RUS** ◆ 34-35 V 4
Ceboruco, Cerro ▲ **MEX** ◇ 28-29 B 2
Cebu ⌒ **RP** ◆ 58-59 H 5
Cebu City ☆ ·· **RP** ◆ 58-59 H 4
Cècèrlèg ☆ **MAU** ◆ 54-55 J 2
Cedar Breaks National Monument · **USA** ◇ 20-21 H 7
Cedar City ○ **USA** ◇ 20-21 H 7 ◆ 16-17 D 3
Cedar Creek Reservoir ⊖ **USA** ◇ 26-27 J 3
Cedar Hill ○ **USA** ◇ 22-23 C 6
Cedar Lake ⊖ **CDN** ◆ 14-15 Q 6
Cedar Lake ⊖ **USA** ◇ 26-27 F 3
Cedar Point ○ **CDN** ◇ 18-19 D 6
Cedar Rapids ○ **USA** ◇ 22-23 C 5 ◆ 16-17 H 2
Cedar River ~ **USA** ◇ 22-23 C 5
Cedartown ○ **USA** ◇ 24-25 F 2
Cedarville ○ **USA** ◇ 20-21 D 5
Cedeño ○ **HN** ◇ 28-29 L 5
Cedral ∴ · **MEX** ◇ 28-29 L 1
Cedro ○ **BR** ◆ 30-31 M 6
Cedros, Isla ⌒ **MEX** ◆ 16-17 C 5
Ceduna ○ **AUS** ◆ 60-61 G 6
Ceelbuur ○ **SP** ◆ 48-49 P 8
Ceerigaabo ☆ **SP** ◆ 48-49 P 6
Cefalù ○ **I** ◇ 46-47 E 5 ◆ 34-35 O 8
Ceheng ○ **CHN** ◆ 54-55 K 7
Ceiba, La ☆ **HN** ◇ 28-29 L 4 ◆ 16-17 J 7
Ceiba, La ○ **YV** ◆ 30-31 E 3
Ceibal, El ∴ · **GCA** ◇ 28-29 J 3
Čekanovskogo, krjaž ⛰ **RUS** ◆ 52-53 V 3
Čekurdah ○ **RUS** ◆ 52-53 a 3
Celaque, Parque Nacional ⊥ **HN** ◇ 28-29 K 4
Celarain, Punta ▲ **MEX** ◇ 28-29 L 1
Celaya ○ **MEX** ◇ 28-29 D 1 ◆ 16-17 F 6
Celebes Basin ▲ ◆ 58-59 H 6
Celebes Sea ≈ ◆ 58-59 H 6
Celestún ○ · **MEX** ◇ 28-29 J 1
Celina ○ **USA** (OH) ◇ 22-23 F 5
Celina ○ **USA** (TN) ◇ 24-25 F 1
Čeljabinsk ☆ **RUS** ◆ 52-53 J 6
Čeljuskin, mys ▲ **RUS** ◆ 52-53 R 2
Čeljuskin, poluostrov ⌒ **RUS** ◆ 52-53 R 2
Celtic Sea ≈ ◇ 38-39 D 6 ◆ 34-35 K 5
Celtic Shelf ≃ ◆ 34-35 K 5
Cenderawasih, Teluk ≈ ◆ 58-59 K 7
Cenotillo ○ **MEX** ◇ 28-29 K 1
Center ○ **USA** ◇ 26-27 K 4
Center Hill Lake ⊖ **USA** ◇ 24-25 F 1
Centerville ○ **USA** ◇ 24-25 E 2
Central ○ **USA** ◇ 26-27 C 3
Central, Cordillera ⛰ **CR** ◇ 28-29 B 6
Central African Republic ■ **RCA** ◆ 48-49 J 7
Central Australia Aboriginal Land X **AUS** ◆ 60-61 F 4
Central Brāhui Range ⛰ **PK** ◆ 56-57 K 5
Central City ○ **USA** ◇ 22-23 E 7
Central Desert Aboriginal Land X **AUS** ◆ 60-61 G 3
Central Eastern Australian Rainforest ⊥ ⋯ **AUS** ◆ 60-61 L 5
Centralia ○ **USA** (IL) ◇ 22-23 D 6
Centralia ○ **USA** (WA) ◇ 20-21 C 2
Central Kalahari Game Reserve ⊥ **RB** ◆ 50-51 F 6
Central Makrān Range ⛰ **PK** ◆ 56-57 J 5
Central'nojakutskaja ravnina ⌣ **RUS** ◆ 52-53 U 5
Central'nosibirskij zapovednik učastok Elogujskij ⊥ **RUS** ◆ 52-53 O 5
Central'nosibirskij zapovednik učastok Enisejsko-Stolbovoj ⊥ **RUS** ◆ 52-53 P 5
Central'no-Tungusskoe, plato ∸ **RUS** ◆ 52-53 R 5
Central Patricia ○ **CDN** ◆ 14-15 S 6
Central Point ○ **USA** ◇ 20-21 C 4
Central Range ⛰ **PNG** ◆ 58-59 M 7
Central Siberian Plateau ∸ **RUS** ◆ 52-53 P 4
Centre □ **F** ◇ 38-39 H 8 ◆ 34-35 M 6
Centreville ○ **USA** ◇ 24-25 E 3
Centro, Cayo ⌒ **MEX** ◇ 28-29 L 2
Centro, El ○ **USA** ◇ 20-21 G 9 ◆ 16-17 C 4
Ceram Sea ≈ ◆ 58-59 J 7
Čerepovec ☆ **RUS** ◇ 42-43 P 2 ◆ 34-35 T 4
Ceres ○ **BR** ◆ 30-31 K 8
Cerf Island ⌒ **SY** ◆ 50-51 M 3
Čerkassy = Čerkasy ☆ **UA** ◆ 34-35 S 6
Čerkasy ☆ **UA** ◆ 34-35 S 6
Čerkessk ☆ **RUS** ◆ 34-35 U 7
Černihiv ○ · **UA** ◆ 34-35 S 5
Černivci ☆ **UA** ◆ 34-35 R 6
Černye Brat'ja, ostrova ⌒ **RUS** ◆ 52-53 b 8
Černyševskij ○ **RUS** ◆ 52-53 T 5
Cerralvo, Isla ⌒ **MEX** ◆ 16-17 E 6
Cerro, El ○ **BOL** ◆ 30-31 G 8
Cerro de Pasco ☆ **PE** ◆ 30-31 D 7
Cerro Mangote ∴ **PA** ◇ 28-29 D 7
Cerro Punta ○ **PA** ◇ 28-29 C 7
Čerskij ○ **RUS** ◆ 52-53 d 4
Čerskogo, hrebet ⛰ **RUS** ◆ 52-53 Y 4
Cervantes ○ **AUS** ◆ 60-61 D 6
Cervati, Monte ▲ **I** ◇ 46-47 E 4 ◆ 34-35 P 7
Cesena ○ **I** ◇ 46-47 D 2 ◆ 34-35 O 7
Cēsis ☆ ·· **LV** ◇ 42-43 J 3 ◆ 34-35 R 4
České Budějovice ○ **CZ** ◇ 40-41 N 4 ◆ 34-35 O 6
Çeşme ☆ **TR** ◆ 34-35 R 8
Čëšskaja guba ≈ ◆ 52-53 F 4
Češt-e Šarīf ○ · **AFG** ◆ 56-57 J 4
Cestos River ~ **LB** ◆ 48-49 D 7
Ceuta ○ **E** ◇ 44-45 E 7 ◆ 34-35 L 8
Cevennen = Cévennes ⛰ **F** ◇ 38-39 J 9 ◆ 34-35 M 7
Cévennes ∸ **F** ◇ 38-39 J 9 ◆ 34-35 M 7
Cévennes, Parc National des ⊥ · **F** ◇ 38-39 J 9 ◆ 34-35 M 7
Chablé ○ **MEX** ◇ 28-29 J 3
Chacahua, Laguna de ≈ · ◇ 28-29 F 4
Chacahua, Parque Natural Laguna de ⊥ **MEX** ◇ 28-29 F 3
Chachapoyas ☆ **PE** ◆ 30-31 D 6
Chacmool ∴ · **MEX** ◇ 28-29 L 2
Chaco □ **RA** ◆ 32-33 K 3
Chaco Austral ∸ **RA** ◆ 32-33 K 3
Chaco Boreal ∸ **PY** ◆ 32-33 K 2
Chaco Central ∸ **PY** ◆ 32-33 K 2
Chaco Culture National Historic Park ⊥ ⋯ **USA** ◇ 26-27 D 1
Chad ■ **TCH** ◆ 48-49 J 5
Chad, Lake = Tchad, Lac ⊖ ◆ 48-49 H 6
Chadayang ○ **CHN** ◆ 54-55 M 7
Chai Nat ○ **THA** ◆ 58-59 D 3
Chala ○ **PE** ◆ 30-31 E 8
Chalais ○ **F** ◇ 38-39 H 9 ◆ 34-35 L 7
Chalatenango ☆ **ES** ◇ 28-29 K 4
Chalchuapa ○ **ES** ◇ 28-29 K 5
Chaleur Bay ≈ ◇ 18-19 M 4 ◆ 14-15 X 7
Chaleurs, Baie des ≈ ◇ 18-19 M 4
Challans ○ **F** ◇ 38-39 G 8 ◆ 34-35 L 6
Challapata ○ **BOL** ◆ 30-31 F 8
Challenger Deep ≃ ◆ 58-59 M 4
Challenger Plateau ≃ ◆ 60-61 O 7
Challis ○ **USA** ◇ 20-21 G 3

70 **Burnie-Somerset — Challis**

Châlons-sur-Marne ☆ • F ◇ 38-39 K 7
◆ 34-35 M 6
Chalon-sur-Saône o F ◇ 38-39 K 8
◆ 34-35 M 6
Chaltel o Fitz Roy, Cerro ▲ RA
◆ 32-33 H 7
Chama o USA ◇ 26-27 D 1
Chama, Río ~ USA ◇ 26-27 D 1
Chamax ∴ • MEX ◇ 28-29 L 2
Chamba o •• IND ◆ 56-57 M 4
Chamberlain Lake ⊂ USA ◇ 22-23 O 2
Chamberlain River ~ AUS ◆ 60-61 F 3
Chambersburg o USA ◇ 22-23 K 6
Chambéry ☆ • F ◇ 38-39 K 9
◆ 34-35 N 6
Chambord o CDN ◇ 18-19 H 4
Chambord, Château ••• F ◇ 38-39 H 8
◆ 34-35 M 6
Chambri Lakes ⊂ PNG ◆ 58-59 M 7
Chame o PA ◇ 28-29 E 7
Chamelecón, Río ~ HN ◇ 28-29 K 4
Chamical o RA ◆ 32-33 J 4
Champagne ⊥ • F ◇ 38-39 K 7
◆ 34-35 M 6
Champagne-Ardenne ▫ F ◇ 38-39 K 8
◆ 34-35 M 6
Champaign o USA ◇ 22-23 D 5
◆ 16-17 J 2
Champasak o LAO ◆ 58-59 E 4
Champerico o GCA ◇ 28-29 J 4
Champlain o USA ◇ 22-23 M 3
Champlain, Lake ⊂ USA ◇ 22-23 M 3
◆ 14-15 W 8
Champotón o • MEX ◇ 28-29 J 2
◆ 16-17 H 7
Chanal Islands ⌒ USA ◇ 20-21 E 9
Chancay o PE ◆ 30-31 D 7
Chandalar River ~ USA ◆ 14-15 G 3
Chandeleur Islands ⌒ USA ◇ 24-25 D 5
◆ 16-17 J 5
Chandeleur Sound ≈ ◇ 24-25 D 5
Chandigarh ☆ •• IND ◆ 56-57 M 4
Chandler o CDN ◇ 18-19 M 4
Chandler o USA ◇ 26-27 K 3
Chandrapur o IND ◆ 56-57 M 7
Changane, Rio ~ MOC ◆ 50-51 H 6
Changara o MOC ◆ 50-51 H 5
Changchun ☆ CHN ◆ 54-55 O 3
Changde o CHN ◆ 54-55 L 6
Changji o CHN ◆ 54-55 F 3
Chang Jiang ~ CHN ◆ 54-55 K 5
Changsha ☆ • CHN ◆ 54-55 L 6
Changtu o CHN ◆ 54-55 N 3
Changzhi o CHN ◆ 54-55 L 4
Changzhou o CHN ◆ 54-55 M 5
Channel Islands ⌒ GB ◇ 38-39 F 7
◆ 34-35 L 6
Channel Islands ⌒ USA ◇ 20-21 D 9
◆ 16-17 B 4
Channel Islands National Park ⊥ USA
◇ 20-21 D 8 ◆ 16-17 B 4
Channel-Port-aux-Basques o CDN
◇ 18-19 P 5 ◆ 14-15 Z 7
Channing o USA ◇ 26-27 F 2
Chanthaburi o THA ◆ 58-59 D 4
Chantrey Inlet ≈ ◆ 14-15 S 3
Chanute o USA ◇ 26-27 K 1
Chany, Ozero = Čany, ozero RUS
◆ 52-53 M 7
Chaohu o CHN ◆ 54-55 M 5
Chaoyang o CHN ◆ 54-55 N 3
Chaozhou o CHN ◆ 54-55 M 7
Chapadinha o BR ◆ 30-31 L 5
Chapais o CDN ◇ 18-19 G 4
Chapala o MEX ◇ 28-29 C 1
Chapala, Lago de ⊂ MEX ◇ 28-29 C 1
◆ 16-17 F 6
Chaparaó, Serra do ▲ BR ◆ 32-33 O 2
Chapeco o BR ◆ 32-33 M 3
Chapel Hill o USA ◇ 24-25 J 2
Chapel Island Indian Reserve ⨯ CDN
◇ 18-19 O 6
Chapleau o CDN ◇ 18-19 C 5
◆ 14-15 U 7
Chapmanville o USA ◇ 22-23 G 7
Chapra o IND ◆ 56-57 N 5
Charagua o BOL ◆ 30-31 G 8
Charcot, Île ⌒ ANT ◆ 13 G 23
Charente ~ F ◇ 38-39 H 8
◆ 34-35 M 6
Charentes ~ F ◇ 38-39 G 9
◆ 34-35 L 6
Chari ~ TCH ◆ 48-49 J 6
Charité-sur-Loire, la o F ◇ 38-39 J 8
◆ 34-35 M 6
Charity o GUY ◆ 30-31 H 3
Charkiv o UA ◆ 34-35 T 6
Charles, Cape ▲ USA ◇ 22-23 L 7
Charlesbourg o CDN ◇ 18-19 J 5
Charles Island ⌒ CDN ◆ 14-15 W 4
Charles Mount ▲ USA ◇ 22-23 C 4
Charleston o USA (IL) ◇ 22-23 D 6
Charleston o USA (MO) ◇ 22-23 D 7
Charleston o • USA (SC) ◇ 24-25 J 3
◆ 16-17 L 4
Charleston ☆ USA (WV) ◇ 22-23 H 6
◆ 16-17 K 3
Charleston Peak ▲ USA ◇ 20-21 G 7
Charlestown o USA ◇ 22-23 F 6
Charleville o AUS ◆ 60-61 K 5
Charleville-Mézières ☆ F ◇ 38-39 K 7
◆ 34-35 M 6
Charlevoix o USA ◇ 22-23 F 3
Charlevoix, Lake ⊂ USA ◇ 22-23 F 3
Charlie Gibbs Fracture Zone ≃
◆ 14-15 c 6
Charliste o USA ◇ 26-27 M 2
Charlotte o USA (MI) ◇ 22-23 F 4
Charlotte o USA (NC) ◇ 24-25 H 2
◆ 16-17 K 3
Charlotte o USA (TX) ◇ 26-27 H 5
Charlotte Amalie ☆ • USA ◆ 16-17 O 7
Charlotte Harbor ≈ ◇ 24-25 G 6
Charlottesville o ••• USA ◇ 22-23 J 6
◆ 16-17 L 3
Charlottetown ☆ • CDN ◇ 18-19 N 5
◆ 14-15 Y 7
Charlton o AUS ◆ 60-61 J 7
Charlton Island ⌒ CDN ◇ 18-19 E 2
◆ 14-15 V 6
Chārsadda o • PK ◆ 56-57 L 4
Charters Towers o • AUS ◆ 60-61 K 4
Chartres ☆ ••• F ◇ 38-39 H 7
◆ 34-35 M 6
Chascomús o RA ◆ 32-33 L 5
Châtaigneraie, la o F ◇ 38-39 G 8
◆ 34-35 L 6
Châteaubriant o F ◇ 38-39 G 8
◆ 34-35 L 6
Château Chambord ••• F ◇ 38-39 H 8
◆ 34-35 M 6
Châteaudun o F ◇ 38-39 H 7
◆ 34-35 M 6
Château-Gontier o F ◇ 38-39 G 8
◆ 34-35 L 6
Châteauguay o CDN ◇ 18-19 H 6
Châteaulin o F ◇ 38-39 E 7
◆ 34-35 L 6
Châteauneuf-sur-Charente o F
◇ 38-39 G 9 ◆ 34-35 L 6
Châteauneuf-sur-Loire o F ◇ 38-39 J 8
◆ 34-35 M 6
Château-Renault o F ◇ 38-39 H 8
◆ 34-35 M 6
Châteauroux ☆ F ◇ 38-39 H 8
◆ 34-35 M 6
Château-Thierry o F ◇ 38-39 J 7
◆ 34-35 M 6
Châtellerault o F ◇ 38-39 H 8
◆ 34-35 M 6
Chatham o CDN (NB) ◇ 18-19 M 5
Chatham o CDN (ONT) ◇ 18-19 C 7
Chatham o USA (LA) ◇ 26-27 L 3
Chatham o USA (VA) ◇ 22-23 J 7
Chatham Island ⌒ NZ ◆ 60-61 R 8
Chatham Rise ≃ ◆ 60-61 Q 8
Châtillon-sur-Seine o • F ◇ 38-39 K 8
◆ 34-35 M 6
Chatsworth o CDN ◇ 18-19 D 6
Chatsworth o USA ◇ 24-25 F 2
Chattahoochee o USA ◇ 24-25 F 4
Chattahoochee River ~ USA
◇ 24-25 F 4 ◆ 16-17 J 4
Chattanooga o • USA ◇ 24-25 F 2
◆ 16-17 J 3
Chaudière, Rivière ~ CDN ◇ 18-19 J 5
Chaumont o F ◇ 38-39 H 8
◆ 34-35 M 6
Chaumont o F ◇ 38-39 K 7
◆ 34-35 M 6
Chautauqua Lake ⊂ USA ◇ 22-23 J 4
Chaves o BR ◆ 30-31 K 5
Cheaha Mountain ▲ USA ◇ 24-25 F 3
Cheat River ~ USA ◇ 22-23 J 6
Cheboksary = Čeboksary ☆ RUS
◆ 34-35 V 4
Cheboygan o USA ◇ 22-23 F 3
◆ 14-15 U 7
Chech, Erg ⊥ DZ ◆ 48-49 E 4
Chechenia ▫ RUS ◆ 34-35 V 7
Checotah o USA ◇ 26-27 K 2
Chedabucto Bay ≈ ◇ 18-19 O 6
Cheektowaga o USA ◇ 22-23 J 4
Chegga o RIM ◆ 48-49 D 3
Chegutu o ZW ◆ 50-51 H 5
Chehalis o USA ◇ 20-21 C 2
Chehalis River ~ USA ◇ 20-21 C 2
Chehaw Indian Monument ∴ USA
◇ 24-25 F 4
Cheju o ROK ◆ 54-55 O 5
Cheju Do ⌒ ROK ◆ 54-55 O 5
Chela, Serra da ▲ ANG ◆ 50-51 D 5
Chelan o USA ◇ 20-21 D 2
Chelan, Lake ⊂ USA ◇ 20-21 D 1
Chelforó o RA ◆ 32-33 J 5
Chelm ☆ PL ◆ 40-41 R 3
◆ 34-35 Q 5
Chelmsford o CDN ◇ 18-19 D 5
Chelyabinsk = Čeljabinsk ☆ RUS
◆ 52-53 J 6
Chemax o MEX ◇ 28-29 L 1
Chemchâm, Sebkhet ⊂ RIM
◆ 48-49 C 4
Chemillé o F ◇ 38-39 G 8
◆ 34-35 L 6
Chemnitz o D ◆ 40-41 M 3
◆ 34-35 O 5
Chemult o USA ◇ 20-21 D 4
Chencoyi o MEX ◇ 28-29 J 2
Cheney o USA ◇ 20-21 F 2
Chengde o ••• CHN ◆ 54-55 M 3
Chengdu ☆ CHN ◆ 54-55 J 5
Chengshan Jiao ▲ CHN ◆ 54-55 N 4
Chenoa o USA ◇ 22-23 D 5
Chenzhou o CHN ◆ 54-55 L 6
Chepes o RA ◆ 32-33 J 4
Chepo o • PA ◇ 28-29 E 7
Chequamegon Bay ⊂ USA ◇ 22-23 C 2
Cheran o MEX ◇ 28-29 D 2
Cheraw o USA ◇ 24-25 J 2
Cherbourg o F ◇ 38-39 G 7
◆ 34-35 L 6
Cherepovets = Čerepovec ☆ RUS
◆ 42-43 P 2 ◆ 34-35 T 4
Cherkasy = Čerkasy ☆ UA ◆ 34-35 S 6
Chernihiv = Černihiv ☆ UA
◆ 34-35 S 5
Chernivtsi = Černivci ☆ UA ◆ 34-35 R 6
Chernobyl = Čornobyl' o UA
◆ 34-35 S 5
Cherokee Indian Reservation ⨯ USA
◇ 24-25 G 2
Cherokee Lake ⊂ USA ◇ 24-25 G 1
Cherry Island ⌒ SOL ◆ 60-61 O 2
Cherryspring o USA ◇ 26-27 H 4
Cherskogo, Khrebet = Čerskogo, hrebet ▲
RUS ◆ 52-53 Y 4
Cherson ☆ • UA ◆ 34-35 S 6
Chesapeake o USA ◇ 22-23 K 7
Chesapeake Bay ≈ ◇ 22-23 K 6
◆ 16-17 L 3
Chesapeake Bay Bridge Tunnel II USA
◇ 22-23 L 7
Chëshskaya Guba = Čëšskaja guba ≈
◆ 52-53 F 4
Chester o CDN ◇ 18-19 M 6
Chester o USA (IL) ◇ 22-23 D 7
Chester o USA (MT) ◇ 20-21 J 1
Chester o USA (PA) ◇ 22-23 L 6
Chester o USA (SC) ◇ 24-25 H 2
Chesterfield, Île ⌒ RM ◆ 50-51 K 5
Chesterfield, Îles ⌒ F ◆ 60-61 M 3
Chesterfield Inlet ≈ ◆ 14-15 S 4
Chesterfield Inlet o CDN ◆ 14-15 S 4
Chestertown o USA ◇ 22-23 K 6
Chesuncook Lake ⊂ USA ◇ 22-23 O 3
Chetek o USA ◇ 22-23 C 3
Chéticamp o CDN ◇ 18-19 O 5
Chetlat Island ⌒ IND ◆ 56-57 L 8
Chetumal ☆ • MEX ◇ 28-29 K 2
◆ 16-17 J 7
Chetumal, Bahía de ≈ ◇ 28-29 K 2
◆ 16-17 J 7
Chewack River ~ USA ◇ 20-21 D 1
Che'w Bahir ⊂ ETH ◆ 48-49 N 8
Chewelah o USA ◇ 20-21 F 1
Cheyenne o USA (OK) ◇ 26-27 H 2
Cheyenne ☆ USA (WY) ◆ 16-17 F 2
Cheyenne River ~ USA ◆ 16-17 F 2
Cheyenne River Indian Reservation ⨯ USA
◆ 14-15 Q 7
Cheyenne Wells o USA ◆ 16-17 F 3
Chhatarpur o IND ◆ 56-57 M 6
Chhindwara o IND ◆ 56-57 M 6
Chiang Mai ☆ THA ◆ 58-59 C 3
Chiang Rai o THA ◆ 58-59 C 3
Chiapa, Río ~ MEX ◇ 28-29 H 3
Chiapa de Corzo o • MEX ◇ 28-29 H 3
Chiapas ▫ MEX ◇ 28-29 H 3
Chiautla o MEX ◇ 28-29 E 2
Chiayi o RC ◆ 54-55 N 7
Chiba ☆ J ◆ 54-55 R 4
Chibabava o MOC ◆ 50-51 H 6
Chibia o ANG ◆ 50-51 D 5
Chibougamau o CDN ◇ 18-19 G 4
◆ 14-15 W 7
Chibougamau, Lac ⊂ CDN ◇ 18-19 G 4
Chibougamau, Rivière ~ CDN
◇ 18-19 G 4
Chicago o USA ◇ 22-23 E 5
◆ 16-17 J 2
Chicago Heights o USA ◇ 22-23 E 5
Chicaná ∴ • MEX ◇ 28-29 K 2
Chicapa ~ ANG ◆ 50-51 F 3
Chicbul o MEX ◇ 28-29 J 2
Chic-Chocs, Monts ▲ CDN ◇ 18-19 L 4
Chic-Chocs, Réserve Faunique des ⊥ CDN
◇ 18-19 M 4
Chichagof Island ⌒ USA ◆ 14-15 J 5
Chichancanab, Laguna ⊂ • MEX
◇ 28-29 K 2
Chichén Itzá ∴ ••• MEX ◇ 28-29 K 1
◆ 16-17 J 6
Chichigalpa o NIC ◇ 28-29 L 5
Chichón, Volcan ▲ MEX ◇ 28-29 H 3
Chickamauga Lake < USA ◇ 24-25 F 2
Chickasha o USA ◇ 26-27 J 2
Chiclayo ☆ PE ◆ 30-31 D 6
Chico o USA ◇ 20-21 D 6
◆ 16-17 B 3
Chico, Río ~ RA ◆ 32-33 J 7
Chicoasén o MEX ◇ 28-29 H 3
Chicoasén, Presa < • MEX ◇ 28-29 H 3
Chicoma Mountain ▲ USA ◇ 26-27 D 1
Chicomuselo o MEX ◇ 28-29 H 4
Chicontepec de Tejeda o MEX
◇ 28-29 E 1
Chicopee o USA ◇ 22-23 M 4
Chicoutimi o CDN ◇ 18-19 J 4
◆ 14-15 W 7
Chicualacuala o MOC ◆ 50-51 H 6
Chidenguele o MOC ◆ 50-51 H 6
Chief Joseph Pass ▲ USA ◇ 20-21 H 3
Chiefland o USA ◇ 24-25 G 5
Chief Menominee Monument • USA
◇ 22-23 F 5
Chifeng o CHN ◆ 54-55 M 3
Chignecto, Cape ▲ CDN ◇ 18-19 M 6
Chignecto Bay ≈ ◇ 18-19 M 6
Chihli, Gulf of = Bo Hai ≈ ◆ 54-55 M 4
Chihuahua ☆ • MEX ◆ 16-17 E 5
Chila o MEX ◇ 28-29 F 3
Chilapa o MEX ◇ 28-29 E 3
Chilapa de Díaz o MEX ◇ 28-29 F 3
Chilca o PE ◆ 30-31 D 7
Chilcoot o USA ◇ 20-21 D 6
Childersburg o USA ◇ 24-25 E 3
Childress o USA ◇ 26-27 G 2
Chile ▪ RCH ◆ 32-33 H 7
Chile Basin ≃ ◆ 32-33 G 2
Chilecito o • RA ◆ 32-33 J 3
Chile Rise ≃ ◆ 32-33 E 6
Chiles, Los o CR ◇ 28-29 B 6
Chililabombwe o Z ◆ 50-51 G 4
Chilko Lake ⊂ CDN ◆ 14-15 M 6
Chillicothe o USA (IL) ◇ 22-23 D 5
Chillicothe o USA (OH) ◇ 22-23 G 6
Chiloé, Isla de ⌒ RCH ◆ 32-33 H 6
Chiloé, Parque Nacional ⊥ RCH
◆ 32-33 H 6
Chiloquin o USA ◇ 20-21 D 4
Chilpancingo de los Bravos ☆ MEX
◇ 28-29 E 3 ◆ 16-17 G 7
Chiltepec o MEX ◇ 28-29 H 2
Chilton o USA ◇ 22-23 D 3
Chilwa, Lake ⊂ MW ◆ 50-51 J 5
Chimaltenango ☆ GCA ◇ 28-29 J 4
Chimán o PA ◇ 28-29 E 7
Chimanimani o • ZW ◆ 50-51 H 5
Chimborazo, Volcán ▲ EC ◆ 30-31 D 5
Chimbote o PE ◆ 30-31 D 6
Chimoio ☆ MOC ◆ 50-51 H 5
China ▪ CHN ◆ 54-55 E 5
Chinandega ☆ NIC ◇ 28-29 L 5
◆ 16-17 J 8
China Point ▲ USA ◇ 20-21 E 9
Chinati Peak ▲ USA ◇ 26-27 E 5
Chincha Alta o PE ◆ 30-31 D 7
Chinchorro, Banco ⌒ MEX ◇ 28-29 L 2
◆ 16-17 J 7
Chincoteague Bay ≈ ◇ 22-23 L 6
Chincultic ∴ • MEX ◇ 28-29 J 3
Chinde o MOC ◆ 50-51 J 5
Chingola o Z ◆ 50-51 G 4
Chinguetti o • RIM ◆ 48-49 C 4
Chinhoyi ☆ • ZW ◆ 50-51 H 5
Chiniot o • PK ◆ 56-57 L 4
Chinko ~ RCA ◆ 48-49 K 7
Chinle o USA ◇ 26-27 C 1
Chinnūr o IND ◆ 56-57 M 7
Chino o USA ◇ 20-21 F 8
Chinon o F ◇ 38-39 H 8
◆ 34-35 M 6
Chino Valley o USA ◇ 20-21 H 8
Chipata ☆ Z ◆ 50-51 H 4
Chipewyan Indian Reserve ⨯ CDN
◆ 14-15 O 5
Chipipa o ANG ◆ 50-51 E 4
Chipman o CDN ◇ 18-19 M 5
Chippewa, Lake ⊂ USA ◇ 22-23 C 3
Chippewa Falls o USA ◇ 22-23 C 3
Chipputneticook Lakes ~ USA
◇ 22-23 P 3
Chiquilá o MEX ◇ 28-29 L 1
Chiquimula ☆ GCA ◇ 28-29 K 4
Chiquimulilla o GCA ◇ 28-29 J 4
Chiquinquirá o CO ◆ 30-31 E 3
Chiquitos, Llanos de ⊥ BOL
◆ 30-31 G 8
Chirfa o RN ◆ 48-49 H 4
Chiricahua Peak ▲ USA ◇ 26-27 C 4
Chirikof Island ⌒ USA ◆ 14-15 E 5
Chiriquí, Golfo de ≈ ◇ 28-29 C 7
Chiriquí, Laguna de ≈ ◇ 28-29 C 7
Chiriquí Grande o PA ◇ 28-29 C 7
Chiri San ▲ ROK ◆ 54-55 O 4
Chirripó, Río ~ CR ◇ 28-29 C 6
Chirripó del Atlántico, Río ~ CR
◇ 28-29 C 7
Chirripó Grande, Cerro ▲ CR
◇ 28-29 C 7
Chisamba o Z ◆ 50-51 G 4
Chisasibi o CDN ◇ 18-19 E 2
◆ 14-15 V 6
Chisec o GCA ◇ 28-29 J 4
Chişinău ★ MD ◆ 34-35 R 6
Chita = Čita ☆ • RUS ◆ 52-53 T 7
Chitado o ANG ◆ 50-51 D 5
Chitāpur o IND ◆ 56-57 M 7
Chitembo o ANG ◆ 50-51 E 4
Chitimacha Indian Reservation ⨯ USA
◇ 26-27 M 5
Chitongo o Z ◆ 50-51 G 5
Chitrāl o • PK ◆ 56-57 L 3
Chitré ☆ PA ◇ 28-29 D 8
Chitre, Serra do ▲ BR ◆ 30-31 L 8
Chittagong o • BD ◆ 56-57 P 6
Chittoor o IND ◆ 56-57 M 8
Chitungwiza o ZW ◆ 50-51 H 5
Chiumbe ~ ANG ◆ 50-51 F 3
Chiume o ANG ◆ 50-51 F 5
Chivay o PE ◆ 30-31 E 8
Chivhu o ZW ◆ 50-51 H 5
Chivicahua National Monument ∴ USA
◇ 26-27 C 3
Chivilcoy o RA ◆ 32-33 L 4
Chixoy o Negro, Río ~ GCA
◇ 28-29 J 4
Chizarira National Park ⊥ ZW
◆ 50-51 G 5
Chlef ☆ DZ ◆ 48-49 F 1
Chmel'nyc'kyj ☆ UA ◆ 34-35 R 6
Chnattisgarh ⊥ IND ◆ 56-57 N 6
Choapan o MEX ◇ 28-29 G 3
Chobe ~ NAM ◆ 50-51 F 5
Chobe National Park ⊥ RB ◆ 50-51 F 5
Chocolate Mountain Gunnery Range xx
USA ◇ 20-21 G 9
Chocolate Mountains ▲ USA
◇ 20-21 G 9
Chocowinity o USA ◇ 24-25 K 2
Choctawhatchee Bay ≈ ◇ 24-25 E 4
Choctawhatchee River ~ USA
◇ 24-25 E 4
Choctaw Indian Reservation ⨯ USA
◇ 24-25 D 3
Choele Choel o RA ◆ 32-33 J 5
Choiseul ⌒ SOL ◆ 58-59 P 8
Choix, Port aux o CDN ◇ 18-19 Q 3
Choke Canyon Lake ⊂ USA
◇ 26-27 H 5
Cholame o USA ◇ 20-21 D 8
Chole • EAT ◆ 50-51 J 3
Cholet o F ◇ 38-39 G 8 ◆ 34-35 L 6
Choluteca ☆ HN ◇ 28-29 L 5
◆ 16-17 J 8
Choluteca, Río ~ HN ◇ 28-29 L 5
Choma o Z ◆ 50-51 G 5
Chon Buri o THA ◆ 58-59 D 4
Chone o EC ◆ 30-31 C 5
Chongjin ☆ KOR ◆ 54-55 O 3
Chongqing o • CHN ◆ 54-55 K 6
Chonos, Archipiélago de los ⌒ RCH
◆ 32-33 G 7
Chontaleña, Cordillera ▲ NIC
◇ 28-29 B 6
Chontalpa o MEX ◇ 28-29 H 3
Choqā Zanbil ∴ •• IR ◆ 56-57 F 4
Chorrera, La o PA ◇ 28-29 E 7
Chos Malal o RA ◆ 32-33 H 5
Choteau o USA ◇ 20-21 H 2
Choûm o RIM ◆ 48-49 C 4
Chouteau o USA ◇ 26-27 K 1
Chowan River ~ USA ◇ 24-25 K 1
Chowchilla o USA ◇ 20-21 D 7
Chowduár o IND ◆ 56-57 O 6
Chrisman o USA ◇ 22-23 E 6
Christchurch o •• NZ ◆ 60-61 P 8
Christian Island ⌒ CDN ◇ 18-19 D 6
Christiansburg o USA ◇ 22-23 H 7
Christie Bay ⊂ CDN ◆ 14-15 O 4
Christmas Creek ~ AUS ◆ 60-61 F 3
Christmas Island ⌒ AUS ◆ 58-59 E 9
Chubut ▫ RA ◆ 32-33 J 6
Chucunaque ~ PA ◇ 28-29 E 7
Chu Dang Sin ▲ VN ◆ 58-59 E 4
Chudleigh o CDN ◇ 18-19 D 5
Chugach Mountains ▲ USA
◆ 14-15 G 4
Chuginadak Island ⌒ USA ◆ 14-15 B 6
Chukchi Plateau ≃ ◆ 13 B 35
Chukchi Sea ◆ 13 C 35
Chukotskiy Poluostrov = Čukotskij
poluostrov ⌒ RUS ◆ 52-53 h 4
Chula Vista o USA ◇ 20-21 F 9
Chulucanas o PE ◆ 30-31 C 6
Chumbicha o RA ◆ 32-33 J 3
Chumphon o THA ◆ 58-59 C 4
Chumpón o MEX ◇ 28-29 L 2
Chumul ∴ • MEX (YUC) ◇ 28-29 K 2
Chumul ∴ • MEX (YUC) ◇ 28-29 K 1
Ch'unch'ŏn o ROK ◆ 54-55 O 4
Chunchura o IND ◆ 56-57 O 6
Chuquicamata o RCH ◆ 32-33 J 2
Churchill o • CDN ◆ 14-15 S 5
Churchill, Cap ▲ CDN ◆ 14-15 S 5
Churchill Falls o CDN ◇ 18-19 M 2
◆ 14-15 Y 6
Churchill River ~ CDN ◆ 14-15 R 5
Churchill River ~ CDN ◇ 18-19 O 2
Churobusco o USA ◇ 22-23 F 5
Churu o IND ◆ 56-57 L 5
Chuska Mountains ▲ USA ◇ 26-27 C 1
Chute-des-Passes o CDN ◇ 18-19 J 4
Chutes Tshunga ~ ZRE ◆ 50-51 G 1
Chuvashia ▫ RUS ◆ 34-35 V 4
Chuxiong o CHN ◆ 54-55 J 6
Chuy o ROU ◆ 32-33 M 4
Ciamis o RI ◆ 58-59 E 8
Cianjur o RI ◆ 58-59 E 8
Ciego de Ávila ☆ C ◆ 16-17 L 6
Ciénaga o CO ◆ 30-31 E 2
Cienfuegos ☆ C ◆ 16-17 K 6
Cihuatlán o MEX ◇ 28-29 B 2
Čikoj ~ RUS ◆ 52-53 S 7
Čikšina ~ RUS ◆ 52-53 H 5
Cilacap o RI ◆ 58-59 E 8
Čil'ći o RUS ◆ 52-53 V 6
Cimarron o USA ◇ 26-27 E 1
Cimarron ~ USA ◇ 26-27 H 1
Cimarron National Grassland ⊥ USA
◇ 26-27 G 1
Cimarron River ~ USA ◇ 26-27 F 1
◆ 16-17 G 3
Cimljanskoe vodohranilišče < RUS
◆ 34-35 U 6
Cincinnati o USA ◇ 22-23 F 6
◆ 16-17 K 3
Cinnabar Mountain ▲ USA ◇ 20-21 F 4
Cintalapa de Figueroa o MEX
◇ 28-29 H 3
Ciotat, la o F ◇ 38-39 K 10
◆ 34-35 M 7
Cipa ~ RUS ◆ 52-53 U 6
Circle o USA ◆ 14-15 H 3
Circleville o USA ◇ 22-23 G 6
Cirebon o • RI ◆ 58-59 E 8
Cisco o USA ◇ 26-27 H 3
Cisne, Islas del = Santanilla, Islas ⌒ HN
◆ 16-17 K 7
Čita ☆ • RUS ◆ 52-53 T 7
Citronelle o USA ◇ 24-25 D 4
Citrus Heights o USA ◇ 20-21 D 6
Città del Vaticano ★ ••• SCV
◇ 46-47 D 4 ◆ 34-35 O 7
Ciudad Altamirano o MEX ◇ 28-29 D 2
Ciudad Bolívar ☆ • YV ◆ 30-31 G 3
Ciudad Camargo o • MEX ◆ 16-17 E 5
Ciudad Colón o CR ◇ 28-29 B 7
Ciudad Constitución o • MEX
◆ 16-17 D 5
Ciudad Cortés o CR ◇ 28-29 C 7
Ciudad Cuauhtémoc o MEX
◇ 28-29 J 4
Ciudad Darío o • NIC ◇ 28-29 L 5
Ciudad de Guatemala ★ GCA
◇ 28-29 J 4
Ciudad del Carmen o • MEX
◇ 28-29 J 2
Ciudad del Este ☆ PY ◆ 32-33 M 3
Ciudad de México ★ ••• MEX
◇ 28-29 E 2
Ciudad Guzmán o • MEX ◇ 28-29 C 2
Ciudad Ixtepec o MEX ◇ 28-29 G 3
Ciudad Juárez o • MEX ◆ 16-17 E 4
Ciudad López Mateos o MEX
◇ 28-29 E 2
Ciudad Madero o MEX ◆ 16-17 G 6
Ciudad Melchor de Mentos o GCA
◇ 28-29 K 3
Ciudad Mutis = Bahía Solano o CO
◆ 30-31 D 3
Ciudad Neily o CR ◇ 28-29 C 7
Ciudad Nezahualcóyotl o MEX
◇ 28-29 E 2
Ciudad Obregón o MEX ◆ 16-17 E 5
Ciudad Ojeda o YV ◆ 30-31 E 2
Ciudad Pemex o MEX ◇ 28-29 H 3
Ciudad Piar o YV ◆ 30-31 G 3
Ciudad Quesada o CR ◇ 28-29 B 6
Ciudad Real o • E ◆ 44-45 F 5
◆ 34-35 L 8
Ciudad Sahagún o MEX ◇ 28-29 E 2
Ciudad Serdán o MEX ◇ 28-29 F 2
Clain ~ F ◇ 38-39 H 8 ◆ 34-35 M 6
Claire, Lake ⊂ CDN ◆ 14-15 O 5
Clairemont o USA ◇ 26-27 G 3
Clair Engle Lake ⊂ USA ◇ 20-21 C 5
Clamecy o F ◇ 38-39 J 8
◆ 34-35 M 6
Clam Lake o USA ◇ 22-23 C 2
Clanton o USA ◇ 24-25 E 3
Clanwilliam o ZA ◆ 50-51 E 8
Claquato Church ∴ USA ◇ 20-21 C 2
Clare o USA ◇ 22-23 F 4
Claremont o USA ◇ 22-23 M 4
Claremore o USA ◇ 26-27 K 1
Clarence, Isla ⌒ RCH ◆ 32-33 H 8
Clarence Island ⌒ ANT ◆ 13 G 31
Clarence Strait ≈ ◆ 60-61 G 2
Clarence Town o • BS ◆ 16-17 M 6
Clarendon o USA ◇ 26-27 G 2
Clarenville o CDN ◇ 18-19 R 4
Clarie, Terre ⊥ ANT ◆ 13 G 14
Clarinda o USA ◆ 16-17 G 2
Clarion o USA ◇ 22-23 J 5
Clarión, Isla ⌒ MEX ◆ 16-17 D 7
Clarion River ~ USA ◇ 22-23 J 5
Clark, Lake ⊂ USA ◆ 14-15 F 4
Clark Canyon Reservoir < USA
◇ 20-21 H 3
Clarkdale o USA ◇ 20-21 H 8
Clarke City o CDN ◇ 18-19 L 3
Clarke River ~ AUS ◆ 60-61 J 3
Clark Fork o USA ◇ 20-21 F 1
Clark Fork River ~ USA ◇ 20-21 G 2
◆ 14-15 N 7
Clark Mountain ▲ USA ◇ 20-21 G 8
Clarksburg o USA ◇ 22-23 H 6
Clarksdale o USA ◇ 26-27 M 2
◆ 16-17 H 4
Clarks Hill Lake ⊂ USA ◇ 24-25 G 3
◆ 16-17 K 4
Clarkston o USA ◇ 20-21 F 2
Clarksville o USA (AR) ◇ 26-27 L 2
Clarksville o USA (TN) ◇ 24-25 E 1
◆ 16-17 J 3
Clarksville o USA (TX) ◇ 26-27 K 3
Clarksville o USA (VA) ◇ 22-23 J 7
Clatsop National Memorial, Fort ∴ USA
◇ 20-21 C 2
Claude o USA ◇ 26-27 G 2
Claxton o USA ◇ 24-25 H 3
Clay Belt ⊥ CDN ◆ 14-15 U 6
Clay City o USA ◇ 22-23 G 7
Clayton o USA (AL) ◇ 24-25 F 4
Clayton o USA (GA) ◇ 24-25 G 2
Clayton o USA (LA) ◇ 26-27 M 4
Clayton o USA (NM) ◇ 26-27 F 1
Clayton o USA (OK) ◇ 26-27 K 2
Clearfield o USA (PA) ◇ 22-23 J 5
Clearfield o USA (UT) ◇ 20-21 H 5
Clear Fork Brazos ~ USA ◇ 26-27 H 3
Clear Hills ▲ CDN ◆ 14-15 N 5
Clear Lake ⊂ USA ◇ 20-21 C 6
Clear Lake Reservoir ⊂ USA
◇ 20-21 D 5
Clearwater o USA (FL) ◇ 24-25 G 6
Clearwater o USA (MT) ◇ 20-21 H 2
Clearwater Lake ⊂ USA ◇ 22-23 C 7
Clearwater Mountains ▲ USA
◇ 20-21 G 2
Clearwater River ~ USA ◇ 20-21 F 2
Cleburne o USA ◇ 26-27 J 3
Cle Elum o USA ◇ 20-21 D 2
Clemson o USA ◇ 24-25 G 2
Clendenin o USA ◇ 22-23 H 6
Clermont o AUS ◆ 60-61 K 4
Clermont o F ◇ 38-39 J 7
◆ 34-35 M 6
Clermont o USA ◇ 24-25 H 5
Clermont-Ferrand ☆ • F ◇ 38-39 J 9
◆ 34-35 M 6
Clermont-l'Hérault o F ◇ 38-39 J 10
◆ 34-35 M 7
Cleveland o USA (GA) ◇ 24-25 G 2
Cleveland o USA (MS) ◇ 26-27 M 3
Cleveland o USA (TN) ◇ 24-25 F 2
Cleveland o USA (TX) ◇ 26-27 K 4
Cleveland o • USA (OH) ◇ 22-23 H 5
◆ 16-17 K 2
Cleveland, Mount ▲ USA ◇ 20-21 H 1
Cleveland Heights o USA ◇ 22-23 H 5
Clewiston o USA ◇ 24-25 H 6
Cliff o USA ◇ 26-27 C 3
Clifton o USA ◇ 26-27 C 3
Clifton Forge o USA ◇ 22-23 J 7
Climax o USA ◇ 24-25 F 4
Clinch Mountains ▲ USA ◇ 24-25 G 1
Cline o USA ◇ 26-27 G 5
Clines Corners o USA ◇ 26-27 E 2
Clingmans Dome ▲ USA ◇ 24-25 G 2
Clint o USA ◇ 26-27 D 4
Clinton o CDN ◇ 18-19 D 7
Clinton o USA (AR) ◇ 26-27 L 2
Clinton o USA (IA) ◇ 22-23 C 5
Clinton o USA (IL) ◇ 22-23 D 5
Clinton o USA (IN) ◇ 22-23 E 6
Clinton o USA (KY) ◇ 22-23 D 7
Clinton o USA (LA) ◇ 26-27 M 4
Clinton o USA (MI) ◇ 22-23 G 4
Clinton o USA (MS) ◇ 26-27 M 3
Clinton o USA (NC) ◇ 24-25 J 2
Clinton o USA (OK) ◇ 26-27 H 2
Clinton o USA (SC) ◇ 24-25 H 2
Clinton, Cape ▲ AUS ◆ 60-61 L 4
Clintonville o USA ◇ 22-23 D 3
Clio o USA ◇ 24-25 F 4
Cloncurry o AUS ◆ 60-61 J 4
Cloridorme o CDN ◇ 18-19 M 4
Cloud River ~ CDN ◇ 18-19 Q 3
Cloverdale o USA ◇ 20-21 C 6
Clovis o USA (CA) ◇ 20-21 E 7
Clovis o USA (NM) ◇ 26-27 F 2
◆ 16-17 F 4
Cloyne o CDN ◇ 18-19 F 6
Cluj-Napoca ☆ • RO ◆ 34-35 Q 6
Clyde o CDN ◆ 14-15 X 2
Clyde Park o USA ◇ 20-21 J 3
Clyde River o CDN ◇ 18-19 M 7
Coachella o USA ◇ 20-21 F 9
Coachella Canal < USA ◇ 20-21 G 9
Coahuayana o MEX ◇ 28-29 C 2
Coahuayutla o MEX ◇ 28-29 D 2
Coalcomán de Matamoros o MEX
◇ 28-29 C 2
Coaldale o USA ◇ 20-21 F 6
Coalinga o USA ◇ 20-21 D 7
Coalville o USA ◇ 20-21 J 5
Coari o BR ◆ 30-31 G 5
Coari, Rio ~ BR ◆ 30-31 G 5
Coast Mountains ▲ CDN ◆ 14-15 K 5
Coast of Labrador ⊥ CDN ◆ 14-15 Y 5
Coast Range ▲ USA ◇ 20-21 C 3
◆ 14-15 M 7
Coatá Laranjal, Área Indígena ⨯ BR
◆ 30-31 H 5
Coatepec o MEX ◇ 28-29 F 2
Coatepeque o GCA ◇ 28-29 J 4
Coatesville o USA ◇ 22-23 L 6
Coaticook o CDN ◇ 18-19 J 6
Coats Island ⌒ CDN ◆ 14-15 U 4
Coats Land ⊥ ANT ◆ 13 F 34
Coatzacoalcos o • MEX ◇ 28-29 G 2
◆ 16-17 H 7
Coatzacoalcos, Río ~ MEX ◇ 28-29 G 3
Coba ∴ • MEX ◇ 28-29 L 1
Cobán ☆ GCA ◇ 28-29 J 4
◆ 16-17 H 7
Cobar o AUS ◆ 60-61 K 6
Cobequid Mountains ▲ CDN
◇ 18-19 M 6
Cobija ☆ BOL ◆ 30-31 F 7
Cobleskill o USA ◇ 22-23 L 4
Coboconk o CDN ◇ 18-19 E 6
Cobourg o CDN ◇ 18-19 E 7
Cobourg Peninsula ⌣ AUS ◆ 60-61 G 2
Coburg Island ⌒ CDN ◆ 14-15 V 1
Coburn Mount ▲ USA ◇ 22-23 N 3
Coca = Puerto Francisco de Orellana o EC
◆ 30-31 D 5
Cochabamba ☆ BOL ◆ 30-31 F 8
Cochagne o CDN ◇ 18-19 M 5
Cochagón, Cerro ▲ NIC ◇ 28-29 B 5
Cochin = Kochi o •• IND ◆ 56-57 M 9
Cochise o USA ◇ 26-27 C 3
Cochran o USA ◇ 24-25 G 3
Cochrane o CDN ◆ 14-15 U 7
Cochrane, Cerro ▲ RCH ◆ 32-33 H 7
Cockburn, Mount ▲ AUS ◆ 60-61 F 5
Cockburn Island ⌒ CDN ◇ 18-19 C 6
Cockburn Town ☆ GB ◆ 16-17 M 6
Cockleiddy Motel o AUS ◆ 60-61 F 6
Coco, El o CR ◇ 28-29 B 6
Coco, Río ~ NIC ◇ 28-29 B 4
Cocoa o USA ◇ 24-25 H 5
Cocobeach o G ◆ 50-51 C 1
Coco Channel ≈ ◆ 58-59 B 4
Coco Island ⌒ MS ◆ 50-51 N 5
Coco o Segovia ~ HN ◇ 28-29 B 4
◆ 16-17 J 8
Cocos Basin ≃ ◆ 58-59 B 6
Cocos Island ⌒ AUS ◆ 58-59 C 9
Cocos Ridge ≃ ◆ 30-31 B 4
Cocula o MEX ◇ 28-29 C 1
Cocuy, Parque Nacional el ⊥ CO
◆ 30-31 E 3
Cod, Cape ▲ USA ◇ 22-23 N 4
Codajás o BR ◆ 30-31 G 5
Codó o BR ◆ 30-31 L 5
Cody o USA ◆ 14-15 P 8
Coen o AUS ◆ 60-61 J 2
Coeroeni o SME ◆ 30-31 H 4
Coëtivy Island ⌒ SY ◆ 50-51 N 3
Coeur d'Alene o USA ◇ 20-21 F 2
◆ 14-15 N 7
Coeur d'Alene Indian Reservation ⨯ USA
◇ 20-21 F 2
Coeur d'Alene Lake ⊂ USA
◇ 20-21 F 2
Coeur d'Alene River ~ USA
◇ 20-21 F 2
Coffeeville o USA ◇ 24-25 D 4
Coffeyville o USA ◇ 26-27 K 1
Coffin Bay ≈ ◆ 60-61 H 6
Coffin Bay National Park ⊥ AUS
◆ 60-61 H 6
Coffs Harbour o AUS ◆ 60-61 L 6
Cognac o • F ◇ 38-39 G 9
◆ 34-35 L 6
Cohoes o USA ◇ 22-23 M 4
Coiba, Isla de ⌒ PA ◇ 28-29 D 8
◆ 16-17 K 9
Coihaique ☆ RCH ◆ 32-33 H 7
Coimbatore o IND ◆ 56-57 M 8
Coimbra ☆ •• P ◇ 44-45 C 4
◆ 34-35 K 7
Coipasa, Salar de ⊂ BOL ◆ 30-31 F 8
Cojbalsan ☆ MAU ◆ 52-53 T 8
Cojudo Blanco, Cerro ▲ RA ◆ 32-33 J 7
Cojutepeque ☆ ES ◇ 28-29 K 5
Cokeville o USA ◇ 20-21 J 4
Colatina o BR ◆ 30-31 L 8
Colbert o USA ◇ 20-21 F 2
Colborne, Port o CDN ◇ 18-19 E 7
Colca, Río ~ PE ◆ 30-31 E 8
Colchester o USA ◇ 22-23 M 3
Cold Bay o USA ◆ 14-15 D 5
Coldwater o USA ◇ 22-23 F 5
Colebrook o USA ◇ 22-23 N 3
Coleman o USA ◇ 26-27 H 4
Coles, Punta ▲ PE ◆ 30-31 E 8
Colesberg o ZA ◆ 50-51 G 8
Coles Island o CDN ◇ 18-19 M 6
Colfax o USA (CA) ◇ 20-21 D 6
Colfax o USA (WA) ◇ 20-21 F 2
Colhué Huapi, Lago ⊂ RA ◆ 32-33 J 7
Colima o MEX ◇ 28-29 B 2
Colima ☆ • MEX (COL) ◇ 28-29 C 2
◆ 16-17 F 7
Colima, Nevado de ▲ MEX ◇ 28-29 C 2
◆ 16-17 F 7
Colin Archer Peninsula ⌣ CDN
◆ 14-15 S 1
Colinas o BR ◆ 30-31 L 6
Colinet o CDN ◇ 18-19 S 5
College Park o USA ◇ 24-25 F 3
College Place o USA ◇ 20-21 E 2
College Station o USA ◇ 26-27 J 4
Collie o AUS ◆ 60-61 D 6
Collier Bay ≈ ◆ 60-61 E 3
Collier Bay Aboriginal Land ⨯ AUS
◆ 60-61 E 3
Collier Range National Park ⊥ AUS
◆ 60-61 D 4
Collierville o USA ◇ 24-25 D 2
Collingwood o CDN ◇ 18-19 D 6
Collins o USA (AR) ◇ 26-27 M 3
Collins o USA (MS) ◇ 24-25 D 4
Collins o USA (MT) ◇ 20-21 J 2
Collinson Peninsula ⌣ CDN
◆ 14-15 Q 2
Collinsville o USA (AL) ◇ 24-25 F 2
Collinsville o USA (OK) ◇ 26-27 K 1
Colmar ☆ • F ◇ 38-39 L 7
◆ 34-35 N 6
Cologne = Köln o D ◆ 40-41 J 3
◆ 34-35 N 5
Coloma o USA ◇ 22-23 D 3
Colombia ▪ CO ◆ 30-31 E 4
Colombia Basin ≃ ◆ 6 G 7
Colombier o CDN ◇ 18-19 K 4
Colombo ☆ CL ◆ 56-57 M 9
Colomiers o F ◇ 38-39 H 10
◆ 34-35 M 7
Colón ☆ PA ◇ 28-29 E 7
Colonel Hill o BS ◆ 16-17 M 6
Colonia ☆ FSM ◆ 58-59 L 5
Colonial Heights o USA ◇ 22-23 K 7
Colonial National Historic Park • USA
◇ 22-23 K 7
Colon Ridge ≃ ◆ 30-31 A 4
Colorado o CR ◇ 28-29 B 6
Colorado ▫ USA ◆ 16-17 E 3
Colorado City o USA ◇ 26-27 G 3
Colorado Desert ⊥ USA ◇ 20-21 F 9
◆ 16-17 C 4
Colorado Plateau ▲ USA ◇ 20-21 H 7
◆ 16-17 D 3
Colorado River ~ USA ◇ 26-27 J 5
Colorado River ~ USA ◇ 20-21 G 8
◆ 16-17 E 3
Colorado River Aqueduct < USA
◇ 20-21 G 8
Colorado River Indian Reservation ⨯ USA
◇ 20-21 G 9
Colorado Springs o • USA ◆ 16-17 F 3
Colotlán o MEX ◆ 16-17 F 6
Colotlipa o MEX ◇ 28-29 E 3
Colquitt o USA ◇ 24-25 F 4
Columbia o USA (KY) ◇ 22-23 F 7
Columbia o USA (LA) ◇ 26-27 L 3

Châlons-sur-Marne — Columbia 71

Columbia o **USA** (MD) ◇ 22-23 K 6
Columbia o **USA** (MO) ◆ 16-17 H 3
Columbia o **USA** (PA) ◇ 22-23 K 5
Columbia o **USA** (MS) ◆ 24-25 E 2
Columbia ☆ **USA** (SC) ◇ 24-25 H 2 ◆ 16-17 K 4
Columbia Beach o **USA** ◇ 20-21 C 2
Columbia Falls o **USA** ◇ 20-21 G 1
Columbia Mountains ▲ **CDN** 14-15 N 6
Columbia Plateau ▲ **USA** ◇ 20-21 F 3 14-15 N 5
Columbia Reach ~ **CDN** 14-15 N 6
Columbia River ~ **CDN** 14-15 N 7
Columbia River ~ **USA** ◇ 20-21 C 3 ◆ 16-17 M 4
Columbus o **USA** (GA) ◇ 24-25 G 3 ◆ 16-17 J 3
Columbus o **USA** (IN) ◇ 22-23 F 6 ◆ 16-17 J 3
Columbus o **USA** (KS) ◇ 26-27 K 1
Columbus o **USA** (MS) ◇ 24-25 F 2 ◆ 16-17 J 4
Columbus o **USA** (NM) ◇ 26-27 D 4
Columbus o **USA** (TX) ◇ 26-27 J 5
Columbus o **USA** (WI) ◇ 22-23 D 4
Columbus ☆ **USA** (OH) ◇ 22-23 G 6 ◆ 16-17 K 3
Columbus Cay o **BH** ◇ 28-29 L 3
Columbus Junction o **USA** ◇ 22-23 C 5
Columna, Pico ▲ **PA** ◇ 20-21 F 1
Colville o **USA** ◇ 20-21 F 1
Colville Channel ≈ **NZ** ◇ 60-61 Q 7
Colville Indian Reservation ✗ **USA** ◇ 20-21 E 1 ◆ 14-15 N 7
Colville River ~ **USA** ◆ 14-15 E 3
Comalcalco o **MEX** ◇ 28-29 H 2
Comalcalco ∴ **MEX** (TAB) ◇ 28-29 H 2
Comanche o **USA** ◇ 26-27 H 4
Comayagua ☆ **HN** ◇ 28-29 L 4
Comayagua, Montañas de ▲ **HN** ◇ 28-29 L 4
Comayaguela o **HN** ◇ 28-29 L 4
Combomune o **MOC** ◇ 50-51 H 6
Comer o **USA** ◇ 24-25 G 2
Comfort o **USA** ◇ 26-27 H 4
Comfort Bight ≈ **CDN** ◇ 18-19 R 2
Comilla o **BD** ◆ 56-57 P 6
Comitán de Domínguez ☆ **MEX** ◇ 28-29 H 4
Commander Islands = Komandorskie ostrova **RUS** ◆ 10-11 Q 3
Commerce o **USA** ◇ 26-27 K 3
Committee Bay ≈ **CDN** 14-15 T 3
Commonwealth Range ▲ **ANT** ◆ 13 E 0
Comoapa o **NIC** ◇ 28-29 B 5
Comodoro Rivadavia o **RA** ◆ 32-33 J 7
Comoé ~ **CI** ◆ 48-49 E 7
Comonfort o **MEX** ◇ 28-29 D 1
Comorin, Cape ▲ **IND** ◆ 56-57 M 9
Comoros **COM** ◆ 50-51 K 4
Comoros ~ **COM** ◆ 50-51 K 4
Compiègne o **F** ◇ 38-39 J 7 ◆ 34-35 M 6
Comstock o **USA** ◇ 26-27 G 5
Comunidad o **CR** ◇ 28-29 B 6
Čona ~ **RUS** ◆ 52-53 S 5
Conakry ★ **RG** ◆ 48-49 B 6
Concarneau o **F** ◇ 38-39 F 8 ◆ 34-35 L 6
Conceição do Araguaia o **BR** ◆ 30-31 K 6
Concepción o **BOL** ◆ 30-31 G 8
Concepción ☆ **PY** ◆ 32-33 J 2
Concepción o **RA** ◆ 32-33 J 3
Concepción ☆ **RCH** ◆ 32-33 H 5
Concepción, La o **PA** ◇ 28-29 C 7
Concepción, La o **YV** ◇ 30-31 E 2
Concepción, Volcán ▲ **NIC** ◇ 28-29 B 6
Concepción de Buenos Aires o **MEX** ◇ 28-29 C 2
Concepción del Oro o **MEX** ◆ 16-17 F 6
Conception Bay ≈ ◇ 18-19 S 5
Conchas o **USA** ◇ 26-27 E 2
Conchas Lake o **USA** ◇ 26-27 E 2
Conchas River ~ **USA** ◇ 26-27 E 2
Concho River ~ **USA** ◇ 26-27 G 4
Conchos, Río ~ **MEX** ◆ 16-17 E 5
Concord o **USA** (CA) ◇ 20-21 C 7
Concord o **USA** (NC) ◇ 24-25 H 2
Concord ☆ **USA** (NH) ◇ 22-23 N 4 ◆ 14-15 N 7
Concordia o **RA** ◆ 32-33 J 4
Concordia, La o **MEX** ◇ 28-29 H 4
Conde o **BR** ◆ 30-31 M 7
Condega o **NIC** ◇ 28-29 L 5
Condobolin o **AUS** ◆ 60-61 K 6
Condom o **F** ◇ 38-39 H 10 ◆ 34-35 M 7
Condon o **USA** ◇ 20-21 D 3
Côn Đao o **VN** ◆ 58-59 E 5
Conecuh River ~ **USA** ◇ 24-25 E 4
Confolens o **F** ◇ 38-39 H 8 ◆ 34-35 L 6
Confusion Bay ≈ ◇ 18-19 R 3
Congo **RCB** ◆ 50-51 D 2
Congo ~ **RCB** ◆ 50-51 D 3
Congo Basin ~ **ZRE** ◆ 50-51 D 2
Congo Fan ~ ◆ 50-51 C 2
Congress o **USA** ◇ 20-21 H 8
Conkal o **MEX** ◇ 28-29 K 1
Conneaut o **USA** ◇ 22-23 H 5
Connecticut **USA** ◇ 22-23 M 5 ◆ 16-17 M 2
Connecticut River ~ **USA** ◇ 22-23 M 4
Connell o **USA** ◇ 20-21 E 2
Connellsville o **USA** ◇ 22-23 J 6
Connersville o **USA** ◇ 22-23 F 6
Conover o **USA** ◇ 24-25 D 2
Conquet o **F** ◇ 38-39 E 7 ◆ 34-35 L 6
Conrad o **USA** ◇ 20-21 J 1
Conroe o **USA** ◇ 26-27 K 4
Conroe, Lake o **USA** ◇ 26-27 K 4
Conselheiro Lafaiete o **BR** ◆ 32-33 O 2
Constança ☆ **RO** ◆ 34-35 R 7
Constantina o **USA** ◇ 22-23 F 6
Constantine ☆ ✶ **DZ** ◆ 48-49 G 1
Constitución o **RCH** ◆ 32-33 H 5
Consuelo Peak ▲ **AUS** ◆ 60-61 K 4

Contact o **USA** ◇ 20-21 G 5
Contagem o **BR** ◆ 30-31 L 8
Contamana o **PE** ◆ 30-31 E 6
Contamana, Sierra ▲ **PE** ◆ 30-31 E 6
Contas, Rio de ~ **BR** ◆ 30-31 M 7
Contoy, Isla ~ **MEX** ◇ 28-29 L 1
Contreras, I ~ **RCH** ◆ 32-33 H 8
Contwoyto Lake o **CDN** ◆ 14-15 O 3
Conway o **USA** (AR) ◇ 26-27 L 2
Conway o **USA** (NH) ◇ 22-23 N 4
Conway o **USA** (SC) ◇ 24-25 J 3
Conway o **USA** (TX) ◇ 26-27 G 2
Cook, Mount ▲ **NZ** ◆ 60-61 P 8
Cook Bay ≈ ◇ 13 G 16
Cookeville o **USA** ◇ 24-25 F 1
Cook Inlet ≈ ◆ 14-15 F 5
Cook Islands ~ **NZ** ◆ 12 L 4
Cooksburg o **USA** ◇ 22-23 L 4
Cook Strait ≈ ◆ 60-61 P 8
Cooktown o ∘ **AUS** ◆ 60-61 K 3
Coolgardie o **AUS** ◆ 60-61 E 6
Cooma o **AUS** ◆ 60-61 K 7
Coonabarabran o **AUS** ◆ 60-61 K 6
Coonamble o **AUS** ◆ 60-61 K 6
Coondapoor o **IND** ◆ 56-57 L 8
Coon Rapids o **USA** ◆ 14-15 S 7
Cooper o **USA** ◇ 26-27 K 3
Cooper Creek ~ **AUS** ◆ 60-61 H 5
Coorabie o **AUS** ◆ 60-61 G 6
Coosa River ~ **USA** ◇ 24-25 E 2
Coos Bay ≈ **USA** ◇ 20-21 B 4
Coos Bay o **USA** ◇ 20-21 B 4 ◆ 14-15 M 8
Cootamundra o **AUS** ◆ 60-61 K 6
Copán ☆ **HN** ◇ 28-29 K 4
Copano Bay ≈ ◇ 26-27 J 5
Copán Ruinas o **HN** ◇ 28-29 K 4
Copé, El o **PA** ◇ 28-29 D 7
Copeland o **USA** ◇ 20-21 H 2
Copenhagen = København ★ • **DK** ◆ 36-37 E 9 ◆ 34-35 O 4
Copiapó ☆ **RCH** ◆ 32-33 H 3
Copperas Cove o **USA** ◇ 26-27 J 4
Copper Harbor o **USA** ◇ 22-23 E 2
Coppermine o **CDN** ◆ 14-15 O 3
Coppermine River ~ **CDN** ◆ 14-15 N 3
Copper River ~ **USA** ◆ 14-15 H 4
Cogén o **CDN** ◆ 54-55 F 5
Coquimatlán o **MEX** ◇ 28-29 C 2
Coquimbo o **RCH** ◆ 32-33 H 4
Coral Basin ~ ◆ 60-61 K 2
Coral Harbour o **CDN** ◆ 14-15 U 4
Coral Sea ≈ ◆ 60-61 L 3
Coral Sea Islands Territory **AUS** ◆ 60-61 K 2
Corbin o **USA** ◇ 22-23 F 7
Corcaigh = Cork o **IRL** ◆ 34-35 K 5
Corcoran o **USA** ◇ 20-21 E 7
Corcovada, Park Nacional ⊥ **CR** ◇ 28-29 C 7
Corcovado, Golfo ≈ ◆ 32-33 H 6
Corcovado, Volcán ▲ **RCH** ◆ 32-33 H 6
Cordele o **USA** ◇ 24-25 G 4
Cordell o **USA** ◇ 26-27 H 2
Cordillera Cantábrica ▲ **E** ◆ 44-45 D 3
Cordillera Central ▲ **BOL** ◆ 30-31 G 8
Cordillera Central ▲ **CO** ◆ 30-31 D 4
Cordillera Central ▲ **E** ◆ 44-45 E 4
Cordillera Central ▲ **PE** ◆ 30-31 D 6
Cordillera Central ▲ **RP** ◆ 58-59 J 3
Cordillera Occidental ▲ **CO** ◆ 30-31 D 4
Cordillera Occidental ▲ **PE** ◆ 30-31 D 6
Cordillera Oriental ▲ **BOL** ◆ 30-31 G 8
Cordillera Oriental ▲ **CO** ◆ 30-31 D 4
Cordillera Oriental ▲ **PE** ◆ 30-31 D 6
Córdoba o ∘∘∘ **E** ◆ 44-45 E 6 ◆ 34-35 L 8
Córdoba o **MEX** ◇ 28-29 F 2
Córdoba o **RA** ◆ 32-33 K 4
Córdoba **RA** (COD) ◆ 32-33 J 4
Córdoba, Sierra de ▲ **RA** ◆ 32-33 J 4
Corfield o **USA** ◇ 60-61 J 4
Corfu = Kérkira ~ **GR** ◆ 46-47 G 5 ◆ 34-35 P 8
Corinth o **USA** (ME) ◇ 22-23 O 3
Corinth o **USA** (MS) ◇ 24-25 D 2
Corinto o **BR** ◆ 30-31 L 8
Corinto o **HN** ◇ 28-29 K 4
Corinto o **NIC** ◇ 28-29 L 5
Corisco, Baie de ≈ ◆ 50-51 C 1
Cork o **IRL** ◆ 34-35 K 5
Çorlu o **TR** ◆ 34-35 P 5
Cornell o **USA** ◇ 22-23 C 3
Corner Brook o **CDN** ◇ 18-19 Q 4 ◆ 14-15 Z 7
Corning o **USA** (AR) ◇ 26-27 M 1
Corning o **USA** (CA) ◇ 20-21 C 6
Corning o **USA** (NY) ◇ 22-23 K 4
Cornouaille ⊥ **F** ◇ 38-39 F 8 ◆ 34-35 L 6
Cornwall o **CDN** ◇ 18-19 M 4
Cornwall o **USA** ◇ 24-25 G 3
Cornwall Island ~ **CDN** ◆ 14-15 R 1
Cornwall Island o **CDN** ◆ 14-15 R 1
Coro ☆ ∘∘∘ **YV** ◆ 30-31 F 2
Coroatá o **BR** ◆ 30-31 L 5
Corocoro o **BOL** ◆ 30-31 F 8
Coroico o **BOL** ◆ 30-31 F 8
Corolla o **USA** ◇ 24-25 K 1
Coromandel Coast ~ **IND** ◆ 56-57 N 8
Coron o **RP** ◆ 58-59 H 4
Corona o **USA** ◇ 26-27 D 3
Corona, Bahía de ≈ ◇ 26-27 C 7 ◆ 16-17 K 9
Coronado National Monument • **USA** ◇ 26-27 B 4
Coronation Gulf ≈ **CDN** ◆ 14-15 O 3
Coronation Island ~ **ANT** ◆ 13 G 32
Coronel Dorrego o **RA** ◆ 32-33 K 5
Coronel Oviedo ☆ **PY** ◆ 32-33 J 2
Coronel Pringles o **RA** ◆ 32-33 K 5
Coropuna, Nevado ▲ **PE** ◆ 30-31 E 8

Corpus Christi o **USA** ◇ 26-27 J 6 ◆ 16-17 H 5
Corpus Christi, Lake ≈ **USA** ◇ 26-27 J 5
Corpus Christi Bay ≈ ◇ 26-27 J 6
Corrente, Rio ~ **BR** ◆ 30-31 L 7
Correntina o **BR** ◆ 30-31 L 7
Corrientes **RA** ◆ 32-33 J 3
Corrientes ☆ **RA** ◆ 32-33 L 3
Corrientes, Cabo ▲ **CO** ◆ 30-31 D 3
Corrientes, Cabo ▲ **MEX** ◇ 28-29 B 1
Corrigan o **USA** ◇ 26-27 K 4
Corry o **USA** ◇ 22-23 J 5
Corryong o **AUS** ◆ 60-61 K 7
Corse, Cap ▲ **F** ◆ 44-45 M 3 ◆ 34-35 N 7
Corse, Parc Naturel Régional de la ⊥ **F** ◆ 46-47 B 3 ◆ 46-47 B 4
Corsica ~ **F** ◆ 34-35 N 7
Corsicana o **USA** ◇ 26-27 J 3
Cortez o **USA** ◇ 26-27 C 1
Cortland o **USA** ◇ 22-23 K 4
Çorum ☆ **TR** ◆ 34-35 S 7
Corumbá o **BR** ◆ 30-31 H 8
Coruña, A ☆ ∘∘∘ **E** ◆ 44-45 C 3 ◆ 34-35 K 7
Corvallis o **USA** ◇ 20-21 B 4
Corvette, Rivière de la ~ **CDN** ◇ 18-19 O 2
Corvo, Ilha do ~ **P** ◆ 34-35 E 8
Corydon o **USA** ◇ 22-23 E 6
Cosamaloapan o **MEX** ◇ 28-29 G 2
Coshocton o **USA** ◇ 22-23 H 5
Cosigüina, Punta ▲ **NIC** ◇ 28-29 L 5
Cosigüina, Volcán ▲ **NIC** ◇ 28-29 L 5
Cosmoledo Atoll ~ **SY** ◆ 50-51 L 3
Cosmo Newberry Mission ✗ **AUS** ◆ 60-61 E 5
Cosne-Cours-sur-Loire o **F** ◇ 38-39 J 8 ◆ 34-35 M 6
Cosoleacaque o **MEX** ◇ 28-29 G 2
Costa, La o **MEX** ◇ 28-29 J 1
Costa Blanca ~ **E** ◆ 44-45 G 6
Costa del Sol ~ **E** ◆ 44-45 E 6 ◆ 34-35 L 8
Costa Marques o **BR** ◆ 30-31 G 7
Costa Rica **CR** ◇ 28-29 B 7
Costera del Pacífico, Llanura ~ **MEX** ◆ 16-17 D 5
Costilla o **USA** ◇ 26-27 E 1
Cotabato City ☆ **RP** ◆ 58-59 H 5
Cotagaita o **BOL** ◆ 32-33 G 2
Cotazar o **MEX** ◇ 28-29 D 1
Coteau des Prairies ▲ **USA** ◆ 14-15 R 7
Coteau du Missouri ▲ **USA** ◆ 14-15 P 7
Côte d'Azur ~ **F** ◇ 38-39 L 10
Côte d'Ivoire **CI** ◆ 48-49 D 7
Côte Nord o **CDN** ◇ 18-19 L 3 ◆ 14-15 X 6
Cotentin ⊥ **F** ◇ 38-39 G 7 ◆ 34-35 L 6
Cotija de la Paz o **MEX** ◇ 28-29 C 2
Cotonou ☆ **DY** ◆ 48-49 F 7
Cotopaxi, Volcán ▲ **EC** ◆ 30-31 D 5
Cottage Grove o **USA** ◇ 20-21 C 4 ◆ 34-35 O 5
Cottbus o **D** ◆ 40-41 N 3
Cottondale o **USA** ◇ 24-25 F 4
Cottonwood o **USA** (AZ) ◇ 20-21 H 8
Cottonwood o **USA** (CA) ◇ 20-21 C 5
Cottonwood o **USA** (ID) ◇ 20-21 F 2
Cotulla o **USA** ◇ 26-27 H 5
Coudres, Île aux ~ **CDN** ◇ 18-19 J 5
Couéron o **F** ◇ 38-39 G 8 ◆ 34-35 L 6
Couhé o **F** ◇ 38-39 H 8 ◆ 34-35 M 6
Coulee City o **USA** ◇ 20-21 E 2
Coulman Island ~ **ANT** ◆ 13 F 18
Coulommiers o **F** ◇ 38-39 J 7 ◆ 34-35 M 6
Coulonge, Rivière ~ **CDN** ◇ 18-19 F 5
Coulterville o **USA** ◇ 22-23 D 6
Council o **USA** ◇ 20-21 F 3
Council Bluffs o **USA** ◆ 16-17 H 2
Counselors o **USA** ◇ 26-27 D 1
Country Force Base Suffield x x **CDN** ◆ 14-15 O 6
Courantyne ~ **GUY** ◆ 30-31 H 4
Cours-sur-Loire, Cosne o **F** ◇ 38-39 J 8
Courtright o **CDN** ◇ 18-19 C 7
Coushatta o **USA** ◇ 26-27 L 3
Coutances o **F** ◇ 38-39 G 7 ◆ 34-35 L 6
Coutras o **F** ◇ 38-39 G 9 ◆ 34-35 L 6
Cove Fort o **USA** ◇ 20-21 H 6
Coventry o **GB** ◆ 34-35 L 4
Cove Palisades State Park, The ⊥ • **USA** ◇ 20-21 C 4
Covington o **USA** (GA) ◇ 24-25 G 3
Covington o **USA** (KY) ◇ 22-23 G 6 ◆ 16-17 K 3
Covington o **USA** (LA) ◇ 26-27 M 4
Covington o **USA** (MI) ◇ 22-23 D 2
Covington o **USA** (TN) ◇ 24-25 D 2
Covington o **USA** (VA) ◇ 22-23 H 7
Cowan, Lake o **AUS** ◆ 60-61 E 6
Cowansville o **CDN** ◇ 18-19 H 6
Cowcowing Lakes o **AUS** ◆ 60-61 D 6
Cow Creek ~ **USA** ◇ 20-21 C 4
Cowlitz River ~ **USA** ◇ 20-21 C 2
Cowra o **AUS** ◆ 60-61 K 6
Coxilha de Santana ▲ **BR** ◆ 32-33 J 4
Coxim o **BR** ◆ 30-31 J 8
Cox's Bazar o **BD** ◆ 56-57 P 6
Cox's Cove o **CDN** ◇ 18-19 P 4
Coyame o **MEX** ◇ 26-27 F 6
Coyoacan o **MEX** ◇ 28-29 E 2
Coyolate, Rio ~ **GCA** ◇ 28-29 J 4
Coyoito o **HN** ◇ 28-29 K 4
Coyuca o **MEX** ◇ 28-29 D 3
Coyuca de Benítez o **MEX** ◇ 28-29 D 3

Cozes o **F** ◇ 38-39 G 9 ◆ 34-35 L 6
Cozumel o **MEX** ◇ 28-29 L 1
Cozumel, Isla de ~ **MEX** ◇ 28-29 L 1 ◆ 16-17 L 6
Cradock o **ZA** ◆ 50-51 G 8
Craig o **USA** ◇ 16-17 E 2
Craigmore o **CDN** ◇ 18-19 O 6
Craiova ☆ **RO** ◆ 34-35 Q 7
Cranbourne o **AUS** ◆ 60-61 K 7
Cranbrook o **CDN** ◆ 18-19 U 6
Crane o **USA** (OR) ◇ 20-21 E 4
Crane o **USA** (TX) ◇ 26-27 F 4
Cranston o **USA** ◇ 22-23 N 5
Crary Mountains ▲ **ANT** ◆ 13 F 25
Crater Lake o **USA** ◇ 20-21 C 4
Crater Lake National Park ⊥ **USA** ◇ 20-21 C 4 ◆ 14-15 M 8
Craters of Diamonds State Park ∴• **USA** ◇ 26-27 L 3
Craters of the Moon National Monument ∴ **USA** ◇ 20-21 H 4
Cratéus o **BR** ◆ 30-31 L 6
Crato o **BR** ◆ 30-31 M 6
Cravo Norte o **CO** ◆ 30-31 E 3
Crawford o **USA** ◇ 24-25 G 3
Crawfordsville o **USA** ◇ 22-23 E 5
Crazy Peak ▲ **USA** ◇ 20-21 J 2
Cree Lake o **CDN** ◆ 14-15 P 5
Creil o **USA** ◇ 38-39 J 7 ◆ 34-35 M 6
Cres ⊥ **HR** ◆ 46-47 E 2 ◆ 34-35 O 7
Crescent o **USA** ◇ 20-21 D 4
Crescent, La o **USA** ◇ 22-23 C 4
Crescent City o **USA** ◇ 20-21 B 5
Crescent City o **USA** (FL) ◇ 24-25 H 4
Crest o **F** ◇ 38-39 K 9 ◆ 34-35 N 6
Crestview o **USA** ◇ 24-25 E 4
Creuse ~ **F** ◇ 38-39 J 8
Cricamola, Reserva Indígena de ✗ **PA** ◇ 28-29 D 7 ◆ 16-17 K 9
Crimea **UA** ◆ 34-35 S 6
Crimea ~ **UA** ◆ 34-35 S 6
Crimea ⊥ **UA** ◆ 34-35 S 7
Crisfield o **USA** ◇ 22-23 L 6
Cristóbal Cólon, Pico ▲ ∘∘ **CO** ◆ 30-31 E 2
Croatia **HR** ◆ 46-47 E 1 ◆ 34-35 P 6
Crockett o **USA** ◇ 26-27 K 4
Croix, Lac à la o **CDN** ◇ 18-19 J 3
Croix-de-Vie, Saint-Gilles o **F** ◇ 38-39 G 8 ◆ 34-35 L 6
Cromwell o **NZ** ◆ 60-61 O 9
Crooked Island o **BS** ◆ 16-17 M 6
Crooked River ~ **USA** ◇ 20-21 D 3
Crosby o **CDN** ◇ 18-19 F 6
Crosbyton o **USA** ◇ 26-27 G 3
Cross City o **USA** ◇ 24-25 G 5
Crosse, La o **USA** ◇ 22-23 C 4
Crossett o **USA** ◇ 26-27 M 3
Crossville o **USA** ◇ 24-25 F 1
Crow Indian Reservation ✗ **USA** ◆ 14-15 P 7
Crowley o **USA** ◇ 26-27 L 4
Crowley, Lake o **USA** ◇ 20-21 E 7
Crownpoint o **USA** ◇ 26-27 C 2
Crown Point o **USA** ◇ 22-23 E 5
Crown Prince Frederik Island ~ **CDN** ◆ 14-15 T 3
Croydon o **AUS** ◆ 60-61 J 3
Crozet, Îles ~ **F** ◆ 9 J 10
Crozon o **F** ◇ 38-39 E 7 ◆ 34-35 L 6
Cruce, Rio o **GCA** ◇ 28-29 K 3
Cruces, Las o **MEX** ◇ 28-29 H 3
Cruces, Las o **USA** ◇ 26-27 D 3 ◆ 16-17 E 4
Cruz, Cabo ▲ **C** ◆ 16-17 L 7
Cruz, La o **USA** ◇ 26-27 H 5
Cruz Alta o **BR** ◆ 32-33 J 3
Cruz del Eje o **RA** ◆ 32-33 K 4
Cruz de Loreto, La o **MEX** ◇ 28-29 B 2
Cruzeiro o **BR** ◆ 32-33 O 2
Cruzeiro do Sul o **BR** ◆ 30-31 E 6
Cruzen Island ~ **ANT** ◆ 13 F 23
Cruz Grande o **MEX** ◇ 28-29 E 3
Crystal Bay ≈ ◇ 24-25 G 5
Crystal City o **USA** ◇ 26-27 H 5
Crystal Falls o **USA** ◇ 22-23 D 2
Crystal Lake Cave • **USA** ◇ 22-23 C 4
Crystal River o **USA** ◇ 24-25 G 5
Crystal River State Archaeological Site ∴• **USA** ◇ 24-25 G 5
Crystal Springs o **USA** ◇ 26-27 M 4
Cʼụʼ Long, Cʼụʼ Sông ⊥ **VN** ◆ 58-59 E 5
Czech Republic **CZ** ◆ 40-41 M 4 ◇ 40-41 O 6
Częstochowa o ∘∘ **PL** ◆ 40-41 P 3

Cuiabá, Rio ~ **BR** ◆ 30-31 H 7
Cuilapa ☆ **GCA** ◇ 28-29 J 4
Cuito ~ **ANG** ◆ 50-51 E 4
Cuito Cuanavale o **ANG** ◆ 50-51 E 4
Culasi o **RP** ◆ 58-59 H 4
Culebra, Isla de ~ **USA** ◆ 24-25 K 6
Culiacán Rosales ☆ **MEX** ◆ 16-17 E 6
Cullmann o **USA** ◇ 24-25 E 2
Culpeper o **USA** ◇ 24-25 K 6
Culuene, Rio ~ **BR** ◆ 30-31 J 7
Culver, Point ▲ **AUS** ◆ 60-61 E 6
Čulym ~ **RUS** (NVS) ◆ 52-53 N 6
Čulym ~ **RUS** ◆ 52-53 N 6
Čulymskaja ravnina ~ **RUS** ◆ 52-53 N 6
Cumana ☆ **YV** ◆ 30-31 G 2
Cumaná ☆ **YV** ◆ 30-31 G 2
Cumberland o **USA** (KY) ◇ 22-23 G 7
Cumberland o **USA** (VA) ◇ 22-23 J 7
Cumberland, Cape = Cape Nahoi ▲ **VAN** ◆ 60-61 O 2
Cumberland, Lake o **USA** ◇ 22-23 F 7
Cumberland Gap ▲ **USA** ◇ 24-25 G 1
Cumberland Gap National Historic Park ∴ **USA** ◇ 22-23 G 7
Cumberland Island ~ **USA** ◇ 24-25 H 4 ◆ 16-17 K 4
Cumberland Island National Seashore ⊥ **USA** ◇ 24-25 H 4
Cumberland Parkway II **USA** ◇ 22-23 F 7
Cumberland Peninsula ~ **CDN** 14-15 X 3
Cumberland Plateau ▲ **USA** ◇ 24-25 F 2 ◆ 16-17 J 4
Cumberland River ~ **USA** ◇ 24-25 F 1
Cumberland Sound ≈ ◆ 14-15 X 3
Cumbres de Majalca, Parque Nacional ∴ **MEX** ◆ 16-17 E 5
Čumikan ☆ **RUS** ◆ 52-53 Y 7
Cuminá, Rio ~ **BR** ◆ 30-31 H 5
Cummings o **USA** ◇ 20-21 C 6
Čuna ~ **RUS** ◆ 52-53 S 6
Cunduacán o **MEX** ◇ 28-29 H 2
Cunene ~ **ANG** ◆ 50-51 D 4
Cúneo ☆ • **I** ◆ 46-47 A 2 ◆ 34-35 N 7
Čunja ~ **RUS** ◆ 52-53 Q 5
Cunnamulla o **AUS** ◆ 60-61 K 5
Čuoksij ~ **RUS** ◆ 52-53 W 3
Curaçá o **BR** ◆ 30-31 M 6
Curaçao ~ **NA** ◆ 16-17 N 8
Curaça ~ **BR** ◆ 30-31 K 5
Curacautín o **RCH** ◆ 32-33 H 5
Curácuaro de Morelos o **MEX** ◇ 28-29 D 2
Curco, La o **USA** ◇ 26-27 K 4
Curicó o **RCH** ◆ 32-33 H 4
Curitiba ☆ • **BR** ◆ 32-33 N 3
Currais Novos o **BR** ◆ 30-31 M 6
Currant o **USA** ◇ 20-21 G 6
Currie o **AUS** ◆ 60-61 J 7
Currie o **USA** ◇ 20-21 G 5
Currituck Sound ≈ ◇ 22-23 L 7
Curuá, Rio ~ **BR** ◆ 30-31 H 6
Curual o **BR** ◆ 30-31 K 5
Curuça o **BR** ◆ 30-31 K 5
Curup o **RI** ◆ 58-59 D 7
Cururupu o **BR** ◆ 30-31 L 5
Curvelo o **BR** ◆ 30-31 L 8
Curwood, Mount ▲ **USA** ◇ 22-23 D 2
Cushing o **USA** ◇ 26-27 J 2
Čusovoj o **RUS** ◆ 34-35 X 4
Cusseta o **USA** ◇ 24-25 F 3
Cusuco, Parque Nacional ⊥ **HN** ◇ 28-29 K 4
Cut Bank o **USA** ◆ 16-17 H 1
Cuthbert o **USA** ◇ 24-25 F 4
Cutzamala de Pinzón o **MEX** ◇ 28-29 D 2
Cuvelai o **ANG** ◆ 50-51 E 4
Cuy, El o **RA** ◆ 32-33 J 5
Cuyahoga Valley National Recreation Area ⊥ **USA** ◇ 22-23 H 5
Cuyo, El o **MEX** ◇ 28-29 L 1
Cuyo Islands ~ **RP** ◆ 58-59 H 4
Cuyuni River ~ **GUY** ◆ 30-31 H 3
Cuzco ☆ • **PE** ◆ 30-31 E 7
Cyclades ~ **GR** ◆ 46-47 K 6 ◆ 34-35 R 8
Cynthiana o **USA** ◇ 22-23 G 6
Cypress o **USA** ◇ 26-27 L 4
Cypress Gardens ∴• **USA** ◇ 24-25 H 6
Cypress Hills ▲ **CDN** ◆ 14-15 O 7
Cyprus **CY** ◆ 34-35 S 9

D

Daaquam o **CDN** ◇ 18-19 J 5
Dabaro o **SP** ◆ 48-49 P 7
Dabba, ad- o **SUD** ◆ 48-49 M 5
Dabeiba o **CO** ◆ 30-31 D 3
Dabola o **RG** ◆ 48-49 C 6
Dacia Seamount ≃ ◆ 34-35 J 9
Dade City o **USA** ◇ 24-25 G 5
Dadra and Nagar Haveli **IND**
Dádu o **PK** ◆ 56-57 K 5
Daet o **RP** ◆ 58-59 H 4
Dafag, Umm o **SUD** ◆ 48-49 K 6
Dagana o **SN** ◆ 48-49 B 5
Dagestan **RUS** ◆ 56-57 F 2
Daggett o **USA** ◇ 20-21 F 8
Dağlıq Qarabağ Muxtar Vilayəti **AZ**
Dáhlia, al-Wáhát ad- ⊥ **ET** ◆ 48-49 L 3
Dahlak Archipelago ~ **ER** ◆ 48-49 O 5
Dahná, ad- ~ **KSA** ◆ 56-57 F 5
Dahná, ad- ⊥ **KSA** ◆ 56-57 G 5
Dáhod o **IND** ◆ 56-57 L 6
Dair az-Zaur ☆ **SYR** ◆ 56-57 E 3
Daingerfield o **USA** ◇ 26-27 K 3
Daintree o **AUS** ◆ 60-61 K 3
Dair az-Zaur ☆ **SYR** ◆ 56-57 E 3

Dairen = Dalian o **CHN** ◆ 54-55 N 4
Dairut o **ET** ◆ 48-49 M 3
Dajarra o **AUS** ◆ 60-61 H 4
Dakar ★ **SN** ◆ 48-49 B 6
Dalälven ~ **S** ◆ 36-37 H 6
Dalat Lat ☆ **VN** ◆ 58-59 E 4
Dalbeg o **AUS** ◆ 60-61 K 4
Dalby o **AUS** ◆ 60-61 L 5
Dale o **USA** ◇ 20-21 E 3
Dale Hollow Lake o **USA** ◇ 24-25 F 1
Dalgaranga Hill ▲ **AUS** ◆ 60-61 D 5
Dalhart o **USA** ◇ 26-27 F 1
Dalhousie o **CDN** ◇ 18-19 L 4
Dalhousie, Cape ▲ **CDN** ◆ 14-15 L 2
Dali o **CHN** ◆ 54-55 J 6
Dalian o **CHN** ◆ 54-55 N 4
Daliang Shan ▲ **CHN** ◆ 54-55 J 6
Dallas o **USA** (OR) ◇ 20-21 C 3
Dallas ☆ **USA** (TX) ◇ 26-27 J 3 ◆ 16-17 G 4
Dallas City o **USA** ◇ 22-23 C 5
Dalles, The o **USA** ◇ 20-21 D 3
Dall Island ~ **USA** ◆ 14-15 K 5
Dalmacija ⊥ **HR** ◆ 34-35 P 7
Dalmas, Lac o **CDN** ◇ 18-19 J 2
Dalmatia = Dalmacija ⊥ **HR** ◆ 46-47 E 3 ◆ 34-35 P 7
Dalnegorsk o **RUS** ◆ 52-53 Y 9
Dálnerečensk o **RUS** ◆ 52-53 X 8
Daloa ☆ **CI** ◆ 48-49 D 7
Dalrymple Lake < **AUS** ◆ 60-61 K 4
Dalton o **USA** ◇ 24-25 F 2
Dalton Ice Tongue ⊂ **ANT** ◆ 13 G 13
Daly River Aboriginal Land ✗ **AUS** ◆ 60-61 F 2
Daly Waters o **AUS** ◆ 60-61 G 3
Damán and Diu **IND** ◆ 56-57 L 6
Damanhûr o **ET** ◆ 48-49 M 2
Damar ~ **Y** ◆ 56-57 E 8
Damar, Pulau ~ **RI** ◆ 58-59 J 8
Damara o **RCA** ◆ 48-49 J 7
Damaraland ⊥ **NAM** ◆ 50-51 D 5
Damascus = Dimašq ★ **SYR** ◆ 56-57 D 4
Damaturu o **WAN** ◆ 48-49 H 6
Dámávand, Kúh-e ▲ ∘∘ **IR** ◆ 56-57 G 3
Damazine o **SUD** ◆ 48-49 M 6
Damba o **ANG** ◆ 50-51 E 2
Damboa o **WAN** ◆ 48-49 H 6
Dámgán o **IR** ◆ 56-57 G 3
Damietta = Dumyát ☆ **ET** ◆ 48-49 M 2
Dámir, Ad- o **SUD** ◆ 48-49 M 5
Dammám, ad- ☆ **KSA** ◆ 56-57 G 5
Damoh o **IND** ◆ 56-57 M 6
Dampier o **AUS** ◆ 60-61 D 4
Dampier Archipelago ~ **AUS** ◆ 60-61 D 4
Damqaut o **Y** ◆ 56-57 G 7
Damrür o **KSA** ◆ 56-57 F 6
Damoh o **IND** ◆ 56-57 M 6
Dana o **USA** ◇ 20-21 D 6
Dana, Mount ▲ **USA** ◇ 20-21 D 6
Dana Barat, Kepulauan ~ **RI** ◆ 58-59 J 8
Danau Toba o **RI** ◆ 58-59 C 6
Danbury o **USA** ◇ 22-23 M 5
Danby Lake o **USA** ◇ 20-21 G 8
Dandong o **CHN** ◆ 54-55 N 3
Dangriga o **BH** ◆ 28-29 K 3 ◆ 16-17 K 7
Dan-Gulbi o **WAN** ◆ 48-49 G 6
Daniel o **USA** ◇ 20-21 J 4
Danjiangkou o **CHN** ◆ 54-55 L 5
Danli o **HN** ◇ 28-29 L 4 ◆ 16-17 J 8
Dan River ~ **USA** ◇ 24-25 J 1
Danube = Donau ~ **D** ◆ 40-41 L 4
Danube = Dunărea ~ **RO** ◆ 34-35 Q 7
Danville o **USA** (AR) ◇ 26-27 L 2
Danville o **USA** (IL) ◇ 22-23 E 5
Danville o **USA** (IN) ◇ 22-23 E 6
Danville o **USA** (KY) ◇ 22-23 F 7
Danville o **USA** (VA) ◇ 22-23 J 7 ◆ 16-17 L 3
Dan Xian o **CHN** ◆ 54-55 K 8
Daoura, Oued ~ **DZ** ◆ 48-49 E 2
Dapaong o **RT** ◆ 48-49 F 6
Da Qaidam o **CHN** ◆ 54-55 H 4
Daqing o **CHN** ◆ 54-55 N 2
Daraj o **LAR** ◆ 48-49 H 2
Darasun o **RUS** ◆ 52-53 T 7
Darbhanga o **IND** ◆ 56-57 O 5
Dardanelle o **USA** ◇ 26-27 L 2
Dardanelle Lake o **USA** ◇ 26-27 L 2
Dar es Salaam ☆ **EAT** ◆ 50-51 J 3
Darfúr ⊥ **SUD** ◆ 48-49 K 6
Darhan o **MAU** ◆ 54-55 K 2
Darién, Parque Nacional de ⊥ ∘∘ **PA** ◇ 28-29 F 8 ◆ 16-17 L 9
Darién, Serranía del ▲ **PA** ◇ 28-29 F 8 ◆ 16-17 L 9
Darjiling o **IND** ◆ 56-57 O 5
Darling Downs ~ **AUS** ◆ 60-61 L 5
Darling Range ▲ **AUS** ◆ 60-61 D 6
Darling River ~ **AUS** ◆ 60-61 J 6
Darlington o **USA** (SC) ◇ 24-25 J 2
Darlington o **USA** (WI) ◇ 22-23 C 4
Darnah ☆ **LAR** ◆ 48-49 K 2
Darnétal o **F** ◇ 38-39 H 7 ◆ 34-35 M 6
Darnick o **AUS** ◆ 60-61 J 6
Darnley, Cape ▲ **ANT** ◆ 13 G 7
Darnley Bay ≈ ◆ 14-15 M 3
Darrington o **USA** ◇ 20-21 D 1
Dartmoor National Park ⊥ **GB** ◇ 38-39 F 6 ◆ 34-35 K 4
Dartmouth o **CDN** ◇ 18-19 U 7
Daru o **PNG** ◆ 58-59 M 8
Darwin o **AUS** ◆ 60-61 F 2
Darwin, Volcán ▲ **EC** ◆ 30-31 A 5
Dashhowuz = Dašhovuz o **TM** ◆ 56-57 H 2
Datil o **USA** ◇ 26-27 D 2
Datil Well National Recreation Site • **USA** ◇ 26-27 D 2
Datong o **CHN** (QIN) ◆ 54-55 J 4
Datong o **CHN** (SHA) ◆ 54-55 L 3

Datu, Tanjung ▲ **RI** ◆ 58-59 E 6
Datu, Teluk ≈ ◆ 58-59 F 6
Daugava ~ **LV** ◆ 42-43 K 3 ◆ 34-35 R 4
Daugavpils o ∘∘∘ **LV** ◆ 42-43 K 4
Dauha, ad- ★ **Q** ◆ 56-57 G 5
Dauka o **OM** ◆ 56-57 G 6
Daund o **IND** ◆ 56-57 L 7
Dauphin o **CDN** ◆ 14-15 Q 6
Dauphiné ⊥ **F** ◇ 38-39 K 9 ◆ 34-35 N 6
Dauphin Island ~ **USA** ◇ 24-25 D 4
Daurkina, poluostrov ▲ **RUS** ◆ 52-53 J 3
Davangere o **IND** ◆ 56-57 L 8
Davao City o **RP** ◆ 58-59 J 5
Davenport o **USA** ◇ 22-23 C 5 ◆ 16-17 H 2
Davenport o **USA** (WA) ◇ 20-21 E 2
David ☆ **PA** ◇ 28-29 C 7 ◆ 16-17 K 9
Davidson o **USA** ◇ 26-27 H 2
Davidson Mountains ▲ **USA** ◆ 14-15 J 3
Davis o **USA** ◇ 20-21 C 6
Davis Bay ≈ ◆ 13 G 14
Davis Dam o **USA** ◇ 20-21 G 8
Davis Mountains ▲ **USA** ◇ 26-27 F 4
Davis National Historic Site, Fort ∴ **USA** ◇ 26-27 F 4
Davison o **USA** ◇ 22-23 G 5
Davis Sea ≈ ◆ 13 G 13
Davis Strait ≈ ◆ 14-15 Z 3
Dawādimi, ad- o **KSA** ◆ 56-57 F 5
Dawson o **USA** ◇ 24-25 G 4
Dawson o **USA** ◆ 14-15 J 4
Dawson Creek o **CDN** ◆ 14-15 M 5
Dawson-Lambton Glacier ⊂ **ANT** ◆ 13 F 33
Dawson Range ▲ **CDN** ◆ 14-15 J 4
Dawu o **CHN** ◆ 54-55 J 5
Dax o **F** ◇ 38-39 G 10 ◆ 34-35 L 7
Da Xian o **CHN** ◆ 54-55 K 5
Daxue Shan ▲ **CHN** ◆ 54-55 J 5
Daylight Pass ⊥ **USA** ◇ 20-21 F 7
Dayton o **USA** (NV) ◇ 20-21 E 6
Dayton o **USA** (OH) ◇ 22-23 F 6 ◆ 16-17 K 3
Dayton o **USA** (TN) ◇ 24-25 F 2
Dayton o **USA** (WA) ◇ 20-21 F 2
Daytona Beach o **USA** ◇ 24-25 H 5 ◆ 16-17 K 5
Dažhovuz ☆ **TM** ◆ 56-57 H 2
Deadman Bay ≈ ◇ 24-25 G 5
Deakin o **AUS** ◆ 60-61 F 6
Deán Funes o **RA** ◆ 32-33 K 4
Dearborn o **USA** ◇ 22-23 G 5
Deary o **USA** ◇ 20-21 F 2
Dease Arm ≈ ◆ 14-15 M 3
Dease Lake o **CDN** ◆ 14-15 K 5
Dease Strait ≈ ◆ 14-15 P 3
Death Valley ~ **USA** ◇ 20-21 F 7 ◆ 16-17 C 3
Death Valley Junction o **USA** ◇ 20-21 F 7
Death Valley National Monument ∴ **USA** ◇ 20-21 F 7
Deauville o **F** ◇ 38-39 H 7 ◆ 34-35 M 6
Debo, Lac o **RMM** ◆ 48-49 E 5
Debre Birhan o **ETH** ◆ 48-49 N 7
Debrecen o **H** ◆ 40-41 Q 5 ◆ 34-35 Q 5
Debre Markos ☆ **ETH** ◆ 48-49 N 6
Decatur o **USA** (AL) ◇ 24-25 E 2
Decatur o **USA** (GA) ◇ 24-25 F 3
Decatur o **USA** (IL) ◇ 22-23 D 6 ◆ 16-17 J 3
Decatur o **USA** (IN) ◇ 22-23 F 5
Decatur o **USA** (TX) ◇ 26-27 J 3
Decazeville o **F** ◇ 38-39 J 9 ◆ 34-35 M 7
Deccan ⊥ **IND** ◆ 56-57 M 7
Decelles, Réservoir o **CDN** ◇ 18-19 F 5 14-15 V 7
Decepción o **ANT** ◆ 13 G 30
Decize o **F** ◇ 38-39 J 8 ◆ 34-35 M 6
Decorah o **USA** ◇ 22-23 C 4
Dédougou o **BF** ◆ 48-49 E 6
Deep River o **CDN** ◇ 18-19 G 5
Deer o **USA** ◇ 26-27 L 2
Deerfield Beach o **USA** ◇ 24-25 H 6
Deer Lake o **CDN** (NFL) ◇ 18-19 Q 4
Deer Lake o **CDN** (NFL) ◇ 18-19 Q 4
Deer Lodge o **USA** ◇ 20-21 H 2
Deer Park o **USA** ◇ 20-21 F 2
Deer Pond o **CDN** ◇ 18-19 R 4
Deerton o **USA** ◇ 22-23 G 5
Deeth o **USA** ◇ 20-21 G 5
Defensores del Chaco, Parque Nacional ⊥ **PY** ◆ 32-33 K 2
Defiance o **USA** ◇ 22-23 F 5
Degeh Bur o **ETH** ◆ 48-49 O 7
Dégelis o **CDN** ◇ 18-19 K 5
Degollado o **MEX** ◇ 28-29 C 1
De Grey River ~ **AUS** ◆ 60-61 D 4
Dehiba o **TN** ◆ 48-49 H 2
Dehra Dun ☆ ∘∘∘ **IND** ◆ 56-57 M 4
Dehri o **IND** ◆ 56-57 N 6
De Jongs, Tanjung ▲ **RI** ◆ 58-59 L 8
Dekese o **ZRE** ◆ 50-51 F 2
Delacroix o **USA** ◇ 24-25 D 5
Delaney o **USA** ◇ 20-21 F 2
Delano o **USA** ◇ 20-21 E 7
Delavan o **USA** ◇ 22-23 D 4
Delaware **USA** ◇ 22-23 L 6 ◆ 16-17 L 2
Delaware Bay ≈ ◇ 22-23 L 6 ◆ 16-17 L 2
Delaware Lake o **USA** ◇ 22-23 G 5 ◆ 16-17 M 2
Del Cano Rise ≃ ◆ 9 H 10
Delegate River o **AUS** ◆ 60-61 K 7
Delgado, Cabo ▲ **MOC** ◆ 50-51 K 4
Delhi ∘∘∘ ★ **IND** ◆ 56-57 M 5
Delhi o **USA** (LA) ◇ 26-27 M 3
Delhi o **USA** (NY) ◇ 22-23 L 4

Ellice Islands = Tuvalu Islands ⌒ TUV ◆ 12 J 3
Elliot o ZA ◆ 50-51 G 8
Elliot Lake o CDN ◇ 18-19 C 5
Elliott o AUS ◆ 60-61 G 3
Elliott Key ⌒ USA ◇ 24-25 H 7
Ellis o USA ◇ 20-21 G 3
Ellisras o ZA ◆ 50-51 G 6
Elliston o AUS ◆ 60-61 G 6
Ellsworth o USA ◇ 22-23 O 3
Ellsworth Highland ⛰ ANT ◆ 13 F 28
Elma o USA ◇ 20-21 C 2
El Mahbas o WSA ◆ 48-49 D 3
El MÃenia o• DZ ◆ 48-49 F 2
Elm Fork Red River ~ USA ◇ 26-27 G 2
Elmira o CDN ◇ 18-19 N 5
Elmira o USA ◇ 22-23 K 4 ◆ 14-15 V 8
El Morro National Monument ∴ USA ◇ 26-27 C 2
Elmwood o USA ◇ 26-27 G 1
El Nido o•• RP ◆ 58-59 G 4
El Obeid = Al-Ubayyiḍ ☆• SUD ◆ 48-49 M 6
Elogujskij, učastok ⊥ RUS ◆ 52-53 N 5
El Oued ☆• DZ ◆ 48-49 G 2
Eloy o USA ◇ 20-21 J 9
El Paso o USA ◇ 26-27 D 4 ◆ 16-17 E 4
El Portal o USA ◇ 20-21 E 7
El Progreso o GCA (JUT) ◇ 28-29 K 4
El Progreso ☆ GCA (PRO) ◇ 28-29 J 4
El Progreso o HN ◇ 28-29 L 4
Elroy o USA ◇ 22-23 C 4
El Salvador ■ ES ◇ 28-29 K 5 ◆ 16-17 J 8
Elsberry o USA ◇ 22-23 C 6
El Tigre o YV ◆ 30-31 G 3
El Triunfo o MEX ◇ 28-29 J 3
Elūru o IND ◆ 56-57 N 7
El Valle o PA ◇ 28-29 D 7
Elvira, Cape ▲ CDN ◆ 14-15 P 2
Elwell, Lake ⊖ USA ◇ 20-21 J 1
Elwood o USA ◇ 22-23 F 5
Elx o E ◇ 44-45 G 5 ◆ 34-35 L 8
Ely o USA (MN) ◇ 22-23 C 2
Ely o USA (NV) ◇ 20-21 G 6 ◆ 16-17 D 3
Elyria o USA ◇ 22-23 G 5
Embarrass River ~ USA ◇ 22-23 E 6
Embi ☆ KZ ◆ 34-35 X 6
Embi ~ KZ ◆ 34-35 X 6
Emden Deep ≃ ◆ 58-59 J 4
Emerald o AUS ◆ 60-61 K 4
Emerald Bank ≃ ◇ 18-19 N 7
Emigrant Gap o USA ◇ 20-21 D 6
Emiliano Zapata o MEX ◇ 28-29 J 3
Emory Peak ▲ USA ◇ 26-27 F 5
Empire o USA ◇ 22-23 E 3
Emporia o USA (KS) ◆ 16-17 G 3
Emporia o USA (VA) ◇ 22-23 K 7
Ems ~ D ◇ 40-41 J 2 ◆ 34-35 N 5
Emu Park o AUS ◆ 60-61 L 4
Emva o RUS ◆ 52-53 G 5
Encarnación ☆ PY ◆ 32-33 L 3
Encinal o USA ◇ 26-27 H 5
Encinitas o USA ◇ 20-21 F 9
Encino o USA (NM) ◇ 26-27 E 2
Encino o USA (TX) ◇ 26-27 H 6
Encontrados o YV ◆ 30-31 E 3
Endeavour Strait ≈ ◆ 60-61 J 2
Endeh o RI ◆ 58-59 H 8
Enderby Land ∸ ANT ◆ 13 G 6
Endicott o USA ◇ 22-23 K 4
Endicott Mountains ⛰ USA ◆ 14-15 F 3
Eneabba o AUS ◆ 60-61 D 5
Enfield o CDN ◇ 18-19 N 6
Enfield o USA (CT) ◇ 22-23 M 5
Enfield o USA (NC) ◇ 24-25 K 1
Engadine o USA ◇ 22-23 F 2
Engelhard o USA ◇ 24-25 L 2
Èngel's o RUS ◆ 34-35 V 5
Engels = Èngel's o RUS ◆ 34-35 V 5
Enggano, Pulau ⌒ RI ◆ 58-59 D 8
England o USA ◇ 26-27 M 2
Englee o CDN ◇ 18-19 Q 3
Englehart o CDN ◇ 18-19 E 5
English Channel ≈ ◇ 38-39 F 7 ◆ 34-35 L 5
English Coast ⌣ ANT ◆ 13 F 29
English Harbour East o CDN ◇ 18-19 R 5
English Harbour West o CDN ◇ 18-19 R 5
Enid o USA ◇ 26-27 J 1 ◆ 16-17 G 3
Enisej ~ RUS ◆ 52-53 O 4
Enisejsk ☆ RUS ◆ 52-53 P 6
Enisejskij zaliv ≈ ◆ 52-53 M 3
Enisejsko-Stolbovoj, učastok ⊥ RUS ◆ 52-53 O 5
Ènkèn, mys ▲ RUS ◆ 52-53 Z 6
Enna o I ◇ 46-47 E 6 ◆ 34-35 O 8
Ennadai Lake ⊖ CDN ◆ 14-15 Q 4
Ennedi ⛰ TCH ◆ 48-49 K 5
Enngonia o AUS ◆ 60-61 K 5
Ennis o USA (MT) ◇ 20-21 J 3
Ennis o USA (TX) ◇ 26-27 J 3
Enochs o USA ◇ 26-27 F 3
Enrekang o RI ◆ 58-59 G 7
Enschede o NL ◇ 40-41 J 2 ◆ 34-35 N 5
Ensenada o• MEX ◆ 16-17 C 4
Enshi o CHN ◆ 54-55 K 5
Ensign o USA ◇ 26-27 G 1
Entebbe o EAU ◆ 50-51 H 1
Enterprise o USA (AL) ◇ 24-25 F 4
Enterprise o USA (OR) ◇ 20-21 F 3
Entiat o USA ◇ 20-21 D 2
Entrecasteaux, Récifs d' ⌒ F ◆ 60-61 N 3
Entrecasteaux Islands, d' ⌒ PNG ◆ 58-59 O 8
Entre-Rios o BR ◆ 30-31 M 7
Entre Ríos ◘ RA ◆ 32-33 L 4
Entre Ríos, Cordillera ⛰ HN ◇ 28-29 B 4
Enugu ☆ WAN ◆ 48-49 G 7
Enumclaw o USA ◇ 20-21 D 2
Enyellé o RCB ◆ 48-49 J 8
Eólie o Lípari, Ísole ⌒ I ◇ 46-47 E 5 ◆ 34-35 O 8
Epatlán o MEX ◇ 28-29 E 2
Épernay o• F ◇ 38-39 J 7 ◆ 34-35 M 6
Ephraim o USA ◇ 20-21 J 6
Ephrata o USA (WA) ◇ 20-21 E 2
Ephrata o• USA (PA) ◇ 22-23 K 5
Epi ⌒ VAN ◆ 60-61 O 3
Épinal ☆• F ◇ 38-39 L 7 ◆ 34-35 N 6
Epizana o BOL ◆ 30-31 F 8
Epupa Falls ~ NAM ◆ 50-51 D 5
Equator ◆ 50-51 B 1
Equatorial Guinea ■ GQ ◆ 48-49 G 8
Equinox Mountain ⛰ USA ◇ 22-23 M 4
Eram o PNG ◆ 58-59 M 7
Eravur o CL ◆ 56-57 N 9
Erāwadi Myit ~ MYA ◆ 54-55 H 7
Erāwadi Myitwanyā ⌣ MYA ◆ 58-59 B 3
Erdi ∸ TCH ◆ 48-49 K 5
Erebus, Mount ▲ ANT ◆ 13 F 17
Erebus and Terror Gulf ≈ ◆ 13 G 31
Erechim o BR ◆ 32-33 M 3
Ereğli ☆ TR ◆ 34-35 S 7
Ereğli ☆ TR ◆ 34-35 S 8
Erejmentau ☆ KZ ◆ 52-53 L 7
Erenhot o CHN ◆ 54-55 L 3
Erevan ★ AR ◆ 34-35 U 7
Erfoud o MA ◆ 48-49 E 2
Erfurt ☆•• D ◇ 40-41 L 3 ◆ 34-35 O 5
Ergun Zuoqi o CHN ◆ 54-55 N 1
Er Hai ⊖ CHN ◆ 54-55 J 6
Eric o CDN ◇ 18-19 M 3
Erick o USA ◇ 26-27 H 2
Erie o USA ◇ 22-23 H 4 ◆ 14-15 U 8
Erie, Lake ⊖ ◇ 22-23 H 4 ◆ 16-17 K 2
Erie Canal < USA ◇ 22-23 L 4
Erimo-misaki ▲ J ◆ 54-55 R 3
Erin o USA ◇ 24-25 E 1
Eritrea ■ ER ◆ 48-49 N 5
Erlangen o D ◇ 40-41 L 4 ◆ 34-35 O 6
Erldunda o AUS ◆ 60-61 G 5
Ernakulam o IND ◆ 56-57 M 9
Ernée o F ◇ 38-39 G 7 ◆ 34-35 L 6
Erode o IND ◆ 56-57 M 8
Eromanga ⌒ VAN ◆ 12 H 4
Eromanga Island = Île Erromango ⌒ VAN ◆ 60-61 O 3
Erongoberg ⛰ NAM ◆ 50-51 E 6
er Raoui, Erg ∸ DZ ◆ 48-49 E 3
Errego o MOC ◆ 50-51 J 5
Er Rîchât, Guelb ▲ RIM ◆ 48-49 C 4
Errol o USA ◇ 22-23 N 3
Ertai o CHN ◆ 54-55 G 2
Ertis ~ KZ ◆ 52-53 M 7
Erzgebirge ⛰ D ◇ 40-41 M 3 ◆ 34-35 O 5
Èrzin ☆ RUS ◆ 52-53 Q 7
Erzincan ☆ TR ◆ 34-35 T 8
Erzurum ☆• TR ◆ 34-35 U 8
Esbjerg o• DK ◇ 36-37 D 9 ◆ 34-35 N 4
Escalante o USA ◇ 20-21 J 7
Escalante River ~ USA ◇ 20-21 J 7
Escambia River ~ USA ◇ 24-25 E 4
Escanaba o USA ◇ 22-23 E 3 ◆ 14-15 T 7
Escanaba River ~ USA ◇ 22-23 E 2
Escárcega o• MEX ◇ 28-29 J 2 ◆ 16-17 H 7
Escondida, Punta ▲ MEX ◇ 28-29 F 4
Escondido o USA ◇ 20-21 F 9
Escondido, Río ~ MEX ◇ 28-29 K 2
Escondido, Río ~ NIC ◇ 28-29 B 5
Escoumins, Les o CDN ◇ 18-19 K 4
Escuintla ☆ GCA ◇ 28-29 J 4
Escuminac o CDN ◇ 18-19 M 5
Escuminac, Point ▲ CDN ◇ 18-19 M 5
Eṣfahān ☆••• IR ◆ 56-57 G 4
Eš̌ger, Kūh-e ⛰ IR ◆ 56-57 H 4
Esil ☆ KZ ◆ 52-53 K 7
Esil ~ KZ ◆ 52-53 K 7
Esker o CDN ◇ 18-19 L 2
Eskimo Lakes ⊖ CDN ◆ 14-15 K 3
Eskişehir ☆ TR ◆ 34-35 S 8
Esmeralda, Isla ⌒ RCH ◆ 32-33 G 7
Esmeralda, La o YV ◆ 30-31 F 4
Esmeraldas ☆• EC ◆ 30-31 D 4
Espalion o F ◇ 38-39 J 9 ◆ 34-35 M 7
Espanola o CDN ◇ 18-19 D 5
Espanola o USA ◇ 26-27 D 2
Española, Isla ⌒ EC ◆ 30-31 B 5
Espaveita o PA ◇ 28-29 D 8
Esperance o AUS ◆ 60-61 E 6
Esperance Bay ≈ ◆ 60-61 E 6
Esperanza o RA ◆ 32-33 H 8
Esperanza, La ☆• HN ◇ 28-29 K 4
Espinal, El o PA ◇ 28-29 D 8
Espino o YV ◆ 30-31 F 3
Espino, El o PA ◇ 28-29 E 7
Espírito Santo ◘ BR ◆ 30-31 L 8
Espiritu Santo ⌒ VAN ◆ 60-61 O 3
Espíritu Santo, Bahía del ≈ ◇ 28-29 L 2
Espita o MEX ◇ 28-29 K 1
Esquel o RA ◆ 32-33 H 6
Essaouira = As-Sawirah ☆• MA ◆ 48-49 D 2
Essej o RUS ◆ 52-53 R 4
Essen o• D ◇ 40-41 J 3 ◆ 34-35 N 5
Essequibo ~ GUY ◆ 30-31 H 4
Essex o USA (CA) ◇ 20-21 G 8
Essex o USA (MT) ◇ 20-21 H 1
Essex Junction o USA ◇ 22-23 M 3
Ésso ☆ RUS ◆ 52-53 c 6
Est, Pointe de l' ▲ CDN ◇ 18-19 O 4
Estacada o USA ◇ 20-21 C 3
Estaca de Bares, Punta de ▲ E ◇ 44-45 D 3 ◆ 34-35 K 7
Estacia Camacho o MEX ◆ 16-17 F 6
Estado Cañitas de Felipe Pescador o MEX ◆ 16-17 F 6
Estado la Calle o MEX ◇ 28-29 D 1
Estados, Isla de los ⌒ RA ◆ 32-33 K 8
Eṣṭahbānāt o• IR ◆ 56-57 G 5
Estância o BR ◆ 30-31 M 7
Estanica o USA ◇ 26-27 D 2
Este, Laguna del ≈ ◇ 28-29 J 2
Estelí ☆ NIC ◇ 28-29 L 5
Estelline o USA ◇ 26-27 G 2
Estero o USA ◇ 24-25 H 6
Estero Bay ≈ ◇ 20-21 D 8
Estill o USA ◇ 24-25 H 3
Estirão do Equador o BR ◆ 30-31 E 5
Estonia ■ EST ◇ 42-43 J 2 ◆ 34-35 Q 4
Estor, El o GCA ◇ 28-29 K 4
Estrondo, Serra do ⛰ BR ◆ 30-31 K 7
Étampes o F ◇ 38-39 J 7 ◆ 34-35 M 6
Etawah o IND ◆ 56-57 M 5
Eternity Range ⛰ ANT ◆ 13 G 30
Ethiopia ■ ETH ◆ 48-49 N 7
Ethiopian Highlands ⛰ ETH ◆ 9 G 4
Etolin Strait ≈ ◆ 14-15 C 4
Eton o AUS ◆ 60-61 K 4
Etosha National Park ⊥ NAM ◆ 50-51 D 5
Etosha Pan ⊖ NAM ◆ 50-51 E 5
Etowah o USA ◇ 24-25 F 2
Etowah Mounds State Historic Site ∴• USA ◇ 24-25 F 2
Etowah River ~ USA ◇ 24-25 F 2
Etzatlan o MEX ◇ 28-29 B 1
Eucla Basin ∸ AUS ◆ 60-61 E 6
Eucla Motels o AUS ◆ 60-61 F 6
Euclid o USA ◇ 22-23 H 5
Euclides da Cunha o BR ◆ 30-31 M 7
Eudistes, Lac des ⊖ CDN ◇ 18-19 M 3
Eudora o USA ◇ 26-27 M 3
Eufaula o USA (AL) ◇ 24-25 F 4
Eufaula o USA (OK) ◇ 26-27 K 2
Eufaula Lake ⊖ USA ◇ 26-27 K 2
Eugene o USA ◇ 20-21 C 4 ◆ 14-15 M 8
Euless o USA ◇ 26-27 J 3
Eulo o AUS ◆ 60-61 K 5
Eungella o AUS ◆ 60-61 K 4
Eunice o USA (LA) ◇ 26-27 L 4
Eunice o USA (NM) ◇ 26-27 F 3
Euphrates ~ SYR ◆ 56-57 E 4
Eupora o USA ◇ 24-25 D 3
Eureka o USA (MT) ◇ 20-21 G 1
Eureka o USA (NV) ◇ 20-21 G 6
Eureka o• USA (CA) ◇ 20-21 B 5 ◆ 16-17 B 2
Eureka Sound ≈ ◆ 14-15 E 1
Eureka Springs o USA ◇ 26-27 L 1
Europa, Picos de ⛰ E ◇ 44-45 E 3 ◆ 34-35 L 7
Eustis o USA ◇ 24-25 H 5
Eutaw o USA ◇ 24-25 E 3
Eva o USA ◇ 26-27 G 1
Eva-Liv, ostrov ⌒ RUS ◆ 52-53 J 1
Evandale o CDN ◇ 18-19 L 6
Evans, Lac ⊖ CDN ◇ 18-19 F 3
Evans, Mount ▲ USA ◇ 20-21 H 2
Evans Strait ≈ ◆ 14-15 U 4
Evanston o USA (IL) ◇ 22-23 E 4
Evanston o USA (WY) ◇ 20-21 J 5
Evansville o CDN ◇ 18-19 C 6
Evansville o USA ◇ 22-23 E 7 ◆ 16-17 J 3
Evant o USA ◇ 26-27 H 4
Èvensk ☆ RUS ◆ 52-53 c 5
Everard, Lake ⊖ AUS ◆ 60-61 G 6
Everett o USA (GA) ◇ 24-25 H 4
Everett o USA (WA) ◇ 20-21 C 2
Everett, Mount ▲ USA ◇ 22-23 M 4
Everglades, The ∸ USA ◇ 24-25 H 7 ◆ 16-17 K 5
Everglades City o USA ◇ 24-25 H 7
Everglades National Park ⊥••• USA ◇ 24-25 H 7 ◆ 16-17 K 5
Evergreen o USA ◇ 24-25 E 4
Évia ⌒ GR ◇ 46-47 J 5 ◆ 34-35 Q 8
Evinayong o GQ ◆ 50-51 D 1
Évora o••• P ◇ 44-45 D 5 ◆ 34-35 K 8
Évreux ☆ F ◇ 38-39 H 7 ◆ 34-35 M 6
Evron o F ◇ 38-39 G 7 ◆ 34-35 L 6
Ewan o USA ◇ 20-21 F 2
Ewaso Ngiro ~ EAK ◆ 50-51 J 1
Ewing o USA ◇ 22-23 C 5
Executive Committee Range ⛰ ANT ◆ 13 F 24
Exeter o CDN ◇ 18-19 D 7
Exeter o USA (CA) ◇ 20-21 E 7
Exeter o USA (NH) ◇ 22-23 N 4
Exeter Sound ≈ ◆ 14-15 Y 3
Exmoor National Park ⊥ GB ◇ 38-39 F 6 ◆ 34-35 L 5
Exmore o USA ◇ 22-23 L 7
Exmouth o AUS ◆ 60-61 C 4
Exmouth Plateau ≃ ◆ 60-61 C 3
Exploits, Bay of ≈ ◇ 18-19 R 4
Exploits Islands ⌒ CDN ◇ 18-19 R 4
Exploits River ~ CDN ◇ 18-19 Q 4
Exuma Cays ⌒ BS ◆ 16-17 L 6
Exuma Sound ≈ ◆ 16-17 L 6
Eyasi, Lake ⊖ EAT ◆ 50-51 H 2
Eyl o SP ◆ 48-49 P 7
Eyre, Lake ⊖ AUS ◆ 60-61 H 5
Eyre North, Lake ⊖ AUS ◆ 60-61 H 5
Eyre Peninsula ⌣ AUS ◆ 60-61 H 6
Ezequiel Montes o MEX ◇ 28-29 E 1
Ezgueret ~ RMM ◆ 48-49 F 5
Ezhou o CHN ◆ 54-55 L 5

F

Fabens o USA ◇ 26-27 D 4
Fachi o RN ◆ 48-49 H 5
Fada o TCH ◆ 48-49 K 5
Fada-N'gourma o BF ◆ 48-49 F 6
Faddeevskij, ostrov ⌒ RUS ◆ 52-53 Z 2
Faddeja, zaliv ≈ ◆ 52-53 S 2
Fadiffolu Atoll ⌒ MV ◆ 56-57 L 9
Fagrinkotti o SUD ◆ 48-49 M 5
Faguibine, Lac ⊖ RMM ◆ 48-49 E 5
Faial, Ilha do ⌒ P ◆ 34-35 F 8
Failaka, Ǧazirat ⌒•• KWT ◆ 56-57 F 5
Fairbank o USA ◇ 22-23 K 6
Fairbanks o USA (MN) ◇ 22-23 C 2
Fairbanks o• USA (AK) ◆ 14-15 G 4
Fairchild o USA ◇ 22-23 C 3
Fairfax o USA ◇ 24-25 H 3
Fairfield o USA (AL) ◇ 24-25 E 3
Fairfield o USA (CA) ◇ 20-21 C 6
Fairfield o USA (ID) ◇ 20-21 G 4
Fairfield o USA (IL) ◇ 22-23 D 6
Fairfield o USA (ME) ◇ 22-23 O 3
Fairfield o USA (MT) ◇ 20-21 J 2
Fairfield o USA (TX) ◇ 26-27 J 4
Fairhaven o CDN ◇ 18-19 S 5
Fairhope o USA ◇ 24-25 E 4
Fairmont o USA ◇ 22-23 H 6
Fair Oaks o USA ◇ 26-27 M 2
Fairoaks o USA ◇ 26-27 M 2
Fairview o USA (MI) ◇ 22-23 F 3
Fairview o USA (OK) ◇ 26-27 H 1
Fairview Peak ▲ USA ◇ 20-21 C 4
Fairweather, Mount ▲ USA ◆ 14-15 J 5
Fais ⌒ FSM ◆ 58-59 M 5
Faisalābād o PK ◆ 56-57 L 4
Faizabad ☆ AFG ◆ 56-57 L 3
Faizābād o IND ◆ 56-57 N 5
Fakfak o RI ◆ 58-59 K 7
Falaise o F ◇ 38-39 G 7 ◆ 34-35 L 6
Falémé ~ SN ◆ 48-49 C 6
Falfurrias o USA ◇ 26-27 H 6 ◆ 16-17 G 5
Falkland Escarpment ≃ ◆ 32-33 M 7
Falkland Islands ⌒ GB ◆ 32-33 K 8
Falkland Plateau ≃ ◆ 32-33 M 8
Fall City o USA ◇ 20-21 D 2
Fall Line Hills ⛰ USA ◇ 24-25 D 2
Fallon o USA ◇ 20-21 E 6
Fall River o USA ◇ 22-23 N 5
Fall River Mills o USA ◇ 20-21 D 5
Falls Creek o AUS ◆ 60-61 K 7
Falls Lake Reservoir < USA ◇ 24-25 J 1
Fallūǧa, al- ☆ IRQ ◆ 56-57 E 4
Falmouth o USA ◇ 22-23 N 5
False Pass o USA ◆ 14-15 D 6
Falster ∸ DK ◇ 36-37 E 9 ◆ 34-35 O 5
Falun o S ◇ 36-37 G 6 ◆ 34-35 P 3
Fama, Ouidi ~ TCH ◆ 48-49 K 5
Famatina, Sierra de ⛰ RA ◆ 32-33 J 3
Fang o THA ◆ 58-59 C 3
Fangak o SUD ◆ 48-49 M 7
Faouët, le o F ◇ 38-39 F 7 ◆ 34-35 L 6
Faradje o ZRE ◆ 48-49 L 8
Farafangana o RM ◆ 50-51 L 6
Farafara Oasis = Farāfira, al-Wāḥāt al- ∸ ET ◆ 48-49 L 3
Farāfira, al-Wāḥāt al- ∸ ET ◆ 48-49 L 3
Farāh ☆ AFG ◆ 56-57 J 4
Farāh Rūd ~ AFG ◆ 56-57 J 4
Farallon de Medinilla ⌒ USA ◆ 58-59 N 3
Farallon de Pajaros ⌒ USA ◆ 58-59 M 2
Faranah ☆ RG ◆ 48-49 C 6
Farasān, Ǧazā'ir ⌒ KSA ◆ 56-57 E 7
Faraulep Atoll ⌒ FSM ◆ 58-59 M 5
Farewell, Cape ▲ NZ ◆ 60-61 P 8
Fargo o USA (GA) ◇ 24-25 G 4
Fargo o USA (ND) ◆ 14-15 R 7
Farīdābād o IND ◆ 56-57 M 5
Farley o USA ◇ 26-27 E 1
Farmer o USA ◇ 20-21 E 2
Farmer City o USA ◇ 22-23 D 5
Farmersville o USA ◇ 26-27 J 3
Farmerville o USA ◇ 26-27 L 3
Farmington o USA (IL) ◇ 22-23 C 5
Farmington o USA (ME) ◇ 22-23 N 3
Farmington o USA (MO) ◇ 22-23 C 7
Farmington o USA (NM) ◇ 26-27 C 1 ◆ 16-17 E 3
Farmville o USA ◇ 22-23 J 7
Farnham o CDN ◇ 18-19 H 6
Faro ~ CAM ◆ 48-49 H 7
Faro o• P ◇ 44-45 D 6 ◆ 34-35 K 8
Faro, Réserve du ⊥ CAM ◆ 48-49 H 7
Faroe Bank ≃ ◇ 38-39 C 1 ◆ 34-35 K 3
Faroe Islands ⌒ FR ◇ 38-39 D 1 ◆ 34-35 K 3
Faroe Shelf ≃ ◆ 34-35 K 3
Farquhar Atoll ⌒ SY ◆ 50-51 M 4
Farquhar Group ⌒ SY ◆ 50-51 M 3
Farrukhābād o IND ◆ 56-57 M 5
Fartak, Ra's ▲ Y ◆ 56-57 G 7
Farvel, Kap = Uummannarsuaq ▲ GRØ ◆ 14-15 c 5
Farwell o USA ◇ 26-27 F 2
Fāshir, Al o• SUD ◆ 48-49 L 6
Fasil Ghebbi ••• ETH ◆ 48-49 N 6
Fastiv o UA ◆ 34-35 R 5
Fatehpur o IND ◆ 56-57 N 5
Fathom Five National Marine Park ⊥ CDN ◇ 18-19 D 6
Fayette o USA (AL) ◇ 24-25 E 3
Fayette o USA (MS) ◇ 26-27 M 4
Fayette, La o USA ◇ 24-25 F 2
Fayetteville o USA (AR) ◇ 26-27 K 1 ◆ 16-17 H 3
Fayetteville o USA (NC) ◇ 24-25 J 2 ◆ 16-17 L 3
Fayetteville o USA (OH) ◇ 22-23 G 6
Fayetteville o USA (TN) ◇ 24-25 E 2
Fayu ⌒ FSM ◆ 58-59 O 5
Fayyūm, al- ☆•• ET ◆ 48-49 M 3
Fāz ☆••• MA ◆ 48-49 E 2
Fdérik ☆ RIM ◆ 48-49 C 4
Fear, Cape ▲ USA ◇ 24-25 K 3 ◆ 16-17 L 4
Fécamp o F ◇ 38-39 H 7 ◆ 34-35 M 6
Federal o RA ◆ 32-33 L 4
Federated States of Micronesia ■ FSM ◆ 58-59 M 5
Feira de Santana o BR ◆ 30-31 M 7
Felipe Carillo Puerto o• MEX ◇ 28-29 K 2 ◆ 16-17 J 7
Felix, Rio ~ USA ◇ 26-27 E 3
Fengcheng o CHN (JXI) ◆ 54-55 M 6
Fengcheng o CHN (LIA) ◆ 54-55 N 3
Fengrun o CHN ◆ 54-55 M 4
Feng Xian o CHN ◆ 54-55 K 5
Feni o BD ◆ 56-57 P 6
Feni Islands ⌒ PNG ◆ 58-59 O 7
Fennimore o USA ◇ 22-23 C 4
Fenton o USA ◇ 22-23 G 4
Feodosija ☆• UA ◆ 34-35 T 6
Ferdo, Le ∸ SN ◆ 48-49 C 6
Ferganskij hrebet ⛰ KS ◆ 56-57 L 2
Fergus Falls o USA ◆ 14-15 R 7
Fergusson Island ⌒ PNG ◆ 58-59 O 8
Ferkessédougou ☆ CI ◆ 48-49 D 7
Fermeuse o CDN ◇ 18-19 S 5
Fernandina, Isla ⌒ EC ◆ 30-31 A 5
Fernandina Beach o USA ◇ 24-25 H 4
Fernando de Magallanes, Parque Nacional ⊥ RCH ◆ 32-33 H 8
Ferokh o IND ◆ 56-57 M 8
Ferrara ☆• I ◇ 46-47 C 2 ◆ 34-35 O 7
Ferreira Gomes o BR ◆ 30-31 J 4
Ferreñafe o PE ◆ 30-31 D 6
Ferris o USA ◇ 26-27 J 3
Ferrol o E ◇ 44-45 C 3 ◆ 34-35 K 7
Ferté-Bernard, la o F ◇ 38-39 H 7 ◆ 34-35 M 6
Fès = Fāz ☆••• MA ◆ 48-49 E 2
Feshi o ZRE ◆ 50-51 E 3
Festus o USA ◇ 22-23 C 6
Feuilles, Rivière aux ~ CDN ◆ 14-15 W 5
Feurs o F ◇ 38-39 K 9 ◆ 34-35 N 6
Fevral'sk o RUS ◆ 52-53 X 7
Fezzan ∸ LAR ◆ 48-49 H 3
Fianarantsoa ☆• RM ◆ 50-51 L 6
Fiatt o USA ◇ 22-23 C 5
Fifi, al- o SUD ◆ 48-49 K 6
Figeac o F ◇ 38-39 J 9 ◆ 34-35 M 7
Figuig o MA ◆ 48-49 E 2
Fiji ■ FJI ◆ 60-61 Q 3
Fiji ⌒ FJI ◆ 60-61 Q 3
Filadelfia o CR ◇ 28-29 B 6
Filchner Ice Shelf ⊂ ANT ◆ 13 E 30
Filer o USA ◇ 20-21 G 4
Fillmore o USA ◇ 20-21 E 8
Finca 7 o CR ◇ 28-29 C 7
Findlay o USA ◇ 22-23 G 5 ◆ 16-17 K 2
Fine o USA ◇ 22-23 L 3
Finger Lakes ⊖ USA ◇ 22-23 K 4 ◆ 14-15 V 8
Finke o AUS ◆ 60-61 G 5
Finke River ~ AUS ◆ 60-61 H 5
Finland ■ FIN ◆ 34-35 Q 3
Finland o USA ◇ 22-23 C 2
Finland, Gulf of ≈ ◇ 36-37 M 7 ◆ 34-35 Q 4
Finlay River ~ CDN ◆ 14-15 M 5
Finnigan, Mount ▲ AUS ◆ 60-61 K 3
Finschhafen o PNG ◆ 58-59 N 8
Fiordland National Park ••• NZ ◆ 60-61 O 9
Fire Island National Seashore ⊥ USA ◇ 22-23 M 5
Firenze ☆••• I ◇ 46-47 C 3 ◆ 34-35 O 7
Firminy o F ◇ 38-39 K 9 ◆ 34-35 N 6
Firozābad o IND ◆ 56-57 M 5
Firth of Forth ≈ ◇ 38-39 F 3 ◆ 34-35 L 4
Fischell o CDN ◇ 18-19 P 4
Fisher Strait ≈ ◆ 14-15 U 4
Fishguard o GB ◇ 38-39 E 6 ◆ 34-35 L 5
Fishing Creek o USA ◇ 22-23 K 6
Fisterra, Cabo ▲ E ◇ 44-45 C 3 ◆ 34-35 K 7
Fitchburg o USA ◇ 22-23 N 4
Fitzgerald o USA ◇ 24-25 G 4
Fitzgerald River National Park ⊥ AUS ◆ 60-61 D 6
Fitzroy Crossing o AUS ◆ 60-61 F 3
Fitzroy River ~ AUS ◆ 60-61 E 3
Fitzwilliam Island ⌒ CDN ◇ 18-19 D 6
Five Cays Settlements o GB ◆ 16-17 M 6
Five Points o USA ◇ 20-21 D 7
Fizi o ZRE ◆ 50-51 G 2
Flagstaff o• USA ◇ 20-21 J 8 ◆ 16-17 D 3
Flagstaff Lake ⊖ USA ◇ 22-23 N 3
Flamingo o USA ◇ 24-25 H 7
Flathead Indian Reservation X USA ◇ 20-21 G 2 ◆ 14-15 O 7
Flathead Lake ⊖ USA ◇ 20-21 G 2 ◆ 14-15 O 7
Flatonia o USA ◇ 26-27 J 5
Flat River o CDN ◇ 18-19 N 5
Flat River o USA ◇ 22-23 C 7
Flattery, Cape ▲ AUS ◆ 60-61 K 2
Flattery, Cape ▲ USA ◇ 20-21 B 1 ◆ 14-15 M 7
Flat Top o USA ◇ 22-23 H 7
Flèche, la o F ◇ 38-39 G 8 ◆ 34-35 L 6
Flemish Cap ≃ ◆ 14-15 b 7
Flenelon Falls o CDN ◇ 18-19 E 6
Flers o F ◇ 38-39 G 7 ◆ 34-35 L 6
Fleurance o F ◇ 38-39 H 10 ◆ 34-35 M 7
Fleur de Lys o CDN ◇ 18-19 Q 3
Fleur-de-May, Lac ⊖ CDN ◇ 18-19 M 3
Fleur-de-May, Lake = Fleur-de-May, Lac ⊖ CDN ◇ 18-19 M 3
Flinders Bay ≈ ◆ 60-61 D 6
Flinders Chase National Park ⊥ AUS ◆ 60-61 H 7
Flinders Island ⌒ AUS (SA) ◆ 60-61 G 6
Flinders Island ⌒ AUS (TAS) ◆ 60-61 K 7
Flinders Ranges ⛰ AUS ◆ 60-61 H 6
Flinders Reef ⌒ AUS ◆ 60-61 K 3
Flinders River ~ AUS ◆ 60-61 J 3
Flin Flon o CDN ◆ 14-15 Q 6
Flint o USA ◇ 22-23 G 4 ◆ 14-15 U 8
Flint Hills ⛰ USA ◇ 26-27 J 1
Flint River ~ USA ◇ 24-25 F 4 ◆ 16-17 K 4
Flomaton o USA ◇ 24-25 E 4
Flora o USA ◇ 22-23 D 6
Florala o USA ◇ 24-25 E 4
Flor de Punga o PE ◆ 30-31 E 6
Florence o USA (AL) ◇ 24-25 E 2
Florence o USA (AZ) ◇ 20-21 J 9
Florence o USA (OR) ◇ 20-21 B 3
Florence o USA (SC) ◇ 24-25 J 2 ◆ 16-17 L 4
Florence o USA (WI) ◇ 22-23 D 3
Florence = Firenze ☆••• I ◇ 46-47 C 3 ◆ 34-35 O 7
Florence Junction o USA ◇ 20-21 J 9
Florencia ☆ CO ◆ 30-31 D 4
Flores ☆• GCA ◇ 28-29 K 3
Flores ⌒ RI ◆ 58-59 H 8
Flores, Ilha das ⌒ P ◆ 34-35 E 8
Flores, Las o RA ◆ 32-33 L 5
Flores Sea ≈ ◆ 58-59 G 8
Floresville o USA ◇ 26-27 H 5
Floriano o BR ◆ 30-31 L 6
Florianópolis ☆• BR ◆ 32-33 N 3
Florida o C ◆ 16-17 L 6
Florida ☆ ROU ◆ 32-33 L 4
Florida ◘ USA ◇ 24-25 H 5 ◆ 16-17 K 5
Florida, Cape ▲ USA ◇ 24-25 H 7
Florida, Estrechos de la = Straits of Florida ≈ ◆ 16-17 K 6
Florida, La ∴• GCA ◇ 28-29 J 3
Florida Bay ≈ ◇ 24-25 H 7 ◆ 16-17 K 5
Florida Keys ⌒ USA ◇ 24-25 H 7 ◆ 16-17 K 6
Florien o USA ◇ 26-27 L 4
Florissant o USA ◇ 22-23 C 6
Floyd, Mount ▲ USA ◇ 20-21 H 8
Floydada o USA ◇ 26-27 G 3
Fly River ~ PNG ◆ 58-59 M 8
Focșani ☆ RO ◆ 34-35 R 6
Fodé o RCA ◆ 48-49 K 7
Fóggia ☆ I ◇ 46-47 E 4 ◆ 34-35 P 7
Fogo o CDN ◇ 18-19 R 4
Fogo Island ⌒ CDN ◇ 18-19 R 4 ◆ 14-15 a 7
Foix o F ◇ 38-39 H 10 ◆ 34-35 M 7
Foley Island ⌒ CDN ◆ 14-15 V 3
Folkston o USA ◇ 24-25 G 4
Follett o USA ◇ 26-27 G 1
Follette, La o USA ◇ 24-25 F 1
Folsom o USA ◇ 26-27 F 1
Fond-du-Lac o CDN ◆ 14-15 P 5
Fond du Lac o USA ◇ 22-23 D 4
Fonseca, Golfo de ≈ ◇ 28-29 L 5 ◆ 16-17 J 8
Fonte Boa o BR ◆ 30-31 F 5
Fontenay, Abbaye de ••• F ◇ 38-39 K 8 ◆ 34-35 M 6
Fontenay-le-Comte o F ◇ 38-39 G 8 ◆ 34-35 L 6
Fonteneau, Lac ⊖ CDN ◇ 18-19 O 3
Fontenelle o USA ◇ 20-21 J 5
Fontenelle Reservoir < USA ◇ 20-21 J 4
Forbes o AUS ◆ 60-61 K 6
Ford o USA ◇ 20-21 F 2
Ford, Cape ▲ AUS ◆ 60-61 F 2
Ford River ~ USA ◇ 22-23 E 2
Fordyce o USA ◇ 26-27 L 3
Forest City o USA ◇ 24-25 H 2
Forest Grove o USA ◇ 20-21 C 3
Forestier, Cape ▲ AUS ◆ 60-61 K 8
Forestville o CDN ◇ 18-19 K 4
Forestville, Parc Provincial de ⊥ CDN ◇ 18-19 K 4
Forgan o USA ◇ 26-27 G 1
Forges-les-Eaux o F ◇ 38-39 H 7 ◆ 34-35 M 6
Forillon, Parc Nacional de ⊥ CDN ◇ 18-19 M 4
Forks o USA ◇ 20-21 B 2
Forli o I ◇ 46-47 D 2 ◆ 34-35 O 7
Formation Cave ∴ USA ◇ 20-21 J 4
Formentera, Illa de ⌒ E ◇ 44-45 H 5 ◆ 34-35 M 8
Formia o I ◇ 46-47 D 4 ◆ 34-35 O 7
Formosa o BR ◆ 30-31 K 8
Formosa ◘ RA ◆ 32-33 K 3
Formosa ☆ RA (FOR) ◆ 32-33 L 3
Formosa do Rio Preto o BR ◆ 30-31 K 7
Föroyar Iceland Ridge ≃ ◆ 34-35 J 3
Forrest o USA ◇ 22-23 D 5
Forrest City o USA ◇ 26-27 M 2
Forrest River Aboriginal Land X AUS ◆ 60-61 F 2
Forsayth o AUS ◆ 60-61 J 3
Fort Albany o CDN ◆ 14-15 U 6
Fortaleza ☆• BR ◆ 30-31 M 5
Fort Amanda State Memorial ∴• USA ◇ 22-23 G 5
Fort Amherst National Historic Park ∴• CDN ◇ 18-19 N 5
Fort Apache Indian Reservation X USA ◇ 26-27 B 2
Fort Atkinson o USA ◇ 22-23 D 4
Fort Beaufort o ZA ◆ 50-51 G 8
Fort Belknap Indian Reservation X USA ◆ 14-15 P 7
Fort Benning xx USA ◇ 24-25 F 3
Fort Benton o USA ◇ 20-21 J 2
Fort Benton Ruins • USA ◇ 20-21 J 2
Fort Bliss Military Reservation xx USA ◇ 26-27 E 3
Fort Bragg o USA ◇ 24-25 J 2
Fort Bragg Military Reservation xx USA ◇ 24-25 J 2
Fort Bridger o USA ◇ 20-21 J 5
Fort Bridger State Historic Site • USA ◇ 20-21 J 5
Fort Chipewyan o CDN ◆ 14-15 O 5
Fort Davis o USA ◇ 26-27 F 4
Fort-de-France ☆ F ◆ 16-17 O 8
Fort Deposit o USA ◇ 24-25 E 4
Fort Dodge o USA ◆ 16-17 H 2
Fort Edward National Historic Site ∴• CDN ◇ 18-19 M 6
Fort Erie o CDN ◇ 18-19 E 7
Fort Fairfield o USA ◇ 18-19 L 5
Fort Fisher • USA ◇ 24-25 K 3
Fort Frances o CDN ◆ 14-15 S 7
Fort Gadsden State Historical Site • USA ◇ 24-25 F 5
Fort Garland o USA ◇ 26-27 E 1
Fort George o CDN ◇ 18-19 E 2
Fort George National Historic Park ∴• CDN ◇ 18-19 E 7
Fort George River = Grande Rivière, La ~ CDN ◇ 18-19 G 2
Fort George River = La Grande Rivière ~ CDN ◇ 18-19 G 2
Fort Gibson Lake ⊖ USA ◇ 26-27 K 1
Fort Good Hope o CDN ◆ 14-15 L 3
Fort Griffin State Historic Park • USA ◇ 26-27 H 3
Fort Hall Indian Reservation X USA ◇ 20-21 H 4 ◆ 14-15 O 8
Fort Hancock o USA ◇ 26-27 E 4
Fort Hunter Liggett Military Reservation xx USA ◇ 20-21 D 7
Fortín de las Flores o MEX ◇ 28-29 F
Fort Jackson xx USA ◇ 24-25 H 2
Fort Jefferson National Memorial • USA ◇ 24-25 G 7
Fort Kent o USA ◇ 22-23 O 2
Fort Kent Historic Site ∴ USA ◇ 22-23 O 2
Fort Knox xx USA ◇ 22-23 F 7
Fort Lauderdale o USA ◇ 24-25 H 6 ◆ 16-17 K 5
Fort Lemhi Monument • USA ◇ 20-21 H 3
Fort Lewis • USA ◇ 20-21 C 2
Fort Liard o CDN ◆ 14-15 M 4
Fort Mackinac • USA ◇ 22-23 F 3
Fort Madison o USA ◇ 22-23 C 5
Fort Matanzas National Monument ∴• USA ◇ 24-25 H 5
Fort McCoy Military Reservation xx USA ◇ 22-23 C 3
Fort McDowell Indian Reservation X USA ◇ 20-21 J 9
Fort McHenry • USA ◇ 22-23 K 6
Fort McKavett State Historic Site • USA ◇ 26-27 G 4
Fort McMurray o• CDN ◆ 14-15 O 5
Fort McPherson o CDN ◆ 14-15 K 3
Fort Mohave Indian Reservation X USA ◇ 20-21 G 8
Fort Munro o• PK ◆ 56-57 K 5
Fort Myers o USA ◇ 24-25 H 6 ◆ 16-17 K 5
Fort Nelson o CDN ◆ 14-15 M 5
Fort Nelson River ~ CDN ◆ 14-15 M 5
Fort Payne o USA ◇ 24-25 F 2
Fort Peck Indian Reservation X USA ◆ 14-15 P 7
Fort Peck Lake ⊖ USA ◆ 14-15 P 7
Fort Pickett xx USA ◇ 22-23 J 7
Fort Pierce o USA ◇ 24-25 H 6 ◆ 16-17 K 5
Fort Portal ☆ EAU ◆ 50-51 H 1
Fort Providence o CDN ◆ 14-15 N 4
Fort Resolution o CDN ◆ 14-15 O 4
Fortress of Louisbourg National History Park ∴• CDN ◇ 18-19 O 6
Fort Rucker xx USA ◇ 24-25 F 4
Fort Rupert o CDN ◇ 18-19 E 3 ◆ 14-15 V 6
Fort-Rupert = Waskaganish o CDN ◇ 18-19 E 3
Fort Rupert (Waskaganish) o CDN ◇ 18-19 E 3 ◆ 14-15 V 6
Fort Saint John o CDN ◆ 14-15 M 5
Fort-Ševčenko o KZ ◆ 56-57 G 2
Fort Severn o CDN ◆ 14-15 T 5
Fort Sheridan • USA ◇ 22-23 E 4
Fort Simpson o CDN ◆ 14-15 M 4
Fort Smith o CDN ◆ 14-15 O 4
Fort Smith o USA ◇ 26-27 K 2 ◆ 16-17 H 3
Fort Stewart xx USA ◇ 24-25 H 3
Fort Stockton o USA ◇ 26-27 F 4 ◆ 16-17 F 4
Fort Sumner o USA ◇ 26-27 E 2
Fort Supply o USA ◇ 26-27 H 1
Fort Témiscamingue National Historic Park ∴• CDN ◇ 18-19 E 5
Fort Thomas o USA ◇ 26-27 C 3
Fort Trois Riviéres ∴• CDN ◇ 18-19 H 5
Fortuna o USA ◇ 20-21 B 5
Fortuna de San Carlos o CR ◇ 28-29 B 6
Fortune o CDN ◇ 18-19 R 5
Fortune Bay ≈ ◇ 18-19 R 5
Fortune Harbour o CDN ◇ 18-19 R 4
Fort Valley o USA ◇ 24-25 G 3
Fort Walton Beach o USA ◇ 24-25 E 4 ◆ 16-17 J 4
Fort Wayne o USA ◇ 22-23 F 5 ◆ 16-17 J 2
Fort Wingate o USA ◇ 26-27 C 2
Fort Worth o USA ◇ 26-27 J 3 ◆ 16-17 G 4
Fort Yukon o USA ◆ 14-15 G 3
Foshan o• CHN ◆ 54-55 L 7
Fosheim Peninsula ⌣ CDN ◆ 14-15 U 1
Foss o USA ◇ 26-27 H 2
Fossil Butte National Monument ∴ USA ◇ 20-21 J 5
Fostoria o USA ◇ 22-23 G 5
Fougamou o G ◆ 50-51 D 2
Fougères o• F ◇ 38-39 G 7 ◆ 34-35 L 6
Foulwind, Cape ▲ NZ ◆ 60-61 P 8
Foumban o•• CAM ◆ 48-49 H 7
Four Corners o USA ◇ 20-21 F 8
Four Mountains, Islands of the ⌒ USA ◆ 14-15 B 6
Foveaux Strait ≈ ◆ 60-61 O 9
Fowlers Bay ≈ ◆ 60-61 G 6
Fowlerton o USA ◇ 26-27 H 5
Foxe Basin ≈ ◆ 14-15 V 3
Foxe Channel ≈ ◆ 14-15 U 3
Foxe Peninsula ⌣ CDN ◆ 14-15 V 4
Fox Islands ⌒ USA (AK) ◆ 14-15 C 6
Fox Islands ⌒ USA (MI) ◇ 22-23 F 3
Fox River ~ USA ◇ 22-23 D 5
Foyn, Cape ▲ ANT ◆ 13 G 30
Foz do Iguaçu o BR ◆ 32-33 M 3
Framingham o USA ◇ 22-23 N 4
Framnesfjella ⛰ ANT ◆ 13 G 7
Franca o BR ◆ 32-33 N 2
Français, Récif des ⌒ F ◆ 60-61 N 3
France ■ F ◇ 38-39 H 8 ◆ 34-35 M 6
Franceses o GCA ◇ 28-29 K 4
Franceville ☆ G ◆ 50-51 D 2
Franche-Comté ◘ F ◇ 38-39 K 8 ◆ 34-35 M 6
Francis Case, Lake ⊖ USA ◆ 16-17 G 2
Francisco Rueda o MEX ◇ 28-29 H 3
Francistown ☆ RB ◆ 50-51 G 6
François o CDN ◇ 18-19 Q 5

74 Ellice Islands — François

Grand Portage National Monument ∴ USA ◇22-23 D2
Grand Pré National Historical Park ∴ CDN ◇18-19 M6
Grand Rapids o CDN ◆14-15 R6
Grand Rapids o USA ◇22-23 F4 ◆14-15 T8
Grand Récif Sud ⌒ F ◆60-61 O4
Grand-Remous o CDN ◇18-19 G5 ◆14-15 V7
Grand River ~ CDN ◇18-19 D7
Grand River ~ USA ◇22-23 F4
Grand Ronde o USA ◇20-21 C3
Grands-Jardins, Parc de Conservation des ⊥ CDN ◇18-19 J5
Grand Teton National Park ⊥ USA ◇20-21 J4 ◆14-15 O8
Grand Teton Peak ▲ USA ◇20-21 J4 ◆14-15 O8
Grand Traverse Bay ≈ USA ◇22-23 F3
Granger, Lake o USA ◇26-27 J4
Grangeville o USA ◇20-21 F3
Granite Lake o CDN ◇18-19 Q4
Granite Peak ▲ USA (MT) ◆14-15 P7
Granite Peak ▲ USA (NV) ◇20-21 F5
Granite Peak ▲ USA (UT) ◇20-21 H5
Gran Sabana, La ⚍ YV ◆30-31 G3
Gran Sasso d'Italia ▲ I ◇46-47 D3 ◆34-35 O7
Grant Birthplace State Memorial ∴ USA ◇22-23 F6
Grant-Kohrs Ranch National Historic Site ∴ USA ◇20-21 H2
Grants o USA ◇26-27 D2 ◆16-17 E3
Grants Pass o USA ◇20-21 C4
Grantsville o USA ◇20-21 H5
Granville o F ◇38-39 G7 ◆34-35 L6
Gras, Lac de o CDN ◆14-15 O4
Grasse o F ◇38-39 L10 ◆34-35 N7
Grasset, Lac o CDN ◇18-19 E4
Grasslands National Park ⊥ CDN ◆14-15 P7
Grass Valley o USA ◇20-21 D6
Grates Cove o CDN ◇18-19 S4
Grates Point ▲ CDN ◇18-19 S4
Gratz o USA ◇22-23 F6
Gravenhurst o CDN ◇18-19 E6
Grave Peak ▲ USA ◇20-21 G2
Gravures rupestres ••• DZ ◆48-49 G3
Gray o F ◇38-39 K8 ◆34-35 M6
Gray o USA (GA) ◇24-25 G3
Gray o USA (ME) ◇22-23 N4
Gray o USA (OK) ◇26-27 G1
Grayling o USA ◇22-23 F3
Grays Harbor ≈ ◇20-21 B2
Grays Lake o USA ◇20-21 J4
Grayson o USA ◇22-23 G6
Grayville o USA ◇22-23 D6
Graz ☆•• A ◇40-41 N5 ◆34-35 P6
Great Abaco Island ⌒ BS ◆16-17 L5
Great America ∴ USA ◇22-23 E4
Great Artesian Basin ⌣ AUS ◆60-61 J4
Great Australian Bight ≈ ◆60-61 F6
Great Bahama Bank ≃ ◆16-17 L6
Great Barrier Island ⌒ NZ ◆60-61 Q7
Great Barrier Reef ⚍ AUS ◆60-61 J2
Great Barrier Reef Marine Park ⊥••• AUS ◆60-61 J2
Great Basin ⌣ USA ◇20-21 F5 ◆16-17 C3
Great Basin National Park ⊥ USA ◇20-21 G6 ◆16-17 D3
Great Bear Lake o CDN ◆14-15 M3
Great Britain ⌒ GB ◇38-39 G3 ◆34-35 L4
Great Coco Island ⌒ MYA ◆58-59 B4
Great Dismal Swamp National Wildlife Refuge ⊥ USA ◇22-23 K7
Great Divide Basin ⌣ USA ◆16-17 E2
Great Dividing Range ▲ AUS ◆60-61 K7
Great Duck Islands ⌒ CDN ◇18-19 C6
Great Eastern Erg ⚍ DZ ◆48-49 F3
Greater Antilles ⌒ ◆16-17 L6
Greater Hinggan Range ▲ CHN ◆54-55 M3
Greater Sunda Islands ⌒ RI ◆58-59 D6
Great Exhibition Bay ≈ ◆60-61 P6
Great Falls o USA (MT) ◇20-21 J2 ◆14-15 O7
Great Falls ∴ USA (MT) ◇20-21 J2
Great Inagua Island ⌒ BS ◆16-17 M6
Great Lake o AUS ◆60-61 K8
Great Nicobar Island ⌒ IND ◆58-59 B5
Great North East Channel ≈ ◆60-61 J2
Great Plains ⚍ ◆14-15 N5
Great Rattling Brook ~ CDN ◇18-19 R4
Great Ruaha ~ EAT ◆50-51 H3
Great Sacandaga Lake o USA ◇22-23 L4
Great Salt Lake o USA ◇20-21 H5 ◆16-17 D2
Great Salt Lake Desert ⚍ USA ◇20-21 H5 ◆16-17 D2
Great Salt Plains Reservoir < USA ◇26-27 H1
Great Sand Sea ⚍ ET ◆48-49 L3
Great Sandy Desert ⚍ AUS ◆60-61 E3
Great Sandy Desert ⚍ USA ◇20-21 D4 ◆14-15 M8
Great Sea Reef ⌒ FJI ◆60-61 Q3
Great Slave Lake o CDN ◆14-15 N4
Great Smoky Mountains ▲ USA ◇24-25 G2
Great Smoky Mountains National Park ⊥••• USA ◇24-25 G2
Great Valley ⌣ USA ◇22-23 K6
Great Victoria Desert ⚍ AUS ◆60-61 F5
Great Wall ••• CHN ◆54-55 M3
Great Western Erg ⚍ DZ ◆48-49 E2
Great Zimbabwe National Monument ∴••• ZW ◆50-51 H6
Gréboun, Mont ▲ RN ◆48-49 G4
Greece ■ GR ◇46-47 H5 ◆34-35 Q8
Greeley o USA ◆16-17 F2
Greem Bell, ostrov ⌒ RUS ◆52-53 J1
Green Bank ≃ ◇18-19 R6
Green Bay ≈ ◇18-19 R4
Green Bay o USA (WI) ◇22-23 D3 ◆14-15 T8
Green Bay o USA (WI) ◇22-23 E3 ◆14-15 T8
Greencastle o USA (IN) ◇22-23 E6
Greencastle o USA (PA) ◇22-23 K6
Greeneville o USA ◇24-25 G1
Greenfield o USA (IL) ◇22-23 C6
Greenfield o USA (IN) ◇22-23 F6
Greenfield o USA (MA) ◇22-23 M4
Greenfield o USA (MO) ◇26-27 L1
Greenfield o USA (TN) ◇24-25 D1
Greenland □ GRØ ◆14-15 b2
Greenland o USA ◇22-23 D2
Greenland-Iceland Rise ≃ ◆34-35 F2
Green Mountain ▲ USA ◇22-23 M4
Greenport o USA ◇22-23 M5
Green River o USA ◇20-21 J6
Green River o USA (WY) ◆16-17 E2
Green River ~ USA ◆16-17 D2
Green River Basin ⌣ USA ◇20-21 J4 ◆16-17 D2
Greensboro o USA (GA) ◇24-25 G3
Greensboro o USA (NC) ◇24-25 J1 ◆16-17 L3
Greensburg o USA (IN) ◇22-23 F6
Greensburg o USA (KS) ◇26-27 H1
Greensburg o USA (PA) ◇22-23 J5
Green Swamp ⌣ USA ◇24-25 J2
Greenup o USA ◇22-23 D6
Greenvale o AUS ◆60-61 J3
Greenville ☆ LB ◆48-49 D7
Greenville o USA (AL) ◇24-25 E4
Greenville o USA (CA) ◇20-21 D5
Greenville o USA (FL) ◇24-25 G4
Greenville o USA (IL) ◇22-23 D6
Greenville o USA (ME) ◇22-23 O3
Greenville o USA (MS) ◇26-27 M3
Greenville o USA (OH) ◇22-23 F5
Greenville o USA (PA) ◇22-23 H5
Greenville o USA (SC) ◇24-25 G2 ◆16-17 K4
Greenville o USA (TN) ◇24-25 K2 ◆16-17 L3
Greenville o USA (TX) ◇26-27 J3
Greenwich o USA ◇22-23 G5
Greenwood o USA (IN) ◇22-23 E6
Greenwood o USA (MS) ◇26-27 M3 ◆16-17 H4
Greenwood o USA (SC) ◇24-25 G2
Greenwood, Lake o USA ◇24-25 G2
Greer o USA ◇24-25 G2
Greers Ferry Lake o USA ◇26-27 L2
Greeson, Lake o USA ◇26-27 L2
Gregorio Méndez o MEX ◇28-29 J3
Grenada o USA ◇24-25 D3
Grenada ■ WG ◆16-17 O8
Grenada ⌒ WG ◆16-17 O8
Grenada Lake o USA ◇24-25 D3
Grenadines, The ⌒ WV ◆16-17 O8
Grenoble ☆ F ◇38-39 K9 ◆34-35 N6
Grenville o USA ◇26-27 F1
Grenville, Cape ▲ AUS ◆60-61 J2
Grey Islands ⌒ CDN ◇18-19 R3 ◆14-15 Z6
Greylock, Mount ▲ USA ◇22-23 M4
Greymouth o NZ ◆60-61 P8
Grey Range ▲ AUS ◆60-61 J5
Grey River o CDN ◇18-19 Q5
Grey River ~ CDN ◇18-19 Q5
Greytown o ZA ◆50-51 H7
Gridley o USA ◇20-21 D6
Griekwastad = Griquatown o ZA ◆50-51 F7
Griffin o USA ◇24-25 F3
Griffith o AUS ◆60-61 K6
Griffiths Point ▲ CDN ◆14-15 M1
Grijalva, Río ~ MEX ◇28-29 H2
Grimmington Bay ≈ ◇18-19 E2
Grimsby o CDN ◇18-19 E7
Grimsey ⌒ IS ◇36-37 e1 ◆34-35 H2
Grinnel Peninsula ⌣ CDN ◆14-15 S1
Griquet o CDN ◇18-19 R3
Grise Fiord o CDN ◆14-15 U1
Groais Island ⌒ CDN ◇18-19 R3
Groix, Île de ⌒ F ◇38-39 F8 ◆34-35 L6
Groningen ☆• NL ◇40-41 J2 ◆34-35 N5
Groote Eylandt ⌒ AUS ◆60-61 H2
Grootfontein ☆ NAM ◆50-51 E5
Groot Karasberge ▲ NAM ◆50-51 E7
Groot Karoo = Great Karoo ⚍ ZA ◆50-51 F8
Groot Waterberg ▲ NAM ◆50-51 E6
Gros Mécatina, Cap du ▲ CDN ◇18-19 P3
Gros Mécatina, Île du ⌒ CDN ◇18-19 P3
Gros Morne ▲ CDN ◇18-19 Q4
Gros Morne National Park ⊥••• CDN ◇18-19 Q4 ◆14-15 Z7
Grosseto ☆ I ◇46-47 C3 ◆34-35 O7
Großglockner ▲•• A ◇40-41 M5 ◆34-35 O6
Groswater Bay ≈ ◆14-15 Z6
Grottes • RCA ◆48-49 J7
Groundhog River ~ CDN ◆14-15 U7
Grouse Creek o USA ◇20-21 H5
Grove City o USA ◇22-23 G6
Grove Hill o USA ◇24-25 E4
Groveland o USA ◇20-21 D7
Grover o USA ◇20-21 J4
Groznyj ☆ RUS ◆34-35 V7
Grullo, El o MEX ◇28-29 B2
Grünau o NAM ◆50-51 E7
Grundy o USA ◇22-23 G7
Grutas de Juxtlahuaca, Parque Natural ⊥ MEX ◇28-29 E3
Gruver o USA ◇26-27 G1
Guabito o PA ◇28-29 C7
Guabo, El o PA ◇28-29 D7
Guadalajara ☆•• MEX ◇28-29 C1 ◆16-17 F6
Guadalquivir, Río ~ E ◇44-45 E6 ◆34-35 K8
Guadalupe o USA ◇20-21 D8
Guadalupe, Isla de ⌒ MEX ◆16-17 C5
Guadalupe Mountains National Park ⊥ USA ◇26-27 E4 ◆16-17 F4
Guadalupe Peak ▲ USA ◇26-27 E4 ◆16-17 F4
Guadalupe River ~ USA ◇26-27 H4
Guadeloupe □ F ◆16-17 O7
Guadiana, Río ~ E ◇44-45 E5 ◆34-35 K8
Guafo, Isla ⌒ RCH ◆32-33 H6
Guainía, Río ~ CO ◆30-31 F4
Guajará-Mirim o BR ◆30-31 F7
Guajira, Península de la ⌣ CO ◆30-31 E2
Gualán o GCA ◇28-29 K4
Gualaquiza o EC ◆30-31 D5
Gualeguaychú o RA ◆32-33 L4
Guam ⌒ USA ◆58-59 M4
Guamblin, Isla ⌒ RCH ◆32-33 G6
Guanabo o C ◆16-17 K6
Guanacaste, Cordillera de ▲ CR ◇28-29 B6
Guanajuato □ MEX ◇28-29 D1
Guanajuato ☆•• MEX (GTO) ◇28-29 D1 ◆16-17 F6
Guanare ☆ YV ◆30-31 F3
Guangdong □ CHN ◆54-55 L7
Guangxi Zhuangzu Zizhiqu □ CHN ◆54-55 K7
Guangyuan o CHN ◆54-55 K5
Guangzhou ☆•• CHN ◆54-55 L7
Guantánamo ☆ C ◆16-17 L6
Guápiles o CR ◇28-29 C6
Guaporé, Reserva Biológica do ⊥ BR ◆30-31 G7
Guaqui o BOL ◆30-31 F8
Guarai o BR ◆30-31 K6
Guarajambala, Río ~ HN ◇28-29 K4
Guarapuava o BR ◆32-33 M3
Guaratinguetá o BR ◆32-33 N2
Guarda ☆• P ◇44-45 D4 ◆34-35 K7
Guarenas o YV ◆30-31 F2
Guaria o CR ◇28-29 C7
Guasave o MEX ◆16-17 E5
Guatemala ■ GCA ◇28-29 J4 ◆16-17 H7
Guatemala = Ciudad de Guatemala ★ GCA ◇28-29 J4
Guatemala = Ciudad de Guatemala ★ GCA ◇28-29 J4 ◆16-17 H8
Guatemala Basin ≃ ◆16-17 H9
Guayape, Río ~ HN ◇28-29 L4
Guayaquil ☆• EC ◆30-31 D5
Guayaquil, Golfo de ≈ ◆30-31 C5
Guaymallén o RA ◆32-33 J4
Guaymas o• MEX ◆16-17 D5
Ğubail, al- o KSA ◆56-57 F5
Guban ⚍ ETH ◆48-49 O6
Guder o ETH ◆48-49 N7
Gudiyattam o IND ◆56-57 M8
Guéckedou o WAL ◆48-49 C7
Guédi, Mont ▲ TCH ◆48-49 J6
Guelph o CDN ◇18-19 D7
Guéra, Pic de ▲ TCH ◆48-49 J6
Guérande o F ◇38-39 F8 ◆34-35 L6
Guéréda o TCH ◆48-49 K6
Guéret ☆ F ◇38-39 H8 ◆34-35 M6
Guernsey ⌒ GBG ◇38-39 F7 ◆34-35 L6
Guerrero □ MEX ◇28-29 D3
Guerrero, Cayos ⌒ NIC ◇28-29 C5
Guerrero, Parque Natural del Estado de ⊥ MEX ◇28-29 E3
Guerrero Negro o• MEX ◆16-17 D5
Guge ▲ ETH ◆48-49 N7
Guguan ⌒ USA ◆58-59 N3
Guiana Basin ≃ ◆30-31 H1
Guiana Highlands ▲ ◆30-31 G3
Guiana Plateau ≃ ◆30-31 J3
Guider o CAM ◆48-49 H7
Guier, Lac de o SN ◆48-49 B5
Guigang o CHN ◆54-55 K7
Guiglo o CI ◆48-49 D7
Guilford Courthouse National Military Park ∴ USA ◇24-25 J1
Guilin o• CHN ◆54-55 L6
Guillestre o F ◇38-39 L9 ◆34-35 N6
Guimarães o BR ◆30-31 L5
Guinea ■ RG ◆48-49 C6
Guinea, Gulf of ≈ ◆48-49 E8
Guinea Basin ≃ ◆9 C5
Guinea-Bissau ■ GNB ◆48-49 B6
Güines o C ◆16-17 K6
Guingamp o F ◇38-39 F7 ◆34-35 L6
Guiones, Punta ▲ CR ◇28-29 B7
Guir, Hamada du ⚍ DZ ◆48-49 E2
Guir, Oued ~ MA ◆48-49 E2
Guiratinga o BR ◆30-31 J8
Güiria o YV ◆30-31 G2
Guiyang ☆ CHN ◆54-55 K6
Guizhou □ CHN ◆54-55 K6
Gujarat □ IND ◆56-57 L6
Gujrānwāla o PK ◆56-57 L4
Gujrāt o PK ◆56-57 L4
Gulbarga o• IND ◆56-57 M7
Gulbin Ka, River ~ WAN ◆48-49 G6
Gulf Islands National Seashore ⊥ USA ◇24-25 D4
Gulfport o USA (FL) ◇24-25 G6
Gulfport o USA (MS) ◇24-25 D4 ◆16-17 J4
Gulf Shores o USA ◇24-25 E4
Guliston ☆ UZ ◆56-57 K2
Gully, The ≃ ◇18-19 P6
Gulmit o PK ◆56-57 L3
Gulu ☆ EAU ◆48-49 M8
Gulwe o EAT ◆50-51 J3
Gumbiro o EAT ◆50-51 J4
Gumel o WAN ◆48-49 G6
Gummi o WAN ◆48-49 G6
Guna o IND ◆56-57 M6
Güneydoğu Toroslar ▲ TR ◆34-35 T8
Gungu o ZRE ◆50-51 E3
Gunnedah o AUS ◆60-61 L6
Gunnison o USA ◇20-21 J6
Guntersville o USA ◇24-25 E2
Guntersville Lake < USA ◇24-25 E2
Guntur o IND ◆56-57 N7
Gununa o AUS ◆60-61 H3
Gunungsitoli o RI ◆58-59 C6
Ğurdaqa, al- ☆• ET ◆48-49 M3
Gurdon o USA ◇26-27 L3
Gurgaon o IND ◆56-57 M5
Gurgei, Ğabal ▲ SUD ◆48-49 K6
Gurguéia, Rio ~ BR ◆30-31 L6
Guri, Embalse de < YV ◆30-31 G3
Gurig National Park ⊥ AUS ◆60-61 G2
Gurupa o BR ◆30-31 J5
Gurupi o BR ◆30-31 K7
Gurupi, Cabo ▲ BR ◆30-31 K5
Gurupi, Serra do ▲ BR ◆30-31 K5
Gurupizinho o BR ◆30-31 K5
Guruve o ZW ◆50-51 H5
Gusau o WAN ◆48-49 G6
Gustavo A. Madero o MEX ◇28-29 E2
Gutenko Mountains ▲ ANT ◆13 F30
Guthrie o USA (AZ) ◇26-27 C3
Guthrie o USA (OK) ◇26-27 J2
Guthrie o USA (TX) ◇26-27 G3
Gutiérrez Zamora o MEX ◇28-29 F1
Guttenberg o USA ◇22-23 C4
Guwahati ☆ IND ◆56-57 P5
Guyana ■ GUY ◆30-31 H3
Guyandot River ~ USA ◇22-23 G6
Guyenne ⚍ F ◇38-39 G9 ◆34-35 L6
Guymon o USA ◇26-27 G1
Guyuan o CHN ◆54-55 K4
Guzman, Ciudad o• MEX ◇28-29 C2 ◆16-17 F7
Gwaai o ZW ◆50-51 G5
Gwabegar o AUS ◆60-61 K6
Gwādar o PK ◆56-57 J5
Gwalior o• IND ◆56-57 M5
Gwanda ☆ ZW ◆50-51 G6
Gwardafuy, Cap = Raas Caseyr ▲ SP ◆48-49 Q6
Gweru ☆ ZW ◆50-51 G5
Gyandzha = Ganca o• AZ ◆56-57 F2
Gyangzê o CHN ◆54-55 F6
Gyda o RUS ◆52-53 M3
Gydanskaja guba ≈ ◆52-53 M3
Gydanskij poluostrov ⌣ RUS ◆52-53 L3
Gydanskiy Poluostrov = Gydanskij poluostrov ⌣ RUS ◆52-53 L3
Gympie o AUS ◆60-61 L5
Győr o H ◇40-41 O5 ◆34-35 P6
Gyrgyčan o RUS ◆52-53 f4

H

Haast o NZ ◆60-61 O8
Haasts Bluff Aboriginal Land X AUS ◆60-61 F4
Habarovsk o RUS ◆52-53 Y8
Hachinohe o J ◆54-55 R3
Hackberry o USA ◇20-21 H8
Hadbaram o OM ◆56-57 H7
Hadbat al-Ğilf al-Kabir ▲ ET ◆48-49 L4
Hadd, Ra's al- ▲ OM ◆56-57 H6
Hadejia o WAN ◆48-49 H6
Hadibū o Y ◆56-57 G8
Hadley Bay ≈ ◆14-15 P2
Hadramaut ⚍ Y ◆56-57 F8
Hadramaut, Wādī ~ Y ◆56-57 F7
Hafar al-Bātin o KSA ◆56-57 F5
Hağar, al- ▲ OM ◆56-57 H6
Hağara, al- ⚍ IRQ ◆56-57 E4
Hağara, al- ▲ KSA ◆56-57 E5
Hagemeister Island ⌒ USA ◆14-15 D5
Hagen, Mount ▲ PNG ◆58-59 N8
Hagerman o USA (ID) ◇20-21 G4
Hagerman o USA (NM) ◇26-27 E3
Hağğa o• Y ◆56-57 E7
Hağğiābād o IR ◆56-57 H5
Ha Giang ☆ VN ◆58-59 D2
Hague, Cap de la ▲ F ◇38-39 G7 ◆34-35 L6
Haguenau o• F ◇38-39 L7 ◆34-35 N6
Haibar o KSA ◆56-57 D5
Haicheng o CHN ◆54-55 N3
Haida o• CDN ◆14-15 K6
Haifa = Hefa ☆• IL ◆56-57 C4
Haikou ☆• CHN ◆54-55 L7
Hā'il ☆• KSA ◆56-57 E5
Hailar o CHN ◆54-55 M2
Hailey o USA ◇20-21 G4
Haima, Ra's al- o UAE ◆56-57 H5
Hainan Dao ⌒ CHN ◆54-55 L8
Hainan Strait = Qiongzhou Haixia ≈ ◆54-55 K7
Haines o USA (AK) ◆14-15 J5
Haines o USA (OR) ◇20-21 F3
Haines Junction o CDN ◆14-15 J4
Haiti ■ RH ◆16-17 M7
Haizhou Wan ≈ ◆54-55 M5
Hajyr o RUS ◆52-53 X3
Hakalau o USA ◇24-25 E8
Hakkari ☆ TR ◆56-57 E3
Hakodate o J ◆54-55 R3
Halab ☆•• SYR ◆56-57 D3
Halā'ib o ET ◆48-49 N4
Halcon, Mount ▲ RP ◆58-59 H4
Hale, Mount ▲ AUS ◆60-61 D5
Haleakala Crater ▲ USA ◇24-25 D7
Haleakala National Park ⊥• USA ◇24-25 D7
Haleiwa o USA ◇24-25 C7
Hale River ~ AUS ◆60-61 H4
Haleyville o USA ◇24-25 E2
Hal Flood Range ▲ ANT ◆13 F23
Halfmoon Bay o NZ ◆60-61 O9
Haliburton Highlands ▲ CDN ◇18-19 E6
Halifax ☆ CDN ◇18-19 N6 ◆14-15 Y8
Halifax Bay ≈ ◆60-61 K3
Halkida o GR ◇46-47 J5 ◆34-35 Q8
Halkidiki ⚍ GR ◇46-47 J4 ◆34-35 Q8
Hallandale o USA ◇24-25 H7
Hallāniyāt, al- ⌒ Y ◆56-57 H7
Hall Beach o CDN ◆14-15 U3
Halle (Saale) o• D ◇40-41 L3 ◆34-35 O5
Hallettsville o USA ◇26-27 J5
Halley Bay o ANT ◆13 F34
Hall Indian Reservation, Fort X USA ◇20-21 H4
Hall Island ⌒ USA ◆14-15 B4
Hall Islands ⌒ FSM ◆58-59 O5
Hall Peninsula ⌣ CDN ◆14-15 X4
Halls Creek o• AUS ◆60-61 F3
Halmahera, Pulau ⌒ RI ◆58-59 J6
Halmahera Sea ≈ ◆58-59 J6
Halmstad o S ◇36-37 F8 ◆34-35 O4
Haltom City o USA ◇26-27 J3
Hamada o J ◆54-55 P5
Hamadah al Hamrā', Al ⚍ LAR ◆48-49 H2
Hamadān o• IR ◆56-57 F4
Hamāh ☆•• SYR ◆56-57 D3
Hamamatsu o J ◆54-55 Q5
Hamāta, Ğabal ▲ ET ◆48-49 M4
Hambantota o CL ◆56-57 N9
Hamburg ☆•• D ◇40-41 L2 ◆34-35 O5
Hamburg o USA (AR) ◇26-27 M3
Hamburg o USA (NY) ◇22-23 J4
Hamelin Pool ≈ ◆60-61 C5
Hamersley Range ▲ AUS ◆60-61 D4
Hamersley Range National Park ⊥••• AUS ◆60-61 D4
Hamhung o KOR ◆54-55 O4
Hami o CHN ◆54-55 G3
Hamilton o AUS ◆60-61 J7
Hamilton o CDN ◇18-19 E7 ◆14-15 V8
Hamilton o NZ ◆60-61 Q7
Hamilton o USA (AL) ◇24-25 E2
Hamilton o USA (MT) ◇20-21 G2
Hamilton o USA (OH) ◇22-23 F6
Hamilton o USA (TX) ◇26-27 H4
Hamilton o USA (WA) ◇20-21 D1
Hamilton Bank ≃ ◆14-15 Z6
Hamilton Hotel o AUS ◆60-61 J4
Hamilton Sound ≈ ◇18-19 R4
Hamirpur o IND ◆56-57 N5
Hamis Mušait o KSA ◆56-57 E7
Hamlin o USA ◇26-27 G3
Hammamet o TN ◆48-49 H1
Hammamet, Golfe de ≈ ◆48-49 H1
Hammerfest o• N ◇36-37 L1 ◆34-35 Q1
Hammon o USA ◇26-27 H2
Hammond o USA (IN) ◇22-23 E5
Hammond o USA (LA) ◇26-27 M4
Hammonton o USA ◇22-23 L6
Hamoyet, Ğabal ▲ SUD ◆48-49 N5
Hampden o CDN ◇18-19 Q4
Hampton o CDN ◇18-19 M6
Hampton o USA (AR) ◇26-27 L3
Hampton o USA (NH) ◇22-23 N4
Hampton o USA (SC) ◇24-25 H3
Hampton o USA (VA) ◇22-23 K7 ◆16-17 L3
Hampton Butte ▲ USA ◇20-21 D4
Hamrat al-Wuzz o SUD ◆48-49 M5
Hamrat as-Shaykh o SUD ◆48-49 L6
Hams Fork ~ USA ◇20-21 J5
Hāmūn-e Ğaz Mūriān o IR ◆56-57 H5
Hana o USA ◇24-25 D7
Hanalei o USA ◇24-25 C6
Hanapepe o USA ◇24-25 C7
Hancheng o CHN ◆54-55 L4
Hancock o USA (MD) ◇22-23 J6
Hancock o USA (NY) ◇22-23 L5
Hancock Summit ▲ USA ◇20-21 G7
Handan o CHN ◆54-55 L4
Handeni o EAT ◆50-51 J3
Handyga ☆ RUS ◆52-53 Y5
Hanford o USA ◇20-21 E7
Hanford Site xx USA ◇20-21 E2
Hangajn Nuruu ▲ MAU ◆54-55 H2
Hangzhou ☆•• CHN ◆54-55 N5
Haniá o GR ◇46-47 K7 ◆34-35 Q8
Hanīš al-Kabīr ⌒ Y ◆56-57 E8
Hank, El ⚍ DZ ◆48-49 D4
Hanka, ozero o RUS ◆52-53 X8
Hanksville o USA ◇20-21 J6
Hann, Mount ▲ AUS ◆60-61 F3
Hanna o CDN ◆14-15 O6
Hannah Bay ≈ ◇18-19 E3
Hannibal o USA ◇22-23 C6 ◆16-17 H3
Hannover ☆• D ◇40-41 K2 ◆34-35 N5
Hà Nội ★• VN ◆58-59 E2
Hanoi = Hà Nội ★• VN ◆58-59 E2
Hanover o CDN ◇18-19 D6
Hanover = Hannover ☆• D ◇40-41 K2 ◆34-35 N5
Hanover, Isla ⌒ RCH ◆32-33 H8
Hansenfjella ▲ ANT ◆13 G6
Han Shui ~ CHN ◆54-55 L5
Hanty-Mansijsk ☆ RUS ◆52-53 K5
Hanzhong o CHN ◆54-55 K5
Happy o USA ◇26-27 G2
Happy Camp o USA ◇20-21 C5
Happy Jack o USA ◇20-21 J8
Happy-Valley-Goose Bay o CDN ◇18-19 O2
Hapur o IND ◆56-57 M5
Harabali ☆ RUS ◆34-35 V6
Harad o KSA ◆56-57 F6
Harağa o KSA ◆56-57 E7
Harare ★•• ZW ◆50-51 H5
Haraze Mangueigne o TCH ◆48-49 K7
Harbin ☆ CHN ◆54-55 O2
Harbor Beach o USA ◇22-23 G4
Harbour Breton o CDN ◇18-19 R5
Harbour Deep o CDN ◇18-19 Q3
Harcourt o CDN ◇18-19 M5
Hardangerfjorden ≈ ◇36-37 C6 ◆34-35 N3
Hardangervidda nasjonalpark ⊥ N ◇36-37 C6 ◆34-35 N3
Hardeeville o USA ◇24-25 H3
Hardin o USA ◇22-23 C6
Harding o ZA ◆50-51 G8
Hardinsburg o USA ◇22-23 E7
Hardwick o USA (GA) ◇24-25 G3
Hardwick o USA (VT) ◇22-23 M3
Hardy o USA ◇26-27 M1
Hare Bay ≈ ◇18-19 Q3
Hārer ☆ ETH ◆48-49 O7
Hārer Wildlife Sanctuary ⊥ ETH ◆48-49 O7
Harewa o ETH ◆48-49 O7
Harğ, al- o KSA ◆56-57 F6
Hargeysa ☆ SP ◆48-49 O7
Hari ~ RI ◆58-59 D7
Hāriğa, al- ☆• ET ◆48-49 M3
Hāriğa, al-Wāḥāt al- ⚍• ET ◆48-49 M4
Harihari o NZ ◆60-61 P8
Harlan o USA ◇22-23 G7
Harlingen o USA ◇26-27 J6 ◆16-17 G5
Harmony o USA ◇22-23 O3
Harney Basin ⌣ USA ◇20-21 E4 ◆14-15 N8
Harney Lake o USA ◇20-21 E4
Harobo o J ◆54-55 R3
Harold Byrd Range ▲ ANT ◆13 E0
Harper ☆ LB ◆48-49 D8
Harper o USA (KS) ◇26-27 H1
Harper o USA (OR) ◇20-21 F4
Harpers Ferry National Historic Park ∴ USA ◇22-23 K6
Harrat Haibar ⚍ KSA ◆56-57 D5
Harricana, Rivière ~ CDN ◇18-19 E3 ◆14-15 V6
Harriman o USA ◇24-25 F2
Harrington o USA (DE) ◇22-23 L6
Harrington o USA (WA) ◇20-21 E2
Harrington Harbour o CDN ◇18-19 P3
Harrisburg o USA (IL) ◇22-23 D7
Harrisburg o USA (OR) ◇20-21 C3
Harrisburg ☆ USA (PA) ◇22-23 K5 ◆16-17 L2
Harrison o USA (AR) ◇26-27 L1
Harrison o USA (MI) ◇22-23 F3
Harrison o USA (OH) ◇22-23 F6
Harrison, Cape ▲ CDN ◆14-15 Z6
Harrisonburg o USA ◇22-23 J6
Harrisville o USA (MI) ◇22-23 G3
Harrisville o USA (WV) ◇22-23 H6
Harrodsburg o USA ◇22-23 F7
Hart o USA ◇26-27 F2
Hartford o USA (AL) ◇24-25 F4
Hartford o USA (KY) ◇22-23 E7
Hartford ☆ USA (CT) ◇22-23 M5 ◆16-17 M2
Hartford City o USA ◇22-23 F5
Hartland o USA ◇22-23 H6
Hart Mountain ▲ USA ◇20-21 E4
Hart Mountain National Antelope Refuge • USA ◇20-21 E4
Hartselle o USA ◇24-25 E2
Hartsville o USA ◇24-25 H2
Hartūm, al- ☆•• SUD ◆48-49 M5
Hartūm Bahrī, al- o SUD ◆48-49 M5
Hartwell o USA ◇24-25 G2
Hartwell Lake < USA ◇24-25 G2
Haruj al Aswad, Al ▲ LAR ◆48-49 J3
Har Us nuur o MAU ◆54-55 G2
Harvard o USA ◇22-23 D4
Harvey Junction o CDN ◇18-19 H5
Harwood o USA ◇26-27 J5
Haryana □ IND ◆56-57 M5
Haš o IR ◆56-57 J5
Hasā', al- ⚍ KSA ◆56-57 F5
Hasaka, al- ☆ SYR ◆56-57 E3
Hasavjurt o RUS ◆34-35 V7
Haskell o USA ◇26-27 H3
Haskovo o BG ◆34-35 R7
Hassan o IND ◆56-57 M8
Hassayampa River ~ USA ◇20-21 H9
Hassi Messaoud o DZ ◆48-49 G2
Hastings o NZ ◆60-61 Q7
Hastings o USA (MI) ◇22-23 F4
Hastings o USA (NE) ◆16-17 G2
Hastings, Port o CDN ◇18-19 O6
Hatanga o RUS ◆52-53 R3
Hatanga ~ RUS ◆52-53 R3
Hatangskij zaliv ≈ ◆52-53 S3
Hatay (Antakya) ☆ TR ◆34-35 T8
Hatch o USA (NM) ◇26-27 D3
Hatch o USA (UT) ◇20-21 H7
Hatchie River ~ USA ◇24-25 D2
Hatgal o MAU ◆54-55 J1
Hathras o IND ◆56-57 M5
Hà Tiên o• VN ◆58-59 D4
Hà Tĩnh ☆ VN ◆58-59 E3
Hatteras o USA ◇24-25 L2
Hatteras, Cape ▲ USA ◇24-25 L2 ◆16-17 L3
Hatteras Abyssal Plain ≃ ◆16-17 M4
Hatteras Island ⌒ USA ◇24-25 L2 ◆16-17 L3
Hattiesburg o USA ◇24-25 D4 ◆16-17 J4
Hattieville o BH ◇28-29 K3
Hat Yai o• THA ◆58-59 D5
Hatyngnah o RUS ◆52-53 b4
Haud ⚍ ETH ◆48-49 O7
Hauraha o SOL ◆60-61 N2
Hauraki Gulf ≈ ◆60-61 Q7
Haur al-Hammār o IRQ ◆56-57 F4
Hauser Lake o USA ◇20-21 J2
Haut, Isle au ⌒ USA ◇22-23 O3
Haute-Normandie □ F ◇38-39 H7 ◆34-35 M6
Hauterive o CDN ◇18-19 K4
Havana o USA ◇22-23 C5
Havana = La Habana ★•• C ◆16-17 K6
Havasu Lake o USA ◇20-21 G8
Havasupai Indian Reservation X USA ◇20-21 H7
Havelock o CDN ◇18-19 H6
Havelock o USA ◇24-25 K2
Haverhill o USA ◇22-23 N4
Havre o USA ◆14-15 P7
Havre, Le o F ◇38-39 H7 ◆34-35 M6
Havre-Aubert o CDN ◇18-19 O5
Havre-Saint-Pierre o CDN ◇18-19 N3
Hawaii □ USA ◇24-25 C7 ◆16-17 b6
Hawaii ⌒ USA (HI) ◇24-25 E8 ◆16-17 b7
Hawaiian Islands ⌒ USA ◇24-25 B6 ◆16-17 b6
Hawaiian Ridge ≃ ◇24-25 B6
Hawaii Volcanoes National Park ⊥••• USA ◇24-25 E8 ◆16-17 b7
Hawātah, al- o SUD ◆48-49 M6
Hawera o NZ ◆60-61 P7
Hawesville o USA ◇22-23 E7
Hawi o USA ◇24-25 E7
Hawke, Cape ▲ AUS ◆60-61 L6
Hawke Bay ≈ ◆60-61 Q7
Hawke Island ⌒ CDN ◇18-19 R2
Hawke River ~ CDN ◇18-19 Q2
Hawkes, Mount ▲ ANT ◆13 E0
Hawke's Bay o CDN ◇18-19 Q3
Hawkesbury o CDN ◇18-19 G6
Hawkins o USA ◇22-23 C3
Hawkinsville o USA ◇24-25 G3
Haw River ~ USA ◇24-25 J2
Hawthorne o USA (FL) ◇24-25 G5
Hawthorne o USA (NV) ◇20-21 E6
Hay o AUS ◆60-61 J6
Haya o SUD ◆48-49 N5
Hayes, Mount ▲ USA ◆14-15 G4
Hayes Halvø ⌣ GRØ ◆14-15 X1
Hayes River ~ CDN ◆14-15 S3
Hay River o CDN (NWT) ◆14-15 N4
Hay River ~ CDN ◆14-15 N5
Hays o USA ◆16-17 G3
Haystack Peak ▲ USA ◇20-21 H6
Haysville o USA ◇26-27 J1
Hayward o USA (CA) ◇20-21 C7
Hayward o USA (WI) ◇22-23 C2
Hazard o USA ◇22-23 G7
Hazāribāg o• IND ◆56-57 O6
Hazel Green o USA ◇22-23 C4
Hazen Strait ≈ ◆14-15 O1
Hazlehurst o USA (GA) ◇24-25 G4
Hazlehurst o USA (MS) ◇26-27 M4
Hazleton o USA ◇22-23 L5
Hazlett, Lake o AUS ◆60-61 F4
Head of Bight ≈ ◆60-61 G6
Headquarters o USA ◇20-21 G2
Head Smashed-in Bison Jump ••• CDN ◆14-15 O7
Heafford Junction o USA ◇22-23 D3
Hearne o USA ◇26-27 J4
Hearst o CDN ◆14-15 U7
Hearst Island ⌒ ANT ◆13 G30
Heart's Content o CDN ◇18-19 S5
Hebbronville o USA ◇26-27 H6
Hebei □ CHN ◆54-55 L4
Hebel o AUS ◆60-61 K5
Heber o USA ◇26-27 B2
Heber City o USA ◇20-21 J5
Heber Springs o USA ◇26-27 M2
Hébertville o CDN ◇18-19 J4
Hebgen Lake o USA ◇20-21 J3
Hebi o CHN ◆54-55 L4
Hebo o USA ◇20-21 C3
Hebrides or Western Isles ⌒ GB ◇38-39 D3 ◆34-35 K4
Hebron o CDN ◆14-15 Y5
Hebron, Mount o USA ◇20-21 C5
Hecate Strait ≈ ◆14-15 K6
Hecelchakán o• MEX ◇28-29 J1
Hechi o CHN ◆54-55 K7
Hecla and Griper Bay ≈ ◆14-15 O1
Hedaru o EAT ◆50-51 J2
Hefa ☆• IL ◆56-57 C4
Hefei ☆ CHN ◆54-55 M5
Hegang o CHN ◆54-55 P2
Heidelberg o USA ◇24-25 D4
Heihe o CHN ◆54-55 O1
Heilbron o ZA ◆50-51 G7
Heilbronn o D ◇40-41 K4 ◆34-35 N6
Heilongjiang □ CHN ◆54-55 N2
Heilong Jiang ~ CHN ◆54-55 O2
Hejaz = Hiğāz, al- ▲ KSA ◆56-57 D5
Hekla ▲ IS ◇36-37 d2 ◆34-35 H3
Helena o USA (AR) ◇26-27 M2
Helena ☆ USA (MT) ◇20-21 H2 ◆14-15 O7
Helena Island ⌒ USA ◇24-25 H3
Helgoland ⌒ D ◇40-41 J1 ◆34-35 N5
Hells Canyon • USA ◇20-21 F3
Helmand, Rūd-e ~ AFG ◆56-57 J4
Helmeringhausen o NAM ◆50-51 E7
Helong o CHN ◆54-55 O3
Helper o USA ◇20-21 J6
Helsingborg o• S ◇36-37 F8 ◆34-35 O4
Helsinki ★•• FIN ◆34-35 Q3
Hemet o USA ◇20-21 F9
Hemlock Grove o USA ◇22-23 L5
Hempstead o USA (NY) ◇22-23 M5
Hempstead o USA (TX) ◇26-27 J4
Henan □ CHN ◆54-55 L5
Henderson o USA (KY) ◇22-23 E7
Henderson o USA (NC) ◇24-25 J1
Henderson o USA (NV) ◇20-21 G7
Henderson o USA (NY) ◇22-23 K4
Henderson o USA (TN) ◇24-25 D2
Henderson o USA (TX) ◇26-27 K3
Hendersonville o USA (NC) ◇24-25 G2
Hendersonville o USA (TN) ◇24-25 E1
Hengduan Shan ▲ CHN ◆54-55 H6
Hengyang o CHN ◆54-55 L6
Hennebont o F ◇38-39 F8 ◆34-35 L6
Hennessey o USA ◇26-27 J1
Henrietta o USA ◇26-27 H3
Henrietta Maria, Cape ▲ CDN ◆14-15 U5
Henry o USA ◇22-23 D5
Henry, Cape ▲ USA ◇24-25 L1
Henryetta o USA ◇26-27 K2
Henry Kater Peninsula ⌣ CDN ◆14-15 X3
Henry's Fork ~ USA ◇20-21 J4
Henvey Inlet Indian Reserve X CDN ◇18-19 D6
Henzada o MYA ◆58-59 C3
Heppner o USA ◇20-21 E3

76 Grand Portage National Monument — Heppner

is, Las ○ RA ♦ 32-33 J 7
t ★ AFG ♦ 56-57 J 4
ert Hoover National Historic Site •
A ◇ 22-23 C 5
ert Wash ○ USA ◇ 20-21 K 9
iers, les ● F ♦ 38-39 G 8
34-35 L 6
da ○ CR ◇ 28-29 B 6
iford ○ USA ◇ 26-27 J 2
age Range ⊾ ANT ♦ 13 F 28
in gol ≃ MAU ♦ 50-51 L 2
n ○ CHN ◇ 22-23 C 4
iniston ○ USA ◇ 20-21 E 3
itage Bay ≈ ♦ 18-19 Q 5
nit Islands ∩ PNG ♦ 58-59 N 7
nosillo ○ MEX ◇ 16-17 D 5
pica Zitácuaro ○ MEX ◇ 28-29 D 4
ero, Punta ⊾ MEX ◇ 28-29 L 2
in ○ USA ◇ 22-23 D 7
schel Island ∩ CDN ♦ 14-15 J 3
vey Bay ≈ ♦ 60-61 L 4
vey Bay ○ AUS ♦ 60-61 L 5
vey Junction ○ CDN ♦ 18-19 H 5
e ○ CHN ♦ 54-55 M 4
eah ○ USA ◇ 24-25 H 4
in ○ GH ♦ 48-49 E 6
ikory ○ USA ◇ 24-25 H 2
kman ○ USA ◇ 22-23 D 7
ikory ○ USA ◇ 24-25 H 2
ks Cays ∩ BH ◇ 28-29 K 3
ialgo ○ MEX (DGO) ◇ 16-17 F 6
ialgo, Ciudad ○ MEX ◇ 28-29 D 2
ialgo del Parral ● MEX ◇ 16-17 L 6
erro ⊾ MEX ◇ 28-29 L 2
jáz, al ⊾ KSA ◇ 56-57 D 5
○ USA ◇ 26-27 G 1
gh Atlas ⊾ MA ♦ 48-49 D 2
ggins ○ USA ◇ 26-27 K 5
ishland Park ○ USA ◇ 22-23 E 4
ighland Peak ⊾ USA ◇ 20-21 F 4
gh Level ○ CDN ♦ 14-15 N 5
gh Plateaus ⊾ DZ ♦ 48-49 F 2
gh Point ⊾ USA ◇ 24-25 H 4
gh Rock Lake < USA ◇ 20-21 E 4
gh Springs ○ USA ◇ 24-25 G 5
gh Uintas Wilderness Area ⊥ USA
20-21 J 5
juerote ○ • YV ◇ 30-31 F 2
iguey ○ DOM ◇ 28-29 L 3
umaa saar ∩ EST ♦ 42-43 H 2
kurangi Trench ≃ ♦ 60-61 Q 8
Idale ○ USA ◇ 20-21 H 7
Idesheim ⁓ D ♦ 40-41 K 2
34-35 N 5
illa, al- ★ IRQ ♦ 56-57 F 4
20-21 F 4
I City ○ USA ◇ 20-21 H 2
illsboro ○ USA (IL) ◇ 22-23 D 6
illsboro ○ USA (NM) ◇ 26-27 D 3
illsboro ○ USA (OH) ◇ 22-23 E 6
illsboro ○ USA (TX) ◇ 26-27 J 3
illsboro Canal < USA ◇ 24-25 J 1
illsborough ○ USA ◇ 24-25 J 1
illsborough Bay ≈ ♦ 18-19 N 5
illside ○ USA ◇ 20-21 H 8
illside ○ CDN ♦ 60-61 K 6
illsville ○ USA ◇ 22-23 H 4
o ○ USA ◇ 24-25 E 6 ◇ 16-17 b 7
illot ⊾ USA ◇ 20-21 C 5
ilok ⊾ USA ♦ 54-55 T 7
imachal Pradesh ● IND ♦ 56-57 M 4
imalaya ⊾ IND ♦ 56-57 M 4
imora ⁓ ETH ♦ 48-49 N 6
ims ⁓ SYR ♦ 56-57 D 4
inche ⁓ RH ◇ 16-17 M 7
60-61 K 3
indaun ○ IND ♦ 56-57 N 7
indmarsh, Lake ≈ AUS ♦ 60-61 J 7
inds Lake ○ CDN ♦ 18-19 Q 4
indu Kush ⊾ ♦ 56-57 K 4
inesville ○ USA ◇ 24-25 H 4
ingol ⁓ PK ♦ 56-57 K 5
inton ○ USA ◇ 22-23 H 7
ios ○ GR ♦ 46-47 L 5 ♦ 34-35 R 8
irakaki ⁓ J ♦ 54-55 R 3
iroshima ● J ♦ 54-55 P 4
iroshima ⁓ J ♦ 38-39 K 7 ♦ 34-35 M 6
ispaniola ∩ ♦ 16-17 M 7
Historic Fort Delaware ∴ USA
22-23 L 5
itachi ⁓ J ♦ 54-55 R 4
Hitachi ∴ USA ◇ 22-23 D 5
itra ⁓ N ♦ 60-61 K 9
iu, Île = Hiw ∩ VAN ♦ 60-61 J 7
ijva-Oa ∩ F ♦ 12 O 3
iwassee Lake < USA ◇ 24-25 G 2
Hjargas nuur ≃ MAU ♦ 54-55 G 2
Hoare Bay ≈ ♦ 14-15 Y 3
hoback Junction ○ USA ◇ 20-21 J 4
Hobart ★ AUS ♦ 60-61 K 8
Hobbs ○ USA ◇ 26-27 F 3
Hobbs Coast ⌣ ANT ♦ 13 F 23
Hobbs Hill ⊾ RIM ♦ 48-49 D 5
Hódmezővásárhely ○ H ♦ 40-41 O 5
34-35 Q 6

Hodna, Chott el ○ DZ ♦ 48-49 F 1
Hodq Shamo ⌣ CHN ♦ 54-55 K 3
Hoedspruit ○ ZA ♦ 50-51 H 6
Hoë Karoo = Upper Karoo ⊾ ZA
50-51 F 8
Hōfu ○ J ♦ 54-55 P 5
Hoggar ⊾ DZ ♦ 48-49 F 3
Hoggar, Tassili du ⊾ DZ ♦ 48-49 F 4
Hohenwald ○ USA ◇ 24-25 E 2
Hohhot ○ CHN ♦ 54-55 L 3
Hoh Xil Shan ⊾ CHN ♦ 54-55 F 4
Hōi Jin ⁓ VN ♦ 58-59 E 2
Hoima ○ EAU ♦ 50-51 H 1
Hokkaidō ∩ J ♦ 54-55 R 3
Holbox, Isla ∩ MEX ◇ 28-29 L 1
Holbrook ○ USA (AZ) ◇ 26-27 K 9
Holbrook ○ USA (ID) ◇ 20-21 H 4
Holbrook ○ USA ◇ 20-21 H 6
Holchit, Punta ⊾ MEX ◇ 28-29 K 1
Holden ○ USA ◇ 20-21 H 6
Holdenville ○ USA ◇ 26-27 J 2
Holguín ○ C ◇ 16-17 L 6
Holland ○ USA ◇ 22-23 E 4
14-15 T 8
Hollick-Kenyon Plateau ⊾ ANT
13 F 26
Hollis ○ USA ◇ 26-27 H 2
Hollister ○ USA (CA) ◇ 20-21 D 7
Hollister ○ USA (MO) ◇ 26-27 L 1
Holly Ridge ○ USA ◇ 24-25 K 2
Holly Springs ○ USA ◇ 24-25 D 2
Hollywood ○ USA (FL) ◇ 24-25 H 6
16-17 K 6
Hollywood •• USA (CA) ◇ 20-21 E 8
Holman Island ○ CDN ♦ 14-15 N 3
Holmsk ○ RUS ♦ 52-53 Z 8
Holsteinsborg = Sisimiut ○ GRØ
14-15 a 3
Holter Lake < USA ◇ 20-21 J 2
Holton ○ CDN ♦ 14-15 Z 6
Holy Cross ○ USA ♦ 14-15 F 6
Holyrood ○ CDN ♦ 18-19 S 9
Hombori ○ RMM ♦ 48-49 E 5
Home Bay ≈ ♦ 14-15 X 3
Homedale ○ USA ◇ 20-21 F 4
Homeł ★ BY ♦ 42-43 M 5
Homer ○ USA (AK) ♦ 14-15 F 5
Homer ○ USA (LA) ◇ 26-27 L 3
Homestead ○ AUS ♦ 60-61 K 4
Homestead ○ USA ◇ 24-25 H 6
Homewood ○ USA ◇ 24-25 E 3
Hominy ○ USA ◇ 26-27 J 1
Homo, Cerro el ⊾ HN ◇ 28-29 L 4
Homyel' = Homeł ★ BY ♦ 42-43 M 5
34-35 S 5
Honda ○ CO ◇ 30-31 E 3
Hondo ○ USA (NM) ◇ 26-27 E 3
Hondo ○ USA (TX) ◇ 26-27 H 5
Hondo, Río ⁓ MEX ◇ 28-29 K 3
Hondo River ⁓ BH ◇ 28-29 K 3
16-17 J 7
Honduras ■ HN ◇ 28-29 K 4
Honduras, Cabo de ⊾ HN ◇ 28-29 L 3
Honduras, Golfo de ≈ ◇ 28-29 L 3
16-17 J 7
Honesdale ○ USA ◇ 22-23 L 5
Honey Lake ≈ USA ◇ 20-21 E 5
Hông Gai ○ VN ♦ 58-59 E 2
Hongguqu ○ CHN ♦ 54-55 M 5
Honghu ○ CHN ♦ 54-55 L 5
Hongjiang ○ CHN ♦ 54-55 K 6
Hong Kong ○ CHN ♦ 54-55 L 7
Hongueedo, Détroit d' ≈ ◇ 18-19 M 4
14-15 X 7
Honiara ★ SOL ♦ 12 G 3
Honningsvåg ○ N ♦ 36-37 M 1
34-35 R 1
Honokaa ○ USA ◇ 24-25 D 7
16-17 b 6
Honokahua ○ USA ◇ 24-25 D 7
Honolulu •• USA ◇ 24-25 D 7
16-17 b 6
Honshū ∩ J ♦ 54-55 P 4
Honuu ○ RUS ♦ 52-53 X 4
Hood, Mount ⊾ USA ◇ 20-21 D 2
14-15 M 7
Hood River ○ USA ◇ 20-21 D 3
Hoods ○ USA ◇ 26-27 G 2
Hool ○ MEX ◇ 28-29 J 2
Hoopa Valley Indian Reservation ⋊ USA
20-21 D 5
Hoopeston ○ USA ◇ 22-23 E 5
Hoop Nature Reserve, De ⊥ ZA ♦ 50-51 F 8
Hoover Dam • USA ◇ 20-21 G 7
Hopa ○ TR ♦ 34-35 U 7
Hope ○ CDN ♦ 14-15 M 7
Hope ○ USA ◇ 26-27 L 3
Hopefield ○ ZA ♦ 50-51 E 8
Hope Island ∩ CDN ♦ 18-19 D 6
Hopelchen ○ MEX ◇ 28-29 K 2
Hoper ⁓ RUS ♦ 34-35 U 5
Hope River ⁓ USA ◇ 24-25 J 1
Hopetown ○ ZA ♦ 50-51 F 7
Hopewell ○ USA ◇ 22-23 K 7
Hopewell Cape ○ CDN ♦ 18-19 M 6
Hopi Indian Reservation ⋊ USA
26-27 B 1 ◇ 20-21 J 8
Hopin ○ MYA ♦ 54-55 H 7
Hopkins, Lake ≈ AUS ♦ 60-61 H 4
Hopkinsville ○ USA ◇ 22-23 E 7
Hopland ○ USA ◇ 20-21 D 6
Hoquiam ○ USA ◇ 20-21 C 2
Hor ⁓ RUS ♦ 52-53 Y 8
Horasan ○ TR ♦ 34-35 U 7
Horinsk ○ RUS ♦ 52-53 T 7
Horlick Mountains ⊾ ANT ♦ 13 E 0
Horlivka ○ UA ♦ 34-35 T 6
Hormuz, Strait of ≈ ♦ 56-57 H 5
Horn, Van ○ USA ◇ 26-27 F 4
16-17 M 2
Hornbjarg ⊾ IS ♦ 36-37 b 1
34-35 G 2
Homconcitos ○ PA ◇ 28-29 N 8
Hornell ○ USA ◇ 22-23 K 4
Horn Islands ∩ PNG ♦ 58-59 N 7
Horn Plateau ⊾ CDN ♦ 14-15 M 4

Horquetas, Las ○ CR ◇ 28-29 C 6
Horrománbád ○ IR ♦ 56-57 F 4
Horramšahr • IR ♦ 56-57 F 4
Horse (Saint Barbe) Islands ∩ CDN
18-19 R 3
Horseshoe Bend ○ USA ◇ 20-21 H 4
Horseshoe Bend National Military Park ∴
USA ◇ 24-25 F 3
Horsham ○ AUS ♦ 60-61 J 7
Horton River ⁓ CDN ♦ 14-15 L 3
Horwood Lake ○ CDN ♦ 18-19 C 5
Horus, Temple of ∴ ET ♦ 48-49 M 4
Hosa'ina ○ ETH ♦ 48-49 N 7
Hose, Pegunungan ⊾ MAL
58-59 F 6
Hospah ○ USA ◇ 26-27 D 2
Hospet ○ IND ♦ 56-57 M 7
Hoste, Isla ∩ RCH ♦ 32-33 J 9
Hotaka-dake ⊾ J ♦ 54-55 Q 4
Hotan ○ CHN ♦ 54-55 D 4
Hotazel ○ ZA ♦ 50-51 F 6
Hot Springs ○ USA (NC) ◇ 24-25 G 1
Hot Springs ○ USA (AR) ◇ 26-27 L 2
16-17 H 4
Hot Springs, Cove ⁓ USA ◇ 20-21 F 3
Hot Springs National Park ⊥ USA
26-27 L 2 ◇ 16-17 H 4
Hottah Lake ○ CDN ♦ 14-15 N 3
Houghton ○ USA ◇ 22-23 D 3
14-15 T 7
Houghton Lake ≈ USA (MI)
22-23 F 3
Houghton Lake ○ USA (MI)
22-23 F 3
Houlton ○ USA ◇ 22-23 P 2
14-15 X 7
Houma ○ CHN ♦ 54-55 L 4
Houma ○ USA ◇ 26-27 M 5
16-17 H 5
Houndé ○ BF ♦ 48-49 E 6
Hourtin et de Carcans, Lac d' ≈ F
38-39 G 9 ♦ 34-35 L 6
Householder Pass ⁓ USA ◇ 20-21 G 8
Houston ○ USA (MS) ◇ 24-25 D 3
Houston ○ • USA (TX) ◇ 26-27 K 5
16-17 H 5
Houston, Lake ≈ USA ◇ 26-27 K 4
Hovd ★ MAU ♦ 54-55 G 2
Hövsgöl nuur ≈ MAU ♦ 54-55 J 1
Howard ○ USA ◇ 22-23 D 3
Howard City ○ USA ◇ 22-23 E 4
Howe, Cape ⊾ AUS ♦ 60-61 K 7
Howell ○ USA ◇ 22-23 G 4
Hoxie ○ USA ◇ 26-27 G 1
Hoy ○ • IR ♦ 56-57 E 3
Hradec Králové ○ CZ ♦ 40-41 N 3
34-35 P 5
Hrodna ○ BY ♦ 42-43 H 5
34-35 Q 5
Hromtau ○ KZ ♦ 34-35 X 5
Hsinchu ○ RC ♦ 54-55 N 7
Hsipaw ○ MYA ♦ 54-55 H 7
Hpai Phong ○ VN ♦ 58-59 E 2
Huacas, Las ∴ CR ◇ 28-29 B 6
Hua Hin ○ THA ♦ 58-59 C 4
Huahua, Río = Wawa, Río ⁓ NIC
28-29 B 4
Huai'an ○ CHN ♦ 54-55 M 5
Huaibei ○ CHN ♦ 54-55 M 5
Huai He ⁓ CHN ♦ 54-55 M 5
Huaihua ○ CHN ♦ 54-55 K 6
Huaiyin ○ CHN ♦ 54-55 M 5
Huajuapan de León ○ MEX
28-29 J 3 ◇ 16-17 G 7
Huaki ○ RI ♦ 58-59 J 8
Hualapai Indian Reservation ⋊ USA
20-21 H 8 ◇ 16-17 D 3
Hualien ○ RC ♦ 54-55 N 7
Huallaga, Río ⁓ PE ◇ 30-31 D 6
Huamantla ○ MEX ◇ 28-29 J 2
Huambo ○ ANG ♦ 50-51 E 4
Huamuxtitlan ○ MEX ◇ 28-29 J 3
Huancabamba ○ PE ◇ 30-31 D 6
Huancane ○ PE ◇ 30-31 F 8
Huancavelica ○ PE ◇ 30-31 D 7
Huancayo ○ PE ◇ 30-31 D 7
Huanchaca, Parque Nacional ⊥ BOL
30-31 G 8
Huang He ⁓ CHN ♦ 54-55 M 4
Huangshan ○ CHN ♦ 54-55 M 6
Huangyuan ○ CHN ♦ 54-55 J 4
Huaniqueo ○ MEX ◇ 28-29 D 2
Huantacareo ○ MEX ◇ 28-29 D 2
Huánuco ○ PE ◇ 30-31 D 6
Huan Xian ○ CHN ♦ 54-55 K 4
Huapi, Serranías ⊾ NIC ◇ 28-29 B 5
Huaraz ○ PE ◇ 30-31 D 6
Huarmey ○ PE ◇ 30-31 D 7
Huasco ○ RCH ◇ 32-33 H 3
Huashixia ○ CHN ♦ 54-55 H 4
Huatabampo ○ MEX ◇ 16-17 E 5
Huatugou ○ CHN ♦ 54-55 G 4
Huatunas, Lago ○ BOL ◇ 30-31 G 7
Huatusco de Chicuellar ○ MEX
28-29 F 2
Huautla de Jiménez ○ MEX ◇ 28-29 E 1
Huayacocotla ○ MEX ◇ 28-29 E 1
Hubbard Creek Reservoir < USA
26-27 H 3
Hubbard Lake ≈ USA ◇ 22-23 G 3
Hubbards ○ CDN ♦ 18-19 M 6
Hubei ● CHN ♦ 54-55 L 5
Hubli ○ IND ♦ 56-57 M 7
Hudaida, al- ○ Y ♦ 56-57 E 8
Hudiksvall ○ S ♦ 42-43 G 3
Hudson ○ USA (MI) ◇ 22-23 F 4
Hudson ○ USA (NY) ◇ 22-23 M 4
Hudson Bay ○ CDN ♦ 14-15 S 6
Hudson Bay ≈ ♦ 14-15 Q 6
Hudson Falls ○ USA ◇ 22-23 M 4
Hudson Mountains ⊾ ANT ♦ 13 E 0
Hudson Strait ≈ ♦ 14-15 W 4
Hudžali ○ UZ ♦ 56-57 H 7
Hué ○ • VN ♦ 58-59 E 3
Hueco ○ USA ◇ 26-27 E 4
Huehuenango ○ MEX ◇ 28-29 E 1
Huehuetán ○ MEX ◇ 28-29 G 4
Huehuetla ○ MEX ◇ 28-29 E 2
Huejotzingo ○ MEX ◇ 28-29 E 2

Huelva ○ • E ♦ 44-45 D 6
34-35 K 8
Huerra, La ○ MEX ◇ 28-29 C 6
Huesca ○ • E ♦ 44-45 G 3
Huetamo de Núñez ○ MEX ◇ 28-29 D 3
Hufūf, al- ○ KSA ♦ 56-57 F 5
Hŭgang ○ TJ ♦ 56-57 K 3
Hughenden ○ AUS ♦ 60-61 J 4
Hughesville ○ USA ◇ 22-23 K 5
Hugo ○ USA ◇ 26-27 K 2
Hugo Reservoir < USA ◇ 26-27 K 2
Huib-Hochplato ⊾ NAM ♦ 50-51 E 7
Huichapan ○ MEX ◇ 28-29 E 1
Huichon ○ KOR ♦ 54-55 O 3
Huila, Nevado del ⊾ CO ◇ 30-31 D 4
Huila, Parque Nacional ⊥ CO ◇ 30-31 D 4
Huilapilan ○ MEX ◇ 28-29 D 5
Huimilpan ○ MEX ◇ 28-29 D 1
Huisne ⁓ F ♦ 38-39 H 7
34-35 M 6
Huitzo ○ MEX ◇ 28-29 F 3
Huixtepec ○ MEX ◇ 28-29 F 3
Huixtla ○ MEX ◇ 28-29 H 4
Huizhou ○ CHN ♦ 54-55 L 7
Hukuntsi ○ RB ♦ 50-51 F 6
Hulah Lake ○ USA ◇ 26-27 J 1
Hull ○ CDN ♦ 18-19 G 6
Hull ○ USA ◇ 22-23 G 4
Hulun Nur ○ CHN ♦ 54-55 M 2
Humaitá ○ BR ◇ 30-31 G 6
Humansdorp ○ ZA ♦ 50-51 F 8
Humble ○ USA ◇ 26-27 K 4
Humboldt ○ USA (NV) ◇ 20-21 E 5
Humboldt ○ USA (TN) ◇ 24-25 D 1
Humboldt ○ CDN ♦ 14-15 O 6
Humboldt Bay ≈ USA ◇ 20-21 B 5
Humboldt Gletscher ⊂ GRØ ♦ 14-15 Y 1
Humboldt River ⁓ USA ◇ 20-21 E 5
16-17 C 2
Humboldt Salt Marsh ○ USA
20-21 F 6
Húmeda, Pampa ⁓ RA ◇ 32-33 K 5
Humphrey ○ USA ◇ 26-27 J 1
Humphreys Peak ⊾ USA ◇ 20-21 J 8
Humptulips ○ USA ◇ 20-21 C 2
Hūn ⁓ LAR ♦ 48-49 J 3
Húnaflói ≈ ♦ 36-37 c 2 ♦ 34-35 G 2
Hunan ● CHN ♦ 54-55 L 6
Hunedoara ○ RO ♦ 34-35 Q 6
Hungary ■ H ♦ 40-41 O 5
34-35 P 6
Hungerford ○ AUS ♦ 60-61 J 5
Hungry Horse Reservoir < USA
20-21 H 1
Hunjiang ○ CHN ♦ 54-55 O 3
Hunter, Île ∩ ♦ 60-61 P 4
Hunter Liggett Military Reservation xx
USA ◇ 20-21 D 8
Hunter River ⁓ CDN ♦ 18-19 N 5
Hunters ○ USA ◇ 20-21 G 2
Huntingdon ○ CDN ♦ 18-19 G 6
Huntington ○ USA (IN) ◇ 22-23 F 5
Huntington ○ USA (OR) ◇ 20-21 F 3
Huntington ○ USA (PA) ◇ 22-23 K 5
Huntington ○ USA (UT) ◇ 20-21 J 6
Huntington ○ USA (WV) ◇ 22-23 G 6
Huntington Beach ○ USA ◇ 20-21 E 9
14-15 V 7
Huntsville ○ CDN ♦ 18-19 E 6
Huntsville ○ USA (AR) ◇ 26-27 L 1
Huntsville ○ USA (TX) ◇ 26-27 K 4
Huntsville ○ USA (AL) ◇ 24-25 E 2
16-17 J 4
Hunucma ○ MEX ◇ 28-29 K 1
Huolingol ○ CHN ♦ 54-55 M 2
Huon Gulf ≈ ♦ 58-59 N 8
Huon Peninsula ⌣ PNG ♦ 58-59 N 8
Hurd, Cape ⊾ CDN ♦ 18-19 D 6
Hurdiyo ○ SP ♦ 48-49 Q 6
Ḩurma, al- ○ KSA ♦ 56-57 E 6
Huron, Lake ≈ ♦ 22-23 G 3
Hurricane ○ USA ◇ 20-21 H 7
Hutchinson ○ USA ◇ 26-27 H 1
Hutchinson Island ∩ USA ◇ 24-25 H 6
Huttonsville ○ USA ◇ 22-23 J 6
Huwār, Wādī ⁓ SUD ♦ 48-49 L 5
Huxi Xincun ○ CHN ♦ 54-55 O 3
Hwange ○ ZW ♦ 50-51 G 5
Hwange National Park ⊥ ZW
50-51 G 5
Hyak ○ USA ◇ 20-21 D 2
Hyannis ○ USA ◇ 22-23 N 5
Hyder ○ USA ◇ 20-21 H 9
Hyderābād ○ IND ♦ 56-57 M 6
Hyderābād ○ PK ♦ 56-57 K 5
Hydrographer Canyon ≃ ♦ 22-23 O 5
Hyères ○ F ♦ 38-39 L 10
34-35 N 7
Hyères, Îles d' ∩ F ♦ 38-39 L 10
34-35 N 7
Hyesan ★ KOR ♦ 54-55 O 3
Hyndman Peak ⊾ USA ◇ 20-21 G 4

I

Iaco, Rio ⁓ BR ◇ 30-31 F 6
Iaguarete ○ BR ◇ 30-31 F 4
Ianthe Shoal ≃ ♦ 58-59 N 5
Iaşi ○ RO ♦ 34-35 R 6
Ibadan ○ WAN ♦ 48-49 F 7
Ibague ○ CO ◇ 30-31 D 4
Ibarra ○ EC ◇ 30-31 D 4
Ibb ○ • Y ♦ 56-57 E 8
Ibera, Esteros del ○ RA ◇ 32-33 L 3
Iberian Basin ≃ ♦ 16-17 H 7
Iberville, Lac d' ≈ CDN ♦ 14-15 W 5
Ibiá ○ BR ◇ 30-31 K 8
Ibiapaba, Serra da ⊾ BR ◇ 30-31 L 5
Ibotirama ○ BR ◇ 30-31 L 7
Içá, Rio = BR ⁓ BR ◇ 30-31 F 5
Içana ○ BR ◇ 30-31 F 4
Ice Caves • USA ◇ 26-27 D 2
İçel (Mersin) ☆ TR ♦ 56-57 C 3
Iceland Basin ≃ ♦ 34-35 F 3

Iceland-Faroe Rise ≃ ♦ 34-35 J 3
Icelandic Plateau ≃ ♦ 34-35 H 2
Ichalkaranji ○ IND ♦ 56-57 L 7
Ichmul ○ MEX ◇ 28-29 K 1
Içhögemskij hrebet ⊾ RUS ♦ 52-53 d 5
Icy Cape ⊾ USA ♦ 14-15 F 2
Idabel ○ USA ◇ 26-27 K 2
Idaho ● USA ◇ 20-21 F 3
Idaho Army National Guard Artillery Range
xx USA ◇ 20-21 F 4
Idaho Falls ○ USA ◇ 20-21 H 4
14-15 O 8
Idaho National Engineering Laboratory xx
USA ◇ 20-21 H 4
'Idd al-Ghanam ○ SUD ♦ 48-49 K 6
Idfū ○ ET ♦ 48-49 M 4
Idhan• Awbārī ⁓ LAR ♦ 48-49 H 3
Idiofa ○ ZRE ♦ 50-51 E 2
Idlib ○ SYR ♦ 56-57 D 3
Ídra ○ GR ♦ 46-47 K 7
34-35 R 8
Ifakara ○ EAT ♦ 50-51 J 3
Ifalik Atoll ∩ FSM ♦ 58-59 M 5
Ife ○ • WAN ♦ 48-49 F 7
Iferouâne ○ RN ♦ 48-49 G 5
Iforhas, Adrar des ⊾ RMM ♦ 48-49 F 4
Igarapé Lourdes, Área Indígena ⋊ BR
30-31 G 7
Igarapé Mirim ○ BR ◇ 30-31 K 5
Igarité ○ BR ◇ 30-31 J 7
Igarka ○ RUS ♦ 52-53 O 4
Ignacio ○ USA ◇ 26-27 D 1
Igoma ○ EAT ♦ 50-51 H 3
Igombe ⁓ EAT ♦ 50-51 H 2
Igornachoick Bay ≈ ♦ 18-19 Q 3
Igrim ○ RUS ♦ 52-53 L 5
Iguache, Mesas de ⁓ CO ◇ 30-31 E 4
Iguaçu, Parque Nacional do ⊥ ⁓ BR
32-33 M 3
Iguala de la Independencia ○ MEX
28-29 E 2 ◇ 16-17 G 7
Iguape ○ BR ◇ 32-33 N 2
Iguatu ○ BR ◇ 30-31 L 6
Iguéla ○ G ♦ 50-51 C 2
Iguetti, Sebkhet ○ RIM ♦ 48-49 D 3
Iguidi, Erg ⁓ DZ ♦ 48-49 D 3
Iharana ○ RM ♦ 50-51 M 4
Ihiala ○ WAN ♦ 48-49 G 7
Ihosy ○ RM ♦ 50-51 M 6
Iljāfene ⁓ RIM ♦ 48-49 D 4
Ijebu-Ode ○ WAN ♦ 48-49 F 7
IJsselmeer ≈ ♦ 40-41 H 2
34-35 N 5
Ikela ○ ZRE ♦ 50-51 F 2
Iki ∩ J ♦ 54-55 O 5
Ik'pikpuk River ⁓ USA ♦ 14-15 F 2
Ilām ○ IR ♦ 56-57 F 4
Ilbenge ○ RUS ♦ 52-53 V 5
Ilebo ○ ZRE ♦ 50-51 F 2
Île-de-France ● F ♦ 38-39 J 7
Ilesa ○ WAN ♦ 48-49 F 7
Ilhéus ○ BR ◇ 30-31 M 7
Ili ⁓ KZ ♦ 56-57 M 2
Ilia ⁓ F ♦ 34-35 J 5
Iliamna Volcano ⊾ USA ♦ 14-15 F 4
Iligan ☆ RP ♦ 58-59 H 5
Ilijara ⁓ EAK ♦ 50-51 K 2
Ill ⁓ F ♦ 38-39 L 7 ♦ 34-35 N 6
Illapel ○ RCH ◇ 32-33 H 4
Illbilee, Mount ⊾ AUS ♦ 60-61 H 5
Iligen City ○ USA ◇ 22-23 C 6
Illinois ● USA ◇ 22-23 C 6
16-17 H 3
Illinois Point ⊾ USA ◇ 20-21 G 2
Illinois River ⁓ USA ◇ 20-21 G 2
Illinois River ⁓ USA ◇ 22-23 C 6
Illizi ○ DZ ♦ 48-49 G 3
Illmo ○ USA ◇ 22-23 D 7
Ilma, Lake ≈ AUS ♦ 60-61 H 5
Il'men', ozero ≈ RUS ♦ 42-43 M 2
34-35 S 4
Ilo ○ PE ◇ 30-31 E 8
Ilobasco ○ ES ◇ 28-29 K 5
Iloilo City ☆ RP ♦ 58-59 H 4
Ilorin ○ WAN ♦ 48-49 F 7
Ilwaco ○ USA ◇ 20-21 C 2
Imanombo ○ RM ♦ 50-51 M 6
Imi ○ ETH ♦ 48-49 O 7
Imlay City ○ USA ◇ 22-23 G 4
Immokalee ○ USA ◇ 24-25 H 6
Imnaha River ⁓ USA ◇ 20-21 F 2
Imperatriz ○ BR ◇ 30-31 K 6
Impfondo ○ RCB ♦ 50-51 E 1
Imphāl ⁓ IND ♦ 56-57 P 5
Imuruan Bay ≈ ♦ 58-59 G 4
Ināl ⁓ RIM ♦ 48-49 C 4
Ince Burnu ⊾ TR ♦ 34-35 S 7
Inch'ŏn ○ ROK ♦ 54-55 O 4
Incudine, Monte ⊾ F ♦ 44-45 M 4
Independence ○ USA (CA) ◇ 20-21 E 7
Independence ○ USA (IA) ◇ 22-23 C 4
Independence ○ USA (KS) ◇ 26-27 K 1
Independence ○ USA ◇ 22-23 H 7
Independence Hall •• USA ◇ 22-23 L 5
Inderborskij ⁓ KZ ♦ 34-35 W 6
India ■ IND ♦ 56-57 M 6
Indiana ● USA ◇ 22-23 J 5
Indiana ○ USA ◇ 22-23 E 6
16-17 J 3
Indianapolis ○ • USA ◇ 22-23 E 6
16-17 J 3
Indiana Trail Caverns • USA
Indian Bay ○ CDN ♦ 18-19 S 4
Indian Ocean ≈ ♦ 58-59 B 6
Indian Ocean ⁓ USA ◇ 26-27 H 3
Indian Point ⊾ USA ◇ 20-21 H 6
Indian River Bay ≈ ♦ 22-23 L 6
Indian Springs ○ USA ◇ 20-21 G 7

Indian Trail Caverns ∴ USA
22-23 G 5
Indian Wells ○ USA ◇ 26-27 B 2
Indigirka ⁓ RUS ♦ 52-53 Z 4
Indio ○ USA ◇ 20-21 F 9
16-17 C 4
Indio, Río ⁓ NIC ◇ 28-29 B 6
Indonesia ■ RI ♦ 58-59 E 7
Indore ○ •• IND ♦ 56-57 M 6
Indre ⁓ F ♦ 38-39 H 8 ♦ 34-35 M 6
Indus ⁓ PK ♦ 56-57 K 6
Indus, Mouths of the ⁓ PK ♦ 56-57 K 6
Indus Fan ≃ ♦ 56-57 J 6
Inegöl ○ TR ♦ 34-35 R 7
Inez ○ USA ◇ 20-21 H 6
Inferior, Laguna ≈ ♦ 28-29 G 3
Infiernillo ○ MEX ◇ 28-29 D 3
Infiernillo, Presa el < MEX ◇ 28-29 D 2
16-17 F 7
Inga • ZRE ♦ 50-51 D 3
Ingeniero Jacobacci ○ RA ◇ 32-33 J 6
Ingham ○ AUS ♦ 60-61 K 3
Inglefield Bredning ≈ ♦ 14-15 X 1
Inglefield Land ⌣ GRØ ♦ 14-15 W 1
Ingoda ⁓ RUS ♦ 52-53 T 7
Ingolstadt ○ D ♦ 40-41 L 4
34-35 O 6
Ingonish Beach ○ CDN ♦ 18-19 O 5
Ingrid Christensen Land ⌣ ANT
13 F 8
Ingushetia ● RUS ♦ 34-35 U 7
Inguškaja Respublika ● RUS
34-35 U 7
Inhambane ○ MOC ♦ 50-51 J 6
Inhambane, Baía de ≈ ♦ 50-51 J 6
Inhaminga ○ MOC ♦ 50-51 J 5
Inharrime ○ MOC ♦ 50-51 J 6
Ininida, Río ⁓ CO ◇ 30-31 F 4
Inja ⁓ RUS ♦ 52-53 O 7
Injune ○ AUS ♦ 60-61 K 5
Inkerman ○ AUS ♦ 60-61 J 3
Inn ⁓ D ♦ 40-41 M 4 ♦ 34-35 O 6
Inner Mongolia ● CHN ♦ 54-55 J 4
Inneston ○ AUS ♦ 60-61 H 7
Innisfail ○ AUS ♦ 60-61 K 3
Innsbruck ☆ A ♦ 40-41 L 5
34-35 O 6
Inongo ○ ZRE ♦ 50-51 E 2
I-n-Quezzam ○ DZ ♦ 48-49 G 4
In Salah ○ DZ ♦ 48-49 F 3
International Amistad Reservoir < USA
26-27 G 5
International Falcon Reservoir < USA
26-27 H 6
International Falls ○ USA ◇ 14-15 S 7
Inukjuak ○ CDN ♦ 14-15 V 5
Inuvik • CDN ♦ 14-15 K 3
Invercargill ○ NZ ♦ 60-61 O 9
Inverell ○ AUS ♦ 60-61 L 5
Inverness ○ CDN ♦ 18-19 O 5
Inverness ○ USA ◇ 24-25 G 5
Inverway ○ AUS ♦ 60-61 H 3
Investigator Ridge ≃ ♦ 12 A 3
Investigator Strait ≈ ♦ 60-61 H 7
Inyangani ⊾ ZW ♦ 50-51 H 5
Inyokern ○ USA ◇ 20-21 F 8
Inyo Mountains ⊾ USA ◇ 20-21 E 7
Inyonga ○ EAT ♦ 50-51 H 3
Inza ⁓ ZRE ♦ 50-51 E 3
Ioánnina ○ GR ♦ 46-47 H 5
Iola ○ USA ◇ 26-27 K 1
Iolotan ○ TM ♦ 56-57 J 3
Iona, Parque Nacional do ⊥ ANG
50-51 D 5
Iones, Cap ⊾ CDN ♦ 14-15 V 6
Ionesport ○ USA ◇ 22-23 P 3
Ionia ○ USA ◇ 22-23 F 4
Ionian Islands ∩ GR ♦ 46-47 H 6
34-35 P 8
Ionian Sea ≈ GR ♦ 42-43 M 2
34-35 S 4
Iony, ostrov ∩ RUS ♦ 52-53 Y 6
Ios ∩ GR ◇ 30-31 M 7
Ió-shima ∩ J ♦ 54-55 R 6
Iowa ● USA ◇ 22-23 H 2
Iowa City ○ USA ◇ 22-23 C 5
16-17 H 3
Iowa Park ○ USA ◇ 26-27 H 3
Ipala ○ GCA ◇ 28-29 K 4
Ipameri ○ BR ◇ 30-31 K 8
Iparia ○ PE ◇ 30-31 D 6
Ipatinga ○ BR ◇ 30-31 L 8
Ipiaú ○ BR ◇ 30-31 M 7
Ipoh • MAL ♦ 58-59 C 5
Ippy ○ RCA ♦ 48-49 K 7
Ipswich ○ AUS ♦ 60-61 L 5
Ipswich ○ GB ♦ 38-39 H 5
34-35 M 5
Ipu ○ BR ◇ 30-31 L 5
Iqaluit ○ CDN ♦ 14-15 X 4
Iqe ○ CHN ♦ 54-55 H 4
Iquique ☆ RCH ♦ 32-33 H 2
Iquitos ☆ PE ◇ 30-31 E 5
Iran ■ IR ♦ 56-57 G 4
Ira Banda ○ RCA ♦ 48-49 K 7
Irako ⁓ J ♦ 30-31 J 3
Irānšahr ○ IR ♦ 56-57 J 5
Irapuato ○ MEX ◇ 28-29 D 1
16-17 F 6
Iran ⁓ IRQ ♦ 56-57 F 4
Irasville ○ USA ◇ 22-23 M 3
Irbid ☆ JOR ♦ 56-57 D 4
Irecê ○ BR ◇ 30-31 L 7
Ireland ■ IRL ◇ 38-39 B 5
34-35 J 5
Irharhar, Oued ⁓ DZ ♦ 48-49 G 3
Irhil M'Goun ⊾ MA ♦ 48-49 E 2
Iriba ○ TCH ♦ 48-49 K 5
Iringa ○ EAT ♦ 50-51 J 3
Iriomote shima ∩ J ♦ 54-55 N 7
Iri, Rio ⁓ BR ◇ 30-31 J 5

Irish Sea ≈ ♦ 38-39 E 5 ♦ 34-35 K 5
Iritua ○ BR ◇ 30-31 K 5
Irkutsk ☆ RUS ♦ 52-53 R 7
Irminger Basin ≃ ♦ 14-15 e 3
Irminger Sea ≈ ♦ 14-15 d 4
Irondequoit ○ USA ◇ 22-23 K 4
Irondro ○ RM ♦ 50-51 L 6
Iron Knob ○ AUS ♦ 60-61 H 6
Iron Mountain ○ USA ◇ 22-23 D 3
Iron River ○ USA (MI) ◇ 22-23 D 3
Iron River ○ USA (WI) ◇ 22-23 C 2
Ironton ○ USA (MO) ◇ 22-23 D 7
Ironton ○ USA (OH) ◇ 22-23 G 6
Ironwood ○ USA ◇ 22-23 C 2
Irrawaddy ⁓ MYA ♦ 58-59 C 3
Irtyš ⁓ RUS ♦ 52-53 M 7
Irtyš ☆ KZ ♦ 52-53 L 6
Irving ○ USA ◇ 26-27 J 3
Irwin Military Reservation, Fort xx USA
20-21 F 8
Isabela, Isla ∩ EC ◇ 30-31 X 4
Isabella ○ USA ◇ 22-23 D 4
Isabella, Cordillera ⊾ NIC ◇ 28-29 B 5
16-17 J 8
Isabella Indian Reservation ⋊ USA
22-23 F 4
Isabella Lake < USA ◇ 20-21 E 8
Isachsen, Cape ⊾ CDN ♦ 14-15 P 1
Ísafjörður ⁓ IS ♦ 36-37 b 1
34-35 G 2
Isalo, Parc National de l' ⊥ RM
50-51 L 6
Isangano National Park ⊥ Z
50-51 H 4
Isbil, Ǧabal ⊾ Y ♦ 56-57 E 8
Iseyin ○ WAN ♦ 48-49 F 7
Isfahan = Eşfahān ☆ IR ♦ 56-57 G 4
Ishigaki shima ∩ J ♦ 54-55 N 7
Ishinomaki ○ J ♦ 54-55 R 4
Ishpeming ○ USA ◇ 22-23 E 2
Isiboro Securé, Parque Nacional ⊥ BOL
30-31 F 8
Isil'kul' ○ RUS ♦ 52-53 L 7
Išim ○ RUS (TMN) ♦ 52-53 K 6
Išim ⁓ RUS ♦ 52-53 L 6
Isimala • EAT ♦ 50-51 J 3
Isiolo ○ EAK ♦ 50-51 J 1
Isiro ○ ZRE ♦ 48-49 L 8
Iskandariya, al- ☆ ET ♦ 48-49 L 2
İskenderun ○ TR ♦ 34-35 T 8
İskenderun Körfezi ≈ ♦ 56-57 C 3
Iskitim ○ RUS ♦ 52-53 N 7
Isla ○ MEX ◇ 28-29 F 2
Isla de Aguada ○ MEX ◇ 28-29 J 2
Isla Grande del Tierra del Fuego ∩
32-33 J 8
Islamabad ★ PK ♦ 56-57 L 4
Isla Magdalena, Parque Nacional ⊥ RCH
32-33 H 6
Islamorada ○ USA ◇ 24-25 H 6
Ísland ■ IS ♦ 36-37 b 2 ♦ 34-35 G 3
Island Lagoon ≈ AUS ♦ 60-61 H 6
Island Lake ○ CDN ♦ 14-15 S 6
Island Park Reservoir < USA
20-21 J 3
Island Pond ○ CDN ♦ 18-19 Q 4
Island Pond ○ USA ◇ 22-23 N 3
Islands, Bay of ≈ ♦ 60-61 P 7
Islands, Bay of ≈ ♦ 18-19 R 4
Isle of Wight ∩ GB ♦ 38-39 G 6
34-35 L 5
Isle Royale National Park ⊥ USA
22-23 D 1 ♦ 14-15 T 7
Isles of Scilly ∩ • GB ♦ 38-39 D 7
34-35 K 6
Isleta ○ USA ◇ 26-27 D 2
Isleta Indian Reservation ⋊ USA
26-27 D 2
Isluga, Parque Nacional ⊥ RCH
30-31 F 8
Ismā'īliya, al- ○ ET ♦ 48-49 M 2
Isoka ○ Z ♦ 50-51 H 4
Isparta ☆ TR ♦ 34-35 S 8
Israel ■ IL ♦ 56-57 C 4
Israelite Bay ≈ AUS ♦ 60-61 G 6
Isseke ○ EAT ♦ 50-51 J 3
Issoire ○ F ♦ 38-39 J 9 ♦ 34-35 M 7
Issoudun ○ F ♦ 38-39 H 8
34-35 M 6
İstanbul ☆ ••• TR ♦ 34-35 R 7
Isthmus of Kra ⁓ THA ♦ 58-59 C 4
Istmina ○ CO ◇ 30-31 D 3
Itaberaba ○ BR ◇ 30-31 L 7
Itaberaí ○ BR ◇ 30-31 K 8
Itabuna ○ BR ◇ 30-31 M 7
Itacaré ○ BR ◇ 30-31 L 7
Itaeté ○ BR ◇ 30-31 L 7
Itaituba ○ BR ◇ 30-31 J 6
Itajaí ○ BR ◇ 32-33 N 3
Itajubá ○ BR ◇ 32-33 N 2
Italy ■ I ♦ 46-47 E 4 ♦ 34-35 O 7
Italy ○ USA ◇ 26-27 J 3
Itanagar ☆ IND ♦ 56-57 P 5
Itapajé ○ BR ◇ 30-31 L 5
Itapebi ○ BR ◇ 30-31 L 7
Itapecurumirim ○ BR ◇ 30-31 L 5
Itapetinga ○ BR ◇ 30-31 L 8
Itapeva ○ BR ◇ 32-33 M 5
Itapicuru, Rio ⁓ BR ◇ 30-31 M 5
Itapipoçá ○ BR ◇ 30-31 L 5
Itaquaí ⁓ BR ◇ 32-33 J 3
Itaqui ○ BR ◇ 30-31 J 7
Itauba ○ BR ◇ 30-31 H 5
Itenes = Guaporé, Rio ⁓ BOL
30-31 G 7
Ithaca ○ USA ◇ 22-23 K 4
Itimbiri ⁓ ZRE ♦ 48-49 K 8
Itiquira ○ BR ◇ 30-31 J 8
Itō ○ J ♦ 54-55 Q 5
Itui, Rio ⁓ BR ◇ 30-31 X 4
Ituiutaba ○ BR ◇ 30-31 K 8
Itula ○ ZRE ♦ 50-51 G 2
Itumbiara ○ BR ◇ 30-31 K 8
Ituni ○ GUY ◇ 30-31 H 3
Iturbide ○ MEX ◇ 28-29 K 2
Ituxi, Rio ⁓ BR ◇ 30-31 F 6
Itzamna ⁓ MEX ◇ 28-29 K 1
Itztapa ○ GCA ◇ 28-29 K 1
Iuka ○ USA ◇ 24-25 D 2
Iul'tin ○ RUS ♦ 52-53 h 4
Ivalo ○ FIN ♦ 34-35 R 2

a o GR ◇46-47 K 4
4-35 Q 7
o IND ◆56-57 N 8
atti o IND ◆56-57 L 8
ng ☆ PNG ◆58-59 O 7
Dašt-e ⩦ IR ◆56-57 G 4
azkij zapovednik ⊥ RUS
34-35 U 7
ihae o USA ◇24-25 E 7
ikini ▲ USA ◇24-25 C 6
akawa o NZ ◆60-61 P 7
embwa o Z ◆50-51 G 3
artha Lakes ⌓ CDN ◇18-19 E 6
assi o RI ◆58-59 J 7
ch Peak ▲ USA ◇20-21 F 7
in o MYA ◆54-55 H 7
Reservoir ⌓ USA ◇26-27 J 1
ar He ~ CHN ◆54-55 D 4
☆ BF ◆48-49 E 6
k Island ⌒ USA ◆14-15 H 5
n ~ RI ◆58-59 G 6
pó, Área Indígena ⚔ BR
30-31 J 6
nta o USA ◇26-27 B 1
s ☆ RMM ◆48-49 C 6
a, Pulau ⌒ RI ◆58-59 J 6
eri ☆• TR ◆34-35 T 8
bazua o CDN ◇18-19 F 6
kh Uplands ⩦ KZ ◆52-53 L 8
kstan ■ KZ ◆52-53 J 8
in' ☆•• RUS ◆34-35 V 4
an River ~ CDN ◆14-15 R 4
erün o IR ◆56-57 G 5
umba o ZRE ◆50-51 F 3
ungula o Z ◆50-51 G 5
au o USA ◇24-25 E 8
hole Point ▲ USA ◇24-25 D 8
inekaise ▲•• S ◇36-37 J 3
34-35 P 2
umen o RI ◆58-59 E 8
h ~ PK ◆56-57 J 5
skemét o H ◇40-41 P 5
34-35 P 6
idie o USA ◇20-21 D 5
gwick o CDN ◇18-19 L 5
iri o RI ◆58-59 F 8
ougou o SN ◆48-49 C 6
le Peak ▲ CDN ◆14-15 L 4
le River ~ CDN ◆14-15 L 4
lung o• RC ◆54-55 N 6
ne o USA ◇22-23 M 4
enjhar Lake ⌓•• PK ◆56-57 K 6
etmannshoop ☆ NAM ◆50-51 E 7
alonia ⌒ GR ◇46-47 H 5
34-35 Q 8
amenanu o RI ◆58-59 H 8
ftya o ETH ◆48-49 N 6
gaska o CDN ◇18-19 O 3
ta ou Douka, Bahr ~ TCH
48-49 J 7
th o AUS ◆60-61 J 7
th Arm o CDN ◆14-15 M 3
thville o USA ◇26-27 L 5
zer o USA ◇20-21 C 3
imkujik National Park ⊥ CDN
18-19 M 6 ◆14-15 X 8
kaha o USA ◇24-25 C 7
lafo o ETH ◆48-49 O 7
lifvun, gora ▲ RUS ◆52-53 e 4
llé o RCB ◆50-51 D 2
ller Lake ⌓ CDN ◆14-15 M 4
llet, Cape ▲ CDN ◆14-15 L 2
llett Strait ≈ ◆14-15 N 1
llogg o USA ◇20-21 F 2
lo o TCH ◆48-49 J 7
lowna o CDN ◆14-15 N 7
lso o USA (CA) ◇20-21 G 8
lso o USA (WA) ◇20-21 C 2
m' o RUS ◆34-35 S 3
mbé o RCA ◆48-49 K 8
mbé, Chutes de ~ RCA ◆48-49 K 8
merovo ☆ RUS ◆52-53 O 6
mi o FIN ◆34-35 Q 2
emijoki ~ FIN ◆34-35 R 2
emkara o RUS ◆52-53 Y 6
emmerer o USA ◇20-21 J 5
emp o USA ◇26-27 J 3
emp, Lake ‹ USA ◇26-27 H 3
emp Land ⩦ ANT ◆13 G 6
emp Peninsula ~ ANT ◆13 F 30
emps Bay o BS ◆16-17 L 6
empt, Lac o CDN ◇18-19 G 5
empten (Allgäu) o• D ◇40-41 L 5
34-35 O 6
emptville o CDN ◇18-19 G 6
enai o USA ◆14-15 F 4
enai Fjords National Park ⊥ USA
14-15 F 5
enai Peninsula ~ USA ◆14-15 F 4
enamu River ~ CDN ◇18-19 O 2
enamu River ~ CDN ◇18-19 P 2
enansville o USA ◇24-25 H 6
endall o USA ◇24-25 H 7
16-17 K 5
endall, Mount ▲ NZ ◆60-61 P 8
endall River ~ AUS ◆60-61 J 2
endallville o USA ◇22-23 F 5
endari ☆ RI ◆58-59 H 7
endawangan o RI ◆58-59 F 7
endégué o TCH ◆48-49 J 6
endujhargarh o IND ◆56-57 O 6
enedy o USA ◇26-27 J 5
enema ☆ WAL ◆48-49 C 7
enge o ZRE ◆50-51 E 2
eng Tung o MYA ◆54-55 H 7
enhardt o ZA ◆50-51 F 7
énitra = Al-Q'nitra ☆ MA ◆48-49 D 2
ennebec River ~ USA ◇22-23 O 3
enner o USA ◇26-27 M 4
ennesaw Mountain National Battlefield
Park ∴• USA ◇24-25 F 3
ennett o USA ◇26-27 M 1
ennewick o USA ◇20-21 E 2
14-15 N 7
eno City o CDN ◆14-15 J 4
enora o CDN ◆14-15 S 7
enosha o USA ◇22-23 E 4
14-15 T 8
ensington o CDN ◇18-19 N 5
Kent o USA (OH) ◇22-23 H 5
Kent o USA (OR) ◇20-21 D 3
Kent o USA (TX) ◇26-27 E 4

Kent o USA (WA) ◇20-21 C 2
Kentau o KZ ◆56-57 K 2
Kent Group ⌒ AUS ◆60-61 K 7
Kent Junction o CDN ◇18-19 M 5
Kentland o USA ◇22-23 E 5
Kenton o USA ◇22-23 G 5
Kent Peninsula ⌣ CDN ◆14-15 P 3
Kentucky ▫ USA ◇22-23 E 7
◆16-17 J 3
Kentucky Lake ⌓ USA ◇22-23 D 7
◆16-17 J 3
Kentucky River ~ USA ◇22-23 F 7
Kentville o CDN ◇18-19 M 6
Kentwood o USA ◇26-27 M 4
Kenya ■ EAK ◆50-51 J 1
Kenya, Mount ▲•• EAK ◆50-51 J 2
Kenya National Park, Mount ⊥ EAK
◆50-51 J 2
Keokuk o USA ◇22-23 C 5
Keowee, Lake ⌓ USA ◇24-25 G 2
Keperveem o RUS ◆52-53 e 4
Kępno o PL ◇40-41 O 3
◆34-35 P 5
Keppel Bay ≈ ◆60-61 L 4
Kerala ▫ IND ◆56-57 M 8
Kéran, Parc National de la ⊥ RT
◆48-49 F 6
Kerby o USA ◇20-21 C 4
Kerč o UA ◆34-35 T 6
Kerch = Kerč o UA ◆34-35 T 6
Kerema ☆ PNG ◆58-59 N 8
Kerens o USA ◇26-27 J 3
Kerinci, Gunung ▲ RI ◆58-59 D 7
Kerkenah, Îles de ⌒ TN ◆48-49 H 2
Kerki o TM ◆56-57 K 3
Kérkira ⌒ GR ◇46-47 G 5
◆34-35 P 8
Kerkouane ∴•• TN ◆48-49 H 1
Kermadec Islands ⌒ NZ ◆12 K 5
Kermadec Ridge ≃ ◆60-61 K 6
Kermān ☆• IR ◆56-57 H 4
Kermit o USA ◇26-27 F 4
Kérouané o RG ◆48-49 D 7
Kerrville o USA ◇26-27 H 4
◆16-17 G 4
Kershaw o USA ◇24-25 H 2
Ket' ~ RUS ◆52-53 O 6
Keta o GH ◆48-49 F 7
Ketapang o RI ◆58-59 E 7
Ketchikan o USA ◆14-15 K 5
Ketoj, ostrov ⌒ RUS ◆52-53 b 8
Ketsko-Tymskaja, ravnina ⌣ RUS
◆52-53 N 5
Kettering o USA ◇22-23 F 6
Kettle Falls o USA ◇20-21 E 1
Kettle Range ▲ USA ◇20-21 E 1
Kettle River ~ USA ◇20-21 E 1
Keuka Lake ⌓ USA ◇22-23 K 4
Kewanee o USA ◇22-23 D 5
Kewaunee o USA ◇22-23 E 3
Keweenaw Bay ⌓ USA ◇22-23 D 2
Keweenaw Bay Indian Reservation ⚔ USA
◇22-23 D 2
Keweenaw Peninsula ⌣ USA
◇22-23 D 2 ◆14-15 T 7
Key Largo o USA ◇24-25 H 7
◆16-17 K 5
Key Like Mine o CDN ◆14-15 P 5
Keyser o USA ◇22-23 J 6
Keystone Lake ⌓ USA ◇26-27 J 1
Keysville o USA ◇22-23 J 7
Key West o• USA ◇24-25 H 7
◆16-17 K 6
Kežma o RUS ◆52-53 R 6
Khadwa o IND ◆56-57 M 6
Khairpur o• PK ◆56-57 K 5
Khakassia ▫ RUS ◆52-53 O 7
Khakhea o RB ◆50-51 F 6
Khalij Surt ≈ ◆48-49 J 2
Khambhat o IND ◆56-57 L 6
Khambhāt, Gulf of ≈ ◆56-57 L 6
Khami Ruins ∴•• ZW ◆50-51 G 6
Khāmis, ash-Shallāl al- = 5th Cataract ~
SUD ◆48-49 M 5
Khānewāl o PK ◆56-57 L 4
Khanka, Ozero = Hanka, ozero ⌓ RUS
◆52-53 X 8
Khānpur o PK ◆56-57 L 5
Kharagpur o IND ◆56-57 O 6
Kharga = al-Ḥāriğa ☆• ET ◆48-49 M 4
Khârga, El = Ḥāriğa, al- ☆• ET
◆48-49 M3
Khargon o IND ◆56-57 M 6
Kharkiv = Charkiv o UA ◆34-35 T 6
Khartoum = al-Ḥarṭūm ★•• SUD
◆48-49 M 5
Khartoum North = Al-Ḥarṭūm Baḥri SUD
◆48-49 M 5
Khashm al-Qirbah o SUD ◆48-49 N 6
Khatt Atoui ~ RIM ◆48-49 B 4
Kherson = Cherson ☆• UA ◆34-35 S 6
Khmel'nyts'kyj = Chmel'nyc'kyj ☆ UA
◆34-35 R 6
Khon Kaen o THA ◆58-59 D 3
Khouribga ☆ MA ◆48-49 D 2
Khudzhand = Ḥuğand ☆ TJ
◆56-57 K 2
Khulna o BD ◆56-57 O 6
Khushāb o PK ◆56-57 L 4
Khuzdār o PK ◆56-57 K 5
Kiambi o ZRE ◆50-51 G 3
Kiamichi Mountain ▲ USA ◇26-27 K 2
Kiamichi River ~ USA ◇26-27 K 2
Kibali ~ ZRE ◆48-49 M 8
Kibangou o RCB ◆50-51 D 2
Kibaya o EAT ◆50-51 J 3
Kibombo o ZRE ◆50-51 G 2
Kibondo o EAT ◆50-51 H 2
Kibris ▫ TR ◆34-35 S 8
Kibwezi o EAK ◆50-51 J 2
Kickapoo Indian Caverns ∴• USA
◇22-23 C 4
Kičmengskij Gorodok ☆ RUS
◆34-35 V 4
Kidal o RMM ◆48-49 F 5
Kidatu o EAT ◆50-51 J 3
Kidepo National Park ⊥ EAU
◆48-49 M 8
Kidira o SN ◆48-49 C 6
Kiel ☆• D ◇40-41 L 1 ◆34-35 O 5
Kielce ☆• PL ◇40-41 Q 3
◆34-35 Q 5

Kiev = Kyjiv ★••• UA ◆34-35 S 5
Kiffa ☆ RIM ◆48-49 C 5
Kigali ★ RWA ◆50-51 H 2
Kigoma ☆ EAT ◆50-51 G 2
Kihei o USA ◇24-25 D 7
Kikori o PNG ◆58-59 M 8
Kikori River ~ PNG ◆58-59 M 8
Kikwit o ZRE ◆50-51 E 3
Kilauea Crater • USA ◇24-25 E 8
Kilauea Lighthouse • USA ◇24-25 C 6
Kilbuck Mountains ▲ USA ◆14-15 D 4
Kilgore o USA ◇26-27 K 3
Kili Bulak o CHN ◆54-55 G 5
Kilifi o EAK ◆50-51 J 2
Kilimanjaro ▲•• EAT ◆50-51 J 2
Kilimanjaro National Park ⊥••• EAT
◆50-51 J 2
Killaloe Station o CDN ◇18-19 F 6
Killarney o CDN ◇18-19 D 6
Killarney Provincial Park ⊥ CDN
◇18-19 D 5
Killeen o USA ◇26-27 J 4
◆16-17 G 4
Killington Peak ▲ USA ◇22-23 M 4
Kilombero ~ EAT ◆50-51 J 3
Kilwa o ZRE ◆50-51 G 3
Kilwa Kisiwani ∴••• EAT ◆50-51 J 3
Kilwa Kivinje o EAT ◆50-51 J 3
Kim o USA ◇26-27 F 1
Kimba o AUS ◆60-61 H 6
Kimbe ☆ PNG ◆58-59 O 8
Kimberley ⩦ AUS ◆60-61 F 3
Kimberley ☆ ZA ◆50-51 F 7
Kimchaek o KOR ◆54-55 O 3
Kinabalu, Gunung ▲•• MAL
◆58-59 G 5
Kincardine o CDN ◇18-19 D 6
Kinchega National Park ⊥ AUS
◆60-61 J 6
Kinchil o MEX ◇28-29 K 1
Kinder o USA ◇26-27 L 4
Kindia ☆ RG ◆48-49 C 6
Kindu o ZRE ◆50-51 G 2
Kineshma = Kinešma ☆ RUS
◇42-43 S 3 ◆34-35 U 4
Kinešma ☆ RUS ◇42-43 S 3
◆34-35 U 4
King, Cayo ⌒ NIC ◇28-29 C 5
King, Lake ⌓ AUS ◆60-61 E 5
Kingaroy o AUS ◆60-61 L 5
King Christian Island ⌒ CDN
◆14-15 Q 1
King Christian IX Land = Kong Christian IX
Land ⩦ GRØ ◆14-15 d 3
King City o USA ◇20-21 D 7
King Edward VIIth Gulf ≈ ◆13 G 6
Kingfisher o USA ◇26-27 J 2
King Frederik IX Land = Kong Frederik IX
Land ⩦ GRØ ◆14-15 a 3
King Frederik VI Coast = Kong Frederik VI
Kyst ⩦ GRØ ◆14-15 c 4
King George Island ⌒ ANT ◆13 G 31
King George Islands ⌒ CDN
◆14-15 V 5
King George Sound ≈ ◆60-61 D 7
King George VIth Sound ≈ ◆13 F 30
King George Vth Land ⩦ ANT
◆13 F 16
King Island ⌒ AUS ◆60-61 J 7
King Island ⌒ USA ◆14-15 C 4
King Lear ▲ USA ◇20-21 E 5
King Leopold Ranges ▲ AUS
◆60-61 E 3
Kingman o USA (AZ) ◇20-21 G 8
Kingman o USA (KS) ◇26-27 H 1
King Mountain ▲ USA ◇26-27 F 4
Kingoonya o AUS ◆60-61 H 6
Kings Canyon National Park ⊥ USA
◇20-21 E 7
Kingscote o AUS ◆60-61 H 7
Kings Cove o CDN ◇18-19 S 4
Kings Landing Historical Settlement ∴•
CDN ◇18-19 L 6
Kings Mountain o USA ◇24-25 H 2
Kings Mountain National Military Park ∴•
USA ◇24-25 H 2
King Sound ≈ ◆60-61 E 3
Kings Peak ▲ USA ◇20-21 J 5
◆16-17 D 2
Kingsport o USA ◇24-25 G 1
Kingston o AUS ◆60-61 K 8
Kingston o CDN ◇18-19 F 6
◆14-15 V 8
Kingston ★• JA ◆16-17 L 7
Kingston o USA (NY) ◇22-23 M 5
Kingston o USA (PA) ◇22-23 L 5
Kingston S.E. o AUS ◆60-61 H 7
Kingston upon Hull o• GB ◇38-39 G 5
◆34-35 L 5
Kingstown ★ WV ◆16-17 O 8
Kingstree o USA ◇24-25 J 3
Kings Trough ≃ ◆34-35 G 7
Kingsville o USA ◇26-27 J 6
◆16-17 G 5
King William Island ⌒ CDN ◆14-15 R 3
Kingwood o USA ◇22-23 J 6
Kinkala ☆ RCB ◆50-51 D 2
Kinmundy o USA ◇22-23 D 6
Kinoosao o CDN ◆14-15 Q 5
Kinshasa ★• ZRE ◆50-51 E 2
Kinston o USA ◇24-25 K 2
◆16-17 L 3
Kintampo o GH ◆48-49 E 7
Kintore, Mount ▲ AUS ◆60-61 G 5
Kinyeti ▲ SUD ◆48-49 M 8
Kiosk o CDN ◇18-19 E 5
Kiowa o USA (KS) ◇26-27 H 1
Kiowa o USA (OK) ◇26-27 K 2
Kipawa, Lac ⌓ CDN ◇18-19 E 5
Kipili o EAT ◆50-51 H 3
Kirbyville o USA ◇26-27 L 4
Kirenga ~ RUS ◆52-53 S 6
Kirensk ☆ RUS ◆52-53 S 6
Kirikkale ☆ TR ◆34-35 S 8
Kirit o SP ◆48-49 P 7
Kiritimati Island ⌒ KIB ◆12 M 2
Kiriwina Island ⌒ PNG ◆58-59 O 8
Kirkenes o N ◇36-37 P 2
◆34-35 S 2
Kirkland Lake o• CDN ◇18-19 E 4
◆14-15 V 7
Kırklareli ☆ TR ◆34-35 R 7

Kirksville o USA ◆16-17 H 2
Kirkük ☆ IRQ ◆56-57 E 3
Kirkwall o• GB ◇38-39 F 2
◆34-35 L 4
Kirkwood o USA ◇22-23 C 6
Kirov o RUS ◆34-35 V 4
Kirovohrad ☆ UA ◆34-35 S 6
Kırşehir ☆ TR ◆34-35 S 8
Kiruna o• S ◇36-37 K 3
◆34-35 Q 2
Kiš, Ğažire-ye ⌒ IR ◆56-57 G 5
Kisangani ☆ ZRE ◆50-51 G 1
Kiselëvsk o RUS ◆52-53 O 7
Kiselevsk = Kiselëvsk o RUS
◆52-53 O 7
Kishtwar o• IND ◆56-57 M 4
Kisi o WAN ◆48-49 F 7
Kisigo Game Reserve ⊥ EAT
◆50-51 H 3
Kisii o EAK ◆50-51 H 2
Kismaanyo ☆ SP ◆50-51 K 2
Kismet o USA ◇26-27 G 1
Kissidougou o RG ◆48-49 C 7
Kissimmee, Lake ⌓ USA ◇24-25 H 6
Kissimmee River ~ USA ◇24-25 H 6
Kisumu ☆ EAK ◆50-51 H 2
Kita o RMM ◆48-49 D 6
Kita-lō-shima ⌒ J ◆54-55 R 6
Kitakyūshū o J ◆54-55 P 5
Kitale o EAK ◆50-51 J 1
Kitami o J ◆54-55 R 3
Kitchener o CDN ◇18-19 D 7
◆14-15 U 8
Kitchigama, Rivière ~ CDN ◇18-19 E 3
Kitgum o EAU ◆48-49 M 8
Kithira ⌒ GR ◇46-47 J 6
◆34-35 Q 8
Kitimat o CDN ◆14-15 L 6
Kittanning o USA ◇22-23 J 5
Kittery o USA ◇22-23 N 4
Kitt Peak National Observatory • USA
◇20-21 J 9
Kitty Hawk o USA ◇24-25 L 1
Kitui o EAK ◆50-51 J 2
Kitwe o Z ◆50-51 G 4
Kiunga o PNG ◆58-59 M 8
Kivu, Lac ⌓ ZRE ◆50-51 G 2
Kızılırmak ~ TR ◆34-35 T 8
Kizilkum ⩦ UZ ◆56-57 J 2
Kizyl Arvat o TM ◆56-57 H 3
Kjustendil o• BG ◆34-35 Q 7
Kladno o CZ ◇40-41 N 3
◆34-35 O 5
Klagenfurt ☆ A ◇40-41 N 5
◆34-35 O 6
Klaipėda ☆•• LT ◇42-43 G 4
◆34-35 Q 4
Klamath o USA ◇20-21 B 5
Klamath Falls o USA ◇20-21 D 4
◆14-15 M 8
Klamath Mountains ▲ USA
◇20-21 C 5 ◆14-15 M 8
Klamath River ~ USA ◇20-21 C 5
◆14-15 M 8
Klang o MAL ◆58-59 D 6
Klarälven ~ S ◇36-37 F 6
◆34-35 O 3
Kle o LB ◆48-49 C 7
Klein Karoo = Little Karoo ⩦ ZA
◆50-51 F 8
Klerksdorp o ZA ◆50-51 G 7
Klickitat River ~ USA ◇20-21 D 2
Klincy o RUS ◇42-43 N 5
◆34-35 S 5
Ključevskaja Sopka, vulkan ▲ RUS
◆52-53 d 6
Ključi o RUS ◆52-53 d 6
Klondike Plateau ▲ CDN ◆14-15 H 4
Kluane Lake ⌓ CDN ◆14-15 J 4
Kluane National Park=Tatshenshini-Alsek
Kluane National Park ⊥••• CDN
◆14-15 H 4
Knewstubb Lake ⌓ CDN ◆14-15 M 6
Knippa o USA ◇26-27 H 5
Knob, Cape ▲ AUS ◆60-61 D 6
Knolls o USA ◇20-21 H 5
Knowles, Cape ▲ ANT ◆13 F 30
Knox o USA ◇22-23 E 5
Knox Land ⩦ ANT ◆13 G 11
Knoxville o USA (PA) ◇22-23 K 5
Knoxville o USA (TN) ◇24-25 G 2
◆16-17 K 3
Knud Rasmussen Land ⩦ GRØ
◆14-15 Z 1
Knysna o ZA ◆50-51 F 8
Koalla o BF ◆48-49 E 6
Kobe ☆ J ◆54-55 Q 5
Kobe o RI ◆58-59 J 6
København ★•• DK ◇36-37 E 9
◆34-35 O 4
Kobroor, Pulau ⌒ RI ◆58-59 K 8
Kobuk River ~ USA ◆14-15 E 3
Kobuk Valley National Park ⊥ USA
◆14-15 E 3
Kocaeli (İzmit) ☆ TR ◆34-35 R 7
Kočečum ~ RUS ◆52-53 R 4
Kōchi ☆• J ◆54-55 P 5
Koch Island ⌒ CDN ◆14-15 V 3
Koch Peak ▲ USA ◇20-21 J 3
Kočubej o RUS ◆34-35 V 7
Kodiak o USA ◆14-15 F 5
Kodiak Island ⌒ USA ◆14-15 F 5
Kodok o SUD ◆48-49 M 7
Koës o NAM ◆50-51 E 7
Koettlitz Glacier ⊂ ANT ◆13 F 16
Kofa National Wildlife Refuge ⊥ USA
◇20-21 G 9
Koforidua ☆ GH ◆48-49 E 7
Kōfu ☆ J ◆54-55 Q 4
Kogalym o RUS ◆52-53 L 5
Kohāt o• PK ◆56-57 L 4
Kohima ☆•• IND ◆56-57 P 5
Kohler Range ▲ ANT ◆13 F 25
Kohtla-Järve o•• EST ◇42-43 K 2
◆34-35 R 4
Kohunlich ∴•• MEX ◇28-29 K 2
Koidu o WAL ◆48-49 C 7
Kojonup o AUS ◆60-61 D 6
Kokkola o FIN ◆34-35 Q 3
Kokomo o USA ◇22-23 E 5
Kökpekti o KZ ◆54-55 E 2
Kökšetau ☆ KZ ◆52-53 K 7

Koksoak, Rivière ~ CDN ◆14-15 X 5
Kokstad o ZA ◆50-51 G 8
Kola, Pulau ⌒ RI ◆58-59 K 8
Kolaka o RI ◆58-59 H 7
Kola Peninsula ⌣ RUS ◆34-35 S 2
Kolbeinsey ⌒ IS ◆34-35 H 2
Kolbio o EAK ◆50-51 K 2
Kolda ☆ SN ◆48-49 C 6
Kolendo, Mount ▲ AUS ◆60-61 H 6
Kolguev, ostrov ⌒ RUS ◆52-53 F 4
Kolhāpur o•• IND ◆56-57 L 7
Koljučinskaja guba ≈ ◆52-53 j 4
Koloa o USA ◇24-25 C 7
Kolokani o RMM ◆48-49 D 6
Kolomna ☆•• RUS ◇42-43 Q 4
◆34-35 T 4
Kolonedale o RI ◆58-59 H 7
Kolonia = Palikir ★ FSM ◆12 G 2
Kolpaševo ☆ RUS ◆52-53 N 6
Kolpino o RUS ◇42-43 M 2
◆34-35 S 4
Kolwezi o ZRE ◆50-51 G 4
Kolyma ~ RUS ◆52-53 b 4
Kolymskaja nizmennost' ⌣ RUS
◆52-53 b 4
Kolymskoe nagor'e ▲ RUS ◆52-53 b 5
Kolymskye Nagor'ye = Kolymskoe nagor'e
▲ RUS ◆52-53 b 5
Komandorskie ostrova RUS ◆10-11 Q 3
Komering ~ RI ◆58-59 D 7
Komi ▫ RUS ◆52-53 G 5
Komono o RCB ◆50-51 D 2
Komoran, Pulau ⌒ RI ◆58-59 L 8
Komotini o GR ◇46-47 K 4
◆34-35 R 7
Komsomolec, ostrov ⌒ RUS
◆52-53 P 1
Komsomol'sk-na-Amure o• RUS
◆52-53 Y 7
Komsomol'sk na Amure = Komsomol'sk-na-
Amure o• RUS ◆52-53 Y 7
Komsomol'skoj Pravdy, ostrova ⌒ RUS
◆52-53 S 2
Kona o RMM ◆48-49 E 6
Konaweha ~ RI ◆58-59 H 7
Konda ~ RUS ◆52-53 K 6
Kondoa o EAT ◆50-51 J 2
Koné ☆• F ◆60-61 N 4
Konebor o RUS ◆52-53 H 5
Köneürgenč ☆ TM ◆56-57 H 2
Kong Christian IX Land ⩦ GRØ
◆14-15 d 3
Kong Frederik IX Land ⩦ GRØ
◆14-15 a 3
Kong Frederik VI Kyst ⩦ GRØ
◆14-15 c 4
Kong Leopold og Dronning Astrid land ⩦
ANT ◆13 F 9
Kongolo o ZRE ◆50-51 G 3
Kongur Shan ▲ CHN ◆54-55 D 4
Koni, poluostrov ⌣ RUS ◆52-53 b 6
Konoša o RUS ◇42-43 R 1
◆34-35 U 3
Konotop o UA ◆34-35 S 5
Konta o IND ◆56-57 N 7
Kontagora o WAN ◆48-49 G 6
Kontcha o CAM ◆48-49 H 7
Kontinemo, Área Indígena ⚔ BR
◆30-31 J 5
Kon Tum o VN ◆58-59 E 4
Konya ☆•• TR ◆34-35 S 8
Konžakovskij Kamen', gora ▲ RUS
◆34-35 X 4
Koocanusa, Lake ⌓ USA ◇20-21 G 1
Kookooligit Mountains ▲ USA
◆14-15 B 4
Koolyanobbing o AUS ◆60-61 D 6
Koosharem o USA ◇20-21 J 6
Kooskia o USA ◇20-21 G 2
Kootenay River ~ CDN ◆14-15 N 6
Ko Phangan ⌒ THA ◆58-59 D 5
Ko Phuket ⌒•• THA ◆58-59 C 5
Koppe Dāg ▲ IR ◆56-57 H 3
K'orahē o ETH ◆48-49 O 7
K'oran, Ē o ETH ◆48-49 O 7
Kora National Park ⊥ EAK ◆50-51 J 2
Korbu, Gunung ▲ MAL ◆58-59 D 6
Korçë ☆•• AL ◇46-47 H 4
◆34-35 Q 7
Kordofan ⩦ SUD ◆48-49 L 6
Korea Bay ≈ ◆54-55 N 4
Korea Strait ≈ ◆54-55 O 5
Korf o RUS ◆52-53 e 5
Korfa, zaliv ≈ ◆52-53 e 5
Korhogo ☆• CI ◆48-49 D 7
Kórinthos o GR ◇46-47 J 6
◆34-35 Q 8
Korjakskaja Sopka, vulkan ▲ RUS
◆52-53 c 7
Korjakskoe nagor'e ▲ RUS ◆52-53 e 5
Korla o CHN ◆54-55 F 3
Koro ⌒ FJI ◆60-61 Q 3
Koroba o PNG ◆58-59 M 8
Koronadal o RP ◆58-59 H 5
Koror ☆ PAL ◆58-59 K 5
Koro Sea ≈ ◆60-61 Q 3
Korosten' o UA ◆34-35 R 5
Korotčaevo o RUS ◆52-53 M 4
Korsakow o RUS ◆52-53 Z 8
Korup, Park National de ⊥ CAM
◆48-49 G 7
Ko Samui ⌒•• THA ◆58-59 D 5
Kosciusko o USA ◇24-25 D 3
Kosciusko, Mount ▲ AUS ◆60-61 K 7
Kosciusko National Park ⊥ AUS
◆60-61 K 7
Kōshetau = Kökšetau ☆ KZ
◆52-53 K 7
Košice o SK ◇40-41 Q 4
◆34-35 Q 6
Koskaecodde Lake ⌓ CDN ◇18-19 R 5
Kosong o KOR ◆54-55 O 4
Kossou, Lac de ⊂ CI ◆48-49 D 7
Kostanaj ☆ KZ ◆52-53 J 7
Kostroma ☆• RUS ◇42-43 R 3
◆34-35 U 4
Kostyantynivka = Južnoukrains'k =
Južnoukrains'k o UA ◆34-35 T 6
Koszalin ☆• PL ◇40-41 O 1
◆34-35 P 5
Kota o IND (MAP) ◆56-57 N 6
Kota o IND (RAJ) ◆56-57 M 5

Kotabaru o RI ◆58-59 G 7
Kota Bharu ☆ MAL ◆58-59 D 5
Kota Bumi o RI ◆58-59 D 7
Kota Kinabalu ☆• MAL ◆58-59 G 5
Kotamobagu o RI ◆58-59 H 6
Kot Diji o•• PK ◆56-57 K 5
Kotel'nyj, ostrov ⌒ RUS ◆52-53 Y 2
Kotido o EAU ◆48-49 M 8
Kotlas ☆ RUS ◆52-53 F 5
Kottagūdem o IND ◆56-57 N 7
Kotto ~ RCA ◆48-49 K 7
Kotuj ~ RUS ◆52-53 R 3
Kotzebue o USA ◆14-15 D 3
Kotzebue Sound ≈ ◆14-15 D 3
Kouango o RCA ◆48-49 J 7
Kouchibouguac o CDN ◇18-19 M 5
Kouchibouguac National Park ⊥ CDN
◇18-19 M 5
Koudougou ☆ BF ◆48-49 E 6
Koukdjuak, Great Plain of the ⩦ CDN
◆14-15 W 3
Koulamoutou ☆ G ◆50-51 D 2
Koulikoro o RMM ◆48-49 D 6
Koundara o RG ◆48-49 C 6
Kountze o USA ◇26-27 K 4
Koupéla o BF ◆48-49 E 6
Kourou o F ◆30-31 J 3
Kouroussa o RG ◆48-49 D 6
Koussi, Emi ▲ TCH ◆48-49 J 5
Koutiala o RMM ◆48-49 D 6
Kouyou ~ RCB ◆50-51 E 2
Kovil' o UA ◆34-35 Q 6
Kovrov ☆ RUS ◇42-43 R 3
◆34-35 U 4
Koyukuk National Wildlife Refuge ⊥ USA
◆14-15 E 3
Koyukuk River ~ USA ◆14-15 E 3
Kozáni ☆• GR ◇46-47 H 4
◆34-35 Q 7
Kpalimé o• RT ◆48-49 F 7
Krâchéh o K ◆58-59 E 4
Kragujevac o• YU ◇46-47 H 2
◆34-35 Q 7
Kraków ☆••• PL ◇40-41 P 3
◆34-35 P 5
Kralendijk o NA ◆16-17 N 8
Kraljevo o YU ◇46-47 H 3
◆34-35 Q 7
Kramators'k o UA ◆34-35 T 6
Kraolândia, Área Indígena ⚔ BR
◆30-31 K 6
Krasneno o RUS ◆52-53 f 5
Krasnodar ☆• RUS ◆34-35 T 6
Krasnoj Armii, proliv ≈ ◆52-53 P 2
Krasnojarsk ☆• RUS ◆52-53 P 6
Krasnojarskoe, vodohranilišče ⌓ RUS
◆52-53 P 7
Krasnokamensk ☆ RUS ◆52-53 U 7
Krasnokamsk o RUS ◆34-35 X 4
Krasnoyarsk = Krasnojarsk ☆• RUS
◆52-53 P 6
Kremenchuk = Kremenčuk o UA
◆34-35 S 6
Kremenčuk o UA ◆34-35 S 6
Krenitzin Islands ⌒ USA ◆14-15 C 6
Kresta, zaliv ≈ ◆52-53 h 4
Kribi o• CAM ◆48-49 G 8
Krishna ~ IND ◆56-57 M 7
Krishnagiri o IND ◆56-57 M 8
Kristiansand ☆ N ◇36-37 C 7
◆34-35 N 4
Kristiansund ☆ N ◇36-37 C 5
◆34-35 N 3
Krivyj Rih o UA ◆34-35 S 6
Krohnwodoke o LB ◆48-49 D 8
Krông Kaôh Kŏng o K ◆58-59 D 4
Kronockij zaliv ≈ ◆52-53 d 7
Kronockij zapovednik ⊥ RUS
◆52-53 d 7
Kronockoe, ozero ⌓ RUS ◆52-53 d 7
Kronprinsesse Mærtha land ⩦ ANT
◆13 F 35
Kronprins Olav land ⩦ ANT ◆13 G 5
Kroonstad o ZA ◆50-51 G 7
Kropotkin o RUS ◆34-35 U 6
Krotz Springs o USA ◇26-27 M 4
Kruger National Park ⊥•• ZA
◆50-51 H 6
Krugersdorp o ZA ◆50-51 G 7
Krui o RI ◆58-59 D 8
Kruis, Kaap = Cross, Cape ▲ NAM
◆50-51 D 6
Kryvyy Rih = Krivyj Rih o UA
◆34-35 S 6
'Ksan Indian Village ••• CDN ◆14-15 L 5
Kuala Dungun o• MAL ◆58-59 D 6
Kualakapus o RI ◆58-59 F 7
Kuala Lumpur ★•• MAL ◆58-59 D 6
Kuala Terengganu ☆• MAL
◆58-59 D 5
Kuantan ☆•• MAL ◆58-59 D 6
Kuching ☆• MAL ◆58-59 F 6
Kudat o MAL ◆58-59 G 5
Kudus o• RI ◆58-59 F 8
Kufra, Wāhāt al ⊥ LAR ◆48-49 K 4
Kūh-e Bahūn ▲ IR ◆56-57 H 5
Kūh-e Vāhān ▲ AFG ◆56-57 L 3
Kuiseb Canyon ⌣•• NAM ◆50-51 E 6
Kuito ☆ ANG ◆50-51 E 4
Kujbyšev ☆• RUS ◆52-53 M 6
Kujdusun o RUS ◆52-53 Z 5
Kukawa o WAN ◆48-49 H 6
Kular, hrebet ▲ RUS ◆52-53 X 4
Kulgera o AUS ◆60-61 G 5
Kulim o MAL ◆58-59 D 5
Kulin o AUS ◆60-61 D 6
Kuljab ☆ TJ ◆56-57 K 3
Kulsary ☆ KZ ◆34-35 W 6
Kulu ☆ TR ◆34-35 S 8
Kulunda ☆ RUS ◆52-53 M 7
Kulungu o ZRE ◆50-51 E 2
Kumakahi, Cape ▲ USA ◇24-25 E 8
Kumamba, Kepulauan ⌒ RI ◆58-59 L 7
Kumamoto ☆• J ◆54-55 P 5
Kumanovo o• MK ◇46-47 H 3
◆34-35 Q 7
Kumarina Roadhouse o AUS
◆60-61 D 4
Kumasi ☆••• GH ◆48-49 E 7
Kumayri = Gjumri o AM ◆34-35 U 7
Kumba o CAM ◆48-49 G 8
Kumbakonam o IND ◆56-57 M 8

Kumbe o RI ◆58-59 M 8
Kumon Taungdan ▲ MYA ◆54-55 H 6
Kumta o IND ◆56-57 L 8
Kumukahi, Cape ▲ USA ◇24-25 E 8
Kuna Cave ∴• USA ◇20-21 F 4
Kunašir, ostrov ⌒ RUS ◆54-55 S 3
Kundelungu, Parc National de ⊥ ZRE
◆50-51 G 4
Kunduz ☆• AFG ◆56-57 K 3
Kunene ~ NAM ◆50-51 D 5
Kŭngirod o UZ ◆56-57 H 2
Kungu o ZRE ◆48-49 J 8
Kungur ☆ RUS ◆34-35 X 4
Kunlun Shan ▲ CHN ◆54-55 D 4
Kunming ☆• CHN ◆54-55 J 6
Kunsan o ROK ◆54-55 O 4
Kununurra o AUS ◆60-61 F 3
Kuonamka, Bol'šaja ~ RUS ◆52-53 T 3
Kuopio ☆ FIN ◆34-35 R 3
Kupang ☆ RI ◆58-59 H 9
Kupiano o PNG ◆58-59 N 9
Kupreanof Island ⌒ USA ◆14-15 K 5
Kuqa o CHN ◆54-55 E 3
Kura ~ AZ ◆34-35 V 7
Kura = Kür ~ AZ ◆34-35 V 7
Küre Dağları ▲ TR ◆34-35 S 7
Kurejka ~ RUS ◆52-53 P 4
Kurejskoe vodohranilišče ‹ RUS
◆52-53 O 4
Kuressaare o•• EST ◇42-43 H 2
◆34-35 Q 4
Kurgan ☆ RUS ◆52-53 K 6
Kurgan-Tjube ☆ TJ ◆56-57 K 3
Kuril Basin ≃ ◆10-11 O 4
Kuril'sk o RUS ◆52-53 a 8
Kuril'skaja kotlovina ≃ ◆52-53 a 8
Kuril Trench ≃ ◆52-53 a 9
Kurinwás, Río ~ NIC ◇28-29 B 5
Kurmuk o SUD ◆48-49 M 6
Kurnool o IND ◆56-57 M 7
Kuror, Ğabal ▲ SUD ◆48-49 M 4
Kursk o RUS ◆34-35 T 5
Kuruktag ▲ CHN ◆54-55 F 3
Kuruman o ZA (CAP) ◆50-51 F 7
Kuruman ~ ZA ◆50-51 F 7
Kurumkan ☆ RUS ◆52-53 T 7
Kurunegala o CL ◆56-57 N 9
Kushiro o J ◆54-55 R 3
Kusiwigasi, Mount ▲ PNG ◆58-59 M 7
Kuskokwim Bay ≈ ◆14-15 D 5
Kuskokwim Mountains ▲ USA
◆14-15 E 4
Kuskokwim River ~ USA ◆14-15 D 4
Kusmuryn o KZ ◆52-53 J 7
Kusti ☆ SUD ◆48-49 M 6
Kūt, al- ☆ IRQ ◆56-57 F 4
Kütahya ☆ TR ◆34-35 R 8
Kutaisi o• GE ◆34-35 U 7
K'ut'aisi = Kutaisi o• GE ◆34-35 U 7
Kutana o RUS ◆52-53 X 6
Kutop'jugan o RUS ◆52-53 L 4
Kutse Game Reserve ⊥ RB ◆50-51 F 6
Kutu o ZRE ◆50-51 E 2
Kuujjuaq o CDN ◆14-15 X 5
Kuusamo o FIN ◆34-35 R 2
Kuwait ■ KWT ◆56-57 F 5
Kuwait, al- ★ KWT ◆56-57 F 5
Kuybyshevskoye Vodokhranilishche =
Samarskoe vodohranilišč ‹ RUS
◆34-35 V 5
Kuytun o CHN ◆54-55 E 3
Kuzneck o RUS ◆34-35 V 5
Kvichak Bay ≈ ◆14-15 E 5
Kvitøya ⌒ N ◆13 A 15
Kwadacha Wilderness Provincial Park ⊥
CDN ◆14-15 L 5
Kwamouth o ZRE ◆50-51 E 2
Kwangju o ROK ◆54-55 O 4
Kwango ~ ZRE ◆50-51 E 3
Kwania, Lake ⌓ EAU ◆50-51 H 1
Kwara ▫ WAN ◆48-49 F 7
Kwekwe o ZW ◆50-51 G 5
Kwenge ~ ZRE ◆50-51 E 3
Kwiambana Game Reserve ⊥ WAN
◆48-49 G 6
Kwilu ~ ZRE ◆50-51 E 3
Kwinana o AUS ◆60-61 D 6
Kyancutta o AUS ◆60-61 H 6
Kyaukme o MYA ◆54-55 H 7
Kyaukpyu o MYA ◆58-59 B 3
Kyjiv ★••• UA ◆34-35 S 5
Kykotsmovi o USA ◇26-27 B 2
Kynuna o AUS ◆60-61 J 4
Kyoga, Lake ⌓ EAU ◆50-51 H 1
Kyōto ☆•• J ◆54-55 Q 5
Kyren o RUS ◆52-53 R 7
Kyrgyzstan ■ KS ◆56-57 L 2
Kystyk, plato ▲ RUS ◆52-53 V 3
Kytyl-Djura o RUS ◆52-53 W 5
Kyūshū ⌒ J ◆54-55 P 5
Kyushu-Palau Ridge ≃ ◆54-55 P 6
Kyzyl ☆ RUS ◆52-53 P 7
Kyzylorda ☆ KZ ◆56-57 K 2
Kyzyltu ☆ KZ ◆52-53 L 7

L

Laascaanood o SP ◆48-49 P 7
Laasqoray o SP ◆48-49 P 6
Laayoune = Al-'Ayun ☆ WSA
◆48-49 C 3
Labasa o FJI ◆60-61 Q 3
Labbezzanga o RMM ◆48-49 F 6
Labdah ∴•• LAR ◆48-49 H 2
Labé ☆ RG ◆48-49 C 6
Labelle o CDN ◇18-19 G 5
Labná ∴• MEX ◇28-29 K 1
Laboulaye o RA ◆32-33 K 4
Labrador ⩦ CDN ◆14-15 W 5
Labrador, Cape ▲ CDN ◆14-15 Y 4
Labrador, Coast of ⩦ CDN ◆14-15 Y 5
Labrador Basin ≃ ◆14-15 a 5
Labrador City o CDN ◇18-19 L 2
◆14-15 X 6
Labrador Sea ≈ ◆14-15 Z 4
Lábrea o BR ◆30-31 G 6
Labrieville o CDN ◇18-19 K 4
Lacanau o F ◇38-39 G 9
◆34-35 L 6

Kavála — Lacanau 79

Lacanau-Océan ○ F ◇ 38-39 G 9 ◆ 34-35 L 6
Lacandón, Sierra del ▲ MEX ◇ 28-29 J 3
Lacanja ○ MEX (CHI) ◇ 28-29 J 3
Lacanjá ∴• MEX (CHI) ◇ 28-29 J 3
Lacantún, Río ~ MEX ◇ 28-29 J 3
Lacassine National Wildlife Refuge ⊥ USA ◇ 26-27 L 5
Lacaune ○ F ◇ 38-39 J 10 ◆ 34-35 M 7
Laccadive Islands = Lakshadweep ⌒ IND ◆ 56-57 L 9
Lac Courte Oreilles Indian Reservation ⚔ USA ◇ 22-23 C 3
Lac du Flambeau Indian Reservation ⚔ USA ◇ 22-23 D 3
Lac-Édouard ○ CDN ◇ 18-19 H 5
Lacey ○ USA ◇ 20-21 C 2
Lac-Humqui ○ CDN ◇ 18-19 L 4
Lachute ○ CDN ◇ 18-19 G 6
Lac-Mégantic ○ CDN ◇ 18-19 J 6
Laconia ○ USA ◇ 22-23 N 4
Lacrosse ○ USA ◇ 20-21 F 2
La Crosse ○ USA ◇ 22-23 C 4 ◆ 16-17 H 2
Lac-Saguay ○ CDN ◇ 18-19 G 5
Lac Seul ○ CDN ◆ 14-15 S 6
La Cueva ○ USA ◇ 26-27 D 2
Lādiqīya, al- ☆ SYR ◆ 56-57 D 3
Ladožskoe ozero ○ RUS ◆ 34-35 S 3
Ladrones, Islas ⌒ PA ◇ 28-29 C 8
Lady Evelyn Lake ○ CDN ◇ 18-19 D 5
Lady Evelyn Smoothwater Provincial Park ⊥ CDN ◇ 18-19 D 5
Lady Newnes Ice Shelf ⊂ ANT ◆ 13 F 18
Ladysmith ○ ZA ◆ 50-51 G 7
Lae ☆ PNG ◆ 58-59 N 8
Lafayette ○ USA (IN) ◇ 22-23 E 5 ◆ 16-17 J 2
Lafayette ○ USA (TN) ◇ 24-25 E 1
Lafayette ○• USA (LA) ◇ 26-27 L 4 ◆ 16-17 H 4
Lafayette, Mount ▲ USA ◇ 22-23 N 3
Lafia ○ WAN ◆ 48-49 G 7
Laflamme, Rivière ~ CDN ◇ 18-19 F 4
Lafoi, Chute de la ~·· ZRE ◆ 50-51 G 4
La Fraternidad, Parque Nacional ⊥ ES ◇ 28-29 K 4
Lagan' ☆ RUS ◆ 34-35 V 6
Lagartero ∴• MEX ◇ 28-29 J 4
Lågen ~ N ◇ 36-37 E 6 ◆ 34-35 N 3
Lages ○ BR ◆ 32-33 M 3
Lage's ○ USA ◇ 20-21 G 5
Laǧǧ, Umm ○ KSA ◆ 56-57 D 5
Laghouat ○• DZ ◆ 48-49 F 2
Lago Piratuba, Parque Natural do ⊥ BR ◆ 30-31 J 4
Lagos ○ P ◇ 44-45 C 6 ◆ 34-35 K 8
Lagos ☆• WAN ◆ 48-49 F 7
Lagossa ○ EAT ◆ 50-51 G 3
La Grande-Deux, Réservoir < CDN ◇ 18-19 F 2
La Grande-Quatre, Réservoir < CDN ◇ 18-19 H 1
La Grande Rivière ~ CDN ◇ 18-19 E 2
La Grande-Trois, Réservoir < CDN ◇ 18-19 G 2
La Grange ⚔ AUS ◆ 60-61 E 3
La Grange ○ USA (GA) ◇ 24-25 F 3
La Grange ○ USA (KY) ◇ 22-23 F 6
La Grange ○ USA (TX) ◇ 26-27 J 5
La Grange Bay ≈ ◆ 60-61 E 3
La Guadeloupe ○ CDN ◇ 18-19 J 6
Laguna ○• BR ◆ 32-33 N 3
Laguna ○ USA ◇ 26-27 D 2
Laguna de Chacahua, Parque Natural ⊥ MEX ◇ 28-29 F 3 ◆ 16-17 G 7
Laguna Indian Reservation ⚔ USA ◇ 26-27 D 2
Laguna San Rafael, Parque Nacional ⊥ RCH ◆ 32-33 H 7
Laguna Yema ○ RA ◆ 32-33 K 2
La Habana ★··· C ◆ 16-17 K 6
Lahaina ○• USA ◇ 24-25 D 7
Lahat ○ RI ◆ 58-59 D 7
Lahontan Reservoir < USA ◇ 20-21 E 6
Lahore ☆··· PK ◆ 56-57 L 4
Lahti ○ FIN ◆ 34-35 R 3
La Huacana ○ MEX ◇ 28-29 D 2
Laï ☆ TCH ◆ 48-49 J 7
Lai Châu ☆ VN ◆ 58-59 D 2
Laila ○ KSA ◆ 56-57 F 6
Laingsburg ○ ZA ◆ 50-51 F 8
Laiwu ○ CHN ◆ 54-55 M 4
Laiyang ○ CHN ◆ 54-55 N 4
Laiyuan ○ CHN ◆ 54-55 L 4
Laizhou Wan ≈ ◆ 54-55 M 4
Lajes ○ BR ◆ 30-31 M 6
Lajitas ○ USA ◇ 26-27 F 5
Lake ○ USA ◇ 20-21 J 3
Lake Arthur ○ USA ◇ 26-27 L 4
Lake Charles ○ USA ◇ 26-27 L 4 ◆ 16-17 H 4
Lake City ○ USA (FL) ◇ 24-25 G 4
Lake City ○ USA (SC) ◇ 24-25 J 3
Lake Clark National Park and Preserve ⊥ USA ◆ 14-15 F 4
Lake District National Park ⊥ GB ◇ 38-39 F 4 ◆ 34-35 L 5
Lake Eyre Basin ⌣ AUS ◆ 60-61 H 5
Lake Eyre National Park ⊥ AUS ◆ 60-61 H 5
Lake Gairdner National Park ⊥ AUS ◆ 60-61 H 6
Lake Geneva ○ USA ◇ 22-23 D 4
Lake George ○ USA ◇ 22-23 M 4
Lake Grace ○ AUS ◆ 60-61 D 6
Lake Harbour ○ CDN ◆ 14-15 X 4
Lake Havasu City ○ USA ◇ 20-21 G 8 ◆ 16-17 D 4
Lake Hughes ○ USA ◇ 20-21 E 8
Lake Isabella ○ USA ◇ 20-21 E 8
Lake Jackson ○ USA ◇ 26-27 K 5
Lakeland ○ USA (FL) ◇ 24-25 H 5
Lakeland ○ USA (GA) ◇ 24-25 G 4
Lake Mackay Aboriginal Land ⚔ AUS ◆ 60-61 F 4
Lake Malawi National Park ⊥··· MW ◆ 50-51 H 4
Lake Mead National Recreation Area ⊥ USA ◇ 20-21 G 7
Lake Mills ○ USA ◇ 22-23 D 4
Lake Placid ○ USA (FL) ◇ 24-25 H 6
Lake Placid ○ USA (NY) ◇ 22-23 M 3
Lake Providence ○ USA ◇ 26-27 M 3
Lakeside ○ USA (NY) ◇ 22-23 J 4
Lakeside ○ USA (OR) ◇ 20-21 B 4
Lakeside ○ USA (VA) ◇ 22-23 K 7
Lake Torrens National Park ⊥ AUS ◆ 60-61 H 6
Lakeview ○ USA (MI) ◇ 22-23 F 4
Lakeview ○ USA (OR) ◇ 20-21 D 4
Lake Wales ○ USA ◇ 24-25 H 6 ◆ 16-17 K 5
Lakewood ○ USA (NJ) ◇ 22-23 L 5
Lakewood ○ USA (NM) ◇ 26-27 E 3
Lake Worth ○ USA ◇ 24-25 H 6
Lakhimpur ○ IND ◆ 56-57 N 5
Lakhpat ○ IND ◆ 56-57 K 6
Lakselv ○ N ◇ 36-37 M 1 ◆ 34-35 Q 1
Lakshadweep ▫ IND ◆ 56-57 L 8
Lakshadweep Sea ≈ ◆ 56-57 L 8
Lalaramau ○ PNG ◆ 58-59 O 7
Lālezār, Kuh-e ▲ IR ◆ 56-57 H 5
Lalibela ○··· ETH ◆ 48-49 N 6
La Libertad ☆ ES ◇ 28-29 K 5
La Libertad ○ HN ◇ 28-29 L 4
Lalindu ~ RI ◆ 58-59 H 7
Lalitpur ○ IND ◆ 56-57 M 6
Lalitpur ○·· NEP ◆ 56-57 O 5
Lamalaga ∸ WSA ◆ 48-49 B 4
Lamanai ∴• BH ◇ 28-29 K 3
Lamanche Valley Provincial Park ⊥ CDN ◇ 18-19 S 5
Lamar ○ USA ◇ 26-27 K 1
Lamasa ○ PNG ◆ 58-59 O 7
Lamballe ○ F ◇ 38-39 F 7 ◆ 34-35 L 6
Lambaréné ☆• G ◆ 50-51 D 2
Lambert Glacier ⊂ ANT ◆ 13 F 8
Lambton, Cape ▲ CDN ◆ 14-15 M 2
Lame Burra Game Reserve ⊥ WAN ◆ 48-49 G 6
La Mesa ○ USA ◇ 20-21 F 9
Lamesa ○ USA ◇ 26-27 G 3
Lamía ○ GR ◇ 46-47 J 5 ◆ 34-35 Q 8
Lamon Bay ≈ ◆ 58-59 H 3
Lamotrek Atoll ⌒ FSM ◆ 58-59 N 5
Lampang ○ THA ◆ 58-59 C 3
Lampasas ○ USA ◇ 26-27 H 4
Lampedusa, Ísola di ⌒ I ◇ 46-47 D 7 ◆ 34-35 O 8
Lamu ○• EAK ◆ 50-51 K 2
Lamu Island ⌒ EAK ◆ 50-51 K 2
Lamy ○ USA ◇ 26-27 E 2
Lana, Río de la ~ MEX ◇ 28-29 G 3
Lanai ⌒ USA ◇ 24-25 D 7 ◆ 16-17 b 6
Lanai City ○ USA ◇ 24-25 D 7
Lancang ○ CHN ◆ 54-55 J 7
Lancang Jiang ~ CHN ◆ 54-55 J 7
Lancaster ○ USA (CA) ◇ 20-21 E 8 ◆ 16-17 C 4
Lancaster ○ USA (NH) ◇ 22-23 N 3
Lancaster ○ USA (OH) ◇ 22-23 G 6
Lancaster ○ USA (PA) ◇ 22-23 K 5
Lancaster ○ USA (SC) ◇ 24-25 H 2 ◆ 16-17 K 4
Lancaster ○ USA (WI) ◇ 22-23 C 4
Lancaster Sound ≈ ◆ 14-15 T 2
Lancaster State Historic Site, Fort ∴ USA ◇ 26-27 G 4
Land, De ○ USA ◇ 24-25 H 5
Land Between The Lakes ⊥ USA ◇ 22-23 D 7
Lander River ~ AUS ◆ 60-61 G 4
Landes de Gascogne, Parc Naturel Régional des ⊥ F ◇ 38-39 G 9 ◆ 34-35 L 7
Land's End ▲·· GB ◇ 38-39 E 6 ◆ 34-35 K 5
Landshut ○·· D ◇ 40-41 M 4 ◆ 34-35 O 6
Lanett ○ USA ◇ 24-25 F 3
Lan'ga Co ○ CHN ◆ 54-55 E 5
Langeac ○ F ◇ 38-39 J 9 ◆ 34-35 M 7
Langfang ○ CHN ◆ 54-55 M 4
Langkawi, Pulau ⌒ MAL ◆ 58-59 C 5
Langlade ○ USA ◇ 22-23 D 3
Langlade, Île ⌒ F ◇ 18-19 Q 5
Langogne ○ F ◇ 38-39 J 9 ◆ 34-35 M 7
Langon ○ F ◇ 38-39 G 9 ◆ 34-35 L 6
Langres ○• F ◇ 38-39 K 8 ◆ 34-35 N 6
Langsa ○ RI ◆ 58-59 C 6
Lang Sơn ☆ VN ◆ 58-59 E 2
Lang Suan ○ THA ◆ 58-59 C 5
Längtans udde ▲ ANT ◆ 13 G 31
Langtry ○ USA ◇ 26-27 G 5
Langudi Rassa National Park ⊥ ETH ◆ 48-49 O 6
Languedoc ∸ F ◇ 38-39 J 10 ◆ 34-35 M 7
Languedoc-Roussillon ▫ F ◇ 38-39 J 10 ◆ 34-35 M 7
Laniel ○ CDN ◇ 18-19 E 5
Lanín, Parque Nacional ⊥ RA ◆ 32-33 H 5
Lankaran ○• AZ ◆ 56-57 F 3
Lannemezan ○ F ◇ 38-39 H 10 ◆ 34-35 M 7
Lannion ○ F ◇ 38-39 F 7 ◆ 34-35 L 6
Lanquín ○• GCA ◇ 28-29 K 4
Lansdale ○ USA ◇ 22-23 L 5
L'Anse ○ USA ◇ 22-23 D 2
L'Anse aux Meadows National Historic Park ⊥··· CDN ◇ 18-19 R 3 ◆ 14-15 Z 6
L'Anse-Pleureuse ○ CDN ◇ 18-19 M 4
Lansing ○ USA (IA) ◇ 22-23 C 4
Lansing ☆ USA (MI) ◇ 22-23 F 4 ◆ 16-17 J 2
Lanthenay, Romorantin- ○ F ◇ 38-39 H 8 ◆ 34-35 M 6
Lantz Corners ○ USA ◇ 22-23 J 5
Lanxi ○ CHN ◆ 54-55 O 2
Lanyu ⌒ RC ◆ 54-55 N 7
Lanzarote ⌒ E ◆ 48-49 C 3
Lanzhou ☆• CHN ◆ 54-55 J 4
Laoag ☆ RP ◆ 58-59 H 3
Laohekou ○ CHN ◆ 54-55 L 5
Laon ☆• F ◇ 38-39 J 7 ◆ 34-35 M 6
Laona ○ USA ◇ 22-23 D 3
Laoong ○ RP ◆ 58-59 J 4
Laos ■ LAO ◆ 58-59 D 3
Lapa ○ BR ◆ 32-33 N 3
Lapalisse ○ F ◇ 38-39 J 8 ◆ 34-35 M 6
La Pampa ▫ RA ◆ 32-33 J 5
La Paz ☆• BOL ◆ 30-31 F 8
La Paz ○ HN (LAP) ◇ 28-29 L 4
La Paz ☆ HN (LAP) ◇ 28-29 L 4
La Paz ☆• MEX ◆ 16-17 D 6
La Paz Centro ○ NIC ◇ 28-29 L 5
La Pérade ○ CDN ◇ 18-19 H 5
La Plata ☆• RA ◆ 32-33 L 4
La Pocatière ○ CDN ◇ 18-19 K 5
La Poile River ~ CDN ◇ 18-19 P 5
La Porte ○ USA (IN) ◇ 22-23 E 5
La Porte ○ USA (TX) ◇ 26-27 K 5
Lappeenranta ○• FIN ◆ 34-35 R 3
Lappland ∸ ◇ 36-37 H 3 ◆ 34-35 P 2
Laptev Sea ≈ ◆ 52-53 U 2
Larache = El-Araich ○ MA ◆ 48-49 D 1
Laramie ○ USA ◆ 16-17 E 2
Laramie Mountains ▲ USA ◆ 16-17 E 2
Larantuka ○ RI ◆ 58-59 H 8
Larder Lake ○ CDN ◇ 18-19 E 4
Laredo ○ USA ◇ 26-27 H 6 ◆ 16-17 G 5
Largeau ☆ TCH ◆ 48-49 J 5
Largo ○ USA ◇ 24-25 G 6
Largo, Cayo ⌒ C ◆ 16-17 K 6
La Rioja ▫ RA ◆ 32-33 J 3
Lárissa ○ GR ◇ 46-47 J 5 ◆ 34-35 Q 8
Larkana ○• PK ◆ 56-57 K 5
Lark Harbour ○ CDN ◇ 18-19 P 4
Larnaka ○• CY ◆ 34-35 S 9
Larocu, Qaşr ○ LAR ◆ 48-49 H 3
La Romaine ○ CDN ◇ 18-19 O 3
La Romana ☆ DOM ◆ 16-17 N 7
la Ronge, Lac ○ CDN ◆ 14-15 P 5
Larrainzar ○ MEX ◇ 28-29 H 3
Larrey Point ▲ AUS ◆ 60-61 D 3
Larrimah ○ AUS ◆ 60-61 G 3
Larry's River ○ CDN ◇ 18-19 O 6
Lars Christensen land ∸ ANT ◆ 13 G 7
Larsen is-shelf ⊂ ANT ◆ 13 G 30
Lascaux, Grotte de ··· F ◇ 38-39 H 9 ◆ 34-35 L 7
Lascelles ○ AUS ◆ 60-61 J 7
Las Choapas ○ MEX ◇ 28-29 G 3
Laškargāh ☆• AFG ◆ 56-57 J 4
Las Palomas ○ USA ◇ 26-27 D 3
La Spézia ○•• I ◇ 46-47 B 2 ◆ 34-35 N 7
Lassen Peak ▲ USA ◇ 20-21 D 5
Lassen Volcanic National Park ⊥ USA ◇ 20-21 D 5 ◆ 16-17 B 2
Lastoursville ○ G ◆ 50-51 D 2
Las Tunas ☆ C ◆ 16-17 L 6
Las Vegas ○ USA (NM) ◇ 26-27 E 2 ◆ 16-17 E 3
Las Vegas ○·· USA (NV) ◇ 20-21 G 7 ◆ 16-17 C 3
Latacunga ☆ EC ◆ 30-31 D 5
Latady Island ⌒ ANT ◆ 13 F 29
Latah Creek ~ USA ◇ 20-21 F 2
Latchford ○ CDN ◇ 18-19 E 5
Laterrière ○ CDN ◇ 18-19 J 4
Latina ☆• I ◇ 46-47 D 4 ◆ 34-35 O 7
Latrobe ○ USA ◇ 22-23 J 5
Lätür ○ IND ◆ 56-57 M 7
Latvia ■ LV ◇ 42-43 J 3 ◆ 34-35 Q 4
Lauca, Parque Nacional ⊥ RCH ◆ 30-31 F 8
Laudar ○ Y ◆ 56-57 F 8
Lauderdale ○ USA ◇ 24-25 D 3
Lauge Koch Kyst ∸ GRØ ◆ 14-15 Y 1
Laughlen, Mount ▲ AUS ◆ 60-61 G 4
Laughlin Peak ▲ USA ◇ 26-27 E 1
Launceston ○ AUS ◆ 60-61 K 8
La Union ○ MEX ◇ 28-29 D 3
Laupahoehoe ○ USA ◇ 24-25 E 8
Laura ○ AUS ◆ 60-61 J 3
Laurel ○ USA (DE) ◇ 22-23 L 6
Laurel ○ USA (MD) ◇ 22-23 K 6
Laurel ○ USA (MS) ◇ 24-25 D 4 ◆ 16-17 J 4
Laurel, Cerro ▲ MEX ◇ 28-29 C 2
Laurens ○ USA ◇ 24-25 G 2
Laurentians ∸ CDN ◇ 18-19 F 5
Laurentides ∸ CDN ◇ 18-19 H 5
Laurentides, Réserve Faunique des ⊥ CDN ◇ 18-19 J 5
Laurie Island ⌒ ANT ◆ 13 G 32
Laurinburg ○ USA ◇ 24-25 J 2
Laurium ○ USA ◇ 22-23 D 2
Lausanne ☆• CH ◇ 40-41 J 5 ◆ 34-35 N 6
Laut, Pulau ⌒ RI ◆ 58-59 G 7
Laut, Pulau ⌒ RI ◆ 58-59 E 6
Lautaret, Col du ▲• F ◇ 38-39 L 9 ◆ 34-35 N 6
Laut Kecil, Kepulauan ⌒ RI ◆ 58-59 G 7
Lautoka ○ FJI ◆ 60-61 Q 3
Lauzon ○ CDN ◇ 18-19 J 5
Lava Beds National Monument ∴ USA ◇ 20-21 D 5
Lavacicle Creek ∴ USA ◇ 20-21 D 4
Laval ○ CDN ◇ 18-19 H 6
Laval ☆• F ◇ 38-39 G 7 ◆ 34-35 L 6
Lāvān, Ğazire-ye ⌒ IR ◆ 56-57 G 5
Lavapié, Punta ▲ RCH ◆ 32-33 H 5
Lavaur ○ F ◇ 38-39 H 10 ◆ 34-35 M 7
La Vérendrye, Réserve Faunique ⊥ CDN ◇ 18-19 F 5
Laverton ○ AUS ◆ 60-61 E 5
La Veta ○ USA ◇ 26-27 E 1
Lavon, Lake ○ USA ◇ 26-27 J 3
Lavras ○ BR ◆ 32-33 O 2
Lavumisa ○ SD ◆ 50-51 H 7
Lawn Bay ≈ ◇ 18-19 R 5
Lawowa ○ RI ◆ 58-59 H 7
Lawrence ○ USA (KS) ◆ 16-17 G 3
Lawrence ○ USA (MA) ◇ 22-23 N 4
Lawrenceburg ○ USA ◇ 24-25 E 2
Lawrenceville ○ USA (GA) ◇ 24-25 G 3
Lawrenceville ○ USA (IL) ◇ 22-23 E 6
Lawrenceville ○ USA (VA) ◇ 22-23 K 7
Lawton ○ USA ◇ 26-27 H 2 ◆ 16-17 G 4
Lawushi Manda National Park ⊥ Z ◆ 50-51 H 4
Lazarev ○ RUS ◆ 52-53 Z 7
Lazarevskoe ○ RUS ◆ 34-35 T 7
Lázaro Cárdenas ○ MEX ◇ 28-29 C 3 ◆ 16-17 F 7
Leading Tickles ○ CDN ◇ 18-19 R 4
Leadore ○ USA ◇ 20-21 H 3
Leahy ○ USA ◇ 20-21 E 2
Leakey ○ USA ◇ 26-27 H 5
Leamington ○ CDN ◇ 18-19 C 7
Leander ○ USA ◇ 26-27 J 4
Learmonth ○ AUS ◆ 60-61 C 4
Leaton State Historic Site, Fort ∴ USA ◇ 26-27 E 5
Leavenworth ○ USA ◇ 20-21 D 2
Lebanon ■ RL ◆ 56-57 D 4
Lebanon ○ USA (IN) ◇ 22-23 E 5
Lebanon ○ USA (KS) ◆ 16-17 G 3
Lebanon ○ USA (KY) ◇ 22-23 F 7
Lebanon ○ USA (MO) ◆ 16-17 H 3
Lebanon ○ USA (NH) ◇ 22-23 M 4
Lebanon ○ USA (OR) ◇ 20-21 C 3
Lebanon ○ USA (PA) ◇ 22-23 K 5
Lebanon ○ USA (TN) ◇ 24-25 E 1
Lebel-sur-Quévillon ○ CDN ◇ 18-19 F 4
Lebo ○ ZRE ◆ 48-49 K 8
Lebu ○ RCH ◆ 32-33 H 5
Lecce ☆• I ◇ 46-47 G 4 ◆ 34-35 P 7
Ledjanaja, gora ▲ RUS ◆ 52-53 f 5
Lednikovaja, gora ▲ RUS ◆ 52-53 S 2
Leeds ○• GB ◇ 38-39 G 5 ◆ 34-35 L 5
Leeds ○ USA ◇ 24-25 E 3
Leesburg ○ USA (FL) ◇ 24-25 H 5
Leesburg ○ USA (VA) ◇ 22-23 K 6
Leesville ○ USA ◇ 26-27 L 4
Leeuwin, Cape ▲ AUS ◆ 60-61 D 6
Leeward Islands ⌒ ◆ 16-17 O 7
Léfini, Réserve de chasse de la ⊥ RCB ◆ 50-51 E 2
Lefkáda ⌒ GR ◇ 46-47 H 5 ◆ 34-35 Q 8
Lefkosia ★·· CY ◆ 34-35 S 8
Lefroy, Lake ○ AUS ◆ 60-61 E 6
Legazpi ☆ RP ◆ 58-59 H 4
Leggett ○ USA ◇ 20-21 C 6
Legnica ☆• PL ◇ 40-41 O 3 ◆ 34-35 P 5
Leh ○• IND ◆ 56-57 M 4
Le Havre ○ F ◇ 38-39 H 7 ◆ 34-35 M 6
Lehman Caves ∴• USA ◇ 20-21 G 6
Lehmann ○ USA ◇ 26-27 F 3
Leiah ○ PK ◆ 56-57 L 4
Leichhardt, Mount ▲ AUS ◆ 60-61 G 4
Leigh Creek ○ AUS ◆ 60-61 H 6
Leighton ○ USA ◇ 24-25 E 2
Leimus ○ HN ◇ 28-29 B 4
Leipzig ○·· D ◇ 40-41 M 3 ◆ 34-35 O 5
Leitchfield ○ USA ◇ 22-23 E 7
Leiyang ○ CHN ◆ 54-55 L 6
Leizhou Bandao ⌣ CHN ◆ 54-55 L 7
Leland ○ USA ◇ 26-27 M 3
Leleque ○ RA ◆ 32-33 H 6
Lelingluang ○ RI ◆ 58-59 K 8
Le Maire, Estrecho de ≈ ◆ 32-33 J 8
Léman, Lac ○ CH ◇ 40-41 J 5 ◆ 34-35 N 6
Lemankoa ○ PNG ◆ 58-59 O 8
Le Mans ○• F ◇ 38-39 H 8 ◆ 34-35 M 6
Lemesos ○• CY ◆ 34-35 S 9
Lemhi, Fort ∴ USA ◇ 20-21 H 3
Lemhi Range ▲ USA ◇ 20-21 H 3
Lemhi River ~ USA ◇ 20-21 H 3
Lemieux Islands ⌒ CDN ◆ 14-15 X 4
Le Mont Saint-Michel ○··· F ◇ 38-39 G 7 ◆ 34-35 L 6
Lempa, Río ~ ES ◇ 28-29 K 5
Lena ~ RUS ◆ 52-53 V 4
Lena ○ USA ◇ 26-27 L 4
Lena River Delta ⌣ RUS ◆ 52-53 W 3
Lençóis ○ BR ◆ 30-31 L 7
Lenge, Bandar-e ○• IR ◆ 56-57 G 5
Lengua de Vaca, Punta ▲ RCH ◆ 32-33 H 4
Lengwe National Park ⊥ MW ◆ 50-51 H 5
Lenin, Qullai ▲ KS ◆ 56-57 L 3
Leningrad = Sankt-Peterburg ☆··· RUS ◆ 42-43 M 2 ◆ 34-35 S 4
Leninogorsk ☆ RUS ◆ 34-35 W 5
Leninsk-Kuzneckij ☆ RUS ◆ 52-53 O 7
Leninsk Kuznetskiy = Leninsk-Kuzneckij ☆ RUS ◆ 52-53 O 7
Leno-Angarskoe plato ∸ RUS ◆ 52-53 R 7
Lenoir ○ USA ◇ 24-25 H 2
Lenoir City ○ USA ◇ 24-25 F 2
Lens ○ F ◇ 38-39 J 6 ◆ 34-35 M 5
Lensk ☆• RUS ◆ 52-53 T 5
Léo ○ BF ◆ 48-49 E 6
León ○• E ◇ 44-45 E 3 ◆ 34-35 K 7
Léon ○ F ◇ 38-39 G 10 ◆ 34-35 L 7
León ○• MEX ◆ 16-17 F 6
León ☆•• NIC ◇ 28-29 L 5 ◆ 16-17 J 8
León, Cerro ▲ MEX ◇ 28-29 F 3 ◆ 16-17 G 7
Leonard ○ USA ◇ 26-27 J 3
Leonardville ○ NAM ◆ 50-51 E 6
Leonora ○ AUS ◆ 60-61 E 5
Leon River ~ USA ◇ 26-27 H 4
León Viejo ∴• NIC ◇ 28-29 L 5
Lepaterique ○ HN ◇ 28-29 L 4
Lepsi ○ KZ ◆ 52-53 M 8
Leptis Magna = Labdah ∴··· LAR ◆ 48-49 H 2
Lerdo de Tejada ○ MEX ◇ 28-29 G 2
Lérida = Lleida ○•• E ◇ 44-45 H 4 ◆ 34-35 M 7
Lerma ○ MEX ◇ 28-29 J 2
Lerwick ○ GB ◇ 38-39 G 1 ◆ 34-35 L 3
Lescoff ○ F ◇ 38-39 E 7 ◆ 34-35 L 6
Leshan ○ CHN ◆ 54-55 J 6
Leskino ○ RUS ◆ 52-53 M 3
Leslie ○ USA (AR) ◇ 26-27 L 2
Leslie ○ USA (ID) ◇ 20-21 H 4
Lesosibirsk ○ RUS ◆ 52-53 P 6
Lesotho ■ LS ◆ 50-51 G 7
Lesperon ○ F ◇ 38-39 G 10 ◆ 34-35 L 7
Lesser Hinggan Range ▲ CHN ◆ 54-55 O 1
Lesser Slave Lake ○ CDN ◆ 14-15 N 5
Lesser Sunda Islands ⌒ RI ◆ 58-59 G 8
Lesvos ⌒ GR ◇ 46-47 L 5 ◆ 34-35 R 8
Leszno ☆• PL ◇ 40-41 O 3 ◆ 34-35 P 5
Lethbridge ○• CDN ◆ 14-15 O 7
Lethem ☆ GUY ◆ 30-31 H 4
Leti, Kepulauan ⌒ RI ◆ 58-59 J 8
Leticia ○ CO ◆ 30-31 F 5
Letohatchee ○ USA ◇ 24-25 E 3
Leupp ○ USA ◇ 26-27 B 2
Levan ○ USA ◇ 20-21 J 6
Levelland ○ USA ◇ 26-27 F 3
Leveque, Cape ▲ AUS ◆ 60-61 E 3
Leverett Glacier ⊂ ANT ◆ 13 E 0
Levick, Mount ▲ ANT ◆ 13 F 17
Lévis ○ CDN ◇ 18-19 J 5
Levittown ○ USA ◇ 22-23 L 5
Levroux ○ F ◇ 38-39 H 8 ◆ 34-35 M 6
Lewes ○ USA ◇ 22-23 L 6
Lewis ⌒ GB ◇ 38-39 D 2 ◆ 34-35 K 4
Lewisburg ○ USA (OR) ◇ 20-21 C 3
Lewisburg ○ USA (TN) ◇ 24-25 E 2
Lewisburg ○ USA (WV) ◇ 22-23 H 7
Lewis Hills ▲ CDN ◇ 18-19 P 4
Lewisporte ○ CDN ◇ 18-19 R 4
Lewis Range ▲ USA ◇ 20-21 H 1 ◆ 14-15 O 7
Lewis River ~ USA ◇ 20-21 C 2
Lewis Smith Lake ○ USA ◇ 24-25 E 3
Lewiston ○ USA (ID) ◇ 20-21 F 2 ◆ 14-15 N 7
Lewiston ○ USA (IN) ◇ 22-23 E 5
Lewiston ○ USA (ME) ◇ 22-23 N 3
Lewiston ○ USA (UT) ◇ 20-21 J 5
Lewistown ○ USA (IL) ◇ 22-23 C 5
Lewistown ○ USA (PA) ◇ 22-23 K 5
Lewisville, Lake ○ USA ◇ 26-27 J 3
Lexington ○ USA (KY) ◇ 22-23 F 6 ◆ 16-17 K 3
Lexington ○ USA (NC) ◇ 24-25 H 2
Lexington ○ USA (TN) ◇ 24-25 D 2
Lexington ○ USA (VA) ◇ 22-23 J 7
Lexington Park ○ USA ◇ 22-23 K 6
Leyte ⌒ RP ◆ 58-59 H 4
LG Deux, Réservoir de ○ CDN ◇ 18-19 F 2 ◆ 14-15 V 6
Lgotny, mys ▲ RUS ◆ 52-53 Y 6
Lhasa ☆··· CHN ◆ 54-55 G 6
Lhokseumawe ○ RI ◆ 58-59 C 5
Lianga ○ RP ◆ 58-59 J 5
Liangpran, Gunung ▲ RI ◆ 58-59 F 6
Lianyuan ○ CHN ◆ 54-55 L 6
Lianyungang ○ CHN ◆ 54-55 M 5
Liaodong Wan ≈ ◆ 54-55 N 3
Liao He ~ CHN ◆ 54-55 N 3
Liaoning ▫ CHN ◆ 54-55 N 3
Liaotung, Gulf of = Liaodong Wan ≈ ◆ 54-55 N 3
Liaoyuan ○ CHN ◆ 54-55 O 3
Liard Plateau ▲ CDN ◆ 14-15 L 4
Liard River ~ CDN ◆ 14-15 M 4
Libby ○ USA ◇ 20-21 G 1
Libenge ○ ZRE ◆ 48-49 J 8
Liberal ○ USA ◇ 26-27 G 1 ◆ 16-17 F 3
Liberia ☆ CR ◇ 28-29 B 6 ◆ 16-17 J 8
Liberia ■ LB ◆ 48-49 C 7
Liberty ○ USA (KY) ◇ 22-23 F 7
Liberty ○ USA (NY) ◇ 22-23 L 5
Liberty ○ USA (TX) ◇ 26-27 K 4
Liboi ○ EAK ◆ 50-51 K 1
Libourne ○ F ◇ 38-39 G 9 ◆ 34-35 L 6
Libreville ☆• G ◆ 50-51 C 1
Libya ■ LAR ◆ 48-49 H 3
Libyan Desert ∸ LAR ◆ 48-49 K 3
Lichinga ☆ MOC ◆ 50-51 J 4
Lichtenburg ○ ZA ◆ 50-51 G 7
Lichteneger, Lac ○ CDN ◇ 18-19 G 2
Licking ○ USA ◇ 22-23 C 7
Licking River ~ USA ◇ 22-23 F 6
Liebig, Mount ▲ AUS ◆ 60-61 G 4
Liechtenstein ■ FL ◇ 40-41 K 5 ◆ 34-35 N 6
Liège ☆• B ◇ 40-41 H 3 ◆ 34-35 N 5
Lienz ○ A ◇ 40-41 M 5 ◆ 34-35 O 6
Liepāja ☆•• LV ◇ 42-43 G 3 ◆ 34-35 Q 4
Lièvre, Rivière du ~ CDN ◇ 18-19 G 5
Lifou ⌒ F ◆ 60-61 O 4
Light, Cape ▲ ANT ◆ 13 F 30
Lighthouse Reef ⌒ BH ◇ 28-29 L 3
Ligonha, Rio ~ MOC ◆ 50-51 J 5
Ligonier ○ USA ◇ 22-23 F 5
Ligua, La ○ RCH ◆ 32-33 H 4
Ligunga ○ EAT ◆ 50-51 J 4
Ligurian Sea ≈ ◇ 46-47 B 3 ◆ 34-35 N 7
Ligurta ○ USA ◇ 20-21 G 9
Lihir Group ⌒ PNG ◆ 58-59 O 7
Lihou Reefs and Cays ⌒ AUS ◆ 60-61 L 3
Lihue ○ USA ◇ 24-25 C 7 ◆ 16-17 b 6
Lijiang ○• CHN ◆ 54-55 J 6
Likasi ○ ZRE ◆ 50-51 G 4
Likati ○ ZRE ◆ 48-49 K 8
Likely ○ USA ◇ 20-21 D 5
Likouala ~ RCB ◆ 50-51 E 1
Lilbourn ○ USA ◇ 22-23 D 7
L'Île-d'Entrée ○ CDN ◇ 18-19 O 5
Lille ☆• F ◇ 38-39 J 6 ◆ 34-35 M 5
Lillehammer ☆ N ◇ 36-37 E 6 ◆ 34-35 O 3
Lilongwe ★• MW ◆ 50-51 H 4
Lima ★··· PE ◆ 30-31 D 7
Lima ○ PY ◆ 32-33 L 2
Lima ○ USA ◇ 22-23 F 5 ◆ 16-17 K 2
Lima, La ○• HN ◇ 28-29 L 4
Limay, Río ~ RA ◆ 32-33 J 5
Limba Limba ~ EAT ◆ 50-51 H 3
Limbé ○• CAM ◆ 48-49 G 8
Limeira ○ BR ◆ 32-33 N 2
Limerick = Luimneach ○ IRL ◇ 38-39 C 5 ◆ 34-35 K 5
Limestone, Lake ○ USA ◇ 26-27 J 4
Limmen Bight River ~ AUS ◆ 60-61 H 3
Límnos ⌒ GR ◇ 46-47 K 5 ◆ 34-35 R 8
Limoges ☆• F ◇ 38-39 H 9 ◆ 34-35 M 6
Limousin ▫ F ◇ 38-39 H 9 ◆ 34-35 L 7
Limoux ○ F ◇ 38-39 J 10 ◆ 34-35 M 7
Limpopo ~ ZA ◆ 50-51 G 6
Limpopo, Rio ~ MOC ◆ 50-51 H 6
Linares ○ E ◇ 44-45 F 5 ◆ 34-35 L 8
Linares ○ MEX ◆ 16-17 G 6
Linares ○ RCH ◆ 32-33 H 5
Lincang ○ CHN ◆ 54-55 J 7
Linchuan ○ CHN ◆ 54-55 M 6
Lincoln ○ RA ◆ 32-33 K 4
Lincoln ○ USA (IL) ◇ 22-23 D 5
Lincoln ○ USA (ME) ◇ 22-23 O 3
Lincoln ○ USA (NH) ◇ 22-23 N 3
Lincoln ☆ USA (NE) ◆ 16-17 G 2
Lincoln Birthplace National Historic Site, Abraham ∴ USA ◇ 22-23 F 7
Lincoln Boyhood National Memorial ∴ USA ◇ 22-23 E 6
Lincoln Caverns ∴ USA ◇ 22-23 J 5
Lincoln City ○ USA ◇ 20-21 C 3
Lincoln Island = Dong Dao ⌒ CHN ◆ 58-59 F 3
Lincoln National Park ⊥ AUS ◆ 60-61 H 6
Lincolnton ○ USA ◇ 24-25 H 2
Linde ~ RUS ◆ 52-53 U 4
Linden ○ USA ◇ 24-25 E 2
Lindi ☆• EAT ◆ 50-51 J 3
Lindi ~ ZRE ◆ 50-51 G 1
Lindi Bay ≈ ◆ 50-51 J 3
Lindsay ○ CDN ◇ 18-19 E 6
Line Islands ⌒ KIB ◆ 12 M 2
Linfen ○ CHN ◆ 54-55 L 4
Lingayen Gulf ≈ ◆ 58-59 H 3
Lingga, Pulau ⌒ RI ◆ 58-59 D 7
Linguère ○ SN ◆ 48-49 B 5
Linh, Ngoc ▲ VN ◆ 58-59 E 3
Linhai ○ CHN ◆ 54-55 N 6
Linhares ○ BR ◆ 30-31 L 8
Linhe ○ CHN ◆ 54-55 K 3
Linköping ☆• S ◇ 36-37 G 7 ◆ 34-35 P 4
Linkou ○ CHN ◆ 54-55 P 2
Linn ○ USA ◇ 22-23 C 6
Lins ○ BR ◆ 32-33 N 2
Linton ○ USA ◇ 22-23 E 6
Linville Caverns ∴ USA ◇ 24-25 H 2
Linxia ○ CHN ◆ 54-55 J 4
Linyanti ~ RB ◆ 50-51 F 5
Linyi ○ CHN ◆ 54-55 M 4
Linz ☆•• A ◇ 40-41 N 4 ◆ 34-35 O 6
Lion, Golfe du ≈ ◇ 38-39 J 10 ◆ 34-35 M 7
Liouesso ○ RCB ◆ 50-51 E 1
Lipantitlan State Historic Site ∴ USA ◇ 26-27 J 6
Lipeck ○ RUS ◇ 42-43 Q 5 ◆ 34-35 T 5
Lipetsk = Lipeck ○ RUS ◇ 42-43 Q 5 ◆ 34-35 T 5
Lipobane, Ponta ▲ MOC ◆ 50-51 J 5
Lira ○ EAU ◆ 48-49 M 8
Liranga ○ RCB ◆ 50-51 E 2
Lisala ○ ZRE ◆ 48-49 K 8
Lisboa ★··· P ◇ 44-45 C 5 ◆ 34-35 K 8
Lisbon ○ USA ◇ 22-23 H 5
Lisbon = Lisboa ★··· P ◇ 44-45 C 5 ◆ 34-35 K 8
Lisburne, Cape ▲ USA ◆ 14-15 C 3
Liscomb Game Sanction ⊥ CDN ◇ 18-19 N 6
Lishui ○ CHN ◆ 54-55 M 6
Lisieux ○• F ◇ 38-39 H 7 ◆ 34-35 M 6
Lisjanskogo, poluostrov ⌣ RUS ◆ 52-53 a 6
Liski ○ RUS ◆ 34-35 T 5
Lismore ○ AUS ◆ 60-61 L 5
Lister, Mount ▲ ANT ◆ 13 F 17
Listowel ○ CDN ◇ 18-19 D 7
Litang ○ CHN ◆ 54-55 J 5
Litchfield ○ USA ◇ 20-21 D 5
Litchfield Beach ○ USA ◇ 24-25 J 3
Lithgow ○ AUS ◆ 60-61 L 6
Lithuania ■ LT ◇ 42-43 G 4 ◆ 34-35 Q 4
Litke, proliv ≈ ◆ 52-53 d 6
Little Andaman ⌒ IND ◆ 58-59 B 4
Little Belt Mountains ▲ USA ◇ 20-21 J 2
Little Colorado River ~ USA ◇ 26-27 C 2 ◆ 16-17 E 4
Little Current ○ CDN ◇ 18-19 D 6
Little Falls ○ USA ◇ 22-23 L 4
Littlefield ○ USA (AZ) ◇ 20-21 H 7
Littlefield ○ USA (TX) ◇ 26-27 F 3
Little Humboldt River ~ USA ◇ 20-21 F 5
Little Lake ○ USA ◇ 20-21 F 8
Little Mecatina River ~ CDN ◇ 18-19 N 2 ◆ 14-15 Y 6
Little Missouri River ~ USA ◆ 14-15 Q 7
Little Nicobar Island ⌒ IND ◆ 58-59 B 5
Little River ~ USA ◇ 26-27 K 3
Littlerock ○ USA ◇ 20-21 F 8
Little Rock ☆ USA ◇ 26-27 L 2 ◆ 16-17 H 4
Little Sable Point ▲ USA ◇ 22-23 E 4
Littleton ○ USA ◇ 22-23 N 3
Little Wabash River ~ USA ◇ 22-23 D 6
Little White River ~ CDN ◇ 18-19 C 5
Liupanshui ○ CHN ◆ 54-55 J 6
Liuwa Plain National Park ⊥ Z ◆ 50-51 F 4
Liuzhou ○• CHN ◆ 54-55 K 7
Livadiá ○• GR ◇ 46-47 J 5 ◆ 34-35 Q 8
Live Oak ○ USA ◇ 24-25 G 4
Livermore, Mount ▲ USA ◇ 26-27 E 4 ◆ 16-17 F 4
Livermore Falls ○ USA ◇ 22-23 N 3
Liverpool ○ CDN ◇ 18-19 M 6
Liverpool ○• GB ◇ 38-39 F 5 ◆ 34-35 L 5
Liverpool Bay ≈ ◆ 14-15 K 3
Livingston ○ USA (AL) ◇ 24-25 D 3
Livingston ○ USA (MT) ◇ 20-21 J 3
Livingston ○ USA (TN) ◇ 24-25 F 1
Livingston ○ USA (TX) ◇ 26-27 K 4
Livingston, Lake ○ USA ◇ 26-27 K 4
Livingstone ☆ Z ◆ 50-51 G 5
Livingston Island ⌒ ANT ◆ 13 G 30
Livonia ○ USA ◇ 22-23 G 4
Livorno ○ I ◇ 46-47 C 3 ◆ 34-35 O 7
Livradois-Forez, Parc Naturel Régional ⊥ F ◇ 38-39 J 9 ◆ 34-35 M 7
Liwale ○ EAT ◆ 50-51 J 3
Liwonde National Park ⊥ MW ◆ 50-51 J 4
Lizarda ○ BR ◆ 30-31 K 6
Lizotte ○ CDN ◇ 18-19 H 4
Ljahovskie ostrova ⌒ RUS ◆ 52-53 Y 3
Ljubljana ★• SLO ◇ 46-47 E 1 ◆ 34-35 O 6
Ljusnan ~ S ◇ 36-37 G 6 ◆ 34-35 P 3
Llano ○ USA ◇ 26-27 H 4
Llano, El ○ PA ◇ 28-29 E 7
Llano Estacado ⌣ USA ◇ 26-27 F 3 ◆ 16-17 F 4
Llano Mariato ○ PA ◇ 28-29 D 8
Llano River ~ USA ◇ 26-27 H 4
Lleida ○•• E ◇ 44-45 H 4 ◆ 34-35 M 7
Lloydminster ○ CDN ◆ 14-15 O 6
Llullaillaco, Volcán ▲ RCH ◆ 32-33 J 2
Loa ○ USA ◇ 20-21 J 6
Loange ~ ZRE ◆ 50-51 F 2
Lobatse ☆ RB ◆ 50-51 F 7
Lobaye ~ RCA ◆ 48-49 J 8
Lobito ○ ANG ◆ 50-51 D 4
Lobos, Cayo ⌒ MEX ◇ 28-29 L 2
Lobuja ○ RUS ◆ 52-53 b 4
Loche, La ○ CDN ◆ 14-15 P 5
Loches ○ F ◇ 38-39 H 8 ◆ 34-35 M 6
Lochinvar National Park ⊥ Z ◆ 50-51 G 5
Lochloosa ○ USA ◇ 24-25 G 5
Lochsa River ~ USA ◇ 20-21 G 2
Locke ○ USA ◇ 20-21 F 1
Lockeport ○ CDN ◇ 18-19 M 7
Lockhart ○ USA ◇ 26-27 J 5
Lockhart River ⚔ AUS ◆ 60-61 J 2
Lock Haven ○ USA ◇ 22-23 K 5
Lockney ○ USA ◇ 26-27 G 2
Lockport ○ USA ◇ 22-23 J 4
Lockwood ○ USA (CA) ◇ 20-21 D 8
Lockwood ○ USA (MO) ◇ 26-27 L 1
Locri ○ I ◇ 46-47 F 5 ◆ 34-35 P 8
Lodève ○ F ◇ 38-39 J 10 ◆ 34-35 M 7
Lodi ○ USA (CA) ◇ 20-21 D 6
Lodi ○ USA (OH) ◇ 22-23 G 5
Lodja ○ ZRE ◆ 50-51 F 2
Lodmalasin ▲ EAT ◆ 50-51 J 2
Łódź ☆•• PL ◇ 40-41 P 3 ◆ 34-35 P 5
Loei ○ THA ◆ 58-59 D 3
Lofoten ⌒• N ◇ 36-37 F 2 ◆ 34-35 O 2
Lofoten Basin ≃ ◆ 16-17 M 2
Logan ○ USA (NM) ◇ 26-27 F 2
Logan ○ USA (OH) ◇ 22-23 G 6
Logan ○ USA (UT) ◇ 20-21 J 5 ◆ 16-17 D 2
Logan ○ USA (WV) ◇ 22-23 H 7
Logan, Mount ▲·· CDN ◆ 14-15 H 4
Logan Mountains ▲ CDN ◆ 14-15 L 4
Logan Pass ▲ USA ◇ 20-21 H 1
Logansport ○ USA ◇ 22-23 E 5
Logaškino ○ RUS ◆ 52-53 b 3
Loge ~ ANG ◆ 50-51 D 3
Logone ~ TCH ◆ 48-49 J 6
Lohéac ○ F ◇ 38-39 G 8 ◆ 34-35 L 6
Lohjanan ○ RI ◆ 58-59 G 7
Loir ~ F ◇ 38-39 H 8 ◆ 34-35 M 6
Loire ~ F ◇ 38-39 H 8 ◆ 34-35 L 6
Loja ☆ EC ◆ 30-31 D 5
Lokichar ○ EAK ◆ 48-49 N 8
Lokitaung ○ EAK ◆ 48-49 N 8
Lokoja ○ WAN ◆ 48-49 G 7
Lokossa ☆ DY ◆ 48-49 F 7
Loks Land ⌒ CDN ◆ 14-15 Y 4
Lol ~ SUD ◆ 48-49 L 7
Loleta ○ USA ◇ 20-21 B 5
Lolland ⌒ DK ◇ 36-37 E 9 ◆ 34-35 O 5
Lolo ○ USA ◇ 20-21 G 2
Lolo Hot Springs ○ USA ◇ 20-21 G 2
Lom ~ CAM ◆ 48-49 H 7
Loma Alta ○ USA ◇ 26-27 G 5
Loma Bonita ○ MEX ◇ 28-29 G 2
Lomami ~ ZRE ◆ 50-51 G 2
Loma Mountains ▲ WAL ◆ 48-49 C 7
Lomas de Arena ○ USA ◇ 26-27 E 4
Lomblen (Kawela), Pulau ⌒ RI ◆ 58-59 H 8
Lombok ⌒ RI ◆ 58-59 G 8
Lombok, Selat ≈ ◆ 58-59 G 8
Lomé ★• RT ◆ 48-49 F 7
Lomela ○ ZRE ◆ 50-51 F 2
Lomela ~ ZRE ◆ 50-51 F 2
Lometa ○ USA ◇ 26-27 H 4
Lomitas, Las ○ RA ◆ 32-33 K 2
Lomonosov Ridge ≃ ◆ 13 A 25
Lompoc ○ USA ◇ 20-21 D 8
Lonävale ○• IND ◆ 56-57 L 7
Loncoche ○ RCH ◆ 32-33 H 5
London ○• CDN ◇ 18-19 D 7 ◆ 14-15 U 8

80 Lacanau-Océan — London

London ★ ••• **GB** ◇ 38-39 G 6
London ○ **USA** (KY) ◇ 22-23 F 7
London ○ **USA** (OH) ◇ 22-23 G 5
Londonderry ☆ ○ **GB** ◇ 38-39 D 4
Londonderry, Cape ▲ **AUS** ◆ 60-61 F 2
Londonderry, Isla ∧ **RCH** ◆ 32-33 H 8
Londrina ○ **BR** ◆ 32-33 M 2
Lone Rock ○ **USA** ◇ 22-23 C 4
Longa ○ **ANG** ◆ 50-51 E 4
Longa, proliv ≈ 52-53 g 3
Long Bay ≈ ◇ 24-25 J 3 ▲ 16-17 L 4
Longa-Mavinga, Coutada Pública do ⊥
  ANG ◆ 50-51 E 5
Long Beach ○ **USA** ◇ 20-21 E 9
Long Branch ○ **USA** (NJ) ◇ 22-23 L 5
Long Branch ○ **USA** ◇ 22-23 M 5
Long Cay ∧ **BH** ◇ 28-29 L 2
Long Creek ○ **CDN** ◇ 18-19 L 6
Long Creek ○ **USA** ◇ 20-21 E 3
Long Harbour ○ **CDN** ◇ 18-19 S 5
Longiram ○ **RI** ◆ 58-59 G 7
Long Island ∧ **BS** ◇ 16-17 L 6
Long Island ∧ **CDN** (NFL) ◇ 18-19 R 5
Long Island ∧ **CDN** (NS) ◇ 18-19 L 6
Long Island ∧ **CDN** (NWT) ◇ 14-15 V 6
Long Island ∧ **PNG** ◆ 58-59 N 7
Long Island ∧ **USA** ◇ 22-23 M 5
  ◇ 16-17 M 2
Long Island Sound ≈ ◇ 22-23 M 5
Longkou ○ **CHN** ◆ 54-55 N 4
Long Point ○ **CDN** (ONT) ◇ 18-19 D 7
Long Point ▲ **CDN** (NFL) ◇ 18-19 P 4
Long Point ○ **CDN** (ONT) ◇ 18-19 D 7
Long Point Bay ≈ **CDN** ◇ 18-19 D 7
Long Range Mountains ▲ **CDN**
  ◆ 14-15 Z 7
Longreach ○ **AUS** ◆ 60-61 J 4
Longs Peak ▲ **USA** ◆ 16-17 E 2
Longue Pointe ▲ **CDN** ◇ 18-19 E 2
Longueuil ○ **CDN** ◇ 18-19 E 2
Long Valley Junction ○ **USA**
  ◇ 20-21 G 6
Longview ○ **USA** (TX) ◇ 26-27 K 3
  ◇ 16-17 H 4
Longview ○ **USA** (WA) ◇ 20-21 C 2
  ◇ 14-15 M 7
Long Xuyên ○ **VN** ◆ 58-59 E 4
Longyan ○ **CHN** ◆ 54-55 N 6
Lons-le-Saunier ○ **F** ◇ 38-39 K 8
  ◆ 34-35 M 6
Lookout, Cape ▲ **USA** ◇ 20-21 C 3
Lookout, Cape ▲ **USA** (NC)
  ◇ 16-17 L 4
Lookout Pass ▲ **USA** ◇ 20-21 G 2
Loon, Pointe à **CDN** ◇ 18-19 E 2
Loongana ○ **AUS** ◆ 60-61 F 6
Lopatina, gora ▲ **RUS** ◆ 52-53 Z 7
Lopatka, mys ▲ **RUS** ◆ 52-53 c 7
Lopez ○ **RP** ◆ 58-59 H 4
Lopez, Cap ▲ **G** ◆ 50-51 C 2
Lop Nur ∴ **CHN** ◆ 54-55 G 3
Lopori ∼ **ZRE** ◆ 50-51 E 2
Lorain ○ **USA** ◇ 22-23 G 5
Loralai ○ **PK** ◆ 56-57 K 4
Lorca ○ **E** ◆ 44-45 G 6 ◆ 34-35 L 8
Lord Howe Island ∧ ••• **AUS**
  ◆ 60-61 M 6
Lord Howe Rise ≃ ◆ 60-61 N 5
Lord-Howe Seamounts ≃ ◆ 60-61 M 5
Lord Mayor Bay ≈ ◆ 14-15 S 3
Lordsburg ○ **USA** ◇ 26-27 C 4
Lorena ○ **BR** ◆ 32-33 N 2
Lorengau ○ **PNG** ◆ 58-59 N 7
Loreto ○ **CO** ◇ 30-31 E 5
Loreto ○ **MEX** ◇ 16-17 D 5
Lorian Swamp ≈ **EAK** ◆ 50-51 J 1
Lorient ○ **F** ◇ 38-39 F 8 ◆ 34-35 L 6
Loring, Port ○ **CDN** ◇ 18-19 E 6
Lorino ○ **RUS** ◆ 52-53 j 4
Lormes ○ **F** ◇ 38-39 J 8
  ◆ 34-35 M 6
Lorneville ○ **CDN** ◇ 18-19 L 6
Lorraine ∼ **F** ◇ 38-39 K 7
  ◆ 34-35 M 6
Losai National Reserve ⊥ **EAK**
  ◆ 50-51 J 1
Los Angeles ○ • **USA** ◇ 20-21 D 4
Los Angeles Aqueduct < **USA**
  ◇ 20-21 E 4
Los Cuchumatanes, Parque Nacional ⊥
  GCA ◇ 28-29 J 4
Los Mochis ○ **MEX** ◇ 16-17 C 5
Lospatos ○ **RI** ◆ 58-59 J 8
Los Roques, Islas ∧ **YV** ◇ 30-31 F 2
Los Santos ○ • **PA** ◇ 28-29 D 8
Lost Hills ○ **USA** ◇ 20-21 E 4
Lost River Range ▲ **USA** ◇ 20-21 G 3
Lost Trail Pass ▲ **USA** ◇ 20-21 H 3
Lot ∼ **F** ◇ 38-39 H 9 ◆ 34-35 M 7
Lothair ○ **USA** ◇ 20-21 J 1
Louangphrabang ○ •• **LAO** ◆ 58-59 D 3
Loubomo ○ **RCB** ◆ 50-51 D 2
Loudéac ○ **F** ◇ 38-39 F 7
  ◆ 34-35 L 6
Loudi ○ **CHN** ◆ 54-55 L 6
Loudun ○ **F** ◇ 38-39 H 8
  ◆ 34-35 M 6
Louga ○ **SN** ◆ 48-49 B 5
Lougheed Island ∧ **CDN** ◆ 14-15 P 1
Louisa ○ **USA** ◇ 22-23 G 6
Louisbourg ○ **CDN** ◇ 18-19 O 6
Louisdale ○ **CDN** ◇ 18-19 O 6
Louise ○ **USA** ◇ 26-27 J 5
Louiseville ○ **CDN** ◇ 18-19 H 5
Louis Trichardt ○ **ZA** ◆ 50-51 G 5
Louisville ○ **CDN** ◇ 18-19 H 5
Louisville ○ **USA** (GA) ◇ 24-25 G 3

Louisville ○ **USA** (KY) ◇ 22-23 F 6
  ◇ 16-17 J 3
Louisville ○ **USA** (MS) ◇ 24-25 D 3
Loup River ∼ **USA** ◇ 16-17 G 2
Lourdes ○ **F** ◇ 38-39 G 10
  ◆ 34-35 L 7
Lousiana ○ **USA** ◇ 26-27 L 4
Louth ○ **AUS** ◆ 60-61 K 6
Louvicourt ○ **CDN** ◇ 18-19 E 5
Louviers ○ **F** ◇ 38-39 H 7
  ◆ 34-35 M 6
Lovelady ○ **USA** ◇ 26-27 K 4
Lovelock ○ **USA** ◇ 20-21 E 5
Loving ○ **USA** ◇ 26-27 H 3
Lovington ○ **USA** ◇ 26-27 F 3
Low ○ **CDN** ◇ 18-19 G 6
Low, Cape ▲ **CDN** ◆ 14-15 T 4
Lowa ∼ **USA** ◇ 22-23 L 4
Lowell ○ **USA** (ID) ◇ 20-21 G 2
Lowell ○ **USA** (MA) ◇ 22-23 N 4
  ◆ 14-15 W 8
Lower Guinea ⊥ ◆ 9 E 5
Lower Hutt ○ **NZ** ◆ 60-61 P 8
Lower Lake ○ **USA** (CA) ◇ 20-21 C 6
Lower Lake ○ **USA** ◇ 20-21 E 5
Lower Pensinula ∼ **USA** ◇ 22-23 F 4
  ◆ 14-15 T 8
Lower Red Lake ○ **USA** ◆ 14-15 R 7
Lower Valley of the Awash •• **ETH**
Lower Zambezi National Park ⊥ **Z**
  ◆ 50-51 G 5
Lowest Point in United States ∴ **USA**
  ◇ 20-21 F 7
Lowman ○ **USA** ◇ 20-21 G 3
Lowville ○ **USA** ◇ 22-23 L 4
Loxton ○ **ZA** ◆ 50-51 F 6
Loyalté, Îles ∧ **F** ◆ 60-61 O 4
Loyds River ∼ **USA** ◇ 18-19 Q 4
Loyoro ○ **EAU** ◆ 48-49 M 8
Lozère, Mont ▲ **F** ◇ 38-39 J 9
Luacano ○ **ANG** ◆ 50-51 F 4
Luachimo ○ **ANG** ◆ 50-51 F 3
Luali ○ **ZRE** ◆ 50-51 D 3
Luama ∼ **ZRE** ◆ 50-51 G 2
Lu'an ○ **CHN** ◆ 54-55 M 5
Luanda ★ **ANG** ◆ 50-51 D 3
Luando, Reserva Natural Integral do ⊥
  ANG ◆ 50-51 E 4
Luanginga ∼ **Z** ◆ 50-51 F 4
Luangue ∼ **ANG** ◆ 50-51 E 3
Luan He ∼ **CHN** ◆ 54-55 M 3
Luanping ○ **CHN** ◆ 54-55 M 3
Luanshya ○ **Z** ◆ 50-51 F 4
Luantun ∴ **BH** ◇ 28-29 K 3
Luarbanhajo ○ **RI** ◆ 58-59 G 8
Lubango ∼ **ANG** ◆ 50-51 D 4
Lubao ○ **ZRE** ◆ 50-51 G 3
Lubbock ○ **USA** ◇ 26-27 G 3
  ◇ 16-17 F 4
Lubec ○ **USA** ◇ 22-23 P 3
Lübeck ○ **D** ◇ 40-41 L 2
  ◆ 34-35 O 5
Lubefu ○ **ZRE** ◆ 50-51 F 2
Lubero ○ **ZRE** ◆ 50-51 G 1
Libero ∼ **ZRE** ◆ 50-51 E 3
Lubilanji ∼ **ZRE** ◆ 50-51 F 3
Lublin ★ **PL** ◆ 40-41 R 3
  ◆ 34-35 Q 5
Lubny ○ **UA** ◆ 34-35 S 6
Lubudi ○ **ZRE** ◆ 50-51 F 3
Lubuklinggau ○ **RI** ◆ 58-59 D 7
Lubumbashi ○ **ZRE** ◆ 50-51 G 4
Lubungu ∼ **Z** ◆ 50-51 F 4
Lubutu ○ **ZRE** ◆ 50-51 G 2
Lucan ○ **CDN** ◇ 18-19 D 7
Lucania ∼ **RI** ◆ 58-59 H 7
Lucedale ○ **USA** ◇ 24-25 D 4
Lucena ☆ **RP** ◆ 58-59 H 4
Lucerne Valley ○ **USA** ◇ 20-21 F 7
Luceville ○ **CDN** ◇ 18-19 K 4
Lucie, Lac < **CDN** ◇ 18-19 J 3
Lucira ○ **ANG** ◆ 50-51 D 4
Lucknow ☆ ○ **IND** ◆ 56-57 N 5
Lucky ○ **USA** ◇ 26-27 L 4
Luçon ○ **F** ◇ 38-39 G 8 ◆ 34-35 L 6
Lucusse ○ **ANG** ◆ 50-51 F 4
Lüderitz ☆ **NAM** ◆ 50-51 E 5
Lüderitzbaai ≈ **NAM** ◆ 50-51 E 7
Ludington ○ **USA** ◇ 22-23 E 4
Ludlow ○ **USA** (CA) ◇ 20-21 F 7
Ludlow ○ **USA** (CO) ◇ 26-27 E 1
Ludowici ○ **USA** ◇ 24-25 H 4
Luebo ○ **ZRE** ◆ 50-51 F 3
Lueders ○ **USA** ◇ 26-27 H 3
Luena ○ **ANG** ◆ 50-51 E 4
Luengué, Coutada Pública do ⊥ **ANG**
Luffin ○ **CHN** ◆ 54-55 M 7
Lufkin ○ **USA** ◇ 26-27 K 4
  ◇ 16-17 H 4
Luganville ○ • **VAN** ◆ 60-61 O 3
Lugenda ∼ **MOC** ◆ 50-51 J 4
Lugo ○ **E** ◆ 44-45 D 3 ◆ 34-35 K 7
Luhans'k ☆ **UA** ◆ 34-35 T 6
Luiana ∼ **ANG** ◆ 50-51 F 5
Luiana, Coutada Pública do ⊥ **ANG**
  ◆ 50-51 F 5
Luilaka ∼ **ZRE** ◆ 50-51 F 2
Luimneach = Limerick ○ **IRL**
  ◆ 34-35 J 5
Luis Moya ○ **MEX** ◇ 16-17 F 6
Luishia ○ **ZRE** ◆ 50-51 G 4
Luiza ○ **ZRE** ◆ 50-51 F 3
Luján ○ **RA** ◆ 32-33 L 4
Lukenie ∼ **ZRE** ◆ 50-51 E 2
Lukeville ○ **USA** ◇ 20-21 H 10
Lukolela ○ **ZRE** ◆ 50-51 E 2
Lukuga ∼ **ZRE** ◆ 50-51 G 3
Lukusuzi National Park ⊥ **Z**
  ◆ 50-51 G 4
Lula ○ **USA** ◇ 24-25 D 2
Luleå ○ **S** ◆ 36-37 J 4 ◆ 34-35 Q 2
Luleälven ∼ **S** ◆ 36-37 J 4

Lulonga ∼ **ZRE** ◆ 50-51 E 1
Lulua ∼ **ZRE** ◆ 50-51 F 2
Lumajang ○ **RI** ◆ 58-59 F 8
Lumbala ○ **ANG** ◆ 50-51 F 4
Lumbala N'guimbo ∼ **ANG** ◆ 50-51 F 4
Lumbardi ∼ **ZRE** ◆ 50-51 F 4
Lumber River ∼ **USA** ◇ 24-25 J 2
Lumberton ○ **USA** (MS) ◇ 24-25 D 4
Lumberton ○ **USA** (NC) ◇ 24-25 J 2
Lumeje ○ **ANG** ◆ 50-51 F 4
Lumi ○ **PNG** ◆ 58-59 M 7
Lumpkin ○ **USA** ◇ 24-25 F 3
Luna ○ **USA** ◇ 26-27 D 3
Lunas, Los ○ **USA** ◇ 26-27 E 3
Lund ○ **USA** ◇ 20-21 H 6
Lundazi ○ **Z** ◆ 50-51 H 4
Lunenburg ○ ••• **CDN** ◇ 18-19 M 6
  ◆ 34-35 M 7
Lunga ∼ **Z** ◆ 50-51 F 4
Lunga ∼ **USA** ◆ 50-51 J 2
Lungué-Bungo ∼ **ANG** ◆ 50-51 F 4
Luohe ○ **CHN** ◆ 54-55 M 5
Luoyang ○ **CHN** ◆ 54-55 L 5
Lúrio, Rio ∼ **MOC** ◆ 50-51 J 4
Lusaka ★ **Z** ◆ 50-51 G 5
Lusambo ○ **ZRE** ◆ 50-51 F 2
Lut, Dašt-e ⊥ **IR** ◆ 56-57 H 4
Luther ○ **USA** ◇ 26-27 J 2
Luts'k ○ **UA** ◆ 34-35 R 5
Lützow-Holm bukt ≈ ◆ 13 G 4
Luuq ○ **SP** ◆ 48-49 O 7
Luverne ○ **USA** ◇ 24-25 E 4
Luvua ∼ **Z** ◆ 50-51 G 3
Luwingu ○ **Z** ◆ 50-51 G 4
Luwuk ○ **RI** ◆ 58-59 H 7
Luxembourg ■ **L** ◆ 40-41 J 4
  ◆ 34-35 N 6
Luxembourg ★ ••• **L** ◆ 40-41 J 4
  ◆ 34-35 N 6
Luxor = al-Uqsur ☆ ••• **ET** ◆ 48-49 M 3
Luz ○ **USA** ◇ 30-31 K 8
Luzern ○ **CH** ◆ 40-41 J 4
  ◆ 34-35 N 6
Luzhou ○ **CHN** ◆ 54-55 K 6
Luziania ○ **BR** ◆ 30-31 K 8
Luzilândia ○ **BR** ◆ 30-31 L 5
Luzon ∧ **RP** ◆ 58-59 H 3
Luzon Strait ≈ ◆ 58-59 H 2
Luzy ○ **F** ◇ 38-39 J 8 ◆ 34-35 M 6
L'viv = Lviv ☆ **UA** ◆ 34-35 Q 6
Lviv ☆ **UA** ◆ 34-35 Q 6
Lvov = Lviv ☆ **UA** ◆ 34-35 Q 6
Lydenburg ○ **ZA** ◆ 50-51 H 5
Lynchburg ○ **USA** ◇ 22-23 J 7
  ◇ 16-17 L 3
Lynches River ∼ **USA** ◇ 24-25 H 2
Lyndon Baines Johnson National Historic
  Park ••• **USA** ◇ 26-27 H 4
Lyndon B. Johnson, Lake < **USA**
  ◇ 26-27 H 4
Lyndonville ○ **USA** (NY) ◇ 22-23 J 4
Lyndonville ○ **USA** (VT) ◇ 22-23 M 3
Lynn ○ **USA** (IN) ◇ 22-23 F 5
Lynn ○ **USA** (MA) ◇ 22-23 N 4
Lynn, Mount ▲ **USA** ◇ 20-21 C 6
Lynndyl ○ **USA** ◇ 20-21 H 6
Lynn Haven ○ **USA** ◇ 24-25 F 4
Lyon ☆ • **F** ◆ 34-35 M 6
Lyons ○ **USA** ◇ 24-25 G 3
Lyra Reef ∼ **PNG** ◆ 58-59 O 7
Lysaja, gora ▲ **RUS** ◆ 52-53 P 6

M

Ma'ān ☆ **JOR** ◆ 56-57 D 4
Ma'arrat an-Nu'mān ○ ∼ **SYR**
  ◆ 56-57 D 3
Maas ∼ **NL** ◆ 40-41 J 3 ◆ 34-35 N 5
Maasin ○ **RP** ◆ 58-59 H 4
Maastricht ○ ∼ **NL** ◆ 40-41 H 3
  ◆ 34-35 N 5
M.A.B., Réserve ⊥ **ZRE** ◆ 50-51 F 4
Mabelle ○ **USA** ◇ 26-27 H 3
Mabote ○ **MOC** ◆ 50-51 H 6
Mabou ○ **CDN** ◇ 18-19 O 5
Mabton ○ **USA** ◇ 20-21 D 2
Mabuasehube Game Reserve ⊥ **RB**
  ◆ 50-51 F 6
Mabuki ○ **EAT** ◆ 50-51 H 2
Macaé ○ **BR** ◆ 32-33 N 2
MacAlpine Lake ○ **CDN** ◆ 14-15 Q 3
Macao ○ **P** ◆ 54-55 L 7
Macapá ☆ **BR** ◆ 30-31 J 4
Macará ○ **EC** ◇ 30-31 C 5
Macaracas ○ **PA** ◇ 28-29 D 8
Macarena, Parque Nacional la ⊥ **CO**
  ◇ 30-31 D 4
Macas ○ **EC** ◇ 30-31 D 5
Macaú ○ **BR** ◆ 30-31 M 6
Macau = Macao ○ • **P** ◆ 54-55 L 7
Macaza, Rivière ∼ **CDN** ◇ 18-19 G 5
Macclesfield Bank ≃ **CHN** ◆ 58-59 F 4
Maccles Lake ○ **CDN** ◇ 18-19 S 5
MacDonald, Lake ○ **AUS** ◆ 60-61 F 4
Macdonnell Ranges ▲ **AUS**
  ◆ 60-61 G 4
Macedonia ■ **MK** ◆ 46-47 H 4
  ◆ 34-35 Q 7
Macenta ○ **RG** ◆ 48-49 D 7
Macachi ○ **EC** ◇ 30-31 D 5
Machakos ○ **EAK** ◆ 50-51 H 2
Machala ☆ **EC** ◇ 30-31 C 5
Machaquilá ∴ **GCA** ◇ 28-29 K 3
Machecoul ○ **F** ◇ 38-39 G 8
Macheng ○ **CHN** ◆ 54-55 M 5
Mācherla ○ **IND** ◆ 56-57 M 7
Machias ○ **USA** ◇ 22-23 P 3
Machilipatnam ○ **IND** ◆ 56-57 N 7
Machu Picchu ∴ **PE** ◇ 30-31 E 7
Mackay ○ **AUS** ◆ 60-61 K 4
Mackay, Lake ○ **AUS** ◆ 60-61 F 4
Mackay Lake ○ **CDN** ◆ 14-15 O 4
Mackenzie Bay ≈ ◆ 14-15 J 3

Mackenzie Delta ⊥ •• **CDN** ◆ 14-15 K 3
Magnolia ○ **USA** ◇ 26-27 L 3
Mackenzie Highway II **CDN** ◆ 14-15 N 3
Mackenzie King Island ∧ **CDN**
  ◆ 14-15 O 1
Mackenzie Mountains ▲ **CDN**
  ◆ 14-15 K 3
Mackenzie River ∼ **CDN** ◆ 14-15 M 4
Mackinac Bridge • **USA** ◇ 22-23 F 3
Mackinac Island State Park • **USA**
  ◇ 22-23 F 3
Mackinaw City ○ **USA** ◇ 22-23 F 3
Mackeys ○ **USA** ◇ 24-25 K 2
Maclean ○ **AUS** ◆ 60-61 L 5
Maclean Strait ≈ ◆ 14-15 P 1
Maclear ○ **ZA** ◆ 50-51 G 6
MacLeod, Lake ○ **AUS** ◆ 60-61 C 4
Macomb ○ **USA** ◇ 22-23 D 5
Macomér ○ **I** ◆ 46-47 B 4
  ◆ 34-35 N 7
Macomia ○ **MOC** ◆ 50-51 K 4
Mâcon ○ ∼ **F** ◇ 38-39 K 8
  ◆ 16-17 K 4
Macon ○ **USA** (GA) ◇ 24-25 G 3
Macon ○ **USA** (OH) ◇ 22-23 G 6
Macondo ○ **ANG** ◆ 50-51 F 4
Macpès ○ **CDN** ◇ 18-19 K 4
Macquarie Harbour ≈ ◆ 60-61 K 8
Macumba River ∼ **AUS** ◆ 60-61 H 5
Macusani ○ **PE** ◇ 30-31 E 7
Madagascar, Arrecife ∼ **MEX**
  ◇ 28-29 J 1
Madagascar Basin ≃ 50-51 M 6
Madagascar Ridge ≃ ◆ 50-51 K 6
Madagasikara ∧ **RM** ◆ 50-51 L 6
Mada'in Salih ∴ **KSA** ◆ 56-57 D 5
Madang ∼ **PNG** ◆ 58-59 N 7
Madaoua ○ **RN** ◆ 48-49 G 6
Madara Canal < **USA** ◇ 20-21 E 7
Madawaska River ∼ **CDN** ◇ 18-19 F 6
Madeira ∼ **USA** ◇ 22-23 J 6
Madeira, Arquipélago de ∼ **P**
  ◆ 48-49 B 2
Madeira, Rio ∼ **BR** ◆ 30-31 G 6
Madeira Rise ≃ ◆ 48-49 B 2
Madeleine, Cap-de-la- ○ **CDN**
  ◇ 18-19 H 5
Madeleine, Îles de la ∧ **CDN**
  ◇ 18-19 O 5 ◆ 14-15 Y 7
Madeline Island ∧ **USA** ◇ 22-23 C 2
Madera ○ **USA** ◇ 20-21 D 7
Madhya Pradesh □ **IND** ◆ 56-57 M 6
Madikeri ○ **IND** ◆ 56-57 M 8
Madill ○ **USA** ◇ 26-27 J 2
Madimba ○ **ZRE** ◆ 50-51 E 2
Madin, al- ☆ ∼ **KSA** ◆ 56-57 D 6
Madison ○ **USA** (IN) ◇ 22-23 F 6
Madison ○ **USA** (SD) ◇ 22-23 H 4
Madison ☆ • **USA** (WI) ◇ 22-23 H 4
  ◇ 14-15 T 8
Madison Bird Refuge ⊥ **USA**
  ◇ 20-21 H 3
Madison Canyon Earthquake Area (1959)
  ∴ **USA** ◇ 20-21 J 3
Madison River ∼ **USA** ◇ 20-21 J 3
Madisonville ○ **USA** (KY) ◇ 22-23 E 7
Madisonville ○ **USA** (TX) ◇ 26-27 K 4
Madiun ○ **RI** ◆ 58-59 F 8
Madley, Mount ▲ **AUS** ◆ 60-61 E 4
Mado Gashi ○ **EAK** ◆ 50-51 J 1
Madrakah, Ra's ∼ **OM** ◆ 56-57 H 7
Madras ☆ **IND** ◆ 56-57 N 8
Madras = Chennai ☆ ○ **IND**
  ◆ 56-57 N 8
Madre, Laguna ○ ◇ 26-27 J 6
  ◇ 16-17 G 5
Madre de Chiapas, Sierra ▲ **MEX**
  ◇ 28-29 H 4 ◇ 16-17 H 5
Madre de Dios, Isla ∧ **RCH**
  ◆ 32-33 G 8
Madre de Dios, Rio ∼ **BOL** ◇ 30-31 F 7
Madre del Sur, Sierra ▲ **MEX**
  ◇ 28-29 D 3
Madrid ★ ••• **E** ◆ 44-45 F 4
  ◆ 34-35 L 7
Madura, Pulau ∧ **RI** ◆ 58-59 F 8
Madura, Selat ≈ ◆ 58-59 F 8
Madurai ○ **IND** ◆ 56-57 M 9
Madura Motel ○ **AUS** ◆ 60-61 F 6
Madurāntakam ○ **IND** ◆ 56-57 M 8
Maebashi ☆ **J** ◆ 54-55 R 4
Mae Hong Son ○ **THA** ◆ 58-59 C 3
Mae Sariang ○ **THA** ◆ 58-59 C 3
Maestra, Sierra ▲ **C** ◇ 16-17 L 6
Maewo = Île Aurora ∧ **VAN**
  ◆ 60-61 O 3
Mafa Channel ≈ ◆ 50-51 J 3
Mafia Island ∧ **EAT** ◆ 50-51 J 3
Mafra ○ **BR** ◆ 32-33 N 3
Mafraq ○ **Y** ◆ 56-57 F 7
Magadan ○ ••• **RUS** ◆ 52-53 c 5
Magadanskoe Ofskoe lesničestvo,
  zapovednik ⊥ **RUS** ◆ 52-53 b 5
Magadanskij Ofskoe lesničestvo,
  zapovednik ⊥ **RUS** ◆ 52-53 b 5
Magadi ○ **EAK** ◆ 50-51 H 2
Magangue ○ **CO** ◇ 30-31 E 3
Magaria ○ **RN** ◆ 48-49 H 6
Magazine Mountain ▲ **USA** ◇ 26-27 L 2
Magburaka ○ **WAL** ◆ 48-49 C 7
Magdalena ○ **BOL** ◇ 30-31 G 7
Magdalena ○ **MEX** ◇ 28-29 D 2
Magdalena ○ **USA** ◇ 26-27 D 2
Magdalena, Isla ∧ **MEX** ◇ 16-17 D 6
Magdalena, Isla ∧ **RCH** ◆ 32-33 G 7
Magdalena, Rio ∼ **MEX** ◇ 16-17 D 4
Magdalena Tequisistlán ○ **MEX**
  ◇ 28-29 D 4
Magdeburg ☆ **D** ◆ 40-41 L 2
  ◆ 34-35 O 5
Magelang ○ **RI** ◆ 58-59 F 8
Magga Range ▲ **ANT** ◆ 13 F 35
Magic Reservoir < **USA** ◇ 20-21 G 3
Magic Valley ∼ **USA** ◇ 20-21 G 4
Magistral'nyj ○ **RUS** ◆ 52-53 V 6
Maǧma'a, al- ○ **KSA** ◆ 56-57 F 5
Magna ○ **USA** ◇ 20-21 H 5
Magnetic Pole Area **ANT** ◆ 14-15 Q 2

Magnitogorsk ○ **RUS** ◆ 34-35 X 5
Magog ○ **CDN** ◇ 18-19 H 6
Magpie, Rivière ∼ **CDN** ◇ 18-19 M 3
Maguari, Cabo ▲ **BR** ◆ 30-31 K 5
Magude ○ **MOC** ◆ 50-51 H 6
Mahābād ○ **IR** ◆ 56-57 F 3
Mahackala ○ **RUS** ◆ 34-35 V 7
Mahād ○ **IND** ◆ 56-57 L 7
Mahaicony ○ **GUY** ◇ 30-31 H 3
Mahajanga ○ **RM** ◆ 50-51 L 5
Mahakam ∼ **RI** ◆ 58-59 G 7
Mahalapye ○ **RB** ◆ 50-51 G 6
Mahānadi ∼ **IND** ◆ 56-57 N 6
Mahanoro ○ **RM** ◆ 50-51 L 5
Maharashtra □ **IND** ◆ 56-57 L 6
Mahavelona ○ **RM** ◆ 50-51 L 5
Mahdia ○ **GUY** ◇ 30-31 H 3
Mahe ○ • **IND** ◆ 56-57 M 8
Mahé Island ∧ **SY** ◆ 50-51 N 2
Mahenge ○ **EAT** ◆ 50-51 J 3
Mahesana ○ **IND** ◆ 56-57 L 6
Mahia Peninsula ∼ **NZ** ◆ 60-61 Q 7
Mahilëv = Mahilev ○ **BY**
  ◆ 42-43 M 5
Mahilyow = Mahilëv ○ **BY**
  ◆ 42-43 M 5 ◆ 34-35 S 5
Mahon Bay ≈ ◇ 18-19 M 6
Mahra, al- ∼ **Y** ◆ 56-57 G 7
Mahuva ○ **IND** ◆ 56-57 L 6
Maiama ○ **RM** ◆ 50-51 L 5
Maica, Rivière ∼ **CDN** ◇ 18-19 N 3
Maiduguri ○ **WAN** ◆ 48-49 H 6
Maiko, Parc National de la ⊥ **ZRE**
  ◆ 50-51 G 2
Maimana ○ **AFG** ◆ 56-57 J 3
Main ∼ **D** ◆ 40-41 L 3 ◆ 34-35 O 5
Main à Dieu ○ **CDN** ◇ 18-19 P 5
Main Brook ○ **CDN** ◇ 18-19 R 4
Main Channel ○ **CDN** ◇ 18-19 Q 4
Maine □ **USA** ◇ 22-23 N 3
  ◇ 14-15 X 7
Maine, Gulf of ≈ ◇ 22-23 P 4
  ◇ 14-15 X 8
Mainé-Soroa ○ **RN** ◆ 48-49 H 6
Maine TPK II **USA** ◇ 22-23 N 4
Mainland ∧ **USA** ◇ 22-23 N 4
Main River ∼ **CDN** ◇ 18-19 Q 4
Maintirano ○ **RM** ◆ 50-51 K 5
Mainz ☆ **D** ◆ 40-41 K 4
  ◆ 34-35 N 6
Maiquetía ○ **YV** ◇ 30-31 F 2
Maisonnette ○ **CDN** ◇ 18-19 L 5
Maitland ○ **AUS** ◆ 60-61 L 6
Maíz, Ciudad del ○ **MEX** ◇ 16-17 G 6
Maíz, Islas del ∧ **NIC** ◇ 28-29 C 7
Maíz Grande, Isla de ∧ **NIC**
  ◇ 28-29 C 7
Maíz Pequeña, Isla de ∧ **NIC**
  ◇ 28-29 C 7
Maja ∼ **RUS** ◆ 52-53 X 5
Majahual ○ **MEX** ◇ 28-29 L 2
Majene ○ **RI** ◆ 58-59 G 7
Majkopçigaj ○ **KZ** ◆ 52-53 K 7
Majkop ○ **RUS** ◆ 34-35 U 7
Majmeča ∼ **RUS** ◆ 52-53 R 3
Majn ∼ **RUS** ◆ 52-53 f 4
Majuro ∼ **MAI** ◆ 12 J 2
Makaha ○ **USA** ◇ 20-21 C 3
Makah Indian Reservation ∧ **USA**
  ◇ 20-21 B 1
Makale ○ **USA** ◆ 58-59 G 7
Makambako ○ **EAT** ◆ 50-51 H 3
Makarov Basin ≃ ◆ 13 A 35
Makasar = Ujung Pandang ☆ **RI**
  ◆ 58-59 G 8
Makassar = Ujung Pandang ☆ **RI**
  ◆ 58-59 G 8
Makassar Strait ≈ ◆ 58-59 G 7
Makeni ○ **WAL** ◆ 48-49 C 7
Makgadikgadi Pans Game Park ⊥ **RB**
  ◆ 50-51 G 6
Makijvka ○ **UA** ◆ 34-35 T 6
Maki National Park ⊥ **ETH** ◆ 48-49 N 7
Makiivka = Makijvka ○ **UA**
  ◆ 34-35 T 6
Makka ☆ ••• **KSA** ◆ 56-57 D 6
Makkovik ○ **CDN** ◆ 14-15 Z 5
Makokou ☆ **G** ◆ 50-51 D 1
Makongolosi ○ **EAT** ◆ 50-51 H 3
Makrān Coast Range ▲ **PK**
  ◆ 56-57 J 5
Makurdi ○ **WAN** ◆ 48-49 G 7
Makuti ○ **ZW** ◆ 50-51 G 5
Makuyuni ○ **EAT** ◆ 50-51 J 2
Mala, Punta ▲ **PA** ◇ 28-29 D 8
Malabar Coast ∼ **IND** ◆ 56-57 L 8
Malabo ★ **GQ** ◆ 48-49 G 8
Malacca, Strait of ≈ ◆ 58-59 D 6
Malad City ○ **USA** ◇ 20-21 H 4
Maladzečna ○ **BY** ◆ 42-43 K 4
  ◆ 34-35 R 5
Mälaga ○ **E** ◆ 44-45 G 6 ◆ 34-35 L 8
Malaga ○ **USA** ◇ 26-27 E 3
Malagarasi ∼ **EAT** ◆ 50-51 H 3
Malaimbandy ○ **RM** ◆ 50-51 L 6
Malaja Heta ∼ **RUS** ◆ 52-53 N 4
Malakāl ☆ **SUD** ◆ 48-49 M 7
Malakhini ○ **NEP** ◆ 56-57 N 5
Malakula = Île Mallicolo ∧ **VAN**
  ◆ 60-61 O 3
Malalaua ○ **PNG** ◆ 58-59 N 8
Malang ○ **RI** ◆ 58-59 F 8
Malanje ☆ **ANG** ◆ 50-51 E 3
Malargüe ○ **RA** ◇ 32-33 J 5
Malartic, Lac ○ **CDN** ◇ 18-19 F 5
Malaspina Glacier ⊂ **USA** ◆ 14-15 H 5
Malatya ☆ **TR** ◆ 56-57 D 3
Malaut ○ **IND** ◆ 56-57 L 4
Malawi ■ **MW** ◆ 50-51 H 4
Malawi, Lake ○ **MW** ◆ 50-51 H 4
Malāyer ○ **IR** ◆ 56-57 F 4
Malaysia ■ **MAL** ◆ 58-59 N 8
Malbaie, La ○ **CDN** ◇ 18-19 J 5
Malden ○ **USA** ◇ 22-23 D 7

Malden Island ∧ **KIB** ◆ 12 M 3
Maldives ∼ **MV** ◆ 10-11 G 8
Maldonado ○ **ROU** ◆ 32-33 M 4
Maldonado, Punta ▲ **MEX** ◇ 28-29 D 4
Málegaon ○ **IND** ◆ 56-57 L 6
Malema ○ **MOC** ◆ 50-51 J 4
Malhär Lake ○ **USA** ◇ 20-21 E 4
Malheur Lake ○ **USA** ◇ 20-21 E 4
Malheur River ∼ **USA** ◇ 20-21 E 3
Mali ■ **RMM** ◆ 48-49 D 6
Malinalco ∴ **MEX** ◇ 28-29 E 2
Malindi ○ **EAK** ◆ 50-51 K 2
Malijamar ○ **USA** ◇ 26-27 F 3
Mallacoota ○ **AUS** ◆ 60-61 K 7
Mallorca ∧ **E** ◆ 44-45 J 5
  ◆ 34-35 O 4
Malone ○ **USA** ◇ 22-23 L 3
Malmesbury ○ **ZA** ◆ 50-51 E 8
Malmö ○ **S** ◆ 36-37 F 9
  ◆ 34-35 O 4
Malonga ○ **ZRE** ◆ 50-51 F 4
Malpelo, Isla de ∧ **CO** ◆ 30-31 C 4
Malpeque Bay ≈ ◇ 18-19 N 5
Mālpura ○ **IND** ◆ 56-57 L 5
Malta ■ **M** ◆ 46-47 E 7 ◆ 34-35 O 8
Maltahöhe ○ **NAM** ◆ 50-51 E 6
Malunda ○ **RI** ◆ 58-59 G 7
Mälvan ○ **IND** ◆ 56-57 L 7
Malvern ○ **USA** ◇ 26-27 L 2
Malyj Ljahovskij, ostrov ∧ **RUS**
  ◆ 52-53 Y 3
Mama ○ **RUS** ◆ 52-53 T 6
Mamasa ○ **RI** ◆ 58-59 G 7
Mambasa ○ **ZRE** ◆ 50-51 G 1
Mamberamo ∼ **RI** ◆ 58-59 L 7
Mamfé ○ **CAM** ◆ 48-49 G 7
Mámi, Ra's ▲ **Y** ◆ 56-57 H 8
Mamiá, Lago ○ **BR** ◆ 30-31 G 5
Mamljutka ○ **KZ** ◆ 52-53 K 7
Mammoth ○ **USA** ◇ 26-27 P 6
Mammoth Cave National Park ⊥ ••• **USA**
  ◇ 22-23 E 7
Mammoth Hot Springs ○ **USA**
  ◇ 20-21 J 3
Mamoré ∼ **BOL** ◇ 30-31 F 7
Mamou ○ **RG** ◆ 48-49 C 6
Mamuju ○ **RI** ◆ 58-59 G 7
Mamuno ○ **RB** ◆ 50-51 F 6
Man ○ **CI** ◆ 48-49 D 7
Manacapuru ○ **BR** ◆ 30-31 G 5
Manado ☆ **RI** ◆ 58-59 H 6
Managua ★ **NIC** ◇ 28-29 L 5
  ◇ 16-17 J 8
Managua, Lago de ○ **NIC** ◇ 28-29 L 5
  ◇ 16-17 J 8
Manáha ○ **Y** ◆ 56-57 E 7
Manakara ○ **RM** ◆ 50-51 L 6
Manali ○ **IND** ◆ 56-57 M 4
Manáma, al- ★ **BRN** ◆ 56-57 G 5
Manamana Avaratra ○ **RM** ◆ 50-51 L 5
Mananjary ○ **RM** ◆ 50-51 L 6
Manantali, Lac de < **RMM** ◆ 48-49 C 6
Manantenina ○ **RM** ◆ 50-51 L 6
Mana Pools National Park ⊥ ••• **ZW**
  ◆ 50-51 G 5
Manapouri, Lake ○ **NZ** ◆ 60-61 O 8
Manas He ∼ **CHN** ◆ 54-55 F 2
Manassas ○ **USA** ◇ 22-23 K 6
Manassas National Battlefield Park ∴ **USA**
  ◇ 22-23 K 6
Manatlán ○ **MEX** ◇ 28-29 C 3
Manaus ☆ **BR** ◆ 30-31 G 5
Mancelona ○ **USA** ◇ 22-23 F 3
Manche = English Channel ≈
  ◇ 38-39 F 6 ◆ **GB** ◇ 38-39 F 5
  ◆ 34-35 L 5
Manchester ○ • **GB** ◇ 38-39 F 5
  ◆ 34-35 L 5
Manchester ○ **USA** (CT) ◇ 22-23 M 5
Manchester ○ **USA** (IA) ◇ 22-23 D 4
Manchester ○ **USA** (KY) ◇ 22-23 G 7
Manchester ☆ **USA** (NH) ◇ 22-23 M 4
  ◇ 14-15 W 8
Manchester ○ **USA** (TN) ◇ 24-25 E 2
Manchester ○ **USA** (VT) ◇ 22-23 M 4
Manchuria ⊥ ∼ **CHN** ◆ 54-55 N 2
Máncora ○ **PE** ◇ 30-31 C 5
Manda, Parc National de la ⊥ **TCH**
  ◆ 48-49 J 7
Mandabe ○ **RM** ◆ 50-51 K 6
Mandal, Puncak ▲ **RI** ◆ 58-59 M 7
Mandalay ☆ **MYA** ◆ 54-55 H 7
Mandalgov' ○ **MAU** ◆ 54-55 K 2
Mandara Mountains ▲ **WAN**
  ◆ 48-49 H 6
Mandasor ○ **IND** ◆ 56-57 M 6
Mandera ○ **EAK** ◆ 50-51 K 1
Mandi ○ **IND** ◆ 56-57 M 4
Mandimba ○ **MOC** ◆ 50-51 J 4
Mandioli, Pulau ∧ **RI** ◆ 58-59 J 7
Mandla ○ **IND** ◆ 56-57 N 6
Mandritsara ○ **RM** ◆ 50-51 L 5
Mandurah ○ • **AUS** ◆ 60-61 D 6
Manfredónia ○ **I** ◆ 46-47 F 4
  ◆ 34-35 P 7
Manga ○ **BR** ◆ 30-31 L 7
Manga ⊥ **RN** ◆ 48-49 H 6
Mangabeiras, Chapada das ▲ **BR**
  ◆ 30-31 K 6
Manga Grande ○ **ANG** ◆ 50-51 E 3
Mangalmé ○ **TCH** ◆ 48-49 J 6
Mangalore ○ **IND** ◆ 56-57 L 8
Mangdzh ∼ **RM** ◆ 50-51 L 5
Mangham ○ **USA** ◇ 26-27 M 3
Mangkalihat, Cabo ▲ **CO** ◇ 30-31 D 4
Mango ○ **RM** ◆ 50-51 L 5
Mangoky ∼ **RM** ◆ 50-51 L 6
Mangole, Pulau ∧ **RI** ◆ 58-59 H 7
Mangueira, Lagoa ○ **BR** ◆ 32-33 M 4
Mangui ○ **CHN** ◆ 54-55 N 1
Mangum ○ **USA** ◇ 26-27 H 2
Mangyshlak, plato ▲ **KZ** ◆ 56-57 G 2
Mangyštau ∼ **KZ** ◆ 56-57 G 2
Manguba, La ○ **CDN** ◇ 18-19 L 6
Mania ∼ **RM** ◆ 50-51 L 6
Manicoré ○ **BR** ◆ 30-31 G 6

Manicouagan ○ **CDN** ◇ 18-19 K 3
  ◆ 14-15 X 6
Manicouagan, Petit Lac ○ **CDN**
  ◇ 18-19 L 3
Manicouagan, Réservoir ⊥ < **CDN** (QUE)
  ◇ 18-19 K 3 ◆ 14-15 X 6
Manicouagan, Réservoir < ••• **CDN** (QUE)
  ◇ 18-19 K 3
Manicouagan, Rivière ∼ **CDN**
  ◇ 18-19 K 3 ◆ 14-15 X 6
Manic-Trois, Réservoir < **CDN**
  ◇ 18-19 J 4
Manila ★ •• **RP** ◆ 58-59 H 4
Manipur □ **IND** ◆ 54-55 P 6
Manisa ☆ **TR** ◆ 34-35 R 8
Manistee ○ **USA** ◇ 22-23 E 4
Manistee River ∼ **USA** ◇ 22-23 F 3
Manistique ○ **USA** ◇ 22-23 F 2
Manistique Lake ○ **USA** ◇ 22-23 F 2
Manistique River ∼ **USA** ◇ 22-23 F 2
Manitoba □ **CDN** ◆ 14-15 Q 5
Manitoba, Lake ○ **CDN** ◆ 14-15 R 6
Manitou, Rivière ∼ **CDN** ◇ 18-19 M 3
Manitou Islands ∧ **USA** ◇ 22-23 E 3
Manitou Lake ○ **CDN** ◇ 18-19 Q 6
Manitoulin Island ∧ **CDN** ◇ 18-19 C 6
  ◆ 14-15 U 7
Manitowoc ○ **USA** ◇ 22-23 E 3
Maniwaki ○ **CDN** (QUE) ◇ 18-19 G 5
Maniwaki X **CDN** (QUE) ◇ 18-19 F 5
Maniwaki Indian Reservation X **CDN**
  ◇ 26-27 K 2
Manizales ○ **CO** ◇ 30-31 D 3
Manjimup ○ **AUS** ◆ 60-61 D 6
Mankanza ○ **ZRE** ◆ 50-51 E 1
Mankato ○ **USA** ◆ 14-15 S 8
Mankins ○ **USA** ◇ 26-27 H 3
Mankono ○ **CI** ◆ 48-49 D 7
Mankyslâk ∼ **KZ** ◆ 56-57 G 2
Mankystau ∼ **KZ** ◆ 56-57 G 2
Manna ○ **RI** ◆ 58-59 D 7
Mannar, Gulf of ≈ **CL** ◆ 56-57 M 9
Mannheim ○ **D** ◆ 40-41 K 4
  ◆ 34-35 N 6
Manning ○ **USA** ◇ 24-25 H 3
Manokwari ○ **RI** ◆ 58-59 K 7
Manombo Atsimo ○ **RM** ◆ 50-51 K 6
Manono ○ **ZRE** ◆ 50-51 G 3
Manosque ○ **F** ◇ 38-39 K 10
  ◆ 34-35 M 7
Manouane ○ **CDN** (QUE)
  ◇ 18-19 G 5
Manouane, Lac ○ **CDN** (QUE)
  ◇ 18-19 J 3
Manouanis, Lac ○ **CDN** ◇ 18-19 J 3
Manresa ○ **E** ◆ 44-45 H 4
  ◆ 34-35 M 7
Mansa ○ **Z** ◆ 50-51 G 4
Mansa Konko ○ **WAG** ◆ 48-49 B 6
Mansel Island ∧ **CDN** ◆ 14-15 V 4
Mansfield ○ **USA** (AR) ◇ 26-27 L 2
Mansfield ○ **USA** (LA) ◇ 26-27 L 3
Mansfield ○ **USA** (MO) ◇ 26-27 L 1
Mansfield ☆ **USA** (OH) ◇ 22-23 G 5
Mansfield ○ **USA** (PA) ◇ 22-23 K 5
Mansfield ○ **USA** (TX) ◇ 26-27 J 3
Mansle ○ **F** ◇ 38-39 H 9 ◆ 34-35 L 7
Mansura ○ **USA** ◇ 26-27 L 4
Mansūra, al- ☆ **ET** ◆ 48-49 K 2
Manta ○ **EC** ◇ 30-31 C 5
Mantalingajan, Mount ▲ **RP**
  ◆ 58-59 G 5
Mante, Ciudad ○ **MEX** ◇ 16-17 G 6
Manteca ○ **USA** ◇ 20-21 D 7
Mantena ○ **BR** ◆ 30-31 L 7
Manteo ○ **USA** ◇ 24-25 L 2
Mantiqueira, Serra da ▲ **BR**
  ◆ 32-33 N 2
Manto ○ **HN** ◇ 28-29 L 4
Manton ○ **USA** ◇ 22-23 F 3
Manú ○ **PE** ◇ 30-31 E 7
Manú, Parque Nacional ⊥ ••• **PE**
  ◇ 30-31 E 7
Manuel ○ **MEX** ◇ 16-17 G 6
Manui, Pulau ∧ **RI** ◆ 58-59 H 7
Manuripi Heath, Reserva Natural ⊥ **BOL**
  ◇ 30-31 F 7
Manus Island ∧ **PNG** ◆ 58-59 N 7
Many ○ **USA** ◇ 26-27 L 4
Manych Depression ∪ **RUS**
  ◆ 34-35 U 6
Manyinga ○ **Z** ◆ 50-51 F 4
Manyoni ○ **EAT** ◆ 50-51 H 3
Manzanillo ○ **C** ◆ 16-17 L 6
Manzanillo ○ **MEX** ◇ 28-29 B 2
  ◇ 16-17 F 7
Manzhouli ○ **CHN** ◆ 54-55 M 2
Manzini ○ **SD** ◆ 50-51 H 6
Maó ○ **E** ◆ 44-45 K 5 ◆ 34-35 M 8
Mao ○ **TCH** ◆ 48-49 J 6
Maoke, Pegunungan ▲ **RI** ◆ 58-59 L 7
Maoming ○ **CHN** ◆ 54-55 L 7
Mapane ○ **RI** ◆ 58-59 H 7
Mapare Island ∧ **MS** ◆ 58-59 N 5
Mapastepec ○ **MEX** ◇ 28-29 H 4
Mapia, Kepulauan ∧ **RI** ◆ 58-59 K 6
Mapinhane ○ **MOC** ◆ 50-51 J 6
Mapire ○ **YV** ◇ 30-31 G 3
Mapleton ○ **USA** ◇ 22-23 L 3
Mappsville ○ **USA** ◇ 22-23 L 7
Maprik ○ **PNG** ◆ 58-59 M 7
Mapuera, Rio ∼ **BR** ◆ 30-31 H 5
Maputo ★ **MOC** ◆ 50-51 H 7
Maputo, Baia do ≈ ◆ 50-51 H 7
Maputo, Reserva de Elefantes do ⊥ **MOC**
  ◆ 50-51 H 7
Maqteïr ∼ **RIM** ◆ 48-49 C 4
Maquatua, Rivière ∼ **CDN** ◇ 18-19 D 3
Maqueze ○ **MOC** ◆ 50-51 H 6
Maquoqua ∼ **RA** ◆ 32-33 J 4
Mar, La ∼ **MEX** ◇ 28-29 F 1
Maraá ○ **BR** ◆ 30-31 F 5
Marabá ○ **BR** ◆ 30-31 K 6
Maracá, Ilha de ∧ **BR** ◆ 30-31 J 4
Maracaiboá ○ **YV** ◇ 30-31 E 2
Maracaibo ☆ **YV** ◇ 30-31 E 2
Maracaibo, Lago de ○ **YV** ◇ 30-31 E 3
Maracaju ○ **BR** ◆ 32-33 L 2
Maracaju, Serra de ▲ **BR** ◆ 30-31 H 8
Maracay ☆ **YV** ◇ 30-31 F 2
Maradah ○ **LAR** ◆ 48-49 J 3

Maradi ☆ RN ◆ 48-49 G 6
Marage ○• IR ◆ 56-57 F 3
Marajó, Baía de ≈ ◆ 30-31 K 5
Marajó, Ilha de ⌒ BR ◆ 30-31 J 5
Maralal ○ EAK ◆ 50-51 J 1
Marale ○ HN ◇ 28-29 L 4
Maralinga ○ AUS ◆ 60-61 G 6
Maralinga -Tjarutja Aboriginal Lands ⚔ AUS ◆ 60-61 G 5
Maramec ○ USA ◇ 26-27 J 1
Marana ○ USA ◇ 20-21 J 9
Maranhão ▫ BR ◆ 30-31 K 6
Marañón, Río ~ PE ◆ 30-31 E 5
Maraoué, Parc National de la ⊥ CI ◆ 48-49 D 7
Marat, Ğabal ▲ Y ◆ 56-57 G 7
Marathon ○ USA (FL) ◇ 24-25 H 7
Marathon ○ USA (TX) ◇ 26-27 F 4
Maravatio ○ MEX ◇ 28-29 D 2
Marawi = Merowe ○ SUD ◆ 48-49 M 5
Marble Bar ○ AUS ◆ 60-61 D 4
Marble Falls ○ USA ◇ 26-27 H 4
Marble Hill ○ USA ◇ 22-23 D 7
Marcala ○ HN ◇ 28-29 K 4
Marceau, Lac ○ CDN ◇ 18-19 L 3
Marche ⊥ F ◇ 38-39 H 8
◆ 34-35 M 6
Marchena, Isla ⌒ EC ◆ 30-31 A 4
Marchinbar Island ⌒ AUS ◆ 60-61 H 2
Mar Chiquita, Laguna ○ RA ◆ 32-33 K 4
Marco ○ USA ◇ 24-25 H 7
Marcona ○ PE ◆ 30-31 D 8
Marcus Baker, Mount ▲ USA ◆ 14-15 G 4
Marcy, Mount ▲ USA ◇ 22-23 M 3
Mar del Plata ○• RA ◆ 32-33 L 5
Mardin ☆ TR ◆ 34-35 U 8
Maré ⌒ F ◆ 60-61 O 4
Mareeba ○ AUS ◆ 60-61 K 3
Maréna ○ RMM ◆ 48-49 C 6
Marennes ○ F ◇ 38-39 G 9
◆ 34-35 L 6
Marfa ○ USA ◇ 26-27 E 4
Margaree Forks ○ CDN ◇ 18-19 O 5
Margarita, Isla de ⌒•• YV ◆ 30-31 G 2
Margaritas, Las ○ MEX ◇ 28-29 J 3
Margate ○ USA ◇ 24-25 H 6
Margeride, Monts de la ▲ F ◇ 38-39 J 9 ◆ 34-35 M 7
Marguerite, Baie ≈ ◆ 13 G 30
Marha ~ RUS ◆ 52-53 U 4
Maria, El ○ PA ◇ 28-29 D 7
Maria Island ⌒ AUS ◆ 60-61 H 2
María Linda, Río ~ GCA ◇ 28-29 J 4
Mariana Trench ≃ ◆ 58-59 M 4
Marianna ○ USA (AR) ◇ 26-27 M 2
Marianna ○ USA (FL) ◇ 24-25 F 4
Mariannes, Îles ⌒ CDN ◇ 18-19 P 3
Marias, Islas ⌒ MEX ◆ 16-17 E 6
Marias Pass ▲ USA ◇ 20-21 H 1
Marias River ~ USA ◇ 20-21 J 1
Ma'rib ○• Y ◆ 56-57 F 7
Maribor ○• SLO ◇ 46-47 E 1 ◆ 34-35 P 6
Marica ~ BG ◆ 34-35 R 7
Maricopa ○ USA (AZ) ◇ 20-21 H 9
Maricopa ○ USA (CA) ◇ 20-21 E 8
Maridi ○ SUD ◆ 48-49 L 8
Marié, Rio ~ BR ◆ 30-31 F 5
Marie-Galante ⌒ F ◆ 16-17 O 7
Mariehamn ☆ FIN ◆ 34-35 P 3
Mariel ○ C ◆ 16-17 K 6
Mari-El ▫ RUS ◆ 34-35 V 4
Mariental ☆ NAM ◆ 50-51 E 6
Marietta ○ USA (GA) ◇ 24-25 F 3
Marietta ○ USA (OH) ◇ 22-23 H 6
Marietta ○ USA (OK) ◇ 26-27 J 3
Marignane ○ F ◇ 38-39 K 10 ◆ 34-35 M 7
Mariinsk ☆ RUS ◆ 52-53 O 6
Marii Prončiščevoj, buhta ≈ ◆ 52-53 T 2
Marijampolė ☆•• LT ◇ 42-43 H 4 ◆ 34-35 Q 5
Marinas River ~ USA ◇ 20-21 H 1
Marinduque Island ⌒ RP ◆ 58-59 H 4
Marine Corps Base Camp Lejeune ✕✕ USA ◇ 24-25 K 2
Marineland of Florida ∴ USA ◇ 24-25 H 5
Marine Museum • USA ◇ 22-23 O 4
Marine National Park ⊥ ER ◆ 48-49 O 5
Marine National Reserve ⊥ EAK ◆ 50-51 K 2
Marinette ○ USA ◇ 22-23 E 3
Maringá ○ BR ◆ 32-33 M 2
Maringa ~ ZRE ◆ 50-51 F 1
Marino Barbareta, Parque Nacional ⊥ HN ◇ 28-29 L 3
Marino Punta Sal, Parque Nacional ⊥ HN ◇ 28-29 L 4
Marion ○ USA (AL) ◇ 24-25 E 3
Marion ○ USA (IA) ◇ 22-23 C 5
Marion ○ USA (IL) ◇ 22-23 D 7
Marion ○ USA (IN) ◇ 22-23 F 5
Marion ○ USA (NC) ◇ 24-25 G 2
Marion ○ USA (OH) ◇ 22-23 G 5
Marion ○ USA (SC) ◇ 24-25 J 2
Marion ○ USA (VA) ◇ 22-23 H 7
Marion, Lake ○ USA ◇ 24-25 H 3 ◆ 16-17 K 4
Marion Reef ⌒ AUS ◆ 60-61 L 3
Maripasoula ○ F ◆ 30-31 J 4
Mariposa ○ USA ◇ 20-21 E 7
Mariscal de Juárez ○ MEX ◇ 28-29 E 3
Mariscal Estigarribia ○ PY ◆ 32-33 K 2
Mariupol' = Maryupol' ○ UA ◆ 34-35 T 6
Mariveles ○ RP ◆ 58-59 H 4
Marj, al ☆•• LAR ◆ 48-49 K 2
Marka ☆ SP ◆ 50-51 K 1
Markam ○ CHN ◆ 54-55 H 6
Marked Tree ○ USA ◇ 26-27 M 2
Markham ○ CDN ◇ 18-19 E 7
Markham, Mount ▲ ANT ◆ 13 E 0
Marktredwitz ○ D ◇ 40-41 M 4 ◆ 34-35 O 5
Mark Twain Lake ○ USA ◇ 22-23 C 6
Marla ○ AUS ◆ 60-61 G 5
Marlborough ○ AUS ◆ 60-61 K 4
Marlborough ○ USA ◇ 22-23 N 4
Marlin ○ USA ◇ 26-27 J 4
Marlinton ○ USA ◇ 22-23 H 6
Marlow ○ USA ◇ 26-27 H 2
Marmande ○ F ◇ 38-39 H 9 ◆ 34-35 L 7
Marmara Denizi ≈ ◆ 34-35 R 7
Marne ~ F ◇ 38-39 K 7 ◆ 34-35 M 6
Marne-au-Rhin, Canal de la < F ◇ 38-39 L 7 ◆ 34-35 N 6
Maroa ○ YV ◆ 30-31 F 4
Maroantsetra ○ RM ◆ 50-51 L 5
Maroni ~ SME ◆ 30-31 J 3
Maroua ☆• CAM ◆ 48-49 H 6
Marovoalavo, Lembalemban'i ▲ RM ◆ 50-51 L 5
Marovoay ○ RM ◆ 50-51 L 5
Marque, La ○ USA ◇ 26-27 K 5
Marquesas Keys ⌒ USA ◇ 24-25 G 7
Marquette ○ USA ◇ 22-23 E 2 ◆ 14-15 T 7
Marquez ○ USA ◇ 26-27 J 4
Marquises, Îles ⌒ F ◆ 12 N 3
Marra, Ğabal ▲•• SUD ◆ 48-49 K 6
Marrakech = Marrakush ☆••• MA ◆ 48-49 D 2
Marrākush ☆••• MA ◆ 48-49 D 2
Marrawah ○ AUS ◆ 60-61 J 8
Marree ○ AUS ◆ 60-61 H 5
Marrero ○ USA ◇ 26-27 M 5
Marromeu ○ MOC ◆ 50-51 J 5
Marromeu, Reserva de ⊥ MOC ◆ 50-51 J 5
Marrupa ○ MOC ◆ 50-51 J 4
Marsá al Burayqah ○ LAR ◆ 48-49 J 2
Marsabit ○ EAK ◆ 48-49 N 8
Marsabit National Reserve ⊥ EAK ◆ 48-49 N 8
Marsá l-'Alam ○ ET ◆ 48-49 M 3
Marsá Maṭruḥ ☆• ET ◆ 48-49 L 2
Marsden ○ AUS ◆ 60-61 K 6
Marseille ☆• F ◇ 38-39 K 10 ◆ 34-35 N 7
Marshall ○ USA (AR) ◇ 26-27 L 2
Marshall ○ USA (IL) ◇ 22-23 E 6
Marshall ○ USA (MI) ◇ 22-23 F 4
Marshall ○ USA (TX) ◇ 26-27 K 3
Marshfield ○ USA (MO) ◇ 26-27 L 1
Marshfield ○ USA (WI) ◇ 22-23 C 3
Marsh Harbour ○ BS ◆ 16-17 L 5
Mars Hill ○ USA ◇ 22-23 P 2
Marsh Island ⌒ USA ◇ 26-27 M 5 ◆ 16-17 H 5
Marsh Pass ▲ USA ◇ 26-27 B 1
Marsoui ○ CDN ◇ 18-19 L 4
Martapura ○ RI ◆ 58-59 F 7
Marte, Rivière à la ~ CDN ◇ 18-19 G 3
Marten River ○ CDN ◇ 18-19 E 5
Martha's Vineyard ⌒ USA ◇ 22-23 N 5 ◆ 16-17 M 2
Martigues ○ F ◇ 38-39 K 10 ◆ 34-35 M 7
Martin ○ USA ◇ 24-25 D 1
Martin, Lake < USA ◇ 24-25 F 3 ◆ 16-17 J 4
Martinas, Las ○ C ◆ 16-17 K 6
Martínez de la Torre ○ MEX ◇ 28-29 F 1
Martinique ▫ F ◆ 16-17 O 8
Martinique Passage ≈ ◆ 16-17 O 8
Martin Peninsula ⌒ ANT ◆ 13 F 25
Martinsburg ○ USA ◇ 22-23 K 6
Martinsville ○ USA (IN) ◇ 22-23 E 6
Martinsville ○ USA (VA) ◇ 22-23 J 7
Martre, Lac la ○ CDN ◆ 14-15 N 4
Maruchin ∴ MEX ◇ 28-29 K 2
Marungu ▲ ZRE ◆ 50-51 G 3
Marvine, Mount ▲ USA ◇ 20-21 J 6
Mary ☆• TM ◆ 56-57 J 3
Mary Anne Passage ≈ ◆ 60-61 D 4
Maryborough ○ AUS ◆ 60-61 L 5
Maryhill ○ USA ◇ 20-21 D 3
Maryland ▫ USA ◇ 22-23 K 6 ◆ 16-17 L 3
Mary River ~ AUS ◆ 60-61 G 2
Marystown ○ CDN ◇ 18-19 R 5
Marysvale ○ USA ◇ 20-21 H 6
Marysville ○ USA (CA) ◇ 20-21 D 6
Marysville ○ USA (OH) ◇ 22-23 G 5
Maryupol' ○ UA ◆ 34-35 T 6
Maryville ○ USA ◇ 24-25 G 2
Marzuq ☆ LAR ◆ 48-49 H 3
Masagua ○ GCA ◇ 28-29 J 4
Masaguara ○ HN ◇ 28-29 L 4
Masai Mara National Reservat ⊥ EAK ◆ 50-51 H 2
Masai Steppe ⊥ EAT ◆ 50-51 J 2
Masaka ☆ EAU ◆ 50-51 H 2
Masalembobesar, Pulau ⌒ RI ◆ 58-59 F 8
Masamba ○ RI ◆ 58-59 H 7
Masan ○ ROK ◆ 54-55 O 4
Masasi ○ EAT ◆ 50-51 J 4
Masatepe ○ NIC ◇ 28-29 L 6
Masawa ○ RI ◆ 58-59 G 7
Masaya ○• NIC ◇ 28-29 L 6
Masbate ☆ RP (MAS) ◆ 58-59 H 4
Masbate ⌒ RP (MAS) ◆ 58-59 H 4
Mascarene Basin ≃ ◆ 50-51 N 4
Mascarene Islands ⌒ ◆ 50-51 N 6
Mascarene Plain ≃ ◆ 50-51 M 5
Mascarene Plateau ≃ ◆ 50-51 O 5
Mascota ○ MEX ◇ 28-29 B 1
Maseru ★ LS ◆ 50-51 G 7
Mašğed-e Soleimān ○• IR ◆ 56-57 F 4
Mašhad ☆•• IR ◆ 56-57 H 3
Mashhad = Mašhad ☆•• IR ◆ 56-57 H 3
Masica, La ○ HN ◇ 28-29 L 4
Masi-Manimba ○ ZRE ◆ 50-51 E 2
Maṣīra, Ğazīrat ⌒ OM ◆ 56-57 H 6
Maṣīra, Gulf of ≈ ◆ 56-57 H 5
Masoala, Tanjona ▲ RM ◆ 50-51 M 5
Mason ○ USA (MI) ◇ 22-23 F 4
Mason ○ USA (TX) ◇ 26-27 H 4
Mason City ○ USA ◆ 16-17 H 2
Masqaṭ ★•• OM ◆ 56-57 H 6
Massaango ○ ANG ◆ 50-51 E 3
Massachusetts ▫ USA ◇ 22-23 M 4 ◆ 14-15 W 8
Massachusetts, Fort ∴ USA ◇ 24-25 D 4
Massachusetts Bay ≈ ◇ 22-23 N 4
Massaguet ○ TCH ◆ 48-49 J 6
Massakory ○ TCH ◆ 48-49 J 6
Massangena ○ MOC ◆ 50-51 H 6
Massena ○ USA ◇ 22-23 L 3 ◆ 14-15 W 8
Massenya ○ TCH ◆ 48-49 J 6
Massey ○ CDN ◇ 18-19 C 5
Massey Sound ≈ ◆ 14-15 R 1
Massiac ○ F ◇ 38-39 J 9 ◆ 34-35 M 7
Massif Central ▲ F ◇ 38-39 J 9 ◆ 34-35 M 6
Massillon ○ USA ◇ 22-23 H 5
Massinga ○ MOC ◆ 50-51 J 6
Masson Island ⌒ ANT ◆ 13 G 10
Mastic Point ○ BS ◆ 16-17 L 5
Mastigouche, Réserve Faunique ⊥ CDN ◇ 18-19 H 5
Mastung ○• PK ◆ 56-57 K 5
Masvingo ☆ ZW ◆ 50-51 H 6
Maswa Game Reservat ⊥ EAT ◆ 50-51 H 2
Matachewan ○ CDN ◇ 18-19 D 5
Maṭadi ☆• ZRE ◆ 50-51 D 3
Matador ○ USA ◇ 26-27 G 2
Matagalpa ☆ NIC ◇ 28-29 B 5
◆ 16-17 J 8
Matagalpa, Río Grande de ~ NIC ◇ 28-29 B 5
Matagami ○ CDN ◇ 18-19 F 4 ◆ 14-15 V 7
Matagami, Lac ○ CDN ◇ 18-19 F 4
Matagorda Bay ≈ ◇ 26-27 J 5 ◆ 16-17 G 5
Matagorda Island ⌒ USA ◇ 26-27 J 5
Matakil, Chutes de ~•• RCA ◆ 48-49 K 7
Matala ○ ANG ◆ 50-51 E 4
Matamoros ○ MEX ◆ 16-17 G 5
Ma'tan as Sarah ○ LAR ◆ 48-49 K 4
Matandu ~ EAT ◆ 50-51 J 3
Matane ○ CDN ◇ 18-19 L 4 ◆ 14-15 X 7
Matane, Réserve Faunique de ⊥ CDN ◇ 18-19 L 4
Matanzas ○•• C ◆ 16-17 K 6
Matapédia ○ CDN ◇ 18-19 L 5
Matapédia, Rivière ~ CDN ◇ 18-19 L 4
Matara ○ CL ◆ 56-57 N 9
Mataram ☆ RI ◆ 58-59 G 8
Mataranka ○ AUS ◆ 60-61 G 2
Matawin, Rivière ~ CDN ◇ 18-19 H 5
Mategua ○ BOL ◆ 30-31 G 7
Matehuala ○ MEX ◆ 16-17 F 6
Mateur ○ TN ◆ 48-49 G 1
Mathis ○ USA ◇ 26-27 J 5
Mathiston ○ USA ◇ 24-25 D 3
Mathura ○•• IND ◆ 56-57 M 5
Mati ☆ RP ◆ 58-59 J 5
Matías Romero ○ MEX ◇ 28-29 G 3 ◆ 16-17 G 7
Matiguás ○ NIC ◇ 28-29 B 5
Matinenda Lake ○ CDN ◇ 18-19 C 5
Matočkin Šar ○ RUS ◆ 52-53 H 3
Mato Grosso ▫ BR ◆ 30-31 H 7
Mato Grosso, Planalto do ⊥ BR ◆ 30-31 H 7
Mato Grosso do Sul ▫ BR ◆ 32-33 L 1
Matrah ○• OM ◆ 56-57 H 6
Matsue ○ J ◆ 54-55 P 4
Matsumoto ○ J ◆ 54-55 Q 4
Matsuyama ☆ J ◆ 54-55 P 5
Matsuzaka ○ J ◆ 54-55 Q 5
Mattagami River ~ CDN ◆ 14-15 U 6
Mattamuskeet Lake ○ USA ◇ 24-25 K 2
Mattawa ○ CDN ◇ 18-19 E 5
Mattawamkeag ○ USA ◇ 22-23 O 3
Matterhorn ▲ USA ◇ 20-21 G 5
Matthews Ridge ○ GUY ◆ 30-31 G 3
Matthew Town ○ BS ◆ 16-17 M 6
Mattoon ○ USA ◇ 22-23 D 6
Matuku ⌒ FJI ◆ 60-61 Q 3
Maturin ☆ YV ◆ 30-31 G 3
Matusadona National Park ⊥ ZW ◆ 50-51 G 5
Maués ○ BR ◆ 30-31 H 5
Maués, Rio ~ BR ◆ 30-31 H 5
Maug Islands ⌒ USA ◆ 58-59 N 2
Maui ⌒ USA ◇ 24-25 D 7 ◆ 16-17 b 6
Maulamyaing ○ MYA ◆ 58-59 C 3
Maumee ○ USA ◇ 22-23 G 5
Maun ☆ RB ◆ 50-51 F 5
Mauna Kea ▲ USA ◇ 24-25 E 8 ◆ 16-17 b 7
Maunaloa ○ USA ◇ 24-25 D 7
Mauna Loa ▲ USA ◇ 24-25 E 8
Maunoir, Lac ○ CDN ◆ 14-15 M 3
Maupertuis, Lac ○ CDN ◇ 18-19 J 3
Maure, Col de ▲ F ◇ 38-39 L 9 ◆ 34-35 N 6
Maurepas, Lake ○ USA ◇ 26-27 M 4
Maurice, Lake ○ AUS ◆ 60-61 G 5
Mauricie, Parc National de la ⊥ CDN ◇ 18-19 H 5
Mauritania ▪ RIM ◆ 48-49 C 5
Mauritius ▪ MS ◆ 50-51 N 6
Mauston ○ USA ◇ 22-23 C 4
Mavinga ○ ANG ◆ 50-51 F 5
Mawa ○ ZRE ◆ 48-49 L 8
Mawlaik ○ MYA ◆ 54-55 G 7
Mawson ○ ANT ◆ 13 G 7
Maxcanú ○ MEX ◇ 28-29 J 1
Maya, Pulau ⌒ RI ◆ 58-59 E 7
Mayaguana Island ⌒ BS ◆ 16-17 M 6
Mayagüez ○ USA ◆ 16-17 N 7
Mayala ○ ZRE ◆ 50-51 E 3
Maya Mountains ▲ BH ◇ 28-29 K 3
Mayapan ∴• MEX ◇ 28-29 K 1
Mayari ○ C ◆ 16-17 L 6
Maych'ew ○ ETH ◆ 48-49 N 6
Maydena ○ AUS ◆ 60-61 K 8
Maydh ⌒ SP ◆ 48-49 P 6
Mayenne ○ F ◇ 38-39 G 7 ◆ 34-35 L 6
Mayenne ~ F ◇ 38-39 G 7 ◆ 34-35 L 6
Mayfield ○ USA (ID) ◇ 20-21 G 4
Mayfield ○ USA (KY) ◇ 22-23 D 7
Mayhill ○ USA ◇ 26-27 E 3
Maymyo ○ MYA ◆ 54-55 H 7
Maynas ⊥ PE ◆ 30-31 D 5
Maynooth ○ CDN ◇ 18-19 F 6
Mayo ○ USA ◇ 24-25 G 4
Mayo, Río ~ RA ◆ 32-33 H 7
Mayombé ▲ G ◆ 50-51 D 2
Mayotte ⌒ F ◆ 50-51 L 4
May Point, Cape ▲ USA ◇ 22-23 L 6
Mayran, Desierto de ⊥ MEX ◆ 16-17 F 5
Maysville ○ USA ◇ 22-23 G 6
Mayumba ○ G ◆ 50-51 D 2
Mazabuka ○ Z ◆ 50-51 G 5
Mazagão ○ BR ◆ 30-31 J 5
Mazama ○ USA ◇ 20-21 D 1
Mazamet ○ F ◇ 38-39 J 10 ◆ 34-35 M 7
Mazār-e Šarīf ☆ AFG ◆ 56-57 K 3
Mazatán ○ MEX ◇ 28-29 H 4
Mazatenango ☆ GCA ◇ 28-29 J 4 ◆ 16-17 H 8
Mazatlán ○• MEX ◆ 16-17 E 6
Mazyr ○ BY ◇ 42-43 L 5 ◆ 34-35 R 5
Mazzamitla ○ MEX ◇ 28-29 C 2
Mbabane ★ SD ◆ 50-51 H 7
Mbaïki ☆ RCA ◆ 48-49 J 8
Mbakaou, Lac de < CAM ◆ 48-49 H 7
Mbala ○• Z ◆ 50-51 H 3
Mbalabala ○ ZW ◆ 50-51 G 6
Mbale ☆• EAU ◆ 50-51 H 1
Mbamba Bay ○ EAT ◆ 50-51 H 4
Mbandaka ☆ ZRE ◆ 50-51 E 1
M'banza Congo ☆ ANG ◆ 50-51 D 3
Mbanza-Ngungu = Thysville ○ ZRE ◆ 50-51 D 3
Mbarara ☆ EAU ◆ 50-51 H 2
Mbari ~ RCA ◆ 48-49 K 7
Mbé ○ RCB ◆ 50-51 D 2
Mbeya ☆ EAT ◆ 50-51 H 3
Mbinda ○ RCB ◆ 50-51 D 2
Mbomou ~ RCA ◆ 48-49 K 8
Mbout ○ RIM ◆ 48-49 C 5
Mbrés ○• RCA ◆ 48-49 J 7
Mbuji-Mayi ☆ ZRE ◆ 50-51 F 3
McAlester ○ USA ◇ 26-27 K 2 ◆ 16-17 G 4
McAllister State Historic Site, Fort ∴• USA ◇ 24-25 H 4
McArthur ○ USA ◇ 22-23 G 6
Mc Arthur River ~ AUS ◆ 60-61 H 3
McCallum ○ CDN ◇ 18-19 Q 5
McCamey ○ USA ◇ 26-27 F 4
McCammon ○ USA ◇ 20-21 H 4
McCarthy ○ USA ◆ 14-15 H 4
McClellanville ○ USA ◇ 24-25 J 3
McClintock Channel ≈ ◆ 14-15 Q 2
McClure Strait ≈ ◆ 14-15 M 1
McComb ○ USA ◇ 26-27 M 4
McConnelsville ○ USA ◇ 22-23 H 6
McCormick ○ USA ◇ 24-25 G 3
McDavid ○ USA ◇ 24-25 E 4
McDonald Peak ▲ USA ◇ 20-21 H 2
McGee Creek Lake ○ USA ◇ 26-27 J 2
McGehee ○ USA ◇ 26-27 M 3
McGill ○ USA ◇ 20-21 G 6
McGivney ○ CDN ◇ 18-19 L 5
McGrath ○ USA ◆ 14-15 E 4
McGuire, Mount ▲ USA ◇ 20-21 G 3
McKay Lake ○ CDN ◇ 18-19 M 2
McKeller ○ CDN ◇ 18-19 E 6
McKenzie ○ USA ◇ 24-25 D 1
McKenzie Bridge ○ USA ◇ 20-21 C 3
McKinlay ○ AUS ◆ 60-61 J 4
McKinley, Mount ▲•• USA ◆ 14-15 F 4
McKinney ○ USA ◇ 26-27 J 3
McKittrick ○ USA ◇ 20-21 E 8
McLaughlin Bank ≃ ◆ 58-59 N 5
McLean ○ USA ◇ 26-27 G 2
McLeansboro ○ USA ◇ 22-23 D 6
McLeod Bay ○ CDN ◆ 14-15 O 4
McLoughlin, Mount ▲ USA ◇ 20-21 C 4
McMasterville ○ CDN ◇ 18-19 H 6
McMillan, Lake ○ USA ◇ 26-27 E 3
McMinnville ○ USA (OR) ◇ 20-21 C 3 ◆ 14-15 M 7
McMinnville ○ USA (TN) ◇ 24-25 F 2
McMurdo ○ ANT ◆ 13 F 17
Mc Murdo Sound ≈ ◆ 13 F 17
McMurray ○ USA ◇ 20-21 C 1
McNary ○ USA ◇ 26-27 C 2
McRae ○ USA ◇ 24-25 G 3
McRobertson Land ⊥ ANT ◆ 13 G 7
McVicar Arm ○ CDN ◆ 14-15 M 4
Mead, Lake ○ USA ◇ 20-21 G 7
Meade ○ USA ◇ 26-27 G 1
Meade Peak ▲ USA ◇ 20-21 J 4
Meadow ○ USA ◇ 26-27 F 3
Meadow Valley Wash ~ USA ◇ 20-21 G 7
Meadville ○ USA ◇ 22-23 H 5
Meaux ○ F ◇ 38-39 J 7 ◆ 34-35 M 6
Mebo, Gunung ▲ RI ◆ 58-59 K 7
Mebridege ~ ANG ◆ 50-51 D 3
Mecca ○ USA ◇ 20-21 G 9
Mecca = Makka ☆•• KSA ◆ 56-57 D 6
Mechanicville ○ USA ◇ 22-23 M 4
Mecheria ○ DZ ◆ 48-49 E 2
Méchins, Les ○ CDN ◇ 18-19 L 4
Mecula ○ MOC ◆ 50-51 J 4
Medan ☆• RI ◆ 58-59 C 6
Medart ○ USA ◇ 24-25 F 4
Médéa ☆ DZ ◆ 48-49 F 1
Medellín ○ CO ◆ 30-31 D 3
Medenine ☆ TN ◆ 48-49 H 2
Medford ○ USA (WI) ◇ 22-23 C 3
Medford ○ USA (OR) ◇ 20-21 C 4 ◆ 14-15 M 8
Mediaş ○• RO ◆ 34-35 Q 6
Medicine Hat ○ CDN ◆ 14-15 O 6
Medicine Lodge ○ USA ◇ 26-27 H 1
Medina ○ USA ◇ 22-23 H 5
Medina = Madina, al- ☆•• KSA ◆ 56-57 D 6
Medina River ~ USA ◇ 26-27 H 5
Mediterranean Sea ≈ ◇ 46-47 E 6 ◆ 34-35 M 8
Mednyj ostrov ⌒ RUS ◆ 52-53 e 7
Medo, El ○ ETH ◆ 48-49 O 7
Médoc ⊥• F ◇ 38-39 G 9 ◆ 34-35 L 6
Medvedica ~ RUS ◆ 34-35 U 5
Medveži ostrova ⌒ RUS ◆ 52-53 d 3
Medvežka ○ RUS ◆ 52-53 d 4
Meekatharra ○ AUS ◆ 60-61 D 5
Meelpaeg Lake ○ CDN ◇ 18-19 Q 4
Meerut ○ IND ◆ 56-57 M 5
Mega ○ ETH ◆ 48-49 N 8
Mega ○ RI ◆ 58-59 K 7
Megantic, Mont ▲ CDN ◇ 18-19 J 6
Meghālaya ▫ IND ◆ 56-57 P 5
Mégiscane, Rivière ~ CDN ◇ 18-19 F 4
Meherrin River ~ USA ◇ 22-23 K 7
Mehrān, Rūd-e ~ IR ◆ 56-57 G 5
Meidānšahr ☆• AFG ◆ 56-57 K 4
Meihekou ○ CHN ◆ 54-55 O 3
Meiktila ○ MYA ◆ 54-55 H 7
Meizhou ○ CHN ◆ 54-55 M 7
Mejillones ○ RCH ◆ 32-33 H 2
Mékambo ○ G ◆ 50-51 D 1
Mek'elē ☆• ETH ◆ 48-49 N 6
Meknès = Miknās ☆ MA ◆ 48-49 D 2
Mekong ~ K ◆ 58-59 E 4
Melaka ☆• MAL ◆ 58-59 D 6
Melanesia ⌒ ◆ 58-59 M 7
Melanesian Basin ≃ ◆ 12 G 2
Melbourne ☆•• AUS ◆ 60-61 J 7
Melbourne ○ USA (AR) ◇ 26-27 M 1
Melbourne ○ USA (FL) ◇ 24-25 H 5 ◆ 16-17 K 5
Melchor, Isla ⌒ RCH ◆ 32-33 H 7
Melchor Múzquiz ○ MEX ◆ 16-17 F 5
Meldrum Bay ○ CDN ◇ 18-19 C 6
Meleck ○ RUS ◆ 52-53 P 6
Mélèzes, Rivière aux ~ CDN ◆ 14-15 W 5
Mélfi ○ TCH ◆ 48-49 J 6
Melilla ○• E ◇ 44-45 F 7 ◆ 34-35 L 8
Melipilla ○ RCH ◆ 32-33 H 4
Melitopol' ○ UA ◆ 34-35 T 6
Mellen ○ USA ◇ 22-23 C 2
Mellish Reef ⌒ AUS ◆ 60-61 M 3
Melo ☆ ROU ◆ 32-33 M 4
Melrhir, Chott ○ DZ ◆ 48-49 G 2
Melrose ○ CDN ◇ 18-19 N 6
Melrose ○ USA (MT) ◇ 20-21 H 3
Melrose ○ USA (NM) ◇ 26-27 F 2
Melton ○ AUS ◆ 60-61 J 7
Melun ☆ F ◇ 38-39 J 7 ◆ 34-35 M 6
Melville ○ USA ◇ 26-27 M 4
Melville, Cape ▲ AUS ◆ 60-61 J 2
Melville, Lake ○ CDN ◇ 18-19 P 2 ◆ 14-15 Z 6
Melville Bay ≈ ◆ 60-61 H 2
Melville Bugt ≈ ◆ 14-15 Y 1
Melville Hills ▲ CDN ◆ 14-15 M 3
Melville Island ⌒ AUS ◆ 60-61 G 2
Melville Island ⌒ CDN ◆ 14-15 O 1
Melville Peninsula ⌒ CDN ◆ 14-15 U 3
Memboro ○ RI ◆ 58-59 G 8
Memphis ∴•• ET ◆ 48-49 M 3
Memphis ○ USA (TN) ◇ 26-27 M 2 ◆ 16-17 H 3
Memphis ○ USA (TX) ◇ 26-27 G 2
Memphrémagog, Lac ○ CDN ◇ 18-19 H 6
Mena ○ USA ◇ 26-27 K 2
Menabe ⊥ RM ◆ 50-51 K 6
Ménaka ○ RMM ◆ 48-49 F 5
Menarandra ~ RM ◆ 50-51 L 6
Ménascouagama, Lac ○ CDN ◇ 18-19 N 3
Menawashei ○ SUD ◆ 48-49 K 6
Mendaña Fracture Zone ≃ ◆ 30-31 A 8
Mendawai ~ RI ◆ 58-59 F 7
Mende ○• F ◇ 38-39 J 9 ◆ 34-35 M 7
Mendenhall ○ USA ◇ 24-25 D 4
Mendī ○ ETH ◆ 48-49 N 7
Mendi ☆ PNG ◆ 58-59 M 8
Mendocino ○ USA ◇ 20-21 C 6
Mendocino, Cape ▲ USA ◇ 20-21 B 5 ◆ 16-17 B 2
Mendota ○ USA (CA) ◇ 20-21 D 7
Mendota ○ USA (IL) ◇ 22-23 D 5
Mendoza ▫ RA ◆ 32-33 J 5
Mendoza ☆• RA (MEN) ◆ 32-33 J 4
Mengzi ○ CHN ◆ 54-55 J 7
Menindee ○ AUS ◆ 60-61 J 6
Menkerja ○ RUS ◆ 52-53 V 4
Menneval ○ CDN ◇ 18-19 L 5
Menominee ○ USA ◇ 22-23 E 3 ◆ 14-15 T 7
Menominee Indian Reservation ⚔ USA ◇ 22-23 D 3 ◆ 14-15 T 7
Menominee River ~ USA ◇ 22-23 E 3
Menomonee Falls ○ USA ◇ 22-23 D 4
Menomonie ○ USA ◇ 22-23 C 3
Menongue ☆ ANG ◆ 50-51 E 4
Menorca ⌒ E ◇ 44-45 J 4 ◆ 34-35 M 7
Mentawai, Kepulauan ⌒ RI ◆ 58-59 C 7
Mentawai Strait ≈ ◆ 58-59 C 7
Menton ○ F ◇ 38-39 L 10 ◆ 34-35 N 7
Menzies ○ AUS ◆ 60-61 E 5
Menzies, Mount ▲ ANT ◆ 13 F 7
Merak ○ RI ◆ 58-59 E 8
Merasheen Island ⌒ CDN ◇ 18-19 R 5
Merauke ○ RI ◆ 58-59 M 8
Mercantour, Parc National du ⊥• F ◇ 38-39 L 9 ◆ 34-35 N 6
Merced ○ USA ◇ 20-21 D 7 ◆ 16-17 B 3
Mercedario, Cerro ▲ RA ◆ 32-33 H 4
Mercedes ○ RA (CO) ◆ 32-33 L 3
Mercedes ○ RA (SLU) ◆ 32-33 J 4
Mercedes ○ USA ◇ 26-27 J 6
Mercer ○ USA (PA) ◇ 22-23 H 5
Mercer ○ USA (WI) ◇ 22-23 C 2
Merchants Bay ≈ ◆ 14-15 Y 3
Mercy, Cape ▲ CDN ◆ 14-15 Y 4
Meredith, Cape ▲ GB ◆ 32-33 K 8
Mergui ○ MYA ◆ 58-59 C 4
Mergui Archipelago ⌒ MYA ◆ 58-59 C 4
Mergui Archipelago = Myeik Kyûnzu ⌒ MYA ◆ 58-59 C 4
Mérida ☆•• MEX ◇ 28-29 K 1 ◆ 16-17 J 6
Mérida ☆• YV ◆ 30-31 E 3
Mérida, Cordillera de ▲ YV ◆ 30-31 E 3
Meriden ○ USA ◇ 22-23 M 5
Meridian ○ USA (MS) ◇ 24-25 D 3 ◆ 16-17 J 4
Meridian ○ USA (TX) ◇ 26-27 J 4
Meridith, Lake ○ USA ◇ 26-27 G 2
Merín, Laguna ○ ROU ◆ 32-33 M 4
Merir ⌒ USA ◆ 58-59 K 6
Merlin ○ USA ◇ 20-21 C 4
Meroe •• SUD ◆ 48-49 M 5
Merredin ○ AUS ◆ 60-61 D 6
Merrill ○ USA (OR) ◇ 20-21 D 4
Merrill ○ USA (WI) ◇ 22-23 D 3
Merrimack River ~ USA ◇ 22-23 N 4
Merritt ○ CDN ◆ 14-15 M 6
Merritt Island ○ USA ◇ 24-25 H 5
Merryville ○ USA ◇ 26-27 L 4
Mersin = İçel ○ TR ◆ 34-35 S 8
Mertz Glacier ⊂ ANT ◆ 13 G 15
Mertzon ○ USA ◇ 26-27 G 4
Meru ○ EAK ◆ 50-51 J 1
Meru ▲•• EAT ◆ 50-51 J 2
Meru National Park ⊥ EAK ◆ 50-51 J 1
Mesa ○ USA (AZ) ◇ 20-21 J 9 ◆ 16-17 D 4
Mesa ○ USA (NM) ◇ 26-27 E 3
Mesa ○ USA (WA) ◇ 20-21 E 2
Mesa Verde National Park ⊥••• USA ◇ 26-27 C 1 ◆ 16-17 E 3
Mescalero Apache Indian Reservation ⚔ USA ◇ 26-27 E 3 ◆ 16-17 E 4
Mesgouez, Lac ○ CDN ◇ 18-19 G 3
Mesick ○ USA ◇ 22-23 F 3
Mesilla, La ○ GCA ◇ 28-29 J 4
Mesopotamia ⊥ IRQ ◆ 56-57 E 3
Mesopotamia ⊥ RA ◆ 32-33 L 4
Mesquite ○ USA ◇ 26-27 J 3
Messalo ~ MOC ◆ 50-51 J 4
Messina ○ I ◇ 46-47 E 5 ◆ 34-35 P 8
Messina ○ ZA ◆ 50-51 H 6
Messina, Stretto di ≈ ◇ 46-47 E 5 ◆ 34-35 O 8
Metaca ○ MOC ◆ 50-51 J 4
Metagama ○ CDN ◇ 18-19 D 5
Meta Incognita Peninsula ⌒ CDN ◆ 14-15 W 4
Metairie ○ USA ◇ 26-27 M 5
Metaline Falls ○ USA ◇ 20-21 F 1
Metán ○ RA ◆ 32-33 K 3
Metangula ○ MOC ◆ 50-51 H 4
Metapán ○ ES ◇ 28-29 K 4
Meteghan ○ CDN ◇ 18-19 L 6
Metema ○ ETH ◆ 48-49 N 6
Metepec ○ MEX (HGO) ◇ 28-29 E 1
Metepec ○ MEX (PUE) ◇ 28-29 E 2
Meteti ○ PA ◇ 28-29 F 7
Metoro ○ MOC ◆ 50-51 J 4
Metropolis ○ USA ◇ 22-23 D 7
Metz ☆• F ◇ 38-39 L 7 ◆ 34-35 N 6
Metztitlán ○ MEX ◇ 28-29 E 1
Meulaboh ○ RI ◆ 58-59 C 6
Meuse ~ F ◇ 38-39 K 7 ◆ 34-35 M 6
Meuse, Côtes de ⊥ F ◇ 38-39 K 7 ◆ 34-35 M 6
Mexia ○ USA ◇ 26-27 J 4
Mexicali ☆ MEX ◆ 16-17 C 4
Mexican Hat ○ USA ◇ 26-27 C 1
Mexican Plateau ▲ MEX ◆ 16-17 F 5
Mexican Water ○ USA ◇ 26-27 C 1
Mexico ▪ MEX ◇ 28-29 C 1 ◆ 16-17 E 5
Mexico ○ USA (ME) ◇ 22-23 N 3
Mexico ○ USA (MO) ◇ 22-23 C 6
Mexico, Gulf of ≈ ◇ 26-27 K 6 ◆ 16-17 H 5
Mexico City = Ciudad de México ★••• MEX ◇ 28-29 E 2
Meyersdale ○ USA ◇ 22-23 J 6
Mezcalapa, Río ~ MEX ◇ 28-29 H 3
Meždurečensk ○ RUS ◆ 52-53 O 7
Mezen' ○ RUS ◆ 52-53 E 4
Mezen' ~ RUS ◆ 52-53 E 4
Mézenc, Mont ▲• F ◇ 38-39 K 9 ◆ 34-35 N 6
Mezenskaja guba ≈ ◆ 52-53 E 4
Mézier, Charleville ☆ F ◇ 38-39 K 7 ◆ 34-35 M 6
Miahuatlán ○ MEX ◇ 28-29 F 3
Miahuatlán, Sierra de ▲ MEX ◇ 28-29 F 3 ◆ 16-17 G 7
Miami ○ USA (AZ) ◇ 26-27 B 3
Miami ○ USA (OK) ◇ 26-27 K 1
Miami ○ USA (TX) ◇ 26-27 G 2
Miami ○• USA (FL) ◇ 24-25 H 7 ◆ 16-17 K 5
Miami Beach ○• USA ◇ 24-25 H 7 ◆ 16-17 K 5
Miami Canal < USA ◇ 24-25 H 6
Miami River ~ USA ◇ 22-23 F 6
Miandrivazo ○ RM ◆ 50-51 L 5
Miangas, Pulau ⌒ RI ◆ 58-59 J 5
Miānwālī ○ PK ◆ 56-57 L 4
Mianyang ○ CHN ◆ 54-55 J 5
Miaodao Qundao ⌒ CHN ◆ 54-55 N 4
Miass ☆ RUS ◆ 52-53 J 6
Miccosukee Indian Reservation ⚔ USA ◇ 24-25 H 6
Michel, Pointe à ▲ CDN ◇ 18-19 K 4
Michelson, Mount ▲ USA ◆ 14-15 H 3
Michigan ▫ USA ◇ 22-23 E 2 ◆ 14-15 T 7
Michigan, Lake ○ USA ◇ 22-23 E 4 ◆ 14-15 T 8
Michigan City ○ USA ◇ 22-23 E 5
Michipicoten Island ⌒ CDN ◆ 14-15 T 7
Michoacán ▫ MEX ◇ 28-29 C 2
Mičurinsk = Mičurinsk ○ RUS ◇ 42-43 R 5 ◆ 34-35 U 5
Mico, Río ~ NIC ◇ 28-29 B 5
Miconge ○ ZRE ◆ 50-51 D 2
Micronesia ⌒ FSM ◆ 58-59 M 5
Mičurinsk ○ RUS ◇ 42-43 R 5 ◆ 34-35 U 5
Midai, Pulau ⌒ RI ◆ 58-59 E 6
Midas ○ USA ◇ 20-21 F 5
Mid-Atlantic Ridge ≃ ◆ 30-31 L 2
Middelburg ○ ZA (CAP) ◆ 50-51 G 8
Middelburg ○ ZA (TRA) ◆ 50-51 G 7
Middle Alkali Lake ○ USA ◇ 20-21 D 5
Middle America Trench ≃ ◇ 28-29 F 4 ◆ 16-17 G 7
Middle Andaman ⌒ IND ◆ 58-59 B 4
Middlebury ○ USA ◇ 22-23 M 3
Middle Fork John Day River ~ USA ◇ 20-21 E 3
Middle Fork Salmon River ~ USA ◇ 20-21 G 3
Middle Gate ○ USA ◇ 20-21 E 6
Middle Ridge ▲ CDN ◇ 18-19 R 4
Middle Sackville ○ CDN ◇ 18-19 N 6
Middlesboro ○ USA ◇ 22-23 G 7 ◆ 16-17 K 3
Middleton ○ AUS ◆ 60-61 J 4
Middleton ○ CDN ◇ 18-19 M 6
Middleton ○ USA (TN) ◇ 24-25 D 2
Middleton ○ USA (WI) ◇ 22-23 D 4
Middleton, Mount ▲ CDN ◇ 18-19 F 3
Middleton Reef ⌒ AUS ◆ 60-61 M 5
Middletown ○ USA (CT) ◇ 22-23 M 5
Middletown ○ USA (NY) ◇ 22-23 L 5
Middletown ○ USA (OH) ◇ 22-23 F 6
Midi, Canal du < F ◇ 38-39 J 10 ◆ 34-35 M 7
Mid-Indian Ridge ≃ ◆ 50-51 O 3
Midi-Pyrénées ▫ F ◇ 38-39 H 10 ◆ 34-35 M 7
Midland ○ CDN ◇ 18-19 E 6
Midland ○ USA (MI) ◇ 22-23 F 4
Midland ○ USA (TX) ◇ 26-27 F 3 ◆ 16-17 F 4
Midouze ~ F ◇ 38-39 G 10 ◆ 34-35 L 7
Mid-Pacific-Seamounts ≃ ◆ 58-59 O 2
Midu ○ CHN ◆ 54-55 J 6
Midway ○ USA ◇ 24-25 F 3
Midwest City ○ USA ◇ 26-27 J 2
Mielec ○• PL ◇ 40-41 Q 3 ◆ 34-35 Q 5
Miguel Alemán, Presa < MEX ◇ 28-29 F 2
Mihajlovka ○ RUS ◆ 34-35 U 5
Miḫrād, al- ⊥ KSA ◆ 56-57 G 6
Mijek ○ WSA ◆ 48-49 C 4
Mikkeli ☆ FIN ◆ 34-35 R 3
Miknās ☆ MA ◆ 48-49 D 2
Mikumi National Park ⊥ EAT ◆ 50-51 J 3
Mikun' ○ RUS ◆ 52-53 G 5
Miladummadulu Atoll ⌒ MV ◆ 56-57 L 9
Milan ○ USA (MI) ◇ 22-23 G 4
Milan ○ USA (TN) ◇ 24-25 D 2
Milan = Milano ☆••• I ◇ 46-47 B 2 ◆ 34-35 N 6
Milando, Reserva Especial do ⊥ ANG ◆ 50-51 E 3
Milange ○ ZRE ◆ 50-51 G 2
Milano ☆••• I ◇ 46-47 B 2 ◆ 34-35 N 6
Milano ○ USA ◇ 26-27 J 4
Milbridge ○ USA ◇ 22-23 P 3
Mildura ○ AUS ◆ 60-61 J 6
Miles ○ AUS ◆ 60-61 L 5
Miles ○ USA ◇ 26-27 G 4
Miles City ○ USA (FL) ◇ 24-25 H 6
Miles City ○ USA (MT) ◆ 14-15 P 7
Mi'lēso ○ ETH ◆ 48-49 O 7
Milford ○ USA (DE) ◇ 22-23 L 6
Milford ○ USA (MA) ◇ 22-23 N 4
Milford ○ USA (NH) ◇ 22-23 N 4
Milford ○ USA (PA) ◇ 22-23 L 5
Milford ○ USA (UT) ◇ 20-21 H 6
Milford Sound ≈ ◆ 60-61 O 8
Milhana ○ MOC ◆ 50-51 J 4
Milim ○ PNG ◆ 58-59 O 8
Milk, Wādī al- ~ SUD ◆ 48-49 M 5
Milk River ~ CDN ◆ 14-15 O 7
Millas ○ F ◇ 38-39 J 10 ◆ 34-35 M 7
Millau ○ F ◇ 38-39 J 9 ◆ 34-35 M 7
Mill City ○ USA ◇ 20-21 C 3
Milledgeville ○ USA ◇ 24-25 G 3
Mille Lacs Lake ○ USA ◆ 14-15 S 7
Millen ○ USA ◇ 24-25 H 3
Millersburg ○ USA (OH) ◇ 22-23 H 5
Millersburg ○ USA (PA) ◇ 22-23 K 5
Millers Creek Reservoir < USA ◇ 26-27 H 3
Millertown ○ CDN ◇ 18-19 Q 4
Millevaches, Plateau de ▲ F ◇ 38-39 H 9 ◆ 34-35 L 7
Millicent ○ AUS ◆ 60-61 J 7
Millington ○ USA ◇ 24-25 D 2
Millinocket ○ USA ◇ 22-23 O 3
Mill Island ⌒ ANT ◆ 13 G 11
Mill Island ⌒ CDN ◆ 14-15 V 4
Millston ○ USA ◇ 22-23 C 3
Millstream Chichester National Park ⊥ AUS ◆ 60-61 D 4
Milltown ○ CDN ◇ 18-19 R 5
Mill Village ○ CDN ◇ 18-19 M 6
Millville ○ USA ◇ 22-23 L 6
Millwood Lake ○ USA ◇ 26-27 K 3
Milner Lake ○ CDN ◇ 18-19 L 2
Milnesand ○ USA ◇ 26-27 F 3
Milo ~ RG ◆ 48-49 D 6
Milos ⌒ GR ◇ 46-47 K 6 ◆ 34-35 Q 8
Milparinka ○ AUS ◆ 60-61 J 5
Milton ○ NZ ◆ 60-61 O 9
Milton ○ USA (FL) ◇ 24-25 E 4
Milton ○ USA (PA) ◇ 22-23 K 5
Milton-Freewater ○ USA ◇ 20-21 E 3
Milwaukee ○• USA ◇ 22-23 E 4 ◆ 14-15 T 8
Milwaukie ○ USA ◇ 20-21 C 3
Mimizan ○ F ◇ 38-39 G 9 ◆ 34-35 L 6
Mimongo ○ G ◆ 50-51 D 2
Mina ○ USA ◇ 20-21 E 6
Minami-Daitō-shima ⌒ J ◆ 54-55 P 6
Minas ☆ ROU ◆ 32-33 L 4
Minas, Cerro las ▲ HN ◇ 28-29 K 4
Minas, Sierra de las ▲ GCA ◇ 28-29 J 4
Minas Basin ≈ ◇ 18-19 M 6
Minas de Matahambre ○ C ◆ 16-17 K 6
Minas Gerais ▫ BR ◆ 30-31 K 8
Minatitlán ○• MEX (COL) ◇ 28-29 B 2
Minatitlán ○• MEX (VER) ◇ 28-29 G 3 ◆ 16-17 H 7
Minbu ○ MYA ◆ 54-55 G 7
Mindanao ⌒ RP ◆ 58-59 J 5
Minden ○ CDN ◇ 18-19 E 6
Minden ○ USA ◇ 26-27 L 3
Mindona Lake ○ AUS ◆ 60-61 J 6
Mindoro ⌒ RP ◆ 58-59 H 4
Mindoro Strait ≈ ◆ 58-59 H 4
Mineola ○ USA ◇ 26-27 K 3
Mineral Wells ○ USA ◇ 26-27 H 3

82 Maradi — Mineral Wells

Minersville o **USA** ◇ 20-21 H 6
Mingaçevir o· **AZ** ◆ 56-57 F 2
Mingan, Îles de ⌒ **CDN** ◇ 18-19 N 3
Minghoshan = Dunhuang o· **CHN** ◆ 54-55 G 3
Mingora o· **PK** ◆ 56-57 L 4
Minh Hþai o **VN** ◆ 58-59 E 5
Minidoka o **USA** ◇ 20-21 H 4
Minigwal, Lake ⊖ **AUS** ◆ 60-61 E 5
Minipi Lake ⊖ **CDN** ◇ 18-19 O 2
Minna ☆ **WAN** ◆ 48-49 G 7
Minneapolis o· **USA** ◆ 14-15 S 8
Minneola o **USA** ◇ 26-27 G 1
Minnesota □ **USA** ◆ 14-15 R 7
Minnesota River ~ **USA** ◆ 14-15 R 8
Minong o **USA** ◇ 22-23 C 2
Minot o **USA** ◆ 14-15 Q 7
Minsk ★ **BY** ◇ 42-43 K 5 ◆ 34-35 R 5
Mint Hill o **USA** ◇ 24-25 H 2
Minto o **CDN** ◆ 14-15 J 4
Minto, Lac ⊖ **CDN** ◆ 14-15 V 5
Minusinsk ☆ **RUS** ◆ 52-53 P 7
Min Xian o **CHN** ◆ 54-55 J 5
Minyā, al- ☆ **ET** ◆ 48-49 M 3
Miquelon o **CDN** ◇ 18-19 F 4
Miquelon, Île ⌒ **F** ◇ 18-19 **I** Q 5
Miracema de Tocantins o **BR** ◆ 30-31 K 6
Mirador o **BR** ◆ 30-31 L 6
Mirador, El ∴· **GCA** ◇ 28-29 K 3
Mirador, Parque Nacional de ⊥ **BR** ◆ 30-31 K 6
Mirador-Dos Lagunas-Río Azul, Parque Nacional ⊥·· **GCA** ◇ 28-29 K 3
Miraflores o **CO** ◆ 30-31 E 4
Miramar o **RA** ◆ 32-33 L 5
Miramichi Bay ≈ ◇ 18-19 M 5
Miramichi River ~ **CDN** ◇ 18-19 L 5
Miranda o **BR** ◆ 32-33 L 2
Miravalles, Volcán ▲ **CR** ◇ 28-29 B 6
Mirğāve o **IR** ◆ 56-57 J 5
Miri o **MAL** ◆ 58-59 F 6
Mirnyj o **ANT** ◆ 13 G 10
Mirnyj ☆· **RUS** ◆ 52-53 T 5
Mirpur Khās o· **PK** ◆ 56-57 K 5
Misaine Bank ≃ ◇ 18-19 P 6
Misantla o **MEX** (VER) ◇ 28-29 F 2
Misantla ∴· **MEX** (VER) ◇ 28-29 F 2
Miscou Centre o **CDN** ◇ 18-19 M 5
Miscou Island ⌒ **CDN** ◇ 18-19 M 5
Mishagomish, Lac ⊖ **CDN** ◇ 18-19 F 3
Misima Island ⌒ **PNG** ◆ 58-59 O 9
Misiones □ **RA** ◆ 32-33 L 3
Miskitos, Cayos ⌒ **NIC** ◇ 28-29 C 4 ◆ 16-17 K 8
Miskolc o **H** ◇ 40-41 Q 4 ◆ 34-35 Q 6
Mismār o **SUD** ◆ 48-49 N 5
Misol-Ha Waterfall · **MEX** ◇ 28-29 H 3
Misool, Pulau ⌒ **RI** ◆ 58-59 K 7
Mişrātah ☆ **LAR** ◆ 48-49 J 2
Missinaibi River ~ **CDN** ◆ 14-15 U 6
Missisagi River ~ **CDN** ◇ 18-19 C 5
Missisicabi, Rivière ~ **CDN** ◇ 18-19 E 3
Mississauga o **CDN** ◇ 18-19 E 7
Mississippi □ **USA** ◇ 24-25 D 4 ◆ 16-17 H 4
Mississippi River ~ **USA** ◆ 16-17 H 4
Mississippi River Delta ᴗ **USA** ◇ 24-25 D 5 ◆ 16-17 J 5
Mississippi Sound ≈ ◇ 24-25 D 4
Missoula o **USA** ◇ 20-21 H 2 ◆ 14-15 O 7
Missouri □ **USA** ◆ 16-17 H 3
Missouri City o **USA** ◇ 26-27 K 5
Missouri River ~ **USA** ◆ 16-17 G 2
Mist o **USA** ◇ 20-21 C 3
Mistassibi, Rivière ~ **CDN** ◇ 18-19 H 3
Mistassini, Lac ⊖ **CDN** ◇ 18-19 H 3 ◆ 14-15 W 6
Mistassini, Réserve de ⊥ **CDN** ◇ 18-19 H 3
Mistassini, Rivière ~ **CDN** ◇ 18-19 H 4
Mistawak, Rivière ~ **CDN** ◇ 18-19 E 4
Mita, Punta ▲ **MEX** ◇ 28-29 B 1
Mitchell o **AUS** ◆ 60-61 K 5
Mitchell o **CDN** ◇ 18-19 D 7
Mitchell o **USA** (OR) ◇ 20-21 D 3
Mitchell o **USA** (SD) ◆ 16-17 G 2
Mitchell, Mount ▲ **USA** ◇ 24-25 G 2 ◆ 16-17 K 3
Mitchell Lake < **USA** ◇ 24-25 E 3
Mitchell River ~ **AUS** ◆ 60-61 J 3
Mitchinamecus, Réservoir ⊖ **CDN** ◇ 18-19 G 5
Mithankot o **PK** ◆ 56-57 L 5
Mithi o **PK** ◆ 56-57 K 6
Mitiaro Island ⌒ **NZ** ◆ 12 M 4
Mitilíni ☆· **GR** ◇ 46-47 L 5 ◆ 34-35 R 8
Mitla ∴· **MEX** ◇ 28-29 F 3
Mitla, Laguna ≈ ◇ 28-29 D 3
Mito ☆ **J** ◆ 54-55 R 4
Mitsinjo o **RM** ◆ 50-51 L 5
Mitsio, Nosy ⌒ **RM** ◆ 50-51 L 4
Mits'iwa o· **ER** ◆ 48-49 N 5
Mitu ☆ **CO** ◆ 30-31 E 4
Mitumba, Monts ⛰ **ZRE** ◆ 50-51 G 2
Mitwaba o **ZRE** ◆ 50-51 G 3
Mitzic o **G** ◆ 50-51 D 1
Mixco o·· **GCA** ◇ 28-29 J 4
Mixquiahuala o **MEX** ◇ 28-29 E 1
Mixteco, Río ~ **MEX** ◇ 28-29 E 2
Mixtlán o **MEX** ◇ 28-29 B 1
Miyako shima ⌒ **J** ◆ 54-55 O 7
Miyāne o· **IR** ◆ 56-57 F 3
Miyazaki ☆ **J** ◆ 54-55 P 5
Mizan Teferi o **ETH** ◆ 48-49 N 7
Mizdah o **LAR** ◆ 48-49 H 2
Mizoram □ **IND** ◆ 56-57 P 6
Mkambati Nature Reserve ⊥ **ZA** ◆ 50-51 G 8
Mkomazi Game Reserve ⊥ **EAT** ◆ 50-51 J 2
Mkuzi Game Reserve ⊥ **ZA** ◆ 50-51 H 7
Mlandizi o **EAT** ◆ 50-51 J 3
Mmabatho ☆ **ZA** ◆ 50-51 F 7
Moa ~ **WAL** ◆ 48-49 C 7
Moa, Pulau ⌒ **RI** ◆ 58-59 J 8
Moa Island ⌒ **AUS** ◆ 60-61 J 2
Moala ⌒ **FJI** ◆ 60-61 Q 3
Moamba o **MOC** ◆ 50-51 H 7
Moanda o **G** ◆ 50-51 D 2
Moapa o **USA** ◇ 20-21 G 7
Móar Bay ≈ ◇ 18-19 E 2
Moba o **ZRE** ◆ 50-51 G 3
Mobaye ☆· **RCA** ◆ 48-49 K 8
Mobile o **USA** ◇ 24-25 D 4 ◆ 16-17 J 4
Mobile Bay ≈ ◇ 24-25 D 4
Mobridge o **USA** ◆ 14-15 Q 7
Mocajuba o **BR** ◆ 30-31 K 5
Moçambique o **MOC** ◆ 50-51 K 5
Moçambique, Ilha de ⌒··· **MOC** ◆ 50-51 K 5
Mocha = al-Muḥā o·· **Y** ◆ 56-57 E 8
Mocha, Isla ⌒ **RCH** ◆ 32-33 H 5
Mochis, Los o **MEX** ◆ 16-17 E 5
Mochudi ☆ **RB** ◆ 50-51 G 6
Mocímboa da Praia o **MOC** ◆ 50-51 K 4
Môco ▲ **ANG** ◆ 50-51 E 4
Mocoa ☆ **CO** ◆ 30-31 D 4
Mocuba o **MOC** ◆ 50-51 J 5
Modane o **F** ◇ 38-39 L 9 ◆ 34-35 N 6
Modena o **I** ◇ 46-47 C 2 ◆ 34-35 O 7
Modena o **USA** ◇ 20-21 H 7
Modesto o **USA** ◇ 20-21 D 7 ◆ 16-17 B 3
Modesto Méndez o **GCA** ◇ 28-29 K 4
Moenkopi Wash ~ **USA** ◇ 20-21 J 7
Moero, Lac = Lake Mweru ⊖ **ZRE** ◆ 50-51 G 3
Moe-Yallourn o **AUS** ◆ 60-61 K 7
Mogadishu = Muqdisho ★ **SP** ◆ 48-49 P 8
Mogincual o **MOC** ◆ 50-51 K 5
Mogoča ☆ **RUS** ◆ 52-53 U 7
Mogotes, Punta ▲ **RA** ◆ 32-33 L 5
Mogotón, Cerro ▲ **NIC** ◇ 28-29 L 5
Mohawk o **USA** ◇ 22-23 D 2
Mohican, Cape ▲ **USA** ◆ 14-15 C 4
Moili ⌒ **COM** ◆ 50-51 K 4
Moin o **CR** ◇ 28-29 C 7
Mo i Rana o **N** ◇ 36-37 G 3 ◆ 34-35 O 2
Moisie o **CDN** ◇ 18-19 L 3
Moisie, Rivière ~ **CDN** ◇ 18-19 L 3 ◆ 14-15 X 6
Moissac o **F** ◇ 38-39 H 9 ◆ 34-35 L 7
Moïssala o **TCH** ◆ 48-49 J 7
Mojave o **USA** ◇ 20-21 E 8
Mojave Desert ∸ **USA** ◇ 20-21 F 8 ◆ 16-17 C 3
Mojave River ~ **USA** ◇ 20-21 F 8
Mojos, Llanos de ∸ **BOL** ◆ 30-31 F 7
Mojynkūm ∸ **KZ** ◆ 52-53 J 8
Mokāma o **IND** ◆ 56-57 O 5
Mokelumne Aqueduct < **USA** ◇ 20-21 D 6
Mokp'o o **ROK** ◆ 54-55 O 5
Môktama Kwe ≈ ◆ 58-59 C 3
Molas del Norte, Punta ▲ **MEX** ◇ 28-29 L 1
Moldova ■ **MD** ◆ 34-35 R 6
Moldoveanu ▲ **RO** ◆ 34-35 Q 6
Mole Lake Indian Reservation X **USA** ◇ 22-23 D 3
Mole National Park ⊥ **GH** ◆ 48-49 E 7
Moline o **USA** (IL) ◇ 22-23 C 5
Moline o **USA** (KS) ◇ 26-27 J 1
Molinos, Los o **USA** ◇ 20-21 C 5
Moliro o **ZRE** ◆ 50-51 H 3
Mollendo o **PE** ◆ 30-31 E 8
Molodežnaja o **ANT** ◆ 13 G 5
Molokai ⌒ **USA** ◇ 24-25 D 7 ◆ 16-17 b 6
Molopo ~ **RB** ◆ 50-51 F 7
Moloundou o **CAM** ◆ 48-49 J 8
Molsheim o· **F** ◇ 38-39 L 7 ◆ 34-35 N 6
Moluccas ⌒ **RI** ◆ 58-59 J 7
Molucca Sea ≈ ◆ 58-59 H 7
Moma o **MOC** ◆ 50-51 J 5
Moma ~ **RUS** ◆ 52-53 Z 4
Mombasa ☆·· **EAK** ◆ 50-51 J 2
Mombasa Marine National Reserve ⊥ **EAK** ◆ 50-51 J 2
Mombetsu o **J** ◆ 54-55 R 3
Mombongo o **ZRE** ◆ 50-51 F 1
Momotombo, Volcán ▲ **NIC** ◇ 28-29 L 5
Momskij hrebet ⛰ **RUS** ◆ 52-53 Z 4
Momskiy Khrebet = Momskij hrebet ⛰ **RUS** ◆ 52-53 Z 4
Mona, Isla ⌒ **USA** ◆ 16-17 N 7
Monaco ■ **MC** ◇ 38-39 L 10 ◆ 34-35 N 7
Monaco Deep ≃ ◆ 34-35 G 9
Monahans o **USA** ◇ 26-27 F 4
Mona Passage ≈ ◆ 16-17 N 7
Monarch o **USA** ◇ 20-21 J 2
Monashee Mountains ⛰ **CDN** ◆ 14-15 N 6
Monastery o **CDN** ◇ 18-19 O 6
Monastir ☆ **TN** ◆ 48-49 H 1
Mončegorsk o **RUS** ◆ 34-35 S 2
Moncks Corner o **USA** ◇ 24-25 H 3
Monclova o **MEX** ◆ 16-17 F 5
Moncton o **CDN** ◇ 18-19 M 5 ◆ 14-15 Y 7
Monett o **USA** ◇ 26-27 L 1
Monga o **ZRE** ◆ 48-49 K 8
Mongala ~ **ZRE** ◆ 48-49 K 8
Monger, Îles ⌒ **CDN** ◇ 18-19 P 3
Mongers Lake ⊖ **AUS** ◆ 60-61 D 5
Mong Hsan o **MYA** ◆ 54-55 H 7
Möng Mit o **MYA** ◆ 54-55 H 7
Mongo ☆ **TCH** ◆ 48-49 J 6
Mongol Altajn Nuruu ⛰ **MAU** ◆ 54-55 F 2
Mongolia ■ **MAU** ◆ 54-55 H 2
Mongu ☆ **Z** ◆ 50-51 F 5
Monico o **USA** ◇ 22-23 D 3
Monida o **USA** ◇ 20-21 H 3
Monida Pass ▲ **USA** ◇ 20-21 H 3
Monitor Range ⛰ **USA** ◇ 20-21 F 6
Monkoto o **ZRE** ◆ 50-51 F 2
Monmouth o **USA** (IL) ◇ 22-23 C 5
Monmouth o **USA** (OR) ◇ 20-21 C 3
Mono ~ **DY** ◆ 48-49 F 7
Mono, Punta del ▲ **NIC** ◇ 28-29 C 6
Mono Lake ⊖ **USA** ◇ 20-21 E 6 ◆ 16-17 C 3
Monroe o **CDN** ◇ 18-19 S 4
Monroe o **USA** (GA) ◇ 24-25 G 3
Monroe o **USA** (LA) ◇ 26-27 L 3 ◆ 16-17 H 4
Monroe o **USA** (MI) ◇ 22-23 G 5
Monroe o **USA** (NC) ◇ 24-25 H 2
Monroe o **USA** (WA) ◇ 20-21 D 2
Monroe o **USA** (WI) ◇ 22-23 D 4
Monroe City o **USA** ◇ 22-23 C 6
Monroe Lake ~ **USA** ◇ 22-23 E 6
Monroeville o **USA** ◇ 24-25 E 4
Monrovia ★· **LB** ◆ 48-49 C 7
Montagne d'Ambre, Parc National de la ⊥ **RM** ◆ 50-51 L 4
Montagne du Pin, Lac de la ⊖ **CDN** ◇ 18-19 G 2
Montague o **CDN** ◇ 18-19 N 5
Montague Island ⌒ **USA** ◆ 14-15 G 4
Montaigu o **F** ◇ 38-39 G 8 ◆ 34-35 L 6
Montalegre o **ANG** ◆ 50-51 E 3
Montalto (Monte Cocuzza) ▲ **I** ◇ 46-47 E 5 ◆ 34-35 P 8
Montana □ **USA** ◇ 20-21 J 2 ◆ 14-15 O 7
Montaña, La ∸ **PE** ◆ 30-31 E 6
Montargis o **F** ◇ 38-39 J 8 ◆ 34-35 M 6
Montauban ☆· **F** ◇ 38-39 H 9 ◆ 34-35 M 7
Montauk o **USA** ◇ 22-23 N 5
Montauk Point ▲ **USA** ◇ 22-23 N 5
Montbard o **F** ◇ 38-39 K 8 ◆ 34-35 M 6
Montbéliard o· **F** ◇ 38-39 L 8 ◆ 34-35 N 6
Mont Blanc ▲·· **F** ◇ 38-39 L 9 ◆ 34-35 N 6
Montceau-les-Mines o **F** ◇ 38-39 K 8 ◆ 34-35 M 6
Mont-de-Marsan ☆ **F** ◇ 38-39 G 10 ◆ 34-35 L 7
Mont-Dore o **F** ◆ 60-61 O 4
Mont-Dore, le o **F** ◇ 38-39 J 9 ◆ 34-35 M 7
Monte Alban ∴··· **MEX** ◇ 28-29 F 3
Monte Alegre o **BR** ◆ 30-31 J 5
Montebello o **CDN** ◇ 18-19 G 6
Montebello, Parque Nacional Lagunas de ⊥ **MEX** ◇ 28-29 J 3
Montebello Islands ⌒ **AUS** ◆ 60-61 D 4
Monte-Carlo o **MC** ◇ 38-39 L 10 ◆ 34-35 N 7
Monte Caseros o **RA** ◆ 32-33 L 4
Monte Comán o **RA** ◆ 32-33 J 4
Monte Cristi ☆ **DOM** ◆ 16-17 M 7
Montecristo, Cerro ▲ **ES** ◇ 28-29 K 4
Monte Dourado o **BR** ◆ 30-31 J 5
Montego Bay o·· **JA** ◆ 16-17 L 7
Monte Grande o **NIC** ◇ 28-29 B 5
Montélimar o **F** ◇ 38-39 K 9 ◆ 34-35 N 6
Montelimar o **NIC** ◇ 28-29 L 6
Montello o **USA** (NV) ◇ 20-21 G 5
Montello o **USA** (WI) ◇ 22-23 D 4
Montemorelos o **MEX** ◆ 16-17 G 5
Monte Pascoal, Parque Nacional de ⊥ **BR** ◆ 30-31 M 8
Montepío o **MEX** ◇ 28-29 G 2
Montepuez o **MOC** ◆ 50-51 J 4
Monte Quemado o **RA** ◆ 32-33 K 3
Monterey o· **USA** ◇ 20-21 D 7 ◆ 16-17 B 3
Monteria ☆ **CO** ◆ 30-31 D 3
Montero o **BOL** ◆ 30-31 G 8
Monte Rosa ⛰ **CH** ◇ 40-41 J 6 ◆ 34-35 N 6
Monterrey ☆· **MEX** ◆ 16-17 F 5
Monterrey Bay ≈ ◇ 20-21 D 7 ◆ 16-17 B 3
Monterrico o **GCA** ◇ 28-29 J 5
Montes Claros o **BR** ◆ 30-31 L 8
Montevideo ★· **ROU** ◆ 32-33 L 4
Monte Vista o **USA** ◇ 26-27 D 1
Montezuma o **USA** ◇ 24-25 F 3
Montezuma Castle National Monument ∴ **USA** ◇ 20-21 J 8
Montezuma Creek o **USA** ◇ 26-27 C 1
Montgomery o **USA** (WV) ◇ 22-23 H 6
Montgomery ☆· **USA** (AL) ◇ 24-25 E 3 ◆ 16-17 J 4
Montgomery City o **USA** ◇ 22-23 C 6
Monticello o **USA** (AR) ◇ 26-27 M 3 ◆ 16-17 H 4
Monticello o **USA** (GA) ◇ 24-25 G 3
Monticello o **USA** (IA) ◇ 22-23 C 4
Monticello o **USA** (KY) ◇ 22-23 F 7
Monticello o **USA** (MS) ◇ 26-27 M 4
Monticello o **USA** (NM) ◇ 26-27 D 3
Monticello o **USA** (NY) ◇ 22-23 L 5
Monticello o **USA** (UT) ◆ 16-17 E 3
Montijo, Golfo de ≈ ◇ 28-29 D 8
Mont-Laurier o **CDN** ◇ 18-19 G 5
Mont-Louis o **F** ◇ 38-39 J 10 ◆ 34-35 M 7
Montluçon o **F** ◇ 38-39 J 8 ◆ 34-35 M 6
Montmagny o **CDN** ◇ 18-19 J 5 ◆ 14-15 W 7
Montmarault o **F** ◇ 38-39 J 8 ◆ 34-35 M 6
Monto o **AUS** ◆ 60-61 L 4
Montpelier o **USA** (ID) ◇ 20-21 J 4
Montpelier ☆ **USA** (VT) ◇ 22-23 M 3 ◆ 14-15 W 8
Montpellier ☆· **F** ◇ 38-39 J 10 ◆ 34-35 M 7
Montréal o· **CDN** ◇ 18-19 H 6 ◆ 14-15 W 7
Montreal River ~ **CDN** ◇ 18-19 D 5
Montrose o **USA** (AR) ◇ 26-27 M 3
Montrose o **USA** (PA) ◇ 22-23 L 5
Mont Saint-Michel, Le o··· **F** ◇ 38-39 G 7 ◆ 34-35 L 6
Montserrat □ **GB** ◆ 16-17 O 7
Mont Tremblant, Parc du ⊥ **CDN** ◇ 18-19 G 5
Monument Hill State Historic Site ∴ **USA** ◇ 26-27 J 5
Monument Pass ▲ **USA** ◇ 26-27 B 1
Monument Valley Navajo Tribal Park ⊥· **USA** ◇ 26-27 B 1
Monza o· **I** ◇ 46-47 B 2 ◆ 34-35 N 6
Monze o **Z** ◆ 50-51 G 5
Moonie o **AUS** ◆ 60-61 L 5
Moora o **AUS** ◆ 60-61 D 6
Moore o **USA** ◇ 26-27 H 5
Moore, Lake ⊖ **AUS** ◆ 60-61 D 5
Moore Home State Memorial ∴· **USA** ◇ 22-23 D 6
Moores Creek National Battlefield · **USA** ◇ 24-25 J 2
Mooresville o **USA** ◇ 24-25 H 2
Moorhead o **USA** ◆ 14-15 R 7
Moose o **USA** ◇ 20-21 J 4
Moosehead Lake ⊖ **USA** ◇ 22-23 O 3
Mooselookmeguntic Lake ⊖ **USA** ◇ 22-23 N 3
Moose River ~ **CDN** ◆ 14-15 U 6
Moosonee o **CDN** ◆ 14-15 U 6
Mopán, Río ~ **GCA** ◇ 28-29 K 3
Mopti ☆ **RMM** ◆ 48-49 E 6
Moquegua ☆ **PE** ◆ 30-31 E 8
Mora o **USA** ◇ 26-27 E 2
Moradabad o **IND** ◆ 56-57 M 5
Morafenobe o **RM** ◆ 50-51 K 5
Moraine State Park ⊥ **USA** ◇ 22-23 H 5
Moramanga o **RM** ◆ 50-51 L 5
Moran o **USA** ◇ 20-21 J 4
Moranbah o **AUS** ◆ 60-61 K 4
Mora River ~ **USA** ◇ 26-27 E 2
Moratuwa o **CL** ◆ 56-57 M 9
Morawa o **AUS** ◆ 60-61 D 5
Moray Firth ≈ ◇ 38-39 E 3 ◆ 34-35 L 4
Morazán o **HN** ◇ 28-29 L 4
Mordvinia □ **RUS** ◇ 42-43 S 4 ◆ 34-35 U 5
Moree o **AUS** ◆ 60-61 K 5
Morehead o **PNG** ◆ 58-59 M 8
Morehead o **USA** ◇ 22-23 G 6
Morehead City o **USA** ◇ 24-25 K 2
Morelia ☆··· **MEX** ◇ 28-29 D 2 ◆ 16-17 F 7
Morell o **CDN** ◇ 18-19 N 5
Morella o **AUS** ◆ 60-61 J 4
Morelos □ **MEX** ◇ 28-29 E 2
Morembe o **RM** ◆ 50-51 K 6
Moremi Wildlife Reserve ⊥ **RB** ◆ 50-51 F 5
Moresby Island ⌒ **CDN** ◆ 14-15 K 6
Moreton Bay ≈ ◆ 60-61 L 5
Moreton Island ⌒ **AUS** ◆ 60-61 L 5
Morfou o **TR** ◆ 34-35 S 8
Morgan o **AUS** ◆ 60-61 H 6
Morgan City o **USA** ◇ 26-27 M 5
Morganfield o **USA** ◇ 22-23 E 7
Morgan Hill o **USA** ◇ 20-21 D 7
Morgan's Corner o **USA** ◇ 24-25 K 1
Morganton o **USA** ◇ 24-25 H 2
Morgantown o **USA** (KY) ◇ 22-23 E 7
Morgantown o **USA** (WV) ◇ 22-23 J 6 ◆ 16-17 L 3
Morhiban, Lac de ⊖ **CDN** ◇ 18-19 N 2
Moriarty o **USA** ◇ 26-27 D 2
Morioka ☆· **J** ◆ 54-55 R 4
Morkoka ~ **RUS** ◆ 52-53 S 4
Morlaix o **F** ◇ 38-39 F 7 ◆ 34-35 L 6
Mormon Print Shop · **USA** ◇ 22-23 F 3
Mornington, Isla ⌒ **RCH** ◆ 32-33 G 7
Mornington Abyssal Plain ≃ ◆ 7 C 10
Mornington Island ⌒ **AUS** ◆ 60-61 H 3
Moro o **USA** ◇ 20-21 D 3
Morocco ■ **MA** ◆ 48-49 D 2
Morogoro ☆ **EAT** ◆ 50-51 J 3
Morokweng o **ZA** ◆ 50-51 F 7
Morón o **C** ◆ 16-17 L 6
Mörön ☆ **MAU** ◆ 54-55 J 2
Morón o **RA** ◆ 32-33 L 4
Morondava o **RM** ◆ 50-51 K 6
Moroni ★· **COM** ◆ 50-51 K 4
Morotai, Pulau ⌒ **RI** ◆ 58-59 J 6
Moroto, Mount ▲ **EAU** ◆ 48-49 M 8
Morrilton o **USA** ◇ 26-27 L 2
Morrinhos o **BR** ◆ 30-31 K 8
Morris o **USA** ◇ 22-23 D 5
Morrisburg o **CDN** ◇ 18-19 G 6
Morristown o **USA** ◇ 24-25 G 1
Morrisville o **USA** ◇ 22-23 M 3
Morro, Punta ▲ **MEX** ◇ 28-29 J 2
Morro Bay o **USA** ◇ 20-21 D 8
Morrumbala o **MOC** ◆ 50-51 J 5
Morteros o **RA** ◆ 32-33 K 4
Mortes, Rio das ~ **BR** ◆ 30-31 J 7
Morton o **USA** ◇ 20-21 C 2
Morton National Park ⊥ **AUS** ◆ 60-61 L 6
Morvan, Parc Naturel Régional du ⊥ **F** ◇ 38-39 K 6 ◆ 34-35 M 6
Morven o **AUS** ◆ 60-61 K 5
Morwell o **AUS** ◆ 60-61 K 7
Mosca o **USA** ◇ 26-27 E 1
Moscow o **USA** (ID) ◇ 20-21 F 2
Moscow o **USA** (KS) ◇ 26-27 G 1
Moscow = Moskva ★··· **RUS** ◇ 42-43 P 4 ◆ 34-35 T 4
Moselle ~ **F** ◇ 38-39 L 7 ◆ 34-35 N 6
Mosers River o **CDN** ◇ 18-19 N 6
Moses Lake o· **USA** ◇ 20-21 E 2 ◆ 14-15 N 7
Moshi ☆ **EAT** ◆ 50-51 J 2
Moskva ★··· **RUS** ◇ 42-43 P 4 ◆ 34-35 T 4
Mosquero o **USA** ◇ 26-27 F 2
Mosquito Lagoon ≈ ◇ 24-25 H 5
Mosquitos, Costa de ᴗ **NIC** ◇ 28-29 C 5 ◆ 16-17 K 8
Mosquitos, Golfo de los ≈ ◇ 28-29 D 7 ◆ 16-17 K 9
Mossaka o **RCB** ◆ 50-51 E 2
Mosselbaai = Mossel Bay o **ZA** ◆ 50-51 F 8
Mossel Bay = Mosselbaai o **ZA** ◆ 50-51 F 8
Mossman o **AUS** ◆ 60-61 K 3
Mossoró o **BR** ◆ 30-31 M 6
Moss Vale o **AUS** ◆ 60-61 L 6
Most o **CZ** ◇ 40-41 M 3 ◆ 34-35 O 5
Mostaganem ☆ **DZ** ◆ 48-49 F 1
Mostar o· **BIH** ◇ 46-47 F 3 ◆ 34-35 P 7
Mostardas o **BR** ◆ 32-33 M 4
Mosul = Al-Mauşil ☆ **IRQ** ◆ 56-57 E 3
Motagua, Río ~ **GCA** ◇ 28-29 K 4
Motihari o **IND** ◆ 56-57 N 5
Motozintla de Mendoza o **MEX** ◇ 28-29 H 4
Motul o **MEX** ◇ 28-29 K 1
Motygino ☆ **RUS** ◆ 52-53 P 6
Mouchalagane, Rivière ~ **CDN** ◇ 18-19 K 2
Moudjéria o **RIM** ◆ 48-49 C 5
Mougalaba, Reserve de la ⊥ **G** ◆ 50-51 D 2
Mouila ☆ **G** ◆ 50-51 D 2
Mould Bay o **CDN** ◆ 14-15 N 1
Moulins ☆· **F** ◇ 38-39 J 8 ◆ 34-35 M 6
Moulmein = Maulamyaing o **MYA** ◆ 58-59 C 3
Moulouya, Oued ~ **MA** ◆ 48-49 E 2
Moulton o **USA** ◇ 24-25 E 2
Moultrie o **USA** ◇ 24-25 G 4
Moultrie, Lake ⊖ **USA** ◇ 24-25 H 3
Mound City Group National Monument ∴ **USA** ◇ 22-23 G 6
Moundou ☆ **TCH** ◆ 48-49 J 7
Moundsville o **USA** ◇ 22-23 H 6
Mountain o **USA** ◇ 22-23 D 3
Mountainair o **USA** ◇ 26-27 D 2
Mountain City o **USA** (NV) ◇ 20-21 G 5
Mountain City o **USA** (TN) ◇ 24-25 H 1
Mountain Gate o **USA** ◇ 20-21 C 5
Mountain Home o **USA** (AR) ◇ 26-27 L 1
Mountain Home o **USA** (ID) ◇ 20-21 G 4
Mountain Springs o **USA** ◇ 20-21 G 7
Mountain View o **USA** ◇ 26-27 L 2
Mountainview o **USA** ◇ 24-25 E 8
Mount Airy o **USA** ◇ 24-25 H 1
Mount Amhurst o **AUS** ◆ 60-61 F 3
Mount Aspiring National Park ⊥ **NZ** ◆ 60-61 O 8
Mount Barker o **AUS** ◆ 60-61 D 6
Mountbatten Indian Reserve X **CDN** ◇ 18-19 C 5
Mount Carleton Provincial Park ⊥ **CDN** ◇ 18-19 L 5
Mount Carmel o **USA** ◇ 22-23 E 6
Mount Carmel Junction o **USA** ◇ 20-21 H 7
Mount Carrol o **USA** ◇ 22-23 D 4
Mount Charleston o **USA** ◇ 20-21 G 7
Mount Clemens o **USA** ◇ 22-23 G 4
Mount Cook National Park ⊥··· **NZ** ◆ 60-61 P 8
Mount Coolon o **AUS** ◆ 60-61 K 4
Mount Desert Island ⌒ **USA** ◇ 22-23 O 3
Mount Dora o **USA** ◇ 24-25 H 5
Mount Forest o **CDN** ◇ 18-19 D 7
Mount Gambier o **AUS** ◆ 60-61 J 7
Mount Garnet o **AUS** ◆ 60-61 K 3
Mount Hagen ☆·· **PNG** ◆ 58-59 N 8
Mount Hope o **AUS** ◆ 60-61 H 6
Mount Ida o **USA** ◇ 26-27 L 2
Mount Isa o·· **AUS** ◆ 60-61 H 4
Mount Magnet o **AUS** ◆ 60-61 D 5
Mount Mulligan o **AUS** ◆ 60-61 J 3
Mount Pleasant o **USA** (IA) ◇ 22-23 C 5
Mount Pleasant o **USA** (MI) ◇ 22-23 F 4
Mount Pleasant o **USA** (TX) ◇ 26-27 K 3
Mount Pleasant o **USA** (UT) ◇ 20-21 J 6
Mount Rainier National Park ⊥ **USA** ◇ 20-21 D 2 ◆ 14-15 M 7
Mount Rogers National Recreation Area ⊥ **USA** ◇ 22-23 H 7
Mount Rushmore National Memorial ∴ **USA** ◆ 16-17 F 2
Mount Saint Helens National Volcanic Monument ⊥ **USA** ◇ 20-21 C 2
Mount Sherrick = Sherrick, Colline ▲ **CDN** ◇ 18-19 E 3
Mount Sterling o **USA** (IL) ◇ 22-23 C 6
Mount Sterling o **USA** (KY) ◇ 22-23 G 6
Mount Trumbull o **USA** ◇ 20-21 H 7
Mount Union o **USA** ◇ 22-23 K 5
Mount Vernon o **USA** (GA) ◇ 24-25 G 3
Mount Vernon o **USA** (IL) ◇ 22-23 D 6 ◆ 16-17 J 3
Mount Vernon o **USA** (IN) ◇ 22-23 E 7
Mount Vernon o **USA** (OH) ◇ 22-23 G 5
Mount Vernon o **USA** (OR) ◇ 20-21 E 3
Mount Vernon o **USA** (WA) ◇ 20-21 C 1
Moura o **BR** ◆ 30-31 G 5
Mourdi, Dépression du ∸ **TCH** ◆ 48-49 K 5
Mourdiah o **RMM** ◆ 48-49 D 6
Moussoro o **TCH** ◆ 48-49 J 6
Moustiers-Sainte-Marie o **F** ◇ 38-39 L 10 ◆ 34-35 N 7
Mouths of the Indus ~ **PK** ◆ 56-57 K 6
Moûtiers o **F** ◇ 38-39 L 9 ◆ 34-35 N 6
Moweaqua o **USA** ◇ 22-23 D 6
Moyale o **EAK** ◆ 48-49 N 8
Moyamba o **WAL** ◆ 48-49 C 7
Moyen Atlas ⛰ **MA** ◆ 48-49 D 2
Moyie Springs o **USA** ◇ 20-21 F 1
Moyobamba ☆ **PE** ◆ 30-31 D 6
Moyogalpa o **NIC** ◇ 28-29 B 6
Mozambique ■ **MOC** ◆ 50-51 H 6
Mozambique Basin ≃ ◆ 50-51 J 7
Mozambique Channel ≈ ◆ 50-51 J 6
Mozambique Plateau ≃ ◆ 50-51 J 8
Mpanda o **EAT** ◆ 50-51 H 3
Mpika o **Z** ◆ 50-51 H 4
Mporokoso o **Z** ◆ 50-51 H 3
Mpume o **ZRE** ◆ 50-51 E 2
Mtwara ☆ **EAT** ◆ 50-51 K 4
Mualama o **MOC** ◆ 50-51 J 5
Muanda o **ZRE** ◆ 50-51 D 3
Muang Khammouan o **LAO** ◆ 58-59 D 3
Muang Không o **LAO** ◆ 58-59 E 4
Muang Pakxan o **LAO** ◆ 58-59 D 3
Muang Sing o **LAO** ◆ 58-59 D 2
Muarabungo o **RI** ◆ 58-59 D 7
Muarateweh o **RI** ◆ 58-59 F 7
Mubarraz o **KSA** ◆ 56-57 F 5
Mubende o **EAU** ◆ 50-51 H 1
Mubi o **WAN** ◆ 48-49 H 6
Mucajaí, Rio ~ **BR** ◆ 30-31 G 4
Mucajaí, Serra ⛰ **BR** ◆ 30-31 G 4
Muchea o **AUS** ◆ 60-61 D 6
Muchinga Mountains ⛰ **Z** ◆ 50-51 H 4
Muconda o **ANG** ◆ 50-51 F 4
Mucusso, Coutada Pública do ⊥ **ANG** ◆ 50-51 F 5
Mudanjiang o **CHN** ◆ 54-55 O 3
Mudgee o **AUS** ◆ 60-61 K 6
Mueda o **MOC** ◆ 50-51 J 4
Muelle de los Bueyes o **NIC** ◇ 28-29 B 5
Muerto, Mar ≈ ◇ 28-29 G 3
Mufulira o **Z** ◆ 50-51 G 4
Mughsail o **OM** ◆ 56-57 G 7
Muğla ☆ **TR** ◆ 56-57 B 3
Muglad, al- o **SUD** ◆ 48-49 L 6
Muḥā, al- o·· **Y** ◆ 56-57 E 8
Muḥammad, Ra's ▲ **ET** ◆ 48-49 M 3
Mühlig-Hofmann Mountains ⛰ **ANT** ◆ 13 F 1
Muhoro o **EAT** ◆ 50-51 J 3
Mũi Cà Mau ▲ **VN** ◆ 58-59 D 5
Mujeres, Isla ⌒·· **MEX** ◇ 28-29 L 1 ◆ 16-17 J 6
Mŭjnoķ ☆ **UZ** ◆ 56-57 H 2
Mukačeve ☆ **UA** ◆ 34-35 Q 6
Mukdahan o **THA** ◆ 58-59 D 3
Mukoshima-rettō ⌒ **J** ◆ 54-55 R 6
Mulailiḥ, al- o **KSA** ◆ 56-57 D 6
Mulanje o **MW** ◆ 50-51 J 5
Mulanje Mountains ⛰ **MW** ◆ 50-51 J 5
Muleshoe o **USA** ◇ 26-27 F 2
Mulhouse o **F** ◇ 38-39 L 8 ◆ 34-35 N 6
Mullan o **USA** ◇ 20-21 G 2
Mullens o **USA** ◇ 22-23 H 7
Müller, Pegunungan ⛰ **RI** ◆ 58-59 F 6
Mullewa o **AUS** ◆ 60-61 D 5
Mullins o **USA** ◇ 24-25 J 2
Mulobezi o **Z** ◆ 50-51 G 5
Mulu, Gunung ▲ **MAL** ◆ 58-59 F 6
Mumbeji o **Z** ◆ 50-51 F 4
Muna o **MEX** ◇ 28-29 K 1
Muna ~ **RUS** ◆ 52-53 U 4
Muncho Lake Provincial Park ⊥ **CDN** ◆ 14-15 L 5
Muncie o **USA** ◇ 22-23 F 5 ◆ 16-17 J 2
Munday o **USA** ◇ 26-27 H 3
Mundelein o **USA** ◇ 22-23 D 4
Mundo Novo o **BR** ◆ 30-31 L 7
Mundubbera o **AUS** ◆ 60-61 L 5
Mundurucânia, Reserva Florestal ⊥ **BR** ◆ 30-31 H 6
Mundurucu, Área Indígena X **BR** ◆ 30-31 H 6
Munfordville o **USA** ◇ 22-23 F 7
Mungbere o **ZRE** ◆ 48-49 L 8
Mungindi o **AUS** ◆ 60-61 K 5
Mungo o **SME** ◆ 30-31 J 3
Munich ☆·· **D** ◇ 40-41 L 4 ◆ 34-35 O 6
Muntok o **RI** ◆ 58-59 E 7
Mupa, Parque Nacional da ⊥ **ANG** ◆ 50-51 E 5
Muqdisho ★ **SP** ◆ 48-49 P 8
Muratus, Pegunungan ⛰ **RI** ◆ 58-59 G 7
Murchison, Cape ▲ **CDN** ◆ 14-15 Y 4
Murchison Falls National Park ⊥ **EAU** ◆ 48-49 M 8
Murchison River ~ **AUS** ◆ 60-61 C 5
Murcia o **E** ◇ 44-45 G 6 ◆ 34-35 L 8
Murdochville o **CDN** ◇ 18-19 M 4
Mureş ~ **RO** ◆ 34-35 Q 6
Muret o **F** ◇ 38-39 H 10 ◆ 34-35 M 7
Murfreesboro o **USA** (AR) ◇ 26-27 L 2
Murfreesboro o **USA** (NC) ◇ 24-25 K 1
Murfreesboro o **USA** (TN) ◇ 24-25 E 2
Murgab ~ **TM** ◆ 56-57 J 3
Muriaê o **BR** ◆ 32-33 O 2
Muritiba o **BR** ◆ 30-31 M 7
Murmansk ☆ **RUS** ◆ 34-35 S 2
Murmanskoye Rise ≃ ◆ 34-35 T 1
Murom ☆ **RUS** ◇ 42-43 S 4 ◆ 34-35 U 4
Muroran o **J** ◆ 54-55 R 3
Murphy o **USA** ◇ 24-25 F 2
Murphy Hot Springs · **USA** ◇ 20-21 G 4
Murphysboro o **USA** ◇ 22-23 D 7
Murray o **USA** ◇ 22-23 D 7
Murray, Lake ⊖ **PNG** ◆ 58-59 M 8
Murray, Lake < **USA** ◇ 24-25 H 2
Murray Bridge o· **AUS** ◆ 60-61 H 7
Murray Harbour o **CDN** ◇ 18-19 N 5
Murray River ~ **AUS** ◆ 60-61 H 6
Murray River Basin ∸ **AUS** ◆ 60-61 J 6
Mururoa ⌒ **F** ◆ 12 O 5
Mururoa Atoll ⌒ **F** ◆ 12 O 5
Murwāra o **IND** ◆ 56-57 N 6
Murwillumbah o **AUS** ◆ 60-61 L 5
Musa Āli Terara ▲ **DJI** ◆ 48-49 O 6
Musai'id o **Q** ◆ 56-57 G 5
Mušbih, Ǧabal ▲ **ET** ◆ 48-49 M 4
Muscat = Masqaț ★·· **OM** ◆ 56-57 H 6
Muscatine o **USA** ◇ 22-23 C 5
Musgrave, Port ≈ ◆ 60-61 J 2
Musgrave Ranges ⛰ **AUS** ◆ 60-61 G 5
Mus-Haja, gora ▲ **RUS** ◆ 52-53 Z 5
Mushie o **ZRE** ◆ 50-51 E 2
Musi ~ **RI** ◆ 58-59 D 7
Musin o **WAN** ◆ 48-49 F 7
Muskegon o **USA** ◇ 22-23 E 4
Muskegon River ~ **USA** ◇ 22-23 F 4
Muskingum River ~ **USA** ◇ 22-23 H 6
Muskogee o **USA** ◇ 26-27 K 2 ◆ 16-17 G 3
Musoma ☆ **EAT** ◆ 50-51 H 2
Musquaro, Lac ⊖ **CDN** ◇ 18-19 O 3
Musquodoboit o **CDN** ◇ 18-19 N 6
Mussau Island ⌒ **PNG** ◆ 58-59 N 7
Musselshell River ~ **USA** ◆ 14-15 P 7
Mussende o **ANG** ◆ 50-51 E 4
Mussolo o **ANG** ◆ 50-51 E 3
Mustang Island ⌒ **USA** ◇ 26-27 J 6
Musún, Cerro ▲ **NIC** ◇ 28-29 B 5
Mūț o **ET** ◆ 48-49 L 3
Mutare ☆· **ZW** ◆ 50-51 H 5
Mutis, Gunung ▲ **RI** ◆ 58-59 H 8
Mutoto o **ZRE** ◆ 50-51 G 3
Mutsamudu o· **COM** ◆ 50-51 K 4
Mutshatsha o **ZRE** ◆ 50-51 F 4
Mutsu o **J** ◆ 54-55 R 3
Muttaburra o **AUS** ◆ 60-61 J 4
Mutton Bay o **CDN** ◇ 18-19 P 3
Mu Us Shamo ∸ **CHN** ◆ 54-55 K 4
Muxima o **ANG** ◆ 50-51 D 3
Muyinga o **BU** ◆ 50-51 H 2
Muy Muy o **NIC** ◇ 28-29 B 5
Muzaffargarh o **PK** ◆ 56-57 L 4
Muzaffarnagar o **IND** ◆ 56-57 M 5
Muzaffarpur o **IND** ◆ 56-57 O 5
Mvuma o **ZW** ◆ 50-51 H 5
Mwanza ☆· **EAT** ◆ 50-51 H 2
Mwanza o **ZRE** ◆ 50-51 G 3
Mweka o **ZRE** ◆ 50-51 F 2
Mwene-Ditu o **ZRE** ◆ 50-51 F 3
Mweru, Lake = Lac Moero ⊖ **Z** ◆ 50-51 G 3
Mweru Wantipa National Park ⊥ **Z** ◆ 50-51 G 3
Mwinilunga o **Z** ◆ 50-51 F 4
Myanmar ■ **MYA** ◆ 54-55 G 7
Myingyan o **MYA** ◆ 54-55 H 7
Myitkyina o **MYA** ◆ 54-55 H 6
Mykolajiv o **UA** ◆ 34-35 S 6
Mykolayiv = Mykolajiv o **UA** ◆ 34-35 S 6
Mymensingh o **BD** ◆ 56-57 P 6
Myohaung o **MYA** ◆ 54-55 G 7
Myrtle o **CDN** ◇ 18-19 E 6
Myrtle Beach o **USA** ◇ 24-25 J 3 ◆ 16-17 L 4
Myrtle Point o **USA** ◇ 20-21 B 4
Mysore o·· **IND** ◆ 56-57 M 8
My Tho ☆· **VN** ◆ 58-59 E 4
Myton o **USA** ◇ 20-21 J 5
M'Zab ∸··· **DZ** ◆ 48-49 F 2
Mziha o **EAT** ◆ 50-51 J 3
Mzimba o **MW** ◆ 50-51 H 4
Mzimkulwana Nature Reserve ⊥ **ZA** ◆ 50-51 G 7
Mzuzu ☆ **MW** ◆ 50-51 H 4

N

Naalehu o **USA** ◇ 24-25 E 8
Nabire o **RI** ◆ 58-59 L 7
Nabouwalu o **FJI** ◆ 60-61 Q 3
Nacala o **MOC** ◆ 50-51 K 4
Nacaome o **HN** ◇ 28-29 L 5
Nacaroa o **MOC** ◆ 50-51 J 4
Naches River ~ **USA** ◇ 20-21 D 2
Naco ∴ **HN** ◇ 28-29 K 4
Nacogdoches o **USA** ◇ 26-27 K 4
Nād-e 'Alī o **AFG** ◆ 56-57 J 4
Nadiād o **IND** ◆ 56-57 L 6
Nadym o **RUS** ◆ 52-53 L 4
Nafūd ad-Daḥī ∸ **KSA** ◆ 56-57 E 6
Nafūd al-Kubrā, an- ∸ **KSA** ◆ 56-57 E 5
Naga o **RP** (CAS) ◆ 58-59 H 4
Naga o **RP** (CEB) ◆ 58-59 H 4
Naǧaf, an- ☆ **IRQ** ◆ 56-57 E 4
Naǧafābād o **IR** ◆ 56-57 G 4
Nagai Island ⌒ **USA** ◆ 14-15 D 5
Nāgāland □ **IND** ◆ 56-57 P 5
Nagano o **J** ◆ 54-55 Q 4
Nagarote o **NIC** ◇ 28-29 L 5
Nagasaki ☆·· **J** ◆ 54-55 O 5
Nāgaur o **IND** ◆ 56-57 L 5
Naǧd ∸ **KSA** ◆ 56-57 E 5
Nāgda o **IND** ◆ 56-57 M 6
Nageezi o **USA** ◇ 26-27 D 1
Nāgercoil o **IND** ◆ 56-57 M 9
Naǧ 'Hammādī o **ET** ◆ 48-49 M 3
Nagornyj ☆ **RUS** ◆ 52-53 g 5
Nagoya ☆· **J** ◆ 54-55 Q 4
Nāgpur o· **IND** ◆ 56-57 M 6
Nagqu o **CHN** ◆ 54-55 G 5
Naǧrān ☆· **KSA** ◆ 56-57 E 7
Naha o **J** ◆ 54-55 O 6
Nahanni National Park ⊥··· **CDN** ◆ 14-15 L 4
Nahodka o **RUS** ◆ 52-53 X 9
Nahualate, Río ~ **GCA** ◇ 28-29 J 4
Nahuatzen o **MEX** ◇ 28-29 D 2
Nahūd, En o **SUD** ◆ 48-49 L 6
Nahuel Huapi, Parque Nacional ⊥ **RA** ◆ 32-33 H 6
Nahunta o **USA** ◇ 24-25 H 4
Nain o **CDN** ◆ 14-15 Y 5
Nāin o· **IR** ◆ 56-57 G 4
Nairai ⌒ **FJI** ◆ 60-61 Q 3
Nairobi ★· **EAK** ◆ 50-51 J 2
Naivasha o **EAK** ◆ 50-51 J 2
Nakanno o **RUS** ◆ 52-53 S 5
Nak'fa o **ER** ◆ 48-49 N 5
Nakhchyvan = Naxçıvan ☆ **AZ** ◆ 56-57 F 3
Nakhon Pathom o **THA** ◆ 58-59 D 4
Nakhon Sawan o **THA** ◆ 58-59 D 3
Nakhon Si Thammarat o·· **THA** ◆ 58-59 C 5
Nakina o **CDN** ◆ 14-15 T 6
Naknek o **USA** ◆ 14-15 E 5
Nakum ∴· **GCA** ◇ 28-29 K 3
Nakuru ☆ **EAK** ◆ 50-51 J 2
Nal'čik ☆· **RUS** ◆ 34-35 U 7
Nālūt o **LAR** ◆ 48-49 H 2
Namacurra o **MOC** ◆ 50-51 J 5
Namak, Daryā-ye ⊖ **IR** ◆ 56-57 G 4
Namaksār ⊖ **AFG** ◆ 56-57 J 4
Namakwaland ∸ **ZA** ◆ 50-51 E 8
Namaland ∸ **NAM** ◆ 50-51 E 7
Namangan o **UZ** ◆ 56-57 L 2
Namapa o **MOC** ◆ 50-51 J 4
Namatanai o **PNG** ◆ 58-59 O 7
Nambe Indian Reservation X **USA** ◇ 26-27 E 2

Minersville — Nambe Indian Reservation 83

Nueces River ∼ USA ◇ 26-27 H 5 ◆ 16-17 G 5
Nueltin Lake ⊖ CDN ◆ 14-15 R 4
Nueva Arcadia o HN ◇ 28-29 K 4
Nueva Coahuila o MEX ◇ 28-29 J 3
Nueva Gerona ☆ C ◆ 16-17 K 6
Nueva Guinea o NIC ◇ 28-29 B 6
Nueva Italia de Ruiz o MEX ◇ 28-29 C 2
Nueva Rosita o MEX ◆ 16-17 F 5
Nueva San Salvador o ES ◇ 28-29 K 5
Nuevo Andoas o PE ◆ 30-31 D 5
Nuevo Campechito o MEX ◇ 28-29 H 2
Nuevo Casas Grandes o MEX ◆ 16-17 E 4
Nuevo Laredo o MEX ◆ 16-17 G 5
Nu Jiang ∼ CHN ◆ 54-55 H 6
Nuku'alofa ★ • TON ◆ 12 K 5
Nuku-Hiva ⌒ F ◆ 12 N 3
Nukulaelae Atoll ⌒ TUV ◆ 12 J 3
Nukus ☆ UZ ◆ 56-57 H 2
Nulato o USA ◆ 14-15 E 4
Nullagine o AUS ◆ 60-61 E 4
Nullarbor National Park ⊥ AUS ◆ 60-61 F 6
Nullarbor Plain ⊥ AUS ◆ 60-61 F 6
Num, Pulau ⌒ RI ◆ 58-59 L 7
Numan o WAN ◆ 48-49 H 7
Nu'mān, Ma'arrat an- o • SYR ◆ 56-57 D 3
Numfor, Pulau ⌒ RI ◆ 58-59 K 7
Nunavik ∪ GRØ ◆ 14-15 a 2
Nunivak Island ⌒ USA ◆ 14-15 C 4
Nunligran o RUS ◆ 52-53 h 5
Nuqay, Jabal ▲ LAR ◆ 48-49 J 4
Nuremberg = Nürnberg o D ◇ 40-41 L 4 ◆ 34-35 O 6
Nuri •• SUD ◆ 48-49 M 5
Nürnberg o D ◇ 40-41 L 4 ◆ 34-35 O 6
Nushki o PK ◆ 56-57 K 5
Nutrioso o USA ◇ 26-27 C 3
Nuuk = Godthåb ☆ GRØ ◆ 14-15 a 4
Nuussuaq Halvø ∪ GRØ ◆ 14-15 a 2
Nuyts Archipelago ⌒ AUS ◆ 60-61 G 6
Nxai Pan National Park ⊥ RB ◆ 50-51 F 5
Nyagassola o RG ◆ 48-49 D 6
Nyainqêntanglha Shan ▲ CHN ◆ 54-55 F 6
Nyala o SUD ◆ 48-49 K 6
Nyamandhlovu o ZW ◆ 50-51 G 5
Nyanga ∼ G ◆ 50-51 D 2
Nyaunglebin o MYA ◆ 58-59 C 3
Nyeri ☆ EAK ◆ 50-51 J 2
Nyima o CHN ◆ 54-55 F 5
Nyingchi o CHN ◆ 54-55 G 6
Nyíregyháza o H ◇ 40-41 Q 5 ◆ 34-35 Q 6
Nykia National Park ⊥ MW ◆ 50-51 H 4
Nykia Plateau ▲ •• MW ◆ 50-51 H 4
Nylstroom o ZA ◆ 50-51 G 6
Nyngan o AUS ◆ 60-61 K 6
Nyong ∼ CAM ◆ 48-49 H 8
Nyons o F ◇ 38-39 K 9 ◆ 34-35 N 6
Nyssa o USA ◇ 20-21 F 4
Nyunzu o ZRE ◆ 50-51 G 3
Nzega o EAT ◆ 50-51 H 2
Nzérékoré o RG ◆ 48-49 D 7
N'Zeto o ANG ◆ 50-51 D 3

O

Oahu ⌒ USA ◇ 24-25 D 7 ◆ 16-17 b 6
Oakdale o USA (CA) ◇ 20-21 D 7
Oakdale o USA (LA) ◇ 26-27 L 4
Oak Grove o USA ◇ 26-27 M 3
Oak Harbor o USA ◇ 20-21 C 1
Oak Hill o USA (FL) ◇ 24-25 H 5
Oak Hill o USA (WV) ◇ 22-23 H 7
Oakhurst o USA ◇ 20-21 E 7
Oakland o USA (CA) ◇ 20-21 C 7
Oakland o USA (MD) ◇ 22-23 J 6
Oakland o USA (MS) ◇ 24-25 D 2
Oak Lawn o USA ◇ 22-23 E 5
Oakley o USA ◇ 20-21 H 4
Oakridge o USA ◇ 20-21 C 4
Oak Ridge o USA (TN) ◇ 24-25 F 1
Oak Ridge o USA (TX) ◇ 26-27 K 4
Oakwood o USA ◇ 26-27 H 2
Oamaru o NZ ◆ 60-61 P 9
Oasis o USA ◇ 20-21 G 5
Oates Land ⊥ ANT ◆ 13 F 17
Oaxaca de Juárez ☆ ••• MEX ◇ 28-29 F 3 ◆ 16-17 G 7
Ob' ∼ RUS ◆ 52-53 K 4
Obamska, Rivière ∼ CDN ◇ 18-19 E 3
Obe o • AFG ◆ 56-57 J 4
Obe = Île Aoba ⌒ VAN ◆ 60-61 O 3
Obera o • RA ◆ 32-33 L 3
Obi, Pulau ⌒ RI ◆ 58-59 J 7
Óbidos o BR ◆ 30-31 H 5
Obihiro o J ◆ 54-55 R 3
Obluč'e o RUS ◆ 52-53 X 8
Obninsk o RUS ◇ 42-43 P 4 ◆ 34-35 T 4
Obo ☆ RCA ◆ 48-49 L 7
Oboa ▲ EAU ◆ 50-51 H 1
Obock o DJI ◆ 48-49 O 6
Obouya o RCB ◆ 50-51 E 2
Obregón, Ciudad o MEX ◆ 16-17 E 5
Obruchev Rise ≃ ◆ 52-53 d 7
Obščij syrt ▲ RUS ◆ 34-35 V 5
Obskaja guba ≈ ◆ 52-53 L 4
Obskaya Guba = Obskaja guba ≈ ◆ 52-53 L 4
Ocala o USA ◇ 24-25 G 5 ◆ 16-17 K 5
Ocaña o CO ◆ 30-31 E 3
Ocapi, Parc National de la ⊥ ZRE ◆ 48-49 L 8
Ocate o USA ◇ 26-27 E 1
Ocean City o USA ◇ 22-23 L 6
Ocean Shores o USA ◇ 20-21 B 2
Oceanside o USA ◇ 20-21 F 9 ◆ 16-17 C 4
Ocean Springs o USA ◇ 24-25 D 4
Očenyrd, gora ▲ RUS ◆ 52-53 K 4
Ochopee o USA ◇ 24-25 H 7
Ocho Rios o • JA ◆ 16-17 L 7
Ocilla o USA ◇ 24-25 G 4
Ocmulgee National Monument ∴ • USA ◇ 24-25 G 3
Ocmulgee River ∼ USA ◇ 24-25 G 3
Oconee, Lake < USA ◇ 24-25 G 3
Oconee River ∼ USA ◇ 24-25 G 3
Oconto o USA ◇ 22-23 E 3
Oconto River ∼ USA ◇ 22-23 D 3
Ocós o GCA ◇ 28-29 H 4
Ocosingo o MEX ◇ 28-29 H 3
Ocotal ☆ NIC ◇ 28-29 L 5 ◆ 16-17 J 8
Ocotepeque, Nueva o HN ◇ 28-29 K 4
Ocotito, El o MEX ◇ 28-29 E 3
Ocotlán o MEX (JAL) ◇ 28-29 C 1 ◆ 16-17 F 6
Ocotlán o • MEX (OAX) ◇ 28-29 F 3
Ocozocoautla o MEX ◇ 28-29 H 3
Ocracoke o USA ◇ 24-25 L 2
Octy, Mount ▲ AUS ◆ 60-61 G 4
Ocú o • PA ◇ 28-29 D 8
Odense o • DK ◆ 36-37 E 9 ◆ 34-35 O 4
Odesa ☆ •• UA ◆ 34-35 S 6
Odessa o USA (TX) ◇ 26-27 F 4 ◆ 16-17 F 4
Odessa o USA (WA) ◇ 20-21 E 2
Odessa = Odesa ☆ •• UA ◆ 34-35 S 6
Odienné ☆ • CI ◆ 48-49 D 7
Odra ∼ PL ◇ 40-41 N 2 ◆ 34-35 O 5
Odzala, Parc National d' ⊥ RCB ◆ 50-51 D 1
Oelwein o USA ◇ 22-23 C 4
Ogaden ⊥ ETH ◆ 48-49 O 7
Oganda, Parc National de l' ⊥ G ◆ 50-51 D 2
Ogasawara shotō ∪ J ◆ 54-55 R 6
Ogascanane, Lac ⊖ CDN ◇ 18-19 E 5
Ogbomoso o WAN ◆ 48-49 F 7
Ogden o USA ◇ 20-21 J 5 ◆ 16-17 D 2
Ogdensburg o USA ◇ 22-23 L 3
Ogeechee River ∼ USA ◇ 24-25 H 3
Ogilvie Mountains ▲ CDN ◆ 14-15 H 3
Ognon ∼ F ◇ 38-39 L 8 ◆ 34-35 N 6
Ogoki Reservoir < CDN ◆ 14-15 T 6
Ogoki River ∼ CDN ◆ 14-15 T 6
Ogooué ∼ G ◆ 50-51 D 2
Ogr o SUD ◆ 48-49 L 6
Oha ☆ • RUS ◆ 52-53 Z 7
Ohau ⌒ USA ◇ 24-25 D 7
Ohio ◻ USA ◇ 22-23 G 5 ◆ 16-17 K 2
Ohio River ∼ USA ◇ 22-23 E 6 ◆ 16-17 K 3
Ohota ∼ RUS ◆ 52-53 Z 5
Ohotsk ☆ • RUS ◆ 52-53 Z 6
Ohotsk, Sea of ≈ ◆ 52-53 a 7
Ohrid o ••• MK ◇ 46-47 H 4 ◆ 34-35 Q 7
Oiapoque ∼ BR ◆ 30-31 J 4
Oiapoque, Reserva Biológica de ⊥ BR ◆ 30-31 J 4
Oil City o USA (LA) ◇ 26-27 L 3
Oil City o USA (PA) ◇ 22-23 J 5
Oildale o USA ◇ 20-21 E 8
Oilton o USA ◇ 26-27 H 6
Oise ∼ F ◇ 38-39 J 7 ◆ 34-35 M 6
Ōita ☆ J ◆ 54-55 P 5
Ojibwa o USA ◇ 22-23 C 3
Ojmjakonskoe nagor'e ▲ RUS ◆ 52-53 Z 5
Ojos del Salado, Nevado ▲ RCH ◆ 32-33 J 3
Oka ∼ RUS ◆ 52-53 R 7
Oka ∼ RUS ◇ 42-43 P 4 ◆ 34-35 T 5
Okahandja ☆ NAM ◆ 50-51 E 6
Okanagan Lake ⊖ CDN ◆ 14-15 N 7
Okano ∼ G ◆ 50-51 D 1
Okanogan o USA ◇ 20-21 E 1
Okanogan River ∼ USA ◇ 20-21 E 1 ◆ 14-15 N 7
Okarche o USA ◇ 26-27 J 2
Okavango ∼ NAM ◆ 50-51 F 5
Okavango Basin ⊥ RB ◆ 50-51 F 5
Okavango Delta ⊥ RB ◆ 50-51 F 5
Okayama o J ◆ 54-55 P 5
Okeechobee o USA ◇ 24-25 H 6
Okeechobee, Lake ⊖ USA ◇ 24-25 H 6 ◆ 16-17 K 5
Okefenokee National Wildlife Refuge ⊥ USA ◇ 24-25 G 4
Okefenokee Swamp ⊖ USA ◇ 24-25 G 4
Okemah o USA ◇ 26-27 J 2
Okhotsk, Sea of ≈ ◆ 52-53 a 7
Okinawa-shima ⌒ J ◆ 54-55 O 6
Okinawa-shotō ⌒ J ◆ 54-55 O 6
Okinoerabu-shima ⌒ J ◆ 54-55 O 6
Okino-Tori-Shima ⌒ J ◆ 54-55 Q 7
Oki-shotō ⌒ J ◆ 54-55 P 4
Oklahoma ◻ USA ◇ 26-27 H 2 ◆ 16-17 G 3
Oklahoma City ☆ USA ◇ 26-27 J 2 ◆ 16-17 G 3
Okmulgee o USA ◇ 26-27 K 2
Oktjabr' ☆ KZ ◆ 34-35 X 6
Oktjabr'skij o RUS (BAS) ◆ 34-35 W 5
Oktjabr'skij o RUS (KMC) ◆ 52-53 c 7
Oktjabr'skoj Revoljucii, ostrov ⌒ RUS ◆ 52-53 P 2
Oktyabr'skiy = Oktjabr'skij o RUS ◆ 34-35 W 5
Okushiri-tō ∪ J ◆ 54-55 Q 3
Okwa ∼ RB ◆ 50-51 F 6
Olá o PA ◇ 28-29 D 7
Ola o USA ◇ 26-27 L 2
Olaf Prydz bukt ≈ ◆ 13 G 8
Olanchito o HN ◇ 28-29 L 4
Öland ⌒ • S ◆ 36-37 H 8 ◆ 34-35 P 4
Olary o AUS ◆ 60-61 J 6
Olavarría o RA ◆ 32-33 K 5
Olbia o I ◇ 46-47 B 4 ◆ 34-35 N 7
Olcott o USA ◇ 22-23 J 4
Old Bohemia Church ∴ USA ◇ 22-23 L 6
Old Crow o CDN ◆ 14-15 J 3
Oldeani ▲ EAT ◆ 50-51 J 2
Oldest Christian Mission Site = Site chrétien ∴ CDN ◇ 18-19 K 4
Old Factory Bay ≈ ◇ 18-19 E 2
Old Faithful Geyser ∴ USA ◇ 20-21 J 3
Old Forge o USA ◇ 22-23 L 4
Old Fort Benton ∴ • USA ◇ 20-21 J 2
Old Fort Henry ∴ • CDN ◇ 18-19 F 6
Old Fort Parker State Historic Site ∴ USA ◇ 26-27 J 4
Old Horse Springs o USA ◇ 26-27 C 3
Old Irontown Ruins ∴ USA ◇ 20-21 H 7
Old Perlican o CDN ◇ 18-19 S 4
Old Woman Mountain ▲ USA ◇ 20-21 G 8
Olean o USA ◇ 22-23 J 4
O'Leary o CDN ◇ 18-19 M 5
Olëkma ∼ RUS ◆ 52-53 V 6
Olëkma ∼ RUS ◆ 52-53 V 6
Olëkminsk ☆ • RUS ◆ 52-53 V 5
Olëkminskij zapovednik ⊥ RUS ◆ 52-53 V 6
Oleksandrivka o UA ◆ 34-35 S 6
Olenëk o RUS (SAH) ◆ 52-53 T 4
Olenëk ∼ RUS ◆ 52-53 S 4
Olenëkskij zaliv ≈ ◆ 52-53 U 3
Olenij, ostrov ⌒ RUS ◆ 52-53 M 3
Oléron, Île d' ⌒ F ◇ 38-39 G 9 ◆ 34-35 L 6
Ol'ga o RUS ◆ 52-53 Y 9
Olga, Lac ⊖ CDN ◇ 18-19 F 4
Ölgij ☆ MAU ◆ 54-55 F 2
Ol'ginsk o RUS ◆ 52-53 X 7
Olifants ∼ NAM ◆ 50-51 E 6
Olifantsrivier ∼ ZA ◆ 50-51 G 6
Olimarao ⌒ FSM ◆ 12 F 2
Olimarao Atoll ⌒ FSM ◆ 58-59 N 5
Ólimpos ▲ GR ◇ 46-47 J 4 ◆ 34-35 Q 7
Olinalá o MEX ◇ 28-29 E 3
Oljutorskij, mys ▲ RUS ◆ 52-53 f 6
Oljutorskij poluostrov ∪ RUS ◆ 52-53 f 5
Oljutorskij zaliv ≈ ◆ 52-53 e 5
Olla o USA ◇ 26-27 L 4
Ollagüe, Volcán ▲ BOL ◆ 32-33 J 2
Olmos o PE ◆ 30-31 D 6
Olney o USA (IL) ◇ 22-23 D 6
Olney o USA (TX) ◇ 26-27 H 3
Oloči o RUS ◆ 52-53 U 7
Ologbo Game Reserve ⊥ WAN ◆ 48-49 G 7
Oloj ∼ RUS ◆ 52-53 d 4
Olojskij hrebet ▲ RUS ◆ 52-53 c 4
Olomane, Rivière ∼ CDN ◇ 18-19 O 3
Olomouc o CZ ◇ 40-41 O 4 ◆ 34-35 P 6
Oloron-Sainte-Marie o • F ◇ 38-39 G 10 ◆ 34-35 L 7
Olsztyn ☆ • PL ◇ 40-41 Q 2 ◆ 34-35 Q 5
Olt ∼ RO ◆ 34-35 Q 6
Oluanpi o RC ◆ 54-55 N 7
Olympia ••• GR ◇ 46-47 H 6 ◆ 34-35 Q 8
Olympia ☆ USA ◇ 20-21 C 2 ◆ 14-15 M 7
Olympic Mountains ▲ USA ◇ 20-21 C 2
Olympic National Park ⊥ ••• USA ◇ 20-21 C 2 ◆ 14-15 M 7
Olympus, Mount ▲ USA ◇ 20-21 C 2
Om' ∼ RUS ◆ 52-53 M 6
Omaha o USA (AR) ◇ 26-27 L 1
Omaha o USA (NE) ◆ 16-17 G 2
Omak o USA ◇ 20-21 E 1
Oman ◼ OM ◆ 56-57 H 7
Oman, Gulf of ≈ ◆ 56-57 H 6
Omapere o NZ ◆ 60-61 P 7
Omaruru ☆ NAM ◆ 50-51 E 6
Omatako ∼ NAM ◆ 50-51 F 5
Omboué o G ◆ 50-51 C 2
Omdurman = Umm Durmān o •• SUD ◆ 48-49 M 5
Omega o USA ◇ 26-27 C 2
Ometepe, Isla de ⌒ NIC ◇ 28-29 B 6 ◆ 16-17 J 8
Ometepec o • MEX ◇ 28-29 E 3
Omgon, mys ▲ RUS ◆ 52-53 c 6
Omineca Mountains ▲ CDN ◆ 14-15 L 5
Ōmiya o J ◆ 54-55 Q 4
Ommanney Bay ≈ ◆ 14-15 Q 2
Omoa o • HN ◇ 28-29 K 4
Omoloj ∼ RUS ◆ 52-53 X 4
Omolon ∼ RUS ◆ 52-53 c 4
Omo National Park ⊥ ETH ◆ 48-49 N 7
Omo Wenz ∼ ETH ◆ 48-49 N 7
Ompah o CDN ◇ 18-19 F 6
Omsk ☆ • RUS ◆ 52-53 L 7
Omsukčan ☆ RUS ◆ 52-53 c 5
Omsukčanskij hrebet ▲ RUS ◆ 52-53 b 5
Omutinskij ☆ RUS ◆ 52-53 K 6
Onancock o USA ◇ 22-23 L 7
Onaping Lake ⊖ CDN ◇ 18-19 D 5
Onaway o USA ◇ 22-23 F 3
Oncócua o ANG ◆ 50-51 D 5
Öndörhaan ☆ MAU ◆ 54-55 L 2
Onega o RUS ◆ 34-35 T 3
Onega ∼ RUS ◆ 34-35 T 3
Oneida o USA (NY) ◇ 22-23 L 4
Oneida o USA (TN) ◇ 24-25 F 1
Oneida Lake ⊖ USA ◇ 22-23 L 4
Onekotan, ostrov ⌒ RUS ◆ 52-53 b 8
Oneonta o USA ◇ 22-23 L 4
Onezhskaya Guba = Onežskaja guba ≈ ◆ 34-35 T 3
Onežskaja guba ≈ ◆ 34-35 T 3
Onežskoe ozero ⊖ RUS ◆ 34-35 T 3
Ongjin o KOR ◆ 54-55 O 4
Ongole o IND ◆ 56-57 N 7
Onitsha ☆ WAN ◆ 48-49 G 7
Onon ∼ RUS ◆ 52-53 U 7
Onslow o AUS ◆ 60-61 D 4
Onslow Bay ≈ ◇ 24-25 K 2 ◆ 16-17 L 4
Ontario ◻ CDN ◆ 14-15 S 6
Ontario o USA (CA) ◇ 20-21 F 8
Ontario o USA (OR) ◇ 20-21 F 3
Ontario o USA (WI) ◇ 22-23 C 4
Ontario, Lake ⊖ ◇ 22-23 J 4 ◆ 14-15 V 8
Ontario Peninsula ∪ CDN ◇ 18-19 D 7
Ontonagon o USA ◇ 22-23 D 2
Onyx Cave ∴ USA ◇ 26-27 L 1
Oodnadatta o AUS ◆ 60-61 H 5
Oologah Lake ⊖ USA ◇ 26-27 K 1
Oos-Londen = East London ☆ • ZA ◆ 50-51 G 8
Opala o ZRE ◆ 50-51 F 2
Opataca, Lac ⊖ CDN ◇ 18-19 G 3
Opava o CZ ◇ 40-41 O 4 ◆ 34-35 P 6
Opawica, Lac ⊖ CDN ◇ 18-19 G 4
Opelika o USA ◇ 24-25 F 3 ◆ 16-17 J 4
Opelousas o USA ◇ 26-27 L 4
Opémisca, Mont ▲ CDN ◇ 18-19 G 4
Opeongo Lake ⊖ CDN ◇ 18-19 E 6
Opichén o MEX ◇ 28-29 K 1
Opienge o ZRE ◆ 50-51 G 1
Opinaca, Réservoir < CDN ◇ 18-19 F 2
Opinaca, Rivière ∼ CDN ◇ 18-19 E 2
Opiscotéo, Lac ⊖ CDN ◇ 18-19 K 2
Opiscotiche, Lac ⊖ CDN ◇ 18-19 L 2
Opocopa, Lac ⊖ CDN ◇ 18-19 L 2
Opole ☆ • PL ◇ 40-41 O 3 ◆ 34-35 P 5
Opopeo o MEX ◇ 28-29 D 2
Opotiki o NZ ◆ 60-61 Q 7
Opp o USA ◇ 24-25 E 4
Opportunity o USA ◇ 20-21 F 2
Opunake o NZ ◆ 60-61 P 7
Opuwo ☆ NAM ◆ 50-51 D 5
Oquossoc o USA ◇ 22-23 N 3
Oracle o USA ◇ 26-27 B 3
Oracle Junction o USA ◇ 26-27 B 3
Oradea ☆ • RO ◆ 34-35 Q 6
Öræfajökull ▲ IS ◇ 36-37 e 2
Orai o IND ◆ 56-57 M 5
Oral ☆ KZ ◆ 34-35 W 5
Oran = Wahrān ☆ •• DZ ◆ 48-49 E 1
Orange o AUS ◆ 60-61 K 6
Orange o • F ◇ 38-39 K 9 ◆ 34-35 N 6
Orange o USA ◇ 26-27 L 4
Orange ∼ ZA ◆ 50-51 E 7
Orange, Cap ▲ F ◆ 30-31 J 4
Orangeburg o USA ◇ 24-25 H 3
Orange Fan ≃ ◆ 50-51 D 8
Orange Park o USA ◇ 24-25 H 4
Orangeville o CDN ◇ 18-19 D 7
Orange Walk o BH ◇ 28-29 K 2
Orango, Ilha de ⌒ GNB ◆ 48-49 B 6
Oranje Gebergte ▲ SME ◆ 30-31 H 4
Oranjerivier ∼ ZA ◆ 50-51 F 7
Oranjestad ☆ ARU ◆ 16-17 M 8
Oratia, Mount ▲ USA ◆ 14-15 D 5
Orb ∼ F ◇ 38-39 J 10 ◆ 34-35 M 7
Orbost o AUS ◆ 60-61 K 7
Orcadas o ANT ◆ 13 G 32
Ord, Mount ▲ AUS ◆ 60-61 F 3
Orderville o USA ◇ 20-21 H 7
Ord River ∼ AUS ◆ 60-61 F 3
Ordu ☆ TR ◆ 34-35 T 7
Örebro ☆ • S ◇ 36-37 G 7 ◆ 34-35 P 4
Oregon o USA (WI) ◇ 22-23 D 4
Oregon ◻ USA ◇ 20-21 C 4 ◆ 14-15 M 8
Oregon Caves National Monument ∴ USA ◇ 20-21 C 4
Orehovo-Zuevo ☆ RUS ◇ 42-43 Q 4 ◆ 34-35 T 4
Orekhovo-Zuyevo = Orehovo-Zuevo ☆ RUS ◇ 42-43 Q 4 ◆ 34-35 T 4
Orel o RUS ◇ 42-43 P 5 ◆ 34-35 T 5
Orem o USA ◇ 20-21 J 5
Orenburg ☆ RUS ◆ 34-35 X 5
Orford, Port o USA ◇ 20-21 B 4
Organ Pipe Cactus National Monument ∴ USA ◇ 20-21 H 9
Orhon gol ∼ MAU ◆ 54-55 J 2
Orica o HN ◇ 28-29 L 4
Orick o USA ◇ 20-21 B 5
Orient o USA ◇ 20-21 E 1
Orillia o CDN ◇ 18-19 E 6 ◆ 14-15 V 8
Orinduik o GUY ◆ 30-31 G 4
Orinoco, Delta del ≈ ◆ 30-31 G 3
Orinoco, Llanos del ⊥ ◆ 30-31 E 4
Orinoco, Río ∼ YV ◆ 30-31 G 3
Orissa ◻ IND ◆ 56-57 N 6
Oristano o • I ◇ 46-47 B 5 ◆ 34-35 N 8
Oriximiná o BR ◆ 30-31 H 5
Orizaba o • MEX ◇ 28-29 F 2 ◆ 16-17 G 7
Orizaba, Parque Nacional Pico de ⊥ MEX ◇ 28-29 F 2
Orizaba, Pico de ▲ MEX ◇ 28-29 F 2
Orkney Islands ⌒ GB ◇ 38-39 F 2 ◆ 34-35 L 4
Orla o USA ◇ 26-27 F 4
Orland o USA ◇ 20-21 C 6
Orlando o • USA ◇ 24-25 H 5 ◆ 16-17 K 5
Orléanais ⌒ F ◇ 38-39 H 8 ◆ 34-35 M 6
Orléans o F ◇ 38-39 H 8 ◆ 34-35 M 6
Orleans, Île d' ⌒ CDN ◇ 18-19 J 5
Orle River Game Reserve ⊥ WAN ◆ 48-49 G 7
Orlik ☆ RUS ◆ 52-53 Q 7
Ormára, Rās ▲ PK ◆ 56-57 J 5
Ormoc o RP ◆ 58-59 H 4
Ormond Beach o USA ◇ 24-25 H 5
Orne ∼ F ◇ 38-39 G 7 ◆ 34-35 L 6
Örnsköldsvik o S ◇ 36-37 J 5 ◆ 34-35 P 3
Orocue o CO ◆ 30-31 E 4
Orofino o USA ◇ 20-21 F 2
Orogrande o USA ◇ 26-27 D 3
Orol dengizi = Aral tenizi ⊖ ◆ 56-57 H 1
Oromocto o CDN ◇ 18-19 L 6
Orondo o USA ◇ 20-21 D 2
Orono o USA ◇ 22-23 O 3
Orosi o USA ◇ 20-21 E 7
Orotina o CR ◇ 28-29 B 7
Orotukan o RUS ◆ 52-53 b 5
Oroville o USA (WA) ◇ 20-21 E 1
Oroville o • USA (CA) ◇ 20-21 D 6
Oroville Reservoir < USA ◇ 20-21 D 6
Oroya, La o PE ◆ 30-31 D 7
Orša ☆ BY ◇ 42-43 M 4 ◆ 34-35 S 5
Orsha = Orša ☆ BY ◇ 42-43 M 4 ◆ 34-35 S 5
Orsk o RUS ◆ 34-35 X 5
Orthez o F ◇ 38-39 G 10 ◆ 34-35 L 7
Orūmīye ☆ • IR ◆ 56-57 F 3
Orūmīye, Daryāče-ye ⊖ IR ◆ 56-57 E 3
Oruro ☆ BOL ◆ 30-31 F 8
Orville Escarpment ▲ ANT ◆ 13 F 30
Orwell o USA ◇ 22-23 H 5
Oš ☆ KS ◆ 56-57 L 2
Osa, Península de ∪ CR ◇ 28-29 C 7 ◆ 16-17 K 9
Ōsaka ☆ • J ◆ 54-55 Q 5
Osasco o BR ◆ 32-33 N 2
Osceola o USA ◇ 24-25 D 2
Oscoda o USA ◇ 22-23 G 3
Osh = Oš ☆ KS ◆ 56-57 L 2
Oshakati o NAM ◆ 50-51 E 5
Oshawa o CDN ◇ 18-19 E 7 ◆ 14-15 V 8
Ōshima ⌒ J ◆ 54-55 Q 5
Ō-shima ⌒ J ◆ 54-55 O 6
Oshivelo o NAM ◆ 50-51 E 5
Oshkosh o USA ◇ 22-23 D 3
Oshwe o ZRE ◆ 50-51 E 2
Osijek ☆ • HR ◇ 46-47 G 2 ◆ 34-35 P 6
Osinniki ☆ RUS ◆ 52-53 O 7
Oskélanéo o CDN ◇ 18-19 G 4
Öskemen o KZ ◆ 52-53 N 8
Os'kino o RUS ◆ 52-53 S 5
Oslo ★ •• N ◇ 36-37 E 7 ◆ 34-35 O 4
Osmaniye ☆ TR ◆ 34-35 T 8
Osnabrück o • D ◇ 40-41 K 2 ◆ 34-35 N 5
Osogbo o • WAN ◆ 48-49 F 7
Osorno o RCH ◆ 32-33 H 6
Osprey Reef ⌒ AUS ◆ 60-61 K 2
Ossa, Mount ▲ AUS ◆ 60-61 K 8
Ossabaw Island ⌒ USA ◇ 24-25 H 4
Osséle o RCB ◆ 50-51 D 2
Osseo o USA ◇ 22-23 C 3
Ossining o USA ◇ 22-23 M 5
Ossokmanuan Lake ⊖ CDN ◇ 18-19 M 2
Ostapazifisches Südpolarbecken ≈ ◆ 13 G 27
Östersund ☆ • S ◇ 36-37 G 5 ◆ 34-35 O 3
Ostrava o CZ ◇ 40-41 P 4 ◆ 34-35 P 6
Ostrowiec Świętokrzyski o PL ◇ 40-41 Q 3 ◆ 34-35 Q 5
Ostsibirische Schwelle ≃ ◆ 13 B 36
Ōsumi-kaikyō ≈ ◆ 54-55 P 5
Oswego o USA (KS) ◇ 26-27 K 1
Oswego o USA (NY) ◇ 22-23 K 4
Otago Peninsula ∪ ••• NZ ◆ 60-61 P 9
Otaki o NZ ◆ 60-61 Q 8
Otaru o J ◆ 54-55 R 3
Otavi o NAM ◆ 50-51 E 5
O'the Cherokees, Lake ⊖ USA ◇ 26-27 K 1
Othello o USA ◇ 20-21 E 2
O'the Pines, Lake < USA ◇ 26-27 K 3
Oti ∼ GH ◆ 48-49 F 7
Otish, Monts ▲ CDN ◇ 18-19 J 2
Otjiwarongo ☆ NAM ◆ 50-51 E 6
Otranto, Canale d' ≈ ◇ 46-47 G 4 ◆ 34-35 P 7
Otselic o USA ◇ 22-23 L 4
Ottawa ★ • CDN ◇ 18-19 G 6 ◆ 14-15 V 7
Ottawa o USA (IL) ◇ 22-23 D 5
Ottawa o USA (OH) ◇ 22-23 F 5
Ottawa Islands ⌒ CDN ◆ 14-15 U 5
Ottawa River ∼ CDN ◇ 18-19 E 5 ◆ 14-15 V 7
Otter, Peaks of ▲ USA ◇ 22-23 J 7
Otter Creek o USA ◇ 24-25 G 5
Ottumwa o USA ◆ 16-17 H 2
Otuzco o PE ◆ 30-31 D 6
Otway, Cape ▲ AUS ◆ 60-61 J 7
Ouachita, Lake ⊖ USA ◇ 26-27 L 2
Ouachita Mountains ▲ USA ◇ 26-27 K 2 ◆ 16-17 G 4
Ouachita River ∼ USA ◇ 26-27 M 4 ◆ 16-17 H 4
Ouadda o RCA ◆ 48-49 K 7
Ouagadougou ★ • BF ◆ 48-49 E 6
Ouahigouya ☆ BF ◆ 48-49 E 6
Oualâta o RIM ◆ 48-49 D 5
Ouanda Djallé o • RCA ◆ 48-49 K 7
Ou'Apelle River ∼ CDN ◆ 14-15 Q 6
Ouarâne ⊥ RIM ◆ 48-49 D 4
Ouareau, Rivière ∼ CDN ◇ 18-19 H 5
Ouargla ☆ • DZ ◆ 48-49 G 2
Ouarkziz, Jbel ▲ MA ◆ 48-49 C 3
Ouarzazate ☆ MA ◆ 48-49 D 2
Oubangui ∼ RCB ◆ 50-51 E 1
Oudâne o • RIM ◆ 48-49 C 4
Oudtshoorn o ZA ◆ 50-51 F 8
Ouémé ∼ DY ◆ 48-49 F 7
Ouessant ⌒ F ◇ 38-39 E 7 ◆ 34-35 L 6
Ouest, Pointe de l' ▲ CDN ◇ 18-19 M 4
Ouezzane o MA ◆ 48-49 D 2
Oujda = Ujdah ☆ MA ◆ 48-49 E 2
Oulu ☆ FIN ◆ 34-35 R 2
Oulujärvi ⌒ FIN ◆ 34-35 R 3
Oum-Chalouba o TCH ◆ 48-49 K 5
Oum-Hadjer o TCH ◆ 48-49 J 6
Oumm ed Droûs Guebli, Sebkhet ⊖ RIM ◆ 48-49 C 4
Oumm ed Droûs Telli, Sebkhet ⊖ RIM ◆ 48-49 C 4
Ounasjoki ∼ FIN ◆ 34-35 Q 2
Ounianga Kébir o TCH ◆ 48-49 K 5
Ourense (Orense) o E ◇ 44-45 D 3 ◆ 34-35 K 7
Ourinhos o BR ◆ 32-33 N 2
Ouro Sogui o SN ◆ 48-49 C 5
Outamba-Kilimbi National Park ⊥ WAL ◆ 48-49 C 7
Outaouais, Rivière des ∼ CDN ◇ 18-19 E 5 ◆ 14-15 V 7
Outardes, Rivière aux ∼ CDN ◇ 18-19 K 3
Outardes Quatre, Réservoir < CDN ◇ 18-19 K 3
Outer Bill Bailey Bank ≃ ◇ 38-39 A 1 ◆ 34-35 J 3
Outer Island ⌒ USA ◇ 22-23 C 2
Outjo ☆ NAM ◆ 50-51 E 6
Ovalau ⌒ FJI ◆ 60-61 Q 3
Ovalle o RCH ◆ 32-33 H 4
Ovamboland ⊥ NAM ◆ 50-51 D 5
Ovana, Cerro ▲ YV ◆ 30-31 F 4
Ovens, The ∴ CDN ◇ 18-19 M 6
Ovens Natural Park ⊥ CDN ◇ 18-19 M 6
Overlander Roadhouse o AUS ◆ 60-61 C 5
Overton o USA ◇ 20-21 G 7
Oviedo = Uviéu ☆ ••• E ◇ 44-45 E 3 ◆ 34-35 K 7
Owando ☆ RCB ◆ 50-51 E 2
Owego o USA ◇ 22-23 K 4
Owen o USA ◇ 22-23 C 3
Owen Fracture Zone ≃ ◆ 50-51 M 1
Owens o USA ◇ 22-23 K 6
Owensboro o USA ◇ 22-23 E 7 ◆ 16-17 J 3
Owens Lake ⊖ USA ◇ 20-21 F 7
Owen Sound o • CDN ◇ 18-19 D 6 ◆ 14-15 U 8
Owens River ∼ USA ◇ 20-21 E 7
Owen Stanley Range ▲ PNG ◆ 58-59 N 8
Owensville o USA ◇ 22-23 C 6
Owerri ☆ WAN ◆ 48-49 G 7
Owo o WAN ◆ 48-49 G 7
Owosso o USA ◇ 22-23 F 4
Owyhee, Lake ⊖ USA ◇ 20-21 F 4
Owyhee Ridge ▲ USA ◇ 20-21 F 4
Owyhee River ∼ USA ◇ 20-21 F 4 ◆ 14-15 N 8
Oxford o CDN ◇ 18-19 N 6
Oxford o USA (IN) ◇ 22-23 E 5
Oxford o USA (MS) ◇ 24-25 D 2
Oxford o USA (NC) ◇ 24-25 J 1
Oxford o USA (OH) ◇ 22-23 F 6
Oxford Junction o USA ◇ 22-23 C 5
Oxford Peak ▲ USA ◇ 20-21 H 4
Oxkutzcab o • MEX ◇ 28-29 K 1
Oxnard o USA ◇ 20-21 E 8
Oyem ☆ G ◆ 50-51 D 1
Oysterville o USA ◇ 20-21 B 2
Ozark o USA (AL) ◇ 24-25 F 4
Ozark o USA (AR) ◇ 26-27 L 2
Ozark National Scenic Riverways ⊥ USA ◇ 22-23 C 7
Ozark Plateau ▲ USA ◇ 26-27 K 1 ◆ 16-17 H 3
Ozarks, Lake of the ⊖ USA ◆ 16-17 H 3
Ozark Wonder Cave ∴ USA ◇ 26-27 K 1
Ozernoj, mys ▲ RUS ◆ 52-53 d 6
Ozernoj, poluostrov ∪ RUS ◆ 52-53 d 6
Ozernoj, zaliv ≈ ◆ 52-53 d 6
Ozernovskij o RUS ◆ 52-53 c 7
Ozette Indian Reservation ⊥ USA ◇ 20-21 B 2
Ožogina ∼ RUS ◆ 52-53 a 4
Ozona o USA ◇ 26-27 G 4

P

Paamiut = Frederikshåb o GRØ ◆ 14-15 b 4
Pabellón, El ∴ • MEX ◇ 28-29 J 3
Pabna o BD ◆ 56-57 O 6
Pab Range ▲ PK ◆ 56-57 K 5
Pacaás Novos, Parque Nacional de ⊥ BR ◆ 30-31 G 7
Pacaás Novos, Serra dos ▲ BR ◆ 30-31 G 7
Pacajus o BR ◆ 30-31 M 5
Pacaraima, Sierra ▲ YV ◆ 30-31 G 4
Pacasmayo o PE ◆ 30-31 D 6
Pacaya-Samiria, Reserva Nacional ⊥ PE ◆ 30-31 E 5
Pachuca de Soto ☆ MEX ◇ 28-29 E 1 ◆ 16-17 G 6
Pacific o USA ◇ 22-23 C 6
Pacific Grove o USA ◇ 20-21 D 7
Pacific House o USA ◇ 20-21 D 6
Pacific Ocean ≈ ◆ 7 A 7
Pacific Ranges ▲ CDN ◆ 14-15 L 6
Packsaddle o AUS ◆ 60-61 J 6
Packwood o USA ◇ 20-21 D 2
Pacora o PA ◇ 28-29 E 7
Pacoval o BR ◆ 30-31 J 5
Padang ☆ RI ◆ 58-59 D 7
Padangpanjang o RI ◆ 58-59 D 7
Padang Sidempuan o RI ◆ 58-59 C 6
Paden City o USA ◇ 22-23 H 6
Padilla o BOL ◆ 30-31 G 8
Padova ☆ • I ◇ 46-47 C 2 ◆ 34-35 O 6
Padre Island ⌒ USA ◇ 26-27 J 6 ◆ 16-17 G 5
Padre Island National Seashore ⊥ USA ◇ 26-27 J 6
Padrón o • E ◇ 44-45 C 3 ◆ 34-35 K 7
Paducah o USA (KY) ◇ 22-23 D 7 ◆ 16-17 J 3
Paducah o USA (TX) ◇ 26-27 G 2
Pafos o ••• CY ◆ 34-35 S 9
Pafúri o MOC ◆ 50-51 H 6
Pagadian ☆ RP ◆ 58-59 H 5
Pagai Selatan, Pulau ⌒ RI ◆ 58-59 D 7
Pagalu, Isla de = Annobón, Isla de ⌒ GQ ◆ 50-51 C 2
Pagan ⌒ USA ◆ 58-59 N 3
Pagatan o RI ◆ 58-59 G 7
Page o USA (AZ) ◇ 20-21 J 7 ◆ 16-17 D 3
Page o USA (OK) ◇ 26-27 K 2
Pageland o USA ◇ 24-25 H 2
Paget, Mount ▲ GB ◆ 32-33 P 8
Pagosa Springs o USA ◇ 26-27 D 1
Pahala o USA ◇ 24-25 E 8
Pahoa o USA ◇ 24-25 E 8
Pahrump o USA ◇ 20-21 G 7
Paia o USA ◇ 24-25 D 7
Paimpol o F ◇ 38-39 F 7 ◆ 34-35 L 6
Painesville o USA ◇ 22-23 H 5
Painted Desert ⊥ USA ◇ 20-21 J 7 ◆ 16-17 D 3
Paintsville o USA ◇ 22-23 G 7
Paisley o USA ◇ 20-21 D 4
Paita o PE ◆ 30-31 C 6
Pajapita o GCA ◇ 28-29 H 4
Pajer, gora ▲ RUS ◆ 52-53 J 4
Pakaá-Nova, Área Indígena ⊥ BR ◆ 30-31 F 7
Pakistan ◼ PK ◆ 56-57 J 5
Pakokku o MYA ◆ 54-55 H 7
Pakwach o EAU ◆ 48-49 M 8
Pakxé o •• LAO ◆ 58-59 E 3
Pala o TCH ◆ 48-49 H 7
Palacios o USA ◇ 26-27 J 5
Palais, le o F ◇ 38-39 F 8 ◆ 34-35 L 6
Palana ☆ RUS ◆ 52-53 c 6
Palangān, Kūh-e ▲ IR ◆ 56-57 J 4
Palangkaraya ☆ RI ◆ 58-59 F 7
Pālanpur o IND ◆ 56-57 L 6
Palapye o RB ◆ 50-51 G 6
Palatka o USA ◇ 24-25 H 5
Palau ⌒ PAL ◆ 12 E 2
Palau = Belau ◼ PAL ◆ 58-59 K 5
Palau Islands ⌒ PAL ◆ 58-59 K 5
Palau Trench ≃ ◆ 58-59 K 5
Palawan ⌒ RP ◆ 58-59 G 5
Palawan Passage ≈ ◆ 58-59 G 5
Palāyankottai o IND ◆ 56-57 M 9
Palembang ☆ RI ◆ 58-59 D 7
Palenque o MEX (CHI) ◇ 28-29 J 3
Palenque ∴ ••• MEX (CHI) ◇ 28-29 H 3
Palenque o PA ◇ 28-29 E 7
Palermo o I ◇ 46-47 D 5 ◆ 34-35 O 8
Palesse ∪ BY ◇ 42-43 J 5 ◆ 34-35 R 5
Palestine o USA ◇ 26-27 K 4
Palestine, Lake o USA ◇ 26-27 K 3
Paletwa o MYA ◆ 54-55 G 7
Palghāt o IND ◆ 56-57 M 8
Palgrave, Mount ▲ AUS ◆ 60-61 D 4
Pāli o IND ◆ 56-57 L 5
Palisades Reservoir < USA ◇ 20-21 J 4
Palizada o MEX ◇ 28-29 H 2
Paljavaam ∼ RUS ◆ 52-53 f 4
Palk Strait ≈ ◆ 56-57 M 9
Palliser, Cape ▲ NZ ◆ 60-61 Q 8
Palma o MOC ◆ 50-51 K 4
Palma, La ⌒ E ◆ 48-49 B 3
Palma, La o MEX ◇ 28-29 J 3
Palma, La ☆ PA ◇ 28-29 E 7
Palma de Mallorca ☆ E ◇ 44-45 J 5 ◆ 34-35 M 8
Palmar, Península El ∪ MEX ◇ 28-29 J 2
Palmar Norte o CR ◇ 28-29 C 7
Palmas, Barra de ≃ ◇ 28-29 F 1
Palmas, Cap ▲ CI ◆ 48-49 D 8
Palmas de Gran Canaria, Las ☆ • E ◆ 48-49 B 3
Palmdale o USA (CA) ◇ 20-21 E 8
Palmdale o USA (FL) ◇ 24-25 H 6
Palm Desert o USA ◇ 20-21 F 9
Palmer o ANT ◆ 13 G 30
Palmer o USA ◆ 14-15 G 4
Palmerston Atoll ⌒ NZ ◆ 12 L 4
Palmerston North o NZ ◆ 60-61 Q 8
Palmerton o USA ◇ 22-23 L 5
Palmetto o USA ◇ 24-25 G 6
Palmira o CO ◆ 30-31 D 4
Palm Islands ⌒ AUS ◆ 60-61 K 3
Palm Springs o • USA ◇ 20-21 F 9
Palmyra o USA ◇ 22-23 E 6
Palmyra Island ⌒ USA ◆ 12 L 2
Palo Alto o USA ◇ 20-21 C 7
Palo Duro Canyon ∴ •• USA (TX) ◇ 26-27 G 2
Palo Duro Canyon ∪ USA ◇ 26-27 G 2
Palomares o MEX ◇ 28-29 G 3
Palomar Mountain ▲ USA ◇ 20-21 F 9 ◆ 16-17 C 4
Palopo o RI ◆ 58-59 H 7
Palouse o USA ◇ 20-21 F 2
Palouse River ∼ USA ◇ 20-21 F 2
Palo Verde o USA ◇ 20-21 G 9
Palpa o PE ◆ 30-31 D 7
Palu ☆ RI ◆ 58-59 G 7
Pama o BF ◆ 48-49 F 6
Pamiers o F ◇ 38-39 H 10 ◆ 34-35 M 7
Pamirs ▲ TJ ◆ 56-57 L 3
Pamlico River ∼ USA ◇ 24-25 K 2
Pamlico Sound ≈ ◇ 24-25 K 2 ◆ 16-17 L 3
Pampa o USA ◇ 26-27 G 2
Pampa, La ◻ RA ◆ 32-33 J 5
Pampa Húmeda ⊥ RA ◆ 32-33 K 5
Pampa Seca ⊥ RA ◆ 32-33 J 4
Pamplona o • CO ◆ 30-31 E 3
Pamplona (Iruña) o •• E ◇ 44-45 G 3 ◆ 34-35 L 7
Pana o USA ◇ 22-23 D 6
Panabá o MEX ◇ 28-29 K 1
Panaca Summit ▲ USA ◇ 20-21 G 7
Panache, Lake ⊖ CDN ◇ 18-19 D 5
Panaji ☆ • IND ◆ 56-57 L 7
Panama ◼ PA ◇ 28-29 E 7 ◆ 30-31 C 3
Panamá ★ •• PA ◇ 28-29 E 7 ◆ 30-31 D 3
Panamá, Bahía de ≈ ◇ 28-29 E 7
Panamá, Golfo de ≈ ◇ 28-29 E 8
Panama Canal < •• PA ◇ 28-29 E 7 ◆ 16-17 L 9
Panama City o USA ◇ 24-25 F 4 ◆ 16-17 J 4
Panamint Range ▲ USA ◇ 20-21 F 7
Panamint Springs o USA ◇ 20-21 F 7
Panay ⌒ RP ◆ 58-59 H 4
Panay ∼ RP ◆ 58-59 H 4
Pandharpur o • IND ◆ 56-57 M 7
Panevėžys o •• LT ◇ 42-43 J 4 ◆ 34-35 Q 4
Pangala o RCB ◆ 50-51 D 2
Pangani ∼ EAT ◆ 50-51 J 2
Pangar Djerem, Réserve ⊥ CAM ◆ 48-49 H 7
Pangkajene o RI ◆ 58-59 G 7
Pangkalanbuun o RI ◆ 58-59 F 7
Pangkalpinang o RI ◆ 58-59 E 7

Nueces River — Pangkalpinang 85

Pontarlier o • F ◇ 38-39 L 8 ◆ 34-35 N 6
Pont-Audemer o F ◇ 38-39 H 7 ◆ 34-35 M 6
Pontchartrain, Lake ⇔ USA ◇ 26-27 M 4 ◆ 16-17 H 4
Pontchâteau o F ◇ 38-39 F 8 ◆ 34-35 L 6
Pont du Gard ••• F ◇ 38-39 K 10 ◆ 34-35 M 7
Pontes e Lacerda o BR ◆ 30-31 H 8
Pontiac o USA (IL) ◇ 22-23 D 5
Pontiac o USA (MI) ◇ 22-23 G 4
Pontianak ☆ RI ◆ 58-59 E 7
Pontic Mountains ▲ TR ◆ 34-35 S 7
Pontivy o F ◇ 38-39 F 7 ◆ 34-35 L 6
Pontoise ☆ F ◇ 38-39 J 7 ◆ 34-35 M 6
Pontorson o F ◇ 38-39 G 7 ◆ 34-35 L 6
Pontotoc o USA ◇ 24-25 D 2
Ponuga o PA ◇ 28-29 D 8
Pools Cove o CDN ◇ 18-19 R 5
Poopó o BOL ◆ 30-31 F 8
Poopó, Lago de ⇔ BOL ◆ 30-31 F 8
Popayan ☆ •• CO ◆ 30-31 D 4
Poplar o USA ◇ 22-23 C 2
Poplar Bluff o USA ◇ 26-27 M 1 ◆ 16-17 H 3
Poplarville o USA ◇ 24-25 D 4
Popocatepetl, Volcán ▲ •• MEX ◇ 28-29 E 2 ◆ 16-17 G 7
Popokabaka o ZRE ◆ 50-51 E 3
Popondetta ☆ PNG ◆ 58-59 N 8
Poptún o GCA ◇ 28-29 K 3
Porangatu o BR ◆ 30-31 K 7
Porbandar o • IND ◆ 56-57 K 6
Porcupine Abyssal Plain ≃ ◆ 34-35 H 5
Porcupine River ~ USA ◆ 14-15 H 3
Porekautimbu, Gunung ▲ RI ◆ 58-59 H 7
Pori o FIN ◆ 34-35 Q 3
Porlamar o YV ◆ 30-31 G 2
Poronajsk o RUS ◆ 52-53 Z 8
Porpoise Bay ≈ ◆ 13 G 13
Portage o CDN ◇ 18-19 M 5
Portage o USA ◇ 22-23 D 4
Portage la Prairie o CDN ◆ 14-15 R 7
Portageville o USA ◇ 22-23 J 4
Portal o USA ◆ 14-15 Q 7
Port Alberni o CDN ◆ 14-15 M 7
Portales o USA ◇ 26-27 F 2
Port Alfred o ZA ◆ 50-51 G 8
Port Allegany o USA ◇ 22-23 J 5
Port Angeles o USA ◇ 20-21 C 1
Port Antonio o • JA ◆ 16-17 L 7
Port Arthur o • AUS ◆ 60-61 K 8
Port Arthur o USA ◇ 26-27 L 5 ◆ 16-17 H 5
Port au Choix o CDN ◇ 18-19 Q 3
Port Augusta o AUS ◆ 60-61 H 6
Port au Port Bay ≈ ◇ 18-19 P 4
Port au Port Peninsula ∪ CDN ◇ 18-19 P 4 ◆ 14-15 Z 7
Port-au-Prince ★ • RH ◆ 16-17 M 7
Port Austin o USA ◇ 22-23 G 3
Port aux Choix National Historic Park ∴ CDN ◇ 18-19 Q 3
Port Blair ☆ IND ◆ 58-59 B 4
Port Blandfort o CDN ◇ 18-19 R 4
Port Bolivar o USA ◇ 26-27 K 5
Port Burwell o CDN ◇ 18-19 D 7 ◆ 14-15 U 8
Port Cartier Sept Îles, Parc Provencial de ⊥ CDN ◇ 18-19 L 3
Port Charlotte o USA ◇ 24-25 G 6
Port Clinton o USA ◇ 22-23 G 5
Port Clyde o USA ◇ 22-23 O 4
Port-Daniel o CDN ◇ 18-19 M 4
Port-de-Paix ☆ RH ◆ 16-17 M 7
Portél o BR ◆ 30-31 J 5
Port Elizabeth o ZA ◆ 50-51 G 8
Porters Corner o USA ◇ 20-21 H 2
Porterville o USA ◇ 20-21 E 7
Porterville o ZA ◆ 50-51 E 8
Port Fourchon o USA ◇ 26-27 M 5
Port-Gentil ☆ G ◆ 50-51 C 2
Port Gibson o USA ◇ 26-27 M 4
Port-Harcourt ☆ WAN ◆ 48-49 G 8
Port Hardy o CDN ◆ 14-15 L 6
Port Hedland o AUS ◆ 60-61 D 4
Port Heiden o USA ◆ 14-15 E 5
Port Hope o CDN ◇ 18-19 E 7
Port Hope Simpson o CDN ◇ 18-19 Q 2
Port Huron o USA ◇ 22-23 G 4
Port Isabel o USA ◇ 26-27 J 6
Port Isabel Lighthouse State Historic Site ∴ • USA ◇ 26-27 J 6
Port Jefferson o USA ◇ 22-23 M 5
Port Jervis o USA ◇ 22-23 L 5
Port Kenny o AUS ◆ 60-61 G 6
Portland o AUS ◆ 60-61 J 7
Portland o USA (IN) ◇ 22-23 F 5
Portland o USA (ME) ◇ 22-23 N 4 ◆ 14-15 W 8
Portland o USA (OR) ◇ 20-21 C 3 ◆ 14-15 M 7
Portland o USA (TX) ◇ 26-27 J 6
Portland, Cape ▲ AUS ◆ 60-61 K 8
Portland Bay ≈ ◆ 60-61 J 7
Portland Creek Pond ⇔ CDN ◇ 18-19 Q 3
Port Lavaca o USA ◇ 26-27 J 5
Port Lincoln o •• AUS ◆ 60-61 H 6
Port Louis ★ • MS ◆ 50-51 N 6
Port Macquarie o AUS ◆ 60-61 L 6
Port Mayaca o USA ◇ 24-25 H 6
Port-Menier o CDN ◇ 18-19 M 4
Port Menier o CDN ◇ 18-19 M 4 ◆ 14-15 Y 7
Port Moresby ★ • PNG ◆ 58-59 N 8
Portneuf, Rivière ~ CDN ◇ 18-19 K 4
Port Nolloth o ZA ◆ 50-51 E 7
Porto ☆ • P ◇ 44-45 C 4 ◆ 34-35 K 7
Porto Alegre ☆ BR ◆ 32-33 M 4
Porto Amboim o ANG ◆ 50-51 D 4
Portobelo o ••• PA ◇ 28-29 E 7
Porto Esperidião o BR ◆ 30-31 H 8
Port of Spain ★ TT ◆ 16-17 O 8
Porto Nacional o BR ◆ 30-31 K 7
Porto-Novo ★ • DY ◆ 48-49 F 7
Port Orchard o USA ◇ 20-21 C 2
Porto Santo ⌒ P ◆ 48-49 B 2
Porto Seguro o • BR ◆ 30-31 M 8
Pôrto Valter o BR ◆ 30-31 E 6
Porto Velho ☆ BR ◆ 30-31 G 6
Portoviejo ☆ EC ◆ 30-31 C 5
Port Pirie o AUS ◆ 60-61 H 6
Port Rowan o CDN ◇ 18-19 D 7
Port Royal National Historic Park ∴ CDN ◇ 18-19 M 6
Port Royal Sound ≈ ◇ 24-25 H 3
Port Said = Būr Sa'īd ☆ ET ◆ 48-49 M 2
Port Saint Joe o USA ◇ 24-25 F 5
Port Saint Johns o ZA ◆ 50-51 G 8
Port-Saint-Louis-du-Rhône o F ◇ 38-39 K 10 ◆ 34-35 M 7
Port Sanilac o USA ◇ 22-23 G 4
Port Shepstone o ZA ◆ 50-51 H 8
Portsmouth o USA (NH) ◇ 22-23 N 4 ◆ 14-15 W 8
Portsmouth o USA (OH) ◇ 22-23 G 6 ◆ 16-17 K 3
Portsmouth o USA (VA) ◇ 22-23 K 7 ◆ 16-17 L 3
Port Sulphur o USA ◇ 24-25 D 5
Port Townsend o • USA ◇ 20-21 C 1
Portugal ■ P ◇ 44-45 B 4 ◆ 34-35 J 8
Port-Vendres o F ◇ 38-39 J 10 ◆ 34-35 M 7
Port-Vila ★ • VAN ◆ 60-61 O 3
Port Wakefield o AUS ◆ 60-61 H 6
Port Washington o USA ◇ 22-23 E 4
Port Welshpool o AUS ◆ 60-61 K 7
Port Wing o USA ◇ 22-23 C 2
Porvenir, El ☆ PA ◇ 28-29 E 7
Posadas ☆ RA ◆ 32-33 L 3
Posito, El ∴ • BH ◇ 28-29 K 3
Poso, Danau ⇔ RI ◆ 58-59 H 7
Posse o BR ◆ 30-31 K 7
Possoš' o RUS ◆ 34-35 T 5
Possum Kingdom Lake ⇔ USA ◇ 26-27 H 3
Post o USA ◇ 26-27 G 3
Post Falls o USA ◇ 20-21 F 2
Postmasburg o ZA ◆ 50-51 F 7
Postville o USA ◇ 22-23 C 4
Potchefstroom o ZA ◆ 50-51 G 7
Poteau o USA ◇ 26-27 K 2
Poteet o USA ◇ 26-27 H 5
Potenza ☆ • I ◇ 46-47 E 4 ◆ 34-35 P 7
Potgietersrus o ZA ◆ 50-51 G 6
Potholes Reservoir ⇔ USA ◇ 20-21 E 2
Poti o • GE ◆ 34-35 U 7
Potiskum o WAN ◆ 48-49 H 6
Pot Mountain ▲ USA ◇ 20-21 G 2
Potomac River ~ USA ◇ 22-23 K 6
Potosí o NIC ◇ 28-29 L 5
Potosi o USA ◇ 22-23 C 7
Potrero Grande o CR ◇ 28-29 C 7
Potrerillos Abajo o PA ◇ 28-29 C 7
Potsdam ☆ ••• D ◇ 40-41 M 2 ◆ 34-35 O 5
Potsdam o USA ◇ 22-23 L 3
Pottstown o USA ◇ 22-23 L 5
Pottsville o USA ◇ 22-23 K 5
Pouch Cove o CDN ◇ 18-19 S 5
Poughkeepsie o USA ◇ 22-23 M 5
Poularies o CDN ◇ 18-19 E 4
Poultney o USA ◇ 22-23 M 4
Poum o F ◆ 60-61 N 4
Pouso Alegre o BR ◆ 32-33 N 2
Pouthisat o K ◆ 58-59 D 4
Poverty Bay ≈ ◆ 60-61 Q 7
Powder River ~ USA ◆ 14-15 P 7
Powder River ~ USA ◇ 20-21 F 3
Powell, Lake ⊂ USA ◇ 20-21 J 7 ◆ 16-17 D 3
Powell River o CDN ◆ 14-15 M 7
Powers o USA ◇ 22-23 E 3
Powhatan o USA ◇ 26-27 L 4
Poxoréo o BR ◆ 30-31 J 8
Poyang Hu ⇔ CHN ◆ 54-55 M 6
Poygan, Lake ⇔ USA ◇ 22-23 D 3
Poza Rica o MEX ◇ 28-29 F 1 ◆ 16-17 G 6
Poznań ☆ •• PL ◇ 40-41 O 2 ◆ 34-35 P 5
Pozo Colorado ☆ PY ◆ 32-33 L 2
Pozos, Los o PA ◇ 28-29 D 8
Prachuap Khirikhan o THA ◆ 58-59 C 4
Prado o BR ◆ 30-31 M 8
Prague = Praha ★ ••• CZ ◇ 40-41 N 3 ◆ 34-35 O 5
Praha ★ ••• CZ ◇ 40-41 N 3 ◆ 34-35 O 5
Praia o BR ◆ 30-31 J 5
Prairie City o USA ◇ 20-21 E 3
Prairie Dog Town Fork of the Red River ~ USA ◇ 26-27 G 2
Prairie du Chien o USA ◇ 22-23 C 4
Prapat o RI ◆ 58-59 C 6
Praslin Island ⌒ SY ◆ 50-51 N 2
Prato o I ◇ 46-47 C 3 ◆ 34-35 O 7
Prats-de-Mollo-la-Preste o F ◇ 38-39 J 10 ◆ 34-35 M 7
Pratt o USA ◇ 26-27 H 1
Prattville o USA ◇ 24-25 E 3
Praya o RI ◆ 58-59 G 8
Precordillera ▲ RA ◆ 32-33 J 4
Predbajkal'skaja vpadina ⊥ RUS ◆ 52-53 S 7
Predporožnyj o RUS ◆ 52-53 Z 4
Premio o CDN ◇ 18-19 M 3
Prentice o USA ◇ 22-23 C 3
Prentiss o USA ◇ 24-25 D 4
Prescott o USA (AR) ◇ 26-27 L 3
Prescott o USA (AZ) ◇ 20-21 H 8 ◆ 16-17 D 4
Prescott o USA (WA) ◇ 20-21 E 2
Prescott Island ⌒ CDN ◆ 14-15 R 2
Presidencia Roque Sáenz Peña o RA ◆ 32-33 K 3
Presidente Barros Dutra o BR ◆ 30-31 L 6
Presidente Epitácio o BR ◆ 32-33 M 2
Presidente Figueiredo o BR ◆ 30-31 G 5
Presidente Prudente o BR ◆ 32-33 M 2
Presidio o USA ◇ 26-27 E 5
Presque Isle o USA ◇ 22-23 P 2 ◆ 14-15 X 7
Preston o USA ◇ 20-21 J 4
Preto, Rio ~ BR ◆ 30-31 L 7
Prêto, Rio ~ BR ◆ 30-31 K 8
Pretoria ★ • ZA ◆ 50-51 G 7
Préveza o GR ◇ 46-47 H 5 ◆ 34-35 Q 8
Priangarskoe plato ⊥ RUS ◆ 52-53 Q 6
Pribilof Islands ⌒ USA ◆ 14-15 B 5
Pribreżnyj hrebet ▲ RUS ◆ 52-53 X 6
Price o USA (MD) ◇ 22-23 L 6
Price o USA (NC) ◇ 24-25 J 1
Price o USA (UT) ◇ 20-21 J 6
Price River ~ USA ◇ 20-21 J 6
Prichard o USA (AL) ◇ 24-25 D 4
Prichard o USA (ID) ◇ 20-21 G 2
Pridnjaprovskaja nizina ∪ BY ◇ 42-43 M 5 ◆ 34-35 S 5
Prieska o ZA ◆ 50-51 F 7
Priest Lake ⇔ USA ◇ 20-21 F 1
Priest River o USA ◇ 20-21 F 1
Prilenskoe, plato ⊥ RUS ◆ 52-53 T 5
Primeira Cruz o BR ◆ 30-31 L 5
Primrose Lake Air Weapons Range xx CDN ◆ 14-15 O 5
Prince Albert o CDN ◆ 14-15 P 6
Prince Albert Mountains ▲ ANT ◆ 13 F 17
Prince Albert Peninsula ∪ CDN ◆ 14-15 N 2
Prince Albert Sound ≈ ◆ 14-15 N 2
Prince Alfred, Cape ▲ CDN ◆ 14-15 L 2
Prince Charles Island ⌒ CDN ◆ 14-15 V 3
Prince Charles Range ▲ ANT ◆ 13 F 7
Prince Edward Island □ CDN ◇ 18-19 N 5 ◆ 14-15 Y 7
Prince Edward Island ⌒ • CDN (PEI) ◇ 18-19 N 5
Prince Edward Island National Park ⊥ CDN ◇ 18-19 N 5
Prince Edward Islands ⌒ ZA ◆ 9 G 10
Prince Edward Peninsula ∪ CDN ◇ 18-19 F 7
Prince Frederick o USA ◇ 22-23 K 6
Prince George o • CDN ◆ 14-15 M 6
Prince Gustav Adolf Sea ≈ ◆ 14-15 P 1
Prince of Wales, Cape ▲ USA ◆ 14-15 C 3
Prince of Wales Island ⌒ AUS ◆ 60-61 J 2
Prince of Wales Island ⌒ CDN ◆ 14-15 R 2
Prince of Wales Island ⌒ USA ◆ 14-15 K 5
Prince of Wales Strait ≈ ◆ 14-15 N 2
Prince Patrick Island ⌒ CDN ◆ 14-15 M 1
Prince Regent Inlet ≈ ◆ 14-15 S 2
Prince Rupert o • CDN ◆ 14-15 K 6
Princess Anne o USA ◇ 22-23 L 6
Princess Charlotte Bay ≈ ◆ 60-61 J 2
Princess Elizabeth Land ⌒ ANT ◆ 13 F 8
Princess Royal Island ⌒ CDN ◆ 14-15 L 6
Princeton o USA (AR) ◇ 26-27 L 3
Princeton o USA (IL) ◇ 22-23 D 5
Princeton o USA (IN) ◇ 22-23 E 6
Princeton o USA (NJ) ◇ 22-23 L 5
Princeton o USA (WV) ◇ 22-23 H 7
Prince William Sound ≈ ◆ 14-15 G 4
Príncipe ⌒ STP ◆ 50-51 C 1
Prindle o USA ◇ 20-21 C 3
Prineville o USA ◇ 20-21 D 3
Prins Christian Sund ≈ ◆ 14-15 c 4
Prinsesse Astrid land ⊥ ANT ◆ 13 F 2
Prinsesse Ragnhild land ⊥ ANT ◆ 13 F 3
Prins Harald land ⊥ ANT ◆ 13 F 4
Prinzapolka, Río ~ NIC ◇ 28-29 B 5
Prinzregent-Luitpold-Land ⊥ ANT ◆ 13 F 3
Priština o •• YU ◇ 46-47 H 3 ◆ 34-35 Q 7
Pritchett o USA ◇ 26-27 F 1
Privolžhskaya Vozvyshennost' = Privolžskaja vozvyšennost' ▲ RUS ◆ 34-35 U 6
Privolžskaja vozvyšennost' ▲ RUS ◆ 34-35 U 6
Prizren o •• YU ◇ 46-47 H 3 ◆ 34-35 Q 7
Proddatūr o IND ◆ 56-57 M 8
Progreso o • MEX ◇ 28-29 K 1
Progreso, El o HN ◇ 28-29 L 4 ◆ 16-17 J 7
Prokop'evsk ☆ RUS ◆ 52-53 O 7
Prokop'yevsk = Prokop'evsk ☆ RUS ◆ 52-53 O 7
Prome o MYA ◆ 58-59 C 3
Promežutočnyj o RUS ◆ 52-53 f 4
Promissão, Represa ⊂ BR ◆ 32-33 N 2
Prončiščeva, bereg ∪ RUS ◆ 52-53 S 2
Propriá o BR ◆ 30-31 M 7
Proserpine o AUS ◆ 60-61 K 4
Protection o USA ◇ 26-27 H 1
Provence ⊥ F ◇ 38-39 K 10 ◆ 34-35 N 7
Provence-Alpes-Côtes d'Azur □ F ◇ 38-39 K 10 ◆ 34-35 M 7
Providence o USA (KY) ◇ 22-23 E 7
Providence ☆ USA (RI) ◇ 22-23 N 5 ◆ 16-17 M 2
Providence Bay o CDN ◇ 18-19 C 6
Providence Island ⌒ SY ◆ 50-51 M 3
Providencia, Isla de ⌒ CO ◇ 28-29 D 5 ◆ 30-31 C 2
Provincetown o USA ◇ 22-23 N 4
Provins o • F ◇ 38-39 J 7 ◆ 34-35 M 6
Provo o USA ◇ 20-21 J 5 ◆ 16-17 D 2
Prudhoe Bay o USA ◆ 14-15 G 2
Prut ~ MD ◆ 34-35 R 6
Prut ~ RO ◆ 34-35 R 6
Prylyky o UA ◆ 34-35 S 5
Pryor, La o USA ◇ 26-27 H 5
Pryor Creek o USA ◇ 26-27 K 1
Prypjac' ~ BY ◇ 42-43 L 5 ◆ 34-35 R 5
Przemyśl ☆ •• PL ◇ 40-41 R 4 ◆ 34-35 Q 6
Prževal'sk ☆ KS ◆ 56-57 M 2
Pskov ☆ •• RUS ◇ 42-43 L 3 ◆ 34-35 R 4
Pubnico o CDN ◇ 18-19 M 7
Pucallpa ☆ PE ◆ 30-31 E 6
Pucaurco o PE ◆ 30-31 E 5
Pucheng o CHN ◆ 54-55 K 5
Pucté o MEX ◇ 28-29 K 2
Pucuro o • PA ◇ 28-29 F 7
Puebla □ MEX ◇ 28-29 E 2
Puebla ☆ ••• MEX (PUE) ◇ 28-29 E 2 ◆ 16-17 G 7
Pueblo o USA ◆ 16-17 F 3
Pueblo Nueva Tiquisate o GCA ◇ 28-29 J 4
Pueblo Nuevo Huesital o PA ◇ 28-29 D 7
Pueblo Pintado o USA ◇ 26-27 D 2
Pueblo Viejo o HN ◇ 28-29 L 4
Puelches o RA ◆ 32-33 J 5
Puente de Ixtla o MEX ◇ 28-29 E 2
Puerco, Rio ~ USA ◇ 26-27 D 2
Puerco River ~ USA ◇ 26-27 C 2
Puerto Acosta o BOL ◆ 30-31 F 8
Puerto Aisén o RCH ◆ 32-33 H 7
Puerto Angel o • MEX ◇ 28-29 F 4 ◆ 16-17 G 7
Puerto Arista o • MEX ◇ 28-29 H 4
Puerto Armuelles o • PA ◇ 28-29 C 7
Puerto Arturo o PE ◆ 30-31 E 5
Puerto Asís o CO ◆ 30-31 D 4
Puerto Ayacucho ☆ YV ◆ 30-31 F 3
Puerto Bahía Negra o PY ◆ 32-33 L 2
Puerto Barrios o GCA ◇ 28-29 K 4 ◆ 16-17 J 7
Puerto Berrío o CO ◆ 30-31 E 3
Puerto Cabezas o NIC ◇ 28-29 C 4 ◆ 16-17 K 8
Puerto Carreño ☆ CO ◆ 30-31 F 3
Puerto Chicxulub o MEX ◇ 28-29 K 1
Puerto Cisnes o RCH ◆ 32-33 H 6
Puerto Cortés o HN ◇ 28-29 L 4
Puerto de Aseses o NIC ◇ 28-29 B 6
Puerto del Rosario o E ◆ 48-49 C 3
Puerto de San José o GCA ◇ 28-29 J 5 ◆ 16-17 H 8
Puerto Deseado o RA ◆ 32-33 J 7
Puerto Escondido o • MEX ◇ 28-29 F 4 ◆ 16-17 G 7
Puerto Gaitan o CO ◆ 30-31 E 4
Puerto Inirida ☆ CO ◆ 30-31 F 4
Puerto Juárez o • MEX ◇ 28-29 L 1
Puerto la Victoria o PY ◆ 32-33 L 2
Puerto Leguizamo o CO ◆ 30-31 E 5
Puerto Limón ☆ •• CR ◇ 28-29 C 7 ◆ 16-17 K 9
Puerto Madero o MEX (CHI) ◇ 28-29 H 4
Puerto Madero o MEX (QR) ◇ 28-29 L 2
Puerto Madryn o RA ◆ 32-33 J 6
Puerto Maldonado ☆ PE ◆ 30-31 F 7
Puerto Masachapa o NIC ◇ 28-29 L 6
Puerto Montt ☆ RCH ◆ 32-33 H 6
Puerto Morazán o NIC ◇ 28-29 L 5
Puerto Natales o RCH ◆ 32-33 H 8
Puerto Obaldia o PA ◇ 28-29 F 7
Puerto Palomas o MEX ◇ 28-29 G 3
Puerto Piña o PA ◇ 28-29 E 8
Puerto Pirámides o RA ◆ 32-33 K 6
Puerto Plata ☆ • DOM ◆ 16-17 M 7
Puerto Portillo o PE ◆ 30-31 E 6
Puerto Princesa ☆ RP ◆ 58-59 G 5
Puerto Quimba o PA ◇ 28-29 E 7
Puerto Rico □ USA ◆ 16-17 N 7
Puerto Rico ⌒ USA ◆ 16-17 N 7
Puerto Rico Trench ≃ ◆ 16-17 N 7
Puerto Rondon o CO ◆ 30-31 E 3
Puerto Sandino o NIC ◇ 28-29 L 5
Puerto San Julián o RA ◆ 32-33 J 7
Puerto Santa Cruz o RA ◆ 32-33 J 8
Puerto Suarez o BOL ◆ 30-31 H 8
Puerto Vallarta o • MEX ◇ 28-29 B 1 ◆ 16-17 E 6
Puerto Victoria o PE ◆ 30-31 E 6
Puerto Viejo o CR (CAR) ◇ 28-29 C 7
Puerto Viejo o CR (HER) ◇ 28-29 B 6
Puerto Villamil o EC ◆ 30-31 A 5
Puerto Williams o RCH ◆ 32-33 J 8
Puget Sound ≈ ◇ 20-21 C 2
Pugwash o CDN ◇ 18-19 N 6
Puig Major ▲ E ◇ 44-45 J 5 ◆ 34-35 M 8
Pujonryong Sanmaek ▲ KOR ◆ 54-55 O 3
Pukalani o USA ◇ 24-25 D 7
Pukaskwa National Park ⊥ • CDN ◆ 14-15 T 7
Pula o HR ◇ 46-47 D 2 ◆ 34-35 O 7
Pulap Atoll ⌒ FSM ◆ 58-59 N 5
Pular, Cerro ▲ RCH ◆ 32-33 J 2
Pulaski o USA (NY) ◇ 22-23 K 4
Pulaski o USA (TN) ◇ 24-25 E 2
Pulaski o USA (VA) ◇ 22-23 H 7 ◆ 16-17 K 3
Pulaski National Monument, Fort ∴ • USA ◇ 24-25 H 3
Pulau ~ RI ◆ 58-59 L 8
Puławy o • PL ◇ 40-41 Q 3 ◆ 34-35 Q 5
Pullman o USA ◇ 20-21 F 2
Pulo Anna ⌒ USA ◆ 58-59 K 6
Puluwat Atoll ⌒ FSM ◆ 58-59 N 5
Puna, Isla ⌒ EC ◆ 30-31 C 5
Punakha o BHT ◆ 56-57 O 5
Puncak Jaya ▲ RI ◆ 58-59 L 7
Puncak Mandala ▲ RI ◆ 58-59 M 7
Pune o • IND ◆ 56-57 L 7
Punia o ZRE ◆ 50-51 G 2
Punilla, Sierra de la ▲ RA ◆ 32-33 J 3
Punjab □ IND ◆ 56-57 L 4
Punjab □ PK ◆ 56-57 L 4
Puno ☆ • PE ◆ 30-31 E 8
Punta Allen o MEX ◇ 28-29 L 2
Punta Arenas ☆ RCH ◆ 32-33 H 8
Punta Chame o PA ◇ 28-29 E 7
Punta Delgada o RCH ◆ 32-33 J 8
Punta Eugenia o MEX ◆ 16-17 C 5
Punta Gorda o BH ◇ 28-29 K 3
Punta Norte o RA ◆ 32-33 K 6
Puntarenas ☆ • CR ◇ 28-29 B 7 ◆ 16-17 K 9
Puntas Negras, Cordon de ▲ RCH ◆ 32-33 J 2
Punto Fijo o YV ◆ 30-31 E 2
Puqi o CHN ◆ 54-55 L 6
Puquina o PE ◆ 30-31 E 8
Puquio o PE ◆ 30-31 E 7
Pur ~ RUS ◆ 52-53 M 4
Puracé, Volcán ▲ CO ◆ 30-31 D 4
Purándiro o MEX ◇ 28-29 D 1
Purari River ~ PNG ◆ 58-59 N 8
Purcell o USA ◇ 26-27 J 2
Purcell Mountains ▲ CDN ◆ 14-15 N 6
Purepero o MEX ◇ 28-29 C 2
Puri o •• IND ◆ 56-57 O 7
Purificación o MEX ◇ 28-29 B 2
Purificacion, Rio ~ MEX ◇ 28-29 B 2
Puruarán o MEX ◇ 28-29 D 2
Purus, Rio ~ BR ◆ 30-31 F 6
Purwakarta o RI ◆ 58-59 E 8
Purwokerto o RI ◆ 58-59 E 8
Pusan o ROK ◆ 54-55 O 4
Puškin o •• RUS ◇ 42-43 M 2 ◆ 34-35 S 4
Pusticamica, Lac ⇔ CDN ◇ 18-19 F 4
Pustunich o MEX (CAM) ◇ 28-29 J 2
Pustunich ∴ • MEX (CAM) ◇ 28-29 J 2
Putao o MYA ◆ 54-55 H 6
Puthein (Bassein) o MYA ◆ 58-59 B 3
Putian o CHN ◆ 54-55 M 6
Puting, Tanjung ▲ RI ◆ 58-59 F 7
Putnam o USA (CT) ◇ 22-23 N 5
Putnam o USA (OK) ◇ 26-27 H 2
Putoničany o RUS ◆ 52-53 P 5
Putorana, plato ▲ RUS ◆ 52-53 P 4
Putoranskij zapovednik ⊥ RUS ◆ 52-53 P 4
Puttalam o CL ◆ 56-57 M 9
Puttur o IND ◆ 56-57 M 8
Putusibau o RI ◆ 58-59 F 6
Puuhonua o Honaunau National Historical Park ⊥ • USA ◇ 24-25 E 8
Puukohola Heiau National Historic Site • USA ◇ 24-25 E 7
Puunahulu o USA ◇ 24-25 E 8
Puuwai o USA ◇ 24-25 B 7
Puyallup o USA ◇ 20-21 C 2
Puyang o CHN ◆ 54-55 L 4
Puy-en-Velay, le ☆ •• F ◇ 38-39 J 9 ◆ 34-35 M 7
Puymorens, Col de ▲ F ◇ 38-39 H 10 ◆ 34-35 M 7
Pweto o ZRE ◆ 50-51 G 3
Pyinmana o MYA ◆ 58-59 C 3
Pymatuning Reservoir ⊂ USA ◇ 22-23 H 5
Pyongyang ★ KOR ◆ 54-55 O 4
Pyote o USA ◇ 26-27 F 4
Pyramid Lake ⇔ USA ◇ 20-21 E 5 ◆ 16-17 C 2
Pyramid Lake Indian Reservation ⅹ USA ◇ 20-21 E 5
Pyrenees ▲ F ◇ 44-45 G 3 ◆ 34-35 L 7
Pyrénées, Parc National des ⊥ • F ◇ 38-39 G 10 ◆ 34-35 L 7
Pyrjatyn o UA ◆ 34-35 S 5

Q

Qa'āmiyāt, al- ⊥ KSA ◆ 56-57 F 7
Qaanaaq = Thule ☆ GRØ ◆ 14-15 X 1
Qadam o SUD ◆ 48-49 L 6
Qadarif, al- o SUD ◆ 48-49 N 6
Qaidam Pendi ⊥ CHN ◆ 54-55 G 4
Qalāt o AFG ◆ 56-57 K 4
Qal'a-ye Nau ☆ AFG ◆ 56-57 J 3
Qamdo o CHN ◆ 54-55 H 5
Qāmišli, al- ☆ SYR ◆ 56-57 E 3
Qandahār ☆ •• AFG ◆ 56-57 K 4
Qandala o SP ◆ 48-49 P 6
Qaqortoq = Julianehåb o GRØ ◆ 14-15 b 4
Qarā', Ğabal al- ▲ OM ◆ 56-57 G 7
Qara Dāġ ▲ IR ◆ 56-57 F 3
Qaraghandy = Karagandy ☆ KZ ◆ 52-53 L 8
Qardho o SP ◆ 48-49 P 7
Qaryah ash Sharqiyah, Al o LAR ◆ 48-49 H 2
Qasr al-Farāfira o ET ◆ 48-49 L 3
Qasr Larocu o LAR ◆ 48-49 H 3
Qatar ■ Q ◆ 56-57 G 5
Qatrūn, Al o LAR ◆ 48-49 H 4
Qattara Depression ⊥ ET ◆ 48-49 L 3
Qawz Rajab o SUD ◆ 48-49 N 5
Qazax o • AZ ◆ 56-57 F 2
Qazvin o • IR ◆ 56-57 F 3
Qeqertarsuaq = Godhavn o GRØ ◆ 14-15 a 3
Qešm, Ğazire-ye ⌒ IR ◆ 56-57 H 5
Qezaltepeque o ES ◇ 28-29 K 5
Qiemo o CHN ◆ 54-55 F 4
Qilian Shan ▲ CHN ◆ 54-55 H 4
Qinā ☆ ET ◆ 48-49 M 3
Qingdao ☆ CHN ◆ 54-55 N 4
Qinghai □ CHN ◆ 54-55 G 4
Qinghai Hu ⇔ CHN ◆ 54-55 H 4
Qingzhang Gaoyuan ⊂ CHN ◆ 54-55 E 5
Qinhuangdao o CHN ◆ 54-55 M 4
Qinzhou o CHN ◆ 54-55 K 7
Qiongzhou Haixia ≈ ◆ 54-55 K 7
Qiqihar o CHN ◆ 54-55 N 2
Qitaihe o CHN ◆ 54-55 P 2
Q'nitra, Al- ☆ MA ◆ 48-49 D 2
Qohrūd, Kūhhā-ye ▲ IR ◆ 56-57 G 4
Qom o •• IR ◆ 56-57 G 4
Qomše o • IR ◆ 56-57 G 4
Qostanay = Kostanaj ☆ KZ ◆ 52-53 J 7
Quabbin Reservoir ⇔ USA ◇ 22-23 M 4
Quakertown o USA ◇ 22-23 L 5
Quamby o AUS ◆ 60-61 J 4
Quanah o USA ◇ 26-27 H 2
Quang Ngãi o •• VN ◆ 58-59 E 3
Quantico Marine Corps xx USA ◇ 22-23 K 6
Quanzhou o • CHN ◆ 54-55 M 7
Quartzsite o USA ◇ 20-21 G 9
Quba o • AZ ◆ 56-57 F 2
Qūčān o • IR ◆ 56-57 H 3
Québec □ CDN ◇ 18-19 F 3 ◆ 14-15 W 6
Québec ☆ ••• CDN (QUE) ◇ 18-19 J 5 ◆ 14-15 W 7
Quebo o GNB ◆ 48-49 C 6
Quebrada Honda o CR ◇ 28-29 B 6
Queen, De o USA ◇ 26-27 K 2
Queen Alexandra Range ▲ ANT ◆ 13 E 0
Queen Charlotte City o CDN ◆ 14-15 K 6
Queen Charlotte Islands ⌒ CDN ◆ 14-15 K 6
Queen Charlotte Sound ≈ ◆ 14-15 L 6
Queen Charlotte Strait ≈ ◆ 14-15 L 6
Queen Elizabeth Islands ⌒ CDN ◆ 13 B 30
Queen Elizabeth National Park ⊥ EAU ◆ 50-51 G 2
Queen Mary Land ⊥ ANT ◆ 13 G 10
Queen Maud Gulf ≈ ◆ 14-15 Q 3
Queens Channel ≈ ◆ 60-61 F 2
Queensland □ AUS ◆ 60-61 H 4
Queensland Plateau ≃ ◆ 60-61 K 3
Queenstown o AUS ◆ 60-61 K 8
Queenstown o ZA ◆ 50-51 G 8
Queets o USA ◇ 20-21 B 2
Quelimane ☆ MOC ◆ 50-51 J 5
Quellón o RCH ◆ 32-33 H 6
Quemado o USA ◇ 26-27 C 2
Quepos o CR ◇ 28-29 B 7
Quepos, Punta ▲ CR ◇ 28-29 B 7
Querendaro o MEX ◇ 28-29 D 2
Querétaro □ MEX ◇ 28-29 D 1
Querétaro ☆ ••• MEX (QRO) ◇ 28-29 D 1 ◆ 16-17 F 6
Quesnel o CDN ◆ 14-15 M 6
Quesso ☆ RCB ◆ 50-51 E 1
Questa o USA ◇ 26-27 E 1
Quetico Provincial Park ⊥ USA ◇ 22-23 C 1
Quetta ☆ • PK ◆ 56-57 K 4
Quevedo o EC ◆ 30-31 D 5
Quévillon, Lac ⇔ CDN ◇ 18-19 F 4
Quezaltenango ☆ • GCA ◇ 28-29 J 4 ◆ 16-17 H 8
Quezon o RP ◆ 58-59 G 5
Quezon City o RP ◆ 58-59 H 4
Quiaca, La o RA ◆ 32-33 J 2
Quiahniztlan • MEX ◇ 28-29 F 2
Quibala o ANG ◆ 50-51 D 4
Quibdó ☆ CO ◆ 30-31 D 3
Quiberon o F ◇ 38-39 F 8 ◆ 34-35 L 6
Quiçama, Parque Nacional do ⊥ ANG ◆ 50-51 D 3
Quicksand o USA ◇ 22-23 G 7
Quijotoa o USA ◇ 20-21 H 9
Quilengues o ANG ◆ 50-51 D 4
Quillagua o RCH ◆ 32-33 J 2
Quillan o F ◇ 38-39 J 10 ◆ 34-35 M 7
Quillayute Indian Reservation ⅹ USA ◇ 20-21 B 2
Quill Lakes ⇔ CDN ◆ 14-15 Q 6
Quilmes o RA ◆ 32-33 L 4
Quilon o • IND ◆ 56-57 M 9
Quilpie o AUS ◆ 60-61 J 5
Quimantag ▲ CHN ◆ 54-55 G 4
Quimili o RA ◆ 32-33 K 3
Quimper ☆ • F ◇ 38-39 E 8 ◆ 34-35 L 6
Quinault o USA ◇ 20-21 C 2
Quinault Indian Reservation ⅹ USA ◇ 20-21 B 2
Quinault River ~ USA ◇ 20-21 C 2
Quince Mil o PE ◆ 30-31 E 7
Quincy o USA (IL) ◇ 22-23 C 6 ◆ 16-17 H 3
Quincy o USA (MA) ◇ 22-23 N 4
Quines o RA ◆ 32-33 J 4
Quinn River ~ USA ◇ 20-21 F 5
Quintana Roo □ MEX ◇ 28-29 K 2
Quintana Roo, Parque Nacional de ⊥ MEX ◇ 28-29 L 1
Quiotepec o MEX ◇ 28-29 F 3
Quirigua ∴ ••• GCA ◇ 28-29 K 4
Quirima o ANG ◆ 50-51 E 4
Quirindi o AUS ◆ 60-61 L 6
Quiroga o MEX ◇ 28-29 D 2
Quissanga o MOC ◆ 50-51 K 4
Quitman o USA (GA) ◇ 24-25 G 4
Quitman o USA (TX) ◇ 26-27 K 3
Quitman Ruins, Fort ∴ USA ◇ 26-27 E 4
Quito ★ ••• EC ◆ 30-31 D 5
Quixadá o BR ◆ 30-31 M 5
Quixeramobim o BR ◆ 30-31 M 6
Qujing o CHN ◆ 54-55 J 6
Qumar Heyan ~ CHN ◆ 54-55 G 4
Qunaiṭira, al- ☆ SYR ◆ 56-57 D 4
Quoin, Du o USA ◇ 22-23 D 6
Qurayyāt, al- ☆ • KSA ◆ 56-57 D 4
Qurdūd o SUD ◆ 48-49 L 6
Qusair, al- o ET ◆ 48-49 M 3
Quyen o AUS ◆ 60-61 J 6
Quy Nho'n ☆ • VN ◆ 58-59 E 4
Qūz, al- o KSA ◆ 56-57 E 7
Quzhou o CHN ◆ 54-55 M 6
Qyzylorda = Kyzylorda ☆ KZ ◆ 56-57 K 2

R

Raanes Peninsula ⌒ CDN ◆ 14-15 T 1
Raba o • RI ◆ 58-59 G 8
Rabat = Ar-Ribāṭ ★ •• MA ◆ 48-49 D 2
Rabaul o • PNG ◆ 58-59 O 7
Rābi', ash-Shallāl ar- = 4th Cataract ~ SUD ◆ 48-49 M 5
Rabun Bald ▲ USA ◇ 24-25 G 2
Rachal o USA ◇ 26-27 H 6
Rachel o USA ◇ 20-21 G 7
Racine o USA ◇ 22-23 E 4
Radama, Nosy ⌒ RM ◆ 50-51 L 4
Radford o USA ◇ 22-23 H 7
Rādhanpur o IND ◆ 56-57 L 6
Radisson o CDN ◇ 18-19 F 2 ◆ 14-15 V 6
Radium Springs o USA ◇ 26-27 D 3
Radom ☆ PL ◇ 40-41 Q 3 ◆ 34-35 Q 5
Radužnyj o RUS ◆ 52-53 M 5
Rae Isthmus ∪ CDN ◆ 14-15 T 3
Rafaela o RA ◆ 32-33 K 4
Rafai o RCA ◆ 48-49 K 8
Rafḥā' o KSA ◆ 56-57 E 5
Rāfit, Ğabal ▲ SUD ◆ 48-49 M 4
Rafsanğān o • IR ◆ 56-57 H 4
Raft River ~ USA ◇ 20-21 H 4
Raft River Mountains ▲ USA ◇ 20-21 H 5
Raga o SUD ◆ 48-49 L 7
Ragaing Yōma ▲ MYA ◆ 58-59 B 3
Ragland o USA ◇ 26-27 F 2
Ragley o USA ◇ 26-27 L 4
Ragueneau o CDN ◇ 18-19 K 4
Ragusa o I ◇ 46-47 E 6 ◆ 34-35 O 8
Raha o RI ◆ 58-59 H 7
Rahad, ar- o SUD ◆ 48-49 M 6
Rahad, ar- ~ SUD ◆ 48-49 M 6
Rahad al-Bardi o SUD ◆ 48-49 K 6
Rahimyār Khān o PK ◆ 56-57 L 5
Rahole National Reserve ⊥ EAK ◆ 50-51 J 1
Raiatea, Île ⌒ F ◆ 12 M 4
Rāichūr o • IND ◆ 56-57 M 7
Raigarh o IND ◆ 56-57 N 6
Railroad Valley ∪ USA ◇ 20-21 G 6
Rainbow Bridge National Monument ∴ USA ◇ 20-21 J 7
Rainbow Lake o CDN ◆ 14-15 N 5
Rainier o USA ◇ 20-21 C 2
Rainier, Mount ▲ USA ◇ 20-21 D 2 ◆ 14-15 M 7
Rainy Lake ⇔ CDN ◆ 14-15 S 7
Raipur o IND ◆ 56-57 N 6
Raivavae, Îles ⌒ F ◆ 12 N 5
Rajada o BR ◆ 30-31 L 6
Rājahmundry o IND ◆ 56-57 N 7
Rajang ~ MAL ◆ 58-59 F 6
Rajasthan □ IND ◆ 56-57 L 5
Rajin o KOR ◆ 54-55 P 3
Rājkot o IND ◆ 56-57 L 6
Ráj-Nándgaon o IND ◆ 56-57 N 6
Rakata, Pulau ⌒ •• RI ◆ 58-59 E 8
Rakiraki o FJI ◆ 60-61 Q 3
Rakops o RB ◆ 50-51 F 6
Rakwa o RI ◆ 58-59 K 7
Raleigh o CDN ◇ 18-19 R 3
Raleigh ☆ USA ◇ 24-25 J 2 ◆ 16-17 L 3
Raleigh Bay ≈ ◇ 24-25 L 2
Raleigh National Historic Site, Fort ∴ USA ◇ 24-25 L 2
Ralls o USA ◇ 26-27 G 3
Rama o NIC ◇ 28-29 B 5 ◆ 16-17 K 8
Rāmabhadrapuram o IND ◆ 56-57 N 7
Ramādi, ar- ☆ IRQ ◆ 56-57 E 4
Ramah o USA ◇ 26-27 C 2
Ramah Navajo Indian Reservation ⅹ USA ◇ 26-27 C 2
Rambouillet o F ◇ 38-39 H 7 ◆ 34-35 M 6
Rambrė ⌒ MYA ◆ 58-59 B 3
Ramea o CDN ◇ 18-19 Q 5
Ramea Island ⌒ CDN ◇ 18-19 Q 5
Ramlat al-Wahiba ⊥ OM ◆ 56-57 H 6
Ramlat as-Sab'atain ⊥ Y ◆ 56-57 F 7
Ramlat Rabyanah ⊥ LAR ◆ 48-49 K 4
Ramon o USA ◇ 26-27 E 2
Ramona o USA ◇ 20-21 F 9
Ramonal ∴ • MEX ◇ 28-29 K 2
Rampur o IND ◆ 56-57 M 5
Ramsay Lake ⇔ CDN ◇ 18-19 C 5
Ramsey o CDN ◇ 18-19 C 5
Ramsey o USA ◇ 22-23 D 6
Ramu River ~ PNG ◆ 58-59 M 7
Rancagua ☆ RCH ◆ 32-33 H 4
Rānchi o •• IND ◆ 56-57 O 6
Rancho California o USA ◇ 20-21 F 9
Rancho Viejo o MEX ◇ 28-29 E 3
Randado o USA ◇ 26-27 H 6
Random Island ⌒ CDN ◇ 18-19 S 4
Rangiora o NZ ◆ 60-61 P 8
Rangkasbitung o RI ◆ 58-59 E 8
Rangnim Sanmaek ▲ KOR ◆ 54-55 O 3
Rangoon = Yangon ★ •• MYA ◆ 58-59 C 3
Rangpur o BD ◆ 56-57 O 5
Ranguana Cay ⌒ BH ◇ 28-29 K 3
Rank, ar- o SUD ◆ 48-49 M 6
Rankin o USA (OK) ◇ 26-27 H 2
Rankin o USA (TX) ◇ 26-27 G 4
Rankins Springs o AUS ◆ 60-61 K 6
Rann of Kachchh ⊥ IND ◆ 56-57 K 6
Ranong o THA ◆ 58-59 C 5
Ransiki o RI ◆ 58-59 K 7
Rantauprapat o RI ◆ 58-59 C 6
Rantoul o USA ◇ 22-23 D 5
Raohe o CHN ◆ 54-55 P 2
Rapa ⌒ F ◆ 12 N 5
Raper, Cape ▲ CDN ◆ 14-15 X 3
Rapid City o USA ◆ 14-15 Q 8
Rapide-Blanc o CDN ◇ 18-19 H 5
Rapid River o USA ◇ 22-23 E 3
Rapids City o USA ◇ 22-23 C 5
Raposa Serra do Sol, Área Indígena ⅹ BR ◆ 30-31 G 4
Raqqa, ar- ☆ SYR ◆ 56-57 D 3
Raquette River ~ USA ◇ 22-23 L 3
Rarotonga Island ⌒ NZ ◆ 12 M 5
Ra's al-Ḥafǧi o KSA ◆ 56-57 F 5
Rashād o SUD ◆ 48-49 M 6
Rās Kōh ▲ PK ◆ 56-57 J 5
Rasmussen Basin ≈ ◆ 14-15 S 3
Rašt ☆ • IR ◆ 56-57 F 3
Rastro ▲ MEX ◆ 16-17 G 6
Ratcha Buri o THA ◆ 58-59 C 4
Ratcliff City o USA ◇ 26-27 J 2
Rāth o IND ◆ 56-57 M 5
Rathdrum o USA ◇ 20-21 F 2
Ratlām o IND ◆ 56-57 M 6
Ratnapura o CL ◆ 56-57 N 9
Raton o USA ◇ 26-27 E 1
Raton Pass ▲ USA ◇ 26-27 E 1
Rattling Brook o CDN ◇ 18-19 Q 4

Pontarlier — Rattling Brook 87

Rauda, ar- o **Y** ❖ 56-57 F 8
Raudales de Malpaso o **MEX**
❖ 28-29 H 3
Raufarhöfn o **IS** ❖ 36-37 f 1
❖ 34-35 H 2
Rauma o••• **FIN** ❖ 34-35 Q 3
Raurkela o **IND** ❖ 56-57 N 6
Ravalli o **USA** ❖ 20-21 G 2
Ravendale o **USA** ❖ 20-21 D 5
Ravenna o• **I** ❖ 46-47 D 2
❖ 34-35 O 7
Ravenshoe o **AUS** ❖ 60-61 K 3
Ravensthorpe o **AUS** ❖ 60-61 E 6
Ràwalpindi o **PK** ❖ 56-57 L 4
Rawlinna o **AUS** ❖ 60-61 F 6
Rawlins o **USA** ❖ 16-17 E 2
Rawson ☆ **RA** ❖ 32-33 J 6
Rawu o **CHN** ❖ 54-55 H 6
Ray, Cape o **USA** ❖ 18-19 P 5
❖ 14-15 Z 7
Raymond o **USA** (IL) ❖ 22-23 D 6
Raymond o **USA** (MS) ❖ 26-27 M 3
Raymond o **USA** (WA) ❖ 20-21 C 2
Rayo ▲ **MEX** ❖ 16-17 E 6
Rayón o **MEX** ❖ 28-29 H 6
Rayong o **THA** ❖ 58-59 D 4
Rayyàn, ar- o **Q** ❖ 56-57 G 5
Raz, Pointe du ⊲ **F** ❖ 38-39 E 7
❖ 34-35 L 6
Ré, Île de ⌒ **F** ❖ 38-39 G 8
Reading o **USA** ❖ 22-23 L 5
❖ 16-17 L 2
Readstown o **USA** ❖ 22-23 C 4
Real, Estero ∼ **NIC** ❖ 28-29 L 5
Real de Santa Maria, El o **PA**
❖ 28-29 E 7
Realico o **RA** ❖ 32-33 K 5
Reardan o **USA** ❖ 20-21 F 2
Rebecca, Lake o **AUS** ❖ 60-61 E 6
Rebun-tò ⌒ **J** ❖ 54-55 R 2
Recherche, Archipelago of the ⌒ **AUS**
❖ 60-61 E 6
Recife ☆ **BR** ❖ 30-31 M 6
Reconquista o **RA** ❖ 32-33 L 3
Recreo o **RA** ❖ 32-33 J 3
Red Bank o **CDN** ❖ 18-19 M 6
Red Bank o **USA** (NJ) ❖ 22-23 L 5
Red Bank o **USA** (TN) ❖ 24-25 F 2
Red Bank 4 Indian Reserve ⋊ **CDN**
❖ 18-19 M 5
Red Bay o **CDN** ❖ 18-19 Q 3
Red Bluff o **USA** ❖ 24-25 D 4
Red Bluff o **USA** ❖ 20-21 C 5
Red Bluff Lake o **USA** ❖ 26-27 F 4
Red Bud o **USA** ❖ 22-23 C 6
Red Butte ▲ **USA** ❖ 20-21 H 8
Red Cliff Indian Reservation ⋊ **USA**
❖ 22-23 C 3
Red Deer o **CDN** ❖ 14-15 O 6
Red Deer River ∼ **CDN** ❖ 14-15 O 6
Redding o **USA** ❖ 20-21 C 5
❖ 16-17 B 2
Redenção o **BR** ❖ 30-31 K 6
Red Hills ▲ **USA** ❖ 26-27 H 1
Redington o **USA** ❖ 26-27 B 3
Red Lake o **USA** ❖ 14-15 S 6
Red Lake Indian Reservation ⋊ **USA**
❖ 14-15 R 7
Redlands o **USA** ❖ 20-21 F 8
Redmond o **USA** (OR) ❖ 20-21 D 3
Redmond o **USA** (WA) ❖ 20-21 C 2
Red Mountain ▲ **USA** (CA)
❖ 20-21 E 7
Red Mountain ▲ **USA** (MT)
❖ 20-21 H 2
Redon o **F** ❖ 38-39 F 8 ❖ 34-35 L 6
Red River ∼ **USA** ❖ 26-27 H 2
❖ 16-17 G 4
Red River of the North ∼ **USA**
❖ 14-15 R 7
Red Rock o **USA** (AZ) ❖ 26-27 C 1
Red Rock o **USA** (OK) ❖ 26-27 G 1
Red Rock River ∼ **USA** ❖ 20-21 H 3
Red Sea ≈ ❖ 56-57 D 5
Redwood Empire ⊥ **USA** ❖ 20-21 C 6
❖ 14-15 M 8
Redwood National Park ⊥••• **USA**
❖ 20-21 B 5 ❖ 14-15 M 8
Redwood Valley o **USA** ❖ 20-21 C 6
Reed City o **USA** ❖ 22-23 F 4
Reedley o **USA** ❖ 20-21 E 7
Reedsport o **USA** ❖ 20-21 B 4
Reedville o **USA** ❖ 24-25 K 7
Reef Islands ⌒ **SOL** ❖ 60-61 O 2
Reese River ∼ **USA** ❖ 24-25 D 3
Reform o **USA** ❖ 24-25 D 3
Regência, Ponta de ▲ **BR** ❖ 30-31 M 8
Regensburg o **D** ❖ 40-41 M 4
❖ 34-35 O 6
Régestan ⊥ **AFG** ❖ 56-57 J 4
Reggane o **DZ** ❖ 48-49 F 3
Reggio o **USA** ❖ 24-25 D 5
Réggio di Calàbria o **I** ❖ 46-47 E 5
❖ 34-35 P 8
Regina ☆ **RA** ❖ 14-15 Q 6
Regina o **F** ❖ 30-31 J 4
Registro o **BR** ❖ 32-33 N 2
Rehoboth o **NAM** ❖ 50-51 H 6
Reidsville o **USA** ❖ 24-25 J 1
Reims o• **F** ❖ 38-39 K 7
❖ 34-35 M 6
Reindeer Lake o **CDN** ❖ 14-15 Q 5
Reine, La o **CDN** ❖ 18-19 G 4
Reinga, Cape o **NZ** ❖ 60-61 P 6
Reinosa o• **E** ❖ 44-45 E 3
❖ 34-35 L 7
Reitoca o **HN** ❖ 28-29 L 5
Reitz o **ZA** ❖ 50-51 H 7
Reliance o **CDN** ❖ 14-15 P 4
Remanso o **BR** ❖ 30-31 L 6
Remedios o **PA** ❖ 28-29 D 7
Remiremont o **F** ❖ 38-39 L 7
❖ 34-35 N 6
Renard, Rivière-au- o **CDN** ❖ 18-19 M 4
Rencontre East o **CDN** ❖ 18-19 R 5
Rend Lake o **USA** ❖ 22-23 D 6
Renfrew o **CDN** ❖ 18-19 G 6
Rengat o **RI** ❖ 58-59 E 7
Renmark o **AUS** ❖ 60-61 J 6
Rennell Island ⌒ **SOL** ❖ 60-61 N 2

Rennes ☆• **F** ❖ 38-39 G 7
❖ 34-35 L 6
Rennick Glacier ⊏ **ANT** ❖ 13 F 17
Reno o **USA** ❖ 20-21 E 6
❖ 16-17 C 3
Reno, El o **USA** ❖ 26-27 J 2
Renous o **CDN** ❖ 18-19 M 5
Renton o **USA** ❖ 20-21 C 2
Reo o **RI** ❖ 58-59 H 8
Réole, la o **F** ❖ 38-39 G 9
❖ 34-35 L 6
Repentigny o **CDN** ❖ 18-19 H 6
Republic o **USA** ❖ 20-21 E 1
Republican River ∼ **USA** ❖ 16-17 G 2
Repulse Bay ≈ ❖ 60-61 E 6
Repulse Bay o **CDN** ❖ 14-15 T 3
Requena o **PE** ❖ 30-31 E 6
Réservoir Manicouagan ⊥••• **CDN**
❖ 18-19 K 3 ❖ 14-15 X 6
Resistencia ☆ **RA** ❖ 32-33 L 3
Reşiţa ☆ **RO** ❖ 34-35 Q 6
Resolution Island ⌒ **CDN** ❖ 14-15 X 4
Respublika Adygeja = Adygệ Respublikèm
⚑ **RUS** ❖ 34-35 T 7
Restigouche Indian Reserve ⋊ **CDN**
❖ 18-19 L 4
Restigouche River ∼ **CDN** ❖ 18-19 L 5
Retalhuleu o **GCA** ❖ 28-29 J 4
Rethel o **F** ❖ 38-39 K 7 ❖ 34-35 N 6
Revelstoke o **CDN** ❖ 14-15 N 6
Revilla Gigedo, Islas ⌒ **MEX**
❖ 16-17 D 7
Revillagigedo Island ⌒ **USA**
❖ 14-15 K 5
Rewa o **IND** ❖ 56-57 M 5
Rewari o **IND** ❖ 56-57 M 5
Rex, Mount ▲ **ANT** ❖ 13 F 29
Rexburg o **USA** ❖ 20-21 J 4
Rey, Isla de ⌒ **PA** ❖ 28-29 E 7
Reyes, Point ⊲ **USA** ❖ 20-21 C 6
Reyes Salgado, Los o **MEX**
❖ 28-29 C 2
Reykjanes Ridge ⌇ ❖ 14-15 e 5
Reykjavík ★• **IS** ❖ 36-37 C 2
❖ 34-35 G 2
Reynolds o **USA** ❖ 22-23 E 5
Reynoldsburg o **USA** ❖ 22-23 G 6
Reynosa o **MEX** ❖ 16-17 G 5
Rēzekne o•• **LV** ❖ 42-43 K 3
❖ 34-35 R 4
Rhea o **USA** ❖ 26-27 H 2
Rhein ∼ **D** ❖ 40-41 K 4 ❖ 34-35 N 6
Rhine = Rhein ∼ **D** ❖ 40-41 K 4
❖ 34-35 N 6
Rhinelander o **USA** ❖ 22-23 D 3
❖ 14-15 T 7
Rhir, Cap ⊲ **MA** ❖ 48-49 D 2
Rhode Island □ **USA** ❖ 22-23 N 5
❖ 16-17 M 2
Rhode Island ⌒ **USA** ❖ 22-23 N 5
Rhodes Matopos National Park ⊥ **ZW**
❖ 50-51 G 6
Rhodope Mountains ▲ **BG** ❖ 34-35 Q 7
Rhône ∼ **F** ❖ 38-39 K 10
❖ 34-35 N 6
Rhône-Alpes ⚑ **F** ❖ 38-39 K 9
❖ 34-35 N 6
Ria Celestun, Parque Natural ⊥ **MEX**
❖ 28-29 J 1 ❖ 16-17 H 6
Ribas do Rio Pardo o **BR** ❖ 32-33 M 2
Ribáuè o **MOC** ❖ 50-51 J 4
Ribeirão Preto o **BR** ❖ 32-33 N 2
Ribérac o **F** ❖ 38-39 H 9
❖ 34-35 L 7
Riberalta o **BOL** ❖ 30-31 F 7
Rice Lake o **CDN** ❖ 18-19 E 6
Rice Lake o **USA** ❖ 22-23 C 3
Richardsbaai = Richards Bay o **ZA**
❖ 50-51 J 7
Richards Bay = Richardsbaai o **ZA**
❖ 50-51 H 7
Richards Island ⌒ **CDN** ❖ 14-15 K 3
Richardson o **USA** ❖ 26-27 H 3
Richardson Mountains ▲ **CDN**
❖ 14-15 J 3
Richfield o **USA** (ID) ❖ 20-21 J 4
Richfield o **USA** (KS) ❖ 26-27 G 1
Richfield o **USA** (UT) ❖ 20-21 H 6
❖ 16-17 D 3
Richgrove o **USA** ❖ 20-21 E 8
Richibucto o **CDN** ❖ 18-19 M 5
Richibucto 15 Indian Reserve ⋊ **CDN**
❖ 18-19 M 5
Richland o **USA** ❖ 20-21 E 2
Richland Center o **USA** ❖ 22-23 C 4
Richlands o **USA** ❖ 22-23 H 7
Richmond o **AUS** ❖ 60-61 J 4
Richmond o **USA** ❖ 18-19 H 6
Richmond o **USA** (AR) ❖ 20-21 C 7
Richmond o **USA** (IN) ❖ 22-23 G 6
Richmond o **USA** (KY) ❖ 22-23 F 7
Richmond o **USA** (VA) ❖ 22-23 K 7
❖ 16-17 L 3
Rich Mountain ▲ **USA** ❖ 26-27 K 2
Richmond ☆ **USA** ❖ 24-25 D 3
Richtersveld National Park ⊥ **ZA**
❖ 50-51 E 7
Richton o **USA** ❖ 24-25 D 4
Richwood o **USA** ❖ 22-23 H 6
Ridder, De o **USA** ❖ 26-27 L 4
Ridge Crest o **USA** ❖ 20-21 F 8
Ridgeland o **USA** ❖ 26-27 M 3
Ridgeway o **USA** ❖ 24-25 J 1
Ridgway o **USA** ❖ 42-43 Q 3
Riding Mountain National Park ⊥ **CDN**
❖ 14-15 Q 6
Rietfontein o **ZA** ❖ 50-51 F 6
Rietstangi ▲ **IS** ❖ 16-17 H 2
Rift Valley National Park ⊥ **ETH**
❖ 48-49 N 7
Riga ★ **LV** ❖ 42-43 J 3
❖ 34-35 Q 4
Riga, Gulf of = Rígas Jūras ≈
❖ 34-35 Q 4 ❖ 42-43 H 3
Rigas Júras Licis ≈ ❖ 42-43 H 3
Riiser-Larsen halvöy ⌒ **ANT** ❖ 13 G 4

Rijeka o **HR** ❖ 46-47 E 2
❖ 34-35 O 6
Riley o **USA** ❖ 20-21 E 4
Rimini o **I** ❖ 46-47 D 2 ❖ 34-35 O 7
Rimouski o **CDN** ❖ 18-19 M 5
Rimouski, Réserve Faunique de ⊥ **CDN**
❖ 18-19 K 4
Rincón o **CR** ❖ 28-29 C 7
Rincón o **USA** ❖ 26-27 D 3
Rinconada o **RA** ❖ 32-33 J 2
Rincón de la Vieja, Parque Nacional ⊥ **CR**
❖ 28-29 B 6
Rincón de la Vieja, Volcán ▲ **CR**
❖ 28-29 B 6
Ringgold o **USA** ❖ 26-27 L 3
Ringling o **USA** ❖ 22-23 G 7
Rinjani, Gunung ▲ **RI** ❖ 58-59 G 8
Rio Abiseo, Parque Nacional ⊥••• **PE**
❖ 30-31 D 6
Rio Acre, Estação Ecologica ⊥ **BR**
Rio Amazonas, Estuário do ≈ **BR**
❖ 30-31 K 4
Rio Azul ∴• **GCA** ❖ 28-29 K 3
Riobamba o **EC** ❖ 30-31 D 5
Rio-Biá, Áreas Indígenas ⋊ **BR**
Rio Branco ☆ **BR** ❖ 30-31 F 6
Rio Branco, Área Indígena ⋊ **BR**
❖ 30-31 F 6
Rio Branco, Parque Nacional do ⊥ **BR**
❖ 30-31 G 4
Rio Bravo o **GCA** ❖ 28-29 K 3
Rio Bravo, Parque Internacional del ⊥
MEX ❖ 16-17 F 5
Rio Claro o **BR** ❖ 32-33 N 2
Rio Conchas ∼ **BR** ❖ 30-31 H 7
Rio de Janeiro ★ **BR** ❖ 32-33 O 2
Rio de Janeiro o•• **BR** (RIO)
❖ 32-33 O 2
Rio de la Plata ≈ ❖ 32-33 L 4
Rio Dulce, Parque Nacional ⊥ **GCA**
❖ 28-29 K 3
Rio Grande o **BR** ❖ 32-33 M 4
Rio Grande o **BR** ❖ 30-31 K 7
Rio Grande ∼ **USA** ❖ 26-27 G 5
❖ 16-17 F 5
Rio Grande do Norte □ **BR** ❖ 30-31 M 6
Rio Grande do Sul □ **BR** ❖ 32-33 M 3
Riohacha o **CO** ❖ 30-31 E 2
Rio Hato o **PA** ❖ 28-29 D 7
Rio Hondo o **GCA** ❖ 28-29 K 4
Rio Hondo, Termas de o• **RA**
❖ 32-33 K 3
Rioja, La o **RA** ❖ 32-33 J 3
Rio Lagartos o• **MEX** ❖ 28-29 K 1
Rio Lagartos, Parque Natural ⊥ **MEX**
❖ 28-29 L 1 ❖ 16-17 H 5
Riom o **F** ❖ 38-39 J 9 ❖ 34-35 M 7
Rio Mulatos o **BOL** ❖ 30-31 F 8
Rio Negro o **RA** ❖ 32-33 J 5
Rio Negro, Pantanal do o **BR**
Rio Negro, Represa del o **ROU**
Rio Negro, Reserva Florestal do ⊥ **BR**
Rio Pardo de Minas o **BR** ❖ 30-31 L 8
Rio Trombetas, Reserva Biológica do ⊥
BR ❖ 30-31 H 4
Rio Verde o **MEX** ❖ 16-17 G 6
Rio Verde o **BR** ❖ 32-33 M 8
Rio Verde de Mato Grosso o **BR**
❖ 30-31 J 8
Ripley o **USA** (KY) ❖ 22-23 G 6
Ripley o **USA** (MS) ❖ 24-25 D 2
Ripley o **USA** (WV) ❖ 22-23 H 6
Risasa o **ZRE** ❖ 50-51 G 2
Rishiri-tò ⌒ **J** ❖ 54-55 R 2
Rising Star o **USA** ❖ 26-27 H 3
Rising Sun o **USA** ❖ 22-23 F 6
Ritter, Mount ▲ **USA** ❖ 20-21 E 7
Ritzville o **USA** ❖ 20-21 E 2
Rivadavia o **RA** ❖ 32-33 K 2
Rivadavia o **RCH** ❖ 32-33 H 3
Rivas ☆ **NIC** ❖ 28-29 B 6
Rivera o **RA** ❖ 32-33 K 4
Rivera ☆ **ROU** ❖ 32-33 L 4
River Cess o **LB** ❖ 48-49 D 7
Riverhead o **USA** ❖ 22-23 M 5
Riverina ⊥ **AUS** ❖ 60-61 J 6
River of No Return Wilderness ⊥ **USA**
❖ 20-21 G 3
Riversdale o **BH** ❖ 28-29 K 3
Riverside o **CDN** ❖ 18-19 D 6
Riverside o **USA** (CA) ❖ 20-21 F 9
Riverside o **USA** (IA) ❖ 22-23 C 5
Rivesaltes o **F** ❖ 38-39 J 10
❖ 34-35 M 7
Riviera o **USA** ❖ 26-27 J 6
Rivière-à-Pierre o **CDN** ❖ 18-19 H 5
Rivière-aux-Saumons o **CDN**
❖ 18-19 N 4
Rivière-Bleue o **CDN** ❖ 18-19 K 5
Rivière-du-Loup o **CDN** ❖ 18-19 K 5
Rivière-Saint-Jean o **CDN** ❖ 18-19 N 3
Rivière-Saint-Paul o **CDN** ❖ 18-19 Q 3
Rivne o **UA** ❖ 34-35 R 5
Rivungo o **ANG** ❖ 50-51 F 5
Riyàd, ar- ★ **KSA** ❖ 56-57 F 6
Riyadh = Riyàd, ar- ★ **KSA**
❖ 56-57 F 6
Rize o **TR** ❖ 34-35 U 7
Rizhao o **CHN** ❖ 54-55 M 4
Rizzuto, Capo ⊲ **I** ❖ 46-47 F 5
❖ 34-35 P 8
 Road Town o• **GB** ❖ 16-17 O 7
Roanne o **F** ❖ 38-39 K 8
Roanoke o **USA** (AL) ❖ 24-25 F 3
Roanoke o **USA** (VA) ❖ 22-23 J 7
❖ 16-17 L 3
Roanoke Island ⌒ **USA** ❖ 24-25 L 2
Roanoke Rapids o **USA** ❖ 24-25 K 1
Roanoke River ∼ **USA** ❖ 22-23 J 7
Roaring Springs o **USA** ❖ 26-27 G 3
Roatán o **HN** ❖ 28-29 L 3
Roatán, Isla de ⌒ **HN** ❖ 28-29 L 3
❖ 16-17 J 7

Roberta o **USA** ❖ 24-25 F 3
Robert's Arm o **CDN** ❖ 18-19 R 4
Roberts Creek Montain ▲ **USA**
❖ 20-21 F 6
Robert S. Kerr Lake o **USA** ❖ 26-27 K 2
Robertson o **USA** (OK) ❖ 26-27 H 2
Roberval, Rio o **BR** ❖ 30-31 G 4
Robertsons Øy ⌒ ❖ 18-19 H 4
❖ 14-15 W 7
Robinson o **USA** ❖ 22-23 E 6
Robinson Island ⌒ **ANT** ❖ 13 G 30
Robinsons River o **CDN** ❖ 18-19 P 4
Robles Junction o **USA** ❖ 20-21 J 9
Robson, Mount ▲ **CDN** ❖ 14-15 N 6
Robstown o **USA** ❖ 26-27 J 6
Roby o **USA** (MO) ❖ 26-27 L 1
Roby o **USA** (TX) ❖ 26-27 G 3
Rocas Aljos ⌒ **MEX** ❖ 16-17 D 7
Rocha ☆ **ROU** ❖ 32-33 M 4
Rochefort o **F** ❖ 38-39 G 9
❖ 34-35 L 6
Rochelle o **USA** (IL) ❖ 22-23 D 5
Rochelle o **USA** (TX) ❖ 26-27 H 4
Rochelle, la ☆• **F** ❖ 38-39 G 8
❖ 34-35 L 6
Rochester o **USA** (IN) ❖ 22-23 E 5
Rochester o **USA** (MI) ❖ 22-23 G 4
Rochester o **USA** (NH) ❖ 22-23 N 4
Rochester o **USA** (NY) ❖ 22-23 K 4
❖ 14-15 V 8
Rochester o **USA** (MN) ❖ 14-15 S 8
Roche-sur-Yon, la ☆• **F** ❖ 38-39 G 8
❖ 34-35 L 6
Rockall ⌒ **GB** ❖ 16-17 J 4
Rockall Plateau ⌇ ❖ 34-35 H 4
Rockall Trough ⌇ ❖ 34-35 H 5
Rockdale o **USA** ❖ 26-27 J 4
Rockefeller National Wildlife Refuge ⊥
USA ❖ 26-27 L 5
Rockefeller Plateau ▲ **ANT** ❖ 13 F 24
Rock Falls o **USA** ❖ 22-23 D 5
Rockford o **USA** (AL) ❖ 24-25 E 3
Rockford o **USA** (IL) ❖ 22-23 D 4
❖ 14-15 T 8
Rockhampton o• **AUS** ❖ 60-61 L 4
Rock Hill o **USA** ❖ 24-25 H 2
Rockingham o **USA** ❖ 24-25 J 2
Rockingham Bay ≈ ❖ 60-61 K 3
Rock Island o **USA** ❖ 22-23 C 5
Rock Lake o **USA** ❖ 20-21 F 2
Rockland o **CDN** ❖ 18-19 G 6
Rockland o **USA** ❖ 22-23 O 3
Rockport o **USA** (TX) ❖ 26-27 J 6
Rockport o **USA** (WA) ❖ 20-21 D 1
Rocksprings o **USA** ❖ 26-27 G 4
Rock Springs o **USA** (WY) ❖ 16-17 E 2
Rockstone o **GUY** ❖ 30-31 H 3
Rockville o **USA** ❖ 22-23 E 6
Rockville o **USA** (MD) ❖ 22-23 K 6
Rockwall o **USA** ❖ 26-27 J 3
Rockwood o **USA** ❖ 24-25 F 2
Rocky Island Lake o **CDN** ❖ 18-19 C 5
Rocky Mount o **USA** (NC) ❖ 24-25 K 2
Rocky Mount o **USA** (VA) ❖ 22-23 J 7
Rocky Mountain National Park ⊥ **USA**
❖ 16-17 E 2
Rocky Mountains ▲ ❖ 14-15 K 4
Rodagua, Lago o **BOL** ❖ 30-31 F 7
Roddickton o **CDN** ❖ 18-19 Q 3
Rodeo o **USA** ❖ 26-27 C 4
Rodeo Viejo o **PA** ❖ 28-29 E 7
Rodez o **F** ❖ 38-39 J 9
❖ 34-35 M 7
Ródos o• **GR** ❖ 46-47 G 5
❖ 34-35 R 8
Ródos ⌒ **GR** ❖ 46-47 M 6
Rodrigues, Ile ⌒ **MS** ❖ 50-51 O 5
Roebourne o **AUS** ❖ 60-61 D 4
Roebuck Bay ≈ ❖ 60-61 E 3
Roes Welcome Sound ≈ ❖ 14-15 T 4
Rogagua, Lago o **BOL** ❖ 30-31 F 7
Rogers, Mount ▲ **USA** ❖ 22-23 H 7
Rogers City o **USA** ❖ 22-23 G 3
Rogerson o **USA** ❖ 20-21 G 4
Rogersville o **CDN** ❖ 18-19 M 5
Roggeveen Basin ⌇ ❖ 7 B 8
Rogoaguado, Lago o **BOL** ❖ 30-31 F 7
Rogue River ∼ **USA** ❖ 20-21 B 4
Rohault, Lac o **CDN** ❖ 18-19 G 4
Roi Et o **THA** ❖ 58-59 D 3
Roll o **USA** ❖ 26-27 C 1
Rolla o **USA** (KS) ❖ 26-27 G 1
Rolla o **USA** (MO) ❖ 22-23 C 7
❖ 16-17 H 3
Rolleston o **AUS** ❖ 60-61 K 4
Rolling Fork o **USA** ❖ 26-27 M 3
Roma o **USA** ❖ 60-61 K 5
Royan o• **F** ❖ 38-39 G 9 ❖ 34-35 L 6
Roma, Pulau ⌒ **RI** ❖ 58-59 J 8
Roma •••• **I** ❖ 46-47 D 4
❖ 34-35 O 7
Roma o **USA** ❖ 26-27 H 6
Roma o **USA** ❖ 24-25 G 2
Romaine, Rivière ∼ **CDN** ❖ 18-19 N 3
❖ 14-15 Y 6
Romania ■ **RO** ❖ 34-35 Q 6
Romano, Cape ⊲ **USA** ❖ 24-25 H 6
Romanovka o **RUS** ❖ 52-53 T 7
Romans-sur-Isère o **F** ❖ 38-39 K 9
Romanzof, Cape ⊲ **USA** ❖ 14-15 C 4
Romblon Island ⌒ **RP** ❖ 58-59 H 4
Rome o **USA** (NY) ❖ 22-23 L 4
Rome = Roma •••• **I** ❖ 46-47 D 4
❖ 34-35 O 7
Romita o **MEX** ❖ 28-29 D 1
Romney o **USA** (VA) ❖ 22-23 J 6
Romney o **USA** (WV) ❖ 22-23 J 6
Romny o **UA** ❖ 34-35 S 5
Romorantin-Lanthenay o **F** ❖ 38-39 H 8
Ronan o **USA** ❖ 20-21 G 2
Roncador, Serra do ▲ **BR** ❖ 30-31 J 7
Ronde, Rivière la ∼ **CDN** ❖ 18-19 H 3
Rondônia □ **BR** ❖ 30-31 G 7
Rondonópolis o **BR** ❖ 30-31 J 8

Ronne Bay ≈ ❖ 13 F 29
Roof Butte ▲ **USA** ❖ 26-27 C 1
Roosevelt o **USA** (AZ) ❖ 20-21 H 8
Roosevelt, Rio ∼ **BR** ❖ 30-31 G 6
Roosevelt Campobello International Park ⊥
CDN ❖ 18-19 L 6
Roosevelt Island ⌒ **ANT** ❖ 13 F 21
Root River ∼ **USA** ❖ 22-23 C 4
Roper Bar o **AUS** ❖ 60-61 G 2
Roper River ∼ **AUS** ❖ 60-61 G 2
Roquefort o **F** ❖ 38-39 G 9
❖ 34-35 L 6
Roques, Islas los ⌒ **YV** ❖ 30-31 F 2
Roraima □ **BR** ❖ 30-31 G 4
Roraima, Mount ▲ **GUY** ❖ 30-31 G 3
Rosalia o **USA** ❖ 20-21 F 2
Rosario o **RA** ❖ 32-33 K 4
Rosario de la Frontera o **RA**
❖ 32-33 K 3
Rosário do Sul o **BR** ❖ 32-33 M 4
Rosas, Las o **USA** ❖ 28-29 H 3
Rosa Zárate o **EC** ❖ 30-31 D 4
Rosburg o **USA** ❖ 20-21 C 2
Roscoff o **F** ❖ 38-39 F 7 ❖ 34-35 L 6
Roscommon o **USA** ❖ 22-23 F 3
Roseau ★ **WD** ❖ 16-17 O 7
Rose-Blanche o **CDN** ❖ 18-19 P 5
Rosebud o **USA** ❖ 26-27 L 2
Rosebud o **USA** ❖ 20-21 J 4
Rosebud Indian Reservation ⋊ **USA**
❖ 16-17 F 2
Roseburg o **USA** ❖ 20-21 C 4
Rosenberg o **USA** ❖ 26-27 K 5
Rosenheim o **D** ❖ 40-41 M 5
❖ 34-35 O 6
Roses o **USA** ❖ 22-23 J 5
Rosiers, Cap-des- o **CDN** ❖ 18-19 M 4
Rosita o **NIC** ❖ 28-29 B 5
Roslawf o **RUS** ❖ 42-43 N 5
❖ 34-35 S 5
Ross Bay Junction o **CDN** ❖ 18-19 L 2
Rosseau, Lake o **CDN** ❖ 18-19 E 6
Rossignol, Lac o **CDN** ❖ 18-19 L 6
Rossignol, Lake o **CDN** ❖ 18-19 M 6
Ross Island ⌒ **ANT** ❖ 13 F 17
Ross Lake o **USA** ❖ 20-21 D 1
Rosslare o **IRL** ❖ 34-35 K 5
Ross River o **CDN** ❖ 14-15 K 4
Ross Sea ≈ ❖ 13 F 19
Rosston o **USA** ❖ 26-27 G 4
Rostock o• **D** ❖ 40-41 M 1
Rostov-na-Donu ☆ **RUS** ❖ 34-35 T 6
Rostraver o **USA** ❖ 22-23 J 5
Rostrenen o **F** ❖ 38-39 F 7
❖ 34-35 L 6
Rota ⌒ **USA** ❖ 58-59 N 4
Roti, Pulau ⌒ **RI** ❖ 58-59 H 9
Roto o **AUS** ❖ 60-61 K 6
Rotorua o **NZ** ❖ 60-61 Q 7
Rotterdam o• **NL** ❖ 40-41 J 3
❖ 34-35 M 5
Rouan o **F** ❖ 38-39 J 6
❖ 34-35 M 5
Roubaix o **F** ❖ 38-39 J 6
❖ 34-35 M 5
Rouen ☆• **F** ❖ 38-39 H 7
❖ 34-35 M 6
Rouge-Matawin, Réserve Faunique ⊥ **CDN**
❖ 18-19 G 5
Rough Rock o **USA** ❖ 26-27 C 1
Roundeyed, Lac o **CDN** ❖ 18-19 J 2
Round Mountain o **USA** ❖ 20-21 F 6
Round Pond o **CDN** ❖ 18-19 R 4
Round Rock o **USA** (AZ) ❖ 26-27 C 1
Round Rock o **USA** (TX) ❖ 26-27 J 4
Round Spring o **USA** ❖ 22-23 C 7
Round Valley Indian Reservation ⋊ **USA**
❖ 20-21 C 6
Rouyn-Noranda o **CDN** ❖ 18-19 E 4
❖ 14-15 V 7
Rovno = Rivne o **UA** ❖ 34-35 R 5
Rovuma, Rio = Ruvuma ∼ **MOC**
❖ 50-51 J 4
Rowan, Port o **CDN** ❖ 18-19 D 6
Rowley Island ⌒ **CDN** ❖ 14-15 V 3
Rowley Shoals ∴ **AUS** ❖ 60-61 D 3
Roxas o **RP** ❖ 58-59 H 4
Roxboro o **USA** ❖ 24-25 J 1
Roy o **USA** (NM) ❖ 26-27 E 2
Roy o **USA** (UT) ❖ 20-21 H 5
Royale, Isle ⌒ **USA** ❖ 22-23 D 2
❖ 14-15 T 7
Royal Society Range ▲ **ANT** ❖ 13 F 16
Royan o• **F** ❖ 38-39 G 9 ❖ 34-35 L 6
Roye o **F** ❖ 38-39 J 6 ❖ 34-35 M 6
Royston o **USA** ❖ 24-25 G 2
Ruacana Falls ∼• **NAM** ❖ 50-51 D 5
Ruaha National Park ⊥ **EAT**
❖ 50-51 H 3
Ruahine Range ▲ **NZ** ❖ 60-61 Q 7
Ruapehu, Mount ▲ **NZ** ❖ 60-61 P 7
Ruawai o **NZ** ❖ 60-61 P 7
Ru'ays, Wàdi ar ∼ **LAR** ❖ 48-49 J 2
Rub' al-Hàli, ar- ⊥ **KSA** ❖ 56-57 F 7
Rubcovsk o **RUS** ❖ 52-53 N 7
Rubeho Mountains ▲ **EAT** ❖ 50-51 J 3
Rubicon River ∼ **USA** ❖ 20-21 D 6
Rubondo National Park ⊥ **EAT**
❖ 50-51 H 2
Ruby Dome ▲ **USA** ❖ 20-21 G 5
Ruby Lake o **USA** ❖ 20-21 G 5
Ruby Mountains ▲ **USA** ❖ 20-21 G 5
Ruby River ∼ **USA** ❖ 20-21 H 3
Rudall River National Park ⊥ **AUS**
❖ 60-61 E 4
Rudnyj o **KZ** ❖ 52-53 J 7
Rudnyy = Rudnyj o **KZ** ❖ 52-53 J 7
Rudolf, Lake = Turkana, Lake o **EAK**
❖ 48-49 N 8
Rudolfa, ostrov ⌒ **RUS** ❖ 52-53 H 1
Rudyard o **USA** ❖ 20-21 J 1
Rufiji ∼ **EAT** ❖ 50-51 J 3
Rufino o **RA** ❖ 32-33 K 4
Rufunsa o **Z** ❖ 50-51 G 5

Rügen ⌒ **D** ❖ 40-41 M 1
❖ 34-35 O 5
Sachs Harbour o **CDN** ❖ 14-15 M 2
Sackville o **CDN** ❖ 18-19 M 6
Saco o **USA** ❖ 22-23 N 4
Sacramento ☆• **USA** ❖ 20-21 D 6
❖ 16-17 B 3
Sacramento, Pampas de ⊥ **PE**
❖ 30-31 E 6
Sacramento Mountains ▲ **USA**
❖ 26-27 E 3 ❖ 16-17 E 4
Sacramento River ∼ **USA** ❖ 20-21 D 6
❖ 16-17 B 3
Sacramento Valley ⌣ **USA** ❖ 20-21 C 6
Sa'da o• **Y** ❖ 56-57 E 7
Sadani o **EAT** ❖ 50-51 J 3
Saddle Mount ▲ **USA**
Sadh o **OM** ❖ 56-57 H 7
Sado-shima ⌒ **J** ❖ 54-55 Q 4
Sádrinsk o **RUS** ❖ 52-53 J 6
Safford o **USA** ❖ 20-21 D 6
Safi = Asfi ☆• **MA** ❖ 48-49 D 2
Safid Kûh, Selsele-ye ▲ **AFG**
❖ 56-57 J 3
Sàga o **CHN** ❖ 54-55 F 6
Sàgar o• **IND** ❖ 56-57 M 6
Sagastyr o **RUS** ❖ 52-53 W 3
Sage o **USA** ❖ 20-21 J 5
Saginaw o **USA** ❖ 22-23 G 4
Saginaw Bay o **USA** ❖ 22-23 G 4
Saglek Bank ⌇ ❖ 14-15 Y 5
Sagua-Baracoa, Grupo ▲ **C** ❖ 16-17 L 6
Sagua National Monument • **USA**
❖ 20-21 J 9
Saguenay, Rivière ∼ **CDN** ❖ 18-19 J 4
❖ 14-15 W 7
Sahalinskij zaliv ≈ ❖ 52-53 Z 7
Sahara ⊥ ❖ 48-49 G 4
Saharan Atlas ▲ **DZ** ❖ 48-49 F 2
Saharanpur o **IND** ❖ 56-57 M 5
Sahel ⊥ ❖ 48-49 E 5
Sáhiwàl o **PK** ❖ 56-57 L 4
Sáhrà' Surt ⊥ **LAR** ❖ 48-49 J 2
Sáhrûd o• **IR** ❖ 56-57 G 3
Sàhtinsk o **KZ** ❖ 52-53 L 8
Sahuaripa o **MEX** ❖ 16-17 E 5
Sahuarita o **USA** ❖ 26-27 B 4
Sahuayo o **MEX** ❖ 28-29 C 1
Sahul Banks ⌇ ❖ 58-59 H 9
Sahul Shelf ⌇ ❖ 60-61 F 1
Saida o **DZ** ❖ 48-49 F 2
Saidor o **PNG** ❖ 58-59 N 8
Saidpur o **BD** ❖ 56-57 O 5
Saigon = Thành Phô Hô Chi Minh o•• **VN**
❖ 58-59 E 4
Saihût o **Y** ❖ 56-57 G 7
Saikhoa Ghât o **IND** ❖ 56-57 Q 5
Saimaa o **FIN** ❖ 34-35 R 3
Saint Albans o **CDN** ❖ 18-19 R 5
❖ 14-15 Z 7
Saint Albans o **USA** ❖ 22-23 H 6
Saint-Alexandre o **CDN** ❖ 18-19 K 5
Saint-Ambroise o **CDN** ❖ 18-19 J 4
Saint-André o **CDN** ❖ 18-19 K 5
Saint-Andrew Bay ≈ ❖ 24-25 F 4
Saint Andrews o **CDN** ❖ 18-19 L 6
Saint Andrew's o **CDN** ❖ 18-19 R 5
Saint Andrew Sound ≈ ❖ 24-25 H 4
Saint Anne o **USA** ❖ 22-23 E 5
Saint Ann's Bay o **CDN** ❖ 18-19 N 5
Saint Anthony o **CDN** ❖ 18-19 R 3
❖ 14-15 Z 6
Saint Anthony o **USA** ❖ 20-21 J 4
Saint-Augustin o **CDN** ❖ 18-19 P 3
Saint-Augustin, Rivière ∼ **CDN**
❖ 18-19 P 3
Saint Augustine o **USA** (IL)
❖ 22-23 C 5
Saint Augustine o••• **USA** (FL)
❖ 24-25 H 4 ❖ 16-17 K 5
Saint Augustin Nord-Ouest, Rivière ∼ **CDN**
❖ 18-19 P 3
Saint Barbe o **CDN** ❖ 18-19 Q 3
Saint-Barthélemy ⌒ **F** ❖ 16-17 O 7
Saint Bernard's o **CDN** ❖ 18-19 R 5
Saint Brendan's o **CDN** ❖ 18-19 R 4
Saint Bride's o **CDN** ❖ 18-19 R 5
Saint-Brieuc ☆• **F** ❖ 38-39 F 7
❖ 34-35 L 6
Saint-Bruno o **CDN** ❖ 18-19 J 4
Saint-Calais o **F** ❖ 38-39 H 8
❖ 34-35 L 6
Saint Catharines o **CDN** ❖ 18-19 E 6
Saint Catherines Island ⌒ **USA**
❖ 24-25 H 4
Saint-Céré o **F** ❖ 38-39 H 9
❖ 34-35 L 7
Saint-Chamond o **F** ❖ 38-39 K 9
❖ 34-35 N 6
Saint Charles o **USA** (ID) ❖ 20-21 J 5
Saint Charles o **USA** (MO) ❖ 22-23 C 6
Saint-Charles-Garnier o **CDN**
❖ 18-19 K 4
Saint-Chély-d'Apcher o **F** ❖ 38-39 J 9
❖ 34-35 M 7
Saint-Chinian o **F** ❖ 38-39 J 10
❖ 34-35 M 7
Saint Clair o **USA** ❖ 22-23 G 4
Saint Clair, Lake o **USA** ❖ 22-23 G 4
❖ 14-15 U 8
Saint Cloud o **CDN** ❖ 18-19 L 6
Saint Cloud o **USA** (MN) ❖ 14-15 S 7
Saint Croix o **CDN** ❖ 18-19 L 6
Saint Croix Island National Monument •
CDN ❖ 18-19 L 6
❖ 34-35 N 6
Saint-Dié o **F** ❖ 38-39 L 7
❖ 34-35 N 6
Saint-Dizier o **F** ❖ 38-39 K 7
❖ 34-35 M 6
Sainte-Agathe-des-Monts o **CDN**
❖ 18-19 G 5
Sainte-Angèle-de-Mérici o **CDN**
❖ 18-19 K 4
Sainte-Anne, Lac o **CDN** ❖ 18-19 L 3
Sainte-Anne-de-Beaupré o **CDN**
❖ 18-19 J 5
Sainte-Anne-des-Monts o **CDN**
❖ 18-19 L 4
Sainte-Anne-du-Lac o **CDN** ❖ 18-19 G 5
Sainte-Croix o **CDN** ❖ 18-19 J 5
Sainte-Eulalie o **CDN** ❖ 18-19 H 5

Santa Rosa ○ **USA** (NM) ◇ 26-27 E 2
Santa Rosa de Copán ☆ **HN** ◇ 28-29 K 4
Santa Rosa Island ⌒ **USA** (CA) ◇ 20-21 D 9
Santa Rosa Island ⌒ **USA** (FL) ◇ 24-25 E 4
Santa Rosalía ○· **MEX** ♦ 16-17 D 5
Santa Rosa Wash ~ **USA** ◇ 20-21 J 9
Šantarskie, ostrova ⌒ **RUS** ♦ 52-53 Y 6
Santa Tecla = Nueva San Salvador ○ **ES** ◇ 28-29 K 5
Santa Terezinha ○ **BR** ♦ 30-31 J 7
Santee River ~ **USA** ◇ 24-25 J 3
Sante Marie Among the Hurons Historic Park · **CDN** ◇ 18-19 E 6
Santiago ○ **BOL** ♦ 30-31 H 8
Santiago ○ **BR** ♦ 32-33 M 3
Santiago ☆ **PA** ◇ 28-29 D 7 ♦ 16-17 K 9
Santiago ★·· **RCH** ♦ 32-33 H 4
Santiago, Cerro ▲ **PA** ◇ 28-29 D 7
Santiago, Río Grande de ~ **MEX** ♦ 16-17 F 6
Santiago Atitlán ○ **GCA** ◇ 28-29 J 4
Santiago Chazumba ○ **MEX** ◇ 28-29 F 2
Santiago de Chuco ○ **PE** ♦ 30-31 D 6
Santiago de Compostela ○··· **E** ◇ 44-45 C 3 ♦ 34-35 K 7
Santiago de Cuba ☆·· **C** ♦ 16-17 L 6
Santiago del Estero □ **RA** ♦ 32-33 K 3
Santiago del Estero ☆ **RA** (SAE) ♦ 32-33 K 3
Santiago de los Cabelleros ☆· **DOM** ♦ 16-17 M 7
Santiago Jamiltepec ○ **MEX** ◇ 28-29 F 3
Santiago Maravatío ○ **MEX** ◇ 28-29 D 1
Santiago Mountains ▲ **USA** ◇ 26-27 F 4
Santiago Tamazola ○ **MEX** ◇ 28-29 E 3
Santiago Tuxtla ○· **MEX** ◇ 28-29 G 2
Santiago Yosondúa ○ **MEX** ◇ 28-29 F 3
San Tiburcio ○ **MEX** ♦ 16-17 F 6
Santo André ○ **BR** ♦ 32-33 N 2
Santo Ângelo ○· **BR** ♦ 32-33 M 3
Santo Antonio ○ **STP** ♦ 50-51 C 1
Santo Corazón ○ **BOL** ♦ 30-31 H 8
Santo Domingo ★··· **DOM** ♦ 16-17 N 7
Santo Domingo ○ **NIC** ◇ 28-29 B 5
Santo Domingo, Río ~ **MEX** ◇ 28-29 F 3
Santo Domingo, Río ~ **MEX** ◇ 28-29 H 3
Santo Domingo, Río ~ **MEX** ◇ 28-29 J 3
Santo Domingo de los Colerados ○ **EC** ♦ 30-31 D 5
Santo Domingo Tehuantepec ○· **MEX** ◇ 28-29 G 3 ♦ 16-17 G 7
Santos ○ **BR** ♦ 32-33 N 2
Santo Tomás ○ **NIC** ◇ 28-29 B 5
Santo Tomas ○ **PA** ◇ 28-29 C 7
Santo Tomás, Punta ▲ **MEX** ♦ 16-17 C 4
Santo Tomás, Volcán ▲ **GCA** ◇ 28-29 J 4
Santo Tomé ○ **RA** ♦ 32-33 L 3
San Vicente ☆ **ES** ◇ 28-29 K 5
San Vito ○ **CR** ◇ 28-29 C 7
San Vito, Capo ▲ **I** ◇ 46-47 D 5 ♦ 34-35 O 8
San Xavier Indian Reservation X **USA** ◇ 20-21 J 9
Sanya ○· **CHN** ♦ 54-55 K 8
San Ysidro ○ **USA** ◇ 26-27 D 2
Sanza Pombo ○ **ANG** ♦ 50-51 E 3
São Amaro ○· **BR** ♦ 30-31 M 7
São Antônio da Abunari ○ **BR** ♦ 30-31 G 5
São Antônio de Jesus ○ **BR** ♦ 30-31 M 7
São Borja ○ **BR** ♦ 32-33 L 3
São Carlos ○ **BR** ♦ 32-33 N 2
São Felix do Araguaia ○ **BR** ♦ 30-31 J 7
São Felix do Xingu ○ **BR** ♦ 30-31 J 6
São Francisco, Rio ~ **BR** ♦ 30-31 M 6
São Francisco do Sul ○ **BR** ♦ 32-33 N 3
São Gabriel ○ **BR** ♦ 32-33 M 4
São Gotardo ○ **BR** ♦ 30-31 K 8
São João, Ilha de ⌒ **BR** ♦ 30-31 L 5
São João del Rei ○· **BR** ♦ 32-33 O 2
São João do Piauí ○ **BR** ♦ 30-31 L 6
São Jorge, Ilha de ⌒ **P** ♦ 34-35 F 8
São José do Rio Preto ○ **BR** ♦ 32-33 N 2
São José dos Campos ○ **BR** ♦ 32-33 N 2
São José do Xingu ○ **BR** ♦ 30-31 J 7
São Lourenço, Rio ~ **BR** ♦ 30-31 H 8
São Luís ☆· **BR** ♦ 30-31 L 5
São Mateus ○ **BR** ♦ 30-31 M 8
São Miguel, Ilha de ⌒ **P** ♦ 34-35 F 8
São Miguel do Araguaia ○ **BR** ♦ 30-31 J 7
São Miguel do Tapuio ○ **BR** ♦ 30-31 L 6
Saona, Isla ⌒ **DOM** ♦ 16-17 N 7
Saône ~ **F** ◇ 38-39 L 7 ♦ 34-35 N 6
São Paulo □ **BR** ♦ 32-33 N 2
São Paulo ☆· **BR** (PAU) ♦ 32-33 N 2
São Raimundo Nonato ○ **BR** ♦ 30-31 L 6
São Sebastião, Ilha de ⌒ **BR** ♦ 32-33 N 2
São Sebastião, Ponta ▲ **MOC** ♦ 50-51 J 6
São Tomé ★ **STP** ♦ 50-51 C 1
São Tomé ⌒ **STP** ♦ 50-51 C 1
São Tomé, Cabo de ▲ **BR** ♦ 32-33 O 2
São Tomé and Príncipe ■ **STP** ♦ 50-51 C 1
Saouayane, Pointe ▲ **CDN** ◇ 18-19 E 3
Saoura, Oued ~ **DZ** ♦ 48-49 E 3
São Vicente ○ **BR** ♦ 32-33 N 2
São Vicente, Cabo de ▲ **P** ◇ 44-45 C 6 ♦ 34-35 K 8
Sape ○ **RI** ♦ 58-59 G 8
Sapele ○ **WAN** ♦ 48-49 G 7
Sapelo Island ⌒ **USA** ◇ 24-25 H 4
Sapo, Serranía del ▲ **PA** ◇ 28-29 E 8
Sapodilla Cays ⌒ **BH** ◇ 28-29 K 3
Sapphire Mountains ▲ **USA** ◇ 20-21 H 2
Sappho ○ **USA** ◇ 20-21 B 1
Sapporo ☆ **J** ♦ 54-55 R 3
Sapri ○ **I** ◇ 46-47 E 4 ♦ 34-35 P 7
Sapulpa ○ **USA** ◇ 26-27 J 1
Sapulut ○ **MAL** ♦ 58-59 G 6
Šaqqat al-Ḩarița ∸ **KSA** ♦ 56-57 F 7
Saqqez ○ **IR** ♦ 56-57 F 3
Šaqrā' ○ **KSA** ♦ 56-57 E 5
Šaqrā' ○ **Y** ♦ 56-57 F 8
Saraar, Bannaanka ∸ **SP** ♦ 48-49 P 7
Saraburi ○ **THA** ♦ 58-59 D 4
Sarajevo ★ **BIH** ◇ 46-47 G 3 ♦ 34-35 P 7
Saraland ○ **USA** ◇ 24-25 D 4
Saranac Lake ○ **USA** ◇ 22-23 L 3
Saransk ○ **RUS** ♦ 34-35 V 5
Sarapul ☆ **RUS** ♦ 34-35 W 4
Sarasota ○ **USA** ◇ 24-25 G 6 ♦ 16-17 K 5
Saratoga National Historic Park ∴ **USA** ◇ 22-23 M 4
Saratoga Springs ○ **USA** ◇ 22-23 M 4
Saratov ☆ **RUS** ♦ 34-35 V 5
Saratovskoe vodohranilišče < **RUS** ♦ 34-35 V 5
Saratovskoye Vodokhranilishche = Saratovskoe vodohr. < **RUS** ♦ 34-35 V 5
Šaraura, aš- ○ **KSA** ♦ 56-57 F 7
Saravan ○ **LAO** ♦ 58-59 E 3
Sarawak □ **MAL** ♦ 58-59 F 6
Šarbakty ○ **KZ** ♦ 52-53 M 7
Šarbitāt, Ra's ▲ **OM** ♦ 56-57 H 7
Sardanga ○ **RUS** ♦ 52-53 U 5
Sardinia ⌒ **I** ◇ 46-47 A 4 ♦ 34-35 N 7
Sardis Lake ⊖ **USA** (MS) ◇ 24-25 D 2
Sardis Lake ⊖ **USA** (OK) ◇ 26-27 K 2
Sar-e Pol-e Ẕahāb ○· **IR** ♦ 56-57 F 4
Sargasso Sea ≈ ♦ 16-17 M 4
Sargodha ○ **PK** ♦ 56-57 L 4
Sarh ☆ **TCH** ♦ 48-49 J 7
Sarḩad ∸ **IR** ♦ 56-57 J 5
Sārī ☆· **IR** ♦ 56-57 G 3
Šarifa, Ğazīrat ⌒ **KSA** ♦ 56-57 E 6
Sarigan ⌒ **USA** ♦ 58-59 N 3
Sarina ○ **AUS** ♦ 60-61 K 4
Šāriqa, aš- ○ **UAE** ♦ 56-57 H 5
Sarir Kalanshiyū ∸ **LAR** ♦ 48-49 K 3
Sariwon ○ **KOR** ♦ 54-55 O 4
Šar'ja ○ **RUS** ♦ 34-35 V 4
Sarlat-la-Canéda ○ **F** ◇ 38-39 H 9 ♦ 34-35 L 7
Šarm aš-Šaiḩ ○· **ET** ♦ 48-49 M 3
Sarmette ○ **VAN** ♦ 60-61 O 3
Sarmi ○ **RI** ♦ 58-59 L 7
Sarmiento ○ **RA** ♦ 32-33 J 7
Sarnia ○ **CDN** ◇ 18-19 C 7 ♦ 14-15 U 8
Sarny ○ **UA** ♦ 34-35 R 5
Sarre ~ **F** ◇ 38-39 L 7 ♦ 34-35 N 6
Sarre, La ○ **CDN** ◇ 18-19 E 4
Sarrebourg ○ **F** ◇ 38-39 L 7 ♦ 34-35 N 6
Sarstoon River ~ **BH** ◇ 28-29 K 4
Sartang ~ **RUS** ♦ 52-53 X 4
Sarthe ~ **F** ◇ 38-39 G 8 ♦ 34-35 L 6
Saryesik Atyrau ∸ **KZ** ♦ 52-53 M 8
Sarygamyš köli ○ **TM** ♦ 56-57 H 2
Saryözek ○ **KZ** ♦ 52-53 M 9
Saryšağan ○ **KZ** ♦ 52-53 L 8
Sarysu ~ **KZ** ♦ 52-53 K 8
Sary-Taš ○ **KS** ♦ 56-57 L 3
Sasabe ○ **USA** ◇ 20-21 J 10
Sasarām ○ **IND** ♦ 56-57 N 6
Sasebo ○ **J** ♦ 54-55 O 5
Saskatchewan □ **CDN** ♦ 14-15 P 6
Saskatchewan River ~ **CDN** ♦ 14-15 Q 6
Saskatoon ○ **CDN** ♦ 14-15 P 6
Saskylah ○ **RUS** ♦ 52-53 T 3
Saslaya, Cerro ▲ **NIC** ◇ 28-29 B 5
Saslaya, Parque Nacional ⊥ **NIC** ◇ 28-29 B 5
Sassafras Mountain ▲ **USA** ◇ 24-25 G 2
Sassandra ☆· **CI** (SAS) ♦ 48-49 D 8
Sassandra ~ **CI** ♦ 48-49 D 7
Sàssari ☆· **I** ◇ 46-47 B 4 ♦ 34-35 N 7
Satadougou-Tintiba ○ **RMM** ♦ 48-49 C 6
Satagaj ○ **RUS** ♦ 52-53 V 5
Satawal Island ~ **FSM** ♦ 58-59 N 5
Satengar, Kepulauan ⌒ **RI** ♦ 58-59 G 8
Satilla River ~ **USA** ◇ 24-25 H 4
Satipo ○ **PE** ♦ 30-31 E 7
Sato ○ **J** ♦ 54-55 O 5
Sātpura Range ▲ **IND** ♦ 56-57 L 6
Satsuma-hantō ⌣ **J** ♦ 54-55 P 5
Satsunan-shotō ⌒ **J** ♦ 54-55 O 6
Satu Mare ☆ **RO** ♦ 34-35 Q 6
Sauce ○ **RA** ♦ 32-33 L 4
Sauce, El ○ **NIC** ◇ 28-29 L 5
Saucier ○ **USA** ◇ 24-25 D 4
Saudi Arabia ■ **KSA** ♦ 56-57 E 6
Sauk City ○ **USA** ◇ 22-23 D 4
Saül ○ **F** ♦ 30-31 J 4
Sauldre ~ **F** ◇ 38-39 J 8 ♦ 34-35 M 6
Saulieu ○ **F** ◇ 38-39 K 8 ♦ 34-35 M 6
Sault Sainte-Marie ○ **CDN** ♦ 14-15 U 7
Sault Sainte Marie ○ **USA** ◇ 22-23 F 2
Saumarez Reef ⌒ **AUS** ♦ 60-61 L 4
Saumlakki ○· **RI** ♦ 58-59 K 8
Saumur ○· **F** ◇ 38-39 G 8 ♦ 34-35 L 6
Sauqira ○ **OM** ♦ 56-57 H 7
Sauqira Bay ≈ ♦ 56-57 H 7
Saurimo ☆ **ANG** ♦ 50-51 F 3
Sausalito ○· **USA** ◇ 20-21 C 7
Sauvolles, Lac ⊖ **CDN** ◇ 18-19 H 2
Sava ~ **BIH** ◇ 46-47 G 2 ♦ 34-35 P 6
Savá ○ **HN** ◇ 28-29 L 4
Savage Cove ○ **CDN** ◇ 18-19 Q 3
Savanna ○ **USA** ◇ 22-23 C 4
Savannah ○ **USA** (TN) ◇ 24-25 D 2
Savannah ○·· **USA** (GA) ◇ 24-25 H 3 ♦ 16-17 K 4
Savannah River ~ **USA** ◇ 24-25 H 3 ♦ 16-17 K 4
Savannah River Plant xx **USA** ◇ 24-25 G 3
Savannakhét ○·· **LAO** ♦ 58-59 D 3
Savanna-la-Mar ○ **JA** ♦ 16-17 L 7
Savant Lake ○ **CDN** ♦ 14-15 S 6
Savè ○ **DY** ♦ 48-49 F 7
Save ~ **F** ◇ 38-39 H 10 ♦ 34-35 M 7
Save, Rio ~ **MOC** ♦ 50-51 H 6
Savoie ∸ **F** ◇ 38-39 L 9 ♦ 34-35 N 6
Savona ☆· **I** ◇ 46-47 B 2 ♦ 34-35 N 7
Savu Sea ≈ ♦ 58-59 H 8
Sawai Mādhopur ○ **IND** ♦ 56-57 M 5
Sawbill ○ **CDN** ◇ 18-19 L 2
Sawmill ○ **USA** ◇ 26-27 C 2
Sawtooth Mountains ▲ **USA** ◇ 20-21 G 3
Sawtooth National Recreation Area ⊥ **USA** ◇ 20-21 G 4
Sawu, Pulau ⌒ **RI** ♦ 58-59 H 9
Saxon ○ **USA** ◇ 22-23 C 2
Sayabec ○ **CDN** ◇ 18-19 L 4
Sayaxché ○ **GCA** ◇ 28-29 J 3
Sayil ∴· **MEX** ◇ 28-29 K 1
Saylor Creek Aerial Gunnery Range xx **USA** ◇ 20-21 G 4
Sayre ○ **USA** (OK) ◇ 26-27 H 2
Sayre ○ **USA** (PA) ◇ 22-23 K 5
Sayula ○ **MEX** ◇ 28-29 C 2
Sayula de Alemán ○ **MEX** ◇ 28-29 G 3
Scaër ○ **F** ◇ 38-39 F 7 ♦ 34-35 L 6
Scandinavia ⌣ ♦ 34-35 O 3
Scarborough ○ **TT** ♦ 16-17 O 8
Sceccai Reba ▲ **ER** ♦ 48-49 N 5
Schefferville ○ **CDN** ♦ 14-15 X 6
Schell Creek Range ▲ **USA** ◇ 20-21 G 6
Schenectady ○ **USA** ◇ 22-23 M 4 ♦ 14-15 W 8
Schoodic Point ▲ **USA** ◇ 22-23 P 3
Schulenburg ○ **USA** ◇ 26-27 J 5
Schwaner, Pegunungan ▲ **RI** ♦ 58-59 F 7
Schwarzwald ▲ **D** ◇ 40-41 K 4 ♦ 34-35 N 6
Schwatka Mountains ▲ **USA** ♦ 14-15 E 3
Schweitzergletscher ⊂ **ANT** ♦ 13 F 33
Schweizerland ∸ **GRØ** ♦ 14-15 d 3
Schwerin ☆· **D** ◇ 40-41 L 2 ♦ 34-35 O 5
Scie, La ○ **CDN** ◇ 18-19 R 4
Scioto River ~ **USA** ◇ 22-23 G 6
Scipio ○ **USA** ◇ 20-21 H 6
Scotia ○ **USA** ◇ 20-21 B 5
Scotia Ridge ≃ ♦ 7 F 10
Scotia Sea ≈ ♦ 7 F 10
Scotstown ○ **CDN** ◇ 18-19 J 6
Scott ○ **ANT** ♦ 13 F 17
Scott, Cape ▲ **CDN** ♦ 14-15 L 6
Scott Glacier ⊂ **ANT** ♦ 13 E 0
Scott Range ▲ **ANT** ♦ 13 G 6
Scott Reef ⌒ **AUS** ♦ 60-61 E 2
Scottsbluff ○ **USA** ♦ 16-17 F 2
Scottsboro ○ **USA** ◇ 24-25 E 2
Scottsburg ○ **USA** ◇ 22-23 F 6
Scottsdale ○ **USA** ◇ 20-21 J 9
Scottsville ○ **USA** ◇ 22-23 E 7
Scottville ○ **USA** ◇ 22-23 E 4
Scotty's Junction ○ **USA** ◇ 20-21 F 7
Scranton ○ **USA** ◇ 22-23 L 5 ♦ 16-17 L 2
Ščučij hrebet ▲ **RUS** ♦ 52-53 e 4
Ščučinsk ☆ **KZ** ♦ 52-53 L 7
Seaford ○ **USA** ◇ 22-23 L 6
Sea Islands ⌒ **USA** ◇ 24-25 H 4 ♦ 16-17 K 4
Seal Cove ○ **CDN** ◇ 18-19 Q 4
Seale ○ **USA** ◇ 24-25 F 3
Seal River ~ **CDN** ♦ 14-15 R 5
Sealy ○ **USA** ◇ 26-27 J 5
Searchlight ○ **USA** ◇ 20-21 G 8
Searcy ○ **USA** ◇ 26-27 M 2 ♦ 16-17 H 3
Seaside ○ **USA** ◇ 20-21 C 3
Seattle ○· **USA** ◇ 20-21 C 2 ♦ 14-15 M 7
Sébaco ○ **NIC** ◇ 28-29 L 5
Sebago Lake ⊖ **USA** ◇ 22-23 N 4
Sebastian ○ **USA** ◇ 24-25 H 6
Sebastián Vizcaíno, Bahía de ≈ ♦ 16-17 D 5
Sebayan, Gunung ▲ **RI** ♦ 58-59 F 7
Sebol ○ **GCA** ◇ 28-29 K 4
Sebree ○ **USA** ◇ 22-23 E 7
Sebring ○ **USA** ◇ 24-25 H 6
Sebta = Ceuta ○ **E** ◇ 44-45 E 7 ♦ 34-35 L 8
Sebuku, Teluk ≈ ♦ 58-59 G 6
Seca, Pampa ∸ **RA** ♦ 32-33 J 5
Sechura ○ **PE** ♦ 30-31 C 6
Sechura, Desierto de ∸ **PE** ♦ 30-31 C 6
Second Mesa ○ **USA** ◇ 26-27 B 2
Secunderābād ○ **IND** ♦ 56-57 M 7
Sedan ○ **AUS** ♦ 60-61 H 6
Sedan ○ **F** ◇ 38-39 K 7 ♦ 34-35 M 6
Sedan ○ **USA** ◇ 26-27 J 1
Sedona ○ **USA** ◇ 20-21 J 8
Sedow Deep ≃ ♦ 13 A 0
Sedro Woolley ○ **USA** ◇ 20-21 C 1
Seeheim ○ **NAM** ♦ 50-51 E 7
Seeley Lake ○ **USA** ◇ 20-21 H 2
Segamat ○ **MAL** ♦ 58-59 D 6
Ségou ☆ **RMM** ♦ 48-49 D 6
Segré ○ **F** ◇ 38-39 G 8 ♦ 34-35 L 6
Seguam Island ⌒ **USA** ♦ 14-15 B 6
Seguedine ○ **RN** ♦ 48-49 H 4
Séguéla ☆ **CI** ♦ 48-49 D 7
Seguin ○ **USA** ◇ 26-27 J 5 ♦ 16-17 G 5
Sehwān ○·· **PK** ♦ 56-57 K 5
Seikan Tunnel ·· **J** ♦ 54-55 R 3
Seiling ○ **USA** ◇ 26-27 H 1
Seille ~ **F** ◇ 38-39 K 8 ♦ 34-35 M 6
Seine ~ **F** ◇ 38-39 H 7 ♦ 34-35 M 6
Sejmčan ☆· **RUS** ♦ 52-53 b 5
Sekondi-Takoradi ☆· **GH** ♦ 48-49 E 8
Šelagskij, mys ▲ **RUS** ♦ 52-53 f 3
Selah ○ **USA** ◇ 20-21 D 2
Selaru, Pulau ⌒ **RI** ♦ 58-59 K 8
Selawik Lake ⊖ **USA** ♦ 14-15 D 3
Selayar, Pulau ⌒ **RI** ♦ 58-59 H 8
Selebi-Phikwe ○ **RB** ♦ 50-51 G 6
Šelek ○ **KZ** ♦ 56-57 M 2
Selemdža ~ **RUS** ♦ 52-53 X 7
Selenga ~ **RUS** ♦ 52-53 S 7
Sèlèngè mörön ~ **MAU** ♦ 54-55 J 2
Selenginsk ○ **RUS** ♦ 52-53 S 7
Sélestat ○· **F** ◇ 38-39 L 7 ♦ 34-35 N 6
Sélibabi ☆ **RIM** ♦ 48-49 C 5
Seligman ○ **USA** (AZ) ◇ 20-21 H 8
Seligman ○ **USA** (MO) ◇ 26-27 L 1
Šelihova, zaliv ≈ ♦ 52-53 c 5
Sélingue, Lac de < **RMM** ♦ 48-49 D 6
Selinsgrove ○ **USA** ◇ 22-23 K 5
Selleck ○ **USA** ◇ 20-21 D 2
Selles-sur-Cher ○ **F** ◇ 38-39 H 8 ♦ 34-35 M 6
Sells ○ **USA** ◇ 20-21 J 10
Selma ○ **USA** (AL) ◇ 24-25 E 3 ♦ 16-17 J 4
Selma ○ **USA** (CA) ◇ 20-21 E 7
Selmer ○ **USA** ◇ 24-25 D 2
Selous Game Reserve ⊥··· **EAT** ♦ 50-51 J 3
Selvagens, Ilhas ⌒ **P** ♦ 48-49 B 2
Selvas ∸ **BR** ♦ 30-31 F 5
Selway-Bitterroot Wilderness ⊥ **USA** ◇ 20-21 G 2
Selway Falls ~ **USA** ◇ 20-21 G 2
Selway River ~ **USA** ◇ 20-21 G 2
Selwyn Mountains ▲ **CDN** ♦ 14-15 K 3
Semarang ☆ **RI** ♦ 58-59 F 8
Semej ○ **KZ** ♦ 52-53 N 7
Semidi Islands ⌒ **USA** ♦ 14-15 E 5
Semillero ○ **GCA** ◇ 28-29 J 4
Seminole ○ **USA** ◇ 26-27 F 3
Seminole, Lake < **USA** ◇ 24-25 F 4
Semitau ○ **RI** ♦ 58-59 F 6
Semnān ☆· **IR** ♦ 56-57 G 3
Senachwine Lake ⊖ **USA** ◇ 22-23 D 5
Senador José Porfírio ○ **BR** ♦ 30-31 J 5
Senador Pompeu ○ **BR** ♦ 30-31 M 6
Sena Madureira ○ **BR** ♦ 30-31 F 6
Senatobia ○ **USA** ◇ 24-25 D 2
Sendai ○ **J** ♦ 54-55 P 5
Seneca ○ **USA** (OR) ◇ 20-21 E 3
Seneca ○ **USA** (SC) ◇ 24-25 G 2
Seneca Caverns ∴ **USA** ◇ 22-23 J 6
Seneca Falls ○ **USA** ◇ 22-23 K 4
Seneca Lake ⊖ **USA** ◇ 22-23 K 4
Senecaville Lake ⊖ **USA** ◇ 22-23 H 6
Senegal ■ **SN** ♦ 48-49 B 6
Sénégal ~ **SN** ♦ 48-49 C 5
Seney ○ **USA** ◇ 22-23 F 2
Senhor do Bonfim ○ **BR** ♦ 30-31 L 7
Sennār ☆· **SUD** ♦ 48-49 M 6
Senneterre ○ **CDN** ◇ 18-19 F 4
Sens ○ **F** ◇ 38-39 J 7 ♦ 34-35 M 6
Sentarum, Danau ⊖ **RI** ♦ 58-59 F 6
Sentinel Range ▲ **ANT** ♦ 13 F 28
Seoni ○ **IND** ♦ 56-57 M 6
Seoul = Sŏul ★ **ROK** ♦ 54-55 O 4
Separ ○ **USA** ◇ 26-27 C 3
Separation Point ○ **CDN** ◇ 18-19 Q 2
Sepik River ~ **PNG** ♦ 58-59 M 7
Sept-Îles ○ **CDN** ◇ 18-19 L 3 ♦ 14-15 X 6
Sept-Îles, Baie des ≈ ◇ 18-19 L 3
Sequoia National Park ⊥ **USA** ◇ 20-21 E 7 ♦ 16-17 C 3
Sequoyah Caverns ∴· **USA** ◇ 24-25 F 2
Sequoyah's Cabin ∴ **USA** ◇ 26-27 K 2
Serafina ○ **USA** ◇ 26-27 E 2
Seram, Pulau ⌒ **RI** ♦ 58-59 J 7
Serang ○ **RI** ♦ 58-59 E 8
Serasan, Pulau ⌒ **RI** ♦ 58-59 E 6
Serasan, Selat ≈ ♦ 58-59 E 6
Serein ~ **F** ◇ 38-39 K 8 ♦ 34-35 M 6
Seremban ☆· **MAL** ♦ 58-59 D 6
Serena, La ☆· **RCH** ♦ 32-33 H 3
Serengeti National Park ⊥··· **EAT** ♦ 50-51 H 2
Serengeti Plain ⌣ **EAT** ♦ 50-51 H 2
Sergeja Kirova, ostrova ⌒ **RUS** ♦ 52-53 O 2
Sergipe □ **BR** ♦ 30-31 M 7
Sermata, Pulau ⌒ **RI** ♦ 58-59 J 8
Serov ☆ **RUS** ♦ 52-53 J 6
Serowe ☆ **RB** ♦ 50-51 G 6
Serpent Mound State Memorial ∴· **USA** ◇ 22-23 G 6
Serpuhov ☆· **RUS** ◇ 42-43 P 4 ♦ 34-35 T 5
Serpukhov = Serpuhov ☆· **RUS** ◇ 42-43 P 4 ♦ 34-35 T 5
Serra da Canastra, Parque Nacional da ⊥ **BR** ♦ 32-33 N 2
Serra do Divisor, Parque Nacional da ⊥ **BR** ♦ 30-31 E 6
Serra do Navio ○ **BR** ♦ 30-31 J 4
Serrana, Banco de ≃ ♦ 16-17 K 8
Serranilla, Banco de ≃ ♦ 16-17 L 7
Serranópolis ○ **BR** ♦ 30-31 J 8
Serres ○ **F** ◇ 38-39 K 9 ♦ 34-35 N 6
Serrinha ○ **BR** ♦ 30-31 M 7
Sertânia ○ **BR** ♦ 30-31 M 6
Sertão ∸ **BR** ♦ 30-31 L 7
Sertão de Camapuã ∸ **BR** ♦ 30-31 J 8
Serule ○ **RB** ♦ 50-51 G 6
Seruyan ~ **RI** ♦ 58-59 F 7
Sese Islands ⌒ **EAU** ♦ 50-51 H 2
Sesepe ○ **RI** ♦ 58-59 J 7
Sesfontein ○ **NAM** ♦ 50-51 D 5
Sesuntepeque ☆ **ES** ◇ 28-29 K 5
Sète ○ **F** ◇ 38-39 J 10 ♦ 34-35 M 7
Sete Lagoas ○ **BR** ♦ 30-31 L 8
Sétif ☆ **DZ** ♦ 48-49 G 1
Settat ☆ **MA** ♦ 48-49 D 2
Sette-Daban, hrebet ▲ **RUS** ♦ 52-53 Y 5
Setúbal ○ **P** ◇ 44-45 C 5 ♦ 34-35 K 8
Setúbal, Baía de ≈ ◇ 44-45 C 5 ♦ 34-35 K 8
Seul, Lac ⊖ **CDN** ♦ 14-15 S 6
Sevan, ozero ⊖ **AR** ♦ 34-35 V 7
Sevastopol' ○·· **UA** ♦ 34-35 S 7
Seven Lakes ○ **USA** ◇ 26-27 D 2
Severnaja Dvina ~ **RUS** ♦ 34-35 U 3
Severnaja Sos'va ~ **RUS** ♦ 52-53 J 5
Severnaya Dvina = Severnaja Dvina ~ **RUS** ♦ 34-35 U 3
Severn River ~ **CDN** ♦ 14-15 T 6
Severnye uvaly ▲ **RUS** ♦ 34-35 V 4
Severobajkal'sk ☆ **RUS** ♦ 52-53 S 6
Severodvinsk ○ **RUS** ♦ 34-35 T 3
Severo-Enisejsk ☆ **RUS** ♦ 52-53 P 5
Severo-Kuril'sk ○ **RUS** ♦ 52-53 c 7
Severy ○ **USA** ◇ 26-27 J 1
Sevier ○ **USA** ◇ 20-21 H 6
Sevier Bridge Reservoir < **USA** ◇ 20-21 H 6
Sevier Desert ∸ **USA** ◇ 20-21 H 6
Sevier Lake ⊖ **USA** ◇ 20-21 H 6 ♦ 16-17 D 3
Sevier River ~ **USA** ◇ 20-21 H 6 ♦ 16-17 D 3
Sevilla ○··· **E** ◇ 44-45 E 6 ♦ 34-35 K 8
Sèvre Niortaise ~ **F** ◇ 38-39 G 8 ♦ 34-35 L 6
Sewa ~ **WAL** ♦ 48-49 C 7
Sewanee ○ **USA** ◇ 24-25 F 2
Seward ○ **USA** ♦ 14-15 G 4
Seward Peninsula ⌣ **USA** ♦ 14-15 C 3
Seychelles ■ **SY** ♦ 50-51 L 4
Seyðisfjörður ☆ **IS** ◇ 36-37 f 2 ♦ 34-35 J 2
Seymour ○ **USA** (IN) ◇ 22-23 F 6
Seymour ○ **USA** (TX) ◇ 26-27 H 3
Sézanne ○ **F** ◇ 38-39 J 7 ♦ 34-35 M 6
Sfax ☆ **TN** ♦ 48-49 H 2
's-Gravenhage = Den Haag ○·· **NL** ◇ 40-41 H 2 ♦ 34-35 M 5
Shaanxi □ **CHN** ♦ 54-55 K 5
Shabeelle, Webi ~ **SP** ♦ 48-49 P 8
Shabogamo Lake ⊖ **CDN** ◇ 18-19 L 2
Shabunda ○ **ZRE** ♦ 50-51 G 2
Shache ○ **CHN** ♦ 54-55 D 4
Shackleton Ice Shelf ⊂ **ANT** ♦ 13 G 10
Shackleton Inlet ≈ ♦ 13 E 0
Shackleton Range ▲ **ANT** ♦ 13 E 0
Shafter ○ **USA** ◇ 26-27 E 5
Shagein ▲ **EAT** ♦ 50-51 J 2
Shahdol ○ **IND** ♦ 56-57 N 6
Shahhāt ∴··· **LAR** ♦ 48-49 K 2
Shakawe ○ **RB** ♦ 50-51 F 5
Shakertown ∴ **USA** ◇ 22-23 F 7
Shallotte ○ **USA** ◇ 24-25 J 3
Shaluli Shan ▲ **CHN** ♦ 54-55 H 5
Shambe ○ **SUD** ♦ 48-49 M 7
Shamokin ○ **USA** ◇ 22-23 K 5
Shamrock ○ **USA** ◇ 26-27 G 2
Shandong □ **CHN** ♦ 54-55 M 4
Shandong Bandao ⌣ **CHN** ♦ 54-55 N 4
Shanghai ☆·· **CHN** ♦ 54-55 N 5
Shanghai Shi □ **CHN** ♦ 54-55 N 5
Shangqiu ○ **CHN** ♦ 54-55 M 5
Shangrao ○ **CHN** ♦ 54-55 M 6
Shangzhi ○ **CHN** ♦ 54-55 O 2
Shanngaw Taungdan ▲ **MYA** ♦ 54-55 H 6
Shantarskiye Ostrova = Šantarskie, ostrova ⌒ **RUS** ♦ 52-53 Y 6
Shantou ○ **CHN** ♦ 54-55 M 7
Shantung Peninsula = Shandong Bandao ⌣ **CHN** ♦ 54-55 N 4
Shanxi □ **CHN** ♦ 54-55 L 4
Shaoguan ○· **CHN** ♦ 54-55 L 7
Shaowu ○ **CHN** ♦ 54-55 M 6
Shaoxing ○ **CHN** ♦ 54-55 N 5
Shaoyang ○ **CHN** ♦ 54-55 L 6
Sharbot Lake ○ **CDN** ◇ 18-19 F 6
Shark Bay ⊥··· **AUS** ♦ 60-61 C 5
Sharon ○ **USA** ◇ 22-23 H 5
Shashemenē ○ **ETH** ♦ 48-49 N 7
Shashi ○ **CHN** ♦ 54-55 L 5
Shasta, Mount ○ **USA** (CA) ◇ 20-21 C 5
Shasta, Mount ▲ **USA** (CA) ◇ 20-21 C 5 ♦ 14-15 M 8
Shasta Caverns, Lake ∴ **USA** ◇ 20-21 C 5
Shasta Lake ⊖ **USA** ◇ 20-21 C 5
Shaw ○ **USA** ◇ 26-27 M 4
Shawano ○ **USA** ◇ 22-23 D 3
Shawinigan ○ **CDN** ◇ 18-19 H 5
Shawnee ○ **USA** ◇ 26-27 J 2
Shawneetown State Historic Site ∴ **USA** ◇ 22-23 D 7
Shawville ○ **CDN** ◇ 18-19 F 6
Shaykh Gok ○ **SUD** ♦ 48-49 M 6
Shea ○ **GUY** ♦ 30-31 H 4
Sheahan ○ **CDN** ◇ 18-19 D 5
Sheboygan ○ **USA** ◇ 22-23 E 4 ♦ 14-15 T 8
Shediac ○ **CDN** ◇ 18-19 M 5
Sheep Springs ○ **USA** ◇ 26-27 C 1
Sheet Harbour ○ **CDN** ◇ 18-19 N 6
Sheffield ○ **CDN** ◇ 18-19 L 6
Sheffield ○ **GB** ◇ 38-39 G 5 ♦ 34-35 L 5
Sheffield ○ **USA** (AL) ◇ 24-25 E 2 ♦ 16-17 J 4
Sheffield ○ **USA** (TX) ◇ 26-27 G 4
Sheffield Lake ⊖ **CDN** ◇ 18-19 Q 4
Shelburne ○ **CDN** (NS) ◇ 18-19 M 7
Shelburne ○ **CDN** (ONT) ◇ 18-19 D 6
Shelburne Bay ≈ ♦ 60-61 J 2
Shelburne Museum ∴ **USA** ◇ 22-23 M 3
Shelby ○ **USA** (MT) ◇ 20-21 J 1
Shelby ○ **USA** (NC) ◇ 24-25 H 2
Shelbyville ○ **USA** (IL) ◇ 22-23 D 6
Shelbyville ○ **USA** (IN) ◇ 22-23 F 6
Shelbyville ○ **USA** (TN) ◇ 24-25 E 2
Shelbyville, Lake ⊖ **USA** ◇ 22-23 D 6
Shelekhova, Zaliv = Šelihova, zaliv ≈ ♦ 52-53 c 5
Shelikof Strait ≈ ♦ 14-15 E 5
Shelter Cove ○ **USA** ◇ 20-21 B 5
Shelton ○ **USA** ◇ 20-21 C 2
Shenandoah National Park ⊥ **USA** ◇ 22-23 J 6 ♦ 16-17 L 3
Shenandoah River ~ **USA** ◇ 22-23 J 6
Shendam ○ **WAN** ♦ 48-49 G 7
Shenyang ☆ **CHN** ♦ 54-55 N 3
Shenzhen ○· **CHN** ♦ 54-55 L 7
Shepahua ○ **PE** ♦ 30-31 E 7
Shepherd Islands = Îles Shepherd ⌒ **VAN** ♦ 60-61 O 3
Shepparton-Mooroopna ○ **AUS** ♦ 60-61 J 7
Sherard, Cape ▲ **CDN** ♦ 14-15 V 2
Sherbo Island ⌒ **WAL** ♦ 48-49 C 7
Sherbrooke ○ **CDN** ◇ 18-19 J 6 ♦ 14-15 W 7
Sheridan ○ **USA** (AR) ◇ 26-27 L 2
Sheridan ○ **USA** (WY) ♦ 14-15 P 8
Sheridan, Fort ∴ **USA** ◇ 22-23 E 4
Sherman ○ **USA** ◇ 26-27 J 3 ♦ 16-17 G 4
Sherman Basin ≈ ♦ 14-15 R 3
Sherman Mills ○ **USA** ◇ 22-23 O 3
Sherman Mountain ▲ **USA** ◇ 20-21 G 5
Sherrick, Colline ▲ **CDN** ◇ 18-19 E 3
Shetland Islands ⌒ **GB** ◇ 38-39 G 1 ♦ 34-35 L 3
Shihezi ○ **CHN** ♦ 54-55 F 3
Shijiazhuang ○ **CHN** ♦ 54-55 L 4
Shikārpur ○ **PK** ♦ 56-57 K 5
Shikoku ⌒ **J** ♦ 54-55 P 5
Shikoku Basin ≃ ♦ 54-55 Q 5
Shiliburi ○ **IND** ♦ 56-57 O 5
Shilka = Šilka ~ **RUS** ♦ 52-53 U 7
Shillong ☆·· **IND** ♦ 56-57 P 5
Shimizu ○ **J** ♦ 54-55 Q 4
Shimoga ○ **IND** ♦ 56-57 M 8
Shimono-shima ⌒ **J** ♦ 54-55 O 5
Shingleton ○ **USA** ◇ 22-23 E 2
Shinnston ○ **USA** ◇ 22-23 H 6
Shinyanga ☆ **EAT** ♦ 50-51 H 2
Ship Bottom ○ **USA** ◇ 22-23 L 6
Shippegan ○ **CDN** ◇ 18-19 M 5
Shippegan Island = Île Lameque ⌒ **CDN** ◇ 18-19 M 5
Shiprock ○ **USA** ◇ 26-27 C 1
Shirazehyōga ▲ **ANT** ♦ 13 F 4
Shirley ○ **USA** ◇ 26-27 L 2
Shishaldin Volcano ▲ **USA** ♦ 14-15 D 6
Shivpuri ○· **IND** ♦ 56-57 M 5
Shivwits Plateau ▲ **USA** ◇ 20-21 H 7
Shiyan ○ **CHN** ♦ 54-55 L 5
Shizuishan ○ **CHN** ♦ 54-55 K 4
Shkodër ☆·· **AL** ◇ 46-47 G 3 ♦ 34-35 P 7
Shoshone ○ **USA** (CA) ◇ 20-21 F 8
Shoshone ○ **USA** (ID) ◇ 20-21 G 4
Shoshone Falls ~ **USA** ◇ 20-21 G 4
Shoshone Ice Caves ∴ **USA** ◇ 20-21 G 4
Shoshone Indian Ice Caves · **USA** ◇ 20-21 G 4
Shoshone Mountains ▲ **USA** ◇ 20-21 F 6 ♦ 16-17 C 3
Show Low ○ **USA** ◇ 26-27 B 2
Shreveport ○ **USA** ◇ 26-27 L 3 ♦ 16-17 H 4
Shrewsbury ○ **USA** ◇ 22-23 K 6
Shuangliao ○ **CHN** ♦ 54-55 N 3
Shuanyashan ○ **CHN** ♦ 54-55 P 2
Shubenacadie Indian Reserve X **CDN** ◇ 18-19 N 6
Shubuta ○ **USA** ◇ 24-25 D 4
Shullsburg ○ **USA** ◇ 22-23 C 4
Shumagin Islands ⌒ **USA** ♦ 14-15 D 5
Shumen = Šumen ○ **BG** ♦ 34-35 R 7
Shurayk, ash- ○ **SUD** ♦ 48-49 M 5
Shymkent = Šymkent ☆· **KZ** ♦ 56-57 K 2
Siāhān Range ▲ **PK** ♦ 56-57 J 5
Sian Ka'an Biosphere Reserve X··· **MEX** ◇ 28-29 L 2 ♦ 16-17 J 7
Šiaškotan, ostrov ⌒ **RUS** ♦ 52-53 b 8
Siau, Pulau ⌒ **RI** ♦ 58-59 J 6
Šiauliai ☆·· **LT** ◇ 42-43 H 4 ♦ 34-35 Q 4
Šibam ○··· **Y** ♦ 56-57 F 7
Sibari ○ **I** ◇ 46-47 F 5 ♦ 34-35 P 8
Siberia □ **RUS** ♦ 52-53 O 5
Sibi ○ **PK** ♦ 56-57 K 5
Sibiloi National Park ⊥ **EAK** ♦ 48-49 N 8
Sibirjakova, ostrov ⌒ **RUS** ♦ 52-53 M 3
Sibiti ~ **EAT** ♦ 50-51 H 2
Sibiti ☆ **RCB** ♦ 50-51 D 2
Sibiu ☆· **RO** ♦ 34-35 Q 6
Sibolga ○ **RI** ♦ 58-59 C 6
Siborongborong ○ **RI** ♦ 58-59 C 6
Sibu ○ **MAL** ♦ 58-59 F 6
Sibut ☆ **RCA** ♦ 48-49 J 7
Sibuyan Island ⌒ **RP** ♦ 58-59 H 4
Sibuyan Sea ≈ ♦ 58-59 H 4
Sichuan □ **CHN** ♦ 54-55 J 5
Sicilia ⌒ **I** ◇ 46-47 E 6 ♦ 34-35 O 7
Sicuani ○ **PE** ♦ 30-31 E 7
Siddhapur ○ **IND** ♦ 56-57 L 6
Sidi Barrānī ○ **ET** ♦ 48-49 L 2
Sidi Bel Abbes ☆ **DZ** ♦ 48-49 E 1
Sidi Ifni ○ **MA** ♦ 48-49 C 3
Sidley, Mount ▲ **ANT** ♦ 13 F 24
Sidney ○ **USA** (NY) ◇ 22-23 L 4
Sidney ○ **USA** (OH) ◇ 22-23 F 5
Sidney Lanier, Lake < **USA** ◇ 24-25 G 2
Sidrolândia ○ **BR** ♦ 32-33 M 2
Siĕmréap ○ **K** ♦ 58-59 D 4
Siena ○·· **I** ◇ 46-47 C 3 ♦ 34-35 O 7
Sierra Blanca ○ **USA** ◇ 26-27 E 4
Sierra Blanca Peak ▲ **USA** ◇ 26-27 E 3
Sierra Colorada ○ **RA** ♦ 32-33 J 6
Sierra de Lacandón, Parque Nacional ⊥· **GCA** ◇ 28-29 J 3 ♦ 16-17 H 7
Sierra Grande ○ **RA** ♦ 32-33 J 6
Sierra Leone ■ **WAL** ♦ 48-49 C 7
Sierra Leone Basin ≃ ♦ 48-49 B 8
Sierra Madre ▲ **RP** ♦ 58-59 H 3
Sierra Madre del Sur ▲ **MEX** ◇ 28-29 D 3 ♦ 16-17 F 7
Sierra Madre Occidental ▲ **MEX** ♦ 16-17 E 5
Sierra Madre Oriental ▲ **MEX** ♦ 16-17 F 5
Sierra Morena ▲ **E** ◇ 44-45 D 6 ♦ 34-35 K 8
Sierra Nevada ▲ **E** ◇ 44-45 F 6 ♦ 34-35 L 8
Sierra Nevada de Santa Marta ▲ **CO** ♦ 30-31 E 2
Sierraville ○ **USA** ◇ 20-21 D 6
Sierra Vista ○ **USA** ◇ 26-27 B 4
Sigli ○ **RI** ♦ 58-59 C 5
Signal Hill National Historic Park ⊥· **CDN** ◇ 18-19 S 5
Signal Peak ▲ **USA** ◇ 20-21 G 9
Signy ○ **ANT** ♦ 13 G 32
Sigsbee Deep ≃ ♦ 16-17 H 6
Siguatepeque ○ **HN** ◇ 28-29 L 4
Siguiri ○ **RG** ♦ 48-49 D 6
Sihotė-Alin' ▲ **RUS** ♦ 52-53 X 9
Sikasso ☆ **RMM** ♦ 48-49 D 6
Sikeston ○ **USA** ◇ 22-23 D 7
Sikkim □ **IND** ♦ 56-57 O 5
Sikonge ○ **EAT** ♦ 50-51 H 3
Sikongo ○ **Z** ♦ 50-51 F 5
Siktjah ○ **RUS** ♦ 52-53 V 4
Silao ○ **MEX** ◇ 28-29 D 1
Silchar ○ **IND** ♦ 56-57 P 6
Siler City ○ **USA** ◇ 24-25 J 2
Silhouette Island ⌒ **SY** ♦ 50-51 N 2
Silifke ○ **TR** ♦ 34-35 S 8
Siling Co ⊖ **CHN** ♦ 54-55 F 5
Silistra ○ **BG** ♦ 34-35 R 7
Šilka ○ **RUS** ♦ 52-53 U 7
Šilka ~ **RUS** ♦ 52-53 U 7
Siloam Springs ○ **USA** ◇ 26-27 K 1
Silsbee ○ **USA** ◇ 26-27 K 4
Silva ○ **USA** ◇ 22-23 C 7
Silvassa ☆ **IND** ♦ 56-57 L 6
Silver Bank ≃ ♦ 16-17 N 6
Silver City ○ **USA** ◇ 26-27 C 3
Silver Creek ~ **USA** ◇ 20-21 E 4
Silver Lake ○ **USA** ◇ 20-21 D 4
Silver Plains ○ **AUS** ♦ 60-61 J 2
Silverton ○ **USA** (OR) ◇ 20-21 C 3
Silverton ○ **USA** (TX) ◇ 26-27 G 2
Silvies River ~ **USA** ◇ 20-21 E 4
Silvituc ○ **MEX** ◇ 28-29 J 2
Šimanovsk ☆ **RUS** ♦ 52-53 W 7
Simao ○ **CHN** ♦ 54-55 J 7
Simard, Lac ⊖ **CDN** ◇ 18-19 E 5
Simbirsk ☆ **RUS** ♦ 34-35 V 5
Simcoe ○ **CDN** ◇ 18-19 D 7
Simcoe, Lake ⊖ **CDN** ◇ 18-19 E 6 ♦ 14-15 V 8
Simdega ○ **IND** ♦ 56-57 N 6
Simēn ▲ **ETH** ♦ 48-49 N 6
Simēn National Park ⊥··· **ETH** ♦ 48-49 N 6
Simeulue, Pulau ⌒ **RI** ♦ 58-59 C 6
Simferopol' ☆·· **UA** ♦ 34-35 S 7
Simikot ○ **NEP** ♦ 56-57 N 5
Simi Valley ○ **USA** ◇ 20-21 E 8 ♦ 16-17 C 4
Simla ☆· **IND** ♦ 56-57 M 4
Simlipal National Park ⊥ **IND** ♦ 56-57 O 6
Simmler ○ **USA** ◇ 20-21 E 8
Simojovel de Allende ○ **MEX** ◇ 28-29 H 3
Simpang ○ **RI** ♦ 58-59 D 7
Simplício Mendes ○ **BR** ♦ 30-31 L 6
Simpson Desert ⌣ **AUS** ♦ 60-61 H 5
Simpson Desert National Park ⊥ **AUS** ♦ 60-61 H 5
Simpson Peninsula ⌣ **CDN** ♦ 14-15 T 3
Simušir, ostrov ⌒ **RUS** ♦ 52-53 b 8
Sinai ⌣ **ET** ♦ 48-49 M 3
Sināwin ○ **LAR** ♦ 48-49 H 2
Sincelejo ☆ **CO** ♦ 30-31 D 3
Sinclair, Lake < **USA** ◇ 24-25 G 3
Šindand ○· **AFG** ♦ 56-57 J 4
Sindangbarang ○ **RI** ♦ 58-59 E 8
Sines ○ **P** ◇ 44-45 C 6 ♦ 34-35 K 8
Siné-Saloum, Parc National du ⊥ **SN** ♦ 48-49 B 6
Singa ○· **SUD** ♦ 48-49 M 6
Singapore ■ **SGP** ♦ 58-59 D 6
Singapore ★·· **SGP** ♦ 58-59 D 6
Singaraja ○ **RI** ♦ 58-59 G 8
Singhamton ○ **CDN** ◇ 18-19 D 6
Singida ☆ **EAT** ♦ 50-51 H 2
Singkawang ○ **RI** ♦ 58-59 E 6
Singkep, Pulau ⌒ **RI** ♦ 58-59 D 7
Singleton ○ **AUS** ♦ 60-61 L 6
Sinjaja ~ **RUS** ♦ 52-53 W 5
Sinkāt ○· **SUD** ♦ 48-49 N 5
Sinkiang = Xinjiang Uygur Zizhiqu □ **CHN** ♦ 54-55 E 3
Sinop ○ **BR** ♦ 30-31 H 7
Sinop ☆· **TR** ♦ 34-35 T 7
Sintang ○ **RI** ♦ 58-59 F 6
Sint Eustatius ⌒ **NA** ♦ 16-17 O 7
Sint Maarten ⌒ **NA** ♦ 16-17 O 7
Sinton ○ **USA** ◇ 26-27 J 5
Sinuiju ☆ **KOR** ♦ 54-55 N 3
Sioma Ngwezi National Park ⊥ **Z** ♦ 50-51 F 5
Sioux City ○ **USA** ♦ 16-17 G 2
Sioux Falls ○· **USA** ♦ 16-17 G 2
Sipacate ○ **GCA** ◇ 28-29 J 5
Siping ○ **CHN** ♦ 54-55 N 3
Siple, Mount ▲ **ANT** ♦ 13 F 24
Sipsey Fork ~ **USA** ◇ 24-25 E 2
Siquerres ○ **CR** ◇ 28-29 C 6
Siquia ○ **NIC** ◇ 28-29 B 5
Siquia, Río ~ **NIC** ◇ 28-29 B 5
Siquijor Island ⌒ **RP** ♦ 58-59 H 5
Šira ☆ **RUS** ♦ 52-53 P 7
Širaāz ☆·· **IR** ♦ 56-57 G 5
Siracusa ○ **I** ◇ 46-47 E 6 ♦ 34-35 P 8
Sir Edward Pellew Group ⌒ **AUS** ♦ 60-61 H 3
Sirena ○ **CR** ◇ 28-29 C 7
Siret ~ **RO** ♦ 34-35 R 6
Sirğān ○ **IR** ♦ 56-57 H 5
Şırnak ☆ **TR** ♦ 34-35 U 8
Sironj ○ **IND** ♦ 56-57 M 6
Sir R. Squires Memorial Provincial Park ⊥ **CDN** ◇ 18-19 Q 4
Sirsova Ridge ≃ ♦ 52-53 f 6
Sir Thomas, Mount ▲ **AUS** ♦ 60-61 F 5
Sir-Wilfrid, Mont ▲ **CDN** ◇ 18-19 G 5
Sisal ○ **MEX** ◇ 28-29 J 1
Sisal, Arrecife ⌒ **MEX** ◇ 28-29 J 1
Sisimiut = Holsteinsborg ○ **GRØ** ♦ 14-15 a 3
Siskiyou Mountains ▲ **USA** ◇ 20-21 C 5
Sisŏphŏn ○ **K** ♦ 58-59 D 4

90 **Santa Rosa — Sisŏphŏn**

eron o F ◆ 38-39 K 9
◆ 34-35 N 6
rs o USA ◇ 20-21 D 3
pur o IND ◆ 56-57 N 5
chrétien ∴ CDN ◇ 18-19 K 4
o GR ◆ 46-47 L 7 ◆ 34-35 R 8
da Abadia (KS) ◇ 26-27 H 1
igi Lake o CDN ◆ 14-15 K 3
o Z ◇ 50-51 F 5
na o NIC ◆ 28-29 B 5
ers'kyj Donec' ∴ UA ◆ 34-35 T 6
čij, mys ☆ TR ◆ 34-35 T 8
iola o ET ◇ 48-49 L 3
iola o CR ◆ 28-29 C 7
iola o PA ◇ 28-29 C 7
Lakes o USA ◇ 22-23 E 4
wang Qi o CHN ◆ 54-55 L 3
eldon o GUY ◆ 30-31 H 4
lland ≐ DK ◇ 36-37 E 9
◆ 34-35 O 4
darsko jezero ≈ YU ◆ 46-47 G 3
◆ 34-35 P 7
gerrak ≈ ◇ 36-37 D 8
◆ 34-35 N 4
ight River ~ USA ◇ 20-21 D 1
sgway o USA ◆ 14-15 J 5
o USA ◇ 52-53 L 9
alistyi Golec, gora ▲ RUS
◆ 52-53 L 9
iirgårdshavets nationalpark ⊥ FIN
◆ 34-35 Q 4
ad o CDN ◇ 18-19 D 5
eena Mountains ▲ CDN ◆ 14-15 L 5
eena River ~ CDN ◆ 14-15 L 6
eldon o GUY ◆ 30-31 H 4
o USA ◇ 50-51 D 5
ellefteälven ~ S ◇ 36-37 J 4
◆ 50-51 P 2
atook Lake o USA ◆ 26-27 J 1
owhegan o USA ◇ 22-23 E 4
ikda o DZ ◆ 48-49 G 1
opje ★ MK ◆ 46-47 H 3
◆ 34-35 Q 7
ovorodino o RUS ◆ 52-53 V 7
owhegan o USA ◇ 22-23 E 4
ull Valley Indian Reservation ⋊ USA
20-21 H 5
odie Mountain ▲ USA ◇ 22-23 J 5
ykomish o USA ◇ 20-21 D 2
ykomish River ~ USA ◇ 20-21 D 2
lunig Caverns ∴ USA ◇ 18-19 J 6
amet, Gunung ▲ RI ◆ 58-59 E 8
o USA ◇ 26-27 G 3
ave Coast ⌄ ◇ 48-49 F 7
ave River ~ CDN ◆ 14-15 O 4
eeping Bear Dunes National Lakeshore ⊥
USA ◇ 22-23 E 3
eeper Islands ~ CDN ◆ 14-15 U 5
eeping Bear Dunes National Lakeshore ⊥
USA ◇ 22-23 E 3
idell o USA ◇ 24-25 D 4
odie Mountain ▲ USA ◇ 22-23 J 5
igeach o USA ◇ 22-23 E 4
◆ 34-35 K 5
igo o USA ◇ 22-23 J 6
ven o BG ◆ 34-35 R 7
lovakia ■ SK ◆ 34-35 P 6
lovenia ■ SLO ◆ 46-47 E 2
◆ 34-35 O 6
lovjans'k o USA ◇ 20-21 J 4
lov'yans'k = Slovjans'k o UA
lupsk ☆ • PL ◆ 40-41 O 1
mackover o USA ◇ 26-27 L 3
mall Point o USA ◇ 22-23 O 4
mallwood Reservoir < CDN
14-15 Y 6
marwa o WSA ◆ 48-49 C 3
methport o USA ◇ 22-23 J 5
milla o USA ◇ 34-35 S 6
mith Arm o CDN ◆ 14-15 M 3
mith Bay ≈ USA ◆ 14-15 V 1
mithfield o USA ◇ 24-25 J 2
mithland o USA ◇ 22-23 E 7
mith Mountain Lake o USA
22-23 J 7
mith River o USA ◇ 20-21 B 5
miths o USA ◇ 24-25 E 3
miths Falls o CDN ◇ 18-19 F 6
miths Ferry o USA ◇ 20-21 F 3
mithton o AUS ◆ 60-61 K 8
mithville o USA ◇ 24-25 F 4
moke Creek Desert ≃ USA
20-21 E 5
moky Cape ▲ AUS ◆ 60-61 L 6
moky Hill River ~ USA ◆ 16-17 F 3
moky Mountains ▲ USA ◇ 20-21 G 4
moky River ~ CDN ◆ 14-15 N 6
molensk ★ RUS ◆ 42-43 N 4
◆ 34-35 S 5
moot o USA ◇ 20-21 J 4
nake River ~ USA ◇ 20-21 J 4
14-15 N 7
nake River Canyon • USA ◇ 20-21 F 4
nake River Plains ⌄ USA ◇ 20-21 H 4
17-21 D 2
nohomish o USA ◇ 20-21 C 2
nolualime Pass ▲ USA ◇ 20-21 G 1
nowdonia National Park ⊥ GB
17 L 5
nowflake o USA ◇ 26-27 B 2
now Hill Island ~ ANT ◆ 13 G 31
now Mount ▲ USA ◇ 20-21 D 6
nowshoe Peak ▲ USA ◇ 20-21 G 1
nyder o USA ◇ 26-27 H 5
oalala o RM ◆ 50-51 L 5
oanierana-Ivongo o RM ◆ 50-51 L 5
oa-Siu o RI ◆ 58-59 J 7
obat ≐ SUD ◆ 48-49 M 7
obradinho, Represa de < BR
30-31 L 7
obral o BR ◇ 30-31 L 5
oc o RUS ◆ 34-35 T 7
ociété, Îles de la ~ F ◆ 12 M 4
ocorro o CO ◇ 30-31 E 2
ocorro o USA ◇ 26-27 D 3
ocorro, Isla ~ MEX ◆ 16-17 D 7
ocotra ~ Y ◆ 56-57 G 8

Sodankylä o FIN ◆ 34-35 R 2
Soda Springs o USA ◇ 20-21 J 4
Söderi o SUD ◆ 48-49 L 6
Sodni ~ RM ◆ 50-51 L 5
Soddy-Daisy o USA ◇ 24-25 F 2
Sofala o MOC ◇ 50-51 H 6
Sofia = Sofija ★ • BG ◆ 46-47 J 3
◆ 34-35 Q 7
Sofija ★ • BG ◆ 46-47 J 3
◆ 34-35 Q 7
Sofijsk o RUS ◇ 52-53 Y 7
Sognefjorden ≈ ◇ 36-37 B 6
◆ 34-35 N 3
Sog Xian o CHN ◆ 54-55 G 5
Šojna o RUS ◇ 52-53 d 6
Šokal'skogo, proliv ≈ ◇ 52-53 R 2
Sokhumi = Suchumi ☆ GE ◆ 34-35 U 7
Sokodé ★ RT ◆ 48-49 F 7
Sokol o RUS ◇ 42-43 S 1
Sokoto ★ WAN ◆ 48-49 G 6
Sokoto ~ WAN ◆ 48-49 G 6
Solana Beach o USA ◇ 20-21 F 9
Solander Island ~ NZ ◆ 60-61 O 9
Solāpur o IND ◆ 56-57 M 7
Soledad o CO ◇ 30-31 E 2
Soledad o USA ◇ 20-21 D 7
Soledad o YV ◇ 30-31 G 3
Soledad de Doblado o MEX
28-29 J 2
Solentiname, Archipiélago de ~ NIC
28-29 B 6
Solikamsk ★ RUS ◆ 34-35 X 4
Sololá o GCA ◇ 28-29 J 4
Soloma o GCA ◇ 28-29 J 4
Solomon Islands ~ ◆ 58-59 O 8
Solomon Islands ■ SOL ◆ 60-61 N 2
Solomon River ~ USA ◆ 16-17 G 3
Solomon Sea ≈ ◆ 58-59 N 8
Solon Springs o USA ◇ 22-23 C 2
Soloveckie ostrova ~ RUS
34-35 T 2
Solwezi o Z ◆ 50-51 G 4
Somalia ■ SP ◆ 50-51 L 1
Somali Basin ≃ ◆ 50-51 L 1
Sombrero, El ~ YV ◇ 30-31 F 3
Somers o USA ◇ 20-21 G 1
Somerset o USA (KY) ◇ 22-23 F 7
16-17 K 3
Somerset o USA (MI) ◇ 22-23 F 4
Somerset o USA (PA) ◇ 22-23 J 5
Somerset-Oos o ZA ◆ 50-51 G 8
Somerville o USA (TN) ◇ 24-25 D 2
Somerville o USA (TX) ◇ 26-27 K 4
Somerville Lake o USA ◇ 26-27 J 4
Somes Bar o USA ◇ 20-21 C 5
Somme ~ F ◇ 38-39 H 6
◆ 34-35 M 5
Sommerton o USA ◇ 20-21 G 9
Somotillo o NIC ◇ 28-29 L 5
Somoto o NIC ◇ 28-29 L 5
Sompeta o IND ◆ 56-57 N 7
Sona ~ PA ◇ 28-29 D 7
Sonag o MAL ◆ 58-59 F 6
Songea o EAT ◆ 50-51 J 3
Songhua Jiang ~ CHN ◆ 54-55 O 3
Songkhla o THA ◆ 58-59 D 5
Songnim o KOR ◆ 54-55 O 4
Songo o ANG ◆ 50-51 D 3
Songo Mnara ∴•• EAT ◆ 50-51 J 3
Songpan o CHN ◆ 54-55 J 5
Sonjol, Sungai ~ RI ◆ 58-59 H 6
Sonmiani Bay ≈ ◆ 56-57 K 5
Sono, Rio do ~ BR ◆ 30-31 K 6
Sonoita o USA ◇ 26-27 B 4
Sonoma Range ▲ USA ◇ 20-21 F 5
Sonora o USA (CA) ◇ 20-21 D 7
Sonora o USA (TX) ◇ 26-27 G 3
Sonora, Rio ~ MEX ◇ 16-17 D 5
Sonora Desert ≃ USA ◇ 20-21 G 9
16-17 C 4
Sonoyta o MEX ◇ 16-17 D 4
Sonsón o CO ◇ 30-31 D 2
Sonsonate o ES ◇ 28-29 J 4
Sonsorol Islands ~ USA ◆ 58-59 K 5
So'n Tây, Thi Xä ~ VN ◆ 58-59 L 7
Sopi o RI ◆ 58-59 J 6
Sopron o H ◆ 40-41 O 5
◆ 34-35 P 5
Sore o F ◇ 38-39 G 9 ◆ 34-35 L 6
Sorel o CDN ◇ 18-19 H 5
Sorell-Midway Point o AUS ◆ 60-61 K 8
Soria o E ◆ 44-45 F 4 ◆ 34-35 L 6
Sorocaba o BR ◇ 32-33 N 2
Sorol Atoll ~ FSM ◆ 58-59 M 5
Sorong o RI ◆ 58-59 K 7
Soroti o EAU ◆ 50-51 H 1
Sør-Rondane ▲ ANT ◆ 13 F 3
Sorsogon o RP ◆ 58-59 J 4
Soscumica, Lac o CDN ◇ 18-19 H 5
Sosnowiec o PL ◆ 40-41 P 3
◆ 34-35 P 5
Sotavento, Islas de ~ ◆ 16-17 N 8
Soto la Marina o MEX ◇ 16-17 G 6
Soutia o MEX ◇ 28-29 K 1
Souanké o RCB ◆ 48-49 H 8
Soubré o CI ◆ 48-49 E 7
Soufflets River ~ CDN ◇ 18-19 O 5
Souk Ahras o DZ ◆ 48-49 G 1
Šoul ~ ROK ◆ 54-55 O 4
Soulis Pond o CDN ◇ 18-19 R 4
Sound Hill Cove o USA ◇ 18-19 O 6
Sources, Mont aux ▲ LS ◆ 50-51 G 7
Souris o USA ◆ 14-15 O 7
Souris River ~ USA ◆ 14-15 O 7
Sousa o BR ◇ 30-31 L 5
Sousse o TN ◆ 48-49 H 1
Souterraine, la o F ◇ 38-39 H 8
◆ 34-35 M 6
South, Tanjung ▲ RI ◆ 58-59 F 7
South Africa ■ ZA ◆ 50-51 F 7
South Alligator River ~ AUS
60-61 G 2
Southampton o CDN ◇ 18-19 F 6
Southampton o • GB ◇ 38-39 G 6
◆ 34-35 L 5
Southampton Island ~ CDN

South Andros Island ~ BS ◆ 16-17 L 6
South Aulatsivik Island ~ CDN
14-15 Y 5
South Australia □ AUS ◆ 60-61 H 5
South Australian Basin ≃ ◆ 60-61 D 8
South Baldy ▲ USA ◇ 26-27 D 3
South Banda Basin ≃ ◆ 58-59 J 8
South Baymouth o CDN ◇ 18-19 F 5
South Bend o USA ◇ 22-23 E 5
South Boston o USA ◇ 22-23 J 7
South Branch o USA ◇ 18-19 P 5
South Branch Potomac ~ USA
22-23 J 6
South Brook o CDN ◇ 18-19 Q 4
South Carolina □ USA ◇ 24-25 H 2
16-17 K 4
South Charleston o USA ◇ 22-23 H 2
South China Basin ≃ ◆ 58-59 G 3
South China Sea ≈ ◆ 58-59 F 5
South Cove o USA ◇ 20-21 G 7
South Dakota □ USA ◆ 14-15 Q 8
South East Cape ▲ AUS ◆ 60-61 K 8
South East Point ▲ AUS ◆ 60-61 K 7
Southeast Indian Ridge ≃ ◆ 50-51 O 7
South End o CDN ◆ 14-15 Q 5
Southern Alps ▲ NZ ◆ 60-61 O 8
Southern Cross o AUS ◆ 60-61 D 6
Southern Indian Lake o CDN
14-15 R 5
Southern Long Cays ~ BH ◆ 28-29 K 3
Southern National Park ⊥ SUD
48-49 L 7
Southern Pines o USA ◇ 24-25 H 2
Southern Ute Indian Reservation ⋊ USA
26-27 D 1
South Fiji Basin ≃ ◆ 60-61 P 5
South Fork o USA ◇ 26-27 D 1
South Fork John Day River ~ USA
20-21 E 3
South Fork Owyhee River ~ USA
20-21 F 4
South Fork Salmon River ~ USA
20-21 F 2
South Georgia ~ GB ◇ 32-33 P 8
South Gut Saint Ann's o CDN
18-19 O 5
South Harbour o CDN ◇ 18-19 O 5
South Haven o USA ◇ 22-23 E 4
South Henik Lake o CDN ◆ 14-15 R 4
South Hill o USA ◇ 22-23 J 7
South Island ~ NZ ◆ 60-61 P 8
South Korea ■ ROK ◆ 54-55 O 4
South Lake Tahoe o USA ◇ 20-21 E 6
South Luangwa National Park ⊥ • Z
50-51 H 4
South Magnetic Pole = Magnetic Pole Area
ANT ◆ 13 G 2
South Malosmadulu Atoll ~ MV
56-57 L 9
South Milford o CDN ◇ 18-19 M 6
South Moresby National Park Reserve ⊥ •••
CDN ◆ 14-15 K 6
South Nahanni River ~ CDN
14-15 L 4
South Orkneys ~ GB ◆ 13 G 32
South Padre Island ~ USA ◇ 26-27 J 6
South Paris o USA ◇ 18-19 M 6
South Platte River ~ USA ◆ 16-17 F 2
South Pole ANT ◆ 13 E 0
Southport o AUS ◆ 60-61 K 8
Southport o CDN ◇ 18-19 S 4
South Saskatchewan River ~ CDN
14-15 O 5
South Shetlands ≐ GB ◆ 13 G 30
South Taranaki Bight ≈ ◆ 60-61 P 8
South Tasman Rise ≃ ◆ 13 F 7
South Teton Wilderness Area ⊥ USA
20-21 J 4
South Tucson o USA ◇ 26-27 B 3
South Turkana National Reservoir ⊥ EAK
50-51 J 1
South Twin Island ~ CDN ◇ 18-19 E 2
South Twin Lake o CDN ◇ 18-19 R 4
South West Cape ▲ AUS ◆ 60-61 K 8
Southwest Cape ▲ NZ ◆ 60-61 O 9
Southwest Gander River ~ CDN
18-19 R 4
Southwest Miramichi River ~ CDN
18-19 N 5
Soutpansberg ▲ ZA ◆ 50-51 G 6
Sovetskaja Gavan' o RUS ◆ 52-53 Y 6
Sowa Pan o RB ◆ 50-51 G 6
Soweto o ZA ◆ 50-51 G 7
Sóya-kaikyō ≈ ◆ 54-55 S 2
Soyaló o MEX ◇ 28-29 H 3
Soyo o ANG ◆ 50-51 D 3
Spain ■ E ◆ 44-45 D 4 ◆ 34-35 K 8
Spaniard's Bay o CDN ◇ 18-19 S 5
Spanish River ~ CDN ◇ 18-19 F 5
Spanish River Indian Reserve ⋊ CDN
18-19 O 5
Spanish Town o ••• JA ◇ 16-17 L 7
Sparks o USA ◇ 20-21 E 6
Sparta o USA (GA) ◇ 24-25 G 3
Sparta o USA (NC) ◇ 22-23 H 1
Sparta o USA (TN) ◇ 24-25 F 1
Sparta o USA (WI) ◇ 22-23 C 4
Spartanburg o USA ◇ 24-25 G 2
Spárti o • GR ◆ 46-47 J 4
Spassk-Dal'nij o RUS ◇ 52-53 X 9
Spearman o USA ◇ 26-27 G 1
Speculator o USA ◇ 22-23 L 4
Speke Gulf ≈ EAT ◆ 50-51 H 2
Spence Bay o CDN ◆ 14-15 S 3
Spencer o USA (IN) ◇ 22-23 E 6
Spencer o USA (WV) ◇ 22-23 H 6
Spencer, Cape ▲ USA ◆ 14-15 H 4
Spencer, Cape ▲ AUS ◆ 60-61 H 7
Spencer Gulf ≈ AUS ◆ 60-61 H 7
Spicer Islands ~ CDN ◆ 14-15 V 3
Spiro o USA ◇ 26-27 K 2
Spitzkoppe ▲•• NAM ◆ 50-51 D 6
Split o • HR ◆ 46-47 F 3
◆ 34-35 O 7
Spofford o USA ◇ 26-27 H 4
Spokane o USA ◇ 20-21 F 2
14-15 N 2
Spokane ~ USA ◇ 20-21 F 2

Spokane House ∴ USA ◇ 20-21 F 2
Spokane Indian Reservation ⋊ USA
20-21 F 2
Spokane River ~ USA ◇ 20-21 F 2
Spooner o USA ◇ 22-23 C 3
Spoon River ~ USA ◇ 22-23 C 5
Sporades ~ GR ◆ 46-47 K 6
◆ 34-35 R 8
Spotted Island o CDN (NFL)
18-19 R 2
Spotted Island ~ CDN (NFL)
Sprague o USA ◇ 20-21 F 2
Sprague River ~ USA ◇ 20-21 D 4
Spratly Islands ~ ◆ 58-59 F 4
Spray o USA ◇ 20-21 E 3
Springbok o ZA ◆ 50-51 E 7
Springdale o CDN ◇ 18-19 Q 4
Springdale o USA (AR) ◇ 26-27 K 1
Springdale o USA (WA) ◇ 20-21 F 1
Springer o USA ◇ 26-27 E 2
Springerville o USA ◇ 26-27 C 2
Springfield o CDN ◇ 18-19 M 6
16-17 J 3
Springfield o USA (CO) ◇ 26-27 F 1
Springfield o USA (IL) ◇ 22-23 D 6
14-15 W 8
Springfield o USA (MO) ◇ 26-27 L 1
16-17 H 3
Springfield o USA (OH) ◇ 22-23 G 6
Springfield o USA (OR) ◇ 20-21 C 4
Springfield o USA (TN) ◇ 24-25 E 1
Springfield o USA (VT) ◇ 22-23 M 4
Springhill o CDN ◇ 18-19 M 6
Spring Hill o USA ◇ 24-25 G 5
Spring Lake o USA ◇ 24-25 J 2
Springlake o USA ◇ 26-27 F 2
Spring Mill State Park ⊥ USA
22-23 E 6
Springs o ZA ◆ 50-51 G 7
Springsure o AUS ◆ 60-61 K 4
Springville o USA (AL) ◇ 24-25 E 2
Springville o USA (NY) ◇ 22-23 J 4
Springville o USA (UT) ◇ 20-21 J 6
Sprucedale o CDN ◇ 18-19 E 6
Spruce Knob ▲ USA ◇ 22-23 J 6
16-17 L 3
Spruce Mountain ▲ USA ◇ 20-21 G 5
Spruce Pine o USA ◇ 24-25 G 2
Spur o USA ◇ 26-27 G 3
Square Islands o CDN ◇ 18-19 R 2
Squires, Mount ▲ AUS ◆ 60-61 F 5
Sredinnyj hrebet ▲ RUS ◆ 52-53 c 7
Srednerusskaja vozvyšennosť ≃ RUS
42-43 Q 5
Sredne russkaja vozvyšennost' ▲ RUS
42-43 Q 5
Sretensk ★ RUS ◆ 52-53 T 5
Sri Dungargarh o IND ◆ 56-57 L 5
Srikakulam o IND ◆ 56-57 N 7
Sri Lanka o CL ◆ 56-57 N 9
Srinagar ★ IND ◆ 56-57 L 4
Staaten River ~ AUS ◆ 60-61 J 3
Staaten River National Park ⊥ AUS
60-61 J 3
Stackpool o CDN ◇ 18-19 D 7
Staked Plain = Llano Estacado ≃ USA
26-27 F 3
Stamford o USA ◇ 22-23 M 5
Stamford, Lake o USA ◇ 26-27 H 3
Stampriet o NAM ◆ 50-51 E 6
Standish o USA ◇ 22-23 F 4
Stanford o USA (KY) ◇ 22-23 F 7
Stanford o USA (MT) ◇ 20-21 J 2
Stanislaus River ~ USA ◇ 20-21 D 7
Stanley o GB ◆ 32-33 L 8
Stanley o USA ◇ 20-21 H 4
Stanley, Port o CDN ◇ 18-19 D 7
Stanovoj hrebet ▲ RUS ◆ 52-53 T 6
Stanovoj Nagor'ye = Stanovoe nagor'e ▲
RUS ◆ 52-53 T 6
Stanovoj Khrebet = Stanovoj hrebet ▲
RUS ◆ 52-53 T 6
Stanton o USA ◇ 26-27 G 3
Stanwix National Monument, Fort ∴ USA
22-23 L 4
Stanwood o USA ◇ 20-21 C 1
Stara Zagora o BG ◆ 34-35 R 7
Starbuck Island ~ KIB ◆ 12 M 3
Star City o USA ◇ 26-27 M 3
Starke o USA ◇ 24-25 G 5
Starkville o USA ◇ 24-25 E 3
◆ 34-35 R 6
State College o USA ◇ 22-23 K 5
Staten Island ~ USA ◇ 22-23 L 5
Statesboro o USA ◇ 24-25 H 3
Statesville o USA ◇ 24-25 H 2
Statue of Liberty ••• USA ◇ 22-23 M 5
16-17 M 3
Staunton o USA ◇ 22-23 J 6
16-17 L 3
Stavanger ☆ • N ◆ 36-37 B 7
◆ 34-35 N 4
Stavropol' ★ RUS ◆ 34-35 U 6
Steamboat o USA ◇ 20-21 E 5
Steele Island ~ ANT ◆ 13 F 30
Steens Mountain ▲ USA ◇ 20-21 E 4
Steenstrup Gletscher ⊂ GRØ
14-15 Z 1
Steep Point ▲ AUS ◆ 60-61 C 5
Stefansson Island ~ CDN ◆ 14-15 P 2
Steinen, Rio ~ BR ◇ 30-31 H 7
Steinkjer ☆ N ◆ 36-37 E 4
Stellarton o CDN ◇ 18-19 N 6
Stephanie Wildlife Reserve ⊥ ETH
48-49 M 7
Stephens o USA ◇ 26-27 L 3
Stephenville o CDN ◇ 18-19 P 4
14-15 Z 7
Stephenville o USA ◇ 26-27 H 3
Stephenville Crossing o CDN
18-19 P 4
Steppe, The ≃ KZ ◆ 52-53 L 7
Sterling o USA ◇ 26-27 F 1
16-17 F 2
Sterling City o USA ◇ 26-27 G 4

Sterling Heights o USA ◇ 22-23 G 4
Sterlitamak ★ RUS ◆ 34-35 X 5
Steubenville o USA ◇ 22-23 H 5
Stevenson o USA ◇ 20-21 D 3
Stevensons Peak ▲ AUS ◆ 60-61 G 5
Stevens Pass ▲ USA ◇ 20-21 D 2
Stevens Point o USA ◇ 22-23 D 3
Stevensville o USA ◇ 20-21 G 2
Stewart Island ~ NZ ◆ 60-61 O 9
Stewart River ~ CDN ◆ 14-15 J 4
Stickney Corner o USA ◇ 22-23 O 3
Stigler o USA ◇ 26-27 K 2
Stikine Plateau ▲ CDN ◆ 14-15 K 5
Stikine River ~ CDN ◆ 14-15 K 5
Stillwater o USA ◇ 26-27 J 1
Stinear Nunataks ▲ ANT ◆ 13 F 7
Stinnett o USA ◇ 26-27 G 2
Stirling o CDN ◇ 18-19 F 6
Stirling North o AUS ◆ 60-61 H 6
Stirling Range National Park ⊥ AUS
60-61 D 6
Stockbridge o USA ◇ 24-25 F 3
Stockbridge Indian Reservation ⋊ USA
22-23 D 3
Stockholm ★ •• S ◆ 36-37 J 7
◆ 34-35 P 4
Stockton o USA (CA) ◇ 20-21 D 7
16-17 B 3
Stockton o USA (FL) ◇ 24-25 G 4
Stockton o USA (IL) ◇ 22-23 C 4
Stockton o USA (OK) ◇ 26-27 H 2
Stockton Island ~ USA ◇ 22-23 C 2
Stockton Lake o USA ◇ 26-27 L 1
Stockton Plateau ≃ USA ◇ 26-27 F 4
Stöng, Rio o K ◇ 52-53 Y 5
Stolbovoj, ostrov ~ RUS ◆ 52-53 X 3
Stones River National Battlefield ∴ • USA
24-25 E 2
Stonington o ANT ◆ 13 G 30
Stonington o USA ◇ 22-23 M 5
Stony Creek o USA ◇ 22-23 K 7
Stony Lake o USA ◆ 14-15 E 4
Stony River o USA ◆ 14-15 E 4
Storkerson Peninsula ∪ CDN
14-15 P 2
Storm Bay ≈ ◆ 60-61 K 8
Stornoway o GB ◇ 38-39 E 4
Storsjön o S ◆ 36-37 G 5
◆ 34-35 O 3
Stoughton o USA ◇ 22-23 D 4
Stout o USA ◇ 22-23 N 3
Stralsund o •• D ◆ 40-41 M 1
◆ 34-35 O 5
Strand o ZA ◆ 50-51 E 8
Stranraer o • GB ◇ 38-39 E 4
Strasbourg ☆ • F ◇ 38-39 L 7
◆ 34-35 N 6
Stratford o CDN ◇ 18-19 D 7
Stratford o USA (CA) ◇ 20-21 E 7
Stratford o USA (TX) ◇ 26-27 F 1
16-17 F 2
Strathroy o CDN ◇ 18-19 D 7
Stratton o USA ◇ 22-23 N 3
Stratton Mountain ▲ USA ◇ 22-23 M 4
Strawberry Reservoir < USA
26-27 D 1
Strawberry River ~ USA ◇ 20-21 J 6
Strawn o USA ◇ 26-27 H 3
Streaky Bay o AUS ◆ 60-61 G 6
Streator o USA ◇ 22-23 D 5
Strevell o USA ◇ 20-21 H 5
Stroeder o RA ◇ 32-33 K 6
Strong o USA ◇ 26-27 L 3
Stroudsburg o USA ◇ 22-23 L 5
Stryj o UA ◆ 34-35 Q 6
Stryker o USA ◇ 20-21 G 1
Stuart o USA (FL) ◇ 24-25 H 6
Stuart o USA (VA) ◇ 22-23 H 7
Stuart Island ~ USA ◆ 14-15 D 4
Stuart Lake o CDN ◆ 14-15 M 6
Sturgeon Bay o USA ◇ 22-23 E 3
Sturgeon Falls o CDN ◇ 18-19 E 6
Sturgeon River ~ CDN ◇ 18-19 D 5
Sturgis o USA ◇ 22-23 F 5
Sturt Creek ~ AUS ◆ 60-61 F 3
Sturt Stony Desert ≃ AUS ◆ 60-61 H 5
Stuttgart o •• D ◆ 40-41 K 4
◆ 34-35 N 6
Stuttgart o USA ◇ 26-27 M 2
Stykkishólmsbær o IS ◆ 36-37 B 2
Su o KZ ◆ 52-53 L 9
Šu o KZ ◆ 52-53 L 9
Suakin o SUD ◆ 48-49 N 5
Suay Riêng o K ◆ 58-59 L 9
Subi, Pulau ~ RI ◆ 58-59 F 6
Sublett o USA ◇ 20-21 H 4
Sublette o USA ◇ 26-27 G 1
Subotica o YU ◆ 46-47 G 1
◆ 34-35 P 6
Subrà al-Ḫaima o ET ◆ 48-49 M 2
Subway Caves ∴ USA ◇ 20-21 D 5
Suceava o RO ◆ 34-35 R 6
Suchiapa, Rio ~ MEX ◇ 28-29 H 3
Suchum o GE ◆ 34-35 U 7
Sucre ★ BOL ◇ 30-31 G 7
Sucua o EC ◇ 30-31 C 4
Sudan ■ SUD ◆ 48-49 L 6
Sudbury o CDN ◇ 18-19 D 5
Sudd ≐ SUD ◆ 48-49 M 7
Suddie o GUY ◇ 30-31 H 3
Sudeten o CZ ◆ 40-41 N 3
◆ 34-35 O 5
Súdpól ▲ ANT ◆ 13 E 0
Sue ~ SUD ◆ 48-49 L 7
Sueco, El o MEX ◇ 16-17 E 5
Suffem o USA ◇ 22-23 M 5
Suffolk o USA ◇ 22-23 K 7
Sugaing o MYA ◆ 54-55 H 6
Sugar River ~ USA ◇ 22-23 D 4

Sutherlin o USA ◇ 20-21 C 4
Sutton o CDN ◇ 18-19 E 6
Sutton o USA ◇ 22-23 J 6
Suva ★ • FJI ◆ 60-61 Q 3
Suwais, Ḫaliǧ as- ≈ ◆ 48-49 M 3
Suwałki o • PL ◆ 40-41 R 1
◆ 34-35 Q 5
Suwannee River ~ USA ◇ 24-25 G 5
Suzdal' o • RUS ◆ 42-43 R 3
Suzhou o CHN (ANH) ◆ 54-55 M 5
Suzhou o CHN (JIA) ◆ 54-55 N 5
Svalbard ~ N ◆ 13 B 17
Svealand ≐ S ◇ 36-37 F 7
Svendsen Peninsula ∪ CDN
14-15 U 1
Sverdlovsk, ostrov ~ RUS ◆ 52-53 M 3
Sverdrup Islands ~ CDN ◆ 14-15 Q 1
Svetlogorsk o RUS ◆ 52-53 O 1
Svetlograd o RUS ◆ 34-35 U 6
Svir' ~ RUS ◆ 42-43 N 1
◆ 34-35 S 3
Svitlovods'k o UA ◇ 34-35 S 6
Svjatoj Nos, mys ▲ RUS ◆ 52-53 Z 3
Svobodnyj o RUS ◆ 52-53 W 7
Svolvær o N ◆ 36-37 G 2
◆ 34-35 O 2
Swain Reefs ~ AUS ◆ 60-61 L 4
Swain's Atoll ~ USA ◆ 12 K 4
Swainsboro o USA ◇ 24-25 G 3
Swakopmund o • NAM ◆ 50-51 D 6
Swan Hill o AUS ◆ 60-61 J 7
Swanquarter o USA ◇ 24-25 K 2
Swan River o CDN ◆ 14-15 Q 6
Swansea o GB ◇ 38-39 F 6
◆ 34-35 L 5
Swansea o USA ◇ 24-25 H 3
Swanton o USA ◇ 22-23 M 3
Swan Valley o USA ◇ 20-21 J 4
Swaziland ■ SD ◆ 50-51 H 7
Sweden ■ S ◆ 36-37 G 7
◆ 34-35 O 4
Sweetgrass o USA ◇ 20-21 J 1
Sweet Home o USA ◇ 20-21 C 3
Sweetwater o USA ◇ 26-27 G 3
Swellendam o • ZA ◆ 50-51 F 8
Świdnica o PL ◆ 40-41 O 3
◆ 34-35 P 5
Swift Current o CDN ◆ 14-15 P 6
Swiss Historic Village • USA
22-23 D 4
Switzerland ■ CH ◆ 40-41 K 5
◆ 34-35 N 6
Sydney ☆ •• AUS ◆ 60-61 L 6
Sydney o CDN ◇ 18-19 O 5
Syktyvkar ★ RUS ◆ 52-53 G 3
Sylacauga o USA ◇ 24-25 E 3
Sylhet o BD ◆ 56-57 P 6
Sylva o USA ◇ 24-25 G 2
Sylvania o USA (GA) ◇ 24-25 H 3
Sylvania o USA (OH) ◇ 22-23 G 5
Sylvan Pass ▲ USA ◇ 20-21 J 4
Sylvester o USA ◇ 24-25 G 4
Şymkent ≐ KZ ◆ 56-57 K 2
Synder o USA ◇ 26-27 J 2
Syowa o ANT ◆ 13 G 4
Syracuse o USA ◇ 22-23 K 4
14-15 V 8
Syrdarija ~ KZ ◆ 52-53 J 8
Syrdar'ja ~ KZ ◆ 56-57 K 2
Syria ■ SYR ◆ 56-57 D 5
Syrian Desert ≃ SYR ◆ 56-57 D 4
Syzran' o RUS ◆ 34-35 V 5
Szczecin o • PL ◆ 40-41 N 2
◆ 34-35 O 5
Szeged o • H ◆ 40-41 Q 5
◆ 34-35 Q 6
Székesfehérvár o • H ◆ 40-41 P 5
◆ 34-35 P 6
Szekszárd o • H ◆ 40-41 P 5
◆ 34-35 P 6
Szolnok o • H ◆ 40-41 Q 5
◆ 34-35 Q 6

T

Tabar Islands ~ PNG ◆ 58-59 O 7
Tabas o • IR ◆ 56-57 H 4
Tabasco □ MEX ◇ 28-29 H 2
Tabatinga o BR ◇ 30-31 F 5
Tabelbala o DZ ◆ 48-49 E 2
Tablas, Las ☆ PA ◇ 28-29 D 8
Tablas Island ~ RP ◆ 58-59 J 3
Table Head ▲ CDN ◇ 18-19 R 2
Table Rock Lake o USA ◇ 26-27 L 1
Tabora o • EAT ◆ 50-51 H 3
Tabor City o USA ◇ 24-25 J 2
Tabou o • CI ◆ 48-49 D 8
Tabríz ☆ •• IR ◆ 56-57 F 3
Tabuaeran ~ KIB ◆ 12 L 2
Tabudarat o RP ◆ 58-59 G 7
Tabūk □ KSA ◆ 56-57 D 5
Tabuk ☆ RP ◆ 58-59 J 3
Tabuk ☆ KSA ◆ 56-57 D 5
Tabusintac Nine Indian Reserve ⋊ CDN
18-19 N 5
Tabwemasana ▲ VAN ◆ 60-61 N 3
Tacana, Volcán ▲ GCA ◇ 28-29 H 4
Tacheng o CHN ◆ 54-55 E 2
Tacinskij o RUS ◆ 34-35 U 6
Tacloban o RP ◆ 58-59 J 4
Tacna o PE ◇ 30-31 E 7
Tacoma o USA ◇ 20-21 C 2
14-15 M 7
Tacora, Volcán ▲ RCH ◇ 30-31 F 7
Tacuarembo o ROU ◇ 32-33 L 4
Tadant, Oued ~ DZ ◆ 48-49 G 2
Tademait, Plateau du ▲ DZ
48-49 F 2
Tadjoura o DJI ◆ 48-49 N 6
Tadmur Palmyra ☆••• SYR ◆ 56-57 D 4
Tadoussac o CDN ◇ 18-19 K 4
Taegu o ROK ◆ 54-55 O 4
Taejon o ROK ◆ 54-55 O 4
Tafassasset, Oued ~ DZ ◆ 48-49 G 3
Tafilalt ≐ MA ◆ 48-49 E 2
Tafiraoute o MA ◆ 48-49 D 2
Taftān, Kūh-e ▲ IR ◆ 56-57 J 5

Taganrog o• RUS ◆ 34-35 T 6
Taguatinga o BR (FED) ◆ 30-31 K 8
Taguatinga o BR (TOC) ◆ 30-31 K 7
Tagula Island ⌒ PNG ◆ 58-59 O 9
Tagum ☆ RP ◆ 58-59 J 5
Tahat ▲ DZ ◆ 48-49 G 4
Tahiti, Île ⌒•• F ◆ 12 N 4
Tahoe, Lake ⊖ USA ◇ 20-21 D 6 ◆ 16-17 B 3
Tahoka o USA ◇ 26-27 G 3
Taholah o USA ◇ 20-21 B 2
Tahoua ☆ RN ◆ 48-49 G 6
Tahquamenon Falls State Park ⊥ USA ◇ 22-23 F 2
Tahtaküpir ☆ UZ ◆ 56-57 J 2
Tahtalı Dağları ▲ TR ◆ 34-35 T 8
Tahulandang, Pulau ⌒ RI ◆ 58-59 J 6
Tahuna o RI ◆ 58-59 J 6
Taï o CI ◆ 48-49 D 7
Tai'an o CHN ◆ 54-55 M 4
Taichung o RC ◆ 54-55 N 7
Ta'if, at o• KSA ◆ 56-57 E 6
Tai Hu ⊖ CHN ◆ 54-55 N 5
Tailai o CHN ◆ 54-55 N 2
Tailem Bend o AUS ◆ 60-61 H 7
Taim o BR ◆ 32-33 M 4
Taima' o• KSA ◆ 56-57 D 5
Tainan o RC ◆ 54-55 N 7
Taipei ★•• RC ◆ 54-55 N 6
Taitao, Peninsula de ⌒ RCH ◆ 32-33 G 7
Taitung o RC ◆ 54-55 N 7
Taiwan ■ RC ◆ 54-55 N 7
Taiwan Strait ≈ ◆ 54-55 M 7
Taiyuan ☆• CHN ◆ 54-55 L 4
Taizhou o CHN ◆ 54-55 M 5
Ta'izz o Y ◆ 56-57 E 8
Tajgonos, poluostrov ⌒ RUS ◆ 52-53 d 5
Tajikistan ■ TJ ◆ 56-57 K 3
Tajín, El ∴•• MEX ◇ 28-29 F 1
Tajmura ~ RUS ◆ 52-53 Q 5
Tajmyr, ozero ⊖ RUS ◆ 52-53 R 3
Tajo, Río ~ E ◇ 44-45 F 4 ◆ 34-35 L 7
Tajšet ☆ RUS ◆ 52-53 Q 6
Tajumulco, Volcán ▲ GCA ◇ 28-29 J 4 ◆ 16-17 H 7
Tak o THA ◆ 58-59 C 3
Takahe, Mount ▲ ANT ◆ 13 F 26
Takengon (Takingeun) o RI ◆ 58-59 C 6
Tākestān o• IR ◆ 56-57 F 3
Takht-i-Bahi ∴•• PK ◆ 56-57 L 4
Takikawa o J ◆ 54-55 R 3
Takiyuak Lake ⊖ CDN ◆ 14-15 O 3
Takla Lake ⊖ CDN ◆ 14-15 L 5
Takla Makan Desert = Taklimakan Shamo ⊥ CHN ◆ 54-55 E 4
Taklimakan Shamo ⊥ CHN ◆ 54-55 E 4
Taksimo o RUS ◆ 52-53 T 6
Takuapa o THA ◆ 58-59 C 5
Tala o MEX ◇ 28-29 C 1
Talacasto o RA ◆ 32-33 J 4
Talamanca, Cordillera de ▲ CR ◇ 28-29 C 7
Talanga o HN ◇ 28-29 L 4
Talara o PE ◆ 30-31 C 5
Talas ☆ KS ◆ 56-57 L 2
Talasea o PNG ◆ 58-59 O 8
Talata Mafara o WAN ◆ 48-49 G 6
Talaud, Kepulauan ⌒ RI ◆ 58-59 J 6
Talawe, Mount ▲ PNG ◆ 58-59 N 8
Talbot, Mount ▲ AUS ◆ 60-61 F 5
Talbotton o USA ◇ 24-25 F 3
Talca ☆• RCH ◆ 32-33 H 5
Talcahuano o RCH ◆ 32-33 H 5
Talcho o RN ◆ 48-49 F 6
Taldykorgan ☆ KZ ◆ 52-53 M 8
Taldyqorghan = Taldykorgan ☆ KZ ◆ 52-53 M 8
Talence o F ◇ 38-39 G 9 ◆ 34-35 L 6
Talequah o USA ◇ 26-27 K 2
Taliabu, Pulau ⌒ RI ◆ 58-59 H 7
Talibon o RP ◆ 58-59 H 4
Talihina o USA ◇ 26-27 K 2
Taliwang o RI ◆ 58-59 G 8
Talkeetna Mountains ▲ USA ◆ 14-15 G 4
Talladega o USA ◇ 24-25 E 3
Tallahassee ☆ USA ◇ 24-25 F 4 ◆ 16-17 K 4
Tallin = Tallinn ★•• EST ◇ 42-43 J 2 ◆ 34-35 Q 4
Tallinn ★•• EST ◇ 42-43 J 2 ◆ 34-35 Q 4
Tallulah o USA ◇ 26-27 M 3
Talnah o RUS ◆ 52-53 O 4
Talon o RUS ◆ 52-53 a 6
Talquin, Lake < USA ◇ 24-25 F 4
Taltal o RCH ◆ 32-33 H 3
Taltson River ~ CDN ◆ 14-15 O 4
Tamala ☆ GH ◆ 48-49 E 7
Tamanrasset ☆•• DZ ◆ 48-49 G 4
Tamanrasset, Oued ~ DZ ◆ 48-49 F 4
Tamarugal, Pampa del ⊥ RCH ◆ 32-33 J 2
Tamatave = Toamasina ☆ RM ◆ 50-51 L 5
Tama Wildlife Reserve ⊥ ETH ◆ 48-49 N 7
Tamazula de Gordiano o MEX ◇ 28-29 C 2
Tamazulapán o MEX ◇ 28-29 F 3
Tamazunchale o• MEX ◆ 16-17 G 6
Tambacounda ☆ SN ◆ 48-49 C 6
Tambej o RUS ◆ 52-53 L 3
Tambelan, Kepulauan ⌒ RI ◆ 58-59 E 6
Tambo o AUS ◆ 60-61 K 4
Tambohorano o RM ◆ 50-51 K 5
Tambora, Gunung ▲ RI ◆ 58-59 G 8
Tambov o RUS ◇ 42-43 R 5 ◆ 34-35 U 5
Tambura o SUD ◆ 48-49 L 7
Tamdytov toglari ▲ UZ ◆ 56-57 J 2
Tamiahua, Laguna de ⊖ MEX ◆ 16-17 G 6
Tamil Nādu ◻ IND ◆ 56-57 M 8
Tammu, Jabal ▲ LAR ◆ 48-49 H 4
Tampa o USA ◇ 24-25 G 6 ◆ 16-17 K 5
Tampa Bay ≈ ◇ 24-25 G 6 ◆ 16-17 K 5
Tampere o• FIN ◆ 34-35 Q 3
Tampico o• MEX ◆ 16-17 G 6
Tamworth o AUS ◆ 60-61 L 6
Tana ~ EAK ◆ 50-51 J 2
Tana = Île Tanna ⌒ VAN ◆ 60-61 O 3
Tana, Lake ⊖ ETH ◆ 48-49 N 6
Tanabe o J ◆ 54-55 Q 5
Tanahgrogot o RI ◆ 58-59 G 7
Tanami Desert ⊥ AUS ◆ 60-61 G 3
Tanana River ~ USA ◆ 14-15 G 4
Tancítaro, Cerro ▲ MEX ◇ 28-29 C 2
Tancítaro, Parque Nacional ⊥ MEX ◇ 28-29 C 2
Tandil o RA ◆ 32-33 L 5
Tanega-shima ⌒ J ◆ 54-55 P 5
Tanezrouft ⊥ DZ ◆ 48-49 E 4
Tanezrouft-Tan-Ahenet ⊥ DZ ◆ 48-49 F 4
Tanga ☆ EAT ◆ 50-51 J 3
Tanga Islands ⌒ PNG ◆ 58-59 O 7
Tanganjika, Lac = Lake Tanganyika ⊖ ZRE ◆ 50-51 G 2
Tanganyika, Lake ⊖ BU ◆ 50-51 G 2
Tanggu o CHN ◆ 54-55 M 4
Tanggula (Dangla) Shan ▲ CHN ◆ 54-55 F 5
Tangier = Tanjah ☆• MA ◆ 48-49 D 1
Tangra Yumco ⊖ CHN ◆ 54-55 F 5
Tangshan o CHN ◆ 54-55 M 4
Taniantaweng Shan ▲ CHN ◆ 54-55 H 5
Tanimbar, Kepulauan ⌒ RI ◆ 58-59 K 8
Tanintharl o MYA ◆ 58-59 C 4
Tanjah ☆• MA ◆ 48-49 D 1
Tanjay o RP ◆ 58-59 H 5
Tanjung o RI ◆ 58-59 G 7
Tanjungbalai o RI ◆ 58-59 C 6
Tanjungpandan o RI ◆ 58-59 E 7
Tanjungpinang o RI ◆ 58-59 D 6
Tanjungredeb o RI ◆ 58-59 G 6
Tanjungselor o RI ◆ 58-59 G 6
Tanjurer ~ RUS ◆ 52-53 f 5
Tank o USA ◇ 26-27 F 4
Tankwa-Karoo National Park ⊥ ZA ◆ 50-51 E 8
Tanna, Île = Tana ⌒ VAN ◆ 60-61 O 3
Tanougou, Cascades de ~•• DY ◆ 48-49 F 6
Tanout o RN ◆ 48-49 G 6
Tantā ☆ ET ◆ 48-49 M 2
Tan-Tan ☆ MA ◆ 48-49 C 3
Tanzania ■ EAT ◆ 50-51 H 3
Taolanaro o• RM ◆ 50-51 L 7
Taonan o CHN ◆ 54-55 N 2
Taos o•• USA ◇ 26-27 E 1 ◆ 16-17 E 3
Taoudenni o RMM ◆ 48-49 E 4
Tapachula o MEX ◇ 28-29 H 4 ◆ 16-17 H 8
Tapaktuan o RI ◆ 58-59 C 6
Tapalpa o• MEX ◇ 28-29 C 2
Tapauá o BR ◆ 30-31 G 6
Tapini o PNG ◆ 58-59 N 8
Tapirapecó, Sierra ▲ YV ◆ 30-31 F 4
Tappahannock o USA ◇ 22-23 K 7
Tapul Group ⌒ RP ◆ 58-59 H 5
Taquari, Pantanal do ⊖ BR ◆ 30-31 H 8
Taquari, Rio ~ BR ◆ 30-31 H 8
Tara ☆ RUS ◆ 52-53 L 6
Tarābulus ★• LAR ◆ 48-49 H 2
Tarābulus ☆• RL ◆ 56-57 D 4
Tarābulus ☆• RL ◆ 56-57 D 4
Tarahumara, Sierra ▲ MEX ◆ 16-17 E 5
Tarakan o RI ◆ 58-59 G 6
Tarangire National Park ⊥ EAT ◆ 50-51 J 2
Táranto ☆• I ◇ 46-47 F 4 ◆ 34-35 P 7
Táranto, Golfo di ≈ ◇ 46-47 F 4 ◆ 34-35 P 7
Tarapoto o PE ◆ 30-31 D 6
Tarare o F ◇ 38-39 K 9 ◆ 34-35 N 6
Tarasa Dwip Island ⌒ IND ◆ 58-59 B 5
Tarascon o•• F ◇ 38-39 K 10 ◆ 34-35 M 7
Tarbagatay Range ▲ KZ ◆ 52-53 N 8
Tarbes ☆ F ◇ 38-39 H 10 ◆ 34-35 M 7
Tarboro o USA ◇ 24-25 K 2
Tarcoola o AUS ◆ 60-61 G 6
Tardoki-Jani, gora ▲ RUS ◆ 52-53 Y 8
Tarfaya o MA ◆ 48-49 C 3
Targhee Pass ▲ USA ◇ 20-21 J 3
Tarija o BOL ◆ 32-33 K 2
Tariku ~ RI ◆ 58-59 L 7
Tarim o• Y ◆ 56-57 F 7
Tarim Basin = Tarim Pendi ⊥ CHN ◆ 54-55 E 4
Tarim He ~ CHN ◆ 54-55 E 3
Tarimoro o MEX ◇ 28-29 D 1
Tarim Pendi ⊥ CHN ◆ 54-55 E 4
Taritatu ~ RI ◆ 58-59 M 7
Tarkio o USA ◇ 20-21 G 2
Tarko-Sale ☆ RUS ◆ 52-53 M 5
Tarlac ☆ RP ◆ 58-59 H 3
Tarn ~ F ◇ 38-39 H 10 ◆ 34-35 M 7
Tarn, Gorges du ~•• F ◇ 38-39 J 9 ◆ 34-35 M 7
Tarnów ☆• PL ◇ 40-41 Q 3 ◆ 34-35 Q 5
Taroom o AUS ◆ 60-61 K 5
Taroudannt ☆• MA ◆ 48-49 D 2
Tarpon Springs o USA ◇ 24-25 G 5
Tarragona o• E ◇ 44-45 H 4 ◆ 34-35 M 7
Tar River ~ USA ◇ 24-25 J 2
Tarso Emissi ▲ TCH ◆ 48-49 J 4
Tarsus ☆• TR ◆ 34-35 S 8
Tartagal o RA ◆ 32-33 K 2
Tartu ☆•• EST ◇ 42-43 K 2 ◆ 34-35 R 4
Tartūs ☆•• SYR ◆ 56-57 D 4
Taschereau o CDN ◇ 18-19 E 4
Tashigang o BHT ◆ 56-57 P 5
Tashkent = Toškent ★•• UZ ◆ 56-57 K 2
Tasikmalaya o RI ◆ 58-59 E 8
Tasman Abyssal Plain ≃ ◆ 60-61 L 7
Tasman Basin ≃ ◆ 60-61 M 7
Tasman Bay ≈ ◆ 60-61 P 8
Tasmania ◻ AUS ◆ 60-61 K 8
Tasmania ⌒ AUS (TAS) ◆ 60-61 J 8
Tasman Peninsula ⌒•• AUS ◆ 60-61 K 8
Tasman Sea ≈ ◆ 60-61 M 7
Tataba o RI ◆ 58-59 H 7
Tatabánya o H ◇ 40-41 P 5 ◆ 34-35 P 6
Tatamagouche o CDN ◇ 18-19 N 6
Tata Mailau, Gunung ▲ RI ◆ 58-59 J 8
Tatarsk ☆ RUS ◆ 52-53 M 6
Tatarskij proliv ≈ ◆ 52-53 Z 7
Tatarskiy Proliv = Tatarskij proliv ≈ ◆ 52-53 Z 7
Tatarstan ◻ RUS ◆ 34-35 V 5
Tateyama o J ◆ 54-55 Q 5
Tathlina Lake ⊖ CDN ◆ 14-15 N 4
Tathra o AUS ◆ 60-61 K 7
Tatnam, Cape ▲ CDN ◆ 14-15 S 5
Tatry ▲ SK ◇ 40-41 P 4 ◆ 34-35 P 6
Tatshenshini-Alsek Kluane National Park ⊥••• CDN ◆ 14-15 H 4
Tatum o USA ◇ 26-27 F 3
Tatvan ☆• TR ◆ 34-35 U 8
Tauá o BR ◆ 30-31 L 6
Taubaté o BR ◆ 32-33 N 2
Taujskaja guba ≈ ◆ 52-53 a 6
Taulabé o HN ◇ 28-29 L 4
Taumaturgo o BR ◆ 30-31 E 6
Taum Sauk Mountain ▲ USA ◇ 22-23 C 7
Taunggyi ☆ MYA ◆ 54-55 H 7
Taunton o USA ◇ 22-23 N 5
Taupo o NZ ◆ 60-61 Q 7
Taupo, Lake ⊖ NZ ◆ 60-61 Q 7
Tauranga o NZ ◆ 60-61 Q 7
Taureau, Réservoir < CDN ◇ 18-19 H 5
Tauria o USA ◇ 26-27 L 1
Taurus Mountains ▲ TR ◆ 34-35 S 8
Tavda ~ RUS ◆ 52-53 K 6
Taveta o EAK ◆ 50-51 J 2
Tavoy o MYA ◆ 58-59 C 4
Tawakoni, Lake ⊖ USA ◇ 26-27 J 3
Tawas City o USA ◇ 22-23 G 3
Tawau o MAL ◆ 58-59 G 6
Tawitawi Island ⌒ RP ◆ 58-59 G 5
Taxco de Alarcon o• MEX ◇ 28-29 E 2 ◆ 16-17 G 7
Taxkorgan o CHN ◆ 54-55 D 4
Tayabamba o PE ◆ 30-31 D 6
Tāyebād o• IR ◆ 56-57 H 4
Taylor o USA ◇ 26-27 J 4
Taylor, Mount ▲ USA ◇ 26-27 D 2
Taylorville o USA ◇ 22-23 D 6
Taymyr, Ozero = Tajmyr, ozero ⊖ RUS ◆ 52-53 R 3
Taymyr Peninsula ⌒ RUS ◆ 52-53 P 2
Tây Ninh o• VN ◆ 58-59 E 4
Taytay o RP ◆ 58-59 G 4
Taz ~ RUS ◆ 52-53 N 4
Taza ☆ MA ◆ 48-49 E 2
Tazewell o USA (TN) ◇ 24-25 G 1
Tazewell o USA (VA) ◇ 22-23 H 7
Tázirbu o LAR ◆ 48-49 K 3
Tazovskaja guba ≈ ◆ 52-53 L 4
Tazovskij ☆ RUS ◆ 52-53 M 4
Tazovskij poluostrov ⌒ RUS ◆ 52-53 L 4
Tazrouk o DZ ◆ 48-49 G 4
Tbilisi ★• GE ◆ 34-35 U 7
Tchad, Lac ⊖ ◆ 48-49 H 6
Tchibanga ☆ G ◆ 50-51 D 2
Tchibemba o ANG ◆ 50-51 D 5
Tchin-Tabaradene o RN ◆ 48-49 G 5
Tcholliré o CAM ◆ 48-49 H 7
Tchula o USA ◇ 26-27 M 3
Te Anau o NZ ◆ 60-61 O 9
Teapa o MEX ◇ 28-29 H 3
Te Araroa o NZ ◆ 60-61 Q 7
Tebingtinggi o RI ◆ 58-59 C 6
Tecalitlán o MEX ◇ 28-29 C 2
Tecamachalco o MEX ◇ 28-29 F 2
Tecámbaro de Collados o MEX ◇ 28-29 D 2
Techia o WSA ◆ 48-49 C 4
Tecka o RA ◆ 32-33 H 6
Tecoh o MEX ◇ 28-29 K 1
Tecojate o GCA ◇ 28-29 J 5
Tecoman o MEX ◇ 28-29 C 2 ◆ 16-17 F 7
Tecozautla o MEX ◇ 28-29 E 1
Tecpan de Galeana o MEX ◇ 28-29 D 3
Tecpatán o MEX ◇ 28-29 H 3
Tecuan, El o MEX ◇ 28-29 B 1
Tedžen o TM ◆ 56-57 J 3
Tegal o RI ◆ 58-59 E 8
Tégouma ~ RN ◆ 48-49 H 5
Tegua = Île Teguan ⌒ VAN ◆ 60-61 O 2
Tegucigalpa ★•• HN ◇ 28-29 L 4 ◆ 16-17 J 8
Tehachapi o USA ◇ 20-21 E 8
Tehachapi Pass ▲ USA ◇ 20-21 E 8
Te Hapua o NZ ◆ 60-61 P 6
Tehek Lake ⊖ CDN ◆ 14-15 R 4
Tehema-Colusa-Canal < USA ◇ 20-21 C 6
Teheran = Tehrān ★•• IR ◆ 56-57 G 3
Tehrān ★•• IR ◆ 56-57 G 3
Tehuacan o• MEX ◇ 28-29 F 2 ◆ 16-17 G 7
Tehuantepec, Golfo de ≈ ◇ 28-29 G 4 ◆ 16-17 G 7
Tehuantepec, Istmo de ⊥ MEX ◇ 28-29 G 3 ◆ 16-17 H 7
Tehuantepec, Rio ~ MEX ◇ 28-29 G 3
Tehuantepec Ridge ≃ ◆ 16-17 G 8
Teide, Parque Nacional del ⊥ E ◆ 48-49 B 3
Tejon Pass ▲ USA ◇ 20-21 E 8
Tejupilco de Hidalgo o MEX ◇ 28-29 D 2
Tekax de Álvaro Obregón o MEX ◇ 28-29 K 1
Tekeze Wenz ~ ETH ◆ 48-49 N 6
Tekirdağ ☆ TR ◆ 34-35 R 7
Tekit o MEX ◇ 28-29 K 1
Tekoa o USA ◇ 20-21 F 2
Tekom o MEX ◇ 28-29 K 1
Tekouiat, Oued ~ DZ ◆ 48-49 F 4
Te Kuiti o NZ ◆ 60-61 Q 7
Tela o HN ◇ 28-29 L 4
Tel Aviv-Yafo ☆ IL ◆ 56-57 C 4
Telchac o MEX ◇ 28-29 K 1
Telefomin o PNG ◆ 58-59 M 8
Telescope Peak ▲ USA ◇ 20-21 F 7
Teles Pires ou São Manuel, Rio ~ BR ◆ 30-31 H 7
Telfer o• AUS ◆ 60-61 E 4
Télimélé o RG ◆ 48-49 C 6
Teller o USA ◆ 14-15 C 3
Tellico Lake < USA ◇ 24-25 F 2
Teloloapan o MEX ◇ 28-29 E 2
Telpoziz, gora ▲ RUS ◆ 52-53 H 5
Telsen o RA ◆ 32-33 J 6
Telukbetung = Bandar Lampung ☆ RI ◆ 58-59 E 8
Temagami o CDN ◇ 18-19 E 5
Temagami, Lake ⊖ CDN ◇ 18-19 D 5
Temascaltepec o MEX ◇ 28-29 D 2
Temax o MEX ◇ 28-29 K 1
Temazcal o MEX ◇ 28-29 F 2
Temazcaltepec o MEX ◇ 28-29 F 3
Tembe Elefant Reserve ⊥ ZA ◆ 50-51 H 7
Tembenči ~ RUS ◆ 52-53 Q 5
Temblador o YV ◆ 30-31 G 3
Tembladoras, Laguna ≈ ◇ 28-29 H 4
Tembo, Chutes ~ ZRE ◆ 50-51 E 3
Temirtau o KZ ◆ 52-53 L 7
Temirtau = Temirtau o KZ ◆ 52-53 L 7
Témiscamie, Rivière ~ CDN ◇ 18-19 H 3
Témiscamingue, Lac ⊖ CDN ◇ 18-19 E 5
Témiscouata, Lac ⊖ CDN ◇ 18-19 K 5
Témistamingue o CDN ◇ 18-19 E 5
Temo o MEX ◇ 28-29 H 3
Tempe o USA ◇ 20-21 J 9
Temple o USA ◇ 26-27 J 4 ◆ 16-17 G 4
Temple Bay ≈ ◆ 60-61 J 2
Tempoal de Sánchez o MEX ◆ 16-17 G 6
Temuco ☆ RCH ◆ 32-33 H 5
Tenabó o MEX ◇ 28-29 J 1
Tenaha o USA ◇ 26-27 K 4
Tenāli o IND ◆ 56-57 N 7
Tenancingo o MEX ◇ 28-29 E 2
Tenasserim = Tanintharl o MYA ◆ 58-59 C 4
Ten Degree Channel ≈ ◆ 58-59 B 5
Tendrara o MA ◆ 48-49 E 2
Ténéré ⊥ RN ◆ 48-49 H 5
Ténéré du Tafassasset ⊥ RN ◆ 48-49 H 4
Tenerife ⌒ E ◆ 48-49 B 3
Ténès o DZ ◆ 48-49 F 1
Tenggarong o• RI ◆ 58-59 G 7
Tengréla ☆ CI ◆ 48-49 D 6
Tenharim/Transamazônica, Área Indígena ⚔ BR ◆ 30-31 G 6
Teniente Matienzo o ANT ◆ 13 G 31
Tenika • RM ◆ 50-51 L 6
Teniz köli ⊖ KZ ◆ 52-53 K 7
Tenke o ZRE ◆ 50-51 G 4
Tenkiller Lake ⊖ USA ◇ 26-27 K 2
Tenkodogo ☆• BF ◆ 48-49 E 6
Ten Mile Lake ⊖ CDN ◇ 18-19 Q 3
Ten Mile Pond ⊖ CDN ◇ 18-19 S 4
Tennant Creek o• AUS ◆ 60-61 G 3
Tennessee ◻ USA ◇ 24-25 D 2 ◆ 16-17 J 3
Tennessee River ~ USA ◇ 24-25 D 2 ◆ 16-17 J 3
Tenochtitlán o MEX ◇ 28-29 G 3
Tenosique de Pino Suárez o MEX ◇ 28-29 J 3
Ten Thousand Islands ⌒ USA ◇ 24-25 H 7
Tentolotianan, Gunung ▲ RI ◆ 58-59 H 6
Teocuitatlán de Corona o MEX ◇ 28-29 C 1
Teófilo Otoni o BR ◆ 30-31 L 8
Teotepec, Cerro ▲ MEX ◇ 28-29 D 3
Teotihuacán ∴•• MEX ◇ 28-29 E 2
Teotitlán del Camino o MEX ◇ 28-29 F 2
Tepalcatepec o MEX ◇ 28-29 C 2
Tepatitlán o MEX ◇ 28-29 C 1
Tepeaca o MEX ◇ 28-29 F 2
Tepecoacuilco o MEX ◇ 28-29 E 2
Tepeji del Río o MEX ◇ 28-29 E 2
Tepic ☆ MEX ◆ 16-17 F 6
Tepich o MEX ◇ 28-29 K 1
Teplice o CZ ◇ 40-41 M 3 ◆ 34-35 O 5
Teques, Los ☆ YV ◆ 30-31 F 2
Tequila o• MEX ◇ 28-29 C 1
Tequisquiapan o MEX ◇ 28-29 E 1
Téra o RN ◆ 48-49 F 6
Terceira, Ilha ⌒ P ◆ 34-35 F 8
Tercero, Rio ~ RA ◆ 32-33 K 4
Teresina ☆ BR ◆ 30-31 L 6
Termez ☆• UZ ◆ 56-57 K 3
Términos, Laguna de ≈ ◇ 28-29 J 2 ◆ 16-17 H 7
Ternate o RI ◆ 58-59 J 6
Ternay, Lac ⊖ CDN ◇ 18-19 K 2
Ternej o RUS ◆ 52-53 Y 9
Terni ☆ I ◇ 46-47 D 3 ◆ 34-35 O 7
Ternopil' ☆ UA ◆ 34-35 R 6
Ternopol' = Ternopil' ☆ UA ◆ 34-35 R 6
Terpenija, mys ▲ RUS ◆ 52-53 Z 8
Terpenija, zaliv ≈ ◆ 52-53 Z 8
Terrace o CDN ◆ 14-15 L 5
Terra Nova National Park ⊥ CDN ◇ 18-19 R 4
Terrebonne o CDN ◇ 18-19 H 6
Terre Haute o USA ◇ 22-23 E 6 ◆ 16-17 J 3
Terrell o USA ◇ 26-27 J 3
Terrenate o MEX ◇ 28-29 F 2
Terrenceville o CDN ◇ 18-19 R 5
Terreton o USA ◇ 20-21 H 4
Teruel o•• E ◇ 44-45 G 4 ◆ 34-35 L 7
Tésécau, Lac ⊖ CDN ◇ 18-19 G 3
Teseny o ER ◆ 48-49 N 5
Teshekpuk Lake ⊖ USA ◆ 14-15 F 2
Tes-Hem ~ MAU ◆ 52-53 Q 8
Teslin River ~ CDN ◆ 14-15 K 4
Tessalit o RMM ◆ 48-49 F 4
Tessaoua o RN ◆ 48-49 G 6
Teste, la o F ◇ 38-39 G 9 ◆ 34-35 L 6
Têt ~ F ◇ 38-39 J 10 ◆ 34-35 M 7
Tetas, Punta ▲ RCH ◆ 32-33 H 2
Tete ☆ MOC ◆ 50-51 H 5
Teton River ~ USA ◇ 20-21 J 2
Tétouan = Titwān ☆• MA ◆ 48-49 D 1
Teuco, Rio ~ RA ◆ 32-33 K 2
Teulada, Capo ▲ I ◇ 46-47 B 5
Tévere ~ I ◇ 46-47 D 3 ◆ 34-35 O 7
Tevriz ☆ RUS ◆ 52-53 L 6
Texana, Lake ⊖ USA ◇ 26-27 J 5
Texarkana o USA ◇ 26-27 K 3 ◆ 16-17 H 4
Texas o AUS ◆ 60-61 L 5
Texas ◻ USA ◇ 26-27 G 4 ◆ 16-17 F 4
Texas City o USA ◇ 26-27 K 5
Texcoco o MEX ◇ 28-29 E 2
Texhoma o USA ◇ 26-27 G 1
Texiguat o HN ◇ 28-29 L 5
Texoma, Lake ⊖ USA ◇ 26-27 J 3 ◆ 16-17 G 4
Teziutlán o MEX ◇ 28-29 F 2
Thabazimbi o ZA ◆ 50-51 G 6
Thailand ■ THA ◆ 58-59 C 4
Thailand, Gulf of ≈ ◆ 58-59 D 4
Thái Nguyên ☆ VN ◆ 58-59 E 2
Thalang o THA ◆ 58-59 C 5
Thale Luang ≈ ◆ 58-59 D 5
Thames ~ GB ◇ 38-39 G 6 ◆ 34-35 M 5
Thames River ~ CDN ◇ 18-19 D 7
Thamesville o CDN ◇ 18-19 D 7
Thana o IND ◆ 56-57 L 7
Thanh Hóa ☆ VN ◆ 58-59 E 3
Thành Phố Hồ Chí Minh ☆•• VN ◆ 58-59 E 4
Thanjavur o•• IND ◆ 56-57 M 8
Thanlwin Myit ~ MYA ◆ 58-59 C 3
Tharād o IND ◆ 56-57 L 6
Thar Desert ⊥ PK ◆ 56-57 K 5
Thargomindah o AUS ◆ 60-61 J 5
Thássos ⌒ GR ◇ 46-47 K 4 ◆ 34-35 Q 7
Thatcher o USA ◇ 26-27 E 1
Thaton o MYA ◆ 58-59 C 3
Thatta o•• PK ◆ 56-57 K 6
Thayer o USA (KS) ◇ 26-27 K 1
Thayer o USA (MO) ◇ 26-27 M 1
Thayetmyo o MYA ◆ 58-59 C 3
Thayne o USA ◇ 20-21 J 4
Thebes ∴•• ET ◆ 48-49 M 3
The Calvados Chain ⌒ PNG ◆ 58-59 O 9
The Johnston Lakes ⊖ AUS ◆ 60-61 E 6
Thelon River ~ CDN ◆ 14-15 Q 4
Theodore o USA ◇ 24-25 D 4
Theodore Roosevelt Lake < USA ◇ 20-21 J 9
Theodore Roosevelt National Park North Unit ⊥ USA ◆ 14-15 Q 7
Theron Range ▲ ANT ◆ 13 E 0
Thessalon o CDN ◇ 18-19 C 5
Thessaloniki ☆•• GR ◇ 46-47 J 4 ◆ 34-35 Q 7
Thetford-Mines o CDN ◇ 18-19 J 5
The Wash ≈ ◇ 38-39 H 5 ◆ 34-35 M 5
Thibodaux o USA ◇ 26-27 M 5
Thiel Mountains ▲ ANT ◆ 13 E 0
Thiès ☆• SN ◆ 48-49 B 6
Thika o EAK ◆ 50-51 J 2
Thimphu ★• BHT ◆ 56-57 O 5
Thio o F ◆ 60-61 O 4
Thionville o F ◇ 38-39 L 7 ◆ 34-35 N 6
Thlewiaza River ~ CDN ◆ 14-15 R 4
Thomas o USA ◇ 22-23 J 6
Thomaston o USA ◇ 24-25 F 3
Thomaston Corner o CDN ◇ 18-19 L 6
Thomasville o USA (AL) ◇ 24-25 E 4
Thomasville o USA (GA) ◇ 24-25 G 4 ◆ 16-17 K 4
Thomasville o USA (NC) ◇ 24-25 H 2
Thompson o CDN ◆ 14-15 R 5
Thompson Falls o USA ◇ 20-21 G 2
Thompson Peak ▲ USA ◇ 20-21 C 5
Thomson o USA ◇ 24-25 G 3
Thomson River ~ AUS ◆ 60-61 J 4
Thonon-les-Bains o• F ◇ 38-39 L 8 ◆ 34-35 N 6
Thoreau o USA ◇ 26-27 C 2
Thorne o CDN ◇ 18-19 E 5
Thorshavn = Tórshavn ☆ FR ◇ 38-39 D 1 ◆ 34-35 K 3
Thouars o F ◇ 38-39 G 8 ◆ 34-35 L 6
Thouet ~ F ◇ 38-39 G 8 ◆ 34-35 L 6
Thousand Islands ⌒ CDN ◇ 18-19 F 6
Three Forks o USA ◇ 20-21 J 3
Three Kings Islands ⌒ NZ ◆ 60-61 P 6
Three Kings Ridge ≃ ◆ 60-61 P 6
Three Points, Cape ▲ GH ◆ 48-49 E 8
Three Rivers o USA (MI) ◇ 22-23 F 5
Three Rivers o USA (NM) ◇ 26-27 D 3
Three Rivers o USA (TX) ◇ 26-27 H 5
Three Sisters ▲ USA ◇ 20-21 D 3
Throckmorton o USA ◇ 26-27 H 3
Throssel, Lake ⊖ AUS ◆ 60-61 E 5
Thủ Dầu Một o VN ◆ 58-59 E 4
Thua ~ EAK ◆ 50-51 J 2
Thule = Qaanaaq ☆ GRØ ◆ 14-15 X 1
Thuli o ZW ◆ 50-51 G 6
Thunder Bay o CDN ◆ 14-15 T 7
Thunder Bay o USA ◇ 22-23 G 3
Thunder Bay River ~ USA ◇ 22-23 G 3
Thung Song o THA ◆ 58-59 C 5
Thurso o GB ◇ 38-39 F 2 ◆ 34-35 L 4
Thurston Island ⌒ ANT ◆ 13 F 27
Thury-Harcourt o F ◇ 38-39 G 7 ◆ 34-35 L 6
Tianjin ☆ CHN ◆ 54-55 M 4
Tianjin Shi ◻ CHN ◆ 54-55 M 4
Tianjun o CHN ◆ 54-55 H 4
Tian Shan ▲ CHN ◆ 54-55 E 3
Tianshui o CHN ◆ 54-55 K 5
Tianyang o CHN ◆ 54-55 K 7
Tiaret ☆• DZ ◆ 48-49 F 1
Tibaji o BR ◆ 32-33 M 2
Tibati o CAM ◆ 48-49 H 7
Tibbuburra o AUS ◆ 60-61 J 5
Tibesti ▲ TCH ◆ 48-49 J 4
Tibesti, Sarir ⊥ LAR ◆ 48-49 J 4
Tibet ◻ CHN ◆ 10-11 H 5
Tibet = Xizang Zizhiqu ◻ CHN ◆ 54-55 E 5
Tiburon o•• RH ◆ 16-17 M 7
Tiburón, Isla ⌒ MEX ◆ 16-17 D 5
Tichît o RIM ◆ 48-49 D 5
Tichkatine, Oued ~ DZ ◆ 48-49 F 4
Ticonderoga o USA ◇ 22-23 M 4
Ticonderoga, Fort ∴ USA ◇ 22-23 M 4
Ticul o MEX ◇ 28-29 K 1
Tidikelt, Plain du ⊥ DZ ◆ 48-49 F 3
Tidjikja ☆ RIM ◆ 48-49 C 5
Tieli o CHN ◆ 54-55 O 2
Tieling o CHN ◆ 54-55 N 3
Tielong o ◆ 56-57 M 3
Tientsin = Tianjin ☆ CHN ◆ 54-55 M 4
Tierra Amarilla o USA ◇ 26-27 D 1
Tierra Blanca o MEX ◇ 28-29 F 2
Tierra Colorada o MEX ◇ 28-29 E 3
Tierra del Fuego ◻ RA ◆ 32-33 J 8
Tierra del Fuego ⌒ RCH ◆ 32-33 H 8
Tiffin o USA ◇ 22-23 G 5
Tiflis = Tbilisi ★• GE ◆ 34-35 U 7
Tifton o USA ◇ 24-25 G 4
Tifu o RI ◆ 58-59 J 7
Tiger o USA ◇ 20-21 F 1
Tignish o CDN ◇ 18-19 M 5
Tigre, El ∴• MEX ◇ 28-29 J 2
Tigre, El o YV ◆ 30-31 G 3
Tigre, Lago del ⊖ GCA ◇ 28-29 J 3
Tigre, Rio ~ PE ◆ 30-31 E 5
Tigre de San Lorenzo, El o PA ◇ 28-29 D 8
Tigris = Diğla ~ IRQ ◆ 56-57 F 4
Tiguent o RIM ◆ 48-49 B 5
Tih, Gabal at- ▲ ET ◆ 48-49 M 3
Tih, Sahrā' at- ⊥ ET ◆ 48-49 M 2
Tihāma ⊥ Y ◆ 56-57 E 7
Tihoreck o RUS ◆ 34-35 U 6
Tihosuco o MEX ◇ 28-29 K 1
Tihuatlán o• MEX ◇ 28-29 F 1
Tihvin ☆ RUS ◇ 42-43 N 2 ◆ 34-35 S 4
Tijeras o USA ◇ 26-27 D 2
Tijuana o• MEX ◆ 16-17 C 4
Tika o CDN ◇ 18-19 M 3
Tikal o GCA (ELP) ◇ 28-29 K 3
Tikal ∴•• GCA (ELP) ◇ 28-29 K 3
Tikal, Parque Nacional ⊥••• GCA ◇ 28-29 K 3 ◆ 16-17 J 7
Tikamgarh o IND ◆ 56-57 M 6
Tiki Basin ≃ ◆ 12 O 4
Tikopia ⌒ SOL ◆ 60-61 O 2
Tiksi ☆ RUS ◆ 52-53 W 3
Tiladummati Atoll ⌒ MV ◆ 56-57 L 9
Tilāl an-Nūba ▲ SUD ◆ 48-49 M 6
Tilantongo o MEX (OAX) ◇ 28-29 F 3
Tilantongo ∴• MEX (OAX) ◇ 28-29 F 3
Tilarán o CR ◇ 28-29 B 6
Tilbury o CDN ◇ 18-19 C 7
Tilden o USA ◇ 26-27 H 5
Tilemsi ~ RMM ◆ 48-49 F 5
Tiličiki ☆ RUS ◆ 52-53 e 5
Tillabéri ☆ RN ◆ 48-49 F 6
Tillamook o USA ◇ 20-21 C 3
Tillamook Bay ≈ ◇ 20-21 C 3
Tiller o USA ◇ 20-21 C 4
Tillsonburg o CDN ◇ 18-19 D 7
Tilly, Lac ⊖ CDN ◇ 18-19 G 2
Timanskij krjaž ▲ RUS ◆ 52-53 G 5
Timanskiy Kryazh = Timanskij krjaž ▲ RUS ◆ 52-53 G 5
Timaru o NZ ◆ 60-61 P 8
Timbalier Bay ≈ ◇ 26-27 M 5
Timbedgha o RIM ◆ 48-49 D 5
Timber o USA ◇ 20-21 C 3
Timber Creek o AUS ◆ 60-61 G 3
Timber Mountain ▲ USA ◇ 20-21 G 6
Timbunke o PNG ◆ 58-59 M 7
Timétrine, Djebel ▲ RMM ◆ 48-49 E 5
Timgad o•• DZ ◆ 48-49 G 1
Timimoun o• DZ ◆ 48-49 F 3
Timiskaming, Lake = Témiscamingue, Lac ⊖ CDN ◇ 18-19 E 5
Timişoara ☆• RO ◆ 34-35 Q 6
Timmins o CDN ◆ 14-15 U 7
Timms Hill ▲ USA ◇ 22-23 C 3
Timor ⌒ RI ◆ 58-59 H 8
Timor Sea ≈ ◆ 58-59 J 9
Timor Trough ≃ ◆ 58-59 H 9
Timoudi o DZ ◆ 48-49 E 3
Timpanogos Cave National Monument ∴ USA ◇ 20-21 J 5
Timpton ~ RUS ◆ 52-53 W 6
Tims Ford Lake ⊖ USA ◇ 24-25 E 2
Tinaja, La o MEX ◇ 28-29 F 2
Tindouf ☆• DZ ◆ 48-49 D 3
Tindouf, Sebkha de ⊖ DZ ◆ 48-49 D 3
Tinfouchy o DZ ◆ 48-49 D 3
Tingal ▲ SUD ◆ 48-49 M 6
Tingambato o MEX ◇ 28-29 D 2
Tinhert, Hamada de ⊥ DZ ◆ 48-49 G 3
Tinian ⌒ USA ◆ 58-59 N 4
Tinkisso ~ RG ◆ 48-49 D 6
Tintina o RA ◆ 32-33 K 3
Tioman, Pulau ⌒ MAL ◆ 58-59 D 6
Tionesta o USA ◇ 22-23 J 5
Tipaza ☆•• DZ ◆ 48-49 F 1
Tipitapa o• NIC ◇ 28-29 L 5
Tipitapa, Rio ~ NIC ◇ 28-29 L 5
Tipton o USA (CA) ◇ 20-21 E 7
Tipton o USA (IA) ◇ 22-23 C 5
Tipton, Mount ▲ USA ◇ 20-21 G 8
Tiptonville o USA ◇ 24-25 D 1
Tiquicheo o MEX ◇ 28-29 D 2
Tiracambu, Serra do ▲ BR ◆ 30-31 K 5
Tirahart, Oued ~ DZ ◆ 48-49 F 4
Tiranë ★• AL ◇ 46-47 G 4 ◆ 34-35 P 7
Tiraspol ☆ MD ◆ 34-35 R 6
Tirband-e Torkestān, Selsele-ye Kūh-e ▲ AFG ◆ 56-57 J 3
Tîrgovişte ☆• RO ◆ 34-35 R 7
Tîrgu Mureş ☆• RO ◆ 34-35 Q 6
Tirich Mir ▲ PK ◆ 56-57 L 3
Tiruchchirappalli o• IND ◆ 56-57 M 8
Tirunelveli o• IND ◆ 56-57 M 9
Tirupati o• IND ◆ 56-57 M 8
Tiruppur o IND ◆ 56-57 M 8
Tishomingo o USA ◇ 26-27 J 2
Tis Isat Fwafwatē = Blue Nile Falls ~ ETH ◆ 48-49 N 6
Tisza ~ H ◇ 40-41 Q 5 ◆ 34-35 …
Titicaca, Lago ⊖ PE ◆ 30-31 F 8
Titishima-rettō ⌒ J ◆ 54-55 R 6
Titiwaifuru o RI ◆ 58-59 L 7
Titov Veles o• MK ◇ 46-47 H 4 ◆ 34-35 Q 7
Titule o ZRE ◆ 48-49 L 8
Titusville o USA (FL) ◇ 24-25 H 5
Titusville o USA (PA) ◇ 22-23 J 5
Titwān ☆• MA ◆ 48-49 D 1
Tivoli o I ◇ 46-47 D 4 ◆ 34-35 …
Tivoli o USA ◇ 26-27 J 5
Tixmul ∴• MEX ◇ 28-29 K 2
Tixtla de Guerrero o MEX ◇ 28-29 …
Tiya ••• ETH ◆ 48-49 N 7
Tizayuca o MEX ◇ 28-29 E 2
Tizimín o MEX ◇ 28-29 K 1 ◆ 16-17 J 6
Tizi Ouzou ☆ DZ ◆ 48-49 F 1
Tiznit ☆ MA ◆ 48-49 D 3
Tjan'-Šan' ▲ KS ◆ 56-57 L 2
Tjukalinsk ☆ RUS ◆ 52-53 L 6
Tjukjan ~ RUS ◆ 52-53 U 4
Tjumen' ☆ RUS ◆ 52-53 K 6
Tjung ~ RUS ◆ 52-53 U 4
Tlacoapa o MEX ◇ 28-29 E 3
Tlacolula o• MEX ◇ 28-29 F 3
Tlacotalpan o• MEX ◇ 28-29 G 2 ◆ 16-17 G 7
Tlacotepec o MEX ◇ 28-29 F 2
Tlacuilotepec o MEX ◇ 28-29 E 1
Tlahuac o MEX ◇ 28-29 E 2
Tlahuiltepa o MEX ◇ 28-29 E 1
Tlalchapa o MEX ◇ 28-29 D 2
Tlalnepantla o MEX ◇ 28-29 E 2
Tlalpan = Tlalnepantla o MEX ◇ 28-29 E 2
Tlapacoyan o MEX ◇ 28-29 F 2
Tlapa del Comonfort o MEX ◇ 28-29 E 3
Tlapaneco, Rio ~ MEX ◇ 28-29 E 3
Tlaquepaque o• MEX ◇ 28-29 C 1
Tlaxcala ◻ MEX ◇ 28-29 E 2
Tlaxcala ☆• MEX (TLA) ◇ 28-29 E 2
Tlaxiaco o MEX ◇ 28-29 F 3
Tlemcen ☆•• DZ ◆ 48-49 E 2
Tmassah o LAR ◆ 48-49 J 3
Toamasina ☆ RM ◆ 50-51 L 5
Tobacco Range ⌒ BH ◇ 28-29 L 3
Tobago ⌒ TT ◆ 16-17 O 8
Toba Kākar Range ▲ PK ◆ 56-57 K
Tobelo o RI ◆ 58-59 J 6
Tobermory o• CDN ◇ 22-23 H 3
Tobin, Mount ▲ USA ◇ 20-21 F 5
Tobique 20 Indian Reserve ⚔ CDN ◇ 18-19 L 5
Tobique River ~ CDN ◇ 18-19 L 5
Toboali o RI ◆ 58-59 E 7
Tobol ~ RUS ◆ 52-53 K 6
Tobol'sk ☆• RUS ◆ 52-53 K 6
Tobyl ~ KZ ◆ 52-53 J 7
Tocantins ◻ BR ◆ 30-31 K 6
Toccoa o USA ◇ 24-25 G 2
Toco o RCH ◆ 32-33 J 2
Tocopilla o RCH ◆ 32-33 H 2
Todeli o RI ◆ 58-59 H 7
Todos Santos o MEX ◆ 16-17 D 6
Toekomstig-stuwmeer ⊖ SME ◆ 30-31 H 4
Toga = Île Toga ⌒ VAN ◆ 60-61 O 2
Togian, Kepulauan ⌒ RI ◆ 58-59 H …
Togo ■ RT ◆ 48-49 F 7
Togo ▲ RUS ◆ 52-53 P 7
Togtoh o CHN ◆ 54-55 L 3
Togwotee Pass ▲ USA ◇ 20-21 J 4
Tohopekaliga, Lake ⊖ USA ◇ 24-25 …
Tōkar o SUD ◆ 48-49 N 5
Tokara-kaikyō ≈ ◆ 54-55 O 5
Tokara-rettō ⌒ J ◆ 54-55 O 6
Tokat ☆• TR ◆ 34-35 T 7
Tokelau Islands ⌒ NZ ◆ 12 K 3
Tok Junction o USA ◆ 14-15 H 4
Tokoroa o NZ ◆ 60-61 Q 7
Tokuno-shima ⌒ J ◆ 54-55 O 6
Tokushima ☆ J ◆ 54-55 P 5
Tōkyō ★• J ◆ 54-55 Q 4
Tol ⌒ FSM ◆ 58-59 O 5
Tolé o PA ◇ 28-29 D 7
Toledo o•• E ◇ 44-45 E 5 ◆ 34-35 L 8
Toledo o USA (OH) ◇ 22-23 G 5 ◆ 16-17 K 2
Toledo o USA (OR) ◇ 20-21 C 3
Toledo Bend Reservoir < USA ◇ 26-27 L 4 ◆ 16-17 H 4
Toliara ☆• RM ◆ 50-51 K 6
Tolimán o MEX ◇ 28-29 E 1
Tolitoli o RI ◆ 58-59 H 6
Tol'jatti = Stavropol-na-Volgi ☆ RUS ◆ 34-35 V 5
Tolija, zaliv ≈ ◆ 52-53 R 2
Tolo, Teluk ≈ ◆ 58-59 H 7
Tolono o USA ◇ 22-23 D 6
Toltén o RCH ◆ 32-33 H 5
Toluca ☆• MEX ◇ 28-29 E 2 ◆ 16-17 G 7
Toluca de Lerdo = Toluca ☆• MEX ◇ 28-29 E 2
Tom' ~ RUS ◆ 52-53 O 7
Tomah o USA ◇ 22-23 C 4
Tomahawk o USA ◇ 22-23 D 3
Tomakomai o J ◆ 54-55 R 3
Tomales Bay ≈ ◇ 20-21 C 6
Tomanivi ▲ FJI ◆ 60-61 Q 3
Tomar o•• P ◇ 44-45 C 5 ◆ 34-35 K 8
Tomás Garrido o MEX ◇ 28-29 K 2
Tomaszów Mazowiecki o PL ◇ 40-41 P 3 ◆ 34-35 P 5
Tomat o SUD ◆ 48-49 N 6
Tomatlán o MEX ◇ 28-29 B 2
Tombador, Serra do ▲ BR ◆ 30-31 H…
Tombigbee River ~ USA ◇ 24-25 D 3 ◆ 16-17 J 4

92 Taganrog — Tombigbee River

Tombouctou o··· RMM ◆ 48-49 E 5
Tombstone o USA ◇ 26-27 B 4
Tombua o ANG ◆ 50-51 D 5
Tomiko o CDN ◇ 18-19 E 5
Tomini, Teluk ≈ ◆ 58-59 H 7
Tomkinson Ranges ▲ AUS ◆ 60-61 F 5
Tommot o RUS ◆ 52-53 W 6
Tomsk ☆· RUS ◆ 52-53 O 6
Toms River o USA ◇ 22-23 L 6
Tonalá o MEX (JAL) ◇ 28-29 C 1
Tonalá o· MEX (CHI) ◇ 28-29 H 3
Tonantins o BR ◆ 30-31 F 5
Tonasket o USA ◇ 20-21 E 1
Tonawanda Indian Reservation ✗ USA ◇ 22-23 J 4
Tondano o RI ◆ 58-59 H 6
Tonga Islands ⌒ TON ◆ 12 K 4
Tongariro National Park ⊥··· NZ ◆ 60-61 Q 7
Tongatapu ⌒ TON ◆ 12 K 5
Tonga Trench ≃ ◆ 12 K 4
Tongchuan o CHN ◆ 54-55 K 4
Tonghua o CHN ◆ 54-55 O 3
Tongjosŏn Man ≈ ◆ 54-55 O 4
Tongling o CHN ◆ 54-55 M 5
Tongren o CHN ◆ 54-55 K 6
Tonila o MEX ◇ 28-29 C 2
Toniná ∴· MEX ◇ 28-29 H 3
Tonk o IND ◆ 56-57 M 5
Tonkawa o USA ◇ 26-27 J 1
Tonkin, Gulf of ≈ ◆ 58-59 E 2
Tônlé Sab o K ◆ 58-59 D 4
Tonnerre o F ◇ 38-39 J 8 ◆ 34-35 M 6
Tonopah o USA ◇ 20-21 F 6 ◆ 16-17 C 3
Tonopah Test Range Atomic Energy Commission xx USA ◇ 20-21 F 7
Tonosí o PA ◇ 28-29 D 8
Tonto, Río ~ MEX ◇ 28-29 F 2
Tonto National Monument ∴· USA ◇ 20-21 J 9
Tooele o USA ◇ 20-21 H 5
Toompine o AUS ◆ 60-61 J 5
Toowoomba o AUS ◆ 60-61 L 5
Topaz Lake o USA ◇ 20-21 E 6
Topeka ☆ USA ◆ 16-17 G 3
Topolovka o RUS ◆ 52-53 d 5
Toppenish o USA ◇ 20-21 D 2
Topsfield o USA ◇ 22-23 P 3
Top Springs o AUS ◆ 60-61 G 3
Toquerville o USA ◇ 20-21 H 7
Tor o ETH ◆ 48-49 M 7
Torbat-e Heidarīye o· IR ◆ 56-57 H 3
Torbay o CDN ◇ 18-19 S 5
Torğaj o KZ (KST) ◆ 52-53 J 8
Torğaj ~ KZ ◆ 52-53 J 7
Torğaj kolaty ⌣ KZ ◆ 52-53 J 7
Torğaj üstirti ▲ KZ ◆ 52-53 J 7
Torino ☆· I ◇ 46-47 A 2 ◆ 34-35 N 6
Tori-shima ⌒ J ◆ 54-55 R 5
Torit o SUD ◆ 48-49 M 8
Torneälven ~ S ◇ 36-37 L 3 ◆ 34-35 Q 2
Torngat Mountains ▲ CDN ◆ 14-15 Y 5
Tornquist o RA ◆ 32-33 K 5
Toro, Cerro del ▲ RA ◆ 32-33 J 3
Toro, Isla del ⌒ MEX ◆ 16-17 G 6
Torola, Río ~ ES ◇ 28-29 K 5
Toronto ☆· CDN ◇ 18-19 E 7 ◆ 14-15 V 8
Toronto o USA ◇ 26-27 K 1
Tororo o EAU ◆ 50-51 H 1
Torrabaai o NAM ◆ 50-51 D 6
Torrance o USA ◇ 20-21 E 9
Torrens, Lake o AUS ◆ 60-61 H 6
Torrens Creek o AUS ◆ 60-61 K 4
Torreón o MEX ◆ 16-17 F 5
Torreon o USA ◇ 26-27 D 2
Torres o· BR ◆ 32-33 N 3
Torres Islands = Îles Torres ⌒ VAN ◆ 60-61 O 2
Torres Strait ≈ ◆ 58-59 M 8
Torres Trench ≃ ◆ 60-61 O 2
Torrey o USA ◇ 20-21 J 6
Torrington o USA ◇ 22-23 M 5
Tórshavn ☆ FR ◇ 38-39 D 1 ◆ 34-35 K 3
Tortuga, Isla La ⌒ YV ◆ 30-31 F 2
Tortuguero, Parque Nacional ⊥ CR ◇ 28-29 C 6
Tory Hill o CDN ◇ 18-19 E 6
Toržok ☆ RUS ◇ 42-43 O 3 ◆ 34-35 S 4
Toškent ☆·· UZ ◆ 56-57 K 2
Tostado o RA ◆ 32-33 K 3
Toston o USA ◇ 20-21 J 2
Toteng o RB ◆ 50-51 F 6
Tôtes o F ◇ 38-39 H 7 ◆ 34-35 M 6
Totness ☆ SME ◆ 30-31 H 3
Totolán o MEX ◇ 28-29 C 1
Totolapan o MEX ◇ 28-29 F 3
Totonicapán ☆· GCA ◇ 28-29 J 4
Tottan Range ▲ ANT ◆ 13 F 35
Totten Glacier ⊂ ANT ◆ 13 G 12
Tottori ☆ J ◆ 54-55 P 4
Touba o CI ◆ 48-49 D 7
Touba o· SN ◆ 48-49 B 6
Toubkal, Jbel ▲ MA ◆ 48-49 D 2
Toucy o F ◇ 38-39 J 8 ◆ 34-35 M 6
Tougan o BF ◆ 48-49 E 6
Touggourt o· DZ ◆ 48-49 G 2
Touho o F ◆ 60-61 O 4
Toul o F ◇ 38-39 K 7 ◆ 34-35 M 6
Toulépleu o CI ◆ 48-49 D 7
Toulnustouc, Rivière ~ CDN ◇ 18-19 K 4
Toulon ☆ F ◇ 38-39 K 10 ◆ 34-35 N 7
Toulouse ☆·· F ◇ 38-39 H 10 ◆ 34-35 M 7
Toungoo o MYA ◆ 58-59 C 3
Tourcoing o F ◇ 38-39 J 6 ◆ 34-35 M 5
Tournus o F ◇ 38-39 K 8 ◆ 34-35 M 6
Tours o F ◇ 38-39 H 8 ◆ 34-35 M 6
Tour Village, De o USA ◇ 22-23 G 3
Touside, Pic ▲ TCH ◆ 48-49 J 4
Towanda o USA ◇ 22-23 K 5
Tower Peak ▲ AUS ◆ 60-61 E 6
Townsend o USA ◇ 20-21 J 2
Townsville o·· AUS ◆ 60-61 K 3
Towot o SUD ◆ 48-49 M 7
Towson o USA ◇ 22-23 K 6
Towuti, Danau o RI ◆ 58-59 H 7
Toxkan He ~ CHN ◆ 54-55 D 3
Toyah o USA ◇ 26-27 F 4
Toyama ☆ J ◆ 54-55 Q 4
Toyohashi o J ◆ 54-55 Q 5
Tozeur ☆· TN ◆ 48-49 G 2
Trabzon ☆·· TR ◆ 34-35 T 7
Tracadie o CDN ◇ 18-19 M 5
Tracy o USA ◇ 20-21 D 7
Trail o CDN ◆ 14-15 N 7
Trá Li = Tralee ☆ IRL ◇ 38-39 C 5 ◆ 34-35 K 5
Tranche-sur-Mer, la o F ◇ 38-39 G 8 ◆ 34-35 L 6
Trang o THA ◆ 58-59 C 5
Trangan, Pulau ⌒ RI ◆ 58-59 K 8
Transhimalaya ▲ ◆ 56-57 M 4
Transylvanian Alps ▲ RO ◆ 34-35 Q 6
Tranzitnyj o RUS ◆ 52-53 h 4
Trápani o I ◇ 46-47 D 5 ◆ 34-35 O 8
Traralgon o AUS ◆ 60-61 K 7
Trârza ⊥ RIM ◆ 48-49 B 5
Travellers Rest ∴ USA ◇ 20-21 G 2
Traverse City o USA ◇ 22-23 F 3 ◆ 14-15 T 8
Travis, Lake o USA ◇ 26-27 H 4
Trego o USA ◇ 22-23 C 3
Treinta y Tres ☆ ROU ◆ 32-33 M 4
Trelew o RA ◆ 32-33 J 6
Tremblant, Mont ▲ CDN ◇ 18-19 G 5
Tremonton o USA ◇ 20-21 H 5
Trenary o USA ◇ 22-23 E 2
Trenche, Rivière ~ CDN ◇ 18-19 H 4
Trenque Lauquen o RA ◆ 32-33 K 5
Trent o USA ◇ 26-27 G 3
Trento ☆· I ◇ 46-47 C 1 ◆ 34-35 O 6
Trenton o CDN ◇ 18-19 F 6
Trenton o USA (MI) ◇ 22-23 G 4
Trenton ☆ USA (NJ) ◇ 22-23 L 5 ◆ 16-17 M 2
Trepassey o CDN ◇ 18-19 S 5
Trepassey Bay ≈ ◇ 18-19 S 5
Tréport, Le o F ◇ 38-39 H 6 ◆ 34-35 M 5
Tres Arroyos o RA ◆ 32-33 K 5
Tres Cruces, Cerro ▲ MEX ◇ 28-29 H 4
Tres Esquinas o CO ◆ 30-31 D 4
Três Ilhas, Cachoeira das ~ BR ◆ 30-31 H 6
Três Lagoas o BR ◆ 32-33 M 2
Tres Lagos o RA ◆ 32-33 H 7
Tres Marías, Represa < BR ◆ 30-31 K 8
Tres Montes, Cabo ▲ RCH ◆ 32-33 G 7
Tres Palos, Laguna ≈ MEX ◇ 28-29 E 3
Tres Piedras o USA ◇ 26-27 E 1
Tres Puntas ▲ GCA ◇ 28-29 K 4
Tres Puntas, Cabo ▲ RA ◆ 32-33 J 7
Três Rios o BR ◆ 32-33 O 2
Tres Valles o MEX ◇ 28-29 F 2
Tres Zapotes ∴· MEX ◇ 28-29 G 2
Trhâza ∴· RMM ◆ 48-49 D 4
Triángulos, Arrecifes ⌒ MEX ◇ 28-29 H 1
Trichur o· IND ◆ 56-57 M 8
Trident Peak ▲ USA ◇ 20-21 E 5
Trier o··· D ◇ 40-41 J 4 ◆ 34-35 N 6
Trieste ☆· I ◇ 46-47 D 2 ◆ 34-35 O 6
Trincomalee o· CL ◆ 56-57 N 9
Trinidad o· BOL ◆ 30-31 G 7
Trinidad o··· C ◆ 16-17 K 6
Trinidad ☆ ROU ◆ 32-33 L 4
Trinidad ⌒ TT ◆ 16-17 O 8
Trinidad o USA ◇ 26-27 E 1 ◆ 16-17 F 3
Trinidad, Isla ⌒ RA ◆ 32-33 K 5
Trinidad and Tobago ■ TT ◆ 16-17 O 8
Trinitaria, La o MEX ◇ 28-29 H 3
Trinity o CDN ◇ 18-19 S 4
Trinity o USA ◇ 26-27 K 4
Trinity Bay ≈ ◇ 18-19 S 5 ◆ 14-15 a 7
Trinity Islands ⌒ USA ◆ 14-15 F 5
Trinity Range ▲ USA ◇ 20-21 E 6
Trinity River ~ USA ◇ 20-21 C 5
Trinity River ~ USA ◇ 26-27 J 3 ◆ 16-17 G 4
Trinkat Island ⌒ IND ◆ 58-59 B 5
Tripoli o GR ◇ 46-47 J 6 ◆ 34-35 Q 8
Tripoli = Tarābulus o· RL ◆ 56-57 D 4
Tripolis = Tarābulus ☆· LAR ◆ 48-49 H 2
Tripolitania ⊥ LAR ◆ 48-49 H 2
Tripura □ IND ◆ 56-57 P 6
Triste, Golfo ≈ ◆ 30-31 F 2
Trivandrum = Thiruvananthapuram ☆· IND ◆ 56-57 M 9
Trobriand Islands ⌒ PNG ◆ 58-59 O 8
Trocatá, Área Indígena ✗ BR ◆ 30-31 K 5
Troick ☆ RUS ◆ 52-53 J 7
Troicko-Pečorsk ☆ RUS ◆ 52-53 H 5
Trois-Pistoles o CDN ◇ 18-19 K 4
Trois-Rivières o CDN ◇ 18-19 H 5 ◆ 14-15 W 7
Trojes, Las o HN ◇ 28-29 B 4
Trombetas, Rio ~ BR ◆ 30-31 H 4
Tromsø ☆· N ◇ 36-37 J 2 ◆ 34-35 P 2
Trona o USA ◇ 20-21 F 8
Tronador, Cerro ▲ RCH ◆ 32-33 H 6
Trondheim ☆·· N ◇ 36-37 E 5 ◆ 34-35 O 3
Trondheimsfjorden ≈ ◇ 36-37 D 5 ◆ 34-35 N 3
Troup o USA ◇ 26-27 K 3
Trout Creek o CDN ◇ 18-19 E 6
Trout Creek o USA ◇ 20-21 G 2
Trout Lake o CDN (NWT) ◆ 14-15 M 4
Trout Lake o CDN (ONT) ◆ 14-15 S 6
Trout Lake o USA (MI) ◇ 22-23 F 2
Trout Lake o USA (WA) ◇ 20-21 D 3
Trout River o CDN ◇ 18-19 P 4
Troy o USA (AL) ◇ 24-25 F 4
Troy o USA (MO) ◇ 22-23 C 6
Troy o USA (MT) ◇ 20-21 G 1
Troy o USA (NY) ◇ 22-23 M 4
Troy o USA (OH) ◇ 22-23 F 5
Troyes ☆· F ◇ 38-39 K 7 ◆ 34-35 M 6
Troy Peak ▲ USA ◇ 20-21 G 6
Truckee o USA ◇ 20-21 D 6
Truckee River ~ USA ◇ 20-21 E 6
Truck Island ⌒ FSM ◆ 58-59 O 5
Truillo ☆ HN ◆ 16-17 J 7
Trujillo ☆· PE ◆ 30-31 D 6
Truk Islands ⌒ FSM ◆ 58-59 O 5
Truro o CDN ◇ 18-19 N 6 ◆ 14-15 Y 7
Truth or Consequences o USA ◇ 26-27 D 3
Tsala Apopka Lake o USA ◇ 24-25 G 5
Tsaratanana o RM ◆ 50-51 L 5
Tsaratanana ▲ RM ◆ 50-51 L 4
Tsau o RB ◆ 50-51 F 6
Tsavo o EAK ◆ 50-51 J 2
Tsavo National Park ⊥ EAK ◆ 50-51 J 2
Tselinograd = Akmola ★ KZ ◆ 52-53 L 7
Tshabong ☆ RB ◆ 50-51 F 7
Tshela o ZRE ◆ 50-51 D 2
Tshikapa o ZRE ◆ 50-51 F 3
Tshimbulu o ZRE ◆ 50-51 F 3
Tshuapa ~ ZRE ◆ 50-51 F 2
Tsiafajavona ▲ RM ◆ 50-51 L 5
Tsimlyanskoye Vodokhranilishche = Cimljanskoe vodohranilišč < RUS ◆ 34-35 U 6
Tsingtao = Qingdao ☆ CHN ◆ 54-55 N 4
Tsingy de Bamaraha Strict Nature Reserve ⊥··· RM ◆ 50-51 K 5
Tsiombe o RM ◆ 50-51 L 7
Tsiroanomandidy o RM ◆ 50-51 L 5
Tsitsikamma National Park ⊥ ZA ◆ 50-51 F 8
Tsugaru Strait ≈ ◆ 54-55 R 3
Tsumeb ☆ NAM ◆ 50-51 E 5
Tsumkwe ☆ NAM ◆ 50-51 F 5
Tsuruga o J ◆ 54-55 Q 4
Tsushima ⌒ J ◆ 54-55 O 5
Tswaane o RB ◆ 50-51 F 6
Tuamotu, Îles ⌒ F ◆ 12 N 4
Tuapse o RUS ◆ 34-35 T 7
Tubac o USA ◇ 20-21 J 10
Tuba City o USA ◇ 20-21 J 7
Tubai, Îles ⌒ F ◆ 12 M 5
Tuban o RI ◆ 58-59 F 8
Tubarão o BR ◆ 32-33 N 3
Tubmanburg o LB ◆ 48-49 C 7
Tubruq ☆ LAR ◆ 48-49 K 2
Tucacas o YV ◆ 30-31 F 2
Tucano o BR ◆ 30-31 M 7
Tucker Bay ≈ ◆ 13 F 18
Tuckerton o USA ◇ 22-23 L 6
Tucson o USA ◇ 26-27 B 3 ◆ 16-17 D 4
Tucumán ⌒ RA ◆ 32-33 J 3
Tucumcari o USA ◇ 26-27 F 2 ◆ 16-17 F 3
Tucupita ☆ YV ◆ 30-31 G 3
Tucuruí o BR ◆ 30-31 K 5
Tufi o PNG ◆ 58-59 N 8
Tuguegarao ☆ RP ◆ 58-59 H 3
Tugur o RUS ◆ 52-53 Y 7
Tukangbesi, Kepulauan ⌒ RI ◆ 58-59 H 8
Tuktoyaktuk o CDN ◆ 14-15 K 3
Tukuyu o EAT ◆ 50-51 H 3
Tula ☆·· RUS ◆ 42-43 P 4 ◆ 34-35 T 5
Tula de Allende o· MEX ◇ 28-29 E 1
Tulalip Indian Reservation ✗ USA ◇ 20-21 C 1
Tulancingo o MEX ◇ 28-29 E 1 ◆ 16-17 G 6
Tulare o USA ◇ 20-21 E 7 ◆ 16-17 C 3
Tulare Lake o USA ◇ 20-21 E 8 ◆ 16-17 D 2
Tularosa o USA ◇ 26-27 D 3
Tulate o GCA ◇ 28-29 J 4
Tulcan ☆ EC ◆ 30-31 D 4
Tuléar = Toliara ☆· RM ◆ 50-51 K 6
Tule River Indian Reservation ✗ USA ◇ 20-21 E 7
Tulia o USA ◇ 26-27 G 2
Tulipan o MEX ◇ 28-29 J 3
Tullahoma o USA ◇ 24-25 E 2
Tulle ☆· F ◇ 38-39 H 9 ◆ 34-35 L 7
Tullos o USA ◇ 26-27 L 4
Tully o AUS ◆ 60-61 K 3
Tulsa o· USA ◇ 26-27 K 1 ◆ 16-17 G 3
Tulua o CO ◆ 30-31 D 4
Tulúm o MEX (QR) ◇ 28-29 L 1 ◆ 16-17 J 6
Tulúm ∴·· MEX (QR) ◇ 28-29 L 1
Tulun ☆ RUS ◆ 52-53 R 7
Tulu Welel ▲ ETH ◆ 48-49 M 7
Tuma, Río ~ NIC ◇ 28-29 B 5
Tumacacori National Monument ∴ USA ◇ 20-21 J 10
Tumaco o CO ◆ 30-31 D 4
Tumbes ☆ PE ◆ 30-31 C 5
Tumen o CHN ◆ 54-55 O 3
Tumkūr o IND ◆ 56-57 M 8
Tumoiscatio del Ruiz o MEX ◇ 28-29 C 2
Tumu o GH ◆ 48-49 E 6
Tumucumaque, Parque Indígena do ✗ BR ◆ 30-31 H 4
Tumucumaque, Serra do ▲ BR ◆ 30-31 H 4
Tumut o AUS ◆ 60-61 K 7
Tunceli ☆ TR ◆ 34-35 T 8
Tunduma o EAT ◆ 50-51 H 3
Tunduru o EAT ◆ 50-51 J 4
Tungaru o SUD ◆ 48-49 M 6
Tungsten o CDN ◆ 14-15 L 4
Tunis ☆··· TN ◆ 48-49 H 1
Tunisia ■ TN ◆ 48-49 G 2
Tunja ☆ CO ◆ 30-31 E 3
Tunkhannock o USA ◇ 22-23 L 5
Tuolumne River ~ USA ◇ 20-21 D 7
Tuotuo Heyan o CHN ◆ 54-55 G 5
Tupã o BR ◆ 32-33 M 2
Tuparro, Parque Nacional El ⊥ CO ◆ 30-31 F 3
Tupelo o USA ◇ 24-25 D 2 ◆ 16-17 J 4
Tupelo National Battlefield ∴ USA ◇ 24-25 D 2
Tupilco o MEX ◇ 28-29 H 2
Tupinambarana, Ilha ⌒ BR ◆ 30-31 H 5
Tupitina o MEX ◇ 28-29 C 2
Tupiza o BOL ◆ 32-33 J 2
Tupper Lake o USA ◇ 22-23 L 3
Tupungato, Cerro ▲ RA ◆ 32-33 J 4
Tuque, La o CDN ◇ 18-19 H 5
Tuquerres o CO ◆ 30-31 D 4
Tura ~ PA ◇ 28-29 F 8
Tura ☆ RUS (EVN) ◆ 52-53 R 5
Tura ~ RUS ◆ 34-35 X 4
Turaif o KSA ◆ 56-57 D 4
Turama River ~ PNG ◆ 58-59 M 8
Turan Lowland ⌣ ◆ 56-57 H 4
Turbat o PK ◆ 56-57 J 5
Turbio, Río ~ RA ◆ 32-33 H 8
Turbo o CO ◆ 30-31 D 3
Turda o RO ◆ 34-35 Q 6
Türgen ▲ MAU ◆ 54-55 G 2
Turgeon, Rivière ~ CDN ◇ 18-19 E 4
Turhal ☆· TR ◆ 34-35 T 7
Turiaçu o BR ◆ 30-31 K 5
Turin = Torino ☆· I ◇ 46-47 A 2 ◆ 34-35 N 6
Turkana, Lake o EAK ◆ 48-49 N 8
Turkey ■ TR ◆ 56-57 B 3
Turkey o USA ◇ 26-27 G 2
Turkey River ~ USA ◇ 22-23 C 4
Türkistan ☆ KZ ◆ 56-57 K 2
Türkmenbaši ☆ TM ◆ 56-57 G 2
Turkmenistan ■ TM ◆ 56-57 H 3
Turks and Caicos Islands □ GB ◆ 16-17 M 6
Turks Islands ⌒ GB ◆ 16-17 M 6
Turku = Åbo ☆· FIN ◆ 34-35 Q 3
Turkwel ~ EAK ◆ 48-49 N 8
Turlock o USA ◇ 20-21 D 7
Turneffe Islands ⌒ BH ◇ 28-29 L 3 ◆ 16-17 J 7
Turpan o CHN ◆ 54-55 F 3
Turrialba o CR ◇ 28-29 C 7
Turuhansk o RUS ◆ 52-53 O 4
Tuscaloosa o USA ◇ 24-25 E 3 ◆ 16-17 J 4
Tuscola o USA (IL) ◇ 22-23 D 6
Tuscola o USA (TX) ◇ 26-27 H 3
Tuskegee o· USA ◇ 24-25 F 3
Tuskegee Institute National Historic Site ∴· USA ◇ 24-25 F 3
Tuticorin o IND ◆ 56-57 M 9
Tuul gol ~ MAU ◆ 54-55 K 2
Tuva □ RUS ◆ 52-53 Q 7
Tuwaiq, Ğabal ▲ KSA ◆ 56-57 F 6
Tuwal o KSA ◆ 56-57 D 6
Tuxcueca o MEX ◇ 28-29 C 1
Tuxpan o· MEX ◇ 28-29 C 2
Tuxpan, Río ~ MEX ◇ 28-29 F 1
Tuxpan de Rodríguez Cano o MEX ◇ 28-29 F 1 ◆ 16-17 G 6
Tuxtla, Sierra de los ▲ MEX ◇ 28-29 G 2
Tuxtla Gutiérrez ☆· MEX ◇ 28-29 H 3 ◆ 16-17 H 7
Tuy Hòa o VN ◆ 58-59 E 4
Tuz Gölü o TR ◆ 34-35 S 8
Tuzigoot National Monument ∴ USA ◇ 20-21 J 8
Tuzla o· BIH ◇ 46-47 G 2 ◆ 34-35 P 7
Tver' ☆·· RUS ◇ 42-43 P 3 ◆ 34-35 T 4
Twentynine Palms o USA ◇ 20-21 F 8
Twentynine Palms Marine Corps Base xx USA ◇ 20-21 F 8
Twilight Cove ≈ ◆ 60-61 F 6
Twillingate o CDN ◇ 18-19 R 4
Twin Bridges o USA ◇ 20-21 H 3
Twin Buttes Reservoir < USA ◇ 26-27 G 4
Twin Falls o USA ◇ 20-21 G 4 ◆ 16-17 D 2
Twin Peaks o AUS ◆ 60-61 D 5
Twofold Bay ≈ ◆ 60-61 K 7
Two Harbors o USA ◇ 22-23 C 2
Two Rivers o USA ◇ 22-23 E 3
Tyara, Cayo ⌒ NIC ◇ 28-29 C 5
Tygh Valley o USA ◇ 20-21 D 3
Tyler o USA ◇ 26-27 K 3 ◆ 16-17 G 4
Tylertown o USA ◇ 26-27 M 4
Tymovskoe ☆ RUS ◆ 52-53 Z 7
Tynda ☆ RUS ◆ 52-53 V 6
Tyner o USA ◇ 22-23 G 7
Tyrma o RUS ◆ 52-53 X 7
Tyrone o USA (NM) ◇ 26-27 C 3
Tyrone o USA (PA) ◇ 22-23 J 5
Tyrrhenian Sea ≈ ◇ 46-47 C 5 ◆ 34-35 O 8
Tyrs Bjerge ▲ GRØ ◆ 14-15 c 4
Tyumen' = Tjumen' ☆ RUS ◆ 52-53 K 6
Tzaneen o ZA ◆ 50-51 H 6
Tzintzel o MEX ◇ 28-29 H 3
Tziscao o MEX ◇ 28-29 J 3
Tzonconejo, Río ~ MEX ◇ 28-29 J 3
Tzucacab o MEX ◇ 28-29 K 1

U

Uaçá, Área Indígena ✗ BR ◆ 30-31 J 4
Uati-Paraná, Área Indígena ✗ BR ◆ 30-31 F 5
Uatuma, Rio ~ BR ◆ 30-31 H 5
Uauá o BR ◆ 30-31 M 6
Uaupés, Rio ~ BR ◆ 30-31 F 4
Uaus, Ra's ▲ OM ◆ 56-57 H 7
Uaxactún ∴· GCA ◇ 28-29 K 3
Ubá o BR ◆ 32-33 O 2
Ubangi ~ ZRE ◆ 50-51 E 1
Ubar ∴· OM ◆ 56-57 G 7
Ubayyid, al- ☆· SUD ◆ 48-49 M 6
Ube o J ◆ 54-55 P 5
Uberaba o BR ◆ 30-31 K 8
Uberlândia o BR (MIN) ◆ 30-31 K 8
Uberlândia o BR (ROR) ◆ 30-31 H 4
Ubirr o AUS ◆ 60-61 G 2
Ubon Ratchathani o THA ◆ 58-59 D 3
Ubundu o ZRE ◆ 50-51 G 2
Učkuduk ☆ UZ ◆ 56-57 J 2
Ucua o ANG ◆ 50-51 D 3
Učur ~ RUS ◆ 52-53 X 6
Uda ~ RUS ◆ 52-53 X 7
Udačnyj o RUS ◆ 52-53 T 4
Udagamandalam o IND ◆ 56-57 M 8
Udaipur o· IND ◆ 56-57 L 6
Udine ☆· I ◇ 46-47 D 1 ◆ 34-35 O 6
Udmurtia □ RUS ◆ 34-35 W 4
Udon Thani o THA ◆ 58-59 D 3
Udupi o IND ◆ 56-57 L 8
Uedinenija, ostrov ⌒ RUS ◆ 52-53 N 2
Uele ~ ZRE ◆ 48-49 K 8
Uelen o RUS ◆ 52-53 k 4
Uere ~ ZRE ◆ 48-49 L 8
Ufa ☆ RUS ◆ 34-35 X 5
Ufa ~ RUS ◆ 34-35 X 4
Uftjuga ~ RUS ◆ 52-53 F 5
Ugalla River Game Reserve ⊥ EAT ◆ 50-51 H 3
Uganda ■ EAU ◆ 50-51 H 1
Ugashik Lake o USA ◆ 14-15 E 5
Ugep o WAN ◆ 48-49 G 7
Uglegorsk o RUS ◆ 52-53 Z 8
Uglič ☆·· RUS ◇ 42-43 Q 3 ◆ 34-35 T 4
Uhrichsville o USA ◇ 22-23 H 5
Uhta o RUS ◆ 52-53 G 5
Uige ☆ ANG ◆ 50-51 E 3
Uintah and Ouray Indian Reservation ✗ USA ◇ 20-21 J 5 ◆ 16-17 D 2
Uinta Mountains ▲ USA ◇ 20-21 J 5
Uis Myn o NAM ◆ 50-51 D 6
Uitenhage o ZA ◆ 50-51 G 8
Ujandina ~ RUS ◆ 52-53 a 4
Ujar ☆ RUS ◆ 52-53 P 6
Ujdah ☆ MA ◆ 48-49 E 2
Ujelang ⌒ MAI ◆ 12 H 2
Ujjain o IND ◆ 56-57 M 6
Ujung Pandang ☆ RI ◆ 58-59 G 8
Ukerewe Island ⌒ EAT ◆ 50-51 H 2
Ukhta = Uhta o RUS ◆ 52-53 G 5
Ukiah o USA (CA) ◇ 20-21 C 6 ◆ 16-17 B 3
Ukiah o USA (OR) ◇ 20-21 E 3
Ukraine ■ UA ◆ 34-35 R 6
'Ulā, al- o·· KSA ◆ 56-57 D 5
Ulaanbaatar ☆ MAU ◆ 54-55 K 2
Ulaangom ☆ MAU ◆ 54-55 G 2
Ulahan-Bom, hrebet ▲ RUS ◆ 52-53 Y 5
Ulamona o PNG ◆ 58-59 O 8
Ulan o CHN ◆ 54-55 H 4
Ulan Bator = Ulaanbaatar ☆ MAU ◆ 54-55 K 2
Ulanhot o CHN ◆ 54-55 N 2
Ulan-Udè ☆· RUS ◆ 52-53 S 7
Ulan Ude = Ulan-Udè ☆· RUS ◆ 52-53 S 7
Uliastaj ☆ MAU ◆ 54-55 H 2
Uliga = Dalap-Uliga-Darrit ☆ MAI ◆ 12 J 2
Ulindi ~ ZRE ◆ 50-51 G 2
Ul'inskij hrebet ▲ RUS ◆ 52-53 Y 6
Ulithi Atoll ⌒ FSM ◆ 58-59 L 4
Ul'janovsk = Simbirsk ☆ RUS ◆ 34-35 V 5
Ulladulla o AUS ◆ 60-61 L 7
Ulm o· D ◇ 40-41 K 4 ◆ 34-35 N 6
Ulm o USA ◇ 20-21 J 2
Ulsan o ROK ◆ 54-55 O 4
Ulu o RUS ◆ 52-53 W 5
Ulúa, Río ~ HN ◇ 28-29 K 4
Uludoruk Tepe ▲ TR ◆ 34-35 U 8
Uluguru Mountains ▲ EAT ◆ 50-51 J 3
Ulungur He ~ CHN ◆ 54-55 F 2
Ulungur Hu o CHN ◆ 54-55 F 2
Ulupalakua o USA ◇ 24-25 D 7
Uluru National Park ⊥··· AUS ◆ 60-61 G 5
Ulysses o USA ◇ 26-27 G 1
Ulz gol ~ MAU ◆ 54-55 L 2
Umán o MEX ◇ 28-29 K 1
Uman' o UA ◆ 34-35 S 6
Umanak Fjord ≈ ◆ 14-15 a 2
Umatilla Indian Reservation ✗ USA ◇ 20-21 E 3
Umatilla River ~ USA ◇ 20-21 E 3
Umbarger o USA ◇ 26-27 G 2
Umboi Island ⌒ PNG ◆ 58-59 N 8
Umeå ☆· S ◇ 36-37 K 5 ◆ 34-35 Q 3
Umeälven ~ S ◇ 36-37 J 4 ◆ 34-35 P 3
Umfolozi Game Reserve ⊥ ZA ◆ 50-51 H 7
Umm al-Hait, Wādī = Ibn Hautar, Wādī ~ OM ◆ 56-57 G 7
Umm al 'Izām, Sabkhat o LAR ◆ 48-49 J 2
Umm Durmān o·· SUD ◆ 48-49 M 5
Umm Sa'ad o LAR ◆ 48-49 L 2
Umnak Island ⌒ USA ◆ 14-15 C 6
Umpqua River ~ USA ◇ 20-21 C 4
Umtata ☆ ZA ◆ 50-51 G 8
Umuarama o BR ◆ 32-33 M 2
Una o BR ◆ 30-31 M 8
Unadilla o USA ◇ 24-25 G 3
Unaí o BR ◆ 30-31 K 8
'Unaiza o KSA ◆ 56-57 E 5
Unalakleet o USA ◆ 14-15 D 4
Unalaska o USA ◆ 14-15 C 6
Unalaska Island ⌒ USA ◆ 14-15 C 6
Uneiuxi, Área Indígena ✗ BR ◆ 30-31 F 5
Unga Island ⌒ USA ◆ 14-15 D 5
Ungava, Péninsule d' ⌣ CDN ◆ 14-15 V 4
Ungava Bay ≈ ◆ 14-15 X 5
Unguz ⊥ TM ◆ 56-57 H 3
Ungwana Bay ≈ ◆ 50-51 K 2
União o BR ◆ 30-31 L 5
União da Vitória o BR ◆ 32-33 M 3
União dos Palmares o BR ◆ 30-31 M 6
Unimak Island ⌒ USA ◆ 14-15 D 6
Unini, Rio ~ BR ◆ 30-31 G 5
Unión o RA ◆ 32-33 J 5
Union o USA (SC) ◇ 24-25 H 2
Union o USA (WV) ◇ 22-23 H 7
Unión, La ☆ ES ◇ 28-29 L 5
Unión, La o HN ◇ 28-29 L 4
Unión, La o MEX ◇ 28-29 K 3
Unión, La o PE ◆ 30-31 D 6
Unión, La o RCH ◆ 32-33 H 6
Union, Mount ▲ USA ◇ 20-21 H 8
Unión, Río La ~ MEX ◇ 28-29 D 2
Union City o USA (PA) ◇ 22-23 J 5
Union City o USA (TN) ◇ 24-25 D 1 ◆ 16-17 J 3
Union Creek o USA ◇ 20-21 C 4
Uniondale o ZA ◆ 50-51 F 8
Unión de Tula o MEX ◇ 28-29 B 2
Unión Hidalgo o MEX ◇ 28-29 G 3
Unión Juárez o MEX ◇ 28-29 H 4
Union National Monument, Fort ∴ USA ◇ 26-27 E 2
Union Springs o USA ◇ 24-25 F 3
Uniontown o USA ◇ 22-23 J 6
United Arab Emirates ■ UAE ◆ 56-57 G 6
United Kingdom ■ GB ◇ 38-39 H 4 ◆ 34-35 L 4
United States ■ USA ◆ 16-17 D 2
United States Military Academy xx USA ◇ 22-23 L 5
United States Naval Weapons Center xx USA ◇ 20-21 F 7
United States Virgin Islands □ USA ◆ 16-17 O 7
Universal City o USA ◇ 26-27 H 5
University Park o USA ◇ 26-27 D 3
Upala o CR ◇ 28-29 B 6
Upata o YV ◆ 30-31 G 3
Upemba, Parc National de l' ⊥ ZRE ◆ 50-51 G 3
Upernavik o GRØ ◆ 14-15 Z 2
Upington o ZA ◆ 50-51 F 7
Upolu Point ▲ USA ◇ 24-25 E 7
Upper Canada Village ∴· CDN ◇ 18-19 G 6
Upper Guinea ⊥ ◆ 9 B 5
Upper Humber River ~ CDN ◇ 18-19 Q 4
Upper Indian Pond o CDN ◇ 18-19 Q 4
Upper Klamath Lake o USA ◇ 20-21 D 4
Upper Lake o USA (CA) ◇ 20-21 C 6
Upper Lake o USA (CA) ◇ 20-21 D 5
Upper Musquodoboit o CDN ◇ 18-19 N 6
Upper Peninsula ⌣ USA ◇ 22-23 E 2 ◆ 14-15 T 7
Upper Sandusky o USA ◇ 22-23 G 5
Uppsala o·· S ◇ 36-37 H 7 ◆ 34-35 P 4
Uqsur, al- ☆·· ET ◆ 48-49 M 3
Ural ~ RUS ◆ 34-35 X 5
Ural Mountains ▲ RUS ◆ 52-53 H 7
Urandi o BR ◆ 30-31 L 7
Uranium City o CDN ◆ 14-15 P 5
Uraricuera, Rio ~ BR ◆ 30-31 G 4
Urbana o USA (IL) ◇ 22-23 D 5
Urbana o USA (OH) ◇ 22-23 G 5
Urbana, La o YV ◆ 30-31 F 3
Urbano Santos o BR ◆ 30-31 L 5
Ureparapara ⌒ VAN ◆ 60-61 O 2
Urewera National Park ⊥ NZ ◆ 60-61 Q 7
Urfa = Şanlı Urfa ☆· TR ◆ 34-35 T 8
Urganč ☆ UZ ◆ 56-57 J 2
Urganch = Urganč ☆ UZ ◆ 56-57 J 2
Urho o CHN ◆ 54-55 F 2
Uriangato o MEX ◇ 28-29 D 1
Uribe o CO ◆ 30-31 D 4
Uribia o CO ◆ 30-31 E 2
Urmi ~ RUS ◆ 52-53 X 8
Ursulo Galván o MEX ◇ 28-29 K 2
Uruaçu o BR ◆ 30-31 K 7
Uruapan del Progreso o· MEX ◇ 28-29 C 2 ◆ 16-17 F 7
Urubamba, Rio ~ PE ◆ 30-31 E 7
Urucará o BR ◆ 30-31 H 5
Uruçuí o BR ◆ 30-31 L 6
Uruguai, Rio ~ BR ◆ 32-33 M 3
Uruguaiana o BR ◆ 32-33 L 3
Uruguay ■ ROU ◆ 32-33 L 4
Ürümqi ☆ CHN ◆ 54-55 F 3
Urup, ostrov ⌒ RUS ◆ 52-53 b 8
'Urūq Hibāka ⊥ KSA ◆ 56-57 F 6
Urville, Île d' ⌒ ANT ◆ 13 G 31
Urville, Mer d' ≈ ◆ 13 G 15
Usa ~ RUS ◆ 52-53 H 4
Uşak ☆ TR ◆ 34-35 R 8
Ušakova, ostrov ⌒ RUS ◆ 52-53 M 1
Ūšaral o KZ ◆ 54-55 E 2
Usborne, Mount ▲ GB ◆ 32-33 L 8
U.S. Energy Research and Development Administration xx USA ◇ 20-21 E 2
'Usfān o KSA ◆ 56-57 D 6
Ushuaia ☆ RA ◆ 32-33 J 8
Üsküdar o TR ◆ 34-35 R 7
Usol'e-Sibirskoe o RUS ◆ 52-53 R 7
Usol'ye Sibirskoye = Usol'e-Sibirskoe o RUS ◆ 52-53 R 7
Uspanapa, Río ~ MEX ◇ 28-29 G 3
Uspero o MEX ◇ 28-29 C 2
Ussel o F ◇ 38-39 J 9 ◆ 34-35 M 7
Ussurijsk o RUS ◆ 52-53 X 9
Ust'-Barguzin o RUS ◆ 52-53 S 7
Ust'-Belaja o RUS ◆ 52-53 f 4
Ust'-Cil'ma o RUS ◆ 52-53 G 4
Ust'-Ilimsk ☆ RUS ◆ 52-53 R 6
Ust'Ilimsk = Ust'-Ilimsk ☆ RUS ◆ 52-53 R 6
Üstirt ▲ KZ ◆ 56-57 G 2
Ust'-Jansk o RUS ◆ 52-53 Y 3
Ustjurt, plato ▲ UZ ◆ 56-57 H 2
Ust'-Kamčatsk ☆ RUS ◆ 52-53 d 6
Ust'-Kujga o RUS ◆ 52-53 Y 3
Ust'-Kut ☆ RUS ◆ 52-53 S 6
Ust'-Lenskij zapovednik (učastok Del'tevyj) ⊥ RUS ◆ 52-53 V 3
Ust'-Maja o· RUS ◆ 52-53 X 5
Ust'-Nera ☆· RUS ◆ 52-53 Z 5
Ust'-Omčug ☆ RUS ◆ 52-53 a 5
Ust'-Ordynskij ☆ RUS ◆ 52-53 R 7
Ust'-Tym o RUS ◆ 52-53 O 6
Ust'-Voja o RUS ◆ 52-53 H 5
Usulután ☆ ES ◇ 28-29 K 5
Usumacinta, Río ~ MEX ◇ 28-29 H 2 ◆ 16-17 H 7
Uta o RI ◆ 58-59 L 7
Utah □ USA ◇ 20-21 H 6 ◆ 16-17 D 3
Utah Lake o USA ◇ 20-21 J 5 ◆ 16-17 D 2
Utatlán ∴· GCA ◇ 28-29 J 4
Ute Creek ~ USA ◇ 26-27 F 1
Ute Mountain Indian Reservation ✗ USA ◇ 26-27 C 1
Uteni o RUS ◆ 52-53 V 7
Ute Peak ▲ USA ◇ 26-27 C 1
Utete o EAT ◆ 50-51 J 3
Utiariti o BR ◆ 30-31 H 7
Utiariti, Área Indígena ✗ BR ◆ 30-31 H 7
Utica o USA (NY) ◇ 22-23 L 4 ◆ 14-15 V 8
Utica o USA (OH) ◇ 22-23 G 5
Utila o HN ◇ 28-29 L 3
Utila, Isla de ⌒ HN ◇ 28-29 L 3
Utrecht ☆· NL ◇ 40-41 H 2 ◆ 34-35 N 5
Utsunomiya ☆ J ◆ 54-55 Q 4
Uttaradit o THA ◆ 58-59 D 3
Uttar Pradesh □ IND ◆ 56-57 M 5
Utupua ⌒ SOL ◆ 60-61 O 2
Uummannarsuaq = Kap Farvel ▲ GRØ ◆ 14-15 c 5
Uvalde o USA ◇ 26-27 H 5
Uvat o RUS ◆ 52-53 K 6
Uviéu = Oviedo ☆· E ◇ 44-45 E 3 ◆ 34-35 K 7
Uvinza o EAT ◆ 50-51 H 3
Uvs nuur o MAU ◆ 54-55 G 1
'Uwaynāt, Al o LAR ◆ 48-49 H 3
Uxmal ∴·· MEX ◇ 28-29 K 1
Uyedineniya, Ostrov = Uedinenija, ostrov ⌒ RUS ◆ 52-53 N 2
Uyuni o BOL ◆ 32-33 J 2
Uyuni, Salar de o BOL ◆ 32-33 J 2
Uzbekistan ■ UZ ◆ 56-57 H 2
Uzerche o· F ◇ 38-39 H 9 ◆ 34-35 L 7
Uzhhorod = Užhorod ☆ UA ◆ 34-35 Q 6
Užhorod ☆ UA ◆ 34-35 Q 6
Užur ☆ RUS ◆ 52-53 O 6

V

Vaalrivier ~ ZA ◆ 50-51 G 7
Vaasa ☆ FIN ◆ 34-35 Q 3
Vacaria o BR ◆ 32-33 M 3
Vacaville o USA ◇ 20-21 C 6
Vader o USA ◇ 20-21 C 2
Vadodara o IND ◆ 56-57 L 6
Vadsø o N ◇ 36-37 O 1 ◆ 34-35 R 1
Vaduz ★· FL ◇ 40-41 K 5 ◆ 34-35 N 6
Vah ~ RUS ◆ 52-53 M 5
Vaiaku ★ TUV ◆ 12 J 3
Vajgač, ostrov ⌒ RUS ◆ 52-53 H 3
Valcheta o RA ◆ 32-33 J 6
Valdajskaja vozvyšennost' ▲ RUS ◇ 42-43 N 3 ◆ 34-35 S 4
Valdayskaya Vozvyshennost' = Valdajskaja vozvyšennost' ▲ RUS ◇ 42-43 N 3 ◆ 34-35 S 4
Valdés, Peninsula ⌣ RA ◆ 32-33 K 6
Valdez o USA ◆ 14-15 G 4
Val-d'Isère o· F ◇ 38-39 L 9 ◆ 34-35 N 6
Valdivia o RCH ◆ 32-33 H 5
Valdivia Fracture Zone ≃ ◆ 7 B 9
Val-d'Or o CDN ◇ 18-19 F 4 ◆ 14-15 V 7
Valdosta o USA ◇ 24-25 G 4 ◆ 16-17 K 4
Vale o USA ◇ 20-21 F 4
Vale do Javari, Área Indígenas do ✗ BR ◆ 30-31 E 6
Valença o BR ◆ 30-31 M 7
Valença do Piauí o BR ◆ 30-31 L 6
Valence ☆· F ◇ 38-39 K 9 ◆ 34-35 N 6
Valence-sur-Baïse o F ◇ 38-39 H 10 ◆ 34-35 M 7
València ☆·· E ◇ 44-45 G 5 ◆ 34-35 L 8
Valencia ☆ YV ◆ 30-31 F 2
València, Golf de ≈ ◇ 44-45 H 5 ◆ 34-35 M 8
Valenciennes o F ◇ 38-39 J 6 ◆ 34-35 M 5
Valentine o USA ◇ 26-27 E 4
Val-Jalbert ∴· CDN ◇ 18-19 H 4
Valladolid o·· E ◇ 44-45 E 4 ◆ 34-35 L 7
Valladolid o· MEX ◇ 28-29 K 1 ◆ 16-17 J 6
Vallard, Lac o CDN ◇ 18-19 K 2
Valle o USA ◇ 20-21 H 8
Valle de Bravo o· MEX ◇ 28-29 D 2
Valle de Guadalupe o MEX ◇ 28-29 C 1
Valle de La Pascua o YV ◆ 30-31 F 3
Valle de Santiago o MEX ◇ 28-29 D 1
Valledupar ☆ CO ◆ 30-31 E 2
Vallée-Jonction o CDN ◇ 18-19 J 5
Valle Hermoso o MEX (QR) ◇ 28-29 K 2
Valle Hermoso o MEX (TAM) ◆ 16-17 G 5
Vallejo o USA ◇ 20-21 C 6
Valle Nacional o· MEX ◇ 28-29 F 3
Vallenar o RCH ◆ 32-33 H 3
Valles, Ciudad o MEX ◆ 16-17 G 6
Valletta ★· M ◇ 46-47 E 7 ◆ 34-35 O 8
Valley East o CDN ◇ 18-19 D 5
Valley Falls o USA ◇ 20-21 D 4
Valley Mills o USA ◇ 26-27 J 4
Valley of the Kings ∴·· ET ◆ 48-49 M 3
Valley Wells o USA ◇ 20-21 G 8
Val-Paradis o CDN ◇ 18-19 E 4
Valparai o IND ◆ 56-57 M 8
Valparaiso o USA (FL) ◇ 24-25 E 4
Valparaiso o USA (IN) ◇ 22-23 E 5

Tombouctou — Valparaiso 93

Vals, Tanjung ▲ RI ◆ 58-59 L 8
Valsbaai ≈ ◆ 50-51 E 8
Van ☆ TR ◆ 34-35 U 8
Van Alstyne o USA ◇ 26-27 J 3
Vanavara ☆ RUS ◆ 52-53 R 5
Van Buren o USA (AR) ◇ 26-27 K 2
Van Buren o USA (ME) ◇ 22-23 P 2
Van Buren o USA (MO) ◇ 26-27 M 1
Vanceboro o USA ◇ 22-23 P 3
Vanceburg o USA ◇ 22-23 G 6
Vancouver o·· CDN ◆ 14-15 M 7
Vancouver o USA ◇ 20-21 C 3
Vancouver Island ⌒ CDN ◆ 14-15 L 7
Vandalia o USA ◇ 22-23 D 6
Vandenberg Air Force Base xx USA ◇ 20-21 D 8
Vanderhoof o CDN ◆ 14-15 M 6
Van Diemen Gulf ≈ ◆ 60-61 G 2
Vänern ⊖ S ◇ 36-37 F 7 ◆ 34-35 O 4
Vangaindrano o RM ◆ 50-51 L 6
Van Gölü ⊖ TR ◆ 34-35 U 8
Vanikolo ⌒ SOL ◆ 60-61 O 2
Vanimo o PNG ◆ 58-59 M 7
Vanne ~ F ◇ 38-39 J 7 ◆ 34-35 M 6
Vannes ☆· F ◇ 38-39 F 8 ◆ 34-35 L 6
Vanoise, Parc National de la ⊥· F ◇ 38-39 L 9 ◆ 34-35 N 6
Van Rees, Pegunungan ▲ RI ◆ 58-59 L 7
Vanrhynsdorp o ZA ◆ 50-51 E 8
Vansittart Bay ≈ ◆ 60-61 F 2
Vansittart Island ⌒ CDN ◆ 14-15 U 3
Vanua Lava ⌒ VAN ◆ 60-61 O 2
Vanua Levu ⌒ FJI ◆ 60-61 Q 3
Vanuatu ■ VAN ◆ 60-61 N 3
Van Vert o USA ◇ 22-23 F 5
Vapor, El o MEX ◇ 28-29 J 2
Varadero o·· C ◆ 16-17 K 6
Varanasi o·· IND ◆ 56-57 N 5
Varangerfjorden ≈ ◇ 36-37 O 1 ◆ 34-35 R 1
Varginha o BR ◆ 32-33 N 2
Varillas, Las o RA ◆ 32-33 K 4
Varna ☆ BG ◆ 34-35 R 7
Varón, Cerro de ▲ MEX ◇ 28-29 B 2
Várzea Grande o BR ◆ 30-31 H 8
Vāsad o IND ◆ 56-57 L 6
Vasconcelos o MEX ◇ 28-29 G 3
Vasjugan ~ RUS ◆ 52-53 N 6
Vasjuganskaja ravnina ⌣ RUS ◆ 52-53 M 6
Vassar o USA ◇ 22-23 G 4
Västerås ☆ S ◇ 36-37 H 7 ◆ 34-35 P 4
Vatican City = Città del Vaticano ★··· SCV ◇ 46-47 D 4 ◆ 34-35 O 7
Vatnajökull ⊂ IS ◇ 36-37 e 2 ◆ 34-35 H 3
Vättern ⊖ S ◇ 36-37 G 7 ◆ 34-35 O 4
Vatulele ⌒ FJI ◆ 60-61 Q 3
Vaughn o USA (MT) ◇ 20-21 J 2
Vaughn o USA (NM) ◇ 26-27 E 2
Vavoua o CI ◆ 48-49 D 7
Vaygach, Ostrov = Vajgač, ostrov ⌒ RUS ◆ 52-53 H 3
Vega o USA ◇ 26-27 F 2
Vega de Alatorre o MEX ◇ 28-29 F 1
Vejle o DK ◇ 36-37 D 9 ◆ 34-35 N 4
Vela, Cabo de la ▲ CO ◆ 30-31 E 2
Velikaja ~ RUS ◆ 52-53 g 5
Velikie Luki ☆ RUS ◇ 42-43 M 3 ◆ 34-35 S 4
Velikiye Luki = Velikie Luki ☆ RUS ◇ 42-43 M 3 ◆ 34-35 S 4
Veliko Tărnovo o BG ◆ 34-35 R 7
Vella Lavella ⌒ SOL ◆ 58-59 P 8
Vellore o· IND ◆ 56-57 M 8
Vel'sk o RUS ◆ 34-35 U 3
Venado, Isla del ⌒ NIC ◇ 28-29 C 6
Venado Tuerto o RA ◆ 32-33 K 4
Vendôme o F ◇ 38-39 H 8 ◆ 34-35 M 6
Venézia ☆··· I ◇ 46-47 D 2 ◆ 34-35 O 6
Venezuela ■ YV ◆ 30-31 F 3
Venezuela Basin ≃ ◆ 16-17 N 8
Veniaminof, Mount ▲ USA ◆ 14-15 E 5
Veniaminof Volcano ▲ USA ◆ 14-15 E 5
Venice o USA (FL) ◇ 24-25 G 6
Venice o USA (LA) ◇ 24-25 D 5
Venice = Venézia ☆··· I ◇ 46-47 D 2 ◆ 34-35 O 6
Venta, La o MEX (TAB) ◇ 28-29 G 2
Venta, La ∴· MEX (TAB) ◇ 28-29 G 2
Ventosa, La o MEX ◇ 28-29 G 3
Ventoux, Mont ▲ F ◇ 38-39 K 9 ◆ 34-35 N 6
Ventspils ☆·· LV ◇ 42-43 G 3 ◆ 34-35 Q 4
Ventuari, Río ~ YV ◆ 30-31 F 3
Ventura o· USA ◇ 20-21 E 8 ◆ 16-17 C 4
Venustiano Carranza o MEX ◇ 28-29 H 3
Venustiano Carranza o MEX ◇ 28-29 C 2
Vera o RA ◆ 32-33 K 3
Veracruz o· MEX (VER) ◇ 28-29 F 2 ◆ 16-17 G 7
Veracruz ▫ MEX ◇ 28-29 E 1
Veraval o IND ◆ 56-57 L 6
Verde, Rio ~ BR ◆ 32-33 M 2
Verde, Río ~ MEX ◇ 28-29 F 3
Verde, Río ~ MEX ◇ 28-29 C 1
Verde River ~ USA ◇ 20-21 J 8 ◆ 16-17 D 4
Verdon ~ F ◇ 38-39 L 10 ◆ 34-35 N 7
Verdon-sur-Mer, le o F ◇ 38-39 G 9 ◆ 34-35 L 6
Verdun o· F ◇ 38-39 K 7 ◆ 34-35 M 6
Vereeniging o ZA ◆ 50-51 G 7
Vereščagino o RUS ◆ 52-53 O 5
Verhalen o USA ◇ 26-27 F 4
Verhneimbatsk o RUS ◆ 52-53 O 5
Verhnetazovskij, zapovednik ⊥ RUS ◆ 52-53 N 5
Verhnjaja Salda ☆ RUS ◆ 52-53 J 6
Verhojansk o RUS ◆ 52-53 X 4
Verhojanskij hrebet ▲ RUS ◆ 52-53 W 4
Verkhoyanskiy Khrebet = Verhojanskij hrebet ▲ RUS ◆ 52-53 W 4
Vermilion o USA ◇ 22-23 G 5
Vermilion Bay ≈ ◇ 26-27 L 5
Vermillon, Rivière ~ CDN ◇ 18-19 H 5
Vermont ▫ USA ◇ 22-23 M 4 ◆ 14-15 W 8
Vernal o USA ◆ 16-17 E 2
Verner o CDN ◇ 18-19 D 5
Verneuil-sur-Avre o F ◇ 38-39 H 7 ◆ 34-35 M 6
Vernia, La o USA ◇ 26-27 H 5
Vernon o F ◇ 38-39 H 7 ◆ 34-35 M 6
Vernon o USA (TX) ◇ 26-27 H 2
Vernon o USA (UT) ◇ 20-21 H 5
Vero Beach o USA ◇ 24-25 H 6
Verona ☆·· I ◇ 46-47 C 2 ◆ 34-35 O 6
Versailles ☆··· F ◇ 38-39 J 7 ◆ 34-35 M 6
Versailles o USA (IN) ◇ 22-23 F 6
Versailles o USA (KY) ◇ 22-23 F 6
Vert, Cap ▲ SN ◆ 48-49 B 6
Vesennij o RUS ◆ 52-53 d 4
Vesoul ☆ F ◇ 38-39 L 8 ◆ 34-35 N 6
Vesterålen ⌒ N ◇ 36-37 G 2 ◆ 34-35 O 2
Vestfjorden ≈ ◇ 36-37 F 3 ◆ 34-35 O 2
Vesuvio ▲ I ◇ 46-47 E 4 ◆ 34-35 O 7
Vetluga ~ RUS ◆ 34-35 V 4
Veyo o USA ◇ 20-21 H 7
Vézelay o··· F ◇ 38-39 J 8 ◆ 34-35 M 6
Vézère ~ F ◇ 38-39 H 9 ◆ 34-35 L 7
Viacha o BOL ◆ 30-31 F 8
Viangchan ★ LAO ◆ 58-59 D 3
Vianópolis o BR ◆ 30-31 K 8
Vicebck o BY ◇ 42-43 M 4 ◆ 34-35 S 4
Vic-en-Bigorre o F ◇ 38-39 H 10 ◆ 34-35 M 7
Vicente Guerrero o MEX (DGO) ◆ 16-17 F 6
Vicente Guerrero o MEX (QR) ◇ 28-29 L 1
Vicente Guerrero o MEX (TLA) ◇ 28-29 E 2
Vichada, Río ~ CO ◆ 30-31 F 4
Vichy o·· F ◇ 38-39 J 8 ◆ 34-35 M 6
Vici o USA ◇ 26-27 H 1
Vicksburg o USA ◇ 26-27 M 3 ◆ 16-17 H 4
Vicksburg National Military Park ∴ USA ◇ 26-27 M 3
Victor o USA (ID) ◇ 20-21 J 4
Victor o USA (NY) ◇ 22-23 K 4
Victor, Lac o CDN ◇ 18-19 O 3
Victor Harbor o AUS ◆ 60-61 H 7
Victoria ▫ AUS ◆ 60-61 J 7
Victoria ☆· CDN ◆ 14-15 M 7
Victoria o RA ◆ 32-33 K 4
Victoria o RCH ◆ 32-33 H 5
Victoria ★· SY ◆ 50-51 N 2
Victoria o USA ◇ 26-27 J 5 ◆ 16-17 G 5
Victoria, Ciudad ☆· MEX ◆ 16-17 G 6
Victoria, Lake ⊖ EAT ◆ 50-51 H 2
Victoria = Limbé o· CAM ◆ 48-49 G 8
Victoria, Mount ▲ MYA ◆ 54-55 G 7
Victoria and Albert Mountains ▲ CDN ◆ 14-15 V 1
Victoria Falls National Park ⊥· ZW ◆ 50-51 G 5
Victoria Island ⌒ CDN ◆ 14-15 O 2
Victoria Lake ⊖ CDN ◇ 18-19 Q 4
Victoria Land ≃ ANT ◆ 13 F 16
Victoria Peak ▲ BH ◇ 28-29 K 3
Victoria River o AUS ◆ 60-61 G 3
Victoria River ~ CDN ◇ 18-19 Q 4
Victoria River Downs o AUS ◆ 60-61 G 3
Victoria Strait ≈ ◆ 14-15 Q 3
Victoriaville o CDN ◇ 18-19 J 5
Victoria West o ZA ◆ 50-51 F 8
Victorica o RA ◆ 32-33 J 5
Victorville o USA ◇ 20-21 F 8
Vidal o USA ◇ 20-21 G 8
Vidalia o USA (GA) ◇ 24-25 G 3
Vidalia o USA (LA) ◇ 26-27 M 4
Vidin o BG ◆ 34-35 Q 7
Vidor o USA ◇ 26-27 L 4
Viedma ☆ RA ◆ 32-33 K 6
Viedma, Lago ⊖ RA ◆ 32-33 H 7
Viejo, El o NIC ◇ 28-29 L 5
Vienna o USA (IL) ◇ 22-23 D 7
Vienna o USA (MO) ◇ 22-23 C 6
Vienna o USA (WV) ◇ 22-23 H 6
Vienna = Wien ★·· A ◇ 40-41 O 4 ◆ 34-35 P 6
Vienne o F ◇ 38-39 K 9 ◆ 34-35 N 6
Vienne ~ F ◇ 38-39 H 8 ◆ 34-35 M 6
Vientiane = Viangchan ★ LAO ◆ 58-59 D 3
Vientos, Los o RCH ◆ 32-33 J 2
Vierzon o F ◇ 38-39 J 8 ◆ 34-35 M 6
Vietnam ■ VN ◆ 58-59 E 3
Vieux-Comptoir, Lac du ⊖ CDN ◇ 18-19 F 2
Vieux-Comptoir, Rivière du ~ CDN ◇ 18-19 E 2
Vigan, le o F ◇ 38-39 J 10 ◆ 34-35 M 7
Vigia o BR ◆ 30-31 K 5
Vigía, El o YV ◆ 30-31 E 3
Vigia Chico o MEX ◇ 28-29 L 2
Vigo o E ◇ 44-45 C 3 ◆ 34-35 K 7
Vijayawada o· IND ◆ 56-57 N 7
Vik ☆ IS ◇ 36-37 d 3 ◆ 34-35 H 3
Vila Bela da Santissima Trinidade o BR ◆ 30-31 H 8
Vila de Sena o MOC ◆ 50-51 J 5
Vilaine ~ F ◇ 38-39 G 8 ◆ 34-35 L 6
Vilanandro, Tanjona ▲ RM ◆ 50-51 K 5
Vila Velha o BR ◆ 32-33 O 2
Vilcabamba, Cordillera ▲ PE ◆ 30-31 E 7
Vilčeka, Zemlja ⌒ RUS ◆ 52-53 J 1
Vilhena o BR ◆ 30-31 G 7
Vilju ~ RUS ◆ 52-53 V 5
Viljujsk ☆· RUS ◆ 52-53 V 5
Viljujskoe vodohranilišče ⊖ RUS ◆ 52-53 T 5
Vil'kickogo, ostrov ⌒ RUS ◆ 52-53 M 3
Vil'kickogo, proliv ≈ ◆ 52-53 R 2
Vil'kitskogo, Proliv = Vil'kickogo, proliv ≈ ◆ 52-53 R 2
Villa Angela o RA ◆ 32-33 K 3
Villa Azueta o MEX ◇ 28-29 G 2
Villach o A ◇ 40-41 M 5 ◆ 34-35 O 6
Villa Corona o MEX ◇ 28-29 C 1
Villa de Cazones o MEX ◇ 28-29 F 1
Villa Dolores o RA ◆ 32-33 J 4
Villa Flores o MEX ◇ 28-29 H 3
Village Cove o CDN ◇ 18-19 R 4
Villagran o MEX ◇ 28-29 D 1
Villaguay o RA ◆ 32-33 L 4
Villa Hermosa o MEX ◇ 28-29 C 1
Villahermosa o MEX (CAM) ◇ 28-29 K 3
Villahermosa ☆· MEX (TAB) ◇ 28-29 H 3 ◆ 16-17 H 7
Villa Hidalgo o MEX ◆ 16-17 E 4
Villa Insurgentes o MEX ◆ 16-17 D 5
Villa María o RA ◆ 32-33 K 4
Villa Mazán o RA ◆ 32-33 J 3
Villa Mills o CR ◇ 28-29 C 7
Villamontes o BOL ◆ 32-33 K 2
Villa Ojo de Agua o RA ◆ 32-33 K 3
Villarrica ☆ PY ◆ 32-33 L 3
Villa Salvadorita o NIC ◇ 28-29 L 5
Villa Tunari o BOL ◆ 30-31 F 8
Villa Unión o RA ◆ 32-33 J 3
Villavicencio ☆ CO ◆ 30-31 E 4
Villefranche-de-Rouergue o F ◇ 38-39 J 9 ◆ 34-35 M 7
Villefranche-sur-Saône o F ◇ 38-39 K 9 ◆ 34-35 N 6
Ville-Marie o CDN ◇ 18-19 E 5
Villeneuve-sur-Lot o F ◇ 38-39 H 9 ◆ 34-35 L 7
Villeroy o CDN ◇ 18-19 J 5
Villeurbanne o F ◇ 38-39 K 9 ◆ 34-35 N 6
Vilnius ★··· LT ◇ 42-43 J 4 ◆ 34-35 R 5
Vilos, Los o RCH ◆ 32-33 H 4
Vilyuyskoye Vodokhranilishche = Viljujskoe vodohranilišče ⊖ RUS ◆ 52-53 T 5
Viña, La o RA ◆ 32-33 J 3
Viña del Mar o RCH ◆ 32-33 H 4
Vinalhaven o USA ◇ 22-23 O 3
Vinalhaven Island ⌒ USA ◇ 22-23 O 3
Vincennes o USA ◇ 22-23 E 6
Vincennes Bay ≈ ◆ 13 G 11
Vindhya Range ▲ IND ◆ 56-57 M 6
Vineland o USA ◇ 22-23 L 6
Vinh ☆ VN ◆ 58-59 E 3
Vinita o USA ◇ 26-27 K 1
Vinnycja ☆ UA ◆ 34-35 R 6
Vinnytsya = Vinnycja ☆ UA ◆ 34-35 R 6
Vinson, Mount ▲ ANT ◆ 13 F 28
Viola o USA (IL) ◇ 22-23 C 5
Viola o USA (KS) ◇ 26-27 J 1
Viphya Mountains ▲ MW ◆ 50-51 H 4
Virac ☆ RP ◆ 58-59 H 4
Viranşehir ☆ TR ◆ 34-35 T 8
Virden o USA ◇ 22-23 D 6
Virgen, La o NIC ◇ 28-29 B 6
Virginia o USA ◆ 14-15 S 7
Virginia ▫ USA ◇ 22-23 J 7 ◆ 16-17 L 3
Virginia Beach o USA ◇ 22-23 K 7 ◆ 16-17 L 3
Virgin River ~ USA ◇ 20-21 G 7
Virudunagar o IND ◆ 56-57 M 9
Virunga, Parc National des ⊥··· ZRE ◆ 50-51 G 2
Visalia o USA ◇ 20-21 E 7
Visayan Sea ≈ ◆ 58-59 H 4
Visby ☆·· S ◇ 36-37 J 8 ◆ 34-35 P 4
Viscount Melville Sound ≈ ◆ 14-15 Q 3
Vishakhapatnam o··· IND ◆ 56-57 N 7
Visrivier Canyon Park, Ai-Ais and ⊥ NAM ◆ 50-51 E 7
Vitiaz Strait ≈ ◆ 58-59 N 8
Vitiaz Trench ≃ ◆ 60-61 P 2
Viti Levu ⌒ FJI ◆ 60-61 Q 3
Vitim ~ RUS ◆ 52-53 T 6
Vitória da Conquista o BR ◆ 30-31 L 7
Vitoria-Gasteiz o· E ◇ 44-45 F 3 ◆ 34-35 L 7
Vitré o F ◇ 38-39 G 7 ◆ 34-35 L 6
Vitry-le-François o F ◇ 38-39 K 7 ◆ 34-35 M 6
Vitsyebsk = Vicebck o BY ◇ 42-43 M 4 ◆ 34-35 S 4
Vittel o· F ◇ 38-39 K 7 ◆ 34-35 M 6
Vivi ~ RUS ◆ 52-53 Q 4
Vizcaíno, Reserva de la Biósfera El ⊥··· MEX ◆ 16-17 D 5
Vize, ostrov ⌒ RUS ◆ 52-53 M 2
Vizeu o BR ◆ 30-31 K 5
Vizianagaram o IND ◆ 56-57 N 7
Vizille o F ◇ 38-39 K 9 ◆ 34-35 N 6
Vjatka ~ RUS ◆ 34-35 W 4
Vjazemskij o RUS ◆ 52-53 X 8
Vjaz'ma ☆ RUS ◇ 42-43 O 4 ◆ 34-35 S 4
Vladikavkaz ☆ RUS ◆ 34-35 U 7
Vladimir ☆··· RUS ◇ 42-43 R 3 ◆ 34-35 U 4
Vladivostok o RUS ◆ 52-53 X 9
Vlorë ☆·· AL ◇ 46-47 G 4 ◆ 34-35 P 7
Vohimena, Tanjona ▲ RM ◆ 50-51 L 7
Voi o EAK ◆ 50-51 J 2
Voinjama ☆ LB ◆ 48-49 D 7
Voiron o F ◇ 38-39 K 9 ◆ 34-35 N 6
Voja, Ust'- o RUS ◆ 52-53 H 5
Vojejkov šelfovyj lednik ⌒ ANT ◆ 13 G 13
Volcán o PA ◇ 28-29 C 7
Volcán Barú, Parque Nacional ⊥·· PA ◇ 28-29 C 7
Volcán de Colima, Parque Nacional ⊥ MEX ◇ 28-29 C 2
Volcano o USA ◇ 24-25 E 8
Volga ~ RUS ◇ 42-43 N 3 ◆ 34-35 V 5
Volgodonsk o RUS ◆ 34-35 U 6
Volgogradskoe vodohranilišče < RUS ◆ 34-35 V 5
Volhov ~ RUS ◇ 42-43 N 2 ◆ 34-35 S 4
Volksrust o ZA ◆ 50-51 G 7
Voločanka o RUS ◆ 52-53 P 3
Vologda ☆· RUS ◇ 42-43 Q 2 ◆ 34-35 T 4
Vólos o· GR ◇ 46-47 J 5 ◆ 34-35 Q 8
Volta ~ GH ◆ 48-49 F 7
Voltaire, Cape ▲ AUS ◆ 60-61 F 2
Volta Lake < GH ◆ 48-49 E 7
Volta Noire ~ BF ◆ 48-49 E 6
Volubilis ∴·· MA ◆ 48-49 D 2
Volyns'kyj, Novohrad- o UA ◆ 34-35 R 5
Volzhskiy = Volžskij o RUS ◆ 34-35 U 6
Volžskij o RUS ◆ 34-35 U 6
Vóries Sporádes ⌒ GR ◇ 46-47 J 5 ◆ 34-35 Q 8
Vöring Plateau ≃ ◆ 34-35 N 2
Vorkuta ☆ RUS ◆ 52-53 J 4
Voroncovo o RUS ◆ 52-53 N 3
Voronež ☆ RUS ◆ 34-35 T 5
Voronezh = Voronež o RUS ◆ 34-35 T 5
Vosburg o ZA ◆ 50-51 F 8
Vosges ▲ F ◇ 38-39 L 8 ◆ 34-35 N 6
Vostok o ANT ◆ 13 F 11
Votkinsk ☆ RUS ◆ 34-35 W 4
Vouga o ANG ◆ 50-51 E 4
Voyageurs National Park ⊥ USA ◆ 14-15 S 7
Vrangelja, ostrov ⌒ RUS ◆ 52-53 g 3
Vredenburg o ZA ◆ 50-51 E 8
Vryburg o ZA ◆ 50-51 F 7
Vryheid o ZA ◆ 50-51 H 7
Vsevidof, Mount ▲ USA ◆ 14-15 C 6
Vui-Uata Nova Itália, Área Indígena ⚔ BR ◆ 30-31 F 5
Vũng Tàu o· VN ◆ 58-59 E 4
Vuranggo o SOL ◆ 58-59 P 8
Vyborg ☆· RUS ◇ 42-43 L 1 ◆ 34-35 R 3
Vyčegda ~ RUS ◆ 52-53 H 5
Vyezžij Log o RUS ◆ 52-53 P 6
Vyšnij Voloček ☆ RUS ◇ 42-43 O 3 ◆ 34-35 S 4
Vytegra ☆· RUS ◆ 34-35 T 3

W

Wa ☆· GH ◆ 48-49 E 6
Waajid o SP ◆ 48-49 O 8
Waar, Pulau ⌒ RI ◆ 58-59 K 7
Wabag ☆· PNG ◆ 58-59 M 8
Wabasca River ~ CDN ◆ 14-15 N 5
Wabash o USA ◇ 22-23 F 5
Wabash River ~ USA ◇ 22-23 F 5 ◆ 16-17 J 2
Wabē Shebelē Wenz ~ ETH ◆ 48-49 O 7
Waccasassa Bay ≈ ◇ 24-25 G 5
Waco o CDN ◇ 18-19 M 3
Waco o USA ◇ 26-27 J 4 ◆ 16-17 G 4
Wad Bandah o SUD ◆ 48-49 L 6
Waddān o· LAR ◆ 48-49 J 3
Waddington, Mount ▲ CDN ◆ 14-15 L 6
Wadesboro o USA ◇ 24-25 H 2
Wadham Islands ⌒ CDN ◇ 18-19 S 4
Wādī Halfā o SUD ◆ 48-49 M 4
Wadley o USA ◇ 24-25 G 3
Wad Madani ☆ SUD ◆ 48-49 M 6
Wadsworth o USA ◇ 20-21 E 6
Wafangdian o CHN ◆ 54-55 N 4
Wager Bay ≈ ◆ 14-15 S 3
Wagga Wagga o AUS ◆ 60-61 K 7
Wagh, al- o KSA ◆ 56-57 D 5
Wağid, Ğabal al- ▲ KSA ◆ 56-57 E 7
Wagin o AUS ◆ 60-61 D 6
Wagon Mound o USA ◇ 26-27 E 1
Wagontire o USA ◇ 20-21 E 4
Wahai o RI ◆ 58-59 J 7
Wah Cantonment o PK ◆ 56-57 L 4
Wahiawa o USA ◇ 24-25 C 7
Wahrān ☆·· DZ ◆ 48-49 E 1
Waialua o USA (HI) ◇ 24-25 D 7
Waialua o USA (HI) ◇ 24-25 C 7
Waianae o USA ◇ 24-25 C 7
Waiāpi, Área Indígena ⚔ BR ◆ 30-31 J 4
Waigeo, Pulau ⌒ RI ◆ 58-59 K 7
Waikiki Beach <· USA ◇ 24-25 D 7
Wailuku o USA ◇ 24-25 D 7
Waimate o NZ ◆ 60-61 P 8
Waimea o USA ◇ 24-25 E 7
Waimiri Atroari, Área Indígena ⚔ BR ◆ 30-31 G 5
Waingapu o RI ◆ 58-59 H 8
Waipara o NZ ◆ 60-61 P 8
Waipukurau o NZ ◆ 60-61 Q 8
Waitsburg o USA ◇ 20-21 E 2
Waiwa o PNG ◆ 58-59 N 8
Wajir o EAK ◆ 50-51 K 1
Wakasa-wan ≈ ◆ 54-55 Q 4
Wakefield o CDN ◇ 18-19 G 6
Wakefield o USA (MI) ◇ 22-23 D 2
Wakefield o USA (RI) ◇ 22-23 N 5
Wakkanai o J ◆ 54-55 R 2
Wakomata Lake ⊖ CDN ◇ 18-19 C 5
Wakulla Springs · USA ◇ 24-25 F 4
Wakunai o PNG ◆ 58-59 P 8
Wałbrzych ☆· PL ◇ 40-41 O 3 ◆ 34-35 P 5
Waldenburg o USA ◇ 26-27 M 2
Walden Ridge ▲ USA ◇ 24-25 F 2
Waldo o USA ◇ 24-25 G 5
Waldorf o USA ◇ 22-23 K 6
Waldport o USA ◇ 20-21 B 3
Waldron o USA ◇ 26-27 K 2
Wales o USA ◆ 14-15 C 3
Wales Island ⌒ CDN ◆ 14-15 T 3
Walfe, Chute ~ ZRE ◆ 50-51 F 3
Walgett o AUS ◆ 60-61 K 6
Walgreen Coast ⌣ ANT ◆ 13 F 26
Walikale o ZRE ◆ 50-51 G 2
Walker o USA ◇ 22-23 F 4
Walker Lake ⊖ USA ◇ 20-21 E 6
Walker Mountains ▲ ANT ◆ 13 F 26
Walker River ~ USA ◇ 20-21 E 6
Walker River Indian Reservation ⚔ USA ◇ 20-21 E 6 ◆ 16-17 C 3
Wallace o USA ◇ 20-21 G 2
Wallaceburg o CDN ◇ 18-19 C 7
Wallal Downs o AUS ◆ 60-61 E 3
Wallaroo o AUS ◆ 60-61 H 6
Walla Walla o USA ◇ 20-21 E 2 ◆ 14-15 N 7
Wallowa Mountains ▲ USA ◇ 20-21 F 3
Wallula o USA ◇ 20-21 E 2
Walmanpa-Warlpiri Aboriginal Land ⚔ AUS ◆ 60-61 G 3
Walnut o USA ◇ 24-25 D 2
Walnut Canyon National Monument ∴ USA ◇ 20-21 J 8
Walnut Cove o USA ◇ 24-25 H 1
Walpole o AUS ◆ 60-61 D 7
Walpole Island Indian Reserve ⚔ CDN ◇ 18-19 C 7
Walsenburg o USA ◇ 26-27 E 1
Walsh o USA ◇ 26-27 F 1
Walt Disney World ·· USA ◇ 24-25 H 5
Walterboro o USA ◇ 24-25 H 3
Waltham Station o CDN ◇ 18-19 F 6
Walton o CDN ◇ 18-19 M 6
Walton o USA ◇ 22-23 F 6
Walvisbaai ≈ ◆ 50-51 D 6
Walvisbaai = Walvis Bay ☆ NAM ◆ 50-51 D 6
Walvis Bay ☆ NAM ◆ 50-51 D 6
Walvis Ridge ≃ ◆ 50-51 B 8
Wamba o ZRE (HAU) ◆ 48-49 L 8
Wamba ~ ZRE ◆ 50-51 E 3
Wami ~ EAT ◆ 50-51 J 3
Wanapitae Lake ⊖ CDN ◇ 18-19 D 5
Wanapitei o CDN ◇ 18-19 D 5
Wanapitei River ~ CDN ◇ 18-19 D 5
Wanganui o NZ ◆ 60-61 Q 7
Wangaratta o AUS ◆ 60-61 K 7
Wangary o AUS ◆ 60-61 H 6
Wangki, Río = Coco o Segovia ~ HN ◇ 28-29 B 4 ◆ 16-17 J 8
Wangpan Yang ≈ ◆ 54-55 N 5
Wanning o CHN ◆ 54-55 L 8
Wan Xian o CHN ◆ 54-55 K 5
Wapanucka o USA ◇ 26-27 J 2
Wapato o USA ◇ 20-21 D 2
Wapello o USA ◇ 22-23 C 5
Wappapello o USA ◇ 22-23 C 7
Wappapello, Lake ⊖ USA ◇ 26-27 M 1
Warangal o· IND ◆ 56-57 M 7
Warburton o AUS (VIC) ◆ 60-61 K 7
Warburton ⚔ AUS (WA) ◆ 60-61 F 5
Warburton Creek ~ AUS ◆ 60-61 H 5
Warburton Range Aboriginal Land ⚔ AUS ◆ 60-61 F 5
Wardha o IND ◆ 56-57 M 6
Ware o CDN ◆ 14-15 L 5
Waren o RI ◆ 58-59 L 7
Warialda o AUS ◆ 60-61 L 5
Warmbad o NAM ◆ 50-51 E 7
Warm Springs o USA (NV) ◇ 20-21 F 6
Warm Springs o USA (OR) ◇ 20-21 D 3
Warm Springs Indian Reservation ⚔ USA ◇ 20-21 D 3 ◆ 14-15 M 8
Warner o USA ◇ 26-27 K 2
Warner Mountains ▲ USA ◇ 20-21 D 4
Warner Range ▲ USA ◇ 20-21 D 5 ◆ 14-15 M 8
Warner Robins o USA ◇ 24-25 G 3
Warrego River ~ AUS ◆ 60-61 K 5
Warren o USA (AR) ◇ 26-27 L 3
Warren o USA (MI) ◇ 22-23 G 4
Warren o USA (NH) ◇ 22-23 N 4
Warren o USA (OH) ◇ 22-23 H 5
Warren o USA (PA) ◇ 22-23 J 5 ◆ 16-17 L 2
Warrendale o USA ◇ 22-23 H 5
Warrenton o USA (GA) ◇ 24-25 G 3
Warrenton o USA (VA) ◇ 22-23 K 6
Warrenton o ZA ◆ 50-51 F 7
Warri o WAN ◆ 48-49 G 7
Warrington o USA ◇ 24-25 E 4
Warrior o USA ◇ 24-25 E 3
Warrior Reefs ⌒ AUS ◆ 60-61 J 2
Warrnambool o AUS ◆ 60-61 J 7
Warsaw o USA (IN) ◇ 22-23 F 5
Warsaw o USA (NC) ◇ 24-25 J 2
Warsaw = Warszawa ★··· PL ◇ 40-41 Q 2 ◆ 34-35 Q 5
Warszawa ★··· PL ◇ 40-41 Q 2 ◆ 34-35 Q 5
Warwick o AUS ◆ 60-61 L 5
Warwick o USA (GA) ◇ 24-25 G 4
Warwick o USA (OK) ◇ 26-27 J 2
Wasatch Plateau ▲ USA ◇ 20-21 J 6
Wasatch Range ▲ USA ◇ 20-21 J 4 ◆ 16-17 D 2
Wasco o USA ◇ 20-21 E 8
Washago o CDN ◇ 18-19 E 6
Washington o USA (GA) ◇ 24-25 G 3
Washington o USA (IA) ◇ 22-23 C 5
Washington o USA (IN) ◇ 22-23 E 6
Washington o USA (MO) ◇ 22-23 C 6
Washington o USA (NC) ◇ 24-25 K 2
Washington o USA (OH) ◇ 22-23 G 6
Washington o USA (PA) ◇ 22-23 H 5 ◆ 16-17 K 2
Washington o USA (WI) ◇ 22-23 E 3
Washington ▫ USA ◇ 20-21 C 2 ◆ 14-15 M 7
Washington, Mount ▲ USA ◇ 22-23 N 3 ◆ 14-15 W 8
Washington Birthplace National Monument, George ∴ USA ◇ 22-23 K 6
Washington D.C. ★· USA ◇ 22-23 K 6 ◆ 16-17 L 3
Washington Island ⌒ USA ◇ 22-23 E 3
Washington National Monument, Booker T. ∴ USA ◇ 22-23 J 7
Washita, Fort ∴ USA ◇ 26-27 J 2
Washita River ~ USA ◇ 26-27 J 2
Washtucna o USA ◇ 20-21 E 2
Waskom o USA ◇ 26-27 K 3
Waspam o NIC ◇ 28-29 B 4
Waspuk, Río ~ NIC ◇ 28-29 B 4
Waswanipi, Lac ⊖ CDN ◇ 18-19 F 4
Waswanipi, Réserve de ⚔ CDN ◇ 18-19 G 4
Waswanipi, Rivière ~ CDN ◇ 18-19 F 4
Watampone o RI ◆ 58-59 H 7
Watarais o PNG ◆ 58-59 N 8
Waterberg Plateau Park ⊥ NAM ◆ 50-51 E 6
Waterbury o USA ◇ 22-23 M 5
Wateree River ~ USA ◇ 24-25 H 3
Watergap o USA ◇ 22-23 G 7
Waterloo o AUS ◆ 60-61 F 3
Waterloo o CDN ◇ 18-19 D 7
Waterloo o USA ◆ 16-17 H 2
Watersmeet o USA ◇ 22-23 D 2
Waterton Glacier International Peace Park ⊥··· USA ◇ 20-21 G 1 ◆ 14-15 O 7
Watertown o USA (NY) ◇ 22-23 L 4 ◆ 14-15 V 8
Watertown o USA (SD) ◆ 14-15 R 8
Watertown o USA (WI) ◇ 22-23 D 4
Water Valley o USA ◇ 24-25 D 2
Waterville o USA ◇ 22-23 O 3
Watonga o USA ◇ 26-27 H 2
Watrous o USA ◇ 26-27 E 2
Watsa o ZRE ◆ 48-49 L 8
Watseka o USA ◇ 22-23 E 5
Watson o AUS ◆ 60-61 G 6
Watson Lake o CDN ◆ 14-15 L 4
Watsonville o USA ◇ 20-21 D 7
Watts Bar Lake ⊖ USA ◇ 24-25 F 2
Watubela, Kepulauan ⌒ RI ◆ 58-59 K 7
Wau o PNG ◆ 58-59 N 8
Wāu o SUD ◆ 48-49 L 7
Waubaushene o CDN ◇ 18-19 E 6
Wauchope o AUS ◆ 60-61 G 4
Waukegan o USA ◇ 22-23 E 4 ◆ 14-15 T 8
Waukesha o USA ◇ 22-23 D 4
Waupaca o USA ◇ 22-23 D 3
Waupun o USA ◇ 22-23 D 4
Waurika o USA ◇ 26-27 H 2
Waurika Lake ⊖ USA ◇ 26-27 H 2
Wausau o USA ◇ 22-23 D 3 ◆ 14-15 T 8
Wausaukee o USA ◇ 22-23 E 3
Wauwatosa o USA ◇ 22-23 D 4
Wave Hill o AUS ◆ 60-61 G 3
Waverly o USA (NY) ◇ 22-23 K 4
Waverly o USA (TN) ◇ 24-25 E 1
Waverly o USA (VA) ◇ 22-23 K 7
Wawa o CDN ◆ 14-15 U 7
Wawa, Río ~ NIC ◇ 28-29 B 4
Wawagosic, Rivière ~ CDN ◇ 18-19 E 4
Wāw al Kabīr o LAR ◆ 48-49 J 3
Waxahachie o USA ◇ 26-27 J 3
Way, Lake ⊖ AUS ◆ 60-61 E 5
Waycross o USA ◇ 24-25 G 4 ◆ 16-17 K 4
Wayerton o CDN ◇ 18-19 M 5
Waynesboro o USA (GA) ◇ 24-25 G 3
Waynesboro o USA (MS) ◇ 24-25 D 4
Waynesboro o USA (TN) ◇ 24-25 E 2
Waynesboro o USA (VA) ◇ 22-23 J 6
Waynesburg o USA ◇ 22-23 H 6
Waynesville o USA ◇ 24-25 G 2
Waynoka o USA ◇ 26-27 H 1
Waza o CAM ◆ 48-49 H 6
Waza, Parc National de ⊥ CAM ◆ 48-49 H 6
Wazirābād o PK ◆ 56-57 L 4
Weatherford o USA (OK) ◇ 26-27 H 2 ◆ 16-17 G 3
Weatherford o USA (TX) ◇ 26-27 J 3
Weaverville o USA ◇ 20-21 C 5
Webequie o CDN ◆ 14-15 T 6
Webster Springs o USA ◇ 22-23 H 6
Weddell Island ⌒ GB ◆ 32-33 K 8
Weddell Sea ≈ ◆ 13 G 32
Wedowee o USA ◇ 24-25 F 3
Weed o USA ◇ 20-21 C 5
Weeki Wachee Spring · USA ◇ 24-25 G 5
Wegener-Inlandeis ⊂ ANT ◆ 13 F 36
Weh, Pulau ⌒ RI ◆ 58-59 C 5
Weichang o CHN ◆ 54-55 M 3
Weifang o CHN ◆ 54-55 M 4
Weinan o CHN ◆ 54-55 K 5
Weining o CHN ◆ 54-55 J 6
Weipa o AUS ◆ 60-61 J 2
Weirton o USA ◇ 22-23 H 5
Weiser o USA ◇ 20-21 F 3
Weiser River ~ USA ◇ 20-21 F 3
Weiss Lake ⊖ USA ◇ 24-25 F 2
Weitchpec o USA ◇ 20-21 C 5
Welch o USA ◇ 22-23 H 7
Weldiya o ETH ◆ 48-49 N 6
Weldon o USA ◇ 24-25 K 1
Weligama o· CL ◆ 56-57 N 9
Welkom o ZA ◆ 50-51 G 7
Welland o CDN ◇ 18-19 E 7
Wellesley Islands ⌒ AUS ◆ 60-61 H 3
Wellington o CDN ◇ 18-19 F 7
Wellington ★ NZ ◆ 60-61 P 8
Wellington o USA (KS) ◇ 26-27 J 1
Wellington o USA (UT) ◇ 20-21 J 6
Wellington, Isla ⌒ RCH ◆ 32-33 H 7
Wellington Channel ≈ ◆ 14-15 S 1
Wellman o USA ◇ 26-27 F 3
Wells o USA ◇ 20-21 G 5 ◆ 16-17 D 2
Wells, Lake ⊖ AUS ◆ 60-61 E 5
Wells Gray Provincial Park ⊥ CDN ◆ 14-15 M 6
Wellston o USA ◇ 22-23 G 6
Wellsville o USA (MO) ◇ 22-23 C 6
Wellsville o USA (NY) ◇ 22-23 K 4
Wels o A ◇ 40-41 N 4 ◆ 34-35 O 6
Welsford o CDN ◇ 18-19 L 6
Wembere ~ EAT ◆ 50-51 H 2
Wemindji o CDN ◇ 18-19 E 2
Wenatchee o USA ◇ 20-21 D 2
Wenatchee Mountains ▲ USA ◇ 20-21 D 2
Wenchang o CHN ◆ 54-55 L 8
Wenden o USA ◇ 20-21 H 9
Wendesi o RI ◆ 58-59 K 7
Wendo o ETH ◆ 48-49 N 7
Wendover o USA ◇ 20-21 H 5
Wendover Range xx USA ◇ 20-21 H 5
Wenge o ZRE ◆ 50-51 F 1
Wentworth o AUS ◆ 60-61 J 6
Wentworth Centre o CDN ◇ 18-19 N 6
Wentzville o USA ◇ 22-23 C 6
Wenzhou o CHN ◆ 54-55 N 6
Werder o ETH ◆ 48-49 P 7
Weser ~ D ◇ 40-41 K 2 ◆ 34-35 N 5
Weslaco o USA ◇ 26-27 H 6
Wesley o USA ◇ 22-23 P 3
Wesleyville o CDN ◇ 18-19 S 4
Wessel, Cape ▲ AUS ◆ 60-61 H 2
Wessel Islands ⌒ AUS ◆ 60-61 H 2
West Bay ≈ ◇ 24-25 D 5
West Bend o USA ◇ 22-23 D 4
West Bengal ▫ IND ◆ 56-57 O 6
Westboro o USA ◇ 22-23 C 3
West Branch o USA ◇ 22-23 F 3
Westbrook o USA ◇ 22-23 N 4
Westby o USA ◇ 22-23 C 4
West Caroline Basin ≃ ◆ 58-59 L 6
West Columbia o USA ◇ 26-27 K 5
Westerly o USA ◇ 22-23 N 5
Western Australia ▫ AUS ◆ 60-61 D 5
Western Desert ⊥ ET ◆ 48-49 L 3
Western Ghāts ⊥ IND ◆ 56-57 L 6
Western Kentucky Parkway II USA ◇ 22-23 E 7
Western Sahara ■ WSA ◆ 48-49 C 4
Western Tasmania National Parks ⊥··· AUS ◆ 60-61 K 8
Westerville o USA ◇ 22-23 G 5
West Falkland ⌒ GB ◆ 32-33 K 8
West Fayu ⌒ FSM ◆ 58-59 N 5
Westfield o USA (MA) ◇ 22-23 M 4
Westfield o USA (NY) ◇ 22-23 J 4
West Frankfort o USA ◇ 22-23 D 7
West Glacier o USA ◇ 20-21 H 1
West Hamlin o USA ◇ 22-23 G 6
West Ice Shelf ⊂ ANT ◆ 13 G 9
West Indies ⊥ ◆ 16-17 L 6
West Liberty o USA ◇ 22-23 G 7
West Lunga National Park ⊥ Z ◆ 50-51 F 4
West Mariana Ridge ≃ ◆ 54-55 M 2
West Memphis o USA ◇ 26-27 M 2
Westmorland o USA ◇ 20-21 G 9
West Nicholson o ZW ◆ 50-51 G 6
Weston o USA (ID) ◇ 20-21 J 4
Weston o USA (WV) ◇ 22-23 H 6
West Ossipee o USA ◇ 22-23 N 4
West Palm Beach o·· USA ◇ 24-25 H 6 ◆ 16-17 K 5
West Plains o USA ◇ 26-27 M 1
West Point o CDN ◇ 18-19 M 5
West Point o USA ◇ 22-23 K 7
West Point Lake < USA ◇ 24-25 F 3
Westport o CDN ◇ 18-19 Q 4
Westport o NZ ◆ 60-61 P 8
Westport o USA (OR) ◇ 20-21 C 2
Westport o USA (WA) ◇ 20-21 B 2
West Siberian Plain ⌣ RUS ◆ 52-53 K 5
West Springfield o USA ◇ 22-23 M 4
West Thumb o USA ◇ 20-21 J 3
West Travaputs Plateau ▲ USA ◇ 20-21 J 6
West Union o USA ◇ 22-23 C 4
West Virginia ▫ USA ◇ 22-23 H 6 ◆ 16-17 K 3
Westwood o USA ◇ 20-21 D 5
West Wyalong o AUS ◆ 60-61 K 6
West Yellowstone o USA ◇ 20-21 J 3 ◆ 14-15 O 8
Wetar, Pulau ⌒ RI ◆ 58-59 J 8
Wetaskiwin o CDN ◆ 14-15 O 6
Wete o EAT ◆ 50-51 J 3
Wewak ☆ PNG ◆ 58-59 M 7
Weyburn o CDN ◆ 14-15 Q 7
Weymouth o CDN ◇ 18-19 M 6
Whale Cove o CDN ◆ 14-15 S 4
Whangarei o NZ ◆ 60-61 P 7
Wharton o USA ◇ 26-27 J 5
Wheatland o USA ◇ 20-21 D 6
Wheeler o USA ◇ 26-27 G 2
Wheeler Lake < USA ◇ 24-25 E 2
Wheeler Peak ▲ USA (NM) ◇ 26-27 E 1
Wheeler Peak ▲ USA (NV) ◇ 20-21 G 6 ◆ 16-17 D 3
Wheeler Ridge o USA ◇ 20-21 E 8
Wheeling o USA ◇ 22-23 H 5
Whewell, Mount ▲ ANT ◆ 13 F 17
Whidbey Island ⌒ USA ◇ 20-21 C 1
Whitbourne o CDN ◇ 18-19 S 5
Whitby o CDN ◇ 18-19 E 7
White, Lake ⊖ AUS ◆ 60-61 F 4
White Bay ≈ ◇ 18-19 Q 3 ◆ 14-15 Z 6
White Bear River ~ CDN ◇ 18-19 Q 4
White Cape Mount ▲ USA ◇ 22-23 O 3
White Cliffs o AUS ◆ 60-61 J 6
White Earth Indian Reservation ⚔ USA ◆ 14-15 R 7
Whitefish o CDN ◇ 18-19 D 5
Whitefish o USA ◇ 20-21 G 1
Whitefish Bay o USA ◇ 22-23 F 2
Whitefish Lake Indian Reserve ⚔ CDN ◇ 18-19 D 5
Whitefish Point o USA ◇ 22-23 F 2
Whitehall o USA (MT) ◇ 20-21 H 3
Whitehall o USA (NY) ◇ 22-23 M 4
Whitehall o USA (WI) ◇ 22-23 C 3
White Hall State Historic Site · USA ◇ 22-23 F 7
Whitehorse ☆· CDN ◆ 14-15 J 4
White Horse Pass ▲ USA ◇ 20-21 G 5
White Island ⌒ CDN ◆ 14-15 T 3
White Lake o USA (WI) ◇ 22-23 D 3
White Lake ⊖ USA (LA) ◇ 26-27 L 5
Whitemark o AUS ◆ 60-61 K 8
White Mountains ▲ USA ◆ 14-15 G 3
White Mountains ▲ USA ◇ 20-21 E 7
White Mountains ▲ USA ◇ 22-23 N 3
White Nile SUD ◆ 48-49 M 6
White Pass ▲ USA ◇ 20-21 D 2
White River ~ USA ◆ 16-17 G 2
White River ~ USA ◇ 22-23 E 6
White River ~ USA ◇ 20-21 D 2
White River ~ USA ◇ 26-27 G 3
White River ~ USA ◇ 20-21 G 6

94 Vals, Tanjung — White River

White River ~ USA ◇ 26-27 M 2 ◆ 16-17 H 3
White River Junction o USA ◇ 22-23 M 4
White River National Wildlife Refuge ⊥ USA ◇ 26-27 M 2
White Salmon o USA ◇ 20-21 D 3
White Sands Missile Range xx USA ◇ 26-27 D 3
White Sands National Monument ∴ USA ◇ 26-27 D 3
White Sands Space Harbor xx USA ◇ 26-27 D 3
White Sea ≈ ◆ 34-35 T 2
White Settlement o USA ◇ 26-27 J 3
Whiteshell Provincial Park ⊥ ·· CDN ◆ 14-15 R 6
White Star o USA ◇ 22-23 F 4
White Sulphur Springs o USA (MT) ◇ 20-21 J 2
White Sulphur Springs o USA (WV) ◇ 22-23 H 7
Whiteville o USA ◇ 24-25 J 2
White Volta ~ GH ◆ 48-49 E 7
Whitewater o USA ◇ 22-23 D 4
Whitewater Baldy ▲ USA ◇ 26-27 C 3 ◆ 16-17 E 4
Whitewater Bay ≈ ◇ 24-25 H 7
Whitewood o AUS ◆ 60-61 J 4
Whitlash o USA ◇ 20-21 J 1
Whitley City o USA ◇ 22-23 F 7
Whitmann Mission National Historic Site ∴ USA ◇ 20-21 E 2
Whitmore Mountains ▲ ANT ◆ 13 E 0
Whitney o CDN ◇ 18-19 E 6
Whitney, Lake ⊖ USA ◇ 26-27 J 4
Whitney, Mount ▲ USA ◇ 20-21 E 7 ◆ 16-17 C 3
Whitney Point o USA ◇ 22-23 L 4
Whittle, Cap ▲ CDN ◇ 18-19 O 3
Whitworth o CDN ◇ 18-19 K 5
Wholdaia Lake ⊖ CDN ◆ 14-15 Q 4
Why o USA ◇ 20-21 H 9
Whyalla o AUS ◆ 60-61 H 6
Whycocomagh o CDN ◇ 18-19 O 6
Whycocomagh Indian Reserve ✕ CDN ◇ 18-19 O 6
Whycocomagh Provincial Park ⊥ CDN ◇ 18-19 O 5
Wiarton o CDN ◇ 18-19 D 6
Wichaway Nunataks ▲ ANT ◆ 13 E 0
Wichita o USA ◇ 26-27 J 1 ◆ 16-17 G 3
Wichita Falls o USA ◇ 26-27 H 3
Wichita Mountains ▲ USA ◇ 26-27 H 2 ◆ 16-17 G 4
Wichita Mountains National Wildlife Refuge · USA ◇ 26-27 H 2
Wickenburg o · USA ◇ 20-21 H 9
Wickes o USA ◇ 26-27 K 2
Wickham, Cape ▲ AUS ◆ 60-61 J 7
Wickliffe o USA ◇ 22-23 D 7
Widyān, al- ⩟ IRQ ◆ 56-57 E 4
Wien ★ ·· A ◇ 40-41 O 4 ◆ 34-35 P 6
Wiesbaden ☆ · D ◇ 40-41 K 3 ◆ 34-35 N 5
Wiggins o USA ◇ 24-25 D 4
Wikwemikong Indian Reserve ✕ CDN ◇ 18-19 D 6
Wilbur o USA ◇ 20-21 E 2
Wilburton o USA ◇ 26-27 K 2
Wilcannia o AUS ◆ 60-61 J 6
Wilderness National Park ⊥ ZA ◆ 50-51 F 8
Wildwood o USA ◇ 22-23 L 6
Wilhelm, Mount ▲ ·· PNG ◆ 58-59 N 8
Wilhelmshaven o D ◇ 40-41 K 2 ◆ 34-35 N 5
Wilkes o ANT ◆ 13 G 12
Wilkes-Barre o USA ◇ 22-23 L 5 ◆ 16-17 L 2
Wilkes Land ⩟ ANT ◆ 13 F 12
Wilkins Strait ≈ ◆ 14-15 O 1
Willamette River ~ USA ◇ 20-21 C 4
Willandra Lakes Region ⊥ ··· AUS ◆ 60-61 J 6
Willapa Bay ≈ ◇ 20-21 B 2
Willapa Hills ▲ USA ◇ 20-21 C 2
Willard o USA ◇ 26-27 D 2
Willcox o USA ◇ 26-27 C 3
Willemstad ☆ NA ◆ 16-17 N 8
Willeroo o AUS ◆ 60-61 G 3
William "Bill" Dannelly Reservoir < USA ◇ 24-25 E 3
Williams o AUS ◆ 60-61 D 6
Williams o USA (AZ) ◇ 20-21 H 8
Williams o USA (CA) ◇ 20-21 C 6
Williamsburg o USA (IA) ◇ 22-23 C 5
Williamsburg o USA (VA) ◇ 22-23 K 7
Williams Lake o CDN ◆ 14-15 M 6
Williamson o USA ◇ 22-23 G 7
Williamsport o USA ◇ 22-23 K 5
Williamston o USA ◇ 24-25 K 2
Williamstown o USA ◇ 22-23 F 6
Williamsville o USA ◇ 26-27 M 1
Willimantic o USA ◇ 22-23 M 5
Williston o USA (FL) ◇ 24-25 G 5
Williston o USA (ND) ◆ 14-15 Q 7
Williston o USA (SC) ◇ 24-25 H 3
Williston o ZA ◆ 50-51 F 8
Williston Lake o CDN ◆ 14-15 M 5
Willmar o USA ◆ 14-15 R 7
Willow Creek ~ USA ◇ 20-21 E 3
Willow Ranch o USA ◇ 20-21 D 5
Willows o USA ◇ 20-21 C 6
Willow Springs o USA ◇ 26-27 M 1
Willsboro o USA ◇ 22-23 M 3
Wilmer o USA ◇ 24-25 D 4
Wilmington o USA (DE) ◇ 22-23 L 6 ◆ 16-17 L 3
Wilmington o USA (OH) ◇ 22-23 G 6
Wilmington o · USA (NC) ◇ 24-25 K 2 ◆ 16-17 L 4
Wilmot o USA ◇ 22-23 H 5
Wilson o USA ◇ 24-25 K 2
Wilson Creek ~ USA ◇ 20-21 E 2
Wilson Lake < USA ◇ 24-25 E 2
Wilson's Creek National Battlefield Park ∴ · USA ◇ 26-27 L 1
Wiltondale o CDN ◇ 18-19 Q 4
Wiluna o AUS ◆ 60-61 E 5
Wimmera ~ AUS ◆ 60-61 J 7
Winamac o USA ◇ 22-23 E 5
Winburg o ZA ◆ 50-51 G 7
Winchester o CDN ◇ 18-19 G 6
Winchester o USA (ID) ◇ 20-21 F 2
Winchester o USA (KY) ◇ 22-23 F 6
Winchester o USA (TN) ◇ 24-25 E 2
Winchester o USA (VA) ◇ 22-23 J 6
Winder o USA ◇ 24-25 G 3
Windermere Lake ⊖ CDN ◇ 18-19 C 5
Windhoek ★ · NAM ◆ 50-51 E 6
Windorah o AUS ◆ 60-61 J 5
Wind River Indian Reservation ✕ USA ◆ 14-15 P 8
Wind River Range ▲ USA ◆ 14-15 P 8
Windsor o CDN (NFL) ◇ 18-19 R 4 ◆ 14-15 Z 7
Windsor o CDN (NS) ◇ 18-19 M 6
Windsor o CDN (ONT) ◇ 18-19 C 7 ◆ 14-15 U 8
Windsor o USA ◇ 24-25 K 1
Windthorst o USA ◇ 26-27 H 3
Windward Islands ⌒ ◆ 16-17 P 7
Windward Passage ≈ ◆ 16-17 M 7
Winfield o USA (AL) ◇ 24-25 E 3
Winfield o USA (KS) ◇ 26-27 J 1 ◆ 16-17 G 3
Wingham o CDN ◇ 18-19 D 7
Winisk o CDN ◆ 14-15 T 5
Winisk Lake ⊖ CDN ◆ 14-15 T 6
Winisk River ~ CDN ◆ 14-15 T 6
Winkelmann o USA ◇ 26-27 B 3
Winnebago, Lake ⊖ USA ◇ 22-23 D 3
Winnemucca o USA ◇ 20-21 E 5
Winnemucca Lake ⊖ USA ◇ 20-21 E 5
Winnfield o USA ◇ 26-27 L 4
Winnie o USA ◇ 26-27 K 5
Winnipeg ☆ CDN ◆ 14-15 R 7
Winnipeg, Lake ⊖ CDN ◆ 14-15 R 6
Winnipegosis, Lake ⊖ CDN ◆ 14-15 Q 6
Winnipesaukee, Lake ⊖ USA ◇ 22-23 N 4
Winnsboro o USA (LA) ◇ 26-27 M 3
Winnsboro o USA (TX) ◇ 26-27 K 3
Winona o USA (AZ) ◇ 20-21 J 8
Winona o USA (MI) ◇ 22-23 D 2
Winona o USA (MN) ◇ 22-23 C 3 ◆ 14-15 S 8
Winona o USA (MO) ◇ 22-23 C 7
Winona o USA (MS) ◇ 24-25 D 3
Winslow o USA (AR) ◇ 26-27 K 2
Winslow o USA (AZ) ◇ 26-27 B 2
Winston o USA ◇ 20-21 C 4
Winston-Salem o USA ◇ 24-25 H 1 ◆ 16-17 K 3
Winter Haven o USA ◇ 24-25 H 5
Winters o USA ◇ 26-27 H 4
Winterville State Historic Site ∴ USA ◇ 26-27 M 3
Winthrop o USA ◇ 20-21 D 1
Winton o AUS ◆ 60-61 J 4
Wirrulla o AUS ◆ 60-61 G 6
Wiscasset o USA ◇ 22-23 O 3
Wisconsin ▫ USA ◆ 14-15 S 7
Wisconsin Dells o · USA ◇ 22-23 D 4
Wisconsin Rapids o USA ◇ 22-23 D 3
Wisconsin River ~ USA ◇ 22-23 C 4 ◆ 16-17 H 2
Wisdom o USA ◇ 20-21 H 3
Wisemen o USA ◆ 14-15 F 3
Wisła ~ PL ◇ 40-41 P 1 ◆ 34-35 P 5
Witt, De o USA (AR) ◇ 26-27 M 2
Witt, De o USA (IA) ◇ 22-23 C 5
Wittenberg o USA ◇ 22-23 D 3
Wittenoom o AUS ◆ 60-61 D 4
Wittman o USA ◇ 20-21 H 9
Witu Islands ⌒ PNG ◆ 58-59 N 7
Witvlei o NAM ◆ 50-51 E 6
Witwatersrand ▲ ZA ◆ 50-51 G 7
W.J. van Blommesteinmeer ⊖ SME ◆ 30-31 H 4
Woburn o CDN ◇ 18-19 J 6
Woëvre ⩟ F ◇ 38-39 K 7 ◆ 34-35 M 6
Wohlthat Mountains ▲ ANT ◆ 13 F 2
Wokam, Pulau ⌒ RI ◆ 58-59 K 8
Wolcott o USA ◇ 22-23 K 4
Woleai Atoll ⌒ FSM ◆ 58-59 M 5
Woleai Island ⌒ FSM ◆ 12 F 2
Wolf Creek o USA (MT) ◇ 20-21 H 2
Wolf Creek o USA (OR) ◇ 20-21 C 4
Wolf Creek Pass ▲ USA ◇ 26-27 D 1
Wolfe Island ⌒ CDN ◇ 18-19 F 6
Wolf River ~ USA ◇ 22-23 D 3
Wollaston, Islas ⌒ RCH ◆ 32-33 J 9
Wollaston Lake ⊖ CDN ◆ 14-15 Q 5
Wollaston Peninsula ⌣ CDN ◆ 14-15 N 3
Wollemi National Park ⊥ AUS ◆ 60-61 L 6
Wollongong o AUS ◆ 60-61 L 6
Wolstenholme, Cap ▲ CDN ◆ 14-15 V 4
Woman River o CDN ◇ 18-19 C 5
Wonga-Wongué, Parc National du ⊥ G ◆ 50-51 C 2
Wŏnju o ROK ◆ 54-55 O 4
Wonsan o KOR ◆ 54-55 O 4
Wonthaggi o AUS ◆ 60-61 K 7
Wood Bay ≈ ◆ 13 F 17
Woodbine o USA ◇ 24-25 H 4
Wood Buffalo National Park ⊥ ··· CDN ◆ 14-15 O 5
Woodburn o USA ◇ 20-21 C 3
Woodbury o USA ◇ 24-25 F 3
Wood Islands o CDN ◇ 18-19 N 6
Woodland o USA (CA) ◇ 20-21 D 6
Woodland o USA (WA) ◇ 20-21 C 3
Woodlark Island = Murua Island ⌒ PNG ◆ 58-59 O 8
Woodroffe, Mount ▲ AUS ◆ 60-61 G 5
Woodruff o USA (UT) ◇ 20-21 J 5
Woodruff o USA (WI) ◇ 22-23 D 3
Woods, Lake of the ⊖ CDN ◆ 14-15 S 7
Woodsboro o USA ◇ 26-27 J 5
Woodsfield o USA ◇ 22-23 H 6
Woodson o USA ◇ 26-27 H 3
Woodstock o CDN (NB) ◇ 18-19 L 5
Woodstock o CDN (ONT) ◇ 18-19 D 7
Woodstock o USA (IL) ◇ 22-23 D 4
Woodstock o USA (VA) ◇ 22-23 J 6
Woodstock 23 Indian Reserve ✕ CDN ◇ 18-19 L 5
Woodsville o USA ◇ 22-23 M 3
Woodville o NZ ◆ 60-61 Q 8
Woodville o USA (MS) ◇ 26-27 M 4
Woodville o USA (TX) ◇ 26-27 K 4
Woodward o USA ◇ 26-27 H 1 ◆ 16-17 G 3
Woody Point o · CDN ◇ 18-19 Q 4
Woollett, Lac ⊖ CDN ◇ 18-19 H 3
Woomera Prohibited Area ✕ AUS ◆ 60-61 G 6
Woonsocket o USA ◇ 22-23 N 5
Wooramel Roadhouse o AUS ◆ 60-61 C 5
Wooster o USA ◇ 22-23 H 5
Worcester o USA ◇ 22-23 N 4 ◆ 14-15 W 8
Worcester o ZA ◆ 50-51 E 8
Worcester Range ▲ ANT ◆ 13 F 17
Worden o USA ◇ 20-21 D 4
Worthington o USA ◆ 16-17 G 2
Wour o TCH ◆ 48-49 J 4
Wrangel Island = Vrangelja, ostrov ⌒ RUS ◆ 52-53 g 3
Wrangell Mountains ▲ USA ◆ 14-15 H 4
Wrangell-Saint Elias N.P. & Preserve & Glacier Bay N.P. ⊥ ··· USA ◆ 14-15 H 4
Wreck Reef ⌒ AUS ◆ 60-61 M 4
Wrens o USA ◇ 24-25 G 3
Wright Brothers National Memorial ∴ USA ◇ 24-25 L 2
Wrightsville o USA ◇ 24-25 G 3
Wrigley o CDN ◆ 14-15 M 4
Wrigley Gulf ≈ ◆ 13 F 24
Wrocław ☆ ·· PL ◇ 40-41 O 3 ◆ 34-35 P 5
Wubin o AUS ◆ 60-61 D 6
Wudu o CHN ◆ 54-55 J 5
Wuhai o CHN ◆ 54-55 K 4
Wuhan ☆ · CHN ◆ 54-55 L 5
Wuhu o CHN ◆ 54-55 M 5
Wu Jiang ~ CHN ◆ 54-55 K 6
Wukari o WAN ◆ 48-49 G 7
Wum o CAM ◆ 48-49 H 7
Wupatki National Monument ∴ USA ◇ 20-21 J 8
Würzburg o ·· D ◇ 40-41 K 4 ◆ 34-35 N 6
Wushan o CHN ◆ 54-55 J 5
Wuvulu Island ⌒ PNG ◆ 58-59 M 7
Wuwei o CHN ◆ 54-55 J 4
Wuxi o CHN ◆ 54-55 N 5
Wuyi Shan ▲ CHN ◆ 54-55 M 6
Wuyunan o CHN ◆ 54-55 K 3
Wuzhong o CHN ◆ 54-55 K 4
Wuzhou o CHN ◆ 54-55 L 7
Wyandotte Caves ∴ · USA ◇ 22-23 E 6
Wyandra o AUS ◆ 60-61 K 5
Wynbring o AUS ◆ 60-61 G 6
Wyndham o AUS ◆ 60-61 F 3
Wynne o USA ◇ 26-27 M 2
Wynniatt Bay ≈ ◆ 14-15 O 2
Wyoming o USA ◇ 22-23 F 4
Wyoming ▫ USA ◆ 16-17 E 2
Wyoming Peak ▲ USA ◇ 20-21 J 4
Wyoming Range ▲ USA ◇ 20-21 J 4
Wyperfeld National Park ⊥ AUS ◆ 60-61 J 7
Wytheville o USA ◇ 22-23 H 7

X

Xaafuun, Raas ▲ SP ◆ 48-49 Q 6
Xai-Xai ☆ MOC ◆ 50-51 H 7
Xalin o SP ◆ 48-49 P 7
Xalpatláhuac o MEX ◇ 28-29 E 3
Xam Hua o LAO ◆ 58-59 D 2
Xandel o ANG ◆ 50-51 E 3
Xangongo o ANG ◆ 50-51 D 5
Xankandi ☆ AZ ◆ 56-57 F 3
Xapuri o BR ◆ 30-31 F 7
Xau, Lake ⊖ RB ◆ 50-51 F 6
Xel-Há ∴ · MEX ◇ 28-29 L 1
Xenia o USA ◇ 22-23 G 6
Xerente, Área Indígena ✕ BR ◆ 30-31 K 6
Xiahe o CHN ◆ 54-55 J 4
Xiamen o · CHN ◆ 54-55 M 7
Xi'an ☆ ·· CHN ◆ 54-55 K 5
Xiangfan o CHN ◆ 54-55 L 5
Xiang Jiang ~ CHN ◆ 54-55 L 6
Xiangkhoang o LAO ◆ 58-59 D 3
Xianning o CHN ◆ 54-55 L 6
Xiantao o CHN ◆ 54-55 L 5
Xianyang o CHN ◆ 54-55 K 5
Xiaogan o CHN ◆ 54-55 L 5
Xiaoshan o CHN ◆ 54-55 N 5
Xichang o CHN ◆ 54-55 J 6
Xicotepec de Juárez o MEX ◇ 28-29 F 1
Xigazê o ·· CHN ◆ 54-55 F 6
Xi Jiang ~ CHN ◆ 54-55 L 7
Xi Liao He ~ CHN ◆ 54-55 N 3
Xilinhot o CHN ◆ 54-55 M 3
Xingcheng o CHN ◆ 54-55 N 3
Xingu, Parque Indígena do ✕ BR ◆ 30-31 J 7
Xinguara o BR ◆ 30-31 K 6
Xingyi o CHN ◆ 54-55 J 6
Xining ☆ CHN ◆ 54-55 J 4
Xinjiang Uygur Zizhiqu ▫ CHN ◆ 54-55 E 3
Xintai o CHN ◆ 54-55 M 4
Xinxiang o CHN ◆ 54-55 L 4
Xinxu o CHN ◆ 54-55 K 7
Xinyu o CHN ◆ 54-55 L 6
Xinzhou o CHN ◆ 54-55 L 4
Xique-Xique o BR ◆ 30-31 L 7
Xishaqundao = Paracel Islands ⌒ ◆ 58-59 F 3
Xi Ujimqin Qi o CHN ◆ 54-55 M 3
Xixón = Gijón o E ◇ 44-45 E 3 ◆ 34-35 K 7
Xizang Zizhiqu ▫ CHN ◆ 54-55 E 5
Xlacah ∴ · MEX ◇ 28-29 K 1
Xochiapa o MEX ◇ 28-29 G 3
Xochicalco ∴ · MEX ◇ 28-29 E 2
Xochimilco o ·· MEX ◇ 28-29 E 2
Xochob ∴ · MEX ◇ 28-29 K 2
X-Pichil o MEX ◇ 28-29 K 2
Xpujil o MEX (CAM) ◇ 28-29 K 2
Xpujil ∴ · MEX (CAM) ◇ 28-29 K 2
Xuanhua o CHN ◆ 54-55 M 3
Xuanzhou o CHN ◆ 54-55 M 5
Xuchang o CHN ◆ 54-55 L 5
Xuddur ☆ SP ◆ 48-49 O 8
Xunantunich ∴ · BH ◇ 28-29 K 3
Xuwen o CHN ◆ 54-55 L 7
Xuzhou o CHN ◆ 54-55 M 5

Y

Yaak o USA ◇ 20-21 G 1
Ya'an o CHN ◆ 54-55 J 6
Yabelo o ETH ◆ 48-49 N 8
Yabelo Wildlife Sanctuary ⊥ ETH ◆ 48-49 N 7
Yacuiba o BOL ◆ 32-33 K 2
Yaghan Basin ≃ ◆ 7 E 10
Yajalón o MEX ◇ 28-29 H 3
Yakeshi o CHN ◆ 54-55 N 2
Yakima o USA ◇ 20-21 D 2 ◆ 14-15 M 7
Yakima Firing Center xx USA ◇ 20-21 D 2
Yakima Firing Range xx USA ◇ 20-21 D 2
Yakima Indian Reservation ✕ USA ◇ 20-21 D 2 ◆ 14-15 M 7
Yakima River ~ USA ◇ 20-21 D 2
Yako o BF ◆ 48-49 E 6
Yaku-shima ⌒ J ◆ 54-55 P 5
Yakutat o USA ◆ 14-15 J 5
Yakutsk = Jakutsk ☆ ·· RUS ◆ 52-53 W 5
Yala o THA ◆ 58-59 D 5
Yalaki o ZRE ◆ 50-51 F 1
Yalata Aboriginal Lands ✕ AUS ◆ 60-61 G 6
Yale o USA ◇ 20-21 C 2
Yale Point ▲ USA ◇ 26-27 C 1
Yalgoo o AUS ◆ 60-61 D 5
Yali o NIC ◇ 28-29 L 5
Yaloké o RCA ◆ 48-49 J 7
Yalong Jiang ~ CHN ◆ 54-55 J 6
Yamagata ☆ J ◆ 54-55 R 4
Yamaguchi ☆ J ◆ 54-55 P 5
Yamal, Poluostrov = Jamal, poluostrov ⌣ RUS ◆ 52-53 K 4
Yamato Basin ≃ ◆ 54-55 P 4
Yamato Rise ≃ ◆ 54-55 P 4
Yamatosammyaku ▲ ANT ◆ 13 F 4
Yambio o SUD ◆ 48-49 L 8
Yamdena, Pulau ⌒ RI ◆ 58-59 K 8
Yamma Yamma, Lake ⊖ AUS ◆ 60-61 J 5
Yamoussoukro ★ · CI ◆ 48-49 D 7
Yamuna ~ IND ◆ 56-57 M 5
Yan'an o CHN ◆ 54-55 K 4
Yandeearra Aboriginal Land ✕ AUS ◆ 60-61 D 4
Yangambi o ZRE ◆ 50-51 F 1
Yangbajain o CHN ◆ 54-55 G 5
Yangjiang o CHN ◆ 54-55 L 7
Yangon ☆ ·· MYA ◆ 58-59 C 3
Yangquan o CHN ◆ 54-55 L 4
Yangshuo o · CHN ◆ 54-55 L 7
Yangtze = Chang Jiang ~ CHN ◆ 54-55 K 5
Yangyuan o CHN ◆ 54-55 L 3
Yangzhou o · CHN ◆ 54-55 M 5
Yanhu o CHN ◆ 54-55 E 5
Yanji o CHN ◆ 54-55 O 3
Yankari Game Reserve ⊥ WAN ◆ 48-49 H 7
Yankton o USA ◆ 16-17 G 2
Yanomami, Parque Indígena ✕ BR ◆ 30-31 G 4
Yantai o CHN ◆ 54-55 N 4
Yaoundé ★ · CAM ◆ 48-49 H 8
Yapacana, Parque Nacional ⊥ YV ◆ 30-31 F 4
Yapen, Pulau ⌒ RI ◆ 58-59 L 7
Yap Islands ⌒ FSM ◆ 58-59 L 5
Yaqui, Río ~ MEX ◆ 16-17 E 5
Yaren ☆ NAU ◆ 12 H 3
Yari, Río ~ CO ◆ 30-31 E 4
Yarkant He ~ CHN ◆ 54-55 D 4
Yarlung Zangbo Jiang ~ CHN ◆ 54-55 G 6
Yarmouth o CDN ◇ 18-19 L 7 ◆ 14-15 X 8
Yaroslavl' = Jaroslavl' ☆ ·· RUS ◆ 42-43 Q 3 ◆ 34-35 T 4
Yarraman o AUS ◆ 60-61 L 5
Yarrowitch o AUS ◆ 60-61 L 6
Yarumal o CO ◆ 30-31 D 3
Yasawa Group ⌒ FJI ◆ 60-61 Q 3
Yasothon o THA ◆ 58-59 D 3
Yass o AUS ◆ 60-61 K 6
Yāsūj ☆ · IR ◆ 56-57 G 4
Yasuni, Parque Nacional ⊥ EC ◆ 30-31 D 5
Yatesville o USA ◇ 24-25 F 3
Yathkyed Lake ⊖ CDN ◆ 14-15 R 4
Yavari, Río ~ PE ◆ 30-31 E 5
Yavatmāl o IND ◆ 56-57 M 6
Yaviza o PA ◇ 28-29 F 7 ◆ 16-17 L 9
Yaxcaba o MEX ◇ 28-29 K 1
Yaxchilan · GCA ◇ 28-29 J 3
Yaxia ∴ · GCA ◇ 28-29 K 3
Yazd ☆ · IR ◆ 56-57 G 4
Yazoo City o USA ◇ 26-27 M 3
Yazoo River ~ USA ◇ 26-27 M 3 ◆ 16-17 H 4
Ye o MYA ◆ 58-59 C 3
Yebbi Souma o TCH ◆ 48-49 J 4
Yecheng o CHN ◆ 54-55 D 4
Yeguada o PA ◇ 28-29 D 7
Yei o SUD ◆ 48-49 M 8
Yekaterinburg = Ekaterinburg ☆ RUS ◆ 52-53 J 6
Yela Island ⌒ PNG ◆ 60-61 L 2
Yelets = Elec o RUS ◆ 42-43 Q 5 ◆ 34-35 T 5
Yellowknife ☆ · CDN ◆ 14-15 O 4
Yellow River = Huang He ~ CHN ◆ 54-55 L 4
Yellow Sea ≈ ◆ 54-55 N 4
Yellowstone Lake ⊖ USA ◇ 20-21 J 3 ◆ 14-15 O 8
Yellowstone National Park ⊥ ··· USA ◇ 20-21 J 3 ◆ 14-15 O 8
Yellowstone River ~ USA ◆ 14-15 P 7
Yellville o USA ◇ 26-27 L 1
Yelm o USA ◇ 20-21 C 2
Yelwa o WAN ◆ 48-49 F 6
Yemassee o USA ◇ 24-25 H 3
Yemen ■ Y ◆ 56-57 F 7
Yenakiyeve = Jenakijeve o UA ◆ 34-35 T 6
Yên Bái ☆ VN ◆ 58-59 D 2
Yendi o GH ◆ 48-49 E 7
Yengisar o CHN ◆ 54-55 D 4
Yeo Lake ⊖ AUS ◆ 60-61 E 5
Yeppoon o AUS ◆ 60-61 L 4
Yerevan = Erevan ★ AR ◆ 34-35 U 7
Yeriho = Arīḥā ☆ ·· AUT ◆ 56-57 D 4
Yerington o · USA ◇ 20-21 E 6
Yĕrüshalayim ★ ·· IL ◆ 56-57 D 4
Yetti ⩟ RIM ◆ 48-49 D 3
Yeu, Île d' ⌒ F ◇ 38-39 F 8 ◆ 34-35 L 6
Yevpatoriya = Jevpatorija ☆ · UA ◆ 34-35 S 6
Yibin o CHN ◆ 54-55 J 6
Yichang o CHN ◆ 54-55 L 5
Yichun o CHN (HEI) ◆ 54-55 O 2
Yichun o CHN (JXI) ◆ 54-55 L 6
Yıldızeli ☆ TR ◆ 34-35 T 8
Yinchuan ☆ · CHN ◆ 54-55 K 4
Yingkou o CHN ◆ 54-55 N 3
Yining o CHN ◆ 54-55 E 3
Yixing o CHN ◆ 54-55 M 5
Yiyang o CHN ◆ 54-55 L 6
Yoakum o USA ◇ 26-27 J 5
Yogyakarta ☆ RI ◆ 58-59 F 8
Yoho National Park ⊥ ··· CDN ◆ 14-15 N 6
Yoko o CAM ◆ 48-49 H 7
Yokohama ☆ · J ◆ 54-55 Q 4
Yola ☆ WAN ◆ 48-49 H 7
Yong'an o CHN ◆ 54-55 M 6
Yonkers o USA ◇ 22-23 M 5
Yonne ~ F ◇ 38-39 J 7 ◆ 34-35 M 6
Yopal o CO ◆ 30-31 E 3
Yorito o HN ◇ 28-29 L 4
York o GB ◇ 38-39 G 5 ◆ 34-35 L 5
York o USA (AL) ◇ 24-25 D 3
York o USA (PA) ◇ 22-23 K 6
York o USA (SC) ◇ 24-25 H 2
York, Cape ▲ AUS ◆ 60-61 J 2
York, Kap ▲ GRØ ◆ 14-15 X 1
Yorke Peninsula ⌣ AUS ◆ 60-61 H 7
Yorketown o AUS ◆ 60-61 H 7
York Factory (abandoned) o CDN ◆ 14-15 S 5
York River ~ USA ◇ 22-23 K 7
York Sound ≈ ◆ 60-61 F 2
Yorkton o CDN ◆ 14-15 Q 6
Yoro ☆ HN ◇ 28-29 L 4
Yoro, Montaña de ▲ HN ◇ 28-29 L 4
Yoro, Parque Nacional Montaña de ⊥ HN ◇ 28-29 L 4
Yoron-shima ⌒ J ◆ 54-55 O 6
Yosemite National Park ⊥ ··· USA ◇ 20-21 E 7 ◆ 16-17 C 3
Yŏsu o ROK ◆ 54-55 O 5
Youdunzi o CHN ◆ 54-55 G 4
Young o AUS ◆ 60-61 K 6
Youngs Cove o CDN ◇ 18-19 M 6
Youngstown o USA (FL) ◇ 24-25 F 4
Youngstown o USA (OH) ◇ 22-23 H 5 ◆ 16-17 K 2
Yozgat ☆ TR ◆ 34-35 S 8
Ypsilanti o USA ◇ 22-23 G 4
Yreka o USA ◇ 20-21 C 5
Ysabel Channel ≈ ◆ 58-59 N 7
Ystannah-Hočo o RUS ◆ 52-53 V 3
Ysyk-Köl, ozero ⊖ KS ◆ 56-57 M 2
Yuanjiang o CHN ◆ 54-55 J 7
Yuan Jiang ~ CHN ◆ 54-55 L 6
Yuan Jiang ~ CHN ◆ 54-55 J 7
Yuat River ~ PNG ◆ 58-59 M 7
Yuba City o USA ◇ 20-21 D 6
Yuba River ~ USA ◇ 20-21 D 6
Yucatán o MEX (YUC) ◇ 28-29 L 1
Yucatán ▫ MEX ◇ 28-29 K 1
Yucatán Basin ≃ ◆ 16-17 J 7
Yucatán Channel ≈ ◆ 16-17 J 6
Yucatán Peninsula ⌣ MEX ◇ 28-29 L 2 ◆ 16-17 J 7
Yucca o USA ◇ 20-21 G 8
Yuci o CHN ◆ 54-55 L 4
Yuendumu ✕ AUS ◆ 60-61 G 4
Yueyang o CHN ◆ 54-55 L 6
Yugorskiy Shar, Proliv = Jugorskij Šar, proliv ≈ ◆ 52-53 H 4
Yugoslavia ■ YU ◆ 46-47 G 3 ◆ 34-35 P 6
Yukon-Charley-Rivers National Preserve ⊥ USA ◆ 14-15 H 4
Yukon Delta ⩟ USA ◆ 14-15 D 4
Yukon Delta National Wildlife Refuge ⊥ USA ◆ 14-15 D 4
Yukon Flats ⩟ USA ◆ 14-15 G 3
Yukon Plateau ▲ CDN ◆ 14-15 J 4
Yukon River ~ USA ◆ 14-15 F 3
Yukon Territory ▫ CDN ◆ 14-15 J 3
Yulara o AUS ◆ 60-61 G 5
Yulee o USA ◇ 24-25 H 4
Yuli o CHN ◆ 54-55 F 3
Yulin o CHN (GXI) ◆ 54-55 L 7
Yulin o CHN (SHA) ◆ 54-55 K 4
Yuma o USA ◇ 20-21 G 9 ◆ 16-17 D 4
Yuma Proving Ground xx USA ◇ 20-21 G 9
Yumen o CHN ◆ 54-55 H 4
Yuna o AUS ◆ 60-61 D 5
Yunaska Island ⌒ USA ◆ 14-15 B 6
Yuncheng o CHN ◆ 54-55 L 4
Yungas ⩟ BOL ◆ 30-31 F 8
Yungui Gaoyuan ⩟ CHN ◆ 54-55 J 7
Yunnan ▫ CHN ◆ 54-55 H 7
Yurécuaro o MEX ◇ 28-29 C 1
Yurimaguas o PE ◆ 30-31 D 6
Yuriria o MEX ◇ 28-29 D 1
Yuscarán ☆ HN ◇ 28-29 L 5
Yushu o CHN (JIL) ◆ 54-55 O 3
Yushu o CHN (QIN) ◆ 54-55 H 5
Yutian o CHN ◆ 54-55 E 4
Yuxi o CHN ◆ 54-55 J 7
Yuzhno Sakhalinsk = Južno-Sahalinsk ☆ RUS ◆ 52-53 Z 8
Yvetot o F ◇ 38-39 H 7 ◆ 34-35 M 6

Z

Zaachila o MEX (OAX) ◇ 28-29 F 3
Zaachila ∴ · MEX (OAX) ◇ 28-29 F 3
Zabid o ··· Y ◆ 56-57 E 8
Zābol o · IR ◆ 56-57 J 4
Zabūt o Y ◆ 56-57 G 7
Zacapa ☆ GCA ◇ 28-29 K 4
Zacapa o HN ◇ 28-29 K 4
Zacapu o MEX ◇ 28-29 D 2
Zacatal o MEX ◇ 28-29 J 2
Zacatecas ☆ · MEX ◆ 16-17 F 6
Zacatecoluca ☆ ES ◇ 28-29 K 5
Zacatepec o MEX ◇ 28-29 E 2
Zacatlán o MEX ◇ 28-29 F 2
Zacoalco de Torres o MEX ◇ 28-29 C 1
Zacualpan o MEX ◇ 28-29 E 2
Zacualtipán o MEX ◇ 28-29 E 1 ◆ 16-17 G 6
Zaculeu ∴ · GCA ◇ 28-29 J 4
Zadar o · HR ◆ 46-47 E 2 ◆ 34-35 P 7
Zafār ∴ · Y ◆ 56-57 E 8
Za'farāna o ET ◆ 48-49 M 3
Zagaoua ⩟ TCH ◆ 48-49 K 6
Zagora o MA ◆ 48-49 D 2
Zagreb ★ · HR ◆ 46-47 E 2 ◆ 34-35 P 6
Zagros Mountains ▲ IR ◆ 56-57 G 4
Zāhedān ☆ IR ◆ 56-57 J 5
Zahrān, az- o KSA ◆ 56-57 G 5
Zahrān al-Ǧanūb o KSA ◆ 56-57 E 7
Zaire ~ ZRE ◆ 50-51 D 3
Zaire = Democratic Republic of Congo ■ ZRE ◆ 50-51 E 2
Zajsan o KZ ◆ 52-53 N 8
Zajsan köli ⊖ KZ ◆ 52-53 N 8
Zákinthos ⌒ GR ◆ 46-47 H 6 ◆ 34-35 Q 8
Zakouma, Parc National de ⊥ TCH ◆ 48-49 J 6
Zalim o KSA ◆ 56-57 E 6
Zalingei o SUD ◆ 48-49 K 6
Zaltan, Bi'r o LAR ◆ 48-49 J 3
Zambeze, Rio ~ MOC ◆ 50-51 H 5
Zambezi o Z (NTW) ◆ 50-51 F 4
Zambezi ~ Z ◆ 50-51 F 5
Zambezi Escarpment ⩟ ZW ◆ 50-51 G 5
Zambia ■ Z ◆ 50-51 F 5
Zamboanga City o · RP ◆ 58-59 H 5
Zambrano o HN ◇ 28-29 L 4
Žambyl ☆ KZ ◆ 52-53 L 9
Zamora o ·· E ◆ 44-45 E 4 ◆ 34-35 K 7
Zamora ☆ EC ◆ 30-31 D 5
Zamora o MEX ◇ 28-29 C 1
Zamość ☆ ·· PL ◇ 40-41 R 3 ◆ 34-35 Q 5
Zanaga o RCB ◆ 50-51 D 2
Žanakazaly ☆ KZ ◆ 52-53 J 8
Žanakorgan ☆ KZ ◆ 52-53 K 9
Žanatas o KZ ◆ 56-57 K 2
Zanderij o SME ◆ 30-31 H 3
Zanesville o USA ◇ 22-23 G 6 ◆ 16-17 K 3
Zanǧān ☆ · IR ◆ 56-57 F 3
Zanthus o AUS ◆ 60-61 E 6
Zanzibar ☆ ·· EAT ◆ 50-51 J 3
Zanzibar Channel ≈ ◆ 50-51 J 3
Zanzibar Island ⌒ EAT ◆ 50-51 J 3
Zaouatanlaz o DZ ◆ 48-49 G 4
Zaozhuang o CHN ◆ 54-55 M 5
Zapadnoe o KZ ◆ 52-53 K 7
Zapadnyj Tannu-Ola, hrebet ▲ RUS ◆ 52-53 O 7
Zapala o RA ◆ 32-33 H 5
Zapata o USA ◇ 26-27 H 6
Zapopan o · MEX ◇ 28-29 C 1 ◆ 16-17 F 6
Zaporižžja ☆ · UA ◆ 34-35 T 6
Zapotlanejo o MEX ◇ 28-29 C 1
Zaragoza o · E ◆ 44-45 G 4 ◆ 34-35 L 7
Zaragoza o MEX ◇ 28-29 F 2
Zarcero o CR ◇ 28-29 B 6
Zarde, Kūh-e ▲ IR ◆ 56-57 G 4
Zare Šaran ☆ AFG ◆ 56-57 K 4
Zarghūn ▲ PK ◆ 56-57 K 4
Zaria o · WAN ◆ 48-49 G 6
Zarizyn = Volgograd ☆ · RUS ◆ 34-35 U 6
Zarqā', az ☆ JOR ◆ 56-57 D 4
Zarzis o TN ◆ 48-49 H 2
Zavhan gol ~ MAU ◆ 54-55 G 2
Zavitinsk o RUS ◆ 52-53 W 7
Zazamt, Wādī ~ LAR ◆ 48-49 J 2
Zazir, Oued ~ DZ ◆ 48-49 G 4
Zebulon o USA ◇ 24-25 J 2
Zeehan o AUS ◆ 60-61 K 8
Zeerust o ZA ◆ 50-51 G 7
Zegher, Hamādat ⩟ LAR ◆ 48-49 H 3
Zeil, Mount ▲ AUS ◆ 60-61 G 4
Zeja ☆ RUS ◆ 52-53 W 7
Zeja ~ RUS ◆ 52-53 X 6
Zejskoe vodohranilišče ⊖ RUS ◆ 52-53 W 7
Želanija, mys ▲ RUS ◆ 52-53 K 2
Železnogorsk o RUS ◆ 42-43 O 5 ◆ 34-35 T 5
Zemio o RCA ◆ 48-49 L 7
Zemlja Bunge, ostrov ⌒ RUS ◆ 52-53 Z 2
Zémongo, Réserve de faune de ⊥ RCA ◆ 48-49 K 7
Zempoala ∴ · MEX ◇ 28-29 F 2
Zenica o BIH ◆ 46-47 F 2 ◆ 34-35 P 7
Zephyrhills o USA ◇ 24-25 G 5
Zeravšanskij hrebet ▲ UZ ◆ 56-57 K 3
Zere, Gōd-e ⊖ AFG ◆ 56-57 J 5
Žeskazgan ☆ KZ ◆ 52-53 K 8
Zhalantun o CHN ◆ 54-55 N 2
Zhambyl = Žambyl ☆ KZ ◆ 52-53 L 9
Zhangbei o CHN ◆ 54-55 L 3
Zhangguangcai Ling ▲ CHN ◆ 54-55 O 3
Zhangjiagang o CHN ◆ 54-55 N 5
Zhangjiakou o CHN ◆ 54-55 L 3
Zhangye o CHN ◆ 54-55 J 4
Zhangzhou o CHN ◆ 54-55 M 7
Zhanjiang o CHN ◆ 54-55 L 7
Zhaojue o CHN ◆ 54-55 J 6
Zhaoqing o · CHN ◆ 54-55 L 7
Zhaotong o CHN ◆ 54-55 J 6
Zharkent o KZ ◆ 56-57 N 2
Zhaxigang o CHN ◆ 54-55 D 5
Zhejiang ▫ CHN ◆ 54-55 M 6
Zhengzhou ☆ · CHN ◆ 54-55 L 5
Zhenjiang o · CHN ◆ 54-55 M 5
Zhezqazghan = Žeskazgan ☆ KZ ◆ 52-53 K 8
Zhob o PK ◆ 56-57 K 4
Zhob ~ PK ◆ 56-57 K 4
Zhongba o CHN ◆ 54-55 E 6
Zhongdian o CHN ◆ 54-55 H 6
Zhongning o CHN ◆ 54-55 K 4
Zhongshan o CHN ◆ 54-55 L 7
Zhoukou o CHN ◆ 54-55 L 5
Zhoushan Dao ⌒ CHN ◆ 54-55 N 5
Zhucheng o CHN ◆ 54-55 M 4
Zhumadian o CHN ◆ 54-55 L 5
Zhuozhou o CHN ◆ 54-55 M 4
Zhuzhou o CHN ◆ 54-55 L 6
Zhytomyr = Žitomyr UA ◆ 34-35 R 5
Zibo o CHN ◆ 54-55 M 4
Zichang o CHN ◆ 54-55 K 4
Žigalovo ☆ RUS ◆ 52-53 S 7
Žigansk o RUS ◆ 52-53 V 4
Zighan o LAR ◆ 48-49 K 3
Zigong o CHN ◆ 54-55 J 6
Ziguinchor ☆ SN ◆ 48-49 B 6
Zihuatanejo o · MEX ◇ 28-29 D 3 ◆ 16-17 F 7
Žilina o SK ◇ 40-41 P 4 ◆ 34-35 P 6
Žilinda o RUS ◆ 52-53 T 3
Zillah o LAR ◆ 48-49 J 3
Zima ☆ RUS ◆ 52-53 R 7
Zimapán o MEX ◇ 28-29 E 1
Zimatlán o MEX ◇ 28-29 F 3
Zimbabwe ■ ZW ◆ 50-51 G 5
Zimnij bereg ⌣ RUS ◆ 34-35 T 2
Zimniy Bereg = Zimnij bereg ⌣ RUS ◆ 34-35 T 2
Zinacatepec o MEX ◇ 28-29 F 2
Zinapécuaro o MEX ◇ 28-29 D 2
Zinave, Parque Nacional de ⊥ MOC ◆ 50-51 H 6
Zinder ☆ · RN ◆ 48-49 G 6
Zion o USA ◇ 22-23 E 4
Zion National Park ⊥ USA ◇ 20-21 H 7 ◆ 16-17 D 3
Zipaquirá o CO ◆ 30-31 E 3
Ziraándaro o MEX ◇ 28-29 D 2
Ziracuaretiro o MEX ◇ 28-29 D 2
Žitomir = Žytomyr o UA ◆ 34-35 R 5
Žitomyr UA ◆ 34-35 R 5
Ziya He ~ CHN ◆ 54-55 M 4
Ziyang o CHN ◆ 54-55 J 5
Žizah ☆ · UZ ◆ 54-55 K 2
Zlatoust ☆ RUS ◆ 34-35 X 4
Zlín o CZ ◇ 40-41 O 4 ◆ 34-35 P 6
Zoar Village State Memorial · USA ◇ 22-23 H 5
Zobué o MOC ◆ 50-51 H 5
Zohlaguna, Meseta de ▲ MEX ◇ 28-29 K 2 ◆ 16-17 J 7
Zohova, ostrov ⌒ RUS ◆ 52-53 b 2
Zolfo Springs o USA ◇ 24-25 H 6
Zomba o · MW ◆ 50-51 J 5
Zongo o ZRE ◆ 48-49 J 8
Zonguldak ☆ TR ◆ 34-35 S 7
Zoró, Área Indígena ✕ BR ◆ 30-31 G 7
Žosaly ☆ KZ ◆ 52-53 J 8
Zouar o TCH ◆ 48-49 J 4
Zouérat o RIM ◆ 48-49 C 4
Zrenjanin o · YU ◆ 46-47 H 2 ◆ 34-35 Q 6
Zufār ⩟ Y ◆ 56-57 G 7
Zugspitze ▲ ·· D ◇ 40-41 L 5 ◆ 34-35 O 6
Zumba o EC ◆ 30-31 D 5
Zumbo o MOC ◆ 50-51 H 5
Zumpango o MEX ◇ 28-29 E 2
Zumpango del Río o MEX ◇ 28-29 E 3
Zuni o USA ◇ 26-27 C 2
Zuni Indian Reservation ✕ USA ◇ 26-27 C 2 ◆ 16-17 E 3
Zunyi o CHN ◆ 54-55 K 6
Zuqur, az- ⌒ Y ◆ 56-57 E 8
Zur o MAU ◆ 54-55 H 2
Zürich ☆ · CH ◇ 40-41 K 5 ◆ 34-35 N 6
Zuruahã, Área Indígena ✕ BR ◆ 30-31 F 6
Zuunharaa o MAU ◆ 54-55 K 2
Zuurberg National Park ⊥ ZA ◆ 50-51 G 8
Zuwārah ☆ LAR ◆ 48-49 H 2
Zuytdorp Cliffs ⩟ AUS ◆ 60-61 C 5
Zvishavane o ZW ◆ 50-51 H 6
Zwedru ☆ LB ◆ 48-49 D 7
Zwickau o D ◇ 40-41 M 3 ◆ 34-35 O 5
Zwolle o USA ◇ 26-27 L 4
Zyrjanka ☆ RUS ◆ 52-53 b 4
Zyrjanovsk o KZ ◆ 52-53 N 8
Žytomyr o UA ◆ 34-35 R 5

White River — Žytomyr 95

Contributors/Credits

MACMILLAN
A Simon & Schuster Macmillan Company
1633 Broadway, New York, NY 10019

Copyright © 1998 RV Reise- und
Verkehrsverlag in der Falk Verlag AG
Munich, Germany
Maps copyright © 1998 GeoData GmbH
& Co. KG.

First United States edition 1998

U.S. Edition

Publisher
Natalie Chapman

Editorial Director
Geoff Golson

Cover Design
Iris Jeromnimon

Cartography

Editors-in-Chief/Project Directors
Dieter Meinhardt, Stuttgart
Eberhard Schäfer, Stuttgart

Editor
Jörg Wagner, Stuttgart

Editorial Staff
Ralf van den Berg, Stuttgart
Klaus Dorenburg, Leipzig
Marion Kästner, Leipzig
Karl-Heinz Klimpel, Leipzig
Rüdiger Werr, Stuttgart

Cartography Relief Artists
Kai Gründler, Leipzig
Eberhard von Harsdorf, Siegsdorf
Prof. Dr. Christian Herrmann, Karlsruhe
Bruno Witzky, Stuttgart

Computer Cartographers
Director: Jörg Wagner, Stuttgart

Natascha Fischer, Stuttgart
Margot Graf, Leipzig
Doris Kordisch, Leipzig
Hannelore Kühsel, Leipzig
Helga Mickel, Leipzig
Karin Oelzner, Leipzig

Technology
Director: Joachim Drück, Stuttgart

Elke Bellstedt, Stuttgart
Bernd Hlawatsch, Stuttgart
Erika Rieger, Stuttgart
Walter Zimmermann, Stuttgart

Index
Gabriele Stuke, Stuttgart

Typesetting
Director: Jörg Wulfes, Stuttgart

Frank Barchet, Stuttgart
Kristine Rischer, Stuttgart

Final Checking
Bernd Hilberer, Stuttgart

**Independent Contributors and
Consultants**
Institut für Angewandte Geodäsie,
Frankfurt/M.
UNESCO, World Heritage Center,
Paris,
Vesna Vujicic
Moscow Aerogeodetic Enterprise,
Moscow,
Dr. Alexander Borodko
Academia Sinica, Nanking,
Prof. Zhang Longsheng
Mrs. Liu Xiaomei

Kartografie Praha A.S., Prague,
Jiri Kucera
Cartographia Ltd, Sofia,
Ivan Petrov
Maplan Warszawa, Warsaw,
H. Michal Siwicki
Prof. Dr. Christian Herrmann, Karlsru
Prof. Dr. Wilfried Fiedler, Munich
Prof. Dr. Heinrich Lamping,
Frankfurt/M.
Kartographisches Büro Messer,
Pfungstadt
Internationales Landkartenhaus,
Stuttgart
Birgit Kapper-Wichtler, Buhlenberg
Beate Siewert-Mayer, Tübingen
Dr. Martin Coy, Tübingen
Dr. Wolfgang Frank, Remshalden
Martin Friedrich, Tübingen
Henryk Gorski, Warsaw
Jörg Haas, Rottenburg
Ernst-Dieter Zeidler, Potsdam

Production

Manufacture
Bernhard Mörk, Stuttgart

General Manufacture
Neef + Stumme, Wittingen

Printed in Germany

10 9 8 7 6 5 4 3 2 1